PSEUDOLAW AND SOVEREIGN CITIZENS

Can you avoid any law you do not consent to? Can you avoid paying taxes by declaring yourself sovereign? Do courts operate under admiralty or maritime law? No. But welcome to the strange world of pseudolaw.

This is the first-ever edited volume solely dedicated to examining pseudolaw and its most prominent adherents, sovereign citizens. Drawing on the expertise of judges, criminologists, legal theorists and political sociologists, this collection offers insights into the global growth and alarming adaptability of pseudolaw. While it might be tempting to laugh at the ridiculousness of pseudolaw, it is a serious matter. People who make these claims rob themselves of meaningful legal opportunities and impose great costs to themselves, the administration of justice, and the community. It is also linked to violent extremism and indicative of growing social insecurity.

Part I offers ways to analyse and differentiate pseudolaw from other forms of conspiracy ideation and fringe legal interpretation. Part II examines the rise of sovereign citizens and the global spread of pseudolaw. Part III explores contemporary issues arising from pseudolaw, including the rise of far-right extremism, laypersons in judicial proceedings, fake claims of indigeneity, and fraudulent "get out of jail" schemes. It concludes by considering how we can respond to this phenomenon.

Pseudolaw and Sovereign Citizens

Edited by
Harry Hobbs
Stephen Young
and
Joe McIntyre

•HART•
OXFORD • LONDON • NEW YORK • NEW DELHI • SYDNEY

HART PUBLISHING

Bloomsbury Publishing Plc

Kemp House, Chawley Park, Cumnor Hill, Oxford, OX2 9PH, UK

1385 Broadway, New York, NY 10018, USA

29 Earlsfort Terrace, Dublin 2, Ireland

First published in Great Britain 2025

A catalogue record for this book is available from the British Library.

A catalogue record for this book is available from the Library of Congress.

Library of Congress Control Number: 2024949832

ISBN: HB: 978-1-50997-891-5
ePDF: 978-1-50997-893-9
ePub: 978-1-50997-892-2

Typeset by Compuscript Ltd, Shannon

FOREWORD

On a sweltering summer day in 1996, I attended a memorial service at a farm nestled in the woods of the Wayne National Forest in rural eastern Ohio in the United States. A year earlier, a police officer had shot and killed Michael Hill, a former officer himself, and at the time one of the leading figures in the sovereign citizen and militia movements in Ohio. Hill had confronted the officer with a gun following a pursuit stemming from a traffic stop over Hill's homemade licence plate. Hill had been the 'chief justice' of 'Our One Supreme Court', the largest so-called 'common law court' in Ohio, and he was viewed as a martyr by the friends and followers who attended his memorial service.[1]

I parked my car in a field – where some of the other parked vehicles also sported counterfeit plates – and walked over to the crowd of people gathering for the service. Several of them, I noticed, were sitting at a folding card table looking through thick books of statutes or case law. They were sovereign citizens, engaged – as I wrote at the time – in 'earnestly discussing the mystical procedures of common law'.[2] It was my first face-to-face encounter with practitioners of pseudolaw, though not my last. I had no idea at the time that I would spend decades studying and writing about the sovereign citizen movement and its sister anti-government extremist movements, as well as encountering them in a variety of contexts, including being cross-examined by sovereigns defending themselves in criminal cases.

For much of that time, few people were even aware of the sovereign citizen movement and the pseudo-legal theories and tactics it practised, despite high-profile events such as the 81-day armed standoff between a group of sovereigns, the Montana Freemen, and the Federal Government in 1996. When I first started providing training on the subject for judges, few in my audiences were aware the movement existed, sometimes assuming the *pro se* defendant who had recently made strange arguments in their court had been an isolated individual. For a long time, the movement remained largely under the radar. Only after a 2010 traffic stop incident in Arkansas, in which a sovereign citizen and his son murdered two police officers, did sustained public attention emerge in the United States, later buttressed by the rise in popularity of sovereign-related traffic stop and courtroom

[1] For an overview of the 'court', see S Braun, 'Meting Out Their Kind of Justice' *Los Angeles Times* (5 September 1995).

[2] M Pitcavage, 'The Martyrdom of Michael Hill: A Description of a Militia Memorial Service' *The Columbus Guardian* (11–17 July 1996), web.archive.org/web/19991109002941/http://www.militia-watchdog.org/memorial.htm.

videos posted to the internet.[3] Even today, despite the worldwide growth of the movement, there remains a shortage of scholarly attention to the subject, especially at book length.[4]

That is why it is such a delight to read this collection of studies on aspects of pseudolaw and its practitioners compiled by Harry Hobbs, Stephen Young and Joe McIntyre. These editors have tapped the expertise of an international array of scholars and authorities from a variety of fields and backgrounds to share their insights on this unfortunately growing phenomenon and the problems it creates. The offerings in this volume go far to enhance our understanding of the concept of pseudolaw itself, as well as movements such as the sovereign citizen movement that embrace its use.

If we think of pseudolaw as the creation and employment of theories and arguments that mimic the outward form and appearance of legitimate legal arguments to the extent that they might be able to convince an untrained layperson, but which in no meaningful way (except rarely and by accident) address or have standing in actual law, then pseudolaw has existed, at least on an individual basis, from the distant time the first misguided *pro se* litigant or defendant entered a courtroom to present a fantastical interpretation of the law that they had convinced themselves would extract them from whatever legal difficulties they faced. Leaving aside the occasional vexatious litigant, such individual concoctors of pseudolaw have never presented any serious challenge or threat to the legal system or society at large. However, the rise in recent decades of entire movements based on and motivated by pseudo-legal arguments, such as the Reichsbürger movement in Germany, described by Anna Löbbert in this volume, or the analogous 'Soviet Citizen' movement in Russia, has allowed pseudolaw to cause many more problems to civic institutions and to society.[5] Unlike an isolated individual who creates and employs a pseudo-legal concept for their own use, movements can create larger and more complex arguments and use them to recruit thousands of people and teach them harmful tactics based on pseudolaw.

Nowhere is this more obvious than in the sovereign citizen movement, the largest pseudolaw-inspired movement by far, with hundreds of thousands of practitioners across many countries. Most of the contributions to this volume deal

[3] M Pitcavage, 'The Lawless Ones: The Resurgence of the Sovereign Citizen Movement' Anti-Defamation League (2012), www.adl.org/sites/default/files/documents/assets/pdf/combating-hate/Lawless-Ones-2012-Edition-WEB-final.pdf; FBI, 'Sovereign Citizens: A Growing Domestic Threat to Law Enforcement' (FBI Law Enforcement Bulletin, September 2011) 20, leb.fbi.gov/file-repository/archives/september-2011-leb.pdf.

[4] Although see Christine M Sarteschi, *Sovereign Citizens: A Psychological and Criminological Analysis* (Springer, 2020). Most academic interest in the sovereign citizen movement and other practitioners of pseudolaw is relatively recent; to date, legal scholars have paid the most attention to the movement, with far fewer contributions from historians, sociologists, anthropologists, criminologists and other disciplines.

[5] On the 'Soviet Citizen' movement, see M Luxmoore, 'Flouting the Law in Nostalgia's Name: Russia's Growing Movement of "Soviet Citizens"' Radio Free Europe/Radio Liberty (25 May 2019), www.rferl.org/a/flouting-law-in-nostalgia-s-name-russia-s-growing-movement-of-soviet-citizens-/29962523.html.

exclusively or primarily with the sovereign citizen movement, simply because of its size and effects. The sovereign citizen movement of today emerged in the late 1970s and early 1980s as the child of two older anti-government movements, the tax protest movement and the Posse Comitatus. The tax protest movement (originally often referred to as the 'tax rebellion' or 'tax strike') originated in the United States in the mid-to-late 1960s, using pseudolaw to argue that people had no legal obligation to pay federal income taxes. The Posse Comitatus arose a few years later, based on the pseudo-legal notion that county officials such as the sheriff (or, if they failed to take action, the people of the county themselves) had the power to thwart the implementation of any federal or state laws, regulations or court orders deemed 'unconstitutional'.[6]

From ideas generated by these two anti-government movements, sovereign citizen 'gurus' in the early 1980s created alternative explanations of history and law that explained why and how people could divorce themselves from the jurisdiction and authority of the government – described as the illegitimate product of a conspiracy – and instead return to obeying only God's law and (their version of) the common law.[7] Sovereign citizens were few in number in the 1980s but saw an increase in the mid-to-late 1990s as part of a general upswell of far-right extremism in the United States, a second surge starting in 2008–09 as a result of the mortgage crisis and recession, and a third surge from 2020 to the present, thanks in part to the pandemic and in part to its penetration of other movements such as QAnon, the anti-vaccine movement and the MAGA movement. Many of the recent sovereign citizens identify as 'American State Nationals', a phenomenon described by Christine M Sarteschi in this volume.[8]

The development of the sovereign citizen movement has allowed numerous arguments and tactics based on pseudolaw to become global in nature and to persist, sometimes for generations. In her analysis in this volume of sovereign citizen litigation, Marilyn McMahon refers to the sovereign tactic of creating fictitious financial instruments with titles such as 'bills of exchange' or 'promissory notes'. The pseudo-legal argument that such instruments are based on – that there is no such thing as lawful money for nations that are not on a gold or silver standard – dates to the 1960s and the early years of the tax protest movement, while the first

[6] This author is currently writing a book on the history of the tax protest movement, the Posse Comitatus, the sovereign citizen movement and the militia movement. The most detailed look at the origins of the Posse Comitatus to date is D Levitas, *The Terrorist Next Door: The Militia Movement and the Radical Right* (Thomas Dunne Books, 2002) 108–67, although it focuses more on the white supremacy of many of its practitioners rather than on pseudolaw.

[7] Examples of early sovereign citizen treatises include WL Avery, 'The Dispatch of Merchants' (Common Sense Publications, 1976), famguardian.org/Subjects/Taxes/Articles/DispatchOfMerchants.htm; 'Common Law to Admiralty' (Barristers' Inn School of Common Law (nd [but circa 1984]); VK Speer, *Pied Pipers of Babylon* (self-published, 1985); and RW Wangrud, *Republic vs. Democracy Redress* (self-published, 1985).

[8] See also K McCarthy, 'Sovereign Citizen Ideology Increasingly Seeping into QAnon' Anti-Defamation League (19 January 2022), www.adl.org/resources/blog/sovereign-citizen-ideology-increasingly-seeping-qanon.

widespread employment of such instruments occurred in the early 1980s with fictitious instruments called 'public office money certificates'.[9] Since then, the use of fictitious financial instruments by sovereign citizens has been unceasing. Other sovereign tactics, including 'paper terrorism' tactics designed to harass and retaliate against public officials, have been equally persistent, as has the employment of force and violence, especially in the United States.[10]

Pseudolaw is at the heart of the sovereign citizen movement. It is both the foundation of their ideology and the tool behind most of their tactics, from tax evasion to fictitious licence plates. Three aspects of sovereign citizen pseudolaw are particularly worth keeping in mind as you read the contributions in this volume:

Magical thinking is at the heart of most sovereign citizen pseudolaw. 'Magical thinking' occurs when people believe that specific words, rituals or actions can affect events in the physical world. Just as a shaman might perform a ritual to heal someone afflicted with a disease, so too do sovereign citizens invoke court cases, statutes and regulations, and legal phrases to free themselves from laws, financial obligations or other unwanted manifestations of government or authority.[11] Bruce Baer Arnold, in his contribution to this volume, describes it as a 'mystification … akin to reciting a spell', while Glen Cash, in his own contribution, emphasises the 'ritual and ceremony' that has 'long been at the heart of pseudolaw ideology'. Practitioners of pseudolaw hope to affect the real law with the homemade arguments they invoke, just as more than a century ago Sioux Ghost Dancers in North America and Boxers in China hoped that their rituals would help them fight the Westerners who oppressed them.

Sovereign citizens do not merely ape legal arguments, but also ape authority. As Maria O'Sullivan notes in her contribution to this work, 'pseudolaw (at least in part) is a tool of dissent, frustration, or alienation by a sector of modern society'. Much of the rank-and-file of the sovereign citizen movement consists of people who believe themselves in financial stress or who find themselves frustrated in their fruitless attempts to push back against some authority perceived as oppressive, such as a tax agency, local zoning commission or child welfare agency. They use pseudolaw to address these concerns and grievances, but they do more: they create their own institutions. Sovereign citizens create their own grand juries, their own courts, their own government agencies ranging from post offices to law enforcement agencies, their own assemblies and presidential offices, their own tribal or Indigenous authorities, and occasionally their own nations.

[9] The creator of public office money certificates, songwriter Tupper Saussy, introduced the concept in a popular book: T Saussy, *The Miracle on Main Street: Saving Yourself and America from Financial Ruin* (Spencer Judd Publishers, 1980). The cheque-like certificates were originally intended largely as a protest, but people soon realised they could use them to attempt to pay fines or debts or for purchases.

[10] For recent trends, criminal incidents and use of violence by the sovereign citizen movement in the United States, see M Pitcavage, 'The Sovereign Citizen Movement in the United States' Anti-Defamation League (21 December 2023), www.adl.org/resources/backgrounder/sovereign-citizen-movement-united-states.

[11] ibid.

Not all authority is governmental authority; sovereign citizens also on occasion create their own medical or banking authorities. Sometimes these creations are in the service of a grift – cons and scams are common within the sovereign citizen movement – but often they are established in the hopes of taking back a power that has been perceived to have been lost. In the United States, sovereign citizens constantly invoke 'we the people' – the first words of the US Constitution – to emphasise their belief that they should have more power. The Wisconsin De Jure General Jural Assembly, for example, describes its goal to

> reestablish self governance and restore our country back to the constitutional republic our Founding Fathers bestowed upon us; one that is of the PEOPLE, by the PEOPLE, and for the PEOPLE. Our voice is to be the voice of WE THE PEOPLE and to hold the de facto government accountable when they overstep their authority.[12]

Much of the sovereign citizen movement and sovereign pseudolaw is about regaining an ostensibly lost authority.

The sovereign citizen movement and its pseudolaw are tremendously flexible. Pseudolaw is inherently flexible, in that it is created as a means to an end – or any end. But it is also flexible in its appeal, with different audiences seeing advantages in adopting and adapting it for their own use. Many of the originators of sovereign citizen ideology were white supremacists, typically adherents of the racist and antisemitic religious sect Christian Identity. But even as early as the 1980s, some activists in the Indigenous Hawai'ian independence movement saw its value and began adopting sovereign citizen ideas, a phenomenon that continues today. In the 1990s, some adherents of an Afrocentric religious sect, the Moorish Science Temple, began merging their beliefs with sovereign citizen beliefs, creating an opening for any Black Americans to participate in the sovereign citizen movement. For much of the 2010s, the US sovereign citizen movement's greatest growth area was within the Black community.[13] Today there are tens of thousands of Black sovereign citizens in the United States, along with people of many other ethnic or racial backgrounds, making the sovereign citizen movement the most multicultural far-right movement in the United States.

Sovereign citizen ideology is also flexible in its ability to take advantage of emerging crises and circumstances, whether the financial crisis of 2008–09 or the pandemic of 2020. As Stephen Young, Harry Hobbs and Rachel Goldwasser note in their discussion of the movement in this volume, sovereign citizen leaders '[take] advantage of novel societal issues and events to promote and spread

[12] 'Welcome to the Wisconsin De Jure General Jural Assembly', wisconsin-dejure.org.

[13] On Moorish sovereigns, see 'Moorish Sovereign Citizens' Southern Poverty Law Center, www.splcenter.org/fighting-hate/extremist-files/group/moorish-sovereign-citizens; 'Moorish Sovereign Citizens' Institute for Strategic Dialogue (10 August 2023), www.isdglobal.org/explainers/moorish-sovereign-citizens; and M Pitcavage, 'The Washitaw Nation and Moorish Sovereign Citizens: What You Need to Know' Anti-Defamation League (18 July 2016), www.adl.org/resources/blog/washitaw-nation-and-moorish-sovereign-citizens-what-you-need-know. Not all people of colour who join the movement adopt 'Moorish' theories; many also adhere to more traditional sovereign citizen beliefs.

pseudolaw … it is highly adaptable to local contexts [and] responsive to social, political, or economic crises'. Flexibility also allowed the sovereign citizen movement to spread internationally, first to Canada, as Donald J Netolitzky describes in this volume, then to the entire English-speaking world; and finally, even to countries in places like continental Europe, where English is not a native tongue, and legal systems are not descended from those of England. Today, one should not be shocked at finding sovereign citizens in virtually any country; I recently discovered there were at least some sovereign citizens now active in far-flung and sparsely populated Namibia, including one who described himself in the following way:

> That the term plaintiff is d.b.a terms JOSEPH GOVEIA is a major mail person, currently is a foreign claimant, non-resident alien, non-neutralized citizen, non-amended citizen residing at [address deleted], Windhoek, Khomas, and Republic of Namibia. The term plaintiff living status is a state Citizen Propria Person, free Preamble Citizenry of sovereign state, free Preamble Citizen of the Land mass Republic for Namibia, De Jure Citizenry, a term Namibian National, sui juris / Lawful capacity free of all legal disability, d.b.a JOSEPH GOVEIA©™® has established as non-resident alien residency, a non-neutralised citizen, non-amendment / non-corporate citizen, non-civilly dead entity citizen in REPUBLIC OF NAMIBIA for over the years.[14]

The flexibility of sovereign citizen ideology and pseudolaw means that the movement is sustainable over the long term and will cause problems for years to come. This is why understanding the concept of pseudolaw and its many different manifestations is so important, and why this volume makes such a contribution to that understanding.

Mark Pitcavage*

[14] *Goveia v Bernard* [2024] NAHCMD 154 (26 March 2024), namiblii.org/akn/na/judgment/nahcmd/2024/154/eng@2024-03-26.

* Mark Pitcavage is a historian and Senior Research Fellow at the Anti-Defamation League Center on Extremism, specialising in far-right extremism. He is presently writing a book on the history of the sovereign citizen movement and its sister anti-government movements.

CONTENTS

LIST OF CONTRIBUTORS

Dr Bruce Baer Arnold is an Associate Professor at the University of Canberra, Australia. Dr Arnold's research explores questions about regulation, identity and high technology.

Glen Cash is a Judge of the District Court of Queensland in Australia where he hears criminal and civil matters. Prior to his appointment, Judge Cash was a Crown Prosecutor for 18 years and conducted trials and appeals in the District Court, Supreme Court and the High Court of Australia.

Dr Jonathan Crowe is Professor, Head of School and Dean of the School of Law and Justice at the University of Southern Queensland, Australia, where he also holds a Research Chair in Law and Justice.

Rachel Goldwasser is a Senior Research Analyst at the Southern Poverty Law Center in the United States where she is an expert on anti-government groups, including sovereign citizens.

David Heilpern is Professor and Dean of Law at Southern Cross University, Australia. Prior to that he was a Judicial Officer in NSW for 22 years, and is admitted as a Barrister in the High Court of Australia.

Dr Harry Hobbs is an Associate Professor in the Faculty of Law and Justice at the University of New South Wales.

Dr Kate Leader is a Senior Lecturer at Queen Mary, University of London. Her work focuses on conspiracy theories, litigants in person, law and performance and access to justice. She holds a PhD in Law from LSE and a PhD in Performance Studies from the University of Sydney.

Anna Löbbert is a DPhil candidate at the Centre for Socio-Legal Studies (CSLS), University of Oxford. Her doctoral research explores law as a tool for state contestation and a vehicle for radical politics. Before joining the CSLS, Anna completed an MSc in Law, Anthropology and Society at LSE and a BA in Social and Cultural Anthropology and Philosophy at Freie Universität Berlin, Germany.

Dr Joe McIntyre is an Associate Professor in Law at the University of South Australia. He has a wide range of research and teaching experiences across the common law world. Dr McIntyre's research focuses on judicial studies and judicial theory.

Dr Marilyn McMahon is a Professor and Dean of Deakin Law School. Her research interests are in the areas of criminal law, criminal procedure, criminal responsibility and evidence. She has published widely in the areas of criminal defences (self-defence and mental state defences) and criminal procedure.

Colin McRoberts is an Associate Teaching Professor at the University of Kansas, School of Business. His research has focused on how individuals avoid legal regulation which has brought him into the world of pseudolaw.

Dr Donald J Netolitzky KC is the former and now retired Complex Litigant Management Counsel for the Alberta Court of King's Bench. Dr Netolitzky's research and publishing focuses on three subjects: (1) investigation and description of pseudolaw concepts, litigation, and communities in Canada; (2) data-based characterisation of abusive litigation and litigants; and (3) measurement and analysis of current and historic court activity from a 'sausage factory' process-oriented perspective.

Dr Maria O'Sullivan is an Associate Professor at Deakin Law School, Australia (BA/LLB (Hons I) Australian National University; LLM, University of Essex; PhD, Monash University). She is the author of a number of international and national publications on the subject of human rights and public law, including papers on the role of human rights in national security laws, and the securitisation of peaceful protest.

Dr Josh Roose is a political sociologist and Associate Professor at the Alfred Deakin Institute for Citizenship and Globalisation in the School of Humanities and Social Sciences at Deakin University, Melbourne. His research focuses primarily on political and religious extremism, populism and the intersection with citizenship, economies, masculinities, and the rule of law.

Dr Christine M Sarteschi, LCSW is a Professor of Social Work and Criminology at Chatham University. Among other things, she is the author of *Sovereign Citizens: A Psychological and Criminological Analysis* and studies extremism and violent crime.

Dr Bridgette Toy-Cronin (LLB(Hons), BA Auckland, LLM Harvard, PhD Otago) is an Associate Professor at the Faculty of Law, University of Otago, the Director of the Civil Justice Centre, and Co-Director of the Otago Centre for Law and Society. Her research has an empirical focus, investigating access to justice, the legal profession, judging, dispute resolution and civil procedure.

Dr Stephen Young is Associate Professor of Law at the University of Otago. He is a socio-legal and critical legal scholar who examines how legal subjects are made and when legal systems clash.

1

Understanding Pseudolaw

HARRY HOBBS, STEPHEN YOUNG AND JOE McINTYRE

I. Introduction

Can a dog be made a legal person by public proclamation? Can a person avoid any law she does not explicitly consent to? Are the government and its agencies merely for-profit trading corporations, with no compulsory jurisdiction? Is the only true law found in one version of the Bible from the seventeenth century?

Welcome to the strange world of pseudolaw – a growing global phenomenon where the forms and methods of legal reasoning are distorted through a fever dream of conspiratorial thinking into a twisted parody of the law. Pseudolaw adherents earnestly believe that they (and often they alone) have access to the 'true' understanding of the law, and by deploying stylised forms of words imbued with magical or mystical meanings, they can avoid what they see as odious and illegitimate state interference.

Many people will have become familiar with pseudolaw adherents – and the most prominent purveyors, sometimes known as 'sovereign citizens' – during the COVID-19 public health emergency. On YouTube, Facebook and other social media sites, adherents upload their interactions with police and other individuals. In these carefully edited confrontations filmed with their mobile phone, they imperialistically dismiss lawful directions to hand over their driver licence or wear a mask before entering a store. The direction is, they decry, unlawful – which they then argue by reference to a diverse range of inapplicable, obsolete and obscure legal instruments and quasi-legal terminology. Such confrontations are only one aspect of this phenomenon. Adherents may intimidate ordinary citizens, harass government officials, market fake legal and consulting services to consumers, and even resort to violence. Increasingly, pseudolaw adherents are also litigating their arguments in courts. It seems that quick dismissals and terse judgments fail to deter the believer.

It is tempting to simply mock or ridicule the individuals making such ridiculous arguments. But the phenomenon is no laughing matter. Pseudolaw adherents rob themselves of meaningful legal opportunity and impose great cost to themselves, their families and the community. The existence and spread of the movement creates opportunities for scammers and charlatans to defraud the innocent. Many believers, particularly those exhibiting tropes and characteristics of sovereign citizens, possess concerning links to violent extremism. The phenomenon of pseudolaw also holds up an (often unflattering) mirror to the legal system itself, highlighting the exclusion and alienation of the public inherent in so many of its mysterious processes. The line between 'law' and 'not-law' can appear incomprehensible to the legal outsider, just as the rules and processes that order the administration of justice can look byzantine and impenetrable to the ordinary citizen. Without sufficient legal literacy, pseudolaw can look an awful lot like, well, law.

The study of pseudolaw requires more than a disinterested examination of a strange form of cultist behaviour and conspiratorial ideation. Rather, it forces us – as scholars of law, history, politics, psychology and criminology – to walk through an uncanny valley of *almost law*, and in doing so reflect upon our own institutions. Not only must we understand pseudolaw as a distinct phenomenon, but we must examine how the legal system contributes to its growth. Ultimately, we must find ways to counter this growing trend. This book takes an important step in our attempt to walk that path.

II. What is Pseudolaw?

In some ways, the best way to understand pseudolaw is to jump right into the cases and stories themselves. While all law is – to some degree – about the stories we tell ourselves, the role of narrative in crafting and creating the phenomenon of pseudolaw is particularly acute. To understand pseudolaw, then, let us begin with an example.

In August 2022, James Jones, a self-represented litigant, appeared in the High Court of New Zealand seeking judicial review of a decision by the District Court at Whanganui. Jones's claim related to an infringement notice he had received for failing to register his dog, a Hungarian Vizsla named Connor. Jones had attempted to explain to the District Court that the whole issue was based on 'mistaken identity'.[1] Connor did not need to be registered with the Council because he is 'a Legal Person, entitled to all the Protection and Privileges afforded a Person under Statute'. This process was purportedly effected by a public proclamation that Jones had placed in a local Whanganui newspaper.[2] As Jones described, one privilege enjoyed by a legal person is that they do 'not have to Register with a Local Authority or wear a collar or be restrained by a leash'.[3] The District Court granted the Council's application to strike out Jones's application on the basis that his claims were 'untenable' and his causes of action 'not reasonably arguable'.[4]

[1] *James v District Court at Whanganui* [2022] NZHC 2196 (31 August 2022) [9].
[2] ibid [21].
[3] ibid [9].
[4] *Jones v Whanganui District Council* [2021] NZDC 3864. See also *James* (n 1) [10].

Jones persisted. In the High Court he widened his claims, asserting that he is a 'Sovereign Man under Common Law' and beyond the jurisdiction of New Zealand courts.[5] Jones appeared to ground his argument on the notion of consent: as a Sovereign Man outside the jurisdiction of the state, Jones could only be subject to New Zealand law – including the Dog Control Act 1996 – if he agreed. Supporting this claim was the assertion that the District Court is a 'for-profit trading entity' that 'relies on contract and consent to "do business" with those that come before it'.[6] Given Jones did not consent to the proceeding, the District Court's judgment should be struck out for want of jurisdiction. Unfortunately for Jones, his case was dismissed, and he was ordered to pay costs. An appeal to the New Zealand Court of Appeal was also struck out.[7]

Perhaps because of its curious facts, *James v District Court at Whanganui* attracted media attention.[8] The case is certainly amusing; one New Zealand journalist joked that the argument made sense, as 'a dog is incapable of signing up to the social contract'.[9] But do not let these absurdities distract from more serious concerns. For Jones, the decision meant that an initial NZD 50 registration fee ballooned considerably. For the administration of justice in New Zealand, it meant the Council, judicial officers across three courts and other state actors were required to spend time and public money engaging with and responding to 'incomprehensible statements' that bore no chance of success.[10] Jones's submissions also hinted at another issue: the intersection and exploitation of Indigenous rights claims. Jones asserted that Connor could be made a legal person 'By the same mechanism that the Whanganui River was made a Person'.[11] That the Whanganui River was given the legal rights of a person by legislation as part of a settlement between the Whanganui iwi and the New Zealand Government aimed at redressing violations of the Treaty of Waitangi was not appreciated.[12]

The facts in *James* may be unique but the style of argument is not. *James* is only one example of a growing number of cases concerning 'pseudolaw'. As *James* illustrates, pseudolaw involves situations where adherents (often litigants) adopt the forms of legal argumentation while advancing strange and fanciful substantive arguments which they genuinely believe reflect the 'true law'. Pseudolaw

[5] *James* (n 1) [14].

[6] ibid [31].

[7] *James v District Court at Whanganui* [2023] NZCA 181 (18 May 2023).

[8] See, for example, J Galuszka, 'Man Ordered to Pay Dog Registration after Court Rejects Idea his Pet is a "Legal Person"' *Stuff* (14 September 2022), www.stuff.co.nz/national/crime/300687962/man-ordered-to-pay-dog-registration-after-court-rejects-idea-his-pet-is-a-legal-person.

[9] @henrycooke (Twitter, 1 September 2022, 8:32AM NZST), twitter.com/henrycooke/status/1565105247009361920.

[10] *James* (n 1) [16], citing *Martin v Chief Executive of the Department of Corrections* [2016] NZHC 2811 [20].

[11] *James* (n 1) [9].

[12] *Te Awa Tupua (Whanganui River Claims Settlement) Act 2017* (NZ). See further T Collins and S Esterling, 'Fluid Personality: Indigenous Rights and the *Te Awa Tupua (Whanganui River Claims Settlement) Act 2017* in Aotearoa New Zealand' (2019) 20 *Melbourne Journal of International Law* 1.

adherents may adopt behaviours that are entirely unacceptable or violent and use their understanding of the law to rationalise their acts as though they are legally justified. In a separate incident, Connor attacked another dog, so Jones drew a knife and began shouting at the other dog's owner.[13] Again, he represented himself in court, claiming 'he had a right to carry the knife and seize or destroy any dog attacking his, under the Dog Control Act', and that his 'folding knife' was not relevantly a 'knife'. This subsequent case also highlights the pick-and-choose nature of pseudolaw. Whereas Jones argued in *James* that he was exempt from the Dog Control Act, in the latter case he relied upon it to excuse his violent behaviour. Where consistency/coherence is in tension with self-interest, pseudolaw shows a strong bias for the latter.

Jones is not alone in arguing that he can legally avoid obligations, or that a 'true' understanding of the law conveniently permits his desired outcome. As this book explores, pseudolaw adherents around the world are relying upon an eclectic and archaic amalgam of genuine legal sources to support a broad range of self-serving 'legal' interpretations.

In Australia, adherents have submitted that Magna Carta discharges them of their obligation to pay their mortgage,[14] that the Constitution ceased to have effect upon Australia signing the Treaty of Versailles,[15] and that the presence of the Royal Coat of Arms above the bench means English common law supersedes Australian statutory law.[16] In one recent case, an applicant sought leave to ask the High Court of Australia to order the Attorney-General to instruct the Crown to grant her the title of 'Sovereign Empress of Australia'.[17] None of these and similar claims has ever succeeded, but it does not stop their repetition. Indeed, it appears that pseudolaw is growing in Australia and New Zealand. In 2023, judicial officers reported a 'sharp rise'[18] in the number of cases brought by litigants asserting that the legal system does not apply to them. Our own study of pseudolaw in New Zealand and Australian courts suggests the COVID-19 pandemic and associated strict public health orders has fuelled the growth of this phenomenon.[19]

[13] L Keith, 'Abusive Knife Wielding Ex-Soldier Terrified Woman Walking her Dog in the Park' *NZ Herald* (4 October 2022), www.nzherald.co.nz/nz/abusive-knife-wielding-ex-soldier-terrified-woman-walking-her-dog-in-the-park/A3WA336FNW2UIY2MUH2TRX7SLA.

[14] *Arnold v State Bank of South Australia* (1992) 38 FCR 484.

[15] *Helljay Investments v Deputy Commissioner of Taxation* (1999) 166 ALR 302. See also Institute of Tax Research, 'Australia: The Concealed Colony' (1999).

[16] *Koteska v Magistrate Manthey* [2013] QCA 105 [15].

[17] *Taylor, In the matter of an application for leave to issue or file* [2023] HCA Trans 63 (18 May 2023).

[18] S Kesteven and D Carrick, 'Magistrates Witness a "Sharp Rise" in Sovereign Citizen Cases brought before the Local Courts' ABC Radio National (8 May 2023), www.abc.net.au/news/2023-05-08/nsw-magistrates-report-sharp-rise-in-sovereign-citizen-cases/102285772.

[19] S Young, H Hobbs and J McIntyre, 'The Growth of Pseudolaw and Sovereign Citizens in Aotearoa New Zealand Courts' (2023) *New Zealand Law Journal* 6; H Hobbs, S Young and J McIntyre, 'The Internationalisation of Pseudolaw: The Growth of Sovereign Citizen Arguments in Australia and Aotearoa New Zealand' (2024) 47 *University of New South Wales Law Journal* 309.

In the United States and Canada, courts are often confronted by arguments that taxes cannot be imposed without the taxpayer's consent, or that the litigant is somehow not subject to the jurisdiction of the court.[20] In other cases, applicants who 'never consented to being governed' seek access to several millions of dollars the Government has apparently held in trust for them since birth.[21] Similar arguments have been run (and lost) in the United Kingdom. In one recent case, several claimants contested foreclosure proceedings by stringing together 'non-existent – or at least considerably adapted – legal terminology' that sought to prove they had been released from their mortgage and the mortgagee 'is now obliged to pay [them] monies'.[22]

Elsewhere across Europe, reports indicate that small but significant numbers of people have attempted to assert their immunity from state law. In Germany, the *Reichsbürger* movement believes that the modern German state is an illegitimate corporation established by the Allied Powers after WWII.[23] In Italy, some people have sought to avoid traffic fines by declaring themselves free citizens of the 'Kingdom of Gaia'.[24] In the Czech Republic, adherents have submitted declarations purporting to terminate a contract with the 'Czech Republic corporation', and argue they remain de jure citizens of Czechoslovakia as its dissolution was illegal.[25]

The preposterousness of these claims might lead many to dismiss them as frivolous and relatively harmless. However, as we have noted, pseudolaw adherents can and do turn violent. In 2011, hundreds of members of the British Constitution Group stormed Birkenhead County Court to attempt a citizens' arrest on a judge in support of a man challenging his council tax bill. One of the organisers announced: 'Today was day one. This is going to happen again and again and again. We have sent a message to this court as one nation and one voice until change comes'.[26]

In the United States, pseudolegal claims are most often associated with sovereign citizens. The Federal Bureau of Investigations has identified sovereign citizens

[20] See for example *Augustinowicz v Nevelson* No 10–cv–564–PB, 2011 WL 6300962 (DNH 16 December 2011). The case was dismissed as defying common sense and 'foreclosed by New Hampshire case law'.

[21] *Zimmer v British Columbia* 2023 BCSC 1235, [3]–[4] (Weatherill J) ('*Zimmer*').

[22] *Lewis v The West Brom* [2023] EWHC 1361 (KB) (7 June 2023) [9].

[23] T Wright, 'Germany's New Mini-Reichs' *Los Angeles Review of Books* (22 June 2019), lareviewofbooks.org/article/germanys-new-mini-reichs.

[24] L Bianchi, 'Dentro l'assurdo mondo dei "sovranisti individuali" italani' Vice (3 June 2017), www.vice.com/it/article/jpn8py/dentro-lassurdo-mondo-dei-sovranisti-individuali-italiani.

[25] Czech Republic Ministersto Vnitra, 'Hnutí Suverénních občanů a jejich aktivity v České republice' (25 May 2023), www.mvcr.cz/chh/clanek/hnuti-suverennich-obcanu-a-jejich-aktivity-v-ceske-republice.aspx.

[26] 'Hundreds of Council Tax Protesters Storm Courtroom in Attempt to Make Citizens' Arrest of Judge' *Daily Mail* (9 March 2011), www.dailymail.co.uk/news/article-1364091/Council-tax-protesters-storm-courtroom-arrest-judge.html.

as 'anti-government extremists'[27] and classified the movement as a 'domestic terrorist threat'.[28] In Australia, the New South Wales Police Force has also described the movement as a potential terrorist threat.[29] In September 2021, a raid by South Australian police on the property of a prominent pseudolaw adherent, found to be a leader of the 100-person strong anti-government group Commonwealth Justice Assembly, uncovered a cache of illegal weapons.[30] Tragically, in December 2022, two police officers and a neighbour were ambushed and murdered by three perpetrators inspired by sovereign citizens beliefs in the Australian state of Queensland.[31] That same month in Germany, around 50 members of the Reichsbürger movement were arrested for planning a *coup d'état* aimed at re-establishing the German monarchy.[32]

Recent internal analysis by the Australian Federal Police has highlighted the risk of violence particularly to public office holders. That report found that:

> We are largely seeing these groups take action in the form of non-violent protest, including co-opting other demonstrations. However, there is also a propensity for fixation on high office holders and public figures, as well as some within the movement urging violence.[33]

As the incidents in Queensland and Germany highlight, this risk of violence should not be minimised. Adherents threaten more than simply the smooth operation of the legal system. They can pose a genuine risk to the safety and wellbeing of judicial officers, police and members of the public.[34] This is a phenomenon that is growing in prevalence and in seriousness of impact. Yet it remains a phenomenon that is understudied in the literature.

[27] The Federal Bureau of Investigation, 'Domestic Terrorism: The Sovereign Citizen Movement' (13 April 2010), perma.cc/L8SQ-2K42.

[28] ibid. See further C Sarteschi, 'Sovereign Citizens: A Narrative Review with Implications of Violence Towards Law Enforcement' (2021) 60 *Aggression and Violent Behaviour* 101509.

[29] J Thomas and J McGregor, 'Sovereign Citizens: Terrorism Assessment Warns of Rising Threat from Anti-Government Extremists' ABC News (30 November 2015), www.abc.net.au/news/2015-11-30/australias-sovereign-citizen-terrorism-threat/6981114.

[30] E Tlozek, 'Man in Custody After Police Raid Alternative Community Meeting Over Public Safety Concerns' ABC News (17 September 2021), www.abc.net.au/news/2021-09-17/sa-police-raid-adelaide-alternative-community-meeting/100472728. The adherent was subsequently convicted and sentenced to jail for a minimum of 14 months: S Fewster, 'Jailed for Firearms Offences' *The Advertiser* (23 November 2022) 11.

[31] K Nguyen and E Gramenz, 'Donald Day Jr, US Sovereign Citizen Linked to Wieambilla Murders, was Prepared for Deadly "Last Stand" with Police, Court Hears' ABC News (29 December 2023), www.abc.net.au/news/2023-12-29/donald-day-jr-wieambilla-shootings-court-transcript/103271920.

[32] K Bennhold and E Solomon, 'Germany Arrests 25 Suspected of Planning to Overthrow Government' *New York Times* (7 December 2022), www.nytimes.com/2022/12/07/world/europe/germany-coup-arrests.html.

[33] S Dametto, 'The Sovereign Citizen Movement in Australia' Australian Federal Police (September 2023) 11, www.afp.gov.au/sites/default/files/2023-09/123-2023.pdf.

[34] C Sarteschi, 'Modern-Day Outlaws, "Sovereign Citizens" Threaten the Rule of Law' *The Conversation* (17 June 2024), www.theconversation.com/modern-day-outlaws-sovereign-citizens-threaten-the-rule-of-law-231352.

III. The Study of Pseudolaw

Pseudolaw is serious, but it has not attracted significant scholarly attention or legal analysis. As Colin McRoberts notes, there have 'been relatively few attempts to seriously manage or even study the ecosystem of harmful, false legal beliefs'.[35] Nonetheless, over the last few years, as the phenomenon has grown, legal scholars have begun to examine the use and misuse of pseudolaw, particularly its invocation by sovereign citizens and other like groups. Given that many of these movements emerged in the United States in the mid-to-late twentieth century, most of this scholarship centres on North America. But, as highlighted above, pseudolaw now has a global reach. It has migrated across the common law world and appears also in a range of civil law countries. It deserves serious scholarly attention.

This is the first book dedicated solely to the study of pseudolaw. We are motivated by the harms caused by pseudolaw as well as the apparent growth and spread of this concerning movement. It is worth stating clearly: *pseudolaw does not work*. Litigants who rely on pseudolegal arguments will fail. Indeed, they will likely find themselves in a more difficult economic and psychological situation because of their interest in and willingness to use pseudolaw. They may grow distant from their families and friends. Pseudolaw is also harmful to the proper administration of justice. Considerable time and resources are wasted disposing of these cases. More seriously, legitimate legal issues may be buried under pseudolegal gibberish and could be dismissed too hastily.[36] Judicial officers may lose patience and rule in error.[37] This can lead to convictions being appealed or even set aside.[38]

Pseudolaw is a response to the state and its judicial systems, but it is also a consequence of the operation of the legal system. Even if pseudolegal arguments are entirely misguided in law, their growth and spread is indicative of social unrest, disaffection and inequality. People experiencing financial or other distress may require legal advice to resolve their challenges. When legal services are expensive and difficult to access, it is understandable that people may seek out alternative advice that promises a solution to their problems. Misinformation and disinformation proliferate online and in conspiratorial communities. Pseudolegal arguments are idiosyncratic. They are taught and reproduced in often stylistically distinct ways by self-described 'gurus'.[39] These charlatans and scammers defraud people

[35] C McRoberts, 'Tinfoil Hats and Powdered Wigs: Thoughts on Pseudolaw' (2019) 58 *Washburn Law Review* 637, 638.

[36] *Republic Arms Ltd v Corporation Trading as New Zealand Police* [2022] NZHC 3185 [3].

[37] *Kelly v Fiander* [2023] WASC 187 (1 June 2023). See further, J McIntyre, H Hobbs and S Young, 'The Strawman Trap: Non-Appearance and the Pitfalls of Pseudolaw' (2024) *Australian Law Journal* (forthcoming).

[38] *Hainaut v Queensland Police Service* [2019] QDC 223 (8 November 2019).

[39] DJ Netolitzky, 'Organized Pseudolegal Commercial Arguments as Magic and Ceremony' (2018) 55 *Alberta Law Review* 1045, 1046; J Tsidulko, 'The Sovereign Citizen Scam' (2013) 18 *Skeptic Magazine* 12, 14–15; N Wallace, '"Messiah-Like Figure" is Doing Own Harvesting' *Sydney Morning Herald* (15 January 2011), www.smh.com.au/world/messiahlike-figure-is-doing-own-harvesting-20110114-19r9v.html.

by selling the legal equivalent of snake oil, peddling 'quick-fix solutions to legal problems'.[40] They hold speaking tours, advertise instructional videos, open online 'universities', and host countless YouTube videos 'teaching' attendees how to opt out of law.[41] In court, adherents submit lengthy documents drawn from templates and recite scripts authored by the guru. Sometimes gurus attend court and provide advice and argument, for an additional fee.[42]

Unsurprisingly, courts are often befuddled and surprised by the claims made. In a magisterial review of pseudolegal arguments, Rooke ACJ of the Alberta Court of Queen's Bench admitted that following their reasoning is difficult: 'I would describe how these documents have the intended effect, except that the … material I have reviewed has never made any sense, so I can only observe the "ingredients" and describe the intended "spell effect".'[43]

Justice Judd of the Supreme Court of Victoria noted in a 2012 case that sovereign citizen pseudolegal arguments are often 'comprised of random, almost incomprehensible, statements, propositions, quotations, argument and references to other material … lifted from other documents and randomly pasted into the pleading'.[44] In another case, Toogood J of the High Court of New Zealand noted:

> There is absolutely no merit in this application and it represents a gross abuse of the Court's procedure … Incomprehensible statements about birthright and being a natural person not susceptible to the laws of this country are regularly and properly rejected by the Courts.[45]

Today, courts are more familiar with the 'incoherent, unintelligible nonsense',[46] and 'the hackneyed argument about the limit of [state] sovereignty which has been rejected summarily so often'.[47] Nevertheless, this does not prevent the recurrence of pseudolegal claims, nor its international influence. How then should we respond to pseudolaw?

IV. The Outline of this Book

Responding appropriately to pseudolaw requires a clear understanding of the phenomenon, including its origins, its evolution, its networks and its manifestations.

[40] C Lee, 'Sovereign Citizens: Sitting on the Docket All Day, Wasting Time' *Minnesota Law Review* De Novo Blog (2 March 2022), minnesotalawreview.org/2022/03/02/sovereign-citizens-sitting-on-the-docket-all-day-wasting-time.

[41] SA Kent, 'Freemen, Sovereign Citizens, and the Challenge to Public Order in British Heritage Countries' (2015) 6 *International Journal of Cultic Studies* 1, 11.

[42] *Meads v Meads* (2012) ABQB 571, [155] (Rooke ACJ).

[43] ibid [536].

[44] *National Australia Bank Ltd v Norman* [2012] VSC 14, [4] (Judd J).

[45] *Martin v Chief Executive of the Department of Corrections* [2016] NZHC 2811 [19]–[20].

[46] *Zimmer* (n 21) [8] (Weatherill J).

[47] P Young, 'Current Issues' (2004) 78 *Australian Law Journal* 763, 767.

This book seeks to make sense of pseudolaw as an increasingly global phenomenon. It is divided into three parts.

To more clearly understand pseudolaw, Part one offers ways to analyse and differentiate the phenomenon from other forms of conspiracy ideation and fringe legal interpretation. To understand where pseudolaw comes from and how it adapts and evolves as it spreads, part two examines the operation and practice of pseudolegal claims in the select jurisdictions of the United States, Canada, Australia and Germany. To understand how the contemporary manifestation of pseudolaw prompts novel challenges, part three explores the impact of pseudolaw across several case studies, including new and emerging organisations, the intersection with Indigenous claims, the impact on non-lawyer advocates, and the risk of violent extremism. In the remainder of this chapter, we introduce the themes and focus of this collection.

A. Theorising Pseudolaw

In part I, contributors theorise pseudolaw as a distinct phenomenon. As the authors explain, pseudolaw is distinguishable from other alternative or conspiracy-minded approaches to law. Indeed, part of what makes pseudolaw unique is the fact that these arguments invariably lose while remaining so attractive to many people looking for legal solutions. A primary reason for this apparent paradox is that although pseudolaw is 'largely incoherent, if not incomprehensible'[48] to outsiders, from the internal perspective there are patterns and semi-coherence behind the impenetrable doctrines, instruments and rules.

First, let us consider the view from the outside. To the casual eye, the style of argument may be familiar. A litigant, ostensibly making legal claims, appears to have 'misread, misconstrue[d], and misunderst[ood]' the law.[49] On closer inspection, however, the situation is different. The litigant has not only relied on 'selective and spurious readings of legal texts to contest state authority' and asserted their own personal claims but has drawn from an impressive and eclectic breadth of sources.[50] They have invoked ancient, historical and international legal instruments like the United States Constitution, Magna Carta, the 1688 English Bill of Rights, the United Nations Declaration on Human Rights, the Bible,[51] divine law, God's law and, of course, the 'true' Common Law.[52] They may also have cited

[48] *R v Sweet* [2021] QDC 216 (6 September 2021) [3].

[49] C Kalinowski IV , 'A Legal Response to the Sovereign Citizen Movement' (2019) 80 *Montana Law Review* 153, 154.

[50] H Hobbs and G Williams, *Micronations and the Search for Sovereignty* (Cambridge University Press, 2022) 69.

[51] *Norman* (n 44) [4] (Judd J); *Zeqaj v Deputy Commissioner of Taxation* [2020] FCA 1270 (4 September 2020); *R v Warman* (2001) BCCA 510 [9] (Hollinrake J).

[52] See *Smith v Keenan* [2022] NZHC 618 [26].

select quotes from a range of statutes, case law and even statements from political leaders. While elements of these instruments may have uses in contemporary legal systems,[53] the litigant has not properly invoked those laws as authority for their claims.

The legal theory underpinning these positions makes little sense to those of us who work within and study state law. While pseudolaw adherents adopt 'legal or legal-sounding language' and their submissions 'appear[] to be law, or related to law' they are not comprehensible to trained lawyers.[54] For this reason, pseudolegal claims are regularly described by courts as 'utterly unsubstantial',[55] and nothing more than 'obvious nonsense',[56] legal 'gibberish'[57] or 'gobbledygook'.[58] It is *pseudo*law because it is obviously not-law, or at least, not-state law. However, for adherents – for those operating within this *nomos* – the movement has an internal coherence. Pseudolaw is not just a misunderstood and misapplied collection of doctrines, instruments and rules. As the authors in part I of this collection explain, pseudolaw constitutes an 'integrated and separate legal apparatus',[59] with its own confounding legal theories. Although much of the source material is originally drawn from conventional law and legal sources, in some circumstances it constitutes a separate, 'parallel world of law'.[60] It is this quality that ensures the transmission and maintenance of pseudolaw.

On our understanding, pseudolaw has three components and can be understood in several ways.[61]

The first component of pseudolaw is that it *coopts the form of more accepted legal argument*. Pseudolaw borrows legal *language* and the *form* of state and international legal argument to appear like accepted legal reasoning.[62] Superficially, the arguments are made in a way that reflects traditional legal methods. Pseudolaw litigants will rely upon statutes and judicial decisions to provide a source-based form of reasoning[63] that, to the untrained eye, appears to mirror 'normal' legal argumentation. As Glen Cash notes, 'ritual and ceremony have long been at the

[53] See eg *Ellis v R* [2011] NZCA 90 (23 March 2011) fn 29. It explains that portions of the Magna Carta apply in Aotearoa New Zealand by virtue of the Imperial Laws Application Act 1988, s 3.

[54] DJ Netolitzky, 'Lawyers and Court Representation of Organized Pseudolegal Commercial Argument [OPCA] Litigants in Canada' (2018) 51 *UBC Law Review* 419, 420.

[55] *Ngola Mbandi v Pangea Ventures*, 2023 WL 4486703 (7th Cir 2023).

[56] *Bradley v The Crown* [2020] QCA 252 (13 November 2020) (Sofronoff P).

[57] *Meads* (n 42) [40].

[58] *Deputy Commissioner of Taxation v Casley* [2017] WASC 161 [15] (Le Miere J).

[59] DJ Netolitzky, 'A Rebellion of Furious Paper: Pseudolaw as a Revolutionary System' (Paper delivered to the Centre d'expertise et de formation sur les intégrismes religieux et la radicalisation (CEFIR) symposium: 'Sovereign Citizens in Canada', Montreal, 3 May 2018) 4; DJ Netolitzky, 'After the Hammer: Six Years of *Meads v. Meads*' (2019) 56 *Alberta Law Review* 1167, 1184.

[60] S Koniak, 'When Law Risks Madness' (1996) 8 *Cardozo Studies in Law and Literature* 65, 67.

[61] For a more fulsome exposition of this conceptual definition of pseudolaw, see Hobbs, Young and McIntyre (n 19) 309.

[62] Netolitzky, 'A Rebellion of Furious Paper' (n 59).

[63] On the nature of 'source based' reasoning in law, see J McIntyre, *The Judicial Function: Fundamental Principals of Contemporary* Judging (Springer, 2019) 104.

heart of pseudolaw ideology',[64] and to a large extent that ritual follows the *form* of mainstream legal methods. Because it employs some formal rituals of mainstream legality, pseudolaw raises unique challenges for judicial systems. For instance, it is not immediately clear how pseudolaw differs from novel argumentation developed from precedent or simple incorrect assertions of the law.

In chapter two, Jonathan Crowe explores this tension by distinguishing pseudolaw from two other legitimate but often overlooked forms of law. As Crowe explains, pseudolaw is dangerous, in part, because it is easily confused with phenomena that play an important role in legal processes: folk law and natural law. Crowe explicates the concepts of folk law and natural law, including their relationship to positive law and their place in legal and administrative decision-making. In doing so, he distinguishes these concepts from pseudolaw, while also explaining why they are often misleadingly cited in pseudolegal discourse. Crowe argues that folk law and natural law, properly understood, are crucial components of social cohesion and the rule of law. Contrarily, pseudolaw is harmful because it obscures and distorts the proper task of these notions in supplementing positive legal enactments.

The second component of pseudolaw is that it involves *contra-narratives that justify alternative, non-orthodox views of law*. To understand why pseudolaw differs from mere novel arguments, it is necessary to appreciate that pseudolaw aims to provide substituting contra-narratives that create an alternative substantive normative legal universe. When analysed from an internal perspective, pseudolaw does not engage with the substantive norms, principles or methods of domestic or international legal reasoning. Instead, pseudolaw relies on its own substantive norms and principles that underlie arguments in a given discrete case. Donald Netolitzky has, for example, identified six core concepts which he argues lie at the heart of the 'pseudolaw memeplex'[65] – the most significant of which is the 'strawman duality'. The core distinction between novel legal arguments and pseudolegal arguments is that the former occurs within the 'conventional legal universe' of substantive coherent norms, while the latter occurs within a parallel 'alternate legal universe'[66] consisting of fundamentally distinct substantive norms. The two approaches bear a superficial similarity, and it may not be possible to draw a clear line between them given the common forms and language. However, the underlying substance is wholly divergent.

In chapter three, Maria O'Sullivan demonstrates this component in her analysis of the use of pseudolaw by members of the anti-vaccination movement in Australia during the COVID-19 pandemic. In exploring legal challenges to vaccine mandates, O'Sullivan seeks to distinguish between litigants who adopted pseudolegal claims and those who misunderstood the remit of actual laws.

[64] G Cash, 'A Kind of Magic: The Origins and Culture of "Pseudolaw"' Paper delivered to the Queensland Magistrates' State Conference 2022, Brisbane (26 May 2022) 9.

[65] Netolitzky, 'A Rebellion of Furious Paper' (n 59).

[66] McRoberts (n 35) 642.

The proliferation of false and misleading claims during the pandemic hampered vaccine take-up rates in many countries. O'Sullivan argues that this demonstrates the need to establish a demarcation between 'pseudolaw' and 'misinterpretation of the law', because that difference determines whether the state should intervene and to what degree. She concludes by providing a framework for defining pseudolaw and how to address it in the context of public health measures.

The third component of pseudolaw is that it involves internalised belief. Pseudolaw adherents seem to genuinely believe that they are upholding the *true law*. In a sense, believers possess an almost endearing commitment to legality and the rule of law. As Chief Justice Quinlan of the Western Australian Supreme Court has observed:

> Significantly, and in something of a paradox, the sovereign citizen almost always has a fervent belief in the importance of the 'rule of law' as they see it. Indeed, the sovereign citizen is deeply committed to the rule of law. It is simply that the 'law' for them happens to be the idiosyncratic subjective opinions that they hold.[67]

For the believer, it is the mainstream law that has departed from that 'legal truth', and they possess the single correct legal answer or approach – a type of legal Protestantism. However, these arguments are, to those with any modicum of understanding of the legal system, entirely without foundation.[68] In a recent case before the High Court of Australia, Justice Edelman identified the hypothetical sovereign citizen litigant as one who would argue by 'genuinely and honestly raising a claim that is utterly hopeless'.[69] This element helps explain the attractiveness of pseudolaw: it allows adherents to simultaneously disregard existing legal norms and disempower state actors, while retaining a self-conception of lawfulness and righteousness.

The notion that pseudolaw recalls a past true and lawful state of community is explored by Bruce Baer-Arnold in chapter four. Baer-Arnold employs literary techniques to draw attention to four perspectives on pseudolaw that may be commonly missed by treating the social phenomenon as simply anti-government 'sovereign citizens'. He argues that pseudolaw is an attempt at realising utopia; that adherents graze among legality as though it is a smorgasbord, selecting and discarding authorities to fit their whims and fancies; that those authorities they select – particularly archaic sources – involve myths, magic and mystification that seek to transcend quotidian processes; and, lastly, that adherents are more likely engaging in a type of rights-talk rather than engaging in revolutionary or terrorist actions. This indicates, for Baer-Arnold, that there are ways of dispelling these myths and strengthening faith in state institutions.

These three components together help to distinguish pseudolaw from other fringe law and law adjacent movements. While conspiracy theorists tend to have

[67] P Quinlan, 'The Rule of Law in a Social Media Age: Sir Francis Burt Oration 2022' (3 November 2022) 18.

[68] *Sill v City of Wodonga* [2018] VSCA 195 (8 August 2018).

[69] *Citta Hobart Pty Ltd & Anor v Cawthorn* [2022] HCATrans 1 (8 February 2022).

a strong internalised belief and a clear contra-narrative, such argumentation lacks the coopting of legal forms common to pseudolaw. In a similar way, pseudolaw can be distinguished from the well-intentioned but misinformed litigant in person who attempts to utilise legal forms and structures but, without the requisite legal training, creates arguments that are substantively nonsense. Such a litigant may believe in their argument and may (to their eyes) be using the appropriate forms and structure, but they do not have the contra-narrative of the pseudolaw adherent. We can also conceive of the *mala fides* actor who adopts the forms of legal argumentation with the content of a contra-narrative to undermine judicial proceedings – out of anger, nihilism or despair. While it may be appealing to place all pseudolaw adherents in this category, pseudolaw adherents are not necessarily bad faith actors trying to destroy or undermine the legal system (though of course, some may be). Rather, many seem deeply misguided in their attempts to restore the 'true law' from a misguided or corrupt modern interpretation.

Elsewhere Kate Leader has explored this tension by highlighting the prevalence of conspiracy theories amongst litigants in persons – including the use of fake judicial templates, accusations of shadowy Freemasons and other cults infiltrating the judiciary, and antisemitic conspiracies.[70] In chapter five Leader examines the roles that lay persons play in legal proceedings and how conspiracist thinking can be developed or aggravated. Drawing on acting theory, Leader argues legal actors are trained to perform in a natural way that appears as though they are not performing. This legal naturalism conceals modes and norms of legal practice that results in separating those who are able to participate (advocates and other legal professionals) from those who lack the skills and training to do so (laypersons). As a result, people without legal training are unable to effectively perform law and are simultaneously derided for their poor performance. Meanwhile, advocates are ambivalent or reluctant to admit that they are performers and law is performative. Because legal actors play these roles without having to articulate or recognise their performances as performances, lay parties who mimic the legal performances and naturalism also mimic the concealed aspects. They observe and then claim to uphold truer, secretive bases for their performances. From a performative perspective, adherents believe they are enacting law correctly, while established legal institutions name 'pseudolaw' as an excluded other.

B. The Operation and Practice of Pseudolaw Around the Globe

In part II, contributors turn their attention to the practice of pseudolaw in select jurisdictions, drilling down into specific movements and manifestations of the

[70] K Leader, 'Conspiracy! Or When Bad Things Happen to Good Litigants in Person' (2024) *Legal Studies*, DOI: https://doi.org/10.1017/lst.2024.18, 1–21.

phenomenon. The pseudolaw movement has been thrust into the mainstream, especially during the COVID-19 pandemic. While many people who engage in pseudolaw are often identified as 'sovereign citizens' – and it appears there is some rhetorical currency in that label – many are not. It is important to note that the sovereign citizen movement is just one that employs pseudolaw.[71] The branches of that broader pseudolaw tree have not been comprehensively examined but seem to include sovereign citizens, freemen-on-the-land, micronations, the 'Detaxers', 'Moorish sovereign citizens', certain species of anti-vaxxers and the anti-tax protestor movement.[72] Other, similar groups exist.

There should be no doubt, though, that currently the most prominent pseudolegal group is the sovereign citizen movement. Sovereign citizens are a group of loosely affiliated individuals who are connected by a shared antagonism towards government and a convoluted and conspiratorial interpretation of the law.[73] Self-identifying 'sovereign citizens' – alongside those that disclaim this terminology[74] – believe that they possess an uncorrupted and true understanding of the legal system: individuals are 'sovereign' and not bound by the laws of the country in which they live unless they waive those rights by accepting a contract with the government. Similar to conspiracy theory ideation with which it shares much in common, the sovereign citizen movement is decentralised and somewhat amorphous: there is no single leader, central catechism or consolidated collection of documents.[75] There is, however, a shared common set of beliefs as to the capacity of the individual to utilise certain legal forms and language to allow themselves to lawfully avoid the application of state law. For example, there is a common belief that by reciting certain phrases (such as 'I am a living being' or 'I do not consent') they *lawfully* avoid any obligation to obey laws and regulations. These phrases purport to deploy a talisman of legal immunity – like a cross presented to a vampire, state actors melt away, immunising the bearer from the need to wear masks, to pay taxes or to hold a driver's licence.[76]

In chapter six, Stephen Young, Harry Hobbs and Rachel Goldwasser document the emergence, origins and growth of sovereign citizen pseudolaw from within the United States. As they explain, the modern phenomenon of pseudolaw – at least the sovereign citizen version – arose out of a confluence of political and religious

[71] DJ Netolitzky, 'A Pathogen Astride the Minds of Men: The Epidemiological History of Pseudolaw' Paper delivered to the Centre d'expertise et de formation sur les intégrismes religieux et la radicalisation (CEFIR) symposium: 'Sovereign Citizens in Canada', Montreal (3 May 2018); Cash (n 64) 6.

[72] For an exploration of various pseudolegal movements in Canada see *Meads* (n 42) [168]–[198].

[73] For more on the sovereign citizen movement, see Hobbs and Williams (n 50) 65–72; F Sullivan, 'The "Usurping Octopus of Jurisdictional Authority": The Legal Theories of the Sovereign Citizen Movement' (1999) 4 *Wisconsin Law Review* 785, 786; J Evans, 'The "Flesh and Blood" Defense' (2012) 53 *William and Mary Quarterly* 1361; J Weir, 'Sovereign Citizens: A Reasoned Response to the Madness' (2015) 19 *Lewis & Clark Law Review* 829; Kalinowski IV (n 49); Koniak (n 60).

[74] Former adherent and now prominent scholar of the pseudolaw phenomenon, Rob Sudy, notes that from within their normative universe, the term 'sovereign citizen' is an oxymoron, because a 'citizen' is a slave of the corporate government. We thank Rob for this valuable insight.

[75] Kalinowski IV (n 49) 155.

[76] Netolitzky (n 71) 15. We thank Donald Netolitzky for this vibrant metaphor.

extremist associations that percolated throughout North America across the twentieth century. While many organisations and individuals contributed to the development of the central tenets and tactics of the movement, three groups stand out. The first is the Posse Comitatus, a loosely organised anti-government militia which spread conspiratorial, racist and antisemitic views across the United States from the 1970s. Over the following years, two organisations branched out of the Posse. Those interested in developing and articulating a legal theory that justified their anti-institutional views coalesced into the Common Law Movement, while others, militia members, sought to build a modern anti-government association, which came to be known as the Patriot Movement. By the 1990s, modern sovereign citizen tropes and views were visible. All that was left was for the movement to go global.

Sovereign citizen pseudolaw was introduced to Canada in the early 2000s. Led by anti-tax protestors and anti-authority freemen-on-the-land, the movement failed to gain much traction. After repeated court failures and public rejection, first-generation pseudolaw movements went extinct, and by the mid-2010s, Canadian social and litigation pseudolaw activity was negligible. However, since 2015, pseudolaw has re-emerged in Canada. In chapter seven, Donald Netolitzky examines how this ideology has adapted in form and audience. Nevertheless, as he explains, pseudolaw remains on the fringes of a fringe, with most modern Canadian pseudolaw adherents' marginal persons embedded in a fantastical alternative-reality conspiratorial space. While pseudolaw has grown in Australia and elsewhere, Netolitzky argues that second wave pseudolaw has made no headway in Canada, thanks to highly informed government and court structures, and well-developed case law. Other jurisdictions should take notice.

Autochthonous versions of pseudolaw have existed for decades in Australia, but the sovereign citizen variant emerged around the time of the Global Financial Crisis in the mid-to-late 2000s. Studies of pseudolaw remain rare in Australia,[77] but contributors in chapters eight and nine seek to rectify this lacuna. In chapter eight, Queensland District Court Judge Glen Cash provides an engaging overview of the culture and argument of pseudolaw and its presence in Australia. Drawing on his own interactions with litigants in court, Cash presents a valuable perspective from the judiciary. His conclusion offers sobering reading; Cash suggests that even though pseudolaw does not work for litigants, we should expect it to continue to spread.

In the following chapter, Marilyn McMahon expands the focal point beyond Queensland. McMahon presents the findings of an empirical review of reported cases in Australia between 2014 and 2023 in which sovereign citizen litigants appeared. In specifically reviewing cases brought, or defended, by sovereign citizens in Australian courts, McMahon identifies common features or tics and relates

[77] *cf* Hobbs, Young and McIntyre (n 19). See also the comprehensive overview developed by former pseudolaw adherent Rob Sudy: R Sudy, 'Australian Pseudolaw Argumentation' (2023), freemandelusion.com/2023/01/08/australian-pseudolaw-argumentation/.

these to the ideology espoused by this group. Her analysis suggests that sovereign citizens are relatively indifferent to the lack of success of their litigation because its primary function is performative and political: courtrooms have become a key public location in which sovereign citizens present their political beliefs. This reality should inform the development of responses.

Pseudolaw and sovereign citizens are not only a creature of the common law English-speaking world. As we have noted, a small but significant number of Germans are members of right-wing organisations such as the Reichsbürger movement. What they all have in common is that they justify resistance to law enforcement as necessary and lawful according to a 'true' understanding of the law. In chapter ten, Anna Löbbert investigates the legal arguments that German sovereign citizens make, based on a review of 250 published judgments. Drawing on interviews with adherents as well as her observation of their interactions with the state, Löbbert argues persuasively that in deciding on coping strategies, legal professionals should look beyond the 'smooth running' of legal processes and consider what motivates sovereign citizen behaviour.

C. Emerging Areas and Issues Involving Pseudolaw

Finally, in part III, the contributors seek to identify emerging areas and novel issues involving pseudolaw. Whereas previous chapters demonstrate that the internationalisation of sovereign citizen-inspired pseudolaw and the growth of the phenomenon manifests differently across jurisdictions, contributors in this part invite us to consider the near future of pseudolaw. The study of pseudolaw is a rapidly developing domain; focus on emergent themes and issues can help anticipate how manifestations may evolve over time.

This swift response of pseudolaw to changing environmental conditions – both in its form and its prevalence – has been evident in the last five years with COVID-19, which provided an opportunity for gurus to spread their teachings on pseudolaw. But this is only one example of evolutionary morphology. Pseudolaw is highly agile and can adapt in light of different contexts and pressures. These include the impact of websites to disseminate claims (such as that anyone can avoid traffic laws), the intersection of Indigenous sovereignty and pseudolaw, and the melding of sovereign citizen beliefs with far-right groups, like My Place in Australia, dedicated to political and ideological action.

Given the amorphous nature of the sovereign citizen movement, groups and individuals relate to and borrow from each other and other anti-government associations. Organisations are also fluid. New groups emerge rapidly, promising freedom from the state, before faltering and disappearing when enough supporters recognise their assurances are ineffective. In chapter eleven, Christine Sarteschi describes one novel, substantial sovereign citizen group in the United States – the American State Nationals (ASNs). Though this group does not consider themselves to be sovereign citizens, they express ideas and tactics that are very similar to those in the movement. Sarteschi focuses on the leaders of the ASN, their strategies for gaining new members, their occasional intermixing of sovereign citizen ideas with QAnon ideology, and their attempts to spread to Canada. She also examines the group's pseudolegal tactics, strategies and beliefs. This chapter is a critical window into how pseudolaw adapts and evolves over time to attract new adherents.

Former Australian Magistrate David Heilpern undertakes a similar study of Australian pseudolaw practitioners. One of the main draws and profit-making arms of the Australian pseudolegal movement is the promise of successfully defending traffic fines. Sites like Aussie Speeding Fines and Know Your Rights profit from these claims and provide 'evidence' for their success with reference to victories in court. In chapter twelve, Heilpern draws on his own experiences as a magistrate to share his analysis of these claims. Unsurprisingly, he finds that all the claimed successes are fictional, deceptive, misdescribed or false. Any claims that sovereign citizen arguments have succeeded in traffic matters in court is incorrect. Given the interaction with traffic law appears to be the start of many adherents interest in pseudolaw, Heilpern concludes with a call for Australian consumer protection authorities to act.

Pseudolaw causes harm to individuals and community, but not all harms are felt in the same manner. One of the more problematic harms occurs where pseudolaw exploits Indigenous rights claims. Indigenous peoples' right to sovereignty is grounded in their status as distinct political communities composed of individuals united by identity and a long history of operating as a distinct society, with a unique economic, religious and spiritual relationship to their land. This right is recognised in international law and also the law of some states, such as the United States of America. Pseudolegal actors have little interest in furthering or supporting Indigenous rights claims, but there is evidence of increasing interconnection and exploitation of Indigenous claims. In chapter thirteen, Colin McRoberts examines the case of a prominent non-Indigenous COVID-19 sceptic who claims to be practising medicine under the First Nations Medical Board, purportedly itself under the auspices of the Crow Tribe (a sovereign Indigenous nation). As McRoberts notes, pseudolaw adherents have taken advantage of a complex and often under-enforced regulatory action, enabling them to fall through legal cracks and avoid the application of both United States federal and state laws. These actions not only diminish the dignity and respect of the Crow Nation but have the potential to endanger patients unwittingly caught up in these scams.

The growth of pseudolaw may indicate broader socio-economic challenges. Navigating a legal dispute without some form of expert advice and assistance is a daunting task. While lawyers are intended to perform this role, space has been left open for non-lawyer advocates to operate in many judicial systems. In chapter fourteen, Bridgette Toy-Cronin explores two common forms of non-lawyer assistants in New Zealand: McKenzie Friends and employment advocates. Unlike lawyers, who owe duties to the administration of justice and the rule of law, non-lawyer advocates are unregulated. This provides an opening for pseudolaw proponents to organise and represent other people in court, potentially creating an industry and further replication. Drawing on evidence about previous movements that have utilised non-lawyer advocates to spread their message, and analysing the current frameworks for non-lawyer advocates, Toy-Cronin considers the practical responses that are available to the courts.

Broad socio-economic challenges manifest in places other than courts. In chapter fifteen, Josh Roose examines how those who use pseudolaw, reject power and sovereignty and claim it for themselves because, for individual and sociological reasons, they are emotionally or psychologically vulnerable. While individuals may be disposed to certain beliefs, sociological factors, like the COVID-19 pandemic, play a critical role in accelerating the growth of sovereign citizen-like movements and the evolution of their ideologies in Australia. During the pandemic, members became highly active in propagating their message – and pseudolaw – over social media, refusing to follow lawful directions, slowing court processes and disrupting the business of local councils. Of most concern to Roose is the melding of sovereign citizen ideologies with conspiratorial and far right anti-government movements with strong violent potential, which is demonstrated in the Australian sovereign citizen group, My Place.

V. Final Thoughts

The forms and manifestations of pseudolaw are in flux. Nevertheless, as this collection demonstrates, underlying themes recur. Those who adopt pseudolaw seek empowerment to lawfully contravene government action, and (more odiously) to prey upon the vulnerabilities and desires of others to pursue personal profit in a legal and political system that often alienates the individual. Studying pseudolaw thus upholds a distorting mirror to law and society. This includes the ways the public understand and interact with the legal system and conspiratorial extremist thinking when individuals engage with the law.

The central ambition of this book is to argue that pseudolaw should be seen as a social phenomenon that demands study in its own right. While there have always been extreme forms of argumentation and behaviour, the social phenomenon described within this volume is not simply a collection of unrelated instances of misinformed citizens from around the globe. Rather, this book examines the common phenomenon underlying the discrete manifestations. It shows that there are benefits in approaching pseudolaw as a discrete phenomenon. It helps understand common pressures, themes and issues. We see that, whether it be the German Sovereignists, US American State Nationals, or MyPlace organisers in Australia, pseudolaw is a shared phenomenon.

This book investigates common themes, trends and concerns. We hope this helps anticipate potential evolutions and refine successful systemic responses. Moreover, it reveals the sheer scale and impact that pseudolaw is having on legal systems around the world. It consumes significant (and scarce) judicial resources, and places large burdens on police, local governments and other public agencies. It imposes substantial costs on adherents, in terms of lost opportunities and increased penalties. It creates a space for the unscrupulous to prey on the vulnerable. Perhaps most concerningly, at the extremes, it can empower those to feel justified in embracing violence.

The chapters in this book also indicate that pseudolaw did not emerge in isolation from law and government. Instead, pseudolaw grew within society and reflects law and society. In this way, it holds a mirror up to lawful society and invites us – practitioners, academics, judges and others – to critically examine our legal system, its institutions and operations. We often presuppose a distinction between law and pseudolaw but, even if there are differences, the distinction is murky. While pseudolaw is full of ritual, performative utterances of 'magical' incantations, and archaic references to obscure sources and texts, so is law. To those untrained (perhaps unindoctrinated) in traditional legal thinking, the line between the rituals of law and pseudolaw is not apparent. For these reasons, we believe that understanding pseudolaw invites a richer and more nuanced understanding of law. We also believe that the legal system has not been a passive participant in the emergence of pseudolaw. It has helped alienate some individuals and can help radicalise adherents. The rise of pseudolaw, then, should act as a catalyst to invite reflection and reform of our legal systems, to democratise our judicial systems and increase accessibility.

PART I

Theorising Pseudolaw

2

Pseudolaw, Folk Law and Natural Law: How to Tell the Difference

JONATHAN CROWE*

I. Introduction

Pseudolaw presents false or distorted, but superficially plausible, claims about legal doctrine. It is a dangerous and costly social phenomenon, with the potential to undermine social cohesion and the rule of law. Pseudolaw is dangerous, in part, because it is easily confused with two other phenomena that play important and legitimate, albeit widely overlooked, roles in legal processes: folk law and natural law.

This chapter explicates the concepts of folk law and natural law, including their relationship to positive law and their place in legal decision-making. It distinguishes these concepts from pseudolaw, while also explaining why they tend to be conflated with it. I argue that folk law and natural law, properly understood, are crucial components of social cohesion and the rule of law; pseudolaw is harmful partly because it obscures and distorts the proper task of these notions in supplementing positive legal enactments.

The term 'law' is most commonly associated in popular discourse with positive law; that is, the law promulgated by public officials who are recognised as having authority by members of the community. Legislation, on this view, is law because it is authoritatively issued by the legislature; judicial decisions are law because they are authoritatively laid down by judges; and so forth. Pseudolaw makes false claims about the content of law; they are false, at least in part, because they do not track the content of the positive law – or do so in superficial or misleading ways. Folk law and natural law, too, do not necessarily correspond to positive law; this sometimes leads them to be dismissed as not really law at all. However, this is a mistake – or so I will argue. Pseudolaw is not law, but folk law and natural law are real and

* Head of School and Dean, School of Law and Justice, University of Southern Queensland; Honorary Adjunct Professor of Law, Bond University. Thanks to Anthony Gray, Harry Hobbs, Nick James, Joe McIntyre, Ian Wright and Steve Young for helpful feedback on earlier drafts.

legitimate kinds of law; indeed, they play a crucial role in upholding the integrity of the legal system.

This chapter begins by exploring two main reasons why pseudolaw is harmful. It imposes costs on the legal system, shifting resources away from meritorious claims, and it undermines law's role in social coordination. I look more closely at law's coordination function and examine precisely why pseudolaw undermines it. Law promotes social coherence because it is generally accepted throughout the community as a salient guide to action; pseudolaw threatens this salience by setting up a rival conception of legal content and seeking to legitimise it by reference to law's positive sources and means of enforcement. Its adherents will fail to do their share for the common good; more significantly, the widespread acceptance of pseudolaw, even if only within small communities, could undermine the integrity and effectiveness of the legal system as a whole.

I then turn to the notion of folk law. Folk law is the law as understood in popular thought and discourse; it corresponds, roughly, to the way that laypeople think and talk about their legal obligations. Folk law need not – and frequently does not – perfectly correspond to the positive law, but it nonetheless plays a necessary role in social coordination. Finally, I introduce natural law, which I define as 'a set of idealised normative inclinations characteristic of humans by virtue of their shared nature'.[1] Humans, I suggest, are naturally inclined to accept certain goods and principles that promote their flourishing. These goods and principles, like folk law, play an important role in social cohesion; they also hold normative legitimacy independently of their role in positive law. It would be both mistaken and harmful to allow our efforts to combat pseudolaw to undermine understanding and acceptance of these two notions.

II. Pseudolaw as a Harmful Social Phenomenon

Pseudolaw features superficially plausible but baseless claims about the content of law. Examples would include someone who claims that Magna Carta absolves them from paying taxes;[2] or that section 115 of the Australian Constitution prohibits the Government from issuing or accepting paper money.[3] These claims have a superficial appeal: after all, Magna Carta has something to do with taxes, and section 115 of the Constitution has something to do with money. However, they

[1] J Crowe, *Natural Law and the Nature of Law* (Cambridge University Press, 2019) 123.

[2] Or, even less plausibly, that it precludes the Parliament from passing gun control laws: *Essenberg v The Queen* [2000] HCATrans 385.

[3] See, for example, M Calligeros, 'It's the Constitution, No Bullion' *Brisbane Times* (10 May 2012), www.brisbanetimes.com.au/national/queensland/its-the-constitution-no-bullion-20120509-1ycw9.html: 'A Queensland driver has tried in vain to argue it is "impossible" for him to pay a speeding fine because the Australian constitution states the government can accept only coins made of gold or silver as payment for debts. … However, Supreme Court Justice Martin Daubney said the basis of Mr Clampett's argument "has long been discredited".' See also *Clampett v Hill* [2007] QCA 394.

are false, having no basis in the legal text or doctrine. These kinds of unfounded claims about law are widely accepted to be harmful for two main reasons. First, they are costly, diverting resources from more legitimate legal claims. And, second, they undermine social cohesion by spreading misinformation about what the law permits or requires.

It is useful to begin our present discussion by unpacking these problems in more detail. First, as to cost: the proponents of pseudolaw will often pursue their claims through litigation or by contesting administrative decisions, sometimes becoming serial vexatious litigants. Judges and administrative decision-makers must respond to these baseless claims, diverting time and resources from more legitimate matters. This increases the workload on decision-makers and adds to the already long wait times people face in having their cases determined.

Pseudolaw, however, is more than an administrative burden. It also undermines law's function in promoting social cohesion. I want to unpack this dimension in more detail. Social cohesion, as I have argued in detail elsewhere,[4] is an important component of human well-being. Human flourishing plausibly consists in participation in a range of goods that humans are inclined to pursue by their nature, such as life, health, friendship, pleasure and aesthetic experience.[5] However, people cannot simply partake in these goods on their own; they require coordinated community support to do so. This is for two reasons.

First, the goods themselves need a community context to define them.[6] What does it mean, after all, to pursue something as apparently amorphous as friendship or beauty? Humans have natural inclinations in this direction, but it is necessary to define what these values mean and what options are open for pursuing them. This is done by means of social practices. All human societies place some value on friendship, play, pleasure and beauty, but they conceptualise these values in substantially different ways. This then presents a range of options for their members to choose in seeking fulfilling lives.

Second, a stable and supportive social structure is needed if all members of a community are to be able to pursue the goods in a reasonable range of ways. I have discussed this topic elsewhere in terms of the idea of the common good.[7] The common good represents the interest all people have in living in a society where all the members can pursue human fulfilment. The common good, however, calls for social coordination; otherwise, people will just pursue the goods for themselves, and perhaps their friends and family, neglecting their duties to others. Conflicts will arise and many people will be unable to enjoy flourishing lives.

[4] Crowe (n 1) ch 4.

[5] ibid ch 2.

[6] ibid 36–39. See also J Crowe, 'Intelligibility, Practical Reason and the Common Good' in J Crowe and CY Lee (eds), *Research Handbook on Natural Law Theory* (Edward Elgar, 2019); J Crowe, 'The Evolution of Natural Law' in W Zaluski, S Bourgeois-Gironde and A Dyrda (eds), *Research Handbook on Legal Evolution* (Edward Elgar, 2024).

[7] Crowe (n 1) ch 4.

Social norms tend to arise as a way of coordinating social action to avoid this predicament. These norms may designate common rules to ensure everyone gets along; for example, people should refrain from attacking each other, respect each other's property, keep their promises and so on. Law plays an important role in this picture.[8] It supplies a mechanism for formalising the social rules so as to promote their coordination function. And it enables the resolution of matters of detail that might otherwise impede social harmony. How much tax should we pay? What side of the road should we drive on? Law can resolve these issues, avoiding needless disputes and ensuring essential social functions are performed.

Social norms, including law, solve problems of social coordination by providing salient solutions. A salient solution, roughly, is one that people prefer to follow in part because they expect that most others will follow it.[9] Law, if its content is generally agreed upon and respected, provides a reliable mechanism for generating salient norms. This power is open to abuse – it can be used to bootstrap unreasonable or inefficient norms into salience, thereby undermining the common good. However, if utilised effectively, it provides a powerful force for social welfare.

We are now in a position to return to pseudolaw. We have seen that law plays an important role in promoting the common good by designating salient solutions to social coordination problems. Law, to play this function well, must be reasonable, fair and efficient. Most fundamentally, however, it must be salient, otherwise it will fail in its basic function of coordinating social behaviour. Pseudolaw, by its nature, poses a threat to law's salience. It serves as a rival to law; worse, it does so by mimicking law's content and seeking to co-opt law's means of enforcement. Those who accept pseudolaw do so, at least in some cases, because they believe it to be law. They will cease to follow law and follow pseudolaw instead.

The result is that a segment of the community will defect from the legal norms that others accept and instead follow their own version of law. This threatens to fragment society and undermine agreed solutions to coordination problems. The taxation system, for example, provides a mechanism – albeit unjust and inefficient – for distributing social resources to ensure that less wealthy members of the community have access to the support they need to lead flourishing lives. Tax law tells us what counts as our share for contributing financially to the common good. However, if a segment of society thinks they do not have to pay taxes due to Magna Carta, then they will defect from this arrangement. They will fail to do their duty to society, unjustly increasing the burden on others; they may even, if their views spread widely enough, undermine the effectiveness of the system as a whole.

The problem is worsened by the individualistic character of pseudolaw. Adherents of pseudolaw often seem to believe that they can pick and choose which aspects of the law to follow. They may think that the law that others observe does

[8] ibid ch 10.

[9] C Bicchieri, *Norms in the Wild: How to Diagnose, Measure and Change Social Norms* (Oxford University Press, 2017) 19.

not apply to them, because they have spotted a loophole that others did not notice. Pseudolaw adherents also commonly maintain that all laws are a form of contract, so they can avoid the application of law by stating that they do not consent to be bound by it. The mindset behind this aspect of pseudolaw discourse is *atomistic* in Charles Taylor's sense;[10] it conceives of society as a constellation of self-sufficient individuals, rather than a community bound together by shared practices and values.

III. Folk Law in Opposition to Pseudolaw

I have focused so far in this chapter on unpacking why pseudolaw poses a threat to legal order. First, it imposes costs on the legal system, diverting much needed resources from more meritorious matters. Second, it undermines law's core function in promoting social coordination. Pseudolaw, for these reasons, is a harmful phenomenon; it should be identified and combated. Nevertheless, care is required in doing so. This is because there are two other phenomena in the vicinity of pseudolaw that could potentially be confused with it. Unlike pseudolaw, however, these phenomena are not harmful to legal order. They are, on the contrary, important components of the legal system that crucially aid its pursuit of the common good.

I will call the first of these phenomena *folk law*. Folk law is, roughly, the way people think and talk about law. The positive law, as discussed previously in this chapter, is the law contained in authoritative legal sources, such as statutes and judicial decisions. However, most people in society lack any direct knowledge of the content of legislation and judgments. The average person has never read a statute or studied a case; they would not know how to do so. Positive law nonetheless manages to guide social action. It does so because people have a rough understanding of what it requires. Positive law, in other words, guides action through the intermediary of folk law. Folk law is the law as understood by non-lawyers.

A. The Role of Folk Law in Securing Law's Coordination Function

Folk law plays a crucial role in securing law's coordination function. I explained in the previous section how law promotes the common good by solving coordination problems. I left the concept of law, for purposes of that discussion, undefined. It is tempting to think that it is the positive law that secures social coordination, but reflection shows that this cannot be the case. After all, as we have just seen,

[10] C Taylor, 'Atomism' in *Philosophy and the Human Sciences: Philosophical Papers 2* (Cambridge University Press, 1985).

most people have no direct knowledge of positive law, defined as the content of legislation, cases and the like. It is, I suggest, folk law, rather than positive law, that primarily discharges law's coordination function. People follow the folk law, which is their understanding of what positive law requires, not the positive law itself.

It is worth noting how the picture of legal coordination I have just outlined differs from the influential account of law as a social practice developed by HLA Hart. Hart famously contended that law is a set of social rules.[11] However, Hart was well aware that most people in society are tenuously acquainted with the positive law. He resolved this issue by arguing that law is a social practice, not of the community at large, but of the community of legal officials. It is legal officials, not citizens generally, who accept the law as conferring binding obligations; they do so because they accept the master rule of recognition as providing an authoritative test for legal validity.[12] Hart's theory can explain why legal officials apply the positive law, but it fails to fully explain how law guides social action more broadly.[13] Folk law helps fill this explanatory gap.

The idea that people's actions are guided by folk law, not positive law as such, has empirical support. One such study, which I co-authored with several collaborators,[14] examined the perceptions of law among participants in family dispute resolution. The study found that most people involved in family disputes gain their understandings of law from relatively informal sources, including online guides, word of mouth and popular culture. Relatively few people involved in such disputes will seek formal legal advice from lawyers; if they do, they do not necessarily find this advice helpful and may prefer to rely on other sources. The result is that family dispute resolution does not occur 'in the shadow of the (positive) law', as has sometimes been claimed; rather, it is more accurate to say that it occurs 'in the shadow of the folk law'.[15]

It is reasonable to think this picture applies not just to family disputes, but to legal disputes generally. People conduct themselves not in the shadow of the positive law, but in the shadow of the folk law; it is the folk law that informs their conception of what they owe legally to others (and what others owe legally to them). What, then, is the relationship of the folk law to the positive law? This is a crucial, but understudied, question. It is crucial, for our present purposes, due to its relevance in determining the relationship between folk law and pseudolaw. If folk law is just what people *think* law says, then how is it different from pseudolaw? Proponents of pseudolaw, after all, may sincerely believe that their claims accurately state the law.

[11] HLA Hart, *The Concept of Law*, 3rd edn (Clarendon Press, 2012) 56–57.

[12] ibid 94–95.

[13] For discussion, see J Crowe and L Agnew, 'Legal Obligation and Social Norms' (2020) 41 *Adelaide Law Review* 217.

[14] J Crowe et al, 'Bargaining in the Shadow of the Folk Law: Expanding the Concept of the Shadow of the Law in Family Dispute Resolution' (2018) 40 *Sydney Law Review* 319.

[15] ibid 335.

B. Distinguishing Folk Law from Pseudolaw

There are, I think, two critical points of distinction between folk law and pseudolaw. The first has to do with the relationship between these forms of law and positive law. Folk law tends to roughly mirror the content of positive law; pseudolaw, by contrast, has no foundation in positive law, although it may superficially appear to do so. This point is illustrated in the family law context by the notorious Alberta case of *Meads v Meads*.[16] Mr Meads, one of the parties in this case, relied upon the following unorthodox submissions:

> He purported to name the case management justice his fiduciary, unilaterally imposed a scheme of fines on anyone who would interact with him or use his name, and detailed a contract between himself (DENNIS LARRY MEADS) and himself (::Dennis-Larry: Meads::), which said Mr. 'Meads' could pay his spousal and child support obligations from Mr. 'MEADS'' $100 billion dollar public treasury bank account.[17]

These arguments, unlike the folk law understandings my collaborators and I observed in family dispute resolution, bear no resemblance to the positive law. Indeed, as Donald Netolitzky notes, they are essentially 'all nonsense'.[18]

What, then, ensures that folk law at least roughly corresponds to positive law – and therefore remains distinct from pseudolaw? The answer lies in formal legal processes. Non-lawyers will, from time to time, deal with lawyers (or legal officials); they will seek legal advice or be subject to formal decisions by police, judges or administrators. These formal processes bring non-lawyers into contact with the positive law; these encounters with positive law, in turn, filter into popular understandings. Furthermore, the stakes in formal legal processes are often high; this tends to ensure people take the information conveyed by them seriously.

It is worth noting here that folk law tends to be *responsive* to formal legal processes in a way that pseudolaw often is not.[19] Suppose a person holds a particular folk understanding of law, but it is then brought to their attention by a reliable source that this understanding does not, in fact, correspond to the positive law. It is likely that, confronted with this information, the person would modify their folk understanding accordingly. Pseudolaw adherents, by contrast, often do not modify their legal beliefs when it is pointed out to them that the positive law says differently. They may persist in believing that their pseudolegal convictions represent, in some sense, the *true* law, leading them to disregard traditional legal sources.

Actually, the picture is more complicated than this account indicates. I said a moment ago that when people are subject to formal legal processes, they encounter positive law. This is not quite right; they do not contact positive law directly, but rather positive law as interpreted by lawyers or legal officials. It is lawyers and

[16] 2012 ABQB 571.

[17] DJ Netolitzky, 'After the Hammer: Six Years of *Meads v Meads*' (2019) 56 *Alberta Law Review* 1167, 1167.

[18] ibid.

[19] Thanks to Nick James for drawing my attention to this point.

legal officials' understandings of positive law that informs the folk law and keeps it grounded in the positive law. However, lawyers and legal officials' understandings of positive law are themselves another more specialised form of folk law. We would expect these understandings to closely correspond to what the positive law actually says, but that correspondence may not be exact. Studies show that even judges sometimes apply their perceptions of law, rather than the law on the books.[20]

We can take this point further and say that positive law, strictly speaking, never guides action – not even in the case of legal officials. Positive law, in and of itself, is causally inert; it is, in the end, just words on paper. What guides action is the *beliefs* about positive law held by legal agents. (Strictly speaking, even beliefs by themselves cannot guide action; they require an accompanying motivation. We will return to this point later.) It is folk law, not positive law, then, that guides social coordination.

This brings us to the second point of distinction between folk law and pseudolaw. Folk law plays an important social coordination function; specifically, it plays that function that I loosely attributed to law in the first part of this chapter. Pseudolaw, however, plays no such role, because unlike folk law it is not salient across the community.

Recall that a standard is salient if people prefer to follow it because they believe most others will follow it. Folk law generally has this attribute, but pseudolaw does not. Some people may follow pseudolaw, but most people do not. Furthermore, even those people who follow pseudolaw do not generally believe it is salient; they do not believe most other people will also follow it. Indeed, adherents of pseudolaw often have the contrary attitude; they may be aware that their understanding of law differs from the general public, but they take pride in this, believing they have some special insight that others lack. They have taken the red pill; others are sheeplike, following the folk law like everyone else.

Some readers might worry that this criterion for distinguishing folk law from pseudolaw is too brittle, as it depends on the empirical question of how many people accept the interpretation in question. Couldn't pseudolaw become folk law, on the view I have outlined, if enough people believe in it? The answer, I think, is yes – and this highlights another kind of danger that pseudolaw poses. If a large enough subgroup within the community comes to believe in pseudolaw, this could result in social fragmentation and undermine respect for law across the community. Susan Koniak's research illustrates this potential, showing how small communities within a larger state can come to share a common belief in particular forms of pseudolaw. These communities may have their own legal doctrines, courts and even militias.[21]

[20] For an example drawn from Australian criminal law, see HM Cockburn, 'The Impact of Introducing an Affirmative Model of Consent and Changes to the Defence of Mistake in Tasmanian Rape Trials' (PhD thesis, University of Tasmania, 2012) 199–204.

[21] S Koniak, 'When Law Risks Madness' (1996) 8 *Cardozo Studies in Law and Literature* 65, 65–67. See also S Koniak, 'The Chosen People in Our Wilderness' (1997) 95 *Michigan Law Review* 1761. See further S Young, H Hobbs and R Goldwasser, ch 6 in this volume.

Pseudolaw, in at least some cases, exhibits its own form of social coherence for those who follow it. The members of the kinds of communities described by Koniak do not see their shared standards as pseudolaw; for them, it is the true law, and may play a genuine coordinating function. Nonetheless, the coordinating role of these kinds of pseudolaw remains inherently limited; these norms may serve to resolve conflicts between adherents, but they will not facilitate conflict-resolution with the wider community, and indeed are more likely to cause or exacerbate conflicts between adherents and other citizens. If enough of the community comes to believe in pseudolaw, it could serve as an alternative locus of social coordination, undermining adherence to positive law and fragmenting society depending on which law people accept. This could happen, for example, if a demagogue and their followers urge acceptance of pseudolegal claims. And those who follow current events need not look far for examples of this danger.

IV. Natural Law in Opposition to Pseudolaw

I turn now to another phenomenon which could be confused with pseudolaw by the unwary: namely, natural law. Pseudolaw adherents regularly reference natural law in support of their arguments, which could lead some people to perceive natural law as a form of pseudolaw. However, this is not only mistaken, but counterproductive. A proper understanding of natural law helps reveal why pseudolaw is harmful, while also supplying legal decision-makers with valuable tools to counteract pseudolaw arguments.

By *natural law*, I mean, as I said at the beginning of this chapter, 'a set of idealised normative inclinations characteristic of humans by virtue of their shared nature'.[22] I have discussed each of the components of this definition in detail elsewhere. Normative inclinations involve two components: a disposition to *act* in a specific way and a disposition to *believe* that the action in question is worthwhile or required.[23] People have many kinds of normative inclinations, but there are some such inclinations that are widely shared by humans across diverse cultural contexts. These include, for example, the inclinations to pursue and value the human goods introduced earlier in this chapter. The existence of these shared normative inclinations can plausibly be explained by reference to facts about human nature.

I use the term *human nature* here to refer to a range of natural facts about humans (that is, the kinds of facts that can be analysed by the natural and social sciences). A narrow view of human nature might confine the concept to biological features of humans as a species. However, I have argued elsewhere for a wide view of human nature that encompasses facts about both human biology and the

[22] Crowe (n 1) 123.
[23] ibid 20.

natural and social environments of human communities.[24] Natural law, then, is a set of normative inclinations that are characteristic of humans by virtue of their shared nature; that is, by virtue of facts about their biology, and natural and social environments. Humans have evolved in such a way as to value and pursue goods such as health, friendship, pleasure and beauty. These values are not arbitrary; they are suitable for humans to pursue, due to their biological, social and ecological characteristics.

It might be objected that shared human normative inclinations are not limited to goods such as health and friendship. Humans across a range of cultural contexts also show less benign normative tendencies, such as the tendency to discriminate against out-group members.[25] This inclination, like the human goods described previously, is plausibly explained by reference to biological and social evolution. However, it is not conducive to a universal condition of human flourishing; rather, it seeks to prioritise the interests of some humans arbitrarily over others. It is for this reason that I have described natural law as 'a set of *idealised* normative inclinations'.[26] A theory of natural law must provide some method from distinguishing those inclinations that serve human flourishing from those that do not. The suggestion I have made elsewhere is that a theory of natural law attempts to capture those normative inclinations humans would hold under conditions of *full imaginative immersion*: that is, the normative inclinations we would hold if we were fully acquainted with their implications for both ourselves and others.[27]

The normative inclinations humans actually hold are not unrelated to natural law in this idealised sense. They can reasonably be viewed as an imperfect manifestation of natural law. This is because full imaginative immersion is modelled, albeit imperfectly, in various actual human decision-procedures and institutional environments.[28] Humans mirror imaginative immersion whenever they engage in moral reasoning; that is, when they reflect upon the impact of their decisions for themselves and others. Dispute resolution procedures mirror imaginative immersion when they seek to bring the interests of parties into dialogue and seek a resolution. And human societies mirror imaginative immersion when they draw upon evolved social norms to shape social practices and institutions, since these norms aggregate the experiences of a wide range of people over time. Each of these mechanisms is deeply flawed, but they tend to ensure that human inclinations are not wholly divorced from natural law in the idealised sense.

[24] J Crowe, 'Philosophical Challenges and Prospects for Natural Law Foundations of Human Rights' in T Angier, IT Benson and M Retter (eds), *The Cambridge Handbook of Natural Law and Human Rights* (Cambridge University Press, 2022).

[25] MB Brewer, 'In-Group Bias in the Minimal Intergroup Situation' (1979) 86 *Psychological Bulletin* 307; DM Taylor and JR Doria, 'Self-Serving and Group-Serving Bias in Attribution' (1981) 113 *Journal of Social Psychology* 201.

[26] Crowe (n 1) 123 (emphasis added).

[27] ibid 25–26.

[28] ibid 125. See also J Crowe, 'The Idea of Small Justice' (2021) 34 *Ratio Juris* 224.

A. The Role of Natural Law in Securing Law's Coordination Function

Natural law, like folk law, plays an important (but often overlooked) role in social coordination. I said earlier that folk law captures people's beliefs about the content of law. It is these beliefs, rather than the technical content of positive law, that guides people's actions. However, strictly speaking, as I noted previously, beliefs alone cannot motivate action. According to the widely accepted Humean picture of motivation, action requires a belief accompanied by an appropriate desire.[29] Suppose, for example, that I am about to go outside, but I look out the window and see it is raining. I therefore pick up an umbrella before heading out. What explains my decision to take the umbrella with me? One factor is clearly my belief that it is raining, along with the belief that the umbrella will keep the rain off. However, these beliefs alone cannot explain my action, unless coupled with a relevant desire – in this case, the desire to stay dry.

Folk law is what people believe the law to be. What motivates them to comply with it? This is a complex question. People obey the law to some extent because they fear punishment. However, this is at best a partial reason. Hart famously pointed out that the fear of sanctions doesn't adequately capture the sense of obligation people feel towards the law.[30] And empirical research backs Hart up: people don't follow the law merely because they feel forced to do so, but also substantially because they see law as a legitimate source of obligations.[31] What, then, makes people feel law is legitimate? Procedural factors are important; people are more likely to view law as legitimate if they feel heard through legal and democratic processes.[32] However, normative inclinations plausibly also play a role: people are more likely to regard law as legitimate if it resonates with their normative inclinations than if it does not.

Natural law is the normative inclinations that humans characteristically hold under ideal conditions. Actual conditions, as we have seen, mirror ideal conditions to some extent. This suggests that a law that resonates with natural law will be more likely, other things being equal, to win adherence than one that does not. Natural law, in the sense of people's inherent inclination to pursue what is good and right, plausibly plays a significant role in ensuring people's adherence to their legal obligations. It is by no means the only factor and its degree of influence will plausibly differ between legal systems, as well as over time. However, any comprehensive account of why people obey the law should take natural law into account.

[29] See M Smith, 'The Humean Theory of Motivation' (1987) 96 *Mind* 36.
[30] Hart (n 11) 82–91.
[31] TR Tyler, *Why People Obey the Law* (Princeton University Press, 2006) ch 5.
[32] ibid ch 6.

Natural law also plays a significant role in legal decision-making. Positive laws are often vague; it may not be clear how they apply to a specific case. I have argued elsewhere that the process of interpreting and applying the law is informed by the wider social context for the law, including social values.[33] These social values, in turn, are shaped by natural law. Judges and other legal decision-makers, like people generally, possess normative inclinations. These normative inclinations will guide their decisions, particularly in cases where the law is unclear. The normative inclinations of judges, for the reasons explored previously, will at least partly reflect natural law. Indeed, the institutional role of the judge includes desiderata, such as impartiality and reflectiveness, that approximate the idealised conditions for forming normative inclinations. This reinforces the likelihood that legal decisions will be guided by natural law.

B. Distinguishing Natural Law from Pseudolaw

Natural law, then, is an important constituent of both social coordination and legal decision-making. It should not be confused with pseudolaw. Unfortunately, as noted previously, proponents of pseudolaw sometimes appeal to natural law, either expressly or implicitly, to support their arguments. So-called sovereign citizens, for example, may claim that they are natural persons with natural rights that cannot be extinguished by law.[34] This rhetoric is somewhat redolent of natural law ideas (although the natural law and natural rights traditions are importantly distinct).[35] However, the natural law tradition, properly understood, gives no basis for the claims of sovereign citizens not to be subjected to the ordinary laws of society. Rather, natural law thinkers have traditionally emphasised the importance of social coordination as discussed previously in this chapter, as well as the role of shared legal rules in achieving this.

Natural law, in the sense of shared normative inclinations, is a crucial driver of social coherence, rather than being opposed to it. It ensures that humans have a shared set of motivations, transcending specific political or legal disputes, that enable them to cooperate and promote the common good. It provides people with a motivation to follow the law, at least when the obligations it imposes are reasonable. And it supplies judges and other decision-makers with a crucial tool in ensuring that interpretation and application of law is not only reasonable, but broadly acceptable to the community. Pseudolaw, as emphasised previously, needs to be clearly rejected, but this does not entail discarding appeals to natural law in

[33] Crowe (n 1) ch 11. See also J Crowe, 'The Narrative Model of Constitutional Implications: A Defence of *Roach v Electoral Commissioner*' (2019) 42 *University of New South Wales Law Journal* 91.

[34] See, for example, *R v Sweet* [2021] QDC 216.

[35] See J Crowe, 'Human Rights in the Natural Law Tradition' in JD Rooney and P Zoll (eds), *Freedom and the Good: Beyond Classical Liberalism* (Routledge, 2024).

social, political or legal contexts. Indeed, natural law, with its emphasis on shared values and coordination through law, provides a strong foundation to challenge the pseudolegal mindset.

V. Conclusion

I began this chapter by unpacking the dangers of pseudolaw in terms of both cost and social coordination. Pseudolaw wastes resources that could otherwise be devoted to resolving legitimate legal claims. More fundamentally, it threatens social coordination by undermining law's function in supplying salient rules. This discussion of law's coordination function then paved the way for the subsequent discussions of folk law and natural law – each of which plays a crucial role in guiding social behaviour. Folk law, I argued, is the law as understood by the general public; it is folk law, rather than positive law as such, which grounds law-abiding conduct. Natural law, on the other hand, is the natural inclinations people have to honour certain values, principles and virtues. It helps motivate people to follow the law, as well as guiding people towards shared and reasonable interpretations of legal materials.

Pseudolaw, for the reasons outlined in this chapter, is a dangerous force in society. It is tempting to respond to pseudolaw through a retreat to positive law. Pseudolaw is wrong, on this view, because it does not correspond to the law on the books; if everyone just follows the positive law, things will be alright. However, this is a mistake. It is not the positive law, but rather folk law and natural law, that primarily guide social action. The most potent response to pseudolaw lies not in legalism, but in fostering a robust culture of respect for shared practices and norms of behaviour. It is in nobody's genuine interests for segments of society to defect arbitrarily from shared understandings of what law requires. Those who advocate such defections should be called out for what they are – not merely disruptors of the positive law, but opponents of the common good. And if the defectors were able to seize control of government institutions, as could conceivably happen, this would not necessarily make their actions legal. Positive law may then become pseudolaw – and folk law and natural law would provide the means to resist it.[36]

How, then, can we effectively resist pseudolaw and foster a robust culture of respect for shared practices and norms? This is a complex question and a full answer lies beyond the scope of this chapter. It is easier to say in general terms what we need to avoid. Pseudolaw adherents often seem to be motivated to defect

[36] For further discussion, see J Crowe, 'Natural Law and Authoritarianism' in R Nate, M Trajkovic and M Egan, *Perspectives on Authoritarianism and Totalitarianism from Literature, Philosophy, Law and History* (Königshausen and Neumann, 2025) (forthcoming).

from community ideas of law due to some personal or group crisis, trauma or sense of exclusion. Therefore, if we wish to discourage resort to pseudolaw in these circumstances, we need to take responsibility as a community for supporting individuals and groups in crisis and seek to include those at the margins. Governments and politicians should avoid the temptation to marginalise or scapegoat vulnerable groups and rather confront the hard work of returning them to the community fold. More broadly, community institutions should seek to foster social belonging, rather than encouraging fragmentation, adversarialism or an atomistic attitude. This prescription goes against contemporary political trends towards polarisation and in group thinking – but the future of law depends on it.

3

Pseudolaw and Legal Fictions: Vaccine Mandate Claims During the COVID-19 Pandemic and Future Implications

MARIA O'SULLIVAN

I. Introduction

The use of pseudolaw online, in courts and in other public fora represent a challenge *to the law* and *for the legal system*. Pseudolaw represents a challenge *to the law* because it requires us to interrogate the true meaning of 'authoritative' law. There is an assumption made in the discourse on the status of law that the ordinary law of the land made by parliament and courts is objective and legitimate and, in contrast, that pseudolaw is 'the other' – that it is imagined, nonsensical and illegitimate. Indeed, pseudolaw has been defined as involving falsity.[1] However, are there in fact clear truths and clear falsities in the law? Is the law truly objective?

Analysing pseudolaw requires placing it within the broader socio-political, economic and legal context in which it operates. As part of this, we must understand the nature of power and how law both utilises and perpetuates power structures within society. The language of law forms part of this power framework, and the very term 'pseudolaw' is emblematic of this. Following on from the question of power and law, one unanswered question is whether *states* can and do use pseudolaw. It is my contention that legal fictions can and have been used by states throughout history and 'real law' can be premised on incorrect and inaccurate foundations. Thus, I argue in this chapter that a defined demarcation between authoritative, state-made law on the one hand and pseudolaw, on the other, is not

[1] Leading pseudolaw scholar Donald J Netolitzky has defined pseudolaw as 'a collection of legal-sounding but false rules that purport to be law': DJ Netolitzky 'The Perfect Weed for this Spoiling Soil: The Ideology, Orientation, Organization, Cohesion, Social Control, and Deleterious Effects of Pseudolaw Social Constructs' (2023) 6 *International Journal of Coercion, Abuse, and Manipulation* 1, 2. The definitions used in this chapter are discussed further below at the text associated with nn 5–6.

sustainable. This is particularly so when one examines the types of legal fictions utilised by states. The delineation between pseudolaw and authoritative law is not clear.

Pseudolaw also represents a challenge *to the legal system* more broadly as its use by groups such as sovereign citizens can result in interference with the operation of courts and other public authorities.[2] Different forms of pseudolaw have been used for many years, but it appears to have increased recently, particularly as part of the rise of online conspiracy theories.[3] Thus, how pseudolaw is defined and how users of pseudolaw are treated by the legal system represent significant issues for social media regulation, court management processes and access to justice policies.

To interrogate the implications of pseudolaw, I analyse its use by members of the anti-vaccination movement during the COVID-19 pandemic. I identify and examine the differences between the use of pseudolaw claims (often marked by references to Magna Carta and the Nuremberg Code) and claims where the individuals misunderstood the remit of actual laws (such as claims that there is a right to conscientious objection to vaccination). This was an issue during the pandemic because some social media users claimed that public health measures imposed by governments violated Magna Carta and/or the Nuremberg Code on the basis that the vaccine was 'experimental'. These claims may have had significant consequences; studies revealed that these types of arguments hampered vaccine take-up rates in a number of countries.[4] However, other people who opposed the COVID-19 health measures did so on the basis of a *misinterpretation of the law* (for instance, that they could claim a conscientious objection to vaccines). How, then, should we demarcate 'pseudolaw' and 'misinterpretation of the law'? This is important because it may be that the state should intervene to limit dissemination of conspiracy theories based on pseudolaw (for example, by removing social media posts), but not if the statement merely reflects a person's misreading of authoritative, operative laws.

In terms of the definition of pseudolaw utilised in this chapter, my starting point is that propounded by leading international expert, Donald Netolitzky, whose work has been extensively cited in existing pseudolaw literature. For Netolitzky, pseudolaw refers to a phenomenon where 'a collection of legal-sounding but false rules that purport to be law'[5] are utilised; pseudolaw 'superficially appears to be

[2] For instance, councils and government departments. On the issue of the difficulties posed by pseudolaw for courts, see the insightful perspective of a judge of the Queensland District Court: G Cash, 'A Kind of Magic: The Origins and Culture of 'Pseudolaw' Paper delivered to the Queensland Magistrates' State Conference 2022 (26 May 2022), archive.sclqld.org.au/judgepub/2022/cash20220526.pdf. See also discussion in H Hobbs, S Young and J McIntyre, 'The Internationalisation of Pseudolaw: The Growth of Sovereign Citizen Arguments in Australia and Aotearoa New Zealand' (2024) 47 *University of New South Wales Law Journal* 309.

[3] Hobbs, Young and McIntyre (n 2) 309.

[4] See for example, SL Wilson and C Wiysonge, 'Social Media and Vaccine Hesitancy' (2020) *BMJ Global Health* 5:e004206.

[5] DJ Netolitzky, 'A Rebellion of Furious Paper: Pseudolaw as a Revolutionary System' Paper delivered to the Centre d'expertise et de formation sur les intégrismes religieux et la radicalisation (CEFIR)

law, or related to law, and usually uses legal or legal-sounding language, but is otherwise spurious'.[6] I accept these definitions but wish to unpack and analyse the classification of pseudolaw as 'false' and 'spurious'. As noted above, authoritative law can also be false or spurious. In this chapter, I use as an example the *terra nullius* doctrine which was applied to the settlement of Australia. This doctrine, which deemed Australia to be 'uninhabited', was based on a falsity. It was a legal fiction. How then does false *authoritative law* differ from pseudolaw? That is, can states use pseudolaw? States can and do. This reality dispels the notion that there is a bright line between pseudolaw and authoritative 'real' law.

In undertaking this analysis, it is important to recognise the alienation and polarisation of individuals in neoliberal states and the difficulties that many face in utilising the legal system and accessing justice. To incorporate these perspectives, I utilise theories relating to power and the lens of epistemic justice to tease out some of the ways in which users of pseudolaw may be seeking to use law as a means of recovering agency and power, and how classifying such uses as 'nonsense' by state authorities may itself be a disempowering act.

The chapter is divided into six sections. I commence in section II by setting out the conceptual framework of language, law and power which is necessary to meaningfully understand the phenomena and implications of pseudolaw. Here I introduce the legal theory frameworks which I use later in my analysis of pseudolaw – literature on law and power and epistemic justice. I then follow this with an examination of the use of pseudolaw by individuals and groups, with a focus on its application during the COVID-19 pandemic in section III. In this part, I do not analyse the forms of pseudolaw which are typically utilised by the sovereign citizen movement (such as claims that the government is illegitimate, and the use of archaic and misapplied symbols and insignia). Rather, my focus is on the manifestations of pseudolaw which emerged during the COVID-19 pandemic, such as claims that vaccine mandates were unlawful under Magna Carta and/or the Nuremberg Code. These will be contrasted to those claims where the individuals *misunderstood* the remit of actual laws (such as that there is a right to conscientious objection to vaccination). In section IV, I compare this to the use of legal fictions by states and query the 'falsity' of these tools. These examples provide the backdrop to section V, where I analyse pseudolaw in the context of power and epistemic justice. In the conclusion to this chapter in section VI, I bring these strands together to address the broader implications of regulating or limiting the

symposium: 'Sovereign Citizens in Canada', Montreal (3 May 2018) cited in Hobbs, Young and McIntyre (n 2) 312.

[6] DJ Netolitzky, 'Lawyers and Court Representation of Organized Pseudolegal Commercial Argument [OPCA] Litigants in Canada' (2018) 51 *University of British Columbia Law Review* 419, 420 cited in Hobbs, Young and McIntyre (n 2) 312. Specifically, Netolitzky states that: 'The rules that make up pseudolaw are framed like law, and use legal language but some of pseudolaw's rules diverge from, and are rejected by, conventional courts and legal systems. In many ways, pseudolaw is a variation on conventional, mainstream legal traditions, rather than a completely novel construct. To date, pseudolaw has grounded most of its rules and structure in a scheme that is recognizable as primarily derived from the historical UK-type "common law" tradition': Netolitzky (n 1) (citations omitted).

use of pseudolaw. I query whether these tools will lead to greater alienation of the alienated and suggest some ideas for future management of pseudolegal adherents.

Before commencing it is important to define the scope of this chapter. I am not revisiting the history of the development of pseudolaw as that has been dealt with comprehensively in existing literature and other chapters in this volume.[7] I also acknowledge that the use of pseudolaw raises a number of important related issues, such as the connection between pseudolegal believers with radicalisation and extremism, and the national security implications arising from that link. The use of pseudolaw by extremist anti-government groups has been identified as a concern by a number of commentators.[8] The security danger presented by this is demonstrated, for example, by the Reichsburger movement in Germany and the actions of Prince Reuss – a prominent sovereign citizen in Germany – who was arrested in 2022 for allegedly taking part in a plot to overthrow the German Government.[9] Whilst I acknowledge the role that alienation and polarisation in society has on the use of pseudolaw, and the implications of regulating its use, the national security implications are a complex issue which warrant a standalone analysis.[10] Thus, although I touch upon this in the conclusions to this chapter, I do not focus on counter-extremism issues in any depth in this paper.

II. Pseudolaw: Language, Law and Power

In order to fully understand and analyse pseudolaw, I wish to situate pseudolaw within its socio-economic context and to examine the broader economic and social push-factors behind the use of pseudolaw today. This is necessary given that the law is both a reflection of power and an instrument of power. As part of this, the language used in law is both an inclusionary and exclusionary tool – the correct language allows the user to be heard, while the incorrect results in exclusion. Applying an understanding of law, language and power to pseudolaw may therefore allow us to determine why it is being used and how legal institutions should respond.

In addressing this question, I should note that there is no clear empirical data on the sort of individuals who use pseudolaw and why they do so.[11] Nonetheless,

[7] See, for example, Netolitzky (n 1); Hobbs, Young and McIntyre (n 2); S Young, H Hobbs and R Goldwasser, ch 6 in this volume; DJ Netolitzky, ch7 in this volume; G Cash, ch 8 in this volume.

[8] See, for example, L Khalil, *Rise of the Extreme Right: The New Global Extremism and the Threat to Democracy* (Lowy Institute for International Policy and Penguin Books, 2022); C Sarteschi, 'Sovereign citizens: A narrative review with implications of violence towards law enforcement' (2021) 60 *Aggression & Violent Behavior* 101509.

[9] See E Campbell, 'How Germany's "Reichsbürger" Sovereign Citizens Movement Became a Threat to the State' ABC Foreign Correspondent (31 August 2023), www.abc.net.au/news/2023-08-31/germany-citizens-of-the-reich-foreign-correspondent/102789818.

[10] J Roose, ch 15 in this volume.

[11] BS Slater, 'Sovereign Citizen Movement: An Empirical Study on the Rise in Activity, Explanations of Growth, and Policy Prescriptions' MA in Security Studies Thesis, Naval Postgraduate School (September 2016), calhoun.nps.edu/bitstream/handle/10945/50485/16Sep_Slater_Brian.pdf.

anecdotal evidence and information gleaned from media reports and the policy and academic literature reflect some trends. First, there is a high usage of pseudolaw by members of the sovereign citizen movement. Whilst it is true that, typically, pseudolaw is used by sovereign citizens as a way of proclaiming their rights, pseudolaw is not only utilised by fringe movements.[12]

Second, the use of pseudolaw internationally has been employed by individuals from a broad range of backgrounds. At one end of the spectrum, Prince Reuss – a descendant of German nobility – has adopted pseudolaw by publicly stating that modern Germany does not exist.[13] Thus, pseudolaw does not appear to be *solely* the tool of the economically disadvantaged or politically disenfranchised.[14] Indeed, one US study on the contemporary sovereign citizen movement found that 'the movement operates broadly, across multiple ethnic and socio-economic backgrounds'.[15]

In Australia, the situation is more opaque. What is clear is that a majority of those using pseudolaw in court proceedings are self-represented.[16] Thus, one can surmise that at least a large cohort of pseudolaw users in the court system in Australia are not able to engage professional legal advice,[17] nor able to adequately represent themselves and therefore may be classified as coming from a certain level of social or economic disadvantage. As Queensland District Court Judge, Glen Cash observes:

> They are persons who feel they are disenfranchised or marginalised. They are in a position of relative disadvantage in society and pseudolaw presents an opportunity to take control. Pseudolaw is the 'inside knowledge' that permits the OPCA [organised pseudolegal commercial arguments] litigant to command a power kept secret from

[12] On this, see Samuel Barrows: 'Pseudolitigants are often confused with "sovereign citizens," and although there is substantial overlap between the groups, they are not one and the same. Sovereign citizens are merely one group of individuals who employ pseudolaw argumentation.': S Barrows, 'Sovereigns, Freemen, and Desperate Souls: Towards a Rigorous Understanding of Pseudolitigation Tactics in United States Courts' (2021) 62 *Boston College Law Review* 905, 908.

[13] Prince Reuss has stated that 'Ever since Germany surrendered it was never sovereign again'; 'Rather, it was an administrative entity of the Allies, the so-called Federal Republic of Germany, in other words, a corporation': Campbell (n 9). See further, M Müller, 'Germany's Growing Reichsbürger Movement' *Deutsche Welle* (8 May 2018), www.dw.com/en/germanys-reichsbürger-movement-out-to-delegitimize-the-state/a-43703824. In December 2022, Prince Reuss was arrested for allegedly taking part in a plot to overthrow the German Government.

[14] For instance, in the landmark pseudolaw case decided by the Alberta Court of Queen's Bench in Canada, Associate Chief Justice Rooke noted that: 'In this Court's experience, there are no stereotypic OPCA litigants. They may be of any age or gender. Some are affluent, while others are not. Canadian caselaw reports OPCA concepts advanced by professionals, 'blue collar' workers, business persons, and retired individuals. Some travel in groups, while others appear to operate by themselves': *Meads v Meads* 2012 ABQB 571 [159]. The Court did note, however, that pseudolaw gurus 'market OPCA schemes to their often desperate, ill-informed, mentally disturbed, or legally abusive customers' [77].

[15] Slater (n 11).

[16] S Kesteven and D Carrick, 'Magistrates Witness a "Sharp Rise" in Sovereign Citizen Cases Brought Before the Local Courts' ABC News (8 May 2023), www.abc.net.au/news/2023-05-08/nsw-magistrates-report-sharp-rise-in-sovereign-citizen-cases/102285772.

[17] Some may also simply wish not to utilise mainstream legal services as law firms may be seen as part of the 'system' or 'problem'.

> others. Such can drive some litigants into a fervent, if not febrile, pursuit of what they perceive as 'justice'.[18]

This is relevant, because pseudolaw (at least in part) is a tool of dissent, frustration or alienation by a sector of modern society. It is no coincidence that the rising use of pseudolaw coincides with evidence of greater economic inequality.[19] To understand pseudolaw then, it is vital to place it within the context of increasing inequality in many societies, increasing polarisation and social alienation, and the difficulties faced by persons who have a legal problem to obtain legal assistance to resolve it.[20] For many, access to power, to influence and to legal redress is increasingly difficult. Indeed, leading international pseudolaw scholars note that a core belief of those using pseudo in the courts is that state authority is defective or incomplete.[21]

The conceptual framework of power and law provided by the epistemic injustice literature provides a valuable means of understanding pseudolaw. Here, 'epistemic' relates to knowledge and the degree of its validation. Thus, epistemic resources form the ideas and language which individuals use to communicate their experiences and problems.

The theory of *epistemic injustice* as a specific doctrine was developed formally by Miranda Fricker in 2007 and has been adapted and refined by other scholars since. In introducing the concept, Fricker proposed that there is a distinctively epistemic kind of injustice and identified two types of epistemic injustice: 'testimonial injustice, in which someone is wronged in their capacity as a giver of knowledge; and hermeneutical injustice, in which someone is wronged in their capacity as a subject of social understanding'.[22] In the context of pseudolaw, testimonial epistemic injustice may occur when a court gives a low level of credibility to a claimant's narrative because the claimant uses the wrong words.

Katherine McDonnel provides a valuable definition of epistemic resources as follows:

> Epistemic resources shape law and policy. … they form both the pool of generally accepted ideas and the language to communicate those ideas and various social experiences. This influences how problems in societies are perceived and defined, and the policies and/or laws developed to address those problems. It provides the conceptual

[18] Cash (n 2) 15.

[19] See Z Qureshi, 'Rising Inequality: A Major Issue of our Time', Brookings Institute (16 May 2023), www.brookings.edu/articles/rising-inequality-a-major-issue-of-our-time/. Qureshi notes that 'Over the past four decades, there has been a broad trend of rising income inequality across countries. Income inequality has risen in most advanced economies and major emerging economies, which together account for about two-thirds of the world's population and 85 percent of global GDP'. See also World Inequality Lab, 'World Inequality Report 2022: Executive Summary' (2021) 11: 'Inequalities within countries are now even greater than the significant inequalities observed between countries'.

[20] See Law Council of Australia, 'Justice Project: Final Report' (2018), lawcouncil.au/justice-project/final-report.

[21] Barrows (n 12) 912, citing Netolitzky (n 5).

[22] M Fricker, *Epistemic Injustice: Power and the Ethics of Knowing* (Oxford University Press, 2007) 8.

> language that individuals can use to communicate their experiences with those problems and their satisfaction with the efforts to address them. Excluding some actors from contributing to these epistemic resources results in a structurally prejudiced pool of knowledge that does not reflect the lived reality of everyone that must operate within it.[23]

Some who employ or use pseudolaw lack the necessary language to properly articulate their grievances.[24] In response to those arguments, they are labelled as using 'pseudolaw' and their claims are (typically) not heard. They are excluded. As McDonnel highlights in the last part of her commentary above, considering the lived reality of persons in the legal system is an important consideration.

Epistemic injustice can also be implemented along class lines. Indeed, Richard Sennett and Jonathan Cobb, who have also written on epistemic knowledge and recognition, speak of the 'hidden injuries of class'.[25] Thus, if pseudolaw is being utilised for the most part by those from a lower socio-economic class who are not heard or do not feel heard by those in power, it is likely that they will feel further marginalised and come to believe that the law does not listen to them. Axel Honneth makes the observation that the literature on epistemic injustice and the theory of social recognition have certain commonalities, one of which is 'their shared assessment that those who are subordinated and disadvantaged in a society are also frequently treated with a certain condescension, disdain, and degradation that has to be conceived as unjust'.[26] He adds that:

> Perhaps one can go a step further and say that both theories begin with the observation that subordinated persons and groups suffer not only from a lack of material goods and opportunities for action but also, and perhaps more severely, from the limited respect and esteem they receive from those enjoying social power.[27]

This underlines the need to consider the operation of pseudolaw against the broader power structures which operate in the economy, society and in the legal system itself.

III. Pseudolaw and Misunderstanding the Law: The COVID-19 Experience

My argument in this chapter is that the delineation between a misreading of the law and pseudolaw is an unclear one, and great care must be taken in classifying

[23] K McDonnel, 'Epistemic Injustice and Remedy: Can BHR [Business and Human Rights] Ever Really "Centre" Rights Holders?' (2023) 29 *Australian Journal of Human Rights* 84, 92.

[24] K Leader, ch 5 in this volume.

[25] Cited in A Honneth 'Two Interpretations of Social Disrespect: A Comparison between Epistemic and Moral Recognition' in P Giladi and N McMillan (eds), *Epistemic Injustice and the Philosophy of Recognition* (Routledge, 2022) 12–13.

[26] ibid 11–12.

[27] ibid (citation omitted).

a statement as 'pseudolaw' simply because it utilises an instrument which is archaic or does not substantiate the claimant's argument. To make this argument, I consider first how members of the anti-vaccination movement dispute vaccine mandates. I then contrast those arguments with the 'best' examples that arose in case law. This shows that the line between authoritative law and pseudolaw in anti-vaccine mandate arguments is not clear, but is, instead, based upon the claimants' access to resources and broader structures of power.

A. Anti-Vaccine Mandates Claims

In this section, I analyse the use of pseudolaw by members of the anti-vaccination movement during the 2020–22 COVID-19 pandemic as a case study. I use one particular issue – mandatory vaccination policies – to examine the differences between the use of pseudolaw claims on one hand and those where individuals misunderstand the remit of authoritative laws on the other. This was an issue during the COVID pandemic because certain individuals and groups made claims about the lawfulness of health measures (such as vaccines) using pseudolaw.

I focus in particular on the legal understanding of *coercion* in the vaccine mandate case study. However, before doing so, it is helpful to set the scene in terms of what types of pseudolegal arguments were made during COVID. These included the following:

- 'I have a right to conscientious objection to vaccines due to Magna Carta';[28]
- 'Vaccine certificates are against the Federal Privacy Act 1988';[29]
- 'The giving of the COVID vaccine constitutes experimental scientific treatment which is prohibited by the Nuremberg Code'.[30]

Alongside these arguments sat other, less 'spurious' claims about mandatory vaccinations. These included claims that a mandatory vaccination policy impacts an individual's right to bodily integrity and that termination from employment

[28] See discussion of such arguments in 'The Anti-Vaxxer's "Sovereign Citizen" Defence Examined' *The Week* (26 January 2022), theweek.com/news/science-health/955535/anti-vax-sovereign-citizen-defence; and H Kesvani 'There's a Darker Side to English Businesses citing Magna Carta to Defy Lockdown' *The Guardian* (2 January 2021), www.theguardian.com/commentisfree/2021/jan/02/english-magna-carta-lockdown-covid-laws-online.

[29] The use of the Commonwealth Privacy Act 1988 in relation to COVID restrictions is discussed in S Moulds, 'No, That's Not the Law: The Danger of Using Pseudolegal Arguments against COVID-19 Rules' The Conversation (3 November 2021), www.theconversation.com/no-thats-not-the-law-the-danger-of-using-pseudolegal-arguments-against-covid-19-rules-170630.

[30] Claims based on the Nuremberg Charter or Code are discussed in AAP Fact Check, 'The Nuremberg Code Doesn't Apply to COVID-19 Vaccinations' (9 June 2021), www.aap.com.au/factcheck/the-nuremberg-code-doesnt-apply-to-covid-19-vaccinations/; and AFP Fact Check, 'Principles in the Nuremberg Code are Compatible with Vaccination', (30 May 2020), factcheck.afp.com/principles-nuremberg-code-are-compatible-vaccination. Many such claims were made on Facebook. See, for example, Lisa Lynn (18 April 2021), www.facebook.com/groups/138599678102481/permalink/184874376808344; Lavonne Lawrence (24 May 2020), perma.cc/8TYL-CXPL.

because a person is unvaccinated constitutes unlawful discrimination. To illustrate this, consider the difference between these two statements:

(a) 'I have a right of conscientious objection to vaccines.'[31]
(b) 'I have a right of conscientious objection to vaccines due to Magna Carta.'[32]

In statement (a), the claimant is arguing that they have a right of conscientious objection to vaccines without naming the particular source of that claim. Is this claim true? Or is it false and completely spurious? As I argued elsewhere during the COVID-19 pandemic, 'There is no recognised right to conscientious objection to vaccinations under Australian law. Therefore, any person who is not willing to be vaccinated cannot merely argue an "objection" to it'.[33] However, there are examples of exemptions being given to certain groups in relation to other vaccines. For instance, the Christian Scientists successfully claimed an exemption to mandatory childhood immunisations by a previous Australian government (an exemption which was later removed).[34] Thus, the claim 'I have a right of conscientious objection to vaccines' is *not* pseudolaw per se. It is simply a statement which does not currently represent the state of the law in Australia.

What, then, of statement (b): 'I have a right of conscientious objection to vaccines due to Magna Carta'? The reference to conscientious objection raises a legal argument of doubtable quality (and unlikely to succeed in a court of law), but the claimant has added to this by sourcing the claim in a document which does not support such a finding. Does this render a doubtful legal argument into a false or spurious claim and therefore a pseudolaw argument? I raise this because a reference to an historical instrument such as Magna Carta is often viewed as an indicator of pseudolaw.[35] However, Magna Carta remains an historical document of foundational significance to common law legal systems. It is regularly referred to as reflecting fundamental principles of human rights and the common law in

[31] This is a paraphrased example of arguments made by various religious and other groups about vaccine mandates and vaccine certificates; see for example arguments by the applicants in *We The Patriots USA, Inc, et al, Applicants v Kathy Hochul, Governor of New York, et al* 17 F 4th 368 (2d Cir 2021). The applicants were devout Christians who claimed to 'object to deriving any benefit – no matter how remote – from a process involving abortion, which they believe is morally wrong. … Since all three currently available COVID-19 vaccinations use cell lines artificially developed from aborted foetal cells in their testing, development, or production, they cannot receive COVID-19 vaccination without violating their consciences'. See also Christian Leaders, 'Open Letter from Christian Leaders to the UK Prime Minister Concerning Vaccine Passport Proposals' (August 2021), vaccinepassportletter.wordpress.com: 'People may have various reasons for being unable or unwilling to receive vaccines currently available including, for some Christians, serious issues of conscience related to the ethics of vaccine manufacture or testing.'

[32] See n 28.

[33] M O'Sullivan, 'Can the Government, or my Employer, Force Me to get a COVID-19 Vaccine Under the Law?' The Conversation (20 August 2020), www.theconversation.com/can-the-government-or-my-employer-force-me-to-get-a-covid-19-vaccine-under-the-law-144739.

[34] See discussion in ibid.

[35] The Secret Barrister, 'Can Magna Carta and "Common Law" Give you Immunity from Covid Regulations? (29 November 2020), thesecretbarrister.com/2020/11/28/can-magna-carta-and-common-law-give-you-immunity-from-covid-regulations/.

various judgments of the High Court of Australia,[36] and is recognised as continuing to have contemporary relevance by judges (writing extra-curially) in the United Kingdom and in Australia,[37] and by various legal academics.[38] Nevertheless, as Judge Cash has, quite rightly, pointed out, 'Whatever the Great Charter's historical significance, it cannot be said to be a piece of functioning legislation that determines rights and obligations today'.[39]

Magna Carta may not protect legal rights and impose obligations in Australian law. My concern, however, is that characterising a person who references or invokes a personal right sourced within Magna Carta differs according to the level of their epistemic resources.[40] That is, we may identify marginalised and disempowered actors invoking Magna Carta as simply pseudolegal adherents or believers, but not judges and others in positions of high esteem. In doing so, the system is elevating those who conform to existing hierarchies of legal power and silencing those who do not. This relates back to my discussion about where power is located – in the hierarchy of courts, not in individuals who struggle to articulate their political opposition to subjection. So, there is a difference in the operation of power.

The substance of the argument – in its 'best' form – must be considered. I now turn to examine this issue by looking in greater depth at a case study involving the legal test for coercion in relation to vaccine mandates. I have chosen this as a case study as recent case law on vaccine mandates in Australia puts into question the line between authoritative law and pseudolaw.

B. Vaccine Mandates Case Study

One issue which has been the subject of both pseudolaw claims on social media and challenges in court has been that vaccine mandates constitute forced medical treatment or unlawful experimentation. Social media users regularly referenced Magna Carta and/or the Nuremberg Code, a set of medical experimentation guidelines drafted after World War II.[41]

[36] For instance, Justice Murphy in *Victoria v Australian Building Construction Employees' and Builders Labourers' Federation* cited the Magna Carta as one of the 'great principles of human rights': (1982) 152 CLR 25, 109; and the High Court in *Ebner v Official Trustee in Bankruptcy* held that 'Fundamental to the common law system of adversarial trial is that it is conducted by an … impartial tribunal … this … can be traced to Magna Carta': (2011) 205 CLR 337, 343.

[37] Lord Irvine, 'The Spirit of the Magna Carta Continues to Resonate in Modern Law' (2003) 119 *Law Quarterly Review* 227, 236; S Crennan, 'Magna Carta, Common Law Values and The Constitution' (2015) 39 *Melbourne University Law Review* 331.

[38] See for example, R Balachandran, 'Magna Carta: Medieval Curiosity or Cornerstone of the Rule of Law?' (2011) 49 *Law Society Journal* 74, 78; D Clark, 'The Icon of Liberty: The Status and Role of Magna Carta in Australian and New Zealand Law' (2000) 24 *Melbourne University Law Review* 866, 868; N Cowdery QC, 'Magna Carta: 800 Years Young' (2015) 40 *Australian Bar Review* 101, 103.

[39] Cash (n 2) 12.

[40] See discussion in ibid.

[41] AAP Fact Check (n 30), reproducing Facebook post from 'Kill the System' stating that the Nuremberg Code means 'They can't force you to get jabbed no matter how hard they try. The law is on your side!': (Facebook, 29 May 2020), archive.md/y1Zhj.

In addition to the expression of such views on social media, certain politicians have also voiced arguments that vaccinations constitute inhuman treatment or non-consensual experimentation. For instance, Australian Liberal National Party (LNP) Senator Gerard Rennick argued that human rights laws protected Australians from being coerced into receiving COVID-19 vaccinations under state mandates.[42] Senator Rennick argued that it was 'intolerably cruel' to tell someone who has had a bad reaction to a first dose of a COVID-19 vaccine that they must have a second shot.[43] He claimed further that the Australian Human Rights Commission Act 1986 (Cth) provided a legal right to refuse in these circumstances. The Act provides relevantly: 'No one shall be subjected to torture or to cruel, inhuman or degrading treatment or punishment. In particular, no one shall be subjected without his free consent to medical or scientific experimentation.'[44] This wording is derived from Article 7 of the International Covenant on Civil and Political Rights ('ICCPR')[45] to which Australia is a party.

What then, is the status of such an argument? As I stated in my expert advice to the Australian Associated Press Fact Check which was carried out in response to that statement, the very high threshold required by Article 7 of the ICCPR means that it would be unlikely to apply to Australian vaccine mandates. This is because the types of actions which have been recognised as meeting this threshold are procedures like forced sterilisation – interventions which are clearly coercive in nature. This can be contrasted to a workplace vaccine requirement which, in my opinion, does not reach that high coercive threshold.

However, was Senator Rennick's statement (a) misguided or inaccurate (and therefore a misreading of the law), or (b) false and spurious (and therefore, pseudolaw)? Some would argue that a statement that vaccine mandates constitute forced medical treatment or scientific experimentation does in fact constitute 'pseudolaw' as it is spurious in nature. Nevertheless, in two recent cases – one from New Zealand in 2022,[46] and one from Queensland in 2024[47] – courts in fact held that a vaccine mandate did involve coercion and thus engaged the protection against forced medical treatment.[48]

[42] AAP Fact Check, 'COVID Vaccination Mandates do not Contravene Australia's Human Rights Laws' (1 December 2021), www.aap.com.au/factcheck/covid-vaccination-mandates-do-not-contravene-australias-human-rights-laws.

[43] ibid.

[44] Australian Human Rights Commission Act 1986 (Cth), Sch 2, Art 7.

[45] International Covenant on Civil and Political Rights, opened for signature 19 December 1966, 999 UNTS 171 (entered into force 23 March 1976) ('ICCPR').

[46] *Four Aviation Security Services Employees* [2022] 2 NZLR 26 (Cooke J).

[47] *Johnston v Carroll (Commissioner of the Queensland Police Service); Witthahn v Wakefield (Chief Executive of Hospital and Health Services and Director General of Queensland Health); Sutton v Carroll (Commissioner of the Queensland Police Service)* [2024] QSC 2.

[48] *Four Aviation Security Services Employees* (n 46) [30]: 'It is a matter of degree whether practical pressure to undergo a medical treatment will be taken to have limited the right to refuse that treatment. Here the level of pressure is significant and amounts to coercion. The employees are forced to be vaccinated or potentially lose their jobs. This involves both economic and social pressure. I accept that the right is accordingly engaged, and that it is limited by the Order.' I note that s 11 of the New Zealand Bill of Rights Act 1990 provides that 'Everyone has the right to refuse to undergo any medical treatment' which is wider language than that used in the ICCPR.

In the Queensland case, *Johnston v Carroll (Commissioner of the Queensland Police Service)*, the Supreme Court found that a vaccine mandate made in relation to the Queensland Police Service[49] engaged the prohibition against cruel, inhuman or degrading treatment, specifically the prohibition against non-consensual medical treatment.[50] It is noteworthy that the challenge was funded in large part by an Australian billionaire, Clive Palmer,[51] a person with power and sufficient resources to engage legal counsel to formulate a challenge to the vaccine policies. The applicants argued that a person cannot give full, free and informed consent to medical treatment if the effect of a mandatory vaccination direction is to force a person to choose between vaccination and employment.[52] The first respondent – the Commissioner of the Queensland Police Service – submitted that the Health Direction did not constitute forced medical treatment 'because it does not forcibly compel a person to be vaccinated'. The Queensland Supreme Court rejected that submission,[53] and found that the right not to be subjected to medical or scientific experimentation or treatment without the person's full, free and informed consent as guaranteed in the State's Human Rights Act was limited.[54] The Court found that 'Non-compliance with those directions could have had life-changing consequences for an employee who declined to comply with the direction'.[55] Although the Court held that the limit was justified given the exigencies posed by COVID-19,[56] it is noteworthy that the argument relating to the element of coercion in relation to the vaccines was *affirmed* by the Court.

What, then, does this say about pseudolaw? The point of this discussion is that the social media post and the statement of the politician above used different *sources* to the successful court cases I summarised above. The social media

[49] Direction No. 14 applied to all QPS officers appointed under s 2.2 of the Police Service Administration Act 1990 (Qld) ('PSAA'). It only exempted those with a medical contraindication, a genuine religious objection, or some other exceptional circumstances: see summary in *Johnston* (n 47) [454].

[50] *Johnston* (n 47). That prohibition, which is in similar terms to the ICCPR, Art 7, is set out in the Human Rights Act 2019 (Qld), s 17 and provides: 'Protection from torture and cruel, inhuman or degrading treatment A person must not be – (a) subjected to torture; or (b) treated or punished in a cruel, inhuman or degrading way; or (c) subjected to medical or scientific experimentation or treatment without the person's full, free and informed consent'.

[51] Clive Palmer reportedly provided between AUD 2.5m and 3m towards the case: see A Messenger, 'Clive Palmer Claims "Great Victory" in Funding Challenge to Queensland's Covid Vaccine Mandate' *The Guardian* (28 February 2024), www.theguardian.com/australia-news/2024/feb/27/clive-palmer-claims-great-victory-in-funding-challenge-to-queenslands-covid-vaccine-mandate.

[52] Applicant's submissions as summarised by Martin J in *Johnston* (n 47) [311].

[53] ibid [324].

[54] ibid [333].

[55] ibid [456].

[56] ibid [459]. I note that, ultimately, the Court declared that the instruments applying the vaccine mandate were held to be unlawful under the Human Rights Act 2019 (Qld), s 58, but this was due to a procedural issue. That is, the Court found it was not satisfied that the Commissioner had demonstrated that she gave proper consideration to the human rights that might have been affected by her decisions: see *Johnston* (n 47) [135]–[139].

post used the Nuremberg Charter, and the Australian senator referenced the Australian Human Rights Commission Act. The two court cases above used human rights legislation. But the *arguments* were very similar – they were focused on the lack of *consent*. The difference was the *speaker* of the claims and their ability to access epistemic resources. In the case of Senator Rennick, his statement received media coverage because he was part of the Government and held power in that regard. In relation to the Queensland challenge, the legal advice Mr Palmer (a billionaire) was able to harness to lodge the proceedings and the power they were therefore able to assert resulted in a proper examination of his claims. The Court agreed with the position that mandatory vaccination constituted forced medical treatment, but ruled that it was nonetheless justified. Nevertheless, the plaintiffs succeeded on procedural grounds.

Following on from these examples of language and power, I note that much of the discourse on pseudolaw focuses on its use by individuals. But can and do *state authorities* use pseudolaw? I turn to this next.

IV. Pseudolaw and States: The Use of Legal Fictions by Courts

This chapter seeks to interrogate the assumption that underpins the discourse on pseudolaw that there is an authoritative 'correct law' (state-made law) and 'pseudolaw' (which is spurious or false). To do so, I draw upon various contestations surrounding the notion that law is 'objective' and focus on the concept of a 'legal fiction' to provide an illustration of how the law has *itself* utilised falsities, that is, pseudolaw.

A. Falsity in Authoritative Law: Legal Fictions

The American legal philosopher Lon Fuller is probably best known as one of the leading scholars on legal fictions. In *Legal Fictions*, published in 1967, Fuller argues that 'there is scarcely a field of the law in which one does not encounter one after another of these conceits of the legal imagination'.[57] His definition of 'legal fiction' includes either:

(1) a statement propounded with a complete or partial consciousness of its falsity, or
(2) a false statement recognised as having utility.[58]

[57] LL Fuller, *Legal Fictions* (Stanford University Press, 1967).
[58] ibid.

Since then, scholars have attempted to define the term further. For instance, Maksymilian Del Mar defines a legal fiction as:

> [A]ny suspension of one or more of the required operative facts leading to the imposition of an associated normative consequence, whether this suspension is introduced because of (i) the absence of proof of some required fact; or (ii) the presence of proof to the contrary.[59]

Many examples of legal fictions have been utilised by legislative drafters and courts. Some have even argued that the maxim 'Everybody knows the law' is an example of a legal fiction. As Liron Shmilovits notes: 'As a statement of fact, the maxim is evidently false. Not even lawyers or judges know all the law. And yet courts apply it, as if it were true, with the result that ignorance of the law is no defence'.[60] Other common legal fictions exist. One commentary in the *Harvard Law Review* noted that '"[the] corporation is a person" remains one of the most enduring and problematic legal fictions'.[61]

To illustrate the use by states of pseudolaw (via legal fictions), I analyse one example of the use of legal fictions by a state authority – the utilisation of the doctrine of *terra nullius* by the British Crown at the time of the 'settlement' of Australia. In addition to this, I briefly discuss a more recent example of a legal fiction – the designation of Rwanda as 'safe' by the UK Government.

B. The Legal Fiction of *Terra Nullius*

The doctrine of *terra nullius* operates where a finding is made that land is unoccupied or uninhabited for legal purposes.[62] It is central to Australian law as it allowed the British Crown to assume sovereignty over Australia as a colony and led to the dispossession of the Indigenous peoples of Australia from their land. The doctrine operated until 1992 when it was overturned in the landmark High Court decision in *Mabo v Queensland (No 2)* ('*Mabo (No 2)*').[63]

[59] M Del Mar 'Legal Fictions and Legal Change' (2013) 9 *International Journal of Law in Context* 442, 442. Del Mar explains: 'This is a broader definition than is commonly found in the literature, because the common trend is to understand fictions as requiring consciousness of falsity, whereas the first reason noted above only requires absence of proof' (442). For other work on legal fictions, see ST Miller, 'The Reasons for Some Legal Fictions' (1910) 8 *Michigan Law Review* 623, 624–25.

[60] L Shmilovits, *Legal Fictions in Private Law* (Cambridge University Press, 2022) 1 (citations omitted).

[61] 'Notes: What We Talk about When We Talk about Persons: The Language of a Legal Fiction' (2001) 114 *Harvard Law Review* 1745, 1750 (citations omitted). See also FS Cohen, 'Transcendental Nonsense and the Functional Approach' (1935) 35 *Columbia Law Review* 809–49.

[62] For a discussion of the development of the concept of '*terra nullius*' and its various definitional interpretations, see D Ritter, 'The "Rejection of Terra Nullius" in Mabo: A Critical Analysis' (1996) 18 *Sydney Law Review* 5.

[63] *Mabo v Queensland (No 2)* (1992) 175 CLR 1.

As Justice Brennan of the High Court noted in *Mabo (No 2)*, the dispossession of Australia's Indigenous population was based on two propositions:

> [T]hat the territory of New South Wales was, in 1788, *terra nullius* in the sense of unoccupied or uninhabited for legal purposes and that full legal and beneficial ownership of all the lands of the Colony vested in the Crown, unaffected by any claims of the Aboriginal inhabitants.[64]

Justice Brennan held that the lands of Australia were not *terra nullius* or 'practically unoccupied' in 1788.[65] Relevantly for this chapter, Brennan J underlined the significance of the *terra nullius* doctrine for the settlement of Australia and explicitly classified it as a 'fiction': 'The fiction by which the rights and interests of indigenous inhabitants in land were treated as non-existent was justified by a policy which has no place in the contemporary law of this country.'[66] His Honour later stated that this 'fictional impediment' to the recognition of Indigenous rights, was centrally significant to the extinguishment of the rights of Australia's Indigenous peoples: 'It was only by fastening on the notion that a settled colony was *terra nullius* that it was possible to predicate of the Crown the acquisition of ownership of land in a colony already occupied by indigenous inhabitants.'[67]

The use of *terra nullius* as a legal fiction – as a falsity – and a tool for the dispossession of land has been recognised by many scholars. For instance, Peter Russell notes that there were, in fact, no lands *globally* which were '*terra nullius*' during European colonisation and calls it a 'legal fiction':

> In reality, in those parts of the world that the European states were interested in colonizing, there simply were no uninhabited lands. Aside from Antarctic ice and a few island atolls, there was no terra nullius. Effective occupation and colonization always involved some combination of European settlement and imposition by force or fraud of European rule over native peoples. The purpose of maintaining the *false distinction* and insisting that there were colonies of pure settlement was to provide legal justification for ignoring the rights and interests of the people who were indigenous to the area. If the settlers and their political leaders came to believe in the truth of this *legal fiction*, it could be potent. And that is what happened in the Australian case – at least up until Eddie Mabo's time.[68]

Danielle Petherbridge also observes that the 'mythical proclamation' of *terra nullius* 'was not only made in 1788 but was also repeated several times throughout the

[64] ibid 109.

[65] ibid.

[66] ibid 42. See also 45: 'Though the rejection of the notion of terra nullius clears away the *fictional impediment* to the recognition of indigenous rights and interests in colonial land, it would be impossible for the common law to recognise such rights and interests if the basic doctrines of the common law are inconsistent with their recognition' (emphasis added).

[67] ibid 45 (emphasis added).

[68] P Russell, *Recognizing Aboriginal Title: The Mabo Case and Indigenous Resistance to English-Settler Colonialism* (University of Toronto Press, 2005) 40 (emphasis added).

19th century in juridical claims and the founding colonial legislature'.[69] It is telling that Petherbridge classifies *terra nullius* as a 'mythical proclamation' here as the mythical aspects of pseudolaw have also been noted by scholars and judges, with some describing them as a magical ritual.[70] This again, underscores the commonalities between legal fictions and pseudolaw. In addition, the use of fictions by courts can be viewed as one of the means by which law avoids analysis of socio-economic or political values.[71]

C. The Continued Use of Legal Fictions

In addition to this important example of the work of legal fictions in the development of authoritative law in Australia, other scholars have provided more contemporary examples of legal fictions by states. For instance, UK constitutional law scholar Adam Tucker recently wrote a commentary on the UK–Rwanda refugee transfer agreement. This agreement, which would allow UK authorities to send certain asylum-seekers to Rwanda for processing, has been highly controversial because the proposed legislation states that Rwanda is safe for certain purposes.[72] Tucker, in his well-reasoned and insightful commentary on this agreement, refers to the definition of a legal fiction by Lon Fuller and states that 'the proposed legislation would qualify under both limbs of this definition'.[73] Tucker argues that legislation which classifies Rwanda as safe 'would not be a truthful statement of the situation on the ground in Rwanda. It would be enacting a falsehood into law. It would be a legal fiction'.[74] More significantly, this fiction would be likely to cause serious harm to those it affected:

> It would involve the deliberate enactment as fact of a dangerous falsehood, designed to empower the executive to evade legal requirements. Its 'utility' (to borrow Fuller's term) would be to exempt the executive from the rule of law, in ways likely to cause serious harm, and indeed deaths.[75]

[69] D Petheridge, 'A Fourth Order of Recognition? Accounting for Epistemic Injustice in Recognition Theory' in P Giladi and N McMillan (eds), *Epistemic Injustice and the Philosophy of Recognition* (Routledge, 2022) 48.

[70] DJ Netolitzky, 'Organised Pseudolegal Commercial Arguments as Magic and Ceremony' (2018) 55 *Alberta Law Review* 1062, 1085.

[71] On this, see Felix Cohen: 'When the vivid fictions and metaphors of traditional jurisprudence are thought of as reasons for decisions, rather than poetical or mnemonic devices for formulating decisions reached on other grounds, then the author, as well as the reader, of the opinion or argument, is apt to forget the social forces which mold the law and the social ideals by which the law is to be judged': Cohen (n 61) 812.

[72] Note that the Bill was eventually passed in April 2024: Safety of Rwanda (Asylum and Immigration) Act 2024 c 8.

[73] A Tucker, 'The Rwanda Policy, Legal Fiction(s), and Parliament's Legislative Authority' UK Constitutional Law Blog (22 November 2023), ukconstitutionallaw.org/2023/11/22/adam-tucker-the-rwanda-policy-legal-fictions-and-parliaments-legislative-authority.

[74] ibid.

[75] ibid.

Tucker starkly underlines the constitutional significance of using such a legal fiction:

> Rwanda is not safe. We cannot simply make it so. Legislation to that effect would be a legal fiction. This particular legal fiction would be a particularly dangerous falsehood – and its enactment would be an abuse of the broad authority that our constitution accords to the Westminster Parliament. It may even be sufficiently abusive to take it outside that legislative authority.[76]

What, then, do we make of the use by states of a form of pseudolaw – of falsities and legal fictions? I would argue that these are emblematic of the power differentials in law and society which are reflected in the classification of individual citizenry's use of pseudolaw as 'spurious' and illegitimate on one hand, and the state's use of legal fictions and falsities as acceptable and legitimate on the other.

It is thereby demonstrative of the critique of law and power which I introduced above. It also reflects theories espoused from Foucault and Marxist scholars about the masked neutrality of the law. For instance, using a Foucauldian perspective, we can say that the legal fictions such as those discussed above which are presented as 'truth' are in fact expressions of power by the maker of the claim and, indeed, that legal fictions are an 'instrument of power'.[77]

V. Analysis of Pseudolaw: Power and Epistemic Injustice

Using the epistemic injustice framework, I emphasise that the arguments posed by some users of pseudolaw outlined in section III – that vaccine mandates are coercive medical treatments rendered unlawful by Magna Carta or the Nuremberg Charter – may contain an element of truth or legitimacy. That is, that vaccine mandates are coercive. However, such claims by individuals are not typically validated by the law because of the position of power of that claimant in society. The users of pseudolaw (unlike the plaintiff in the successful Queensland Supreme Court challenge) do not usually have access to power to influence or legal assistance in order to frame their claims in an acceptable way so that they may be validated by the legal system. It could also be argued that whilst some might not have access to power, others may in fact be 'oppositional' to legal uses of power. That cohort of pseudolaw users who are unwilling to submit and be subject to legal institutions (in a Foucauldian sense), draw on odd legal sources and are, therefore, marginalised.[78]

[76] ibid.

[77] M Foucault, 'Two Lectures' in C Gordon (ed), *Power/Knowledge: Selected Interviews and Other Writings 1972–1977* (Vintage 1980).

[78] I wish to acknowledge Stephen Young for this valuable insight.

As I noted in my Introduction to this chapter, the use of pseudolaw must be understood and assessed in light of structural factors such as economic inequality, the social alienation suffered by some in our society and the feelings of powerlessness that these factors engender in a segment of modern societies (in Australia, the USA, Canada, New Zealand and many European countries). Coupled with these social and economic developments is the increasing use of automation (by companies and governments) which leads to further isolation and has a propensity to dehumanise citizens. For instance, people are increasingly interacting with companies and governments via phone apps and chatbots. It is subsequently more difficult for people affected by a government decision to seek advice and be heard by another human. It should not be surprising that many in our society feel powerless and unheard. Using pseudolaw is a means for reclaiming some power and being 'heard'.

The claims of pseudolaw must also be considered against the reality that law is opaque, expensive and impenetrable for many. As noted in section II, law is used as an instrument of power and part of the power of the law is in the language it uses. As Richard Susskind observes: 'From a lay perspective, as well as appearing to be unaffordable, the courts seem to be excessively time-consuming, unjustifiably combative, and inexplicably steeped in opaque procedure and language.'[79]

The rise in the use of pseudolaw is (partly) explainable by the significant access to justice barriers in our legal system. There has been an increase in self-represented litigants in Australia.[80] Thus, in addition to dealing with pseudolaw in the courtroom itself, I would argue that there are also access to justice issues that need to be addressed to improve structural inequality and alienation in society.

I do not wish, in this analysis, to downplay the difficulties posed by the use of pseudolaw in the courts, which has been well documented by judges faced by such cases.[81] I also acknowledge that the legal system quite rightly sets out rules for the operation of litigation and implements case management procedures to ensure the efficient and proper functioning of the court system. However, it should be acknowledged that this decides whose voice will be heard and who will shape legal precedent and discourse. Whilst I do not question the imperative of ensuring an efficient and proper operation of justice, I underline that there are access to justice and power issues behind the operation of the law which should be borne in mind by those dealing with pseudolaw (whether as a scholar, practitioner or judicial officer) and that classifying a claim as 'pseudolaw' is not a neutral term – it is an exercise of power and exclusion.

[79] R Susskind, *Tomorrow's Lawyers: An Introduction to Your Future* (Oxford University Press, 2017) 94.

[80] Law Council of Australia (n 20) 42: 'The efficiency and fairness of the justice system depends upon ready access to legal assistance. The growing numbers of self-represented litigants, in part due to the reduced capacity of legal assistance services to meet demand, are causing enormous strain on court resources and are diminishing the overall efficiency of the justice system.'

[81] See, for example, Cash (n 2).

In terms of power, pseudolaw can also be viewed as an act of resistance. As Hugh Collins quite rightly points out: 'one of the crucial distinguishing features of law is the belief of subjects that the rules and institutions of the legal system have legitimate authority'.[82] The use of pseudolaw by litigants and in other fora demonstrates that increasing numbers of people in societies across the world do *not* believe that the rules and institutions of the legal system have legitimate authority. This has been noted in the work of Netolitzky:

> Pseudolaw's not-law rules and its conspiratorial narratives have a clear purpose and social function. Pseudolaw rebalances authority, removing and rejecting 'conventional' state and institutional authority, and shifting that balance of power to individuals. As such, pseudolaw is an anti-authority tool. Pseudolaw purports to subvert and/or negate government rule-making, and de-legitimizes authority over 'subject' populations.[83]

Thus, some care needs to be taken that the use of pseudolaw as resistance to the law is dealt with carefully and fairly so as to avoid further alienation of the claimant and maintain public confidence in the legal system.

In analysing these issues, we can also draw on the many works of legal philosophy and theory which deal with law and power and the objectivity of law, including Marxist critiques of law, the writings of Foucault[84] and Unger.[85] For instance, the work of Raymond Belliotti on the contemporary application of Marxism is helpful in considering the social and political dynamics underpinning the use of pseudolaw. Belliotti highlights the need to interrogate the notion of 'law as neutral':

> Marxists view the rule of law as a primary culprit in the liberal-capitalist legitimation of the status quo … Behind the rule of law's mask of formal neutrality lies a conglomeration of processes, doctrines, and structures that serve generally to advance certain class interests and to defeat or marginalize other class interests … Thus, Marxists tend not to praise the rule of law, but to interrogate it.[86]

Belliotti also touches upon the feelings of alienation that are often experienced by workers, noting that 'Regardless of whether workers self-consciously announce the requisite feelings of estrangement, the objective social condition of the proletariat is pervaded by alienation'.[87] These observations are highly relevant to the contemporary use of pseudolaw which is typically by those disenfranchised or marginalised as a way of claiming back a voice and level of power.[88]

[82] H Collins, 'Roberto Unger and the Critical Legal Studies Movement' (1987) 14 *Journal of Law and Society* 387, 393.
[83] Netolitzky (n 1) 1, 6 (citations omitted).
[84] Foucault (n 77).
[85] RM Unger, *What Should Legal Analysis Become?* (Verso, 1996).
[86] RA Bellioti, 'The Legacy of Marxist Jurisprudence' in DS Caudill and SJay Gold, *Radical Philosophy of Law: Contemporary Challenges to Mainstream Legal Theory and Practice* (Humanities Press, 1995) 12–13.
[87] ibid 4.
[88] See discussion in Cash (n 2).

VI. Conclusions and Future Directions

As I noted at the outset of this chapter, the increased use of pseudolaw in many jurisdictions poses a challenge to the law and to the operation of the legal system more generally. This chapter has sought to address some of the nuances of this issue by situating pseudolaw within the context of the development of authoritative law and to question the conceptual difference between pseudolaw and legal fictions. The chapter has used the claims made about mandatory vaccinations during the COVID-19 pandemic as a case study to illustrate the difference between pseudolaw and misinterpretations of the law and to interrogate the assumption that there is a clear boundary between 'pseudolaw' and the actual 'law' (that is, that passed by Parliament or handed down by a court). I have also used the comparison of pseudolaw with state use of legal fictions to illustrate that there is no clear, bright line between accepted, authoritative law (made by state authorities) and pseudolaw (used by individuals). This demonstrates the need to be more nuanced in our approach to pseudolaw and incorporate an understanding that considers law and power (and law *as* power).

I have suggested that pseudolaw should be viewed in its socio-political context – in light of the distribution of wealth and power in our societies – and its operation with respect to people experiencing disadvantage. It is generally acknowledged that we are increasingly facing problems of inequality and alienation. Pseudolaw is a symptom of economic inequality, social polarisation and alienation in our society and in the law. For a certain cohort of society who feel disempowered and alienated, pseudolaw is a means to reclaim power, to claim a voice and be heard by 'the system'.

In light of this and in terms of the way forward, a number of measures should be taken to alleviate some of the more pressing dangers and concerns arising from the increasing use of pseudolaw. First, a special unit should be established in courts dealing with a pronounced number of pseudolaw claims (for instance, in Australia in the Magistrates Court). Those units should incorporate therapeutic justice measures and a more holistic approach to the problems encountered by the claimant in order to make those people feel heard by 'the system'. Other possible reforms could include clearer 'plain English' explanations of court rulings that speak to users from diverse backgrounds, greater community legal education, and increased resourcing of legal aid. Further, a rethinking of the digitalisation of government information and resources which has contributed to the disconnection that some in the community are experiencing should be considered. More broadly, we must recognise the existence of the feelings of alienation by the users of pseudolaw and address the root causes of that alienation (by, for instance, implementing social cohesion measures, particularly to address the sovereign citizen movement). A holistic approach to this issue, which recognises the power dynamic behind pseudolaw and the role of law in legitimating some voices and not others, will be an important step in this endeavour.

4

Pseudolaw as Utopia and Legal Smorgasbord

BRUCE BAER ARNOLD

I. Introduction

Contemporary pseudolaw, such as Organised Pseudolegal Commercial Argument (OPCA),[1] 'freeman on the land,[2] ego-centred sovereignism[3] or sovereign citizen[4] claims, has been variously characterised as 'nonsensical',[5] 'bafflegab',[6] 'mischievous', an incoherent 'common law constitutionalism',[7] an 'expression of magic'[8] or a potential precursor of 'lone wolf terrorism'.[9] It frequently features assertions – meant

[1] DJ Netolitzky, 'The History of the Organized Pseudolegal Commercial Argument Phenomenon in Canada' (2016) 53 *Alberta Law Review* 609; and G Sammon, '"Organised Pseudo-Legal Commercial Argument" Litigation: Challenges for the Administration of Justice in Ireland' (2015) 38 *Dublin University Law Journal* 85.

[2] See for example DC Hofmann, 'Breaking Free: A Socio-Historical Analysis of the Canadian Freemen-on-the-Land Movement' in J Littlewood, L Dawson and SK Thompson (eds), *Terrorism and Counterterrorism in Canada* (University of Toronto Press, 2020) 77; and SA Kent, 'Freemen, Sovereign Citizens, and the Challenge to Public Order in British Heritage Countries' (2015) 6 *International Journal of Cultic Studies* 1. Examples of Australians self-identifying as Freemen on the Land are noted in *Australian Competition & Consumer Commission v Rana* [2008] FCA 374; and *Van den Hoorn v Ellis* [2010] QDC 451. Use of the same characterisation in courts includes *State of New South Wales v Gavin* [2022] NSWSC 84 [39].

[3] D Walkenhorst and M Ruf, 'Violent Ego-Centered Sovereignism as a Global Threat? The Case of the German "Reichsbürger" and Implications for P/CVE Research' in F Atamuradova and S Zeiger (eds), *Researching the Evolution of Countering Violent Extremism* (Hedayah, 2021) 224.

[4] CM Sarteschi, *Sovereign Citizens: A Psychological and Criminological Analysis* (Springer, 2020).

[5] See, for example, *Glew v White* [2012] WASCA 138; *Attorney General (WA) v Glew* [2014] WASC 100; *Woodley v Cipolla*, 2022 ONSC 7096; *Meads v Meads*, 2012 ABQB 571; and *Rambaldi and Anor v Rice Bar Restaurant and Anor* [2018] VSC 218.

[6] *R v Cooper* 2023 BCPC 69.

[7] BB Arnold and E Mikus-Fletcher, 'Whose Constitution: Sovereign Citizenship, Rights Talk and Rhetorics of Constitutionalism in Australia' (2023) 14 *Jindal Global Law Review* 1.

[8] G Cash, 'A Kind of Magic: The Origins and Culture of "Pseudolaw"' Paper delivered to the Queensland Magistrates' State Conference (26 May 2022); and DJ Netolitzky, 'Organized Pseudolegal Commercial Arguments as Magic and Ceremony' (2017) 55 *Alberta Law Review* 1045.

[9] P Jarzabkowski, C Unger and K Meissner, 'Extremist Movements in Australia: A Study of Individual Ideology' University of Queensland Business School (2023), espace.library.uq.edu.au/view/UQ:a9a66f3.

to be legally efficacious – that polities lack authority because there has been a constitutional rupture,[10] duties of obedience have dissolved because the polities have become United States corporations[11] or civil/criminal law enforcement is invalid because businesses and governments incorrectly identify individuals by using conventional orthography.[12]

Pseudolaw also features assertions that polities lack legitimacy in civil and criminal law because they disregard the sovereignty of contract between an individual and other entities – an individualism resulting in a legal smorgasbord whose consumers are ostensibly entitled to reject inconvenient obligations while enjoying the benefits provided by the state. More colourfully, on occasion it includes discoveries by individuals that they are the rightful head of state and therefore our rulers,[13] enjoy immunities as the head of an unrecognised nation,[14] are a 'Galactic Emissary' supposedly authorised by the 'Moot Court of Terra Australis Incognito'[15] or the claim by self-identified witch Eilish D'Avalon that 'I'm a being from another world and don't require' a driver's licence. When pulled over for speeding she informed the police officer that 'Your laws and penalties don't apply to me. I'm not accepting them, I'm sorry, I must go, thank you', accordingly leaving the scene with that officer's arm caught in her driver's side window, dragging him nearly 200 metres.[16]

The following pages seek to complement other chapters in this collection by offering four perspectives on pseudolaw in Australia, a federal liberal democratic state that traces its origins to both English law and mythologies about individual/collective identity.[17] These perspectives are: pseudolaw as utopias, grazing a smorgasbord, mystification, and rights talk. These are primarily

[10] For perspectives on the notion of constitutional rupture, typically involving a radical political change, see NJ Brown and JG Waller, 'Constitutional Courts and Political Uncertainty: Constitutional Ruptures and the Rule of Judges' (2016) 14 *International Journal of Constitutional Law* 817; *Milton Jones (a pseudonym) v DPP* [2015] VSCA 272; *Joosse v Australian Securities and Investment Commission* (1998) 159 ALR 260 [11], [19]; and *Chia Gee v Martin* (1906) 3 CLR 649.

[11] See for example *Hedley v Spivey* [2011] WASC 325.

[12] See for example *Bradley v The Crown* [2020] QCA 252 and *Royal Bank of Canada v Anderson*, 2022 ABQB 354 [4].

[13] A Sloan, *King Alan 1st: The Miraculous and True King of England* (New Generation Publishing, 2020).

[14] H Hobbs and G Williams, *How To Rule Your Own Country* (NewSouth, 2022). See also *Avram v Official Trustee in Bankruptcy* [2001] FCA 1480; *Australian Prudential Regulation Authority v Siminton (No 6)* [2007] FCA 1608; *Australian Competition and Consumer Commission v Purple Harmony Plates Pty Ltd (No 3)* [2002] FCA 1487; and *Roman v Commonwealth of Australia* [2004] NTSC 9.

[15] *Ms Julia Elana Miroch v Powercor Australia Ltd* [2022] FWC 1880 [3].

[16] K Matthews, 'Geelong Cop-Dragging "Witch" Eilish De Avalon says she's Not from Here' *Geelong Advertiser* (27 July 2010), www.news.com.au/breaking-news/geelong-cop-dragging-witch-eilish-de-avalon-says-shes-not-from-here/news-story/3826816de8294e8ad63fb03ed9438781; and 'Witch "Declines" Jail for Dragging Cop with Car' ABC News (23 June 2011), www.abc.net.au/news/2011-06-23/witch-declines-jail-for-dragging-cop-with-car/2769250.

[17] R Ward, 'Australian Legend Re-visited' (1978) 18 *Australian Historical Studies* 171; J Carniel, 'Richard White's Inventing Australia: Revisiting the Invention Forty Years Later' (2021) 18 *History Australia* 156.

aesthetic interventions that seek to understand pseudolaw. They are presented to highlight the misplaced idealism and artifices that exist in the varieties of pseudolaw.

Section II provides the justification for these perspectives. Beginning by noting the multiplicity of pseudolaw in Australia, it reflects on how analysis can condense or obscure that diversity leading to a narrow and misguided view of pseudolaw. The four perspectives noted above are then offered to provide broader insight into the totality of this phenomenon. In section III, it is suggested that pseudolaw can be understood as an expression of a legal utopia, an ideal and unrealisable state that privileges individuals rather than communities, and valorises rights while eliding responsibilities. As section IV notes, this attitude means that many pseudolaw adherents appear to treat law as a matter of consumption, a smorgasbord from which 'consumers' of the legal system are entitled to idiosyncratically take or reject elements (typically on the basis of convenience) without regard for coherence or the rights of other entities.

Section V highlights the mystification inherent in many pseudolaw claims. This can include, for instance, assertions regarding a common law constitutionalism founded on a misreading (wilful or otherwise) of Magna Carta (assumed to override any inconvenient subsequent law) or the belief that the magical expression common in straw man claims – for example use of upper case surnames – will persuade courts. Section VI offers a further perspective, suggesting that contemporary pseudolaw often exists within a broader 'rights talk' influenced by popular rhetoric in the United States and identitarian politics.

These perspectives provide the basis for interpretation through a hermeneutic circle;[18] in other words, recursive examination of aspects of a text or other entity to gain insights about both those aspects and that of which they are part. Pseudolaw is conceptually incoherent. From the perspective of 'law on the ground' (that is, the legal system that is both enforced within Australia and similar jurisdictions and that is taken as a given by most people) individual aspects of pseudolaw are indeed nonsensical. Read together they appear to reinforce each other and to accommodate the incorporation of disparate beliefs (such as the meaning of flags) that non-adherents would regard as irrelevant or meaningless. They offer an alternate view of the world to one that requires coherence and stability.

Having offered these four perspectives, the chapter concludes in section VII by offering several reflections on potential responses to some instances of Australian pseudolaw. In particular, it explores the importance of public education on and about legal systems, and the scope for restricting 'gurus' who propagate pseudolaw mechanisms on a commercial basis. The focus is on Australia but the analysis

[18] HG Gadamer, *Truth and Method*, 2nd edn (J Weinsheimer trans) (Continuum, 2004) 271; HG Gadamer, 'Hermeneutics and Social Science' (1975) 2 *Cultural Hermeneutics* 307. See also J Grondin, *Introduction to Philosophical Hermeneutics* (Yale University Press, 1997) 1; M Foster, 'Hermeneutics' in B Leiter and M Rosen (eds), *The Oxford Handbook of Continental Philosophy* (Oxford University Press, 2007) 30.

is applicable to other jurisdictions, noting the spread of pseudolaw in Canada, New Zealand, the United Kingdom and other nations.[19]

II. 32 Flavours of Failed Authority

Food giant Campbell's historically advertised 32 flavours of soup: each different but on a taxonomic basis ultimately all the same, a consumable in a can appropriated by pop artist Andy Warhol.[20] This chapter expressly recognises the diversity of pseudolaw, which, for example, encompasses assertions of rights that are broader than claims of sovereign citizenship or the identitarianism underlying the Reichsbürger movements in Germany,[21] ethnostate militias in the United States[22] or Australian separatist micronations[23] such as the Sovereign Yidindji Government.[24] Like Campbell's 32 flavours of soup, the diversity of pseudolaw is obscured by scholars (who wish they were Warhol) as 'sovereign citizens'.

The chapter does not offer what Skinner might describe as a 'Grand Theory' of pseudolaw.[25] Nor does it critique a wide-ranging and coherent body of doctrine articulated by leading pseudolaw theorists. The absence of such a critique is pragmatic, as there are no persuasive theorists and very little theorisation – as distinct

[19] H Hobbs, S Young and J McIntyre, 'The Internationalisation of Pseudolaw: The Growth of Sovereign Citizen Arguments in Australia and Aotearoa New Zealand' (2024) 47 *University of New South Wales Law Journal* 309.

[20] G Indiana, *Andy Warhol and the Can that Sold the World* (Basic Books, 2010).

[21] D Juling, 'Reichsbürger: An Old German Ideology in New Clothing?' George Washington University, Institute for European, Russian, and Eurasian Studies, Illiberalism Studies Program Working Papers 16 (2023) and F Hartleb, P Schliefsteiner and C Schiebel, 'From Anti-Measure Activism to Anti-State Extremism? The "Querdenker" Protest-Movement and Its Interrelation and Dynamics with the "Reichsbürger" in Germany and Austria' (2023) 17 *Perspectives on Terrorism* 123.

[22] EA Schlatter, *Aryan Cowboys: White Supremacists and the Search for a New Frontier, 1970–2000* (University of Texas Press, 2006); and JL Smith, *Saints, Sinners, and Sovereign Citizens: The Endless War Over the West's Public Lands* (University of Nevada Press, 2021).

[23] See in particular the discussion of the *Montevideo Convention on the Rights and Duties of States* and other frameworks of recognition in H Hobbs and G Williams, *Micronations and the Search for Sovereignty* (Cambridge University Press, 2022) and TD Grant, 'Defining Statehood: The Montevideo Convention and its Discontents' (1998) 37 *Columbia Journal of Transnational Law* 403, alongside Hobbs and Williams (n 14).

[24] H Hobbs and G Williams, 'The Demise of the "Second Largest Country in Australia": Micronations and Australian Exceptionalism' (2021) 56 *Australian Journal of Political Science* 206. For legally unrecognised micronations – pseudostates – see generally BB Arnold, 'Pseudo-States and Sovereign Citizens' in K Gray (ed), *Global Encyclopedia of Territorial Rights* (Springer, 2022). BB Arnold and E Mikus-Fletcher, 'Whose Constitution: Sovereign Citizenship, Rights Talk and Rhetorics of Constitutionalism in Australia' (2023) 14 *Jindal Global Law Review* 1 differentiates sovereign citizenship from assertion of sovereignty by First Nations in Australia and elsewhere. It also differentiates sovereign citizenship from purported microstates, addressed in for example *Purple Harmony Plates* (n 14); *Siminton* (n 14); *Casley v Commissioner of Taxation* [2007] HCATrans 590 and *Deputy Commissioner of Taxation v Casley* [2017] WASC 161; *Roman* (n 14); *Williamson v Hodgson* [2010] WASC 95; and *Maxwell (also known as Harley Robert Williamson) v Bruse* [2012] WASC 12.

[25] Q Skinner, 'The Return of Grand Theory' in Q Skinner (ed), *The Return of Grand Theory in the Human Sciences* (Cambridge University Press, 1985) 1.

from unfounded assertions and statements that are often voluminous but unintelligible. What adherents of some types of pseudolaw characterise as their gurus (individuals who sell do-it-yourself pseudolaw kits, offer paid pseudolaw seminars and unsuccessfully appear in tribunals as advocates or mentors) do not articulate a credible theorisation of wrongs, immunities or remedies and have not been successful in litigation. One implication, noted below, is that their activity might be usefully crimped under Australian and overseas consumer protection regimes.

If pseudolaw is not a matter of systematic theorisation, a contention in this chapter is instead that – to borrow the observation of a scholar in another field – it is ultimately 'not a coherent doctrine or body of systematically interrelated ideas, but rather a vaguer worldview made up of a number of prejudices with varied appeals to different audiences which could scarcely be dignified with the term "ideology"'.[26]

A corollary is that we should be cautious about the reductionism in referring to pseudolaw as a 'movement'[27] (discussed below), both because of the diversity of its expression and because it is rarely organised through, for example, recognised leaders and administrative bodies. It lacks a theoretician such as Kautsky, Lenin, Bernstein or Hayek.[28] The 'gurus' who feature in Australian and Canadian judgments are not intellectuals or ostensible politicians; their credibility in the minds of believers is likely to be that they offer a populist 'truth' that is perceived as more authentic than that from academia, 'old media' and practitioners of 'politics as usual'.

The absence of a discrete organised pseudolaw movement is unsurprising given the emphasis on individualism evident in social media use by many pseudolaw adherents and the opportunity for those people to express consonant beliefs, for example about vaccination and fluoridation conspiracies, through membership of fringe political parties, groups such as the antisemitic League of Rights[29] and in ad hoc events such as protests during COVID-19 lockdowns in Australia.[30] In the

[26] M Fulbrook, *The Divided Nation: A History of Germany 1918–1990* (Oxford University Press, 1991) 51.

[27] D Baldino and K Lucas, 'Anti-Government Rage: Understanding, Identifying and Responding to the Sovereign Citizen Movement in Australia' (2019) 14 *Journal of Policing, Intelligence and Counter Terrorism* 245; M Ligon, 'The Sovereign Citizen Movement: A Comparative Analysis with Similar Foreign Movements and Takeaways for the United States Judicial System' (2021) 35 *Emory International Law Review* 297; E Hodge, 'The Sovereign Ascendant: Financial Collapse, Status Anxiety, and the Rebirth of the Sovereign Citizen Movement' (2019) 4 *Frontiers in Sociology* 76; CL Matheson, 'Psychotic Discourse: The Rhetoric of the Sovereign Citizen Movement' (2018) 48 *Rhetoric Society Quarterly* 187–206; and RM Valeri, 'The Sovereign Citizens Movement' in RM Valeri and K Borgeson (eds), *Terrorism in America* (Routledge, 2018) 118.

[28] Sovereign citizenship in Australia is not an agenda of 'What Is To Be Done' (akin to Lenin's 1902 'skeleton plan' with that title). It is instead an expression of what cannot be done by the state, for example implement traffic rules or taxation obligations, on an instance by instance basis.

[29] K Campion, 'A "Lunatic Fringe"? The Persistence of Right Wing Extremism in Australia' (2019) 13 *Perspectives on Terrorism* 2; S Encel, 'Antisemitism and Prejudice in Australia' (1989) 23 *Patterns of Prejudice* 16.

[30] G Martin, 'Protest, Policing and Law During COVID-19: On the Legality of Mass Gatherings in a Health Crisis' (2021) 46 *Alternative Law Journal* 275–81; EJR Clarke, A Klas and E Dyos, 'The Role

absence of large-scale data it is conceivable that many of the people have weak social bonds and that a substantial number are either socially marginal or susceptible to 'bafflegab' claims because of economic distress.

That hypothesis is offered cautiously, given indications that much connection between people attracted to some types of pseudolaw appears to centre on private channels such as Telegram, Parler, Gab, 8kun or 4chan that host extremist statements, serve to obfuscate scrutiny and affirm the identity of participants as having a QAnon-style elite understanding denied to ordinary people.[31] Much of the pseudolaw exposition in less-hermetic social media is telegraphic. It does not offer a coherent, fact-based and extended explanation of principles. It often appears to be directed at fellow adherents rather than the world at large, group reinforcement rather than conversion.

One conclusion might therefore be that although courts consider pseudolaw expression as nonsensical – a collection of words that is bewildering because it employs an unrecognisable legal syntax – scholars such as the author of this chapter who rely on judgments, discussion with judicial staff and scrutiny of media coverage do not have a comprehensive view of how pseudolaw adherents understand their place in the world. Such a conclusion justifies examining pseudolaw from various perspectives. Another conclusion is that if we look beyond what differentiates each flavour of pseudolaw (for example, the invocation that Australian polities lack legitimacy because they have become 'Delaware corporations' or that law does not apply to witches) we can see a commonality: pseudolaw is a matter of a failed claim to authority, irrespective of obfuscation regarding orthography, red ink or fictions about the Statute of Westminster.[32] On this understanding, pseudolaw can be construed as an expression of belief rather than feasible agenda for systematic law reform, a form of utopia or even magic. It is to this, our first perspective on pseudolaw, that we now turn.

III. Pseudolaw as Utopias

Utopias – visions of a perfect state, often understood as a regime in which all desires are effortlessly satisfied – are a recurrent feature of Western literature, predating the satirical work by lawyer Thomas More.[33] The genre includes the

of Ideological Attitudes in Responses to COVID-19 Threat and Government Restrictions in Australia' (2021) 175 *Personality and Individual Differences* 110734; and L Khalil and J Roose, 'Anti-Government Extremism in Australia: Understanding the Australian Anti-Lockdown Freedom Movement as a Complex Anti-Government Social Movement' (2023) 17 *Perspectives on Terrorism* 144.

[31] L Munn, 'Sustainable Hate: How Gab Built a Durable "Platform for the People"' (2022) 47 *Canadian Journal of Communication* 219; and AE Marwick and WC Partin, 'Constructing Alternative Facts: Populist Expertise and the QAnon Conspiracy' (2024) 26 *New Media & Society* 2535.

[32] *Joosse* (n 10); *Helljay Investments Pty Ltd v Deputy Commissioner of Taxation* [1999] HCA 56; *DCT v Palmer (No 2)* [2022] VCC 2001; and *Butterfield v LeBlanc* 2007 BCSC 235.

[33] J Carey (ed), *The Faber Book of Utopia* (Faber, 1999); MJ Lasky, *Utopia and Revolution* (Macmillan, 1976); and G Claeys (ed), *Utopias of the British Enlightenment* (Cambridge University Press, 1994).

hobo paradise in the ballad of *The Big Rock Candy Mountains*, perhaps inspired by the mediaeval Land of Cockayne[34] in which roast chickens drop from the skies to feed the unfranchised poor and fish obligingly jump out of the rivers onto dinner plates. Cockayne was an expression of populist resentment and legal incomprehension in multiple jurisdictions across Europe. It was a land where a miraculous regime change benefitted the formerly downtrodden – much like the vision of the sugar-lump and horse-ribbon heaven in Orwell's *Animal Farm*. There were no rats and mice or lawyers. Cows milked themselves. Every man (although apparently not women) had unrestricted ownership of houses and gardens. No taxes, coinage, heretics, heathen, lords, masters. The genre also includes More's austere *Utopia* (complete with slave labour),[35] Campanella's theocratic 1623 *The City of the Sun*[36] and recent work such as Ayn Rand's *Atlas Shrugged*[37] or behaviourist pieces from John Watson and BF Skinner, such as *Walden Two*.[38]

Some contemporary utopians desire a strong comprehensive legal system. The Reichsbürger, for example, want a return to the Wilhelmine regime in Imperial Germany, apparently claiming that contemporary law enforcement agencies and courts have somehow failed to recognise that the Kaiser's law is still in place.[39] Others, such as some of the self-identified sovereign citizens and Indigenous separatists discussed below, want a minimalist state.

Unlike standard utopias, pseudolaw is neither satirical nor a concerted call for action, instead resembling the mindset in belief systems such as QAnon with which it is sometimes associated.[40] The preceding part cautioned that there are uncertainties about how sovereign citizens and other exponents of pseudolaw understand the world, on occasion relying on mythologised understandings of Magna Carta or international human rights agreements as establishing social norms, causes of action and legal rights that override Australian state/territory and national statute law. Much sovereign citizen communication in social media and in representations to courts or tribunals appears to be a matter of a utopia founded on a mythologised past of yeoman farmers, state incapacity and small self-ordered homogenous communities: a prelapsarian world of Robin Hood

[34] H Pleij, *Dreaming of Cockaigne: Medieval Fantasies of the Perfect Llife* (Columbia University Press, 2003).

[35] LT Sargent, 'More's "Utopia": An Interpretation of its Social Theory' (1984) 5 *History of Political Thought* 195; and AR Heiserman, 'Satire in the Utopia' (1963) 78 *PMLA* 163.

[36] An overview is provided in N Malcolm, 'The Crescent and the City of the Sun: Islam and the Renaissance Utopia of Tommaso Campanella' (2004) 125 *Proceedings of the British Academy* 41. An echo of Campanella's work is found in the theocratic New Westralia secessionists considered in Arnold and Mikus-Fletcher (n 7) and noted in CM Sarteschi, 'Sovereign Citizens: A Narrative Review with Implications of Violence Towards Law Enforcement' (2021) 60 *Aggression and Violent Behavior* 101509.

[37] A Rand, *Atlas Shrugged* (Random House, 1957).

[38] BF Skinner, *Walden Two* (Hackett, 1948).

[39] A Löbbert, ch 10 in this volume. See also Walkenhorst and Ruf (n 3).

[40] PL Forberg, '"No Cult Tells You to Think for Yourself": Discursive Ideology and the Limits of Rationality in Conspiracy Theory QAnon' (2023) 67 *American Behavioral Scientist* 649; M Rothschild, *The Storm is Upon us: How QAnon became a Movement, Cult, and Conspiracy Theory of Everything* (Melville House, 2021); and CT Conner and N MacMurray, 'The Perfect Storm: A Subcultural Analysis of the QAnon Movement' (2022) 48 *Critical Sociology* 1049.

where lawyers were either absent or rightly challenged because 'lawyer law' is both false and oppressive. That vision is both anachronistic and dysfunctional. As the following section notes, pseudolaw proponents are apparently unaware of the realities of Magna Carta or admiralty law, often deeply committed to demonstrably inefficacious legal procedures and, in contrast to libertarian theorists such as Nozick, tacitly assume an entitlement to 'free riding' of public goods.

If the perfect state can be effected simply by a pseudolaw believer denying the authority of the state on a systematic or selective basis and relying on magical mechanisms such as name changes and notions of two personalities, we are in the land of Gilbert and Sullivan's *Utopia Limited*, a smash hit from 131 years ago.[41] That work by former lawyer William Schwenk Gilbert and composer Arthur Sullivan satirised corporate law and anxieties about national identity. Gilbert's libretto about absurdity and the erasure of legal liability is not far removed from some of the varieties of pseudolaw. In it, good King Paramount, ruler of a tropical island that is presumably located east of Australia, embraces law reform in the UK by incorporating the kingdom as a private corporation, free of liabilities but unregistered in Delaware. Every citizen becomes a separate company. So perfect is the new regime that crime all but disappears, emptying the courts and – oh horror – leaving lawyers jobless until reality intervenes. Reviews of the opening night in 1893 appreciated the piece for what it was: splendid costumes, engaging music, witty dialogue, a tale for entertainment rather than an exposition of law's possibilities.

The critics did not anticipate the range of pseudolaw claims apparent in Australia, the United Kingdom, Canada and New Zealand in recent years or what this chapter characterises as a legal smorgasbord. This leads to our second perspective.

IV. Grazing a Smorgasbord

Many manifestations of pseudolaw, in particular claims by sovereign citizens, are founded on conceptualising public administration as a sort of legal smorgasbord: citizens are consumers who get to graze what is on offer, entitled to take what they like and reject what is inconvenient. Court and tribunal reports (alongside advice by the sovereigns to each other in social media) thus feature litigants rejecting speed limits, obligations to have a current driver's licence or to register the vehicle in which they are travelling, comply with environmental protection regimes or child support obligations, or repay loans from financial institutions.

At an administrative level that selectivity might be obfuscated through mechanisms noted above, for example that law made by Australian governments have no effect because the governments at some stage became corporations registered in

[41] J Snape, 'Utopia, Limited or a Limited Utopia?' in I Ward (ed), *A Cultural History of Law in the Age of Reform* (Bloomsbury, 2019) 35.

Delaware (although apparently not in corporate havens such as the Caymans) or the individual is immunised from liability by expressing a surname in upper case letters.

At a deeper level the selectivity presents three conundrums. The first is a sovereign as the head of a recognised polity might have the discretion to choose which of that individual's own laws might be relied upon in any instance and given the often-misunderstood Westphalian Principle has discretion about adherence to law made by other polities. As Harry Hobbs and George Williams and others have noted,[42] recognition as a sovereign state (with a consequent ability to disregard another state's law) requires more than self-identification by an individual who wishes to exercise a fictive right to reject obligations without experiencing adverse consequences.

The second conundrum is that law reports indicate that many pseudolaw exponents in Australia are relying on pseudolaw claims that deny the authority of judicial fora while appearing in those fora.[43] Courts have recurrently taken considerable pains to explain to such litigants that the claims are unrecognisable and on occasion have eventually addressed a litigant's repeated denial of authority by identifying that individual as a vexatious litigant.[44] The third conundrum, irrespective of whether pseudolaw lacks both legitimacy and effect because it fails HLA Hart's rules, is that it purportedly legitimises free riding contrary to the notions of fairness articulated by figures such as John Rawls and rationales for community obedience noted by Tom Tyler in answering why ordinary people obey the law without regard to convenience.[45]

Sovereign citizens and other pseudolaw litigants who claim an immunity from driver/vehicle licensing or speed restrictions appear to assume that they have a unique self-elected right to travel using community infrastructure. Presumably they consider that while law regarding taxation obligations or responsibility for repaying loans to financial institutions is not applicable to them, they are entitled to enjoy the benefits of community goods (such as law enforcement, emergency services, roads, hospitals, aged care support and subsidised pharmaceuticals) funded through public revenue, and can expect financial institutions to lend on the basis of contracts that the sovereigns can disavow when inconvenient. Few litigants appear to be living 'off grid' in a contemporary version of Sherwood Forest without any use of public services. They instead embrace what Wolin characterised as Foucault's aesthetic decisionism in which individual subjectivity disregards rationality and subjugates social goods to personal gratification.[46] This leads to the third perspective offered, that of mystification.

[42] Hobbs and Williams (n 23); Arnold (n 24).

[43] This is explored by M McMahon, ch 9 in this volume.

[44] See, for example, *Gargan v Magistrate Dillon* [2005] NSWSC 1106; *Gargan v Director of Public Prosecutions* (2004) 144 A Crim R 296; *Official Trustee in Bankruptcy v Gargan (No 2)* [2009] FCA 398; and *Lohe v Gargan* [2000] QSC 140.

[45] TR Tyler, *Why People Obey The Law* (Princeton University Press, 1990).

[46] R Wolin, 'Foucault's Aesthetic Decisionism' (1986) 67 *Telos* 71.

V. Mystification

Australian pseudolaw believers recurrently invoke misread mediaeval and early modern law as having transcendent legal and cultural authority.[47] This mystification, perhaps attributable to not reading the law and to not understanding the place of particular statutes, arises from a belief that invocation – akin to reciting a spell – is efficacious and that contemporary ills can be alleviated (if not ended) by calling on a better but non-existent past. The Magna Carta is oft-invoked in this endeavour.

Krygier challenges such romanticism about the 'Great Charter', commenting that:

> It was not the first document of its type, though that is often alleged; it was ineffectual, its first incarnation quickly provoking civil war rather than restraining the king; and it was not, he [Tom Ginsburg] insists, the 'ringing endorsement of liberty' it is so often claimed to be. Instead, some of its less hallowed but more precise clauses include one preventing Jews from charging interest on certain debts, another barring a woman's testimony from leading to the imprisonment of anyone for killing anyone except her husband, and another removing fish traps from the Thames and other waterways (save on the sea coast). Even its most famous clauses that grant 'the lawful judgment of his peers or … the law of the land' and timely legal justice to every 'free man', particularly chapters 39 and 40, are limited in their substantive scope and social reach. They didn't enunciate habeas corpus or found trial by jury, still less representative government or democracy. They certainly had little to say for those, most of the population then and now, who lacked any of the privileges of those dead white male barons who did the deal.[48]

Pseudolaw adherents might assume that references to inextinguishable but not universal rights under Magna Carta are persuasive. That belief is not founded on a scrutiny of the various Cartas. It is not based on an understanding of how an agreement between early English elites and the monarch in an era of state incapacity has been assimilated in subsequent law that is a foundation of our own administrative state.[49] An irony of self-identified sovereign citizens seeking legitimacy for selective disregard of inconvenient law through reference to Magna Carta or the Bill of Rights is that those enactments were meant to bind sovereigns. Partaking of a legal

[47] For broader discussions of misreadings and valorisation see D Clark, 'The Icon of Liberty: The Status and Role of *Magna Carta* in Australian and New Zealand Law' (2000) 24 *Melbourne University Law Review* 866; P Linebaugh, *The Magna Carta Manifesto: Liberties and Commons for All* (University of California Press, 2009); J Atkins, '(Re) Imagining Magna Carta: Myth, Metaphor and the Rhetoric of Britishness' (2016) 69 *Parliamentary Affairs* 603; and P Coss, 'Presentism and the "Myth" of Magna Carta' (2017) 234 *Past and Present* 227. A detailed itemisation of 'Magna Carta Lawful Rebellion' pseudolaw is provided in *AVI v MHVB* 2020 ABQB 790 [38]–[91].

[48] M Krygier, 'Magna Carta and the Rule of Law Tradition' (2016) 65 *Papers on Parliament* 11, 13 (citations omitted).

[49] Clark (n 47); JC Holt, *Magna Carta*, 2nd edn (Cambridge University Press, 1992); and Z Elkins, T Ginsburg and J Melton, 'On the Influence of *Magna Carta* and other Cultural Relics' (2016) 47 *International Review of Law and Economics* 3.

smorgasbord on the basis of convenience, fashion or other arbitrary attribute gives the pseudolaw adherent a status as someone beyond the law that would have been envied by most mediaeval monarchs. This mystification does considerable work.

Somewhat more bleakly, the 'citizen' aspect in their self-identification as sovereign citizens is problematical. Supposed rights under Magna Carta are not necessarily perceived by pseudolaw adherents as universal – no Kantian cosmopolitanism – given that social media statements by adherents are often nativist, in other words associated with groups that embrace rhetoric about 'white replacement' or otherwise call for radical restrictions on migration. That is a reflection of the 'citizen movements' extremism on the left and right explored by Matthew Cunningham's 1992 *Mobilising the Masses: Populist Conservative Movements in Australia and New Zealand During the Great Depression*, or in studies of the contemporary Reichsbürger phenomenon in Germany and Austria that note advocacy for excluding or criminalising minorities.

One consequence is that reading social media and judgments in Australia and overseas is both bewildering and on occasion more frightening than watching Gilbert and Sullivan. It is frightening given what might be reasonably construed as incitements to violence – an echo of Shakespeare's 'first hang all the lawyers' – rather than amicable civil disobedience.

It is also frightening because, if we look at claims in the Fair Work Commission and Australian courts, we can see that some pseudolaw adherents appear to be deeply committed to a belief system that will provide them with frustration rather than the desired outcomes. The strength of commitment is such that recurrent failure by some claimants and their 'for profit' representatives does not dissuade them from using the same claims in an appeal or in similar circumstances. It is tempting to compare that resistance to disillusionment to the belief systems evident among some contemporary and long-running millenarian groups. Believers have eagerly awaited the End Times, when all ills will be cured and the legal lion will sit down with the disempowered lamb. The day of judgment has been recurrently announced – sometimes to a specific day, hour and minute – and true believers have recommitted rather than abandon the faith when nothing happened and onlookers mocked their credulity.

Gilbert and Sullivan captured some of the magic of words and procedure, law as a matter of form rather than content and thus coherence. Reference to form, utopias and religious belief is relevant because much pseudolaw appears to be a matter of faith. An article on pseudolaw and common law constitutionalism thus characterised some adherents as engaging in spellmaking, believing that saying the correct words – irrespective of content – will achieve their desired ends and command the court, tribunal or other decision-maker.[50] Some language use is so unstable as to be meaningless, with Netolitzky quoting a 'Red Queen' disclaimer that 'The below signed retains the right to define all words in the above notice and

[50] Arnold and Mikus-Fletcher (n 7). See also Cash (n 8); Netolitzky (n 8).

to change the definition of any/all words at any time without notice'.[51] Unilateral changes for a party's convenience are not necessarily endorsed in contract, consumer protection and other law; they are likely to foster distrust or merely derision that exacerbates the marginality of the individual who asserts a 'right' to do what they want, whenever they want.

One point of reference for pseudolaw exponents regarding law as a matter of abracadabra – now used by this author to enchant toddlers but traditionally functioning as part of an efficacious spell – is that content does not matter. The word 'abracadabra', for example, has no meaning in itself but supposedly has power when spoken aloud in conjunction with other language as part of a performance by the practitioner. Just say the magic words and something will happen. Such an understanding of reality that would presumably allow a large language model system such as ChatGPT to command either the spirits or public revenue agencies such as the Australian Taxation Office.

We see some of that misunderstanding of law and public administration, the focus on form rather than content and context, in pseudolaw claims where adherents disclaim liability on the basis that Australian governments are Delaware corporations or that adherents should receive entitlements but disavow obligations by expressing their name in upper case characters. In doing so, the fourth perspective – rights talk – is offered as a means of clarifying the mystification.

VI. Rights Talk

This chapter began by noting reference to pseudolaw as a movement, often framed in terms of a risk of violence and by extension of what has come to be characterised as domestic terrorism through action that harms individuals and/or infrastructure, with a consequent incapacitation of the state and alienation of communities from the state. That characterisation is unsurprising given renewed public attention to terrorism and the potential opportunities for academics, law enforcement and other stakeholders who engage with terrorism.

The conflation of pseudolaw with violence is, however, problematic when we consider the long history of terror. Merriman and others have, for example, identified histories of violence that eschewed abracadabra or notions of a conceptual rupture, instead reflecting detailed agendas for regime change and coherent theorisation about legal relationships that would be ended or amended through the action of adherents.[52] A 2023 report from the University of Queensland Business School stated that the:

> Sovereign Citizen movement, originating overseas but rapidly diffusing to many countries, including Australia, [has] already been described as a form of domestic

[51] @DNetolitzky (Donald J Netolitzky) (X, 13 December 2023, 7:54am MST), twitter.com/DNetolitzky/status/1734678146916794741.

[52] J Merriman, *The Dynamite Club: How a Bombing in the Fin-De-Siecle Paris Ignited the Age of Modern Terror* (Houghton Mifflin, 2009); D Sweetman, *Explosive Acts: Toulouse-Lautrec, Oscar Wilde,*

> terrorism. More recently their profile was raised during disruptive protests in response to COVID-19 public health orders that imposed restrictions on Australian communities. The disruption created by this movement has been magnified by its ability to coalesce with other causes; especially conspiracy theorists, right wing extremists, and those with extreme religious beliefs. This magnification has led to media scrutiny, calling into question the legitimacy of the Sovereign Citizen movement and its potential links to extremism.[53]

This chapter suggests caution in a reductive and condensed characterisation of sovereign citizens (and more broadly pseudolaw per se) as a movement and as a precursor of violence.

Instead, most pseudolaw can be understood as a pernicious type of identitarian 'rights talk'.[54] But it is not a paradigmatic example, because, as a legal discourse, it typically has three incoherent features. First it relies on an assertion of rights founded on ancient authority unrecognised by courts. Second, the purported rights-holder often expects a discretionary personal right – what Isaiah Berlin would describe as a negative liberty[55] – to be free from duties – for example paying taxes that enable the construction of community goods such as roads (which the holder tacitly regards as entitlements). The holder's rights are superior to that of peers, who on occasion are dismissed as ignorant or sheep because they do not exercise or even identify such rights. Third, the exercise of that supposed superiority as a matter of ego-centered sovereignism might directly harm peers, for instance through a claimed immunity from environmental regimes that protect the rights-holder's neighbours from pollution or exacerbation of disasters such as bushfires and floods. It also might indirectly harm peers through, for example, supposed immunity after damaging Indigenous cultural property, significant given settler state histories in which First Nations peoples were denied legal sovereignty and full citizenship,[56] or appropriation of Indigenous identities.[57]

Even though it involves rights talk, pseudolaw disregards what Hohfeld usefully characterised as correlates: the reciprocity of rights being matched by

Felix Feneon and the Art & Anarchy of the Fin De Siecle (Simon & Schuster, 1999); VH Sundquist, 'Political Terrorism: An Historical Case Study of the Italian Red Brigades' (2010) 3 *Journal of Strategic Security* 53; and S Aust, *Baader-Meinhof: The Inside Story of the RAF* (Oxford University Press, 2009).

[53] Jarzabkowski, Unger and Meissner (n 9).

[54] MA Glendon, *Rights Talk: The Impoverishment of Political Discourse* (The Free Press, 1991); N Milner, 'The Denigration of Rights and the Persistence of Rights Talk: A Cultural Portrait' (1989) 14 *Law & Social Inquiry* 631; M Ignatieff, *Human Rights as Politics and Idolatry* (Princeton University Press, 2011); PA Djupe et al, 'Rights Talk: The Opinion Dynamics of Rights Framing' (2014) 95 *Social Science Quarterly* 652; and J Bakan, *Just Words: Constitutional Rights and Social Wrongs* (University of Toronto Press, 1997).

[55] A useful introduction is provided in B Baum and R Nichols (eds), *Isaiah Berlin and the Politics of Freedom: 'Two Concepts of Liberty' 50 Years Later* (Routledge, 2012).

[56] Commonwealth Director of Public Prosecutions, 'CDPP Prosecutes 'Sovereign Citizens' After Desecrating Ancient Uluru Cave' (2023), www.cdpp.gov.au/case-reports/cdpp-prosecutes-sovereign-citizens-after-desecrating-ancient-uluru-cave.

[57] M Day and B Carlson, 'So-Called Sovereign Settlers: Settler Conspirituality and Nativism in the Australian Anti-Vax Movement' (2023) 12 *Humanities* 112.

obligations.[58] Robert Nozick's theorisation of a minimalist state and aspiration to a utopia[59] – unrecognised by most pseudolaw exponents – assumed that citizenship was an aspect of a collective and that as a matter of practicality – unlike roast chickens or Teslas dropping from the sky – people would contribute to community goods such as roads and water supplies.[60] Neither Nozick nor John Locke assumed that everyone could accept or reject law on an instance-by-instance basis just because an individual wanted the equivalent of the cheese and disliked the pickled vegetables on a smorgasbord. If pseudolaw is a selectively endorsed utopia involving mystification and rights talk, how precisely can we engage with those who wish to cast spells?

VII. Disenchantment

James Allan criticised much rights talk with the comment that:

> [P]roponents often talk about human rights and their side of an issue as though they are the superbly well-informed, altruistic side with a mystical and ineffable pipeline to God while the other side is best understood as being motivated by reactionary, borderline racist, and certainly stupid sentiments that could do with a few months in a re-education camp.[61]

In seeking to address concerns regarding the varieties of pseudolaw, for instance, given anxieties about frustration escalating to terrorism or the unnecessary load on courts and tribunals, one response is to identify how sovereign citizens and other pseudolaw adherents understand the world and why they have a misplaced commitment to that belief. Four perspectives have been provided here to help explain it. That identification is a potential basis for processes of disenchantment.

A starting point might be a recognition that much pseudolaw is not a matter of a 'movement', particularly an 'organised movement', but is instead individualistic, disorganised and likely to remain so.[62] Agitation in Australian social media and in face-to-face protests regarding COVID-19-related public health measures appears to have momentarily brought together a range of actors (including neo-nazis and

[58] WN Hohfeld, 'Fundamental Legal Conceptions as Applied in Judicial Reasoning' (1913) 23 *Yale Law Journal* 16.

[59] See for example the critiques in RM Bader and J Meadowcroft (eds), *The Cambridge Companion to Nozick's Anarchy, State, and Utopia* (Cambridge University Press, 2011).

[60] R Nozick, *Anarchy, State, and Utopia* (Basic Books, 1974). See also BH Fried, 'Begging the Question with Style: *Anarchy, State, and Utopia* at Thirty Years' (2005) 22 *Social Philosophy and Policy* 221.

[61] JFP Allan, 'The idea of human rights' (2013) 25 *Bond Law Review* 1, 3.

[62] J McSwiney, *Far-Right Political Parties in Australia: Disorganisation and Electoral Failure* (Routledge, 2024). TR Rochon, 'Political Movements and State Authority in Liberal Democracies' (1990) 42 *World Politics* 299 discusses the features of political movements that might include people who embrace sovereign citizenship values and understandings but do not specifically further claims regarding sovereign citizenship per se. See also D Baldino and M Balnaves, 'Sticky Ideologies And Non-Violent Heterodox Politics' in E Orofino and W Allchorn (eds), *Routledge Handbook of Non-Violent Extremism: Groups, Perspectives and New Debates* (Routledge, 2023) 15.

adherents of various sovereign citizen arguments) with differing commitments and often no discernable hierarchy or other structure.[63]

Legal scholars might be sceptical about how we can dispel the magic underlying some of the pseudolegal claims and their faith in a utopia that addresses resentment about taxation, environmental protection, the disobedience and unhappiness of young people, economic uncertainty or the ongoing disengagement from the state highlighted in the 2019 Australian National University Election Study.[64] That study, for example, reported satisfaction with democracy is at its lowest level since the 1970s constitutional crisis, with trust in the Australian Government having reached its lowest level on record.

The ANU data indicated that fewer than 26 per cent of Australians believe people in government can be trusted, with 56 per cent believing government is run for 'a few big interests' and only 12 per cent believing government is run for 'all the people'. Such disquiet is increasing, with for example a 27 per cent decline since 2007 in stated satisfaction with how Australia's democracy is working. Overall trust in government has declined by nearly 20 per cent since 2007. Three-quarters of respondents believe that people in government are looking after themselves. One implication is that those engaging in pseudolaw are expressing what these statistics reveal. They are dissatisfied with government, society and the status quo. They are searching or grazing among the smorgasbord for a utopia. A corollary is that building social solidarity through a government that is seen to address growing inequalities,[65] rather than through the civics courses and consumer protection or contempt action noted below, will reduce susceptibility to the 'pseudolaw virus'.

Nevertheless, strengthening the teaching of civics education at primary school and high school likely remains part of the solution. However, educational design should bear in mind that some audiences are either choosing not to hear or are interpreting what they hear in ways influenced by their cohort's anxieties and misinformation on TikTok and other social media apps. In fact, TikTok was recently reported as a dominant source of information for the 18-to-29-year demographics.[66]

Another response, unlikely to be embraced by free speech advocates, is to explore scope for restriction under the Australian Consumer Law of commercial pseudolaw guides and workshops by pseudolaw gurus.[67] Other criminal action might be available. Courts in Canada have stated that 'OPCA guru activities are

[63] J Roose, ch15 in this volume, explores this point further.

[64] S Cameron and I McAllister, *The 2019 Australian Federal Election: Results from the Australian Election Study* (Australian National University, 2020).

[65] A Rebechi and N Rohde, 'Poverty and Inequality in Australia, 2001–2018' in J Silber (ed), *Research Handbook on Measuring Poverty and Deprivation* (Edward Elgar, 2023) 663.

[66] KE Matsa, 'More Americans are Getting News on TikTok, Bucking the Trend Seen on Most Other Social Media Sites' (Pew Research Center, 15 November 2023), www.pewresearch.org/short-reads/2023/11/15/more-americans-are-getting-news-on-tiktok-bucking-the-trend-seen-on-most-other-social-media-sites.

[67] D Heilpern, ch 12 in this volume.

prima facie criminal contempt, given their rejection and public denial of Canadian legislation and court authority'.[68] In *AVI v MHVB*, the Court held:

> [G]urus who promote OPCA schemes that purportedly defeat legitimate court authority are engaged in criminal contempt of court. This may appear to be the use of a sledgehammer to crush an ant. I would instead use the analogy of an inoculation to stop a virus. OPCA and MCLR [Magna Carta Lawfull Rebellion] gurus harm people. These gurus teach illusions that will predictably fail. They promise much, but their clientele gets less than nothing. These schemes are nothing more than cons, led by people who rely and feed on the oft-quoted statement attributed to P.T. Barnum (of circus fame): a sucker is born every minute. That is as true now as it was when spoken more than 150 years ago. The Courts are not suckers. And the Courts will not be intimidated.[69]

That both can and should be reinforced by restriction under Australian law of online incitements to violence by pseudolaw adherents. We do have scope to crimp the expression of hate speech by figures such as Elon Musk and to require greater responsibility on the part of digital platforms operated by the likes of Meta.

A final response, in conclusion, is that the state has its own magic and should prioritise enforcement on a strategic basis – for public good – of law covering currency, taxation, fraud, environmental and other offences that are supposedly justified by pseudolaw believers. In 2023, the Supreme Court of British Columbia stated:

> When viewed exclusively from a government and court perspective, pseudolaw is nothing but a waste of state and institutional resources. That perspective misses something important. Pseudolaw leads to self-inflicted injury by those who advance these toxic ideas, including increased litigation damages and costs, criminal sanctions, psychiatric detention, foreclosed homes, and broken families. In a very real sense, OPCA litigants are the victims of the conman gurus who sell supposed secrets to the real but concealed law. Worse, OPCA theories authorize unorthodox and illegal actions against government, police, and court workers, including violence. Pseudolaw is a form of legal quackery or snake oil. Much as doctors and scientists are the most effective critics of pseudomedical and pseudoscience frauds, courts are the expert bodies logically and functionally positioned to refute OPCA misconceptions with clear, substantive, and responsive court decisions.[70]

In some instances exemplary action will fall on deaf ears or foster the resentment of adherents who consider that they have been martyred by an illegitimate judicial system, but it is worth discussion. That deafness is not a definitive metric of failure, given that enlightenment is just as much about persuading the unconverted from embracing pseudolaw as it about correcting existing believers.

[68] *Royal Bank of Canada v Anderson* 2022 ABQB 525 [27] and *Fearn v Canada Customs*, 2014 ABQB 114 [215]–[256]; See also *Yap v Matic [No 7]* [2023] WASC 55.

[69] *AVI v MHVB* (n 47) [52]–[54].

[70] *R v Hardy* 2023 BCPC 65 [10].

5

Failure to Perform: How can Theatre and Performance Studies Help us Understand Conspiracy Theories?

KATE LEADER

> You get people turning up and looking like idiots, when in actual fact they're not, they just haven't been given the, there's no guidance for them to find anywhere.
>
> 'Tim'

> The barristers are behind you and they've got a nice big space, desks and everything like that. They've got you at the front, you're sitting there, you've got about that much room to sit in, your knees are up against the front of it. There's a desk there, little, about that wide in front of you like that to put your papers on. So if you've got to stand up and address the judge, you can't do it without tipping the thing up and all your papers fall on the floor. Deliberate this is, absolutely deliberate.
>
> 'Neil'

I. Introduction

Why do some lay litigants turn to conspiracy theories? And what does this have to do with theatre, performance and pseudolaw? This chapter seeks to shed light on these questions by exploring the relationship between litigation and conspiracy theories through the lens of what I call 'failure to perform'. In this chapter I suggest that there are parallels to be drawn between the performative practices of pseudolaw process and the behaviour of litigants in person (LiPs). Drawing on research into LiPs in legal proceedings,[1] I argue that an important and overlooked factor

[1] Laypersons here primarily include LiPs, which formed the empirical research for my book: K Leader, *Litigants in Person in the Civil Justice System: In Their Own Words* (Hart, 2024). However, this work is also informed by more recent research I have undertaken in collaboration with Dr Lucy Welsh into lay benches in magistrates courts (decision-making in the lower criminal courts in England and

in developing a belief in conspiracy theories is the experience of repeated failure when lay litigants try to pursue or defend claims.

But while the fact that lay litigants may be more likely to fail than legally represented parties has long been recognised, what is *not* sufficiently recognised is the degree to which this failure is rooted in the lack of a *clear role for laypersons* when they try to participate in legal proceedings. This becomes particularly apparent in the context of pseudolaw, where there is a disconnect between the role pseudolaw adherents see for themselves (as experts capable of influencing the judge) and the role they are perceived to hold (disruptive and difficult litigants). By analysing the behaviour of LiPs and pseudolaw adherents through the lens of theatricality and performance, the importance of a clear role conception becomes apparent.

In this chapter, I argue that this lack of a role is rooted in a broader normalisation of legal specialism that works to naturalise and conceal modes of performance that separate those who are able to participate (legal professionals) from those who lack the skills and training to do so (laypersons). This process is, as I will show, an essential part of the broader project of reinforcing dependence on legal professionals and in keeping with Bordieuan ideas about the juridical field.[2] The *result* of this lack of role is that laypersons end up unable to access how to effectively perform as they are not legal professionals and are, simultaneously, derided for their poor performance. But this is, I argue, not due to litigants' inherent defects, but largely due to the mystification of the way in which legal actors acquire their skills.

Drawing on theatre and performance studies, and in particular acting theory, section II of this chapter argues that advocates, despite being ambivalent or reluctant to admit what they do is performative, have always been trained in performance. This is often misrecognised as natural behaviour, but is in fact what I call *legal naturalism* – a performance style that has become habitual. I go on to show that legal naturalism, the perception that advocates are *not acting*, does two critical things for the purposes of this chapter: first, it perpetuates a naturalised dominance over laypersons fundamental to the adversarial model of evidence testing. Secondly, because this performance process is unarticulated (and unrecognised, largely, by the advocates themselves), this means it is inaccessible to lay parties who seek to participate in proceedings.

In section III of this chapter, I will show that this means that when laypersons attempt to mimic legal performance, they will fail to understand that their inability to perform is inevitable as there is no way for them to perform well. Drawing on materials that provide guidance for laypersons in legal proceedings I will show how their contradictory performative demands and unclear expectations evidence that this is not a properly conceptualised role.

Wales is made by either a bench of volunteer magistrates, advised by a legal advisor, or by a district judge sitting alone): C Baksi, 'Some Magistrates Behave like "Little Emperors"' *The Times* (21 March 2024), www.thetimes.co.uk/article/some-magistrates-behave-like-little-emperors-zzqjq3x9m.

[2] P Bourdieu, *The Field of Cultural Production: Essays on Arts and Literature* (Columbia University Press, 1993); P Bourdieu, 'The Force of Law: Towards a Sociology of the Juridical Field' (1987) 38 *Hastings Law Journal* 805, 833–34.

Finally, section IV will ultimately show how this can lead to conspiracy theories: laypersons who try to repeatedly practise to become competent are prevented from doing so because they cannot succeed in a system that does not understand how laypersons can perform successfully. Such failure provides the fertile ground to develop conspiracy theories. In addition, such 'failures of performance' can become their own peculiar performative specialty: the rise of pseudolaw, and the phenomenon of the 'freemen of the land' is, arguably, a misjudged performance that has become its own iteration.[3]

While the focus in this particular paper is on 'failure to perform' and, thinking specifically about how not being able to achieve 'legal naturalism' can drive litigants to conspiracy theories, there is another way in which performance can help illuminate the phenomenon of pseudolaw. As Harry Hobbs et al define it: 'Pseudolaw refers to the phenomenon whereby adherents adopt the forms and structures of legal argumentation while substituting the substantive content and underlying principles for a distinct and parallel set of beliefs.'[4] Thomas Scheffer argues that the case file in legal proceedings – the bundle – is the 'organised memory' of the case: 'The circulation of case-information relies on the file's completeness. Everything that enters the file is supposed to remain in it. As a result, it swells with each file-work session.'[5] As Scheffer argues, however, putting together such a file is a manifestation of specialised knowledge and activity: knowing how to use it and access it relies on legal skills. Litigants in person, who do not grasp this 'bundle as organised memory', observe legal professionals and fixate on what they take away from the bundle – its materiality as a growing bundle of paper – and associate this with legal skills. LiPs therefore accumulate paperwork, mistaking its materiality for the 'materiality' of what it is to be a legal professional.[6] This leads to one of the stereotypical images of LiPs: individuals who carry around hordes of folders or paper in plastic bags or suitcases.

I suggest in this chapter that there is a parallel process at play in the formation of the performative practices of pseudolaw. Lay litigants attempt to imitate and reproduce modes of legal discourse *as they perceive them* without having the relevant skill to understand their complexity – indeed, their specific history, as all forms of language in legal proceedings are highly specialised and refer to previous iterations in a way that could not be understood by an outsider.[7] Instead pseudolaw

[3] I explain this idea at greater length in K Leader, 'Conspiracy! Or, when bad things happen to good litigants in person' *Legal Studies* (2 September 2024), www.cambridge.org/core/journals/legal-studies/article/conspiracy-or-when-bad-things-happen-to-good-litigants-in-person/B1AE515EFE1256C401737C477F7D713F.

[4] H Hobbs, S Young and J McIntyre, 'The Internationalisation of Pseudolaw: The Growth of Sovereign Citizen Arguments in Australia and Aotearoa New Zealand' (2024) 47 *University of New South Wales Law Journal* 309, 309.

[5] T Scheffer, 'Materialities of Legal Proceedings' (2004) 17 *International Journal of the Semiotics of Law* 365, 379.

[6] ibid 380.

[7] Marvin Carlson writes about the repetition of performance as a kind of 'ghosting' in the theatre: when one stages *Hamlet* one does so with a very clear sense of it having been done countless times

becomes a form of 'mimicry' where litigants adopt language they perceive to sound like what they are hearing and this becomes, through pseudolaw networks, developed into a fully imbricated kind of performative practice: *bad acting*. So, what do I mean by bad acting or good acting and how is it relevant?

II. Legal Naturalism as the *Mode* of Legal Performance

During my research for my first PhD nearly 20 years ago, I spent several months at Sydney University Law School sitting in on advocacy training classes. I wrote up one such observation below:

> It is April 2005 at a moot at Sydney University Law School. The prosecution begins:
>
> May it please the court … er … I … sorry, I withdraw that.
>
> Looking around the classroom there is no Clarence Darrow in sight. There is not even a Law and Order McCoy, a Johnnie Cochran, or a Geoffrey Robertson. Instead, there is a terrified 22-year-old wearing what looks like his father's too big blazer, trousers that ride up far above his sock-line, and who is carrying a large red umbrella and a slightly cheap looking mock-leather briefcase. His choice of clothing, clearly meant to make him look professional, instead renders him looking more like a 14-year-old extra from Modern Times. Perhaps, of course, it is the location as well. I am in Lecture Room 6, two storeys underground. We are in a small dark classroom, and the entire building smells like damp washing.[8] It is hard to take anyone seriously under these conditions. This frightened 22-year-old man in his father's blazer wants to be a barrister, like many other law graduates who every year sit for their Bar exams and try to make their way into the profession. Yet this student is so far removed from the advocates of popular imagination it seems an impossible leap. So how can a law student with a golfing umbrella in a basement improve? What does this young law student need to do to become an effective advocate?

This question has followed me ever since. How do legal advocates get good? And what is good?

A. Theatricality and the Legal Performance

Advocacy training – methods and advice for advocates on how to improve their courtroom skills – has existed in one way or another for (literally) ages. As far back as the 1500s, there were printed English manuals of advice for legal practice.[9]

before and it therefore always contains the ghosts of its previous incarnations that people bring with them. I have always thought this 'ghosting' was also apposite for legal proceedings. See M Carlson, *The Haunted Stage: Theatre as Memory Machine* (University of Michigan Press, 2003).

[8] The law school at Sydney University has now moved to the main campus and smells much better.

[9] A Fraunce, *The lavviers logike exemplifying the praecepts of logike by the practise of the common lawe, by Abraham Fraunce* (London, Imprinted by William How, for Thomas Gubbin, and T Newman, 1588);

These manuals themselves often drew on ancient Greek and Roman advice for pleaders that date back thousands of years, and there has been a steady stream of books on decorum and procedure through the centuries. This material has also boomed since the 1970s.[10] The more recent material has become increasingly multidisciplinary, with a multitude of material whose focus is on performance and persuasion.[11] This includes a growing body of work directly focused on perceived affinities between acting and advocacy. But alongside the long history of guides and techniques of how to be a good advocate, there has been a concurrent resistance to any association of advocacy with explicit performance. Milner Ball draws attention to this underlying pejorative attitude towards acting in his classic article from 1972, 'The Play's the Thing':

> The identification of juridical proceedings as theatre requiring live presentation would seem unexceptional but for the fact that the label has been rejected, as though theatrics were an expendable, intrusive embarrassment to the scientific and businesslike austerities of the courts.[12]

Anti-theatrical prejudice dogs any discussion of lawyers as actors.[13] This can be most simply summarised as due to the implication that acting and theatre are forms of artifice and falsehood, which runs counter to the claim (however dubious) that legal proceedings attempt to determine forms of truth.[14] As such, it is an undesirable comparison. But as Elizabeth Burns noted in *Theatricality:* '[D]egrees of theatricality are culturally determined … theatricality itself is determined by a particular viewpoint, a mode of perception'.[15] Burns continues:

> Behaviour can be described as 'theatrical' only by those who know what drama is, even if their knowledge is limited to the theatre in their own country and period … Behaviour is not therefore theatrical because it is of a certain kind but because the

T Powell, *The attourneys academy, or, The manner and forme of proceeding practically vpon any suite, plaint or action whatsoever, in any court of record whatsoever, within this kingdome : especially in the great courts at Westminster, to whose motion all other court of law or equitie … are diurnally mooued : with the moderne and most vsuall fees of the officers and ministers* of such courts publisht by his Maiesties speciall priuiledge (London: Printed for Beniamin Fisher: and are to be sold at his Shop in Pater-noster Row, at the signe of the Talbot, 1623).

[10] See for example R Fine, *The How-to-Win Trial Manual: A No-Holds-Barred Sure-Fire Way to Win*, 6th eden (Juris Publishing, 2024). See also the resources linked on the website of the National Institute of Trial Advocacy: www.nita.org/s/category/products/books/0ZG4W000000Pb1xWAC?c__results_layout_state=%7B%7D.

[11] P Lahav, 'Theatre in the Courtroom' (2004) 16 *Law and Literature* 451; R Harbinger, 'Trial by Drama' (1971) 55 *Judicature* 122; D Larner, 'Justice and Drama: Historical Ties and "Thick" Relationships' (1998) 22 *Legal Studies Forum* 3; D Larner, 'Teaching Justice: The Idea of Justice in the Structure of Drama' (1999) 23 *Legal Studies Forum* 201; A Tow, 'Teaching Trial Practice and Dramatic Technique' (1997) 13 *Journal of Paralegal Education and Practice* 59; MI Milstein and LR Bernstein, 'Trial as Theater' (1997) 33 *Trial* 64.

[12] MS Ball, 'The Play's the Thing: An Unscientific Reflection on the Rubric of Courtroom-as-Theater' (1975) 28 *Stanford Law Review* 84.

[13] J Barish, *The Antitheatrical Prejudice* (University of California Press, 1981).

[14] See J Langbein, *The Origins of Adversary Criminal Trial* (Oxford University Press, 2003).

[15] E Burns, *Theatricality: A Study of the Convention in Theatre and Social Life* (Harper and Row, 1973) 3–4.

> observer recognises certain patterns and sequences which are analogous to those with which he [sic] is familiar in the theatre.[16]

If theatre is not constituted by specific and static signs, but rather by the 'double relationship between theatre and social life', a pejorative conception of theatricality can therefore only exist if there is an implicit dichotomy being made between natural and theatrical behaviour.[17] What is theatrical, therefore, is what transgresses or deviates from convention.

For laypersons, courtroom proceedings may seem theatrical because of shared conventions such as costume and staging. However, for advocates, the theatrical may signify behaviour that deviates from habituated courtroom practice: individuals who represent themselves, for example, will fall into this category. This is because they do not know how to behave whereas advocates (hopefully) will; crucially, though, this behaviour is perceived as the *opposite* of theatrical or 'not-performing'. For many advocates, then, acting is more like 'acting up' – emotional and inappropriate.[18] This means that explicit advocacy training material can be unwelcome as it fails to be in keeping with the perception of 'not-performing'.[19] As Marett Leiboff cogently puts it:

> [T]heatre, which has no actual consequence of the kind law has, expects its participants, actors, directors and dramaturgs, to be deeply inured in forms of training that expect them to be both self-aware and aware beyond the self. Law, by and large, doesn't care, meaning that whilst we are expected to be technically capable, there is next to no consideration of self-awareness or awareness of worlds beyond the self.[20]

B. Legal Naturalism as the Style of Legal Performance

But *what* appropriate advocacy looks like will always be difficult to firmly establish in large measure because it is not historically static. Conventions and expectations of an advocate will change in different situations and will also change over time.[21] As such, what is recognised as appropriate behaviour is a particular style that advocates must learn through induction into the social universe of the law.

[16] ibid 3–4.

[17] ibid 12–13.

[18] Overt 'theatricality' by an advocate also signifies to his or her colleagues that he or she does not understand the proper decorum of the courtroom. I will unpack the underlying assumptions behind this later in the chapter. See also Toy-Cronin, ch 14 in this volume.

[19] Certainly, in Australia and the UK, there is limited tolerance for any kind of flamboyancy that might be permitted in US advocacy. There is also, literally, less room for manoeuvre, as in Australia (and the UK) an advocate is confined to questioning a witness from behind the Bar table whereas in the US an advocate may move around the space between the Bar table, jury box and judge's bench. Linda Mulcahy writes on this 'segmentation' and 'segregation' in her work on courtroom architecture. See: L. Mulcahy, *Legal Architecture Justice, Due Process and the Place of Law* (Routledge, 2012).

[20] M Leiboff, *Towards a Theatrical Jurisprudence* (Routledge, 2019).

[21] On what appropriate advocacy looks like, see L McCrimmon and I Maxwell, 'Teaching Trial Advocacy: Inviting the Thespian into Blackstone's Tower' (1999) 33 *Law Teacher* 44.

This nebulous area of appropriate behaviour is what I call *legal naturalism*: a performance style that indicates competence and skill to other legal practitioners and to a trier of fact (whether judge, lay bench or jury, although it may differ before each) and whose parameters alter over time.

Legal naturalism functions on a largely unconscious level whereby advocates habituate what they have learned (as well as absorb relatively unconsciously how to behave) to the point where their behaviour feels, to an experienced advocate, like it is natural and looks, from an outside perspective, like it is simply a professional persona. So, although many legal agents consciously associate acting with artificiality and construct a dichotomy between acting and their own practice of 'not performing' (being 'natural'), this is a form of misrecognition, resulting from advocates' failure to recognise their own embodied courtroom behaviour as a performance style.[22] Legal naturalism is, in the courtroom context, simply a case of 'good acting' rather than 'over-acting'.

i. Naturalism and the Internalisation of the Performance

This concept of legal naturalism owes much to the work of Pierre Bourdieu.[23] Bourdieu uses the term *habitus* to describe this acquisition and embodiment of belief systems. *Habitus* is a concept to help explain how we acquire and naturalise life-knowledge obtained through education and socialisation. This knowledge takes the form of unconscious dispositions towards things and plays a large role in what we value. What we choose to value will depend on our background, but we will value participation in certain areas or *fields* and therefore gravitate towards them.[24] Bourdieu argues that agents internalise the logics of fields unconsciously through education and socialisation. Because this process works on a largely pre-cognitive level, the actual field-specific logics become 'naturalised', and agents rarely reflect upon them as a way of being in the world. So those coming into the field are unlikely to question the field logic itself.[25]

[22] *Misrecognition* is a term coined by sociologist Pierre Bourdieu. Bourdieu argues that those working within a particular area of endeavour (or *field*) internalise and naturalise the logics of that field relatively unconsciously. This unconscious embodiment means they may misrecognise what they are doing. For example, a barrister learns that lawyers facilitate conflict resolution and represent clients in court. However, a barrister also unconsciously naturalises (and does not question) the dominance of the lawyer in a courtroom process. Consequently, the power and control a barrister has over lay participants is not something of which he/she is (usually) consciously aware. This is a form of misrecognition. See Bourdieu, *The Field of Cultural Production* (n 2).

[23] ibid.

[24] A field for Bourdieu is a site of struggle in which people (*social agents*, in Bourdieu's terms) compete with one another for capital of shared value that is not necessarily monetary yet not entirely unrelated to money (as all fields sit within and are autonomous – by degree – to the field of economy). The process of accruing capital is strategic, and because our primary desire is for recognition we must invest in the field we move towards, and we must 'play the game'. See ibid.

[25] This is not absolutely the case. Again, Bourdieu uses these terms as conceptual aids, rather than structural absolutes. Bourdieu also argues that those newly entering the field have less to lose and may in fact benefit from challenging the implicit rules as they can then set themselves up in opposition: ibid.

But these field logics are inherently, as Bourdieu would argue, symbolically violent. *Symbolic violence* is the exploitation of and dominance by those in a relatively powerful position over those who have less capital. As Bourdieu notes:

> In reality, the institution of a 'judicial space' implies the establishment of a borderline between actors. It divides those qualified to participate in the game and those who, though they may find themselves in the middle of it, are in fact excluded by their inability to accomplish the conversion of mental space – and particularly of linguistic stance – which is presumed by entry into this social space.[26]

Bourdieu's field theory is therefore richly performative and legal naturalism builds on this framework, but also thinks more specifically about naturalistic acting to consider *what* this role looks like. For an actor, playing another character naturalistically involves adapting one's way of being in the world, one's habitus, to 'sign another'.[27]

Naturalistic acting involves an actor not only attempting to become conscious of, and modify one's own 'symptoms' of *habitus*, but is also an attempt to understand and navigate a different way of being in the world and concomitant sign system. Naturalistic actors do not only mimic external characteristics; rather they attempt to present themselves as fully embodied characters. The effort behind this accurate representation is ideally invisible in an effective performance, where an audience does not notice the disjunction between an actor and the character they are playing. The enormous effort and high level of preparation for an actor involved in naturalistic performance is transformed by an audience's experience, where they simply seem 'natural'.

ii. *Litigative Performance and Legal Naturalism*

Legal Naturalism as I am defining it is similar to naturalistic acting. Both actors and advocates must neutralise symptoms of their *habitus* – reducing obvious markers of their past that may jar with audience reception. To their peers (and superiors), advocates must seem competent, professional and disinterested. Legal naturalism is necessary not only to be persuasive in a case, but more largely to ensure an advocate's competence. Legal naturalism, then, is not natural; rather it is a form of performance habituated by legal practitioners. But if legal naturalism is a habituated performance style, how is it acquired?

As outlined above, Pierre Bourdieu argues that agents' naturalisation of the internal logics of particular fields happens through processes of education and

[26] Bourdieu, 'Towards a Sociology' (n 2) 828.

[27] Paul Moore writes on such a process: 'Although not by name, the *habitus* as an idea is one that many actors may be familiar with. A good deal of training, which typically spans three or four years and continues into professional life, involves rigorous exercises aimed at neutralising physical expressions of this conceptual apparatus. "Symptoms" of *habitus*, such as accent, colloquialisms and bodily expression, all of which help to locate our past in the present, are suppressed, allowing the actor to temporarily sign another. The more completely actors master the ability to do this on a precognitive level, the more successful and comfortable their attempts at performance are likely to be': P Moore, 'Longing to Belong: Trained Actors' Attempts to Enter the Profession' (PhD Thesis, University of Sydney, 2005) 46.

socialisation.[28] Traditionally, the primary means of advocacy training was pupillage, which was effectively a form of apprenticeship.[29] This mode of training derived from English practice and continues today as pupillage in the UK and in various derivative forms (usually called 'readership') in Australia.[30] Pupillage is therefore more than learning how to handle briefs or stand in court: it is an introduction to the social universe in which legal agents operate. To make a living, advocates require referrals of briefs from solicitors and clerks within chambers.[31] Consequently, the importance of networking and establishing good working relationships with colleagues and superiors is essential to job survival. Pupillage is the ground-level entry to this world, where the novice advocate can demonstrate their competence and/or reliability with the specific goal of creating a good reputation and consequently obtaining work.

Pupillage also formalises a hierarchy where the senior advocate's abilities are the model for the junior. This, of course, is a form of role play: the acquisition of knowledge by an advocate through pupillage is consequently a form of modelling that is similar to repertory theatre, whereby a novice actor is attached to a company and improves his or her skills through imitation, rather than consciously absorbed verbal instruction. This form of education is in the doing, rather than in explicit training. An advocate's imitation over time becomes part of his or her *habitus*. Law graduates do not leave law school and turn into gifted advocates after passing the Bar exam – they *rehearse*.

Acquisition of legal naturalism, then, is a gradual 'becoming' of practice and familiarity, akin to the way one learns a trade.[32] This performativity of self echoes Erving Goffman's idea of presenting the best aspect of oneself to others so as to position oneself for advantage. However, Goffman's concentration on the conscious aspect and preparation for this overstates how aware an advocate is of

[28] The acquisition of *habitus* occurs over a lifetime and is, as previously noted, a flexible and adaptable series of dispositions whereby our previous experience of what we value will determine how we interpret and receive certain situations: what Bourdieu terms a 'structuring structure'. Bourdieu emphasises this flexibility and complexity, pointing out: 'there is nothing mechanical about the relationship between the field and the habitus. The space of available positions does indeed help to determine the properties expected and even demanded of possible candidates … but the perception of the space of possible positions and trajectories and the appreciation of the value each of them derives from its location in the space depend on these dispositions'. Bourdieu, *The Field of Cultural Production* (n 2) 65.

[29] In Australia, Queensland still uses the term 'pupillage'.

[30] Pupillage in one of the Inns of Courts in the UK has been in place for hundreds of years. Prior to the expansion of the role of the university degree, apprenticeship was accepted as the most important means of legal training. However, the proportion of students undergoing it has varied considerably. In the 19th century in the UK, almost all barristers underwent pupillage for two years. Yet by the 1950s, it was estimated that only one-fifth underwent pupillage. Consequently, it became mandatory in 1959 to complete 12 months of pupillage. See RL Abel, *The Making of the English Legal Profession 1800–1988* (Beard Books, 1998) 52–54.

[31] As noted earlier, this is the case in the UK and most states in Australia, however the move towards a 'fused profession' of solicitor/barrister in Australia may mean that barristers are increasingly directly approached by clients.

[32] In an article about Australian advocacy training, Marcus Priest calls the legal profession 'one of the last great trade guilds': M Priest, 'Raising the Bar' *The Australian Financial Review* (27 April 2007), www.afr.com/politics/raising-the-bar-20070427-jk7gs.

what they are doing.[33] Ultimately, advocates who undergo pupillage no longer see the skills learnt over a period of years as specific. Instead, advocates will see themselves as having navigated their way normally in the legal universe. This means that although the importance of apprenticeship is recognised, what is learned is less easy to quantify, as it may come to be seen as networking, and 'common sense' rather than acquiring highly specialised skills.

Those advocates who undergo pupillage consequently see their practice as either an 'art' in the classical sense (oratory and rhetoric) or as 'natural'. John Mortimer's lawyer character in *A Voyage Round My Father* claims that being a great advocate relies primarily on 'common sense' rather than brilliance.[34] Mortimer's student, Geoffrey Robertson (a Sydney University Law School graduate), says 'advocacy courses … now affect to teach a trade which comes instinctively or not at all'.[35] Justice Edward Parry states (rather loftily) that: 'the high privilege of lighting the torch at the lamp of eloquence is a gift of the gods, for orators are born, and not made'.[36]

As Bourdieu notes, part of the mastery of any 'art' form is an obscuring of the conditions through which this mastery was made possible:

> Ignoring the social and cultural conditions underlying such an experience, and at the same time treating as a birthright the virtuosity acquired through long familiarization or through the exercises of a methodical training … for the acquisition of art competence in the sense of mastery of all the means for the specific appropriation of works of art is a self-seeking silence because it is what makes it possible to legitimatize a social privilege by pretending that it is a gift of nature.[37]

So what does all this mean? Legal naturalism is simultaneously all pervasive and unrecognised. While legal professionals have a strong sense of what is appropriate or inappropriate – what crosses the border from effective advocacy into overt theatricality, for example – such ideas are so naturalised as to feel completely normal and not something that can be consciously recognised, let alone articulated. So even though such a process is highly dependent on role play, imitation and rehearsal, the concept of acting or performance becomes not only alien, but often actively rejected: to act is a form of fakery, a form of overt theatrics, an intrusion into the nebulous world of appropriate behaviour.

III. The Failure to Perform

So far I have argued that advocates are performers: that *legal naturalism* is an unconsciously absorbed and reproduced performance style that goes misrecognised as

[33] E Goffman, *The Presentation of Self in Everyday Life* (Anchor Books & Doubleday, 1959).

[34] 'No brilliance is required in law, just common sense and relatively clean fingernails': J Mortimer, *A Voyage Round My Father* (Penguin Plays, 1982) Act 1.12.

[35] G Robertson, *The Justice Game* (Vintage, 1998) 24.

[36] EA Parry, *Seven Lamps of Advocacy* (T Fisher Unwin, 1923) 72.

[37] Bourdieu, *The Field of Cultural Production* (n 2) 234.

basic competence or, at times, as a 'gift of nature'. This conception of the litigative performance poses some fundamental questions for those unversed in the legal habituation. What does legal naturalism mean for lay litigants? And what does it have to do with conspiracy theories?

A. The Expected Role of Litigants in Person

We have talked about the *role* of the advocate and what it might look like. But what is the role of the litigant in person (LiP)? Here we might, as LiPs will, turn to guidance provided for litigants in person and see what it says. The Bar Council guide suggests:

> Speak in short sentences. You might be tempted to speak like lawyers speak on television. Resist this temptation. Lawyers do not really speak like that. Some bad lawyers do, but judges hate it. Judges just want you to say what you mean in plain English.[38]

The Citizens Advice Bureau guide talks along similar lines:

> Forget everything you see on the telly. Most court hearings in TV programmes are about crime – and that is not what we are talking about here and anyway they focus on the drama of the story rather than reality.[39]

It seems clear from the above, at least, that LiPs' role involves not imitating what they see on television. The implication there is that because many LiPs will not have participated in legal proceedings before, they are unlikely to have experience of them and should not substitute this experience for what they see on TV.

But are they meant to behave like lawyers? On the one hand, the Bar Council guide suggests *yes*: to be a good LiP is to be *like* a *real* lawyer who speaks 'simply' and in 'short sentences'. By suggesting 'lawyers do not really speak like that' they are implying the goal for LiPs *is* to speak like real lawyers, not the 'fake' TV lawyers they fear LiPs will imitate. This view is echoed by the 'Handbook for Litigants in Person', produced by judges: they explicitly suggest LiPs should observe barristers and solicitors to learn how to behave: 'It is a very good idea to visit a court and watch a hearing in advance of the day of your trial or hearing and see how a trial is conducted and how a barrister or solicitor behaves in court'.[40] Indeed, this is what Toy-Cronin also notes in her research into behavioural guidance:

> We can see the indications that this is supposedly the role that the insiders want the LiP to fulfil. In handbooks and guides for LiPs, LiPs are exhorted to ensure what is put before the court is concise and relevant: to behave 'quietly, courteously, and respectfully', and not to waste the court's time. A LiP who adopts this lawyer-like role may indeed be well regarded by the court. Such a LiP will engage in rules-based argument, be careful with court time, ask for no assistance from the opposing counsel, court staff or judge,

[38] The Bar Council, 'A Guide to Representing Yourself in Court (2016) 23.
[39] Citizens Advice Bureau, 'Going to Court' (2011).
[40] E Bailey et al, 'A Handbook for Litigants in Person' (Courts and Tribunals Judiciary, 2012) 114.

> and to play to role well, mirror the social class and education of the majority of lawyers through dress, presentation, reasoning, and style of interaction.[41]

But at the same time the guides also seem to be quite clear that LiPs are *not* meant to try to be lawyers.

> Sometimes, the other side will make arguments about what the law is. Before the Hearing, you might have tried to understand the law as well as you can. If you feel that you understand it and have a point to make, make it clearly and simply. However, you are not expected to be a lawyer. The judge will try hard to think about the arguments that you would be making if you were a lawyer. The lawyers for the other side should talk to the judge about any law that is damaging to their case (and supports your arguments). In that way, the judge and the other lawyers will be aware that you are not a qualified lawyer and will make allowances for that.[42]

The guide goes on to suggest that litigants 'keep it simple. Throughout the Hearing, use simple, non-legal language as much as you can'.[43] So perhaps LiPs should not behave like lawyers. So where does that leave them? As Toy-Cronin notes, acting like a lawyer

> is an error that is made by both the insiders who imagine this is what they want from LiPs, and LiPs who guess that this is the role expected of them. A performance of the benchmark lawyer by a LiP is not practically achievable, but even if it were, it is not permitted by the insiders in the social world of the court.[44]

This is because the distinctions being made between being 'lawyerly' and 'non lawyerly' actually *both* require legal naturalism. For example, how 'simply' are lawyers ever actually speaking? As Lucy Welsh notes in her research into magistrates courts, the perception that the lower courts are a 'law-free zone' is a misrecognition of the seemingly simple but legally specific shorthand being employed in the language used. It may *sound* like simple language, but it has highly specific and precise meaning to those who are legally trained, which will be entirely missed by those who are not.[45] In this respect, the 'short sentences' advocated by these guides similarly risk a misunderstanding of how legally precise this language might need to be. And this means there isn't an understood or recognised role for non-lawyers.

Such guidance also misunderstands just how specific the performative skills are practised by advocates: in my study into litigants in person one of my research participants did as the guides suggested and attended court to observe the behaviour of the barristers and solicitors:

> I went down to court and quite, quite funny, I just, I wanted to see how the barristers, where they sat in court, and how they addressed the court, and what they did. So I remember, a particularly funny case, there were about six defendants in this one case

[41] B Toy-Cronin, 'The Role of the Litigant in Person in Civil Courts' *Social and Legal Studies* (forthcoming).
[42] The Bar Council (n 38) 25.
[43] ibid 23.
[44] Toy-Cronin (n 41).
[45] L Welsh, *Access to Justice in Magistrates Courts* (Hart, 2022).

> and each one had got their own barrister and they were all bobbing up and down, they were all sat on the same row all with the wigs and the black thing on, they looked like pistons in a car, bobbing up, bobbing, when one sat down, the other one … in no particular order, it was sort of random bobbing up and down.

Any litigant in person who tries to act like a lawyer is therefore likely to fail because these are specific performative and linguistic skills that denote extensive practice, socialisation and legal knowledge.

So, litigants in person cannot speak simply and clearly without having to translate their experiences into legally accepted ones: even where this is not a case of using legal words, it is still asking for coherence based on legal skills. The upshot is that even when LiPs are told *not* to be lawyers, there are still implicit expectations that they will behave liked skilled professionals, because lawyers *do not recognise that this is what they are asking them.*

And underlying this confusion is the need to restrain the perceived likely behavioural deviance of LiPs: to manage the risk they are expected to bring into the courtroom. The 'Handbook for Litigants in Person' has a single paragraph that exemplifies this strange mix of encouragement and distrust. It starts with encouragement: 'All judges are aware that trials and hearings can be very stressful and are often emotional occasions', before sounding a warning to LiPs about the need to behave themselves: 'That is why it is essential that everyone in court should try as hard as they can to behave properly so that all parties have an equal opportunity to present their respective cases'. The language then returns to supportive, noting that judges understand that LiPs 'may be overawed by too much formality and may become tongue-tied unable to say all that they need to in giving evidence or advancing argument'. But it then switches again, warning them not to be manipulative due to this: 'do not take advantage of any informality'. It finally concludes the paragraph warning LiPs that 'serious or persistent misbehaviour in a court room or chambers may be a contempt of court punishable by up to 2 years' imprisonment'.[46]

B. The Doomed Outsider: *LiPs and Unobtainable Legal Naturalism*

So where does that leave LiPs? They have a series of inconsistent sources of advice that range from 'imitate lawyers' to explicitly *do not* imitate lawyers. They must speak 'simply', but that 'simple' is a field-specific construction that goes unrecognised as complex by legal agents who have naturalised how they behave. So the distinction between 'non-lawyerly' behaviour and 'lawyer like behaviour' is actually an artificial one: *both* are founded in skills of legal naturalism. And this confusion plays out in an environment where this very gap between the two

[46] Bailey (n 40) 114.

performances of lay and law is an essential component in reproducing the legitimacy of this gap and reinforcing the need for representation.

As Toy-Cronin argues, the legal profession 'maintains the fiction that the ideal LiP is one who performs the lawyer's role. This role is neither possible nor desired by the high-status actors; LiPs must remain differentiated'.[47] So, ultimately this means there is a lack of clear role for LiPs and underlying this is the fact that such a role is not possible: laypersons cannot do well because they are not meant to.[48] As Bourdieu expressed it:

> The difference between the vulgar vision of the person who is about to come under the jurisdiction of the court, that is to say, the client, and the professional vision of the expert witness, the judge, the lawyer, and other juridical actors, is far from accidental. Rather it is essential to a power relation upon which two systems of presuppositions, two systems of expressive intention – two world-views – are grounded.[49]

For our lay litigants, then, it means that they are doomed either way. They can extensively prepare in as lawyerly a manner as they can and risk failing because they have not acquired *legal naturalism*. This leads to 'bad acting' – a poor imitation of lawyerly behaviour, epitomised in the LiP who sees the centrality of the bundle to litigation and therefore acquires voluminous files they bring to court in plastic bags: a mistaking of the material appearance of voluminous paper from the skill of understanding the role of the bundle as a 'locus of specialised knowledge and activity'.[50]

This failure of performance will be doubly resented by legal agents who, as Toy-Cronin notes, 'maintain the fiction' that acting like a lawyer is desirable but in fact do not want this.[51] Or LiPs can come to court without trying to behave in a lawyerly way and their performance will be deemed inadequate because they will not be able to adequately or coherently express themselves in a way that makes their claim or defence understandable (because they lack the very legal skills they need to do this and which they have been explicitly told are not necessary): either way, they will 'fail to perform'.

IV. Conspiracy Theories, Pseudolaw and Legal Performance

As I suggested in the introduction, the formation of the performative practices of conspiracy theories parallels those of pseudolaw. While the exact relationship between conspiracy theory and pseudolaw is a topic that warrants further

[47] Toy-Cronin (n 41).

[48] See, for example, the potential to crack down on other non-legally qualified individuals: Toy-Cronin, ch 14 in this volume.

[49] Bourdieu, 'Towards a Sociology' (n 2) 828.

[50] Scheffer (n 5) 356; L Reed, 'Pink Tape' (blog), www.pinktape.co.uk.

[51] Toy-Cronin (n 41).

exploration, it is clear that some LiPs who use conspiracy theories are engaging in pseudolaw, and that some, perhaps even most, pseudolaw is a type of conspiracy theory. But because my research has focused on the performance of LiPs, the following primarily analyses the legal performance and constitution of conspiracy theories. I suggest this analysis has implications for some pseudolaw adherents, as similar formations are at work in the social construction of pseudolaw. So, what does failure to perform have to do with conspiracy theories?

In Bridgette Toy-Cronin's article examining how the role of LiPs is proscribed through boundary work, she relates the experience of a litigant who attempts to put things on the Bar table, but who is told to leave by the opposing party. The judge then invites the LiP to use the table and this, it becomes clear, is an established practice:

> As a judge explained: "Our court takers always ensure they sit at the back and I invite them to come and sit up at the front, at counsel's table … It is just courtesy. They are not entitled to be seated on counsel's benches because they are not counsel, but because they are appearing for themselves, they are being heard, we allow them in".[52]

This anecdote bears similarity to the experience of 'Neil' related at the beginning of this chapter, which I reproduce here:

> The barristers are behind you and they've got a nice big space, desks and everything like that. They've got you at the front, you're sitting there, you've got about that much room to sit in, your knees are up against the front of it. There's a desk there, little, about that wide in front of you like that to put your papers on. So if you've got to stand up and address the judge, you can't do it without tipping the thing up and all your papers fall on the floor. Deliberate this is, absolutely deliberate.

The distinction between how the two anecdotes are differently understood is the explanation given to them. Neil becomes a conspiracy theorist because he cannot understand his differential treatment nor why, despite his best efforts to prepare, he is never considered to be performing properly. And it is here that failure to perform can lead to conspiracy theory: conspiracy theories can provide an explanation for what otherwise cannot be adequately articulated – either by the legal professionals or by the LiPs – that successful performance depends on *legal naturalism* and this is inherently inaccessible for laypersons.

A. Divergent Approaches to Understanding Conspiracy Theories

Whilst there has been a huge growth in interest in conspiracy theories in the past decade, my argument that repeated failure can lead to conspiracy theory is grounded in a specific conception of conspiracy theories. Conspiracy theory research has tended to fall under two umbrellas: (1) the pathological; and (2) the sociological.

[52] ibid.

The first, and oldest, of these approaches is rooted in psychology whereby conspiracy theory is seen as a form of pathology, or a product of conspiracist ideation. Such a conception sees conspiracy theory as an individualised phenomenon to which people are more or less susceptible depending on their particular characteristics.[53] Such an approach to conspiracy theory remains the most common, and while there has been until recently no specific work on conspiracy theories and law and litigation,[54] there is a body of work on 'obsessive' litigants that draws on psychological research to argue that there is such a personality type as a 'querulent litigant'.[55]

However, while I do not wholly reject the pathological aspects of attraction to conspiracy theory, I find this approach far less convincing than the alternative approach rooted in social science, which focuses on conspiracy theories as a collective phenomenon. As Michael Butter and Peter Knight suggest, the 'starting point' for such an approach 'would need to be the recognition that no matter what psychological traits are involved, conspiracy theories are essentially social constructs'.[56] In this respect, to claim that conspiracy theories – and pseudolaw as a similar social formation – are essentially social constructs and to approach them in this way does not preclude the possibility that pathology or predispositions *can* play a role in determining who may and may not be susceptible to such ideas, it simply does not automatically focus on this alone.

In this respect, as Butter and Knight argue, focusing on conspiracy theories as social phenomenon allows us to ask different types of questions: rather than saying 'what kind of person believes in conspiracy theories?', we might instead ask 'under what conditions do conspiracy theories emerge?' And 'What work do they do?' Here we can state two general equally important qualifiers: first, conspiracy theories are *social*; and secondly, they are explanatory – conspiracy theories are therefore, at root, a collective explanation for what otherwise eludes understanding.[57] Individuals deploying them, then, will reach for a shared conspiracy theory to explain something in their lives they cannot explain otherwise.

[53] See for example KM Douglas et al, 'The Psychology of Conspiracy Theories' (2017) 26 *Current Directions in Psychological Science* 538–42; MJ Wood and M Karen, 'Conspiracy Theory Psychology: Individual Differences, Worldviews, and States of Mind' in JE Uscinski (ed), *Conspiracy Theories and the People Who Believe Them* (Oxford University Press, 2018) 245.

[54] See Hobbs, Young and McIntyre (n 4); S Young, H Hobbs and J McIntyre, 'The Growth of Pseudolaw and Sovereign Citizens in Aotearoa New Zealand Courts' (2023) *New Zealand Law Journal* 6; DJ Netolitzky, 'The Dead Sleep Quiet: History of the Organized Pseudolegal Commercial Argument Phenomenon in Canada – Part II' (2023) 60 *Alberta Law Review* 795, 797.

[55] See for example I Freckelton, 'Querulent Paranoia and the Vexatious Complainant' (1988) 11 *International Journal of Law and Psychiatry* 127; N Bedford and M Taylor, 'Model No More: Querulent Behaviour, Vexatious Litigants and the *Vexatious Proceedings Act 2005* (Qld)' (2014) 24 *Journal of Judicial Administration* 46.

[56] M Butter and P Knight, 'Bridging the Great Divide: Conspiracy Theory Research for the 21st Century' (2015) 62 *Diogenes* 6.

[57] D Groh, 'The Temptation of Conspiracy Theory, or: Why Do Bad Things Happen to Good People? Part 1: Preliminary Draft of a Theory of Conspiracy Theories' in CF Graumann and S Moscovici (eds), *Changing Conceptions of Conspiracy* (Springer, 1987) 3.

Defining what a conspiracy theory is can be challenging. As Joseph Uscinski points out, there is no reliable method to distinguish between things that are 'totally out there' from 'ideas experts have yet to endorse as true': so what is and is not a conspiracy theory is a porous border.[58] In addition, as Michael Wood points out 'Calling something a conspiracy theory (or someone a conspiracy theorist) is seen as an act of rhetorical violence, a way of dismissing reasonable suspicion as irrational paranoia'.[59] In this respect, it might be more useful to think about what a conspiracy theory *does* rather than trying to nail down what one is. What a conspiracy theory *does* is provide an explanation of a negative experience or a failure. Those who believe in conspiracy theories simply use a different explanation for why failure takes place; or rather, because they have a desire *for* a unified explanation of why this takes place.[60] Conspiracy theories also provide simple explanations for experiences that do not have obvious explanations and provide reassurance.[61]

B. Conspiracy Theory and Litigants in Person

This definition may not fully account for *who* will become a conspiracy theorist but, in this context, thinking about lay litigants, moving away from pathologisation allows us to steer clear of two key problems. First, avoiding pathologisation stops us from falling into the trap of dismissing any complaints by litigants because they are 'difficult'. LiPs have historically been perceived as more difficult, or vexatious, and needing to be managed (as seen above, the 'Handbook for Litigants in Person' threatens imprisonment for contempt for such behaviours).[62] But as Michael Wood notes, labelling someone a conspiracy theorist, enables attention to shift from the substance of their claims towards their credibility, and so we fail to take them seriously.[63] This is similar to the experience of a claimant drawing on pseudolaw: this label will move the focus away from any underlying claim towards the fact that they are a pseudolaw adherent and, therefore, not to be taken seriously.

In addition to not dismissing LiP claims, though, avoiding pathologisation also allows for more careful reflection on what is, and is not, a conspiracy theory. As Joseph Uscinski pointed out (see above), we do not always know what is

[58] J Uscinski, *Conspiracy Theories: A Primer* (Rowman and Littlefield, 2020) 38.

[59] MJ Wood, 'Some Dare Call It Conspiracy: Labelling Something a Conspiracy Theory Does Not Reduce Belief in It' (2016) 37 *Political Psychology* 695.

[60] D Aaronovitch, *Voodoo Histories: How Conspiracy Theory Has Shaped Modern History* (Vintage Books, 2009) 5.

[61] Groh (n 57) 3. See also Leader (n 3).

[62] Bailey (n 40) 114; K Leader, 'From Bear Gardens to the County Court: Creating the Litigant in Person' (2020) 79 *Cambridge Law Journal* 260.

[63] Wood (n 59) 695.

conspiracy theory ('totally out there') from what is not ('ideas experts have yet to endorse as true').[64] And here, while 'Neil' may be wrong that legal professionals are *consciously* setting out to disadvantage him by making his papers fall on the ground, he is not wrong that this *is* part of a broader field-wide strategy of distinguishing between lay and law, just one that is not necessarily done consciously.

And it is here I want to suggest, following Butter and Knight's lead, that the work conspiracy theories *do* for litigants is that it allows them an explanation for why they cannot seem to succeed despite repeated practice. Marc Galanter, in his influential article 'How the Haves Come out Ahead' argued that a key factor in obtaining better outcomes in litigation is repeated practice.[65] Those 'repeat players' (RPs), who included legal professionals but also repeat defendants, for example, would generally do better in proceedings because they had multiple chances to practise and familiarise themselves. For the purpose of this chapter, we might say they had the opportunity to rehearse. But this theory runs aground when it comes to LiPs because effective rehearsal is only possible if there is a coherent role someone can learn to perform. And because LiPs do not have this, repeat experience does not lead to improved outcomes or better performance. It is *this* repeated 'failure to perform', rooted in the explicit differential treatment LiPs receive, that can help to fuel, aggravate and, at times, cause litigants to turn to conspiracy theory. More than this, such repeated failures can also fuel the development of pseudolaw performance: failed imitations of legal practice become their own kind of ritualised behaviour where litigants may, as in my research study, walk into a courtroom and challenge the judge on 'what kind of law' the court operated under or claim that they do not have, or will not give, a legal name.[66]

The turn to conspiracy theory through repeated failure of performance was observable in my study into LiPs where a significant portion of a small sample size (5–7 out of 15) expressed conspiracy theories about the courts.[67] These conspiracy theories grouped into different themes of Freemasonry, antisemitism, corruption and shadow courts.[68] But what was *shared* across all of these experiences was that those who believed in them had repeated experiences of litigation where, despite their significant effort to acquire the requisite skill to do well, this was not recognised, or was explicitly rejected by the court. As one interviewee recounted:

> I didn't expect some judges not to, uh, implement the *Civil Procedure Rules* which are rules, I mean they're, they're laid down in law, um, I really didn't expect them, um, not

[64] See Uscinski (n 58) 38.

[65] M Galanter, 'Why the "Haves" Come out Ahead: Speculations on the Limits of Legal Change' (1974) 9 *Law & Society Review* 95.

[66] This practice has become common enough in King's Lynn to cause the local council to issue specific guidance about how to deal with so called 'freemen'. See Borough Council of King's Lynn and West Norfolk, '"Freeman on the Land" and Challenges to the Legality of Council Tax' (2024), www.west-norfolk.gov.uk/info/20117/your_council_tax_explained/1035/freeman_on_the_land_and_challenges_to_the_legality_of_council_tax.

[67] Leader (n 1).

[68] Leader (n 3).

> to implement at all or only to implement the ones that favoured the over-mighty claimant. If, if a litigant in person as I'm finding just makes, you know, fails to comply with something or other, the other side will exploit it to the nth degree but the, certainly in my case, the other side has completely ignored timescales in a way that prejudices my uh rights in law, and no one has pulled them up at all!

Similarly, another LiP noted the only explanation for his failure had to be because he was a LiP:

> It was very, very, very distressing because they had a barrister supplied by the *Solicitor's Indemnity Fund* and even though I think I held my own very well, well obviously I did because I won the case, I did very, very well considering that I was a complete amateur but I think because of the masons and all that sort of stuff, masonic lodges and all these people knowing each other, it would be very embarrassing for a solicitor, the thing is if I had won, it would have been in the press, and it would have been very embarrassing for them and they didn't want that so that's how they cover up to keep litigants in person down to make sure that you don't rock the boat.

Another believer in the Freemasonry conspiracy felt that legal professionals (masons) signalled to each other in court, and this is how outcomes were determined:

> [A] freemason, if he is in difficulties, say in a court, and you see it in a court, they go up like that, I just don't know what to do your Honour, so he's saying (finger signals) I'm a widow's son, see that's a fraud, you see, passing themselves off as something they're not. Yeah, they do all sorts of other tricks like you know, turn their head away and that means it stinks, this case stinks.

These litigants felt themselves to be prepared and to have acquired the required skills, but they misrecognised that this simply was not possible. The experience of differential treatment was expressed by others who also expressed conspiracy theories. As another interviewee noted: 'it's a rigged game, there's no level playing field, and woe betide anyone who goes in there'.

C. Conspiracy Theories and the Failure to Perform

It is worth pausing to reflect on the implications of this. Litigants in my study *knew* they were treated differently and *felt* that equality of arms was routinely violated. They also felt that their attempt to acquire expertise was rejected. This is all in keeping with both 'boundary work' and more specifically, the role of *legal naturalism* in obscuring the conditions under which skills are acquired and naturalised within the legal field.[69]

So, while the conspiracy theories the litigants expressed may be fictitious, the conspiracy theory that LiPs are not being treated fairly is not a conspiracy

[69] Toy-Cronin (n 41).

theory at all. As recent research from the United States has shown, *pro se* litigants are both consciously and unconsciously discriminated against because LiPs are punished for either trying to be a lawyer, or for *not* being one: they are denied the ability to acquire performative competence and simultaneously derided *for* this inadequacy.[70] And all these conscious and unconscious biases translate into what Richard Moorhead described as a 'strong perceptual cocktail of unfairness'.[71]

LiPs have no clear role, suffer contradictory guidance on how to behave and when they do attempt to acquire or mimic legal skills, they are prevented from doing so or dismissed as bad actors. Such negative experiences foster and aggravate conspiracist ideas around legal process to help explain what has happened to them. And this turn to conspiracy theory will only compound the likelihood of their being dismissed and not taken seriously.

V. Conclusion

So where do we end up? This lack of a clear role for LiPs, indicative of a highly specialised and semiautonomous legal field, fuels conspiracy theory. Like pseudolaw, such conspiracy theory can be highly offensive, and is mistaken in its targets. But two important points remain: first, such conspiracy theory is *not* the product of the pathology of serial litigants – while it is often painted as such, such an analysis serves to dismiss what is genuinely rooted differential treatment. Instead, it is the product of genuine unfairness foundational to the experience of LiPs pursuing and defending claims. And secondly, while the target of the conspiracy theories is mistaken, the 'conspiracy theory' of the courts treating LiPs unfairly is, arguably, not a 'conspiracy theory' at all. Until we conceptualise a way for LiPs to perform well, to make *space* for them, they will continue to fail, and continue to turn to conspiracy theories for explanation.

[70] V Quintanilla et al, 'The Signaling Effect of Pro Se Status' (2017) 42 *Law & Social Inquiry* 1091.

[71] R Moorhead, 'The Passive Arbiter: Litigants in Person and the Challenge to Neutrality' (2007) 16 *Social and Legal Studies* 405, 410.

PART II

The Operation and Practice of Pseudolaw Around the Globe

6

The Rise of Sovereign Citizen Pseudolaw in the United States of America

STEPHEN YOUNG, HARRY HOBBS AND
RACHEL GOLDWASSER

I. Introduction

Individuals express sovereign citizen pseudolaw when they claim they are not subject to the jurisdiction of a national government and, instead, assert they are 'freemen', 'natural men/women' or 'citizens of a sovereign state'. They do so to disclaim any authority held by a government they view as corrupt and illegitimate. Today, there are numerous ways that individuals express and justify these claims. They may point to archaic and obsolete legal instruments that they insist still represent the good or true law. They may destroy and renounce any state-issued identification document they possess, believing its existence constitutes their acceptance of a contract. They may also sign their names in non-standard ways or file paperwork with the courts self-identifying as sovereign or outside the court's jurisdiction. These actions are understood to comprise sovereign citizen tropes. For this reason, individuals acting in this way are characterised as sovereign citizens and their legal arguments as sovereign citizen pseudolaw.

This characterisation may be imprecise. Many who engage in these actions deny that they are 'sovereign citizens', recognising the reputation the term holds.[1] Others embellish or adorn their legal claims with supplementary conspiratorial and anti-institutional ideas, making it difficult to precisely source and classify their beliefs.[2] At the same time, there is not and has never been an isolated and unified 'sovereign citizen movement', but rather a diffuse and interconnected

[1] Christine Sarteschi, ch 11 in this volume. From an internal perspective the term is also oxymoronic, as a citizen is a slave to a corporate government. We thank Rob Sudy for this insight.

[2] DJ Netolitzky, 'The Dead Sleep Quiet: History of the Organized Pseudolegal Commercial Argument Phenomenon in Canada – Part II' (2023) 60 *Alberta Law Review* 795, 797.

network of individuals and groups that speak a similar language and practise many like activities. Given there is no official sovereign citizen doctrine, no codification of principles and positions, no catechism, or movement, individuals often adopt and adapt various theories, narratives and schemes to suit their own purposes. The internationalisation of these beliefs has spurred further modifications.[3] But the core of these beliefs emerged somewhere.

In this chapter, we explain the formation and development of a particular style of pseudolaw from within the United States that we call sovereign citizen pseudolaw. As we illustrate, this primarily legalistic phenomenon arose from a confluence of right-wing and religious extremist associations and social clubs that percolated throughout North America across the twentieth century. Chief among these are the Posse Comitatus, the Common Law Movement and the anti-government Patriot Movement.[4] The influence of each movement and organisation on contemporary sovereign citizen pseudolaw is not linear. Nor are these 'movements' uniform or cohesively formed or controlled, which our analysis might appear to suggest. Instead, like Wittgenstein's concept of family resemblances,[5] individuals associated with these groups share overlapping similarities but differ according to whether they more heavily emphasise religious, political, economic, legalistic or militaristic views, attitudes and approaches. In this way, modern sovereign citizen tropes and views emerged as a gradual accretion of legalistic concepts, rituals and claims that developed and adapted from earlier organisations.

In providing a generalist history, we clarify three aspects of modern sovereign citizen pseudolaw. First, contemporary sovereign citizen pseudolaw derives or emerged from these earlier movements. These 'movements' (for lack of a better word) were loosely organised around a core but diffuse set of extremist religious, political and economic beliefs. Second, this organisational structure facilitated (and still facilitates) experimentation, allowing individual leaders or gurus to modify and adapt their tactics and specific beliefs in search of followers. Third, given this dynamic, growth and expansion occur primarily during periods of crisis, with particularly adept leaders taking advantage of novel societal issues and events to promote and spread their unique models of pseudolaw. We maintain that, because sovereign citizen pseudolaw gradually emerged in this way, it is highly adaptable to local contexts; responsive to social, political or economic crises; spreads in unforeseen ways while recycling core claims or tropes; and may involve extremist religious, political and economic beliefs.

[3] H Hobbs, S Young and J McIntyre, 'The Internationalisation of Pseudolaw: The Growth of Sovereign Citizen Arguments in Australia and Aotearoa New Zealand' (2024) 47 *University of New South Wales Law Journal* 309.

[4] The influence of the Tax Protestor movement is also visible: see H Hobbs and G Williams, *Micronations and the Search for Sovereignty* (Cambridge University Press, 2022) 66.

[5] L Wittgenstein, *Philosophical Investigations* (Blackwell Publishing, 2001) § 67.

This chapter is divided into three substantive sections. In section II, we provide a history of the Posse Comitatus, locating its materialisation in the peculiar influence of British Israelism and the right-wing Christian Identity movement. Unlike those earlier religious-political groups, the Posse focused more on government and law, developing the foundation for what became 'sovereign citizen pseudolaw'. In section III, we examine two outgrowths of the Posse. We first explore how the Common Law Movement emerged as a more legalistic-focused branch roughly between 1980 and 1995, before describing a more militaristic and violent extension that operated under the auspices of the Patriot Movement. The core beliefs and claims integral to sovereign citizen pseudolaw were firmly established by the 1990s and self-identifying 'sovereign citizens' first appeared during this period. The most significant elaboration in the years since has been the national and international spread of this phenomenon. In section IV, we briefly note this development, outlining how sovereign citizen pseudolaw has metastasised across the United States. Other chapters in this volume examine specific manifestations in different countries.

II. Origins

The primary precursor of contemporary sovereign citizen pseudolaw is the Posse Comitatus, a loosely organised far-right social movement with a militia component that emerged in the early 1970s in the United States.[6] Translated as 'power of the county',[7] its members drew on a misreading and misunderstanding of an 1878 Act of Congress to argue that there is no legitimate government beyond the county, and no higher authority than the local sheriff.[8] But the Posse Comitatus was more than simply an anti-government militia; as an outgrowth of the white supremacist Christian Identity movement, its members believed they were the 'true Israelites', chosen by God, and spread conspiratorial, racist and antisemitic views. In fact, many of their core beliefs can be traced back to a peculiar pseudo-religious movement called British Israelism.[9] In this part, we provide a brief introduction to British Israelism and Christian Identity, before detailing the formation of the Posse Comitatus under the leadership of William Potter Gale.

[6] F Sullivan, 'The Usurping Octopus of Jurisdictional/Authority: The Legal Theories of the Sovereign Citizen Movement' (1999) 4 *Wisconsin Law Review* 785; J Corcoran, *Bitter Harvest: Gordon Kahl and the Posse Comitatus: Murder in the Heartland* (Viking, 1990).

[7] L Zeskind, *Blood and Politics: The History of the White Nationalist Movement from the Margins to the Mainstream* (Macmillan, 2009) 72.

[8] *Posse Comitatus Act 1878*, 18 USC § 1385. See further JM Berger, 'Without Prejudice: What Sovereign Citizens Believe' George Washington University Project on Extremism (June 2016) 8.

[9] M Barkun, *Religion and the Racist Right: The Origins of the Christian Identity Movement*, revd edn (University of North Carolina Press, 1997) 3. Evelyn Schlatter argues that the US's 'agrarian myth' promotes populism and leads to organisations that seek to wrest control from the corrupt few. See E Schlatter, *Aryan Cowboys: White Supremacists and the Search for a New Frontier* (University of Texas Press, 2006) ch 4.

A. British Israelism and Christian Identity

British Israelism is a belief that the people of Great Britain are the 'lineal descendants of the "ten lost tribes" of Israel'.[10] Although elements of this idea can be traced to the late sixteenth century,[11] the movement first emerged 'as an identifiable religious force' in the 1880s 'when the circumstances of the time were particularly propitious for the appearance of a movement so imperialistically-orientated'.[12] The movement drew large crowds. Even in the 1960s, up to '20,000 people attended the annual national congress of the leading Israelist organisation in Britain'.[13]

The quasi-religious movement also found fertile soil in Britain's former colonies, including those in North America. Although arriving across the Atlantic in the late nineteenth century, British Israelism grew significantly in the years following the Great Depression. As it matured, an important distinction emerged. At its core, British Israelism, in seeking to establish a glorious history for the Anglo-Saxon people, fostered 'racial chauvinism'.[14] Nevertheless, its mainstream proponents considered Jewish people essentially a brother race, as both the Jews and Anglo-Saxons were descended from the original tribes of Israel. The budding American variant, however, explicitly adopted the latent antisemitism within the US.[15] In the 1930s, it also drew on a more radical conservative milieu forming in opposition to President Franklin D Roosevelt's New Deal.

One of the more important British Israelite organisations in shepherding this transition was established in Detroit in 1930. That year, lawyer Howard Rand and newspaper editor William J Cameron formed the Anglo-Saxon Federation of America.[16] Together Rand and Cameron supported the growth of affiliated clubs across the US, facilitating a link between their pseudo-religious views, antisemitism and the political right. The Federation denied that Jews were descendants of the Tribe of Judah or the inheritors of the lands of Israel.[17] Alarmed by the Federal Government's response to the Great Depression – which saw the growth of federal power to stabilise the economy – they also sought to ground their preferred law and policy within the ideology of British or Anglo-Israelism.

[10] Barkun (n 9) 4.

[11] See TG Dedon, 'From Julius Evola to Anders Breivik: the Invented Tradition of Far-Right Christianity' in G Mannion, D Doyle and T Dedon (eds), *Ecumenical Perspectives Five Hundred Years After Luther's Reformation* (Palgrave MacMillan, 2021) 93 (identifying ML Loyer's, *The Ten Lost Tribes* as generating the idea that Anglo-Saxons and others are descendants of ancient Israelites).

[12] J Wilson, 'British Israelism' (1968) 16 *Sociological Review* 41, 41.

[13] A Cottrell-Boyce, 'British-Israelists and the "State of Israeli" in the Twentieth Century' (2020) 44 *Journal of Religious History* 269, 297.

[14] W Ingram, 'God and Race: British-Israelism and Christian Identity' in T Miller (ed), *America's Alternative Religions* (State University of New York Press, 1995) 119, 121–22.

[15] Barkun (n 9) 51.

[16] RL Roy, *Apostles of Discord: A Study of Organized Bigotry and Disruption on the Fringes of Protestantism* (Beacon Press, 1953) 91.

[17] LT Talbot, *What's Wrong with Anglo-Israelism?* (Dunham Publishing Company, 1956) 10.

In 1933, for example, Cameron promoted the concept of 'Biblical economics' or the 'God-given principles of taxation and credit', where:

> Land and by extension other forms of property, must not be taxed, nor must that part of the land's produce that its owners consume. 'Only the surplus over and above a livelihood was taxed, and that in a slight degree'.[18]

Although tax protests have a long history in the United States, an expert on the Posse Comitatus, Daniel Levitas, situates this development as a 'conservative reaction to Roosevelt and the Democrats'.[19]

Rand and Cameron were not alone. Around this same time, another British Israelite, Wesley Swift, strengthened the links between the pseudo-religious movement and political extremism. A key figure in the emerging white supremacist Christian Identity movement, the former Methodist minister established the Anglo-Saxon Christian Congregation, which later became the Church of Jesus Christ Christian.[20] Based on the West Coast in California, Swift and his supporters were 'at liberty to borrow, modify, and discard doctrine as their own idiosyncrasies dictated'.[21] Active in the Ku Klux Klan and friends with prominent antisemite and leader of the Christian Nationalist Crusade, Gerald LK Smith, Swift connected the early Christian Identity movement to political actors and extremist right-wing ideologies.[22]

Christian Identity emerged as a loosely structured sect that embraced a theology premised on a variety of ideas rather than an orthodox series of beliefs.[23] They developed two central claims that are important for our purposes. First, the movement advanced the antisemitic 'two-seed' doctrine which asserted that the children of Eve – Cain and Abel – had different fathers.[24] Abel was fathered by Adam, and his descendants became the true Israelites of the Bible.[25] On the other hand, Jews were children of Cain's father, Satan.[26] Second, because the

[18] Barkun (n 9) 204.

[19] 'Hate Group Expert Daniel Levitas Discusses Posse Comitatus, Christian Identity Movement and More' Southern Poverty Law Center Intelligence Report (15 June 1998), www.splcenter.org/fighting-hate/intelligence-report/1998/hate-group-expert-daniel-levitas-discusses-posse-comitatus-christian-identity-movement-and.

[20] M Durham, 'Christian Identity and the Politics of Religion' (2008) 9 *Totalitarian Movements and Political Religions* 79, 80.

[21] Barkun (n 9) 55.

[22] ibid; D Levitas, *The Terrorist Next Door: The Militia Movement and the Radical Right* (St Martin's Press, 2002) 36–37; Anti-Defamation League, 'Backgrounder: Christian Identity' (5 April 2017), www.adl.org/resources/backgrounder/christian-identity.

[23] Anti-Defamation League (n 22).

[24] See J Schamber and S Stroud, 'Mystical Anti-Semitism and the Christian Identity Movement: A Narrative Criticism of Dan Gayman's "The Two Seeds of Genesis 3:15"' Paper presented at the Annual Meeting of the National Communication Association, Seattle, WA (9–12 November 2000) 4.

[25] A Cottrell-Boyce, 'British Israelism' in J Crossley and A Lockhart (eds), *Critical Dictionary of Apocalyptic and Millenarian Movements* (2021), www.cdamm.org/articles/british-israelism; Southern Poverty Law Center, 'Christian Identity' www.splcenter.org/fighting-hate/extremist-files/ideology/christian-identity.

[26] Durham (n 20) 81; Cottrell-Boyce (n 25). See also Zeskind (n 7) 62.

Anglo-Saxon people are the racial and biological descendants of Israel, it is vital to ensure American law 'conform to the law presented in the Bible'.[27] The movement's right-wing economic vision was thus a product of its antisemitism, but this was also combined with growing fears about communism and race relations in the 1960s.[28] Levitas explains that 'For Smith and Swift, communism was synonymous with Judaism, and Jews were the masterminds of a global conspiracy to undermine Christian civilization'.[29] Borrowing from Rand and Cameron's biblical economics, Swift's Christian Identity interpreted the Bible as a means for ensuring individuals retained nearly all the money they made free from taxation and excused any debts they incurred.[30]

B. Christian Identity and the Rise of the Posse Comitatus

Swift remained at the heart of Christian Identity, but as a loosely organised and decentralised movement, various ministries arose across the country.[31] In the late 1960s, two of Swift's more prominent disciples, William Potter Gale and Richard Butler, began to develop their own doctrines and precepts. When Swift died in 1970, Butler moved Swift's church to Idaho and rebranded as the Aryan Nations, which remains an active neo-Nazi group.[32] In contrast, Gale – a United States veteran and Reverend – clothed Christian Identity's pseudo-religious and far-right political ideology in a quasi-legalistic vision that focused on protecting and promoting his interpretation of the natural rights of individuals.[33] Over time and with Gale's guidance, this legal, political and religious amalgamation developed into sovereign citizen pseudolaw. It began, however, with an organisation led by Gale that was far more militia-like.

Gale had been particularly active in paramilitary groups in the 1950s and 1960s. In 1957, he first discussed the idea of creating a posse.[34] The concept of posse comitatus dates to ninth-century England.[35] It refers to a group of people mobilised by a peace officer, such as a chief or sheriff, to resist invasion, suppress lawlessness and protect property and the public welfare.[36] Gale appropriated this concept and tied 'it directly to [Christian] Identity theology'.[37] While Gale adopted the interpretive techniques of Christian Identity, he applied them in a far

[27] Barkun (n 9) 200–01.

[28] A Bochicchio, 'Justification by Race: Wesley Swift's White Supremacy and Anti-Semitic Theological Views in His Christian Identity Sermons' (2021) 17 *Journal of Hate Studies* 35, 35.

[29] Levitas (n 22) 28.

[30] Barkun (n 9) 205.

[31] Durham (n 20) 81.

[32] Levitas (n 22) 110; Anti-Defamation League (n 22).

[33] Levitas (n 22) 3.

[34] ibid 108.

[35] DB Kopel, 'The *Posse Comitatus* and the Office of Sheriff: Armed Citizens Summoned to the Aid of Law Enforcement' (2015) 104 *The Journal of Criminal Law and Criminology* 761.

[36] ibid 772–74. See Sheriffs Act 1887, s 8.

[37] Barkun (n 9) 221.

more legalistic manner. No longer so focused on religious claims, his embrace of legalism led to the gradual development of sovereign citizen pseudolaw. Over the following years he helped found the white supremacist Christian Defence League and the anti-tax California Rangers.[38] In 1971, Gale published a manifesto, or what he called a 'guide', recommending that citizens create local posse groups.[39] Implementing his own advice, Gale formed the United States Christian Posse Association.[40]

In melding these beliefs into a concept that people could enact, Gale created another loosely formed institution that would spread in diffuse ways. Gale would approve a charter for a posse in a county as long as it contained at least seven 'Christian citizens',[41] and contended each militia was 'doing the Lord's word when it acted against evildoers'.[42] Who constituted 'evildoers' was capacious, encompassing any officials that were against the local Posse's aims. If the county sheriff refused to support the Posse, perhaps by seeking to enforce federal laws,

> he shall be removed by the Posse to the most populated intersection of streets in the township and at high noon be hung by the neck, the body remaining until sundown as an example to those who would subvert the law.[43]

Around the same time, Henry 'Mike' Beach, a former dry cleaner and member of the pro-Nazi group the Silver Shirts, also formed a group called the Sheriff's Posse Comitatus.[44] It appears these two Posse groups arose nearly simultaneously, but it is generally accepted that Gale is responsible for the Posse Comitatus as we know it today.[45]

Fundamental to the Posse Comitatus belief system is that each county would be 'independent, a veritable law unto itself, subject only to its own understanding of what God required in a particular time and place'.[46] The highest authority was the county sheriff, which would later give rise to the term 'constitutional sheriff', used to describe sheriffs who approved of this fabricated hierarchy. Engaging with other levels of law or government – even simply by possessing state identification or a federal social security number, or paying income tax – would violate their ideology and be illegal.[47]

38 Levitas (n 22) 108.
39 ibid 108–09; Interview with Daniel Levitas (n 19). See further G Cash, ch 8 in this volume.
40 Barkun (n 9) 69, 207; Schlatter (n 9) 105.
41 M Barkun, Violence and Democracy: Justifications for Separatism on the Radical Right' (2000) 12 *Terrorism and Political Violence* 193, 195.
42 Barkun (n 9) 222.
43 B Smith, *Terrorism in America: Pipe Bombs and Pipe Dreams* (State University of New York Press, 1995) 58.
44 M Pitcavage, 'Common Law and Uncommon Courts: An Overview of the Common Law Court Movement' Militia Watchdog (25 July 1997) 2.
45 Barkun (n 9) 221; *cf* Schlatter (n 9) 106 (claiming that Gale created Posse and Beach set himself up as the founder); Levitas (n 22) 114 (asserting that Beach stole Gale's Posse guide and republished it as his own).
46 Barkun (n 9) 222.
47 Schlatter (n 9) 108.

Gale's Posse started in California, spread up the coast, and then into the Midwest. As it spread in the 1970s, they immediately began causing problems in almost every state. The Posse exploited disaffected farmers in 'the early 1980s, when inflation, falling land values, rising interest rates, and poor lending practices combined to create a financial crisis that threatened to overwhelm farmers of little or moderate means'.[48] The radicalisation of economically vulnerable individuals, such as those facing evictions, foreclosure or bankruptcy, would later become a hallmark of sovereign citizen pseudolaw. Although farmers were organising as a political force through the American Agricultural Movement, the Posse provided a convenient narrative that pointed to a clear villain: an 'international (Jewish) banking conspiracy which had destroyed the Constitutional/Biblical monetary system and replaced it with one based on credit designed to suck people dry'.[49] Expanding the arguments from Christian Identity, the Posse embraced a quasi-legalism. They argued that 'taxes need not be paid because "Federal Reserve bank notes" weren't backed by gold and silver, [and] farmers were told they should ignore their debts because bank loans were not "real money"'.[50] Gale broadcast his sermons from a high-powered radio in Kansas.[51] This hooked some disaffected farmers, and his ideology spread throughout the United States.

The most inventive legalistic aspects of the Posse began to develop at this time. To help 'remedy' the farm crisis,[52] Gale formed the Committee of the States (COS) in 1984. In doing so, he demonstrated how the most successful gurus will reappropriate real legal instruments and history to suit their immediate objectives and spread their views. The Articles of Confederation – a precursor to the United States Constitution – was an agreement signed in 1777 between the original 13 states of the United States. The Articles empowered a body called the COS, comprising one member from each state, and which was intended to carry out the functions of government while the Continental Congress was in recess. It never achieved a quorum and was disbanded after one year. The Articles of Confederation were later replaced with the adoption of the United States Constitution. Gale, however, inaccurately claimed that the Articles 'remained in effect',[53] and argued that the COS's role of managing the nation's affairs extended to times when Congress overstepped its constitutional authority.[54] Given their belief that all government above the county level was illegitimate, Gale's COS had a lot of work to do.

These claims are particularly important for understanding the quasi-legal aspects visible within sovereign citizen pseudolaw. Gale claimed that the Articles of Confederation 'contains God's law for his people, for their nations and their

[48] Pitcavage (n 44) 5; Zeskind (n 7) 73.
[49] Pitcavage (n 44) 5.
[50] Levitas (n 22) 180.
[51] J Tsidulko, 'The Sovereign Citizen Scam' (2012) 18 *Skeptic Magazine* 12, 13.
[52] Levitas (n 22) 287.
[53] Barkun (n 9) 207; Pitcavage (n 44) 5.
[54] Barkun (n 9) 208.

governments … The source is the Bible, otherwise known as the common law'.[55] The valorisation of the common law as associated with God's law was a theme developed throughout the Common Law Movement, discussed below. The claim persists today. It explains why the Articles of Confederation remain a popular component of sovereign citizen beliefs since the instrument is God's law, and God's law is irrevocable.[56]

Gale's legalism contributed to contemporary sovereign citizen pseudolaw, but it drew from and overlapped with Christian Identity's claims. Gale linked law and government to religion, but his unorthodox legal interpretations were, essentially, the same religious interpretations within Christian Identity ideology. For Michael Barkun, Gale's political fundamentalism was 'not unlike his religious fundamentalism' as 'he believed a complete, inerrant account of American government could be derived from the literal text of charter documents' that had been 'concealed or misrepresented by malevolent forces'.[57]

Religious, political and legal claims overlapped in the COS, and these so-called 'malevolent forces' make these beliefs conspiratorial. They are what Mark Pitcavage calls the 'hidden history' justification for their ideology – the belief 'that the true history of the United States – and thus the true laws, the true obligations, the true government – had been hidden from the American citizens by a massive, long-lasting conspiracy'.[58] Most Americans, they claim, do not realise the truth because they are under the power of malevolent forces, such as shadowy cabals of Jewish bankers, the British monarchy, or the Vatican, which have taken over or influenced law, government and the media.[59] Unsurprisingly, the FBI has stated that COS was an 'anti-[B]lack, anti-Jewish, anti-government organization' and tied Gale to 'liaisons with the Aryan Nations … and other white hate groups'.[60]

As Gale and his supporters maintained that the Articles of Confederation and COS were still in effect, they also claimed that federal laws such as the Internal Revenue Code were not legal. They were nothing but 'a string of unconstitutional abuses which attempt to require a citizen's consent to the repudiation and violation of his God-given and Constitutional rights'.[61] Any attempt to interfere with the operations of the COS was also illegal. The Posse planned to remove any person from office who 'commit criminal acts or who violate their oath of office', including attempts to enforce taxation because the 'states are sovereign in this

[55] ibid 207.
[56] Barkun (n 41) 196.
[57] Barkun (n 9) 207.
[58] Pitcavage (n 44) 4.
[59] See, for example, AV Reitz, 'Dear Monique – The Nature of My Work with the Vatican', annavonreitz.com/natureofmywork.pdf; K Weill, 'Sovereign Citizen Tells Judge "Fuck You" After Allegedly Stalking Mayor Over 5G Conspiracy Theory' The Daily Beast (18 June 2019), www.thedailybeast.com/sovereign-citizen-tells-judge-fuck-you-after-allegedly-stalking-mayor-over-5g-conspiracy-theory: 'On his blog, Bruce supported some core sovereign citizen claims, including that the U.S. is actually a corporation run by the Queen of England, and that its laws do not apply to him'.
[60] Federal Bureau of Investigation, 'FBI Records: The Vault – William Potter Gale Part 01 of 02' 6, vault.fbi.gov/william-potter-gale/william-potter-gale-part-01-of-02/view.
[61] Barkun (n 9) 207.

Republic' and Congress has 'no jurisdiction over that sovereign citizen, who is a citizen of a state and a county in a state'.[62] In this way, the core beliefs of sovereign citizen pseudolaw crystallised: individuals are citizens of a county in a state who follow the common law; they are not subject to Federal Government they consider corrupt.

By the mid-1980s, the Posse had become a national movement. Around 12–15,000 'hard-core activists' embraced the Posse's view of the Constitution, revelled in their 'hatred of the banking system, the income tax, national government, and the welfare state' and remained 'fixated on age-old myths about Jewish plots for world domination and the inherent supremacy of white Anglo-Saxon culture'.[63] The movement began attracting increasing attention from federal, state and local authorities. In 1981, Missouri farmer Wayne Cryts confronted federal marshals seeking to enforce a court order, stating: 'I am a sovereign individual and a citizen of the state of Missouri and am operating under common law. The court order is without the weight of law and does not have jurisdiction over me.'[64] When the marshals stepped aside, Cryts became a 'hero to desperate farmers'.[65]

Nevertheless, it was only a matter of time before violent incidents would break out.[66] In 1983, Posse leader and North Dakota farmer, Gordon Kahl, killed two federal marshals, leading to a national manhunt, and a shootout that ended in his death.[67] Emboldened by the growth of this movement, Gale and his associates not only refused to pay tax but began sending 'indictments' (ie death threats) to IRS employees for trespassing their 'local sovereignty'.[68] In 1986, several were arrested and charged with threatening IRS agents.[69] Gale was convicted but died before he could serve his term.

The power and appeal of Posse Comitatus significantly declined in the late 1980s 'largely through loss of leadership'.[70] Some were imprisoned. Gale passed away, as did Henry Beach. Kahl died violently. Pitcavage explains that:

> [T]he Posse did not really survive. But the Posse had never been simply an organization – indeed, it was hardly ever well-organized. The Posse Comitatus was much more durable as an ideology … The belief system survived even as the group faded.[71]

The Posse's ideology was a mixture of beliefs established in British Israelism and Christian Identity. These movements differed but share family resemblances.

[62] ibid.
[63] Levitas (n 22) 9.
[64] 'Farmers Take Impounded Soybeans' *The New York Times* (17 February 1981) 14. See further Pitcavage (n 44) 5.
[65] Pitcavage (n 44) 5.
[66] ibid 2–3; Levitas (n 22) 192–200, 217–20.
[67] Corcoran (n 6); Pitcavage (n 44) 2–3.
[68] Barkun (n 9) 208.
[69] ibid 4.
[70] Pitcavage (n 44) 3.
[71] ibid.

The main difference is that the Posse clearly embraced legal discourse in ways previous groups had not. This core difference would lead to an explosion of pseudolaw. Attractive and influential to a growing Common Law Movement, constitutional sheriffs who believed in the supremacy it enshrined upon them, and private militias, their growing pseudolegal ideology permitted individuals to vilify the Government and seek redress of grievance through fringe or violent means.

III. Transformation and Emergence

The growth and spread of the Posse throughout the United States inspired regional variation and offshoots. As Gale's Posse decreased in power and influence, other groups arose. Those interested in the legal theories underpinning the organisations' vision focused on justifying their actions and educating new members. The Common Law Movement developed novel pseudolegal theories that remain central to modern sovereign citizen pseudolaw. Alongside this more legalistic approach were those who were well-armed and keen to stand their ground against the state and Federal Government. These militia members came to form a modern anti-government Patriot Movement. In this section we explore these two descendants of the Posse Comitatus. Although the two movements appear different – one legalistic and one more violent – they are interrelated, incestuous siblings. Both embraced the underlying pseudolegal ideology of the Posse, both contained individuals who identified as 'sovereign citizens', and both contributed to the development of the theories, narratives, and tactics that we can retrospectively describe as sovereign citizen pseudolaw.

A. The Common Law Movement

The dissemination of Posse ideology across the United States, alongside the diminution of the Posse itself, affected the development of this anti-government ideology. Over time, a modified form emerged as the Common Law Movement. It was not initially separate from the Posse. Rather, given their shared attitudes and beliefs, these groups shared members. Nevertheless, the common law offshoot began to formally coalesce in the 1980s and eventually became a much larger movement independent of the Posse itself.

Mark Pitcavage identifies Posse member and Christian Identity preacher James Wickstrom from Wisconsin,[72] Gordon Kahl in North Dakota[73] and George Gordon from Idaho as 'an excellent example of how the common law philosophy

[72] For more on Wickstrom, see Schlatter (n 9) 110–12.
[73] See Corcoran (n 6).

was used in practice'.[74] Although initially a tax protestor, Gordon began studying the 'common law' in the early 1980s to find a basis to avoid paying taxes. He developed a following and established the Barristers Inn School of Common Law, where he lectured on common law ideology to audiences. Throughout the 1980s and into the 1990s, Gordon was active in spreading his vision and practice of invoking the common law to avoid state law. This encompassed a wide range of activities, including refusing to adhere to traffic stops that he saw as breaching his right to travel, filing a USD 700,000 claim against a collection agency, leading tax protests, filing suits against a hospital for treating his daughter 'without permission and violat[ing] his civil rights in trying to collect $2,000 for care expenses', and setting up other common law schools where he taught students not to make 'contracts' with the state.[75] Throughout the 1980s, individuals like Gordon founded numerous common law schools, including, among others, the John Doe School of Law, and the Universal Life University School of Law.[76]

Common law practitioners also formed their own sham courts, removed from the United States legal system, which only they considered legitimate. By the mid-1990s, common law courts operated in as many as 20 states.[77] These courts arose, in part, as a Common Law Movement response to state and federal legislation aimed at undermining the influence of the Posse Comitatus. At one point, Gale commented that they should hang a legislator who was attempting to pass an anti-Posse bill, and James Wickstrom replied that he deserved a hearing 'by a "citizen's grand jury" first'.[78] Thus, the first citizen grand jury was created, and the first common law courts were formed in Wisconsin.[79] In Texas, common law practitioners began setting up 'townships'. After several altercations, Texas Rangers raided a township court and arrested the members. The adherents responded by filing financial liens claiming millions of dollars in debt against the state actors who were involved.[80] We see another example of this, although in a more militia-like form, discussed below as the Republic of Texas.

The Posse had popularised the idea of filing false liens during the farm crisis. As many farmers lost their land, the Posse blamed international (Jewish) bankers and presented farmers with their contorted interpretation of the common law. They turned the legal mechanisms that dispossessed them into a weapon against those they saw as their enemies.[81] Initially, the Posse encouraged those fighting foreclosure to file liens against their own properties, often for the 'labor, service and material' they put into the land in 'order to frustrate banks attempting to

[74] Pitcavage (n 44) 9.
[75] ibid 10.
[76] ibid.
[77] S Koniak, 'When Law Risks Madness' (1996) 8 *Cardozo Studies in Law and Literature* 65, 67.
[78] Pitcavage (n 44) 10.
[79] ibid 10–11; for more information on the Wisconsin Common Law Court, see Koniak (n 77) 71–73, fns 55–57; 96–97.
[80] Pitcavage (n 44) 11.
[81] Koniak (n 77).

foreclose', or file liens against each other's properties.[82] Although aggravating in the short term, the efforts could not frustrate foreclosure forever.

Members also relied on their own common law court systems. Typically made up of sovereign citizen judges and grand juries willing to hear the plaintiff's grievances and mete out pseudolegal 'judgments', including sentencing some to death. Individuals began to file their own 'Quiet Title Actions'.[83] Adherents presented their birth certificate as evidence they were born in a particular American state and as such were sovereign citizens of that state.[84] This purifying act sought to remove what they perceived as the Federal Government's claim against their identity. They believed that through these actions they could own themselves and secure a clear, unencumbered identity. Adherents also used their court systems as weapons against non-members, filing 'liens against outsiders … charged with violating the rights of community members as conceived by their law'.[85] These liens designated who their enemies were, those 'who are not God's Chosen People do not have clear title to the land'.[86]

As the Posse grew in influence, some members experimented with more aggressive approaches. In a tactic now characterised as 'paper terrorism', members filed numerous documents 'to clog up the legal and financial systems of the nation and to intimidate, harass and coerce the agents of those systems'.[87] This included filing fraudulent financial liens against individuals they perceived as enemies, which were listed as unresolved debt on credit reports. The tactic worked, at least initially. County clerks occasionally did not recognise these fraudulent liens as false, or did not have the authority to question them, while those who did and refused to file the applications 'found themselves subject to fake liens, threats and other forms of harassment'.[88] Posse adherents filed countless liens against banks, bankers, lenders, corporations and attorneys associated with those acts, and other unlucky individuals who stood in their way. They did so in Iowa, Wisconsin, Oregon, Colorado, Utah, Arizona, New Mexico, California, Florida, Montana, Washington and elsewhere.[89]

The rhetoric, claims and legal theories underpinning the Common Law movement derived from the Posse Comitatus. Like the Posse, members maintained that the county is the ultimate level of government, and state and federal laws were

[82] M Pitcavage, 'Paper Terrorism's Forgotten Victims: The Use of Bogus Liens against Private Individuals and Businesses' The Militia Watchdog (29 June 1998), web.archive.org/web/20020918011634/http:/www.adl.org/mwd/privlien.asp, referencing *Federal Land Bank of Omaha v Boese*, 373 NW 2d 118 (Iowa 1985).

[83] A quiet title action is a lawsuit that seeks to establish the party's title to real property and thus 'quiet' any challenges or alternative claims to title.

[84] Koniak (n 77) 68; see also, Netolitzky (n 2) 818.

[85] Koniak (n 77) 68.

[86] ibid 77.

[87] Pitcavage (n 82).

[88] Naval Criminal Investigative Service, 'Anti-Government Extremists: An Information Project' Criminal Intelligence Unit (August 1999) 30.

[89] Pitcavage (n 82).

necessarily subordinate.[90] Over time, the movement developed new terminology. Adherents participating in the common law courts characterised themselves as 'sovereign citizens' or 'freemen' because, having proven their unencumbered identities, they asserted they are citizens of sovereign states, not citizens of the Federal Government.[91] This minor terminological shift is important; although largely adopting the ideology of the Posse, the nomenclature of 'sovereign citizens' persists.

Throughout this period, common law adherents also developed a range of new theories and claims. Roger Elvick, the 'national spokesperson for the Committee of States' founded by Gale,[92] and founder of the Inns of Law of Wisconsin,[93] utilised a scheme involving 'sight drafts' called the 'redemption' scheme. These documents are similar to credit and can be used to pay off debt or purchase items or property upfront, where the seller would receive their payment through redemption of the sight draft. It is called the redemption scheme because Elvick's company, Common Title Bond & Truth, issued sight drafts to desperate farmers in the 1980s in exchange for their property deeds. Farmers would use the sight drafts to pay off debt or make a purchase, but instead of following legitimate sight draft procedures Elvick's company did not pay out the holders of the sight draft, instead hoarding the deeds.[94] With Elvick's assistance, his associate Emil Wiley conspired to defraud the Internal Revenue Service by having individuals fraudulently claim large monetary refunds on their tax returns, while Elvick and Wiley produced sight drafts fraudulently purported to be from the IRS and payable to them, then attempted to exchange them for legitimate financial instruments.[95] Elvick was arrested and charged with conspiracy to impede justice.[96] By the time he was imprisoned in 1990, Elvick was advising Redemption groups in '30 states and several provinces of Canada, and had tried to pass more than $15 million in bad sight drafts'.[97]

While incarcerated, Elvick also started developing new ideas and spreading them to other prisoners. In 1999, he developed perhaps the most notable feature of contemporary sovereign citizen pseudolaw – the strawman theory.[98] The theory declares that the United States went bankrupt after it abandoned the

[90] Naval Criminal Investigative Service (n 88) 29.

[91] ibid.

[92] Southern Poverty Law Center, 'His "Straw Man" Free, A Scammer Finds The Rest of Him Isn't', Intelligence Report (27 July 2005) www.splcenter.org/fighting-hate/intelligence-report/2005/his-straw-man-free-scammer-finds-rest-him-isnt.

[93] DJ Netolitzky, 'The History of the Organized Pseudolegal Commercial Argument Phenomenon in Canada' (2016) 53 *Alberta Law Review* 609, 617.

[94] 'Farmers' Hopes Bounce as U.S. Rejects Finance Plan' *Chicago Tribune* (20 September 1987).

[95] *US v Wiley*, 979 F 2d 365 (5th Cir 1992).

[96] *US v Elvick*, No 1:90-CR-01570-ACK (D Haw 1991).

[97] Southern Poverty Law Center (n 92).

[98] DJ Netolitzky, 'A Rebellion of Furious Paper: Pseudolaw as a Revolutionary System' Conference Paper, Sovereign Citizens in Canada Symposium, Centre d'expertise et de formation sur les intégrismes religieux et la radicalisation (3 May 2018) 4; Netolitzky (n 93).

gold standard in 1933. It then transformed itself into a corporation and tethered its currency to the value of its citizens by taking a USD 630,000 loan out in each citizen's name and placing it in a secret bank account.[99] The accounts are said to be held in the United States Treasury Department, 'under the corporate shell names of each citizen'.[100] These paper doppelgangers are termed 'strawmen'. The strawman, Elvick explained, is distinct from flesh and blood, sovereign citizens of a state, who follow the common law. This distinction allows sovereign people to disassociate from their strawman and draw on the bank account, called Treasury Direct Accounts, associated with that strawman identity to pay debts or taxes simply by writing 'Accepted for Value' on bills.[101]

As Donald Netolitzky and Christine Sarteschi note in their chapters in this volume, variations of the redemption theory remain prominent.[102] The strawman theory has spread around the world. It is promoted online,[103] and used widely (without success).[104] It is now the hallmark of sovereign citizen pseudolaw even if the person using it denies that they are a 'sovereign citizen'.[105]

This section has identified key developments in sovereign citizen pseudolaw that emerged from the Common Law Movement. However, while some individuals focused on building the legal theories underpinning this manifestation of pseudolaw, the more violent aspects associated with this ideology did not dissipate. Various groups and militias continued to use and develop budding pseudolaw alongside more armed and confrontational responses. It is to the anti-government Patriot Movement that we now turn.

B. The Patriot Movement

As the Posse Comitatus fell apart, the Common Law Movement began developing new quasi-legal approaches when engaging with the state. The Posse's more violent elements appeared to be slowly receding. That is, however, until several catalysts reinvigorated the militia movement that was once central to the Posse.

In 1992, federal agents killed members of the Weaver family following a siege at Ruby Ridge in Idaho. The following year, federal agents invaded a Branch Davidian compound in Waco, Texas, during a stand-off between the religious cult and the Government, resulting in the death of four officers, and 82 cult members,

[99] Southern Poverty Law Center (n 92); S Smith, 'An Analysis of the Sovereign Citizen Movement: Demographics and Trial Behaviors' (University of Arkansas, MA Thesis, 2016) 14–15.

[100] Southern Poverty Law Center (n 92); Smith (n 99) 16.

[101] DJ Netolitzky, 'Organized Pseudolegal Commercial Arguments as Magic and Ceremony' (2018) 55 *Alberta Law Review* 1045, 1072.

[102] DJ Netolitzky, ch 7 in this volume; C Sarteschi, ch 11 in this volume.

[103] L Storey, 'Common Law School: Escape the Tax Slave Matrix w/ Brandon Joe Williams' YouTube (19 March 2024), www.youtube.com/watch?v=VU7rlz25H7E&t=891s.

[104] JE Evans, 'The Flesh and Blood Defense' (2012) 53 *William & Mary Law Review* 1361, 1362–64.

[105] C Sarteschi, ch 11 in this volume; G Cash, ch 8 in this volume; Netolitzky (n 98); Hobbs, Young and McIntyre (n 3).

including 26 children.[106] The next year, federal legislation was introduced to regulate gun control.[107] Some segments of the population saw these events as confirming that the United States Government was overreaching and tyrannical, or ascending towards it, which gave 'renewed energy to the "patriot" movement, as it now called itself'.[108] Members of this movement would engage in paper terrorism, as mentioned above, against the Federal Government, but others were willing to conduct firearms and paramilitary-style training, utilising fortifications and immense firepower, in preparation for offensive or defensive civilian warfare. In this section, we highlight two significant groups.

Sovereign members of this 'patriot movement' included the Montana Freemen:

> In January, 1993, a group of 'sovereign citizens,' or 'freemen,' ordered the county attorney of Garfield County, MT to prosecute the county director of the Farmers Home Administration for fraud. The county attorney refused and 36 armed 'freemen' seized the Garfield County Courthouse and set up a 'Supreme Court of Garfield/Comitatus.' The county attorney filed charges against 15 of the Freemen who seized the courthouse. On 15 July 94, the 'Garfield County Freemen' mailed letters threatening the jurors if any of the defendants were convicted.[109]

That was only the beginning. Eight of the 15 who were arrested did not show up for trial. As sovereign citizens, they did not recognise the court's authority. Instead, in 1995, when the Sheriff went to arrest them, they barricaded themselves in Justus Township, a ranch that had become a 'sanctuary' for common law followers, including farmers who were attempting to forestall foreclosure and others who taught classes on common law techniques,[110] and claimed that their Posse Comitatus law derives from the Holy Scriptures.[111] Following an 81-day stand-off, the members eventually surrendered; nearly all were indicted or convicted on federal conspiracy charges of various sorts.

The Montana Freeman retained the Posse's racist beliefs but with a more developed sovereign citizen ideology. They believed that when the 14th Amendment was ratified in 1868, the Federal Government – a corporation in disguise – secretly replaced state citizenship with federal, corporate citizenship, undermining their true constitutional protection.[112] As a result, the Freeman claimed the 'United States is peopled by two nations, not one', drawing a distinction 'between "American

[106] Pitcavage (n 82).
[107] Levitas (n 22) 301, 304.
[108] Pitcavage (n 44) 12. Zeskind identifies aspects of the 'patriots' earlier, with the formation of the Christian-Patriots Defense League, a paramilitary organisation that adhered to Christian Identity doctrine. Zeskind (n 7) 64. See also D Lewis, 'Twenty Years Ago Today, the Montana Freemen Started Its 81-Day Standoff' *Smithsonian Magazine* (25 March 2016), www.smithsonianmag.com/smart-news/twenty-years-ago-today-the-montana-freeman-started-its-81-day-standoff-180958568.
[109] Naval Criminal Investigative Service (n 88) 32. Zeskind (n 7) 357–58.
[110] Naval Criminal Investigative Service (n 88) 32.
[111] Zeskind (n 7) 358.
[112] Sullivan (n 6).

nationals" (or "organic sovereigns") and "U.S. citizens".[113] Of course, because the 14th Amendment granted citizenship to former slaves and naturalised citizens, their views on the organic sovereign nation they claimed to reside within were explicitly predicated on racial superiority. The Freeman believed that: 'For themselves and their Aryan kin, there is a republic where whites enjoy rights superior to those held by people of color and Jews. The latter are the unfortunate denizens of a "corporation" headquartered in Washington, D.C.'.[114]

Similar actions by other sovereign citizens and sovereign citizen-inspired groups continued to occur throughout the United States. Another prominent incident occurred in Texas. In the 1980s and well into the 1990s, Richard McLaren, a resident of Davis Mountains Resort, a community in West Texas, sued the land developers of Davis Mountains Resort, claiming the land surveys had previously been cancelled, so that the purchasers did not have title.[115] He then began filing liens against the title company and his neighbours' properties causing some neighbours to simply forfeit their land while others spent up to USD 100,000 to fight off his liens.[116]

McLaren developed grander ambitions. Relying on historical misinformation which he characterised as the 'diligent research [of] a para-legal [sic] in Fort Davis, Texas', McLaren 'discovered' that the United States annexation of the Republic of Texas (ROT) in 1846 was illegal.[117] Believing that the Federal Government's assertion of jurisdiction over Texas was illegitimate, he sought to resuscitate the independent Republic which had existed between 1836 and 1846. McLaren repeatedly sued the Federal Government seeking 'proof' that 'the Sovereign People of the Republic of Texas' had assented to annexation.[118] The group even made a claim to the International Court of Justice to have the ROT recognised as an independent nation-state.

The ROT purported to offer a significant benefit to its supporters. As the ROT considered itself a sovereign state and the State of Texas under (illegitimate) federal control, its citizens would not be subject to United States tax, fees or regulations.[119] In a short amount of time, hundreds of people joined the nascent

[113] L Zeskind, 'Basis of Freemen's Philosophy is Racism' Southern Poverty Law Center, Intelligence Report (15 June 1998), www.splcenter.org/fighting-hate/intelligence-report/1998/basis-freemen%E2%80%99s-philosophy-racism.

[114] ibid.

[115] RH Brock, 'The Republic of Texas is No More: An Answer to the Claim that Texas Was Unconstitutionally Annexed to the United States' (1997) 28 *Texas Tech Law Review* 679, 694. See generally, DM Miller, *Texas Secessionists Standoff: the 1997 Republic of Texas "War"* (Texas A&M University Press, 2023).

[116] Pitcavage (n 82).

[117] Brock (n 115) 682; Pitcavage (n 82). Texas did legally join the Union. See JW Paulsen, 'If at First You Don't Secede: Ten Reasons Why the Republic of Texas Movement is Wrong' (1997) 38 *South Texas Law Review* 801, 803–07.

[118] For more details on the specific arguments and claims, see Brock (n 115) 695–722.

[119] R Monroe, 'Surviving the Standoff with the Republic of Texas' *The New Yorker* (12 April 2022), www.newyorker.com/news/letter-from-the-southwest/surviving-the-standoff-with-the-republic-of-texas.

republic and some began filing fake liens and money orders through the redemption scheme.[120] They even filed financial statements with a forged signature of the state's governor, George W Bush.[121] As a result, McLaren and the ROT ran into direct conflict with state and legal authorities.[122] That conflict would only intensify.

In April 1997, Joe and his wife Margaret Rowe – inhabitants of Davis Mountain Resorts – reported some suspicious activity to Jefferson Davis county sheriffs.[123] Sheriffs investigated and ended up arresting a ROT member.[124] In retaliation, three ROT members broke into the Rowes' home, and declared the Rowes 'prisoners of war'.[125] ROT members shot Joe, and held the Rowes for 13 hours before negotiating their release in exchange for the release of the arrested ROT member.[126] After releasing the Rowes, the members of the ROT convened at McLaren's trailer, which he called the ROT 'embassy'.[127] Following a seven-day stand-off with state law enforcement officers, the ROT members and its followers surrendered.[128] McLaren was sentenced to 99 years in prison for kidnap.[129]

McLaren's imprisonment ended that iteration of the ROT, but the group re-emerged, calling themselves Texians and formed a member-led pseudo-government. Their core claims – that the Government has been replaced by a corporation planning on enforcing martial law, that taxation is unconstitutional, that only gold and silver are legal tender – continue to have traction internally and among those who apply sovereign citizen pseudolaw.[130] McLaren would also continue pressing his legal arguments, appealing his convictions and arguing that the United States did not have jurisdiction over the 'sovereign nation bordered by the United States of America and Mexico', the ROT.[131]

The Montana Freeman and the ROT are emblematic of the Patriot Movement that arose to prominence in the mid-1990s. They were 'unorganized militias' who threatened and executed violence and engaged in filing fake liens and bank drafts.[132] The practical impact was significant. The Montana Freeman, for instance, were convicted of federal conspiracy and bank fraud, involving 3,432 cheques totalling USD 15.5 billion and creating 'actual losses of USD 1.8 billion'.[133] Of course, this

[120] Pitcavage (n 82).
[121] Monroe (n 119).
[122] Brock (n 115) 702–04; Pitcavage (n 83).
[123] Monroe (n 119); *McLaren v State*, 2 SW 3d 595, 596 (1999).
[124] Monroe (n 119).
[125] ibid.
[126] ibid; *McLaren v US Inc*, 2 F Supp 2d 48, 49 (1998).
[127] Monroe (n 119).
[128] *McLaren v US Inc*, 2 F Supp 2d 48, 49 (1998).
[129] Pitcavage (n 83).
[130] Paulsen (n 117) 802–03.
[131] *McLaren v US Inc*, 2 F Supp 2d 48, 49 (1998).
[132] Pitcavage (n 83).
[133] Southern Poverty Law Center 'Four Montana Freemen Found Guilty' Intelligence Report (15 September 1998), www.splcenter.org/fighting-hate/intelligence-report/1998/four-montana-freemen-found-guilty.

was not the extent of criminal damage. Many sovereign patriots engaged in violent acts. Most infamous was Terry Nichols who helped Timothy McVeigh bomb the Alfred P Murrah Federal Building in Oklahoma City in 1995.[134]

Terry Nichols is representative of an important shift. Over the course of the 1990s his anti-government views increasingly intertwined with ideologies from the Posse Comitatus and nascent sovereign citizen pseudolaw. In 1992, he twice unsuccessfully sought to renounce his United States citizenship, and declared in court that the corrupt United States Government had no jurisdiction over him.[135] Further radicalised by the sieges at Ruby Ridge and Waco, Nichols – and McVeigh – began to plot revenge. The Oklahoma City bombing killed 168 people, but from the 1990s onwards, more common were incidents of individual and small-scale violence in confrontations with police and other state actors.

The Oklahoma City bombing, the ROT and the Montana Freemen captured national attention. They also demonstrated that sovereign citizen pseudolaw and ideology had begun to spread throughout the United States. Given its extreme anti-government and anti-institutional vision, it should not be surprising that members could erupt into violence.

IV. Establishment and Spread

In the mid-to-late 1990s, sovereign citizen pseudolaw emerged as its own phenomenon. Its broad contours – including the notion that the Government is corrupt or a corporation, that 'free' or 'flesh and blood' individuals are not subject to state law, that they uphold the true common law – and the primary tactics and methodologies adopted – issuing fake bank notes or liens, refusing to possess state identification documents, and confronting state actors – had been established. While some of these tropes and strategies can be directly linked to earlier individuals and organisations, it is more accurate to describe their development as a part of an evolutionary accretion.

Evolutionary processes influenced the phenomenon in other ways. Sovereign citizen pseudolaw is highly adaptive and responsive to local contexts, spreads in unanticipated but recognisable ways, grows in times of societal disaffections, and may continue to involve extremist religious, political and economic beliefs.[136] It has also spread in the absence of any uniform movement. Instead, so-called 'gurus' or 'modern legal alchemists' present pseudolegal information 'in seminars, books, website, and instructional DVDS and other records' to their 'followers'.[137]

[134] Levitas (n 22) 315–16.

[135] S Rimer, 'The Second Suspect: With Extremism and Explosives, A Drifting Life Found a Purpose' *The New York Times* (28 May 1995) 1.

[136] DJ Netolitzky, 'A Pathogen Astride the Minds of Men: The Epidemiological History of Pseudolaw' Conference Paper, CEFIR Symposium: Sovereign Citizens in Canada (3 May 2018) 3.

[137] *Meads v Meads* [2012] ABQB 571 [78]–[79] ('*Meads*').

Sovereign citizen pseudolaw can quickly transform, catalyse ephemeral social movements, and inspire violence. In this final section, we identify a few ways that contemporary sovereign citizen pseudolaw adapted and spread throughout the United States. We start with the example of the strawman argument to illustrate how sovereign citizen pseudolaw adapts as it spreads. We then demonstrate how sovereign citizen pseudolaw has expanded through networks, specifically by tapping into prisons, taking advantage of socio-economic crises, and making full use of the Internet. This provides some insight into how this 'pathogen' has infected the United States and the globe.[138]

Despite seeing many of their sovereign citizen contacts jailed throughout the 1990s, militia members and those involved in various common law movements continued practicing and promoting pseudolaw. Many employed the strawman argument, which has become the most identifiable and widespread aspect of sovereign citizen pseudolaw. Today, contemporary pseudolaw advocates from around the world treat it as gospel. One group on Facebook explains:

> As a child, you have had an imaginary friend. You may be surprised to learn that evidence exists that you have had a make-believe twin from the time your mother and father permitted a Birth Certificate to be filed for you. This make-believe friend is not real, but artificial. It is a straw man, an artificial entity that has a name very similar to yours.[139]

Strawman theory is justified in very formalistic ways. Consider the purportedly significant revelation visible by cross-referencing a style guide and legal dictionary. From Australia, it is claimed that the *Chicago Manual of Style* states that the name of corporations should be written in capital letters.[140] Meanwhile, the Facebook group cited above asserts that *Black's Law Dictionary* apparently describes a 'strawman' as a '"front"; a third party who is put up in name only to take part in a transaction'.[141] Collating these two ideas, believers claim this means that when your name is written in all capital letters (such as in a birth certificate or court document), the sender is addressing a corporate strawman rather than the flesh and blood individual. One sovereign explains: '"Your" all capitalized name on a credential – or any other government document – is not a proper noun. IT IS NOT YOU. It is a government creature, created by government, that is an artificial entity, a legal fiction.'[142]

[138] Netolitzky (n 136) 3.

[139] 'BIRTH CERTIFICATE Equals Chattel Property' Facebook, www.facebook.com/groups/623134387814835.

[140] *R v Sweet* [2021] QDC 216 (6 September 2021) [2] (Cash DCJ). While the *Chicago Manual of Style* does say that the names of institutions, groups and companies should be capitalised – ie, the University of Otago, the Faculty of Law, or Captain Beefheart and His Magic Band – it remains unclear why sovereign citizens believe the entire word should be capitalised. See *Chicago Manual of Style*, 17th edn (University of Chicago Press, 2017) s 8.68.

[141] See 'BIRTH CERTIFICATE Equals Chattel Property (n 139).

[142] Do Not Be Fooled by Government, 'Your ALL CAPITALIZED NAME', notfooledbygovernment.com/all-capitalized-name.

As a conspiracy theory that purports to uncover hidden information, adherents believe that most people never realise they can opt out. Correspondingly, adherents assert that when people are educated or discover this knowledge about the common law, they can use law to disassociate their real sovereign citizen self from the fictional identity. They also work under the belief that this process of dissociating enables them to assert that legal creations or contracts belong to their strawman, especially those where their names are listed in capital letters, a standard United States legal practice that has spread internationally. Thus, they illegitimately deny personal responsibility for debt they amassed or crimes they committed.

Because sovereign citizen pseudolaw is so adaptable, sovereign citizens have employed the strawman in numerous ways to establish themselves as 'free men and women' outside the jurisdiction of the Government. Often individuals place a copyright or trademark sign after their name, in red ink, or a thumbprint.[143] There are other ways too. A notable figure here is the late David Wynn Miller, who created a language called CORRECT-SENTENCE-STRUCURE-COMMUNICATION-PARSE-SYNTAX-GRAMMAR, a mathematical language that purports to guarantee legal outcomes. A former machinist and welder who dubiously claimed to be 'fluent in numerous languages, has an IQ of 200, and that he has not aged since he died and was resurrected at age 25', Miller developed a new way of distinguishing 'PLENIPOTENTIARY JUDGE David-Wynn: Miller', as he called his sovereign self from his legal 'corporate' personality.[144] As Netolitzky explains, this 'variation on a name transforms a human into a "prepositional phrase," which is purportedly outside state authority'.[145] Miller was active in spreading his ideas into Canada,[146] and, as Glen Cash discusses in his chapter, Australia.[147] After Miller's death in 2018, Russell Jay Gould, Miller's one-time protégé, continued to market these ideas throughout the United States.[148]

The strawman argument remains the hallmark of sovereign citizen pseudolaw. Unfortunately, sovereign citizen pseudolaw's other most well-known feature – the capacity for violence – has also spread throughout the United States. In the

[143] See J Williams, 'Why Some Far-Right Extremists think Red Ink can Force the Government to Give Them Millions' Vox (9 February 2016), www.vox.com/2016/2/9/10942860/sovereign-citizens-movement; A Conti, 'Learn to Spot the Secret Signals of Far-Right "Sovereign Citizens"' Vice (1 May 2018), www.vice.com/en/article/8xkp74/learn-to-spot-the-secret-signals-of-far-right-sovereign-citizens.

[144] *Meads* (n 137) [143]; C McRoberts, 'Tinfoil Hats and Powdered Wigs: Thoughts on Pseudolaw' (2019) 58 *Washburn Law Review* 637, 638–41; M Potok, '"Full Colon Miller"' Southern Poverty Law Center Intelligence Report (15 April 2003), www.splcenter.org/fighting-hate/intelligence-report/2003/full-colon-miller.

[145] Netolitzky (n 93) 630.

[146] ibid.

[147] SA Kent, 'Freemen, Sovereign Citizens, and the Challenge to Public Order in British Heritage Countries' (2015) 6 *International Journal of Cultic Studies* 1; G Cash, ch 8 in this volume. See, for example *Wollongong City Council v Falamaki* [2009] FMCA 1204 and *Wollongong City Council v Falamaki* [2010] NSWLEC 66.

[148] See, for example, *Brooker v Gould*, Civil Case No 12-cv-00093-REB-KMT (D Colo Apr 19, 2012).

late 1990s, for instance, John Joe Gray was stopped for speeding by a police officer. After being removed from the car following an altercation, officers found that he was driving with a 'cache of firearms'.[149] Gray was convicted, but while free on bond, he barricaded himself and his family on their property.[150] A former member of the ROT, Gray found new avenues and connections for spreading pseudolaw. He became a 'leader in the Texas Constitutional Militia' and associated with the 'Embassy of Heaven'.[151] Without phones or electricity, Gray and his family continued their stand-off until it 'officially ended in 2014 when a district attorney dropped charges'.[152] Throughout the 2000s, stand-offs with armed individuals exhibiting sovereign citizen beliefs continued. In 2007, for example, Ed and Elaine Brown were finally arrested in their New Hampshire home after a five-month stand-off following a conviction for evading USD 1.9 million in taxes.[153] Many of these stand-offs concluded in imprisonment.

Imprisonment did not stop the spread of sovereign citizen pseudolaw, nor did it inoculate vulnerable people. Instead, it metastasised, as prisons proved an ideal environment to educate disaffected individuals about the 'Common Law' and spread pseudolaw techniques.[154] Throughout this period, *The America's Bulletin* – a publisher and online outlet for sovereign citizen content – sold 'The Prison Packet' to inmates.[155] This document recycled information about the redemption scheme and other sovereign citizen pseudolaw for inmates.[156] In doing so, it adapted and developed its own theories; rather than drawing on sight drafts, it claimed to teach prisoners how to enrich themselves by drawing on 'prison bonds' that underwrite their incarceration.[157]

As sovereign citizen pseudolaw remained tenuously connected to religion, others took advantage of religious services surrounding prisons. For example, one individual claiming to be a dentist established a church in Jacksonville, Texas called

[149] C Stowers, 'Between Heaven and Hell' *Dallas Observer* (27 July 2000). See further: Embassy of Heaven, 'John Joe Gray' (27 July 2000), media.embassyofheaven.com/johnjoegray/johnjoe1.php.

[150] Stowers (n 149); J Henderson, 'Family Holes up in Bunker, Evades Court' *Houston Chronicle* (8 August 2000), media.embassyofheaven.com/johnjoegray/johnjoe2.php.

[151] Henderson (n 150).

[152] M Fernandez, 'Lesson for Stalemated Sides in Oregon: A Texas Standoff Without End *The New York Times* (7 January 2016), www.nytimes.com/2016/01/08/us/lesson-for-stalemated-sides-in-oregon-a-texas-standoff-without-end.html. It unofficially continued until 2016 as neither side involved in the stand-off realised that the charges had been dropped.

[153] Southern Poverty Law Center, 'NH Tax Protesters Arrested Without Shot' Intelligence Report (1 December 2007), www.splcenter.org/fighting-hate/intelligence-report/2007/nh-tax-protesters-arrested-without-shot; Southern Poverty Law Center, 'Law Officials Pursue Differing Standoff Policies' Intelligence Report (1 July 2007), www.splcenter.org/fighting-hate/intelligence-report/2007/law-officials-pursue-differing-standoff-policies.

[154] C Sanchez, 'Sovereign Citizens Movement Resurging' Southern Poverty Law Center, Intelligence Report (26 February 2009), www.splcenter.org/fighting-hate/intelligence-report/2009/sovereign-citizens-movement-resurging.

[155] Anti-Defamation League, 'The America's Bulletin' (Glossary of Extremism and Hate), extremismterms.adl.org/glossary/americans-bulletin.

[156] The America's Bulletin, 'The Prison Packer', americansbulletin.com/product/prisoner-packet.

[157] Sanchez (n 154).

the House of Israel – a distant echo of British Israelism – that purported to operate as a prison ministry. After several 'House of Israel' members ran afoul of the law, Jacksonville police raided the ministry. They found a store of drugs marked with 'The Republic of Texas', as well as pornography, antisemitic, neo-confederate, and anti-government publications. The church and ministry claimed to help inmates but was essentially 'a crash pad for fugitives from justice and a secretive guild of "sovereign citizens"'.[158]

As the Farm Crisis in the early 1980s demonstrated, sovereign citizen pseudolaw has developed, spread and grown in times of emergency. The 2007 Global Financial Crisis thus presented a perfect opportunity for sovereign citizen gurus to develop new ways of exploiting vulnerable people by selling pseudolegal schemes. Many were directed towards financial institutions. In 2009, Angel Cruz and his supporters, calling themselves the United Cities and, wearing counterfeit United States Treasury badges, cordoned off a Miami, Florida branch of the Bank of America.[159] Drawing inspiration from the Common Law Movement, Cruz attempted to 'evict' the Bank with a 'court order' from 'The United Cities Private Court'.[160] The 'order' referenced a USD 15.25 billion lawsuit that Cruz filed against Bank of America, as well as the bank's 'wrongful' refusal to cash out USD 14 million in phony bank drafts.[161] Cruz's direct approach may have been novel, but the underlying theory supposedly justifying his actions recycled well-established sovereign citizen pseudolaw arguments.

Older methods of spreading misinformation continued. Gurus saw the Global Financial Crisis as an opportunity to travel the country – and internationally – selling information and hosting seminars on sovereign citizen pseudolaw.[162] Although it is not possible to accurately identify the number or extent of these 'educational' lecture tours, there are a number of prominent cases. In 2010, for instance, Jerry Kane was travelling with his son, Joe, lecturing on alleged solutions to mortgage and foreclosure problems. He claimed that money and home loans are fictitious, and that people could live in their houses mortgage-free by signing certain legal instruments. When two Arkansas police officers pulled over the Kanes' van, a verbal argument turned violent, and both officers were killed. It was the first known homicide of an officer committed by sovereign citizens since Gordon Kahl killed federal marshals in 1983.[163] This is one example of violence perpetrated by sovereign citizens. A close follower of the movement, Christine

[158] S Scherr, '"Sovereign Citizens" Outfit Raided in Jacksonville, Texas' Southern Poverty Law Center, Intelligence Report (30 November 2008), www.splcenter.org/fighting-hate/intelligence-report/2008/%E2%80%98sovereign-citizens%E2%80%99-outfit-raided-jacksonville-texas.

[159] Sanchez (n 154).

[160] ibid.

[161] ibid.

[162] Kent (n 147).

[163] JJ MacNab, '"Sovereign" Citizen Kane' Southern Poverty Law Center, Intelligence Report (1 August 2010), www.splcenter.org/fighting-hate/intelligence-report/2010/sovereign-citizen-kane; S Dewan and J Hubbel, 'Arkansas Suspects Had Rage Toward Government' *The New York Times* (24 May 2010), www.nytimes.com/2010/05/24/us/24arkansas.html.

Sarteschi, has researched and collected data on 'at least 250 cases of violence, including arson, child abuse, rape, sexual assault, attempted kidnapping, mass shootings, and homicides'.[164]

Individuals and gurus have taught sovereign citizen pseudolaw in seminars and in prisons successfully for decades, but the most effective tool has been the Internet and social media. A 2011 report from the United States Federal Bureau of Investigation on sovereign citizens has proved prescient:

> The sovereign-citizen threat likely will grow as the nationwide movement is fueled by the Internet, the economic downturn, and seminars held across the country that spread their ideology and show people how they can tap into funds and eliminate debt through fraudulent methods. As sovereign citizens' numbers grow, so do the chances of contact with law enforcement and, thus, the risks that incidents will end in violence.[165]

Countless websites contain and promote this information.[166] Social media sites, including Facebook, X, YouTube, Telegram, TikTok and others, have numerous groups dedicated to teaching the intricacies and nuances of their supposed legal approaches.[167] Several authors in this volume have also noted the importance of the Internet and social media for recruitment, education and socialisation.[168]

Militia groups have also used the Internet to attract new audiences. In 2014, for example, cattle rancher Cliven Bundy sent an open invitation to the patriot movement to visit his Nevada Ranch. Fuelled with sovereign citizen pseudolaw and the belief that the Government had no right to charge him grazing fees for letting his cattle roam and feed on federally owned land – and supported by a number of well-armed recruits including the Oath Keepers and other militias – the Bundy family entered into a tense armed stand-off with Bureau of Land Management Agents.[169] Two attendees, Jared and Amanda Miller, later travelled to a 'Las Vegas

[164] C Sarteschi, 'Sovereign Citizens: More than Paper Terrorists' Just Security (5 July 2021), www.justsecurity.org/77328/sovereign-citizens-more-than-paper-terrorists; C Sarteschi, 'Sovereign Citizens: A Narrative Review with Implications of Violence towards Law Enforcement' (2021) 60 *Aggression and Violent Behaviour* 101509.

[165] Federal Bureau of Investigation, 'Sovereign Citizens: A Growing Domestic Threat to Law Enforcement' Law Enforcement Bulletin (1 September 2011), leb.fbi.gov/articles/featured-articles/sovereign-citizens-a-growing-domestic-threat-to-law-enforcement.

[166] BS Slater, 'Sovereign Citizen Movement: An Empirical Study on the Rise in Activity, Explanations of Growth, and Policy Prescriptions' MA Thesis, Naval Postgraduate School (September 2016) 14, discussing The Freedom School (thefreedomschool.com), Sovereignty Education and Defense Ministry (SEDM) (sedm.org) and Sovereignty Press (sovereigntypress.com/-l9ONK4sSEnO59MhxsmXXex-).

[167] See, for example, 'BIRTH CERTIFICATE Equals Chattel Property (n 139); Storey (n 103); One Stupid Fuck (www.instagram.com/one.stupid.fuck).

[168] Christine Sarteschi documents the reach of one contemporary movement involving sovereign citizen pseudolaw, the American State Nationals in person and on telegram, while David Heilpern details how two websites sell misleading and legally incorrect information to people hoping to avoid traffic fines: C Sarteschi, ch 11 in this volume; D Heilpern, ch 12 in this volume.

[169] JJ MacNab, 'Context Matters: The Cliven Bundy Standoff – Part 3' Forbes (6 May 2014), www.forbes.com/sites/jjmacnab/2014/05/06/context-matters-the-cliven-bundy-standoff-part-3/?sh=41176a5e6599; R Lenz and M Potok, 'War in the West: The Bundy Ranch Standoff and the American Radical Right' Southern Poverty Law Center (10 July 2014), www.splcenter.org/20140709/war-west-bundy-ranch-standoff-and-american-radical-right.

pizzeria and without any provocation or warning, shot and killed two police officers sitting in a booth eating lunch'.[170] JJ MacNab, an expert on sovereign citizens, explains that Jared and Amanda, at age 31 and 22, were part of a new generation emboldened by sovereign citizen pseudolaw:

> [They] belong to [the] youngest subgroup within the Sovereign world. This group is racially diverse, both male and female, urban and rural, and usually self-identified as libertarians … a person in this group likely entered the movement as an angry veteran who has recently left the military, as a child raised by Sovereigns, or through seemingly unrelated groups such as Anonymous, the 9/11 'Truth' movement, the Occupy movement, or the legalized marijuana community.[171]

Sovereign pseudolaw is inter-generational. In 2016, Ammon and Ryan Bundy, who were involved in the 2014 stand-off at their father Cliven's Nevada ranch, led an armed group to the headquarters of the federally owned Malheur National Wildlife Refuge in Oregon.[172] They occupied the Refuge for over a month before surrendering. During the stand-off, one participant, Robert 'Lavoy' Fincum was killed by federal law enforcement after evading their roadblock and commands.

The accessibility of sovereign citizen pseudolaw via the Internet and social media channels has transformed it in curious ways. Indeed, in its adaptations and mutations, it has even been adopted by African American communities who were once scorned by the movement's founders based on their white supremacist Christian Identity beliefs. In the 1990s, for example, some members of the Moorish Science Temple, a religious sect of primarily African Americans, branched into sovereign citizen pseudolaw. The Temple later denounced sovereign citizenship, but the impact of the ideology among Moors was ongoing. Moorish sovereign citizens claim that they are descendants of Moroccan Moors subject to the 1786 United States–Morocco Treaty of Friendship and thus supposedly exempt from United States law.[173] This belief has led to numerous altercations between Moors and the police. Another group whose members refer to themselves as Back Hebrew Israelites, who like the Christian Identity adherents from the original Posse, believe they are the true Israelites, invokes the Foreign Sovereign Immunities Act and the *Holy Bible* as supposedly allowing them to avoid having to pay vehicle registration fees.[174] Sovereign citizen pseudolaw has not jettisoned its racist, white supremacist

[170] JJ MacNab, 'What Las Vegas Police Killings Show About Evolving Sovereign Movement' Forbes (13 June 2014), www.forbes.com/sites/jjmacnab/2014/06/13/what-las-vegas-police-killings-show-about-evolving-sovereign-movement/?sh=4079576a2a28.

[171] ibid.

[172] C Gallaher, 'Placing the Militia Occupation of the Malheur National Wildlife Refuge in Harney County, Oregon' (2016) 15 *ACME: An International Journal for Critical Geographies* 293.

[173] M Ligon, 'The Sovereign Citizen Movement: A Comparative Analysis with Similar Foreign Movements and Takeaways for the United States Judicial System' (2021) 35 *Emory International Law Review* 297; C Fiandaca, 'Rise of the Moors Highway Standoff: Where the Cases Stand Now' CBS News (1 July 2022), www.cbsnews.com/boston/news/rise-of-the-moors-wakefield-highway-standoff.

[174] *Ngola Mbandi v Pangea Ventures*, 2023 WL 4486703 (7th Cir 2023).

and antisemitic origins, but it has proven sufficiently malleable for all manner of disaffected or marginalised individuals and communities to become radicalised and adopt and experiment with it. This flexibility has facilitated its proliferation across the United States and the globe.

V. Conclusion

Confronted by claims that the Government is illegitimate, and the laws of the land do not apply, judges, police officers and ordinary people may struggle not only to comprehend these arguments but to understand where this phenomenon originated and why it has spread so widely. In this chapter, we have sought to answer these questions. We have explained that the origins of sovereign citizen pseudolaw developed in the United States out of a potent mix of racially motivated, extremist political and religious organisations that jostled for attention and members throughout the twentieth century. These loosely organised groups allowed for experimentation, ensuring adept leaders could adapt and invent new theories and strategies to take advantage of social crises and emergencies, facilitating the spread of sovereign citizen pseudolaw.

The underlying theories and narratives that propel sovereign citizen pseudolaw can be traced to three primary, loosely organised groups. They are William Potter Gale's Posse Comitatus, the more legalistic Common Law Movement, and the more militaristic antigovernment Patriot Movement. Exploiting socioeconomic crises, these groups thrived on the disaffected and marginalised citizens who were often desperate enough to believe there was a way to hold on to their property by accessing a secret bank account or retaliating against those they thought had harmed them using pseudolegal methods. The pattern has continued in the new millennium, but expanded its grasp to include disaffected voters, people prone to believing conspiracy theories, and those angry about vaccine mandates or public health guidelines put in place during the COVID-19 pandemic. The Internet and social media have only increased opportunities for dissemination and transmission of pseudolaw. On Telegram, Facebook and other platforms, individuals learn, adapt and transform sovereign citizen pseudolaw to their immediate interests.

We have limited our review to a pre-history of sovereign citizen pseudolaw rather than a contemporary examination of its reach. We have not examined the significant and sustained social and economic crises caused by the COVID-19 pandemic and the necessary public health response that proved a catalytic explosion for sovereign citizen gurus and ideologues to spread their beliefs. It is our hope that understanding the background and origins of the phenomenon can assist in developing appropriate responses to this concerning phenomenon.

7

The Sun Only Shines on YouTube: The Marginal Presence of Pseudolaw in Canada

DONALD J NETOLITZKY*

I. Introduction

Pseudolaw is a collection of not-law concepts[1] typically deployed to purportedly:

(1) shift the balance of authority away from government and institutional actors and to individuals, in the process providing extraordinary authority and immunity from legal obligations;[2] and
(2) eliminate debts and obtain money for nothing.[3]

This chapter surveys the arrival in Canada of modern pseudolaw circa 2000, and the subsequent rise and collapse of a range of Canadian pseudolaw host communities.

Pseudolaw has never been successful in Canada, and historically has only been adopted in small and marginal groups, usually oriented around a key organising individual, commonly called 'gurus'. Canada in that sense differs from United States pseudolaw communities, which are typically described as amorphous or leaderless.

* Donald J Netolitzky (PhD Microbiology, University of Alberta, 1995; LLB, University of Alberta, 2005; LLM, University of Alberta, 2020; KC, Alberta, 2022) is the now-retired Complex Litigant Management Counsel for the Alberta Court of King's Bench. The views expressed in this publication are those of the author, and not those of any member of the Court of King's Bench, or the Court itself.

[1] H Hobbs, S Young and J McIntyre, 'The Internationalisation of Pseudolaw: The Growth of Sovereign Citizen Arguments in Australia and Aotearoa New Zealand' (2024) 47 *University of New South Wales Law Journal* 309, 311–16.

[2] DJ Netolitzky, 'A Revolting Itch: Pseudolaw as a Social Adjuvant' (2021) 22 *Politics, Religion & Ideology* 164.

[3] DJ Netolitzky, 'After the Hammer: Six Years of Meads v Meads' (2019) 56 *Alberta Law Review* 1167, 1175–82.

No reliable data precisely indicates how many individuals in Canada have associated with or taken steps to engage pseudolaw. However, data from pseudolaw scheme records, the volume and type of pseudolaw documents that are directed to public institutions, and known instances of pseudolaw litigation suggest the pseudolaw-adherent population in Canada has always been small, probably nothing more than a few thousand at any time,[4] and shows strong region-to-region variation, with maximum activity in western provinces, particularly British Columbia.[5]

As this chapter reviews Canada's diverse pseudolaw landscape, factors that contribute to pseudolaw's marginal status in Canadian society will be identified and evaluated. Although pseudolaw has been observed to expand broadly during periods of public crisis, such as the United States 1980s farm crisis and 2010 financial disruptions, and the Republic of Ireland 2010 property bubble,[6] in Canada pseudolaw never achieved any significant public acceptance, even during the recent COVID-19 pandemic and amidst the otherwise broad and unprecedented spread of conspiratorial belief.[7] These environmental factors might favour pseudolaw becoming more broadly disseminated and applied, as has been observed in certain other jurisdictions. However, in Canada that did not happen.

II. Pseudolaw Concepts in Canada

Since 2000, the core pseudolaw concepts identified in Canada belong to the usual six-part United States-sourced 'pseudolaw memeplex':[8]

(1) government authority is limited and/or defective;
(2) everything is a contract;

[4] See DJ Netolitzky, 'The History of the Organized Pseudolegal Commercial Argument Phenomenon in Canada' (2016) 53 *Alberta Law Review* 609, 612; DJ Netolitzky, 'The Dead Sleep Quiet: History of the Organized Pseudolegal Commercial Argument Phenomenon in Canada – Part II' (2023) 60 *Alberta Law Review* 795, 807–13. Unfortunately, US-sourced commentary on Canadian pseudolaw phenomena has mischaracterised the nature of these groups, and inaccurately extrapolated that Canada has 30,000 'sovereign citizens'. That both misdescribes the political and cultural objectives of Canadian pseudolaw actors, and almost certainly grossly exaggerates the frequency of this phenomenon.

[5] Netolitzky (2023) (n 4) 811.

[6] SA Kent, 'Freemen, Sovereign Citizens, and the Challenge to Public Order in British Heritage Countries' (2015) 6 *International Journal of Cultic Studies* 1; E Hodge, 'The Sovereign Ascendant: Financial Collapse, Status Anxiety, and the Rebirth of the Sovereign Citizen Movement' (2019) 4 *Frontiers in Sociology* 1; DJ Netolitzky, 'A Pathogen Astride the Minds of Men: The Epidemiological History of Pseudolaw' CEFIR Symposium Sovereign Citizens in Canada, Montreal (3 May 2018) 10–12.

[7] Netolitzky (2023) (n 4); DJ Netolitzky, 'New Hosts for an Old Disease: History of the Organized Pseudolegal Commercial Argument Phenomenon in Canada – Part III' (2023) 60 *Alberta Law Review* 971.

[8] DJ Netolitzky, 'A Rebellion of Furious Paper: Pseudolaw as a Revolutionary Legal System' CEFIR Symposium Sovereign Citizens in Canada, Montreal (3 May 2018) 14–15; Netolitzky (n 2); see also *Meads v Meads* [2012] ABQB 571.

(3) silence means consent;
(4) an enforceable right in law requires an injured party;
(5) the 'Strawman Theory' duality; and
(6) monetary and banking conspiracy theories directed to debt elimination and 'money for nothing'.

Pseudolaw schemes in Canada are almost always either copied or derived from foreign examples. Very few pseudolaw concepts or motifs are truly 'Canadian', and those few that are uniquely Canadian typically relate to a purported defect in Canadian government authority, such as that Canada ceased to exist in 1931 as a consequence of the Statute of Westminster,[9] or narrow Canada-specific pseudolaw claims to eliminate debts.[10]

Canada's chief role in an international pseudolaw context is as a conceptual epidemiological bridge between the United States and Commonwealth jurisdictions. Prior to 2000, United States-sourced pseudolaw was very nation-specific, for example linking its theories to specific United States constitutional amendments, the 'weak Federal/strong state' structure of that country, events in United States monetary history, and 'Redemption' Strawman Theory claims specific to that nation. Canada was the jurisdiction where a single individual, Eldon Warman, in the late 1990s 'localised' United States-style pseudolaw concepts so as to replace United States-specific motifs with those more compatible with Canadian and Commonwealth history, government structures and legal principles.[11] For example, Warman pointed to historical 'Anglo-Saxon Common Law' and the Magna Carta as supraconstitutional authorities, rather than United States foundational documents, and adapted Strawman Theory to focus on birth documentation instead of social security numbers. Other imported pseudolaw concepts, such as fractional reserve banking 'money for nothing' claims, remained largely unaltered as those Canadian and United States arguments were compatible and/or interchangeable.

Once introduced into Canada and now 'localised', United States-sourced concepts rapidly displaced pre-existing Canadian pseudolaw. From Canada, the now evolved and acclimatised pseudolaw memeplex was transferred to many other jurisdictions.[12]

Very little new pseudolaw has subsequently appeared in Canada, though why is opaque.[13] One indisputable point is Canadian pseudolaw users are mesmerised by Strawman Theory.[14] Briefly, Strawman Theory claims that what is usually

[9] Netolitzky (2016) (n 4) 615–16; Netolitzky (n 7) 976–77.
[10] eg, misinterpretation of the Bills of Exchange Act, RSC 1985, c B-4 'consumer purchase' provisions, reviewed in Netolitzky (n 3) 1178–79.
[11] Netolitzky (n 6) 6–8.
[12] ibid.
[13] Netolitzky (n 3) 1182–85.
[14] Reviewed in C Kalinowski IV, 'A Legal Response to the Sovereign Citizen Movement' (2019) 80 *Montana Law Review* 153; Netolitzky (n 8) 6–7; DJ Netolitzky, 'Organized Pseudolegal Commercial

thought of as a single entity instead has two separable halves: a 'flesh and blood' human being, and an immaterial legal entity, often called 'the Strawman', the 'legal fiction', 'the person', or a corporation or estate. According to Strawman Theory, human beings are not born with a strawman, but, rather, that the strawman is created by government documentation as a concealed trickster contract, and then attached to the human being as a kind of dark legal doppelganger. The strawman is identified by a name in all capital letters, eg 'FIRSTNAME LASTNAME' while the proper identifier for a human is a mixed or all lower case name, or a name with an atypical structure and/or punctuation, such as ':Firstname-Lastname:', or 'Firstname of the Lastname Family'.

According to Strawman Theory, governments have no authority over human beings, but instead chain that authority via contracts from the government to the strawman, then through the strawman to the flesh-and-blood individual. To escape state authority and law, one needs to sever the contract-based strawman to human linkage, and/or denounce and reject the strawman's obligations as not one's own. In Canada Strawman Theory appears in myriad variations and permutations, but those different forms are consistently grounded on the same underlying conceptual structure. Differences are limited: changes to language, or the purported legal(ish) nature and character of the strawman.

A related pseudolegal misconception is that the strawman is associated with a secret government-operated bank account that exists to monetise citizen/slaves. Pseudolaw gurus teach this pool of funds may be accessed or seized by special paperwork and processes known as 'Accept for Value' (A4V) and 'Redemption'.[15]

Foreign (typically United States- or United Kingdom-sourced) pseudolaw continues to appear in Canada, even where the outsider scheme is either crudely or not at all 'localised' into a form that might make sense outside the United States[16] or United Kingdom.[17] For example, Canadian pseudolaw adherents often advance what are purely United States A4V and Redemption schemes, addressing documents to United States government actors and institutions. Sometimes application of United States-native schemes is explained by unsophisticated claims that Canada is a corporation registered in and/or owned by the United States.[18]

Arguments as Magic and Ceremony' (2018) 55 *Alberta Law Review* 1045 1069–78; Hobbs, Young and McIntyre (n 1).

[15] *Meads* (n 8) [531]–[543].

[16] For example, the documents attached to *Docken v Anderson* [2023] ABKB 291; *Docken v Anderson* [2023] ABKB 313 that purport a Canadian pseudolaw litigant's strawman is a trust registered with the US Securities and Exchange Commission.

[17] For example, *AVI v MHVB* [2020] ABQB 489; DJ Netolitzky, 'Ten Seconds to Implosion: The Magna Carta Lawful Rebellion' (2023) 6 *International Journal of Coercion, Abuse, and Manipulation*, DOI: 10.54208/1000/0006/003.

[18] For example, *Fearn v Canada Customs* [2014] ABQB 114 [66]–[69]; *Girard v The Queen* [2014] TCC 107 [25]; *R v Gerlitz* [2014] ABQB 247 [6].

In summary, the Canadian pseudolaw conceptual space and resources toolkit is unremarkable. Canadian pseudolaw adherents advance the same not-law schemes as their equivalents worldwide.

III. Early Influences

Prior to Warman localising the United States pseudolaw memeplex, Canada had independently developed locally sourced instances of pseudolaw. Our understanding of this 'PreDetaxer'[19] period, roughly 1950–2000, is very likely incomplete, but from what is known, most pseudolaw adherents focused on negating personal income tax obligations. Several pseudolaw theories in use at this time were purely Canadian in origin, such as that Constitution Act,[20] sections 91–92 division of federal and provincial authorities meant Canada had no tax authority,[21] and that Canada had ceased to exist as a country due to purported defects in the 1931 Statute of Westminster.[22] Curiously, the latter argument was developed and advanced by elected members of Parliament belonging to the monetary theory oriented Social Credit Party of Canada.[23]

Limited and narrow transfers of pseudolaw from the United States did occur during this period. For example, leading Detaxer guru David Kevin Lindsay in 1999 published a text, *Rights Denied! How Your government has stolen Your Right to use the Highways You pay for!*,[24] that paralleled and localised United States motor vehicle 'travelling' pseudolaw schemes. Similarly, another Social Credit politician, Joseph A Thauberger, introduced United States fractional reserve banking conspiracy concepts into Canada by publishing a Canadian variant of the United States Christian Identity pamphlet, 'Billions for the Banks, Debts for the People'.[25]

PreDetaxer characteristics, organisation and communications are poorly documented. This population appears small, socially conservative and politically marginal. In addition to Social Credit affiliations, a Quebec-based highly conservative Roman Catholic sect called the Pilgrims of St-Michael 'White Berets',[26]

[19] Named for its chronological position in advance of the first modern anti-tax pseudolaw movement, the Detaxers, see section IV.A below.

[20] The Constitution Act 1867 (Imp) 30 & 31 Vict, c 3.

[21] Netolitzky (2016) (n 4) 614–15.

[22] Statute of Westminster 1931 (Imp) 22 & 23 Geo 5.

[23] Netolitzky (2016) (n 4) 615–16.

[24] DK Lindsay, *Rights Denied! How Your government has stolen Your Right to use the Highways You pay for!* (AAA Publishing, 1999).

[25] This document existed in multiple versions, for example: JA Thauberger, 'Billions for the Bankers; Debts for the People' (Freedom Foundations Inc, 6th edn), www.web.archive.org/web/20160331230736/http://somagardens.com/billions/b-toc.htm.

[26] M Geoffroy, 'The Pilgrims of Saint-Michael: Preserving Quebec's Traditional "Intégriste"' in SJ Palmer, M Geoffroy and PL Gareau (eds), *The Mystical Geography of Quebec: Catholic Schisms and New Religious Movements* (Palgrave MacMillan, 2020) 85–108.

spread these ideas via organised speaking engagements and Canada-wide bulk mailing of *The Michael Journal* newspaper.[27] Usenet, particularly the 'can.taxes' newsgroup, appears to have been a major forum and hub where PreDetaxer ideas were disseminated, as well as personal websites.

PreDetaxer activities led to a limited record of reported court judgments that rejected their arguments. Canada-specific concepts that emerged and evolved during the PreDetaxer period have gone extinct, displaced by the United States pseudolaw memeplex imported by Warman, with the exception of the Statute of Westminster 'there is no Canada' theory, which, unexpectedly resurfaced two decades later.

IV. The First Wave of Modern Canadian Pseudolaw

Around the beginning of the century, the United States-type pseudolaw, as localised by Warman, was adopted by two very different populations: the anti-income tax 'Detaxer' movement, and the criminal and social parasite 'Freemen-on-the-Land'. In this instance the 'chain of transmission' is clear since the founder of the Freeman phenomenon, Robert Arthur Menard, explicitly identified Warman, and Warman devotee and Detaxer guru, Rev Alex Muljiani, as his pseudolaw sources.[28]

The arrival of United States-style pseudolaw in Canada marks the point Canada became part of a worldwide phenomenon: a nation with two duelling legal systems, one conventional, the other an unorthodox scheme wielded by diverse social groups and populations. This transition was largely centred on broad adoption of Strawman Theory. The following sections briefly outline the rise and fall of these variations on Canadian pseudolaw and their host populations.

A. Detaxers

The demarcation point between the PreDetaxer and Detaxer phenomena is chiefly a question of pseudolegal theory: local Canadian pseudolaw was displaced by United States concepts and the 'Canadianised' narrative developed by Warman. Many of the anti-tax personalities on either side of that divide are the same.[29] Both argument types coexisted in the early 2000s. However, there is a clear demarcation line in the forms of argumentation and concepts used, and that transition was remarkably rapid. For example, circa 2000 Detaxer promoter Patrick Ellis recorded seminars that made sophisticated Constitution Act,

[27] Netolitzky (2016) (n 4) 615–16.
[28] Netolitzky (n 6) 9.
[29] Netolitzky (2016) (n 4) 613–24.

sections 91–92 separation of power arguments. Within a year, Ellis had switched to Warman-style pseudolaw.[30] Leading Detaxer guru Russell Porisky advanced classic Strawman Theory duality and name structures in court in 2000.[31] Newly arrived Strawman Theory was typically applied to argue that Canada's taxation authority only applied to corporations, including the strawman, and not flesh-and-blood humans. These claims were often meshed with how the Canadian Income Tax Act[32] defined 'income', 'taxpayer' and 'person'.

Much Detaxer activity occurred on now inaccessible and/or deleted Internet message groups, some private, others public, with some personal websites. The primary Detaxer message groups reveal that the early Detaxers were a small population, numbering in the low hundreds at most, who operated less in a commercial 'guru-follower' context, than as a community of peer investigators, puzzling through legislation and case law, and tracking each other's litigation and filings as Canadian tax authorities prosecuted these individuals. This community was comparatively sophisticated, and cooperative rather than competitive or hierarchical.

Detaxers were politically flexible, accepting both highly conservative, libertarian and sometimes racist elements, but also hardline socialist participants, such as Daniel Lavigne.[33] While pseudolaw is sometimes described as law used by economically marginal people, that was not true of Canadian Detaxers, who included many wealthy professionals and business owners.[34]

A winnowing process occurred over time, as Detaxer activity coalesced around several larger schemes:

(1) *The Porisky-led Paradigm Education Group (PEG)* (2002–08)[35] that used formal instruction and extensive documentary and video materials presented via a multilevel structure by 30 trained 'Educators' to 800 students. When PEG pseudolaw was rejected by Canadian courts, Porisky formally abandoned his scheme. Much criminal litigation followed.

(2) *Fiscal Arbitrators* (2005–11) and *Demara Consulting* (2009–12) operated unsophisticated parallel schemes where the strawman was claimed as a business expense. Jointly these Detaxer products, that were marketed as legally valid but little-known accounting strategies, had several thousand customers.[36]

[30] *Ellis v Canada (Office of the Prime Minister)* [2001] SKQB 378.

[31] *R v Porisky* (18 January 2000), Chilliwack 40082-1 (BCPC).

[32] Income Tax Act, RSC 1985, c 1 (5th Supp).

[33] Netolitzky (2016) (n 4) 613–24.

[34] DJ Netolitzky, 'Lawyers and Court Representation of Organized Pseudolegal Commercial Argument [OPCA] Litigants in Canada' (2018) 51 *University of British Columbia Law Review* 419; DJ Netolitzky, 'A Ride With My Best Friend: The Fiscal Arbitrator Pseudolaw Tax Evasion Scheme, Recruitment, and Litigation' (2023) *International Journal of Coercion, Abuse, and Manipulation*, DOI: 10.54208/1000/0006/005.

[35] Netolitzky (2016) (n 4) 623–24; Netolitzky (2018) (n 34) 441–48.

[36] Netolitzky (2023) (n 34).

The Public Prosecution Service of Canada successfully obtained criminal convictions against Porisky, PEG Educators, high-income PEG customers and the Fiscal Arbitrators and Demara Consulting lead promoters.[37] Other taxpayer followers received Canada Revenue Agency 'gross negligence' penalties of 50 per cent of the tax sought to be avoided.

Over a decade later, this litigation is now concluding. The promoters' defences ran the full gamut of pure pseudolaw argument to conventional, usually evidentiary and procedural, arguments.[38] The PEG criminal defendants were particularly sophisticated and networked in private to share privileged disclosure and incrementally develop strategies to sabotage their prosecutions. The PEG defendants' trials are textbook illustrations of how Canadian criminal proceedings are vulnerable to manipulation by skilled and calculating self-represented litigants who applied both conventional and pseudolaw strategies, often in multiple jurisdictions, to frustrate prosecution on technical 'get out of jail free' grounds. In contrast, most Detaxer customers abandoned pseudolaw for conventional law and court processes. They engaged a pragmatic 'damage control' response, often retained lawyers, and only disputed narrow issues, such as liability for gross negligence penalties.[39]

The degree of commitment to pseudolaw and its narrative varied widely among the Detaxers. Early Detaxers and promoter/gurus may not always have been 'true believers', but certainly were 'eagerly hopeful'. In contrast, the broad customer base of PEG, Fiscal Arbitrators, and Demara Consulting were often goal-oriented 'mercenaries'. For example, an investigation of Fiscal Arbitrators customers determined the majority had no understanding of or interest in the strawman business expense scheme itself.[40] Their only objective was a fast buck, by any means.

The Detaxers generally maintained a low profile, and to varying degrees held their pseudolaw as privileged, secret, 'for-pay only' knowledge. Except for specific legal and court circles, the Detaxers were basically unknown to the Canadian public, and the subject of only limited media reporting that usually simply echoed Canada Revenue Agency public announcements.

The Detaxer phenomenon is now dead. The Detaxers were ultimately results-oriented, rather than a political or cultural movement. Once Detaxer techniques failed in practice, and its participants were sanctioned, the movement collapsed. Furthermore, after court adjudication of their claims most Detaxer leader figures acknowledged they were wrong in law. In Canada pseudolaw has not been employed for tax avoidance/evasion in the past decade. Canada Revenue Agency actors on rare occasions encounter pseudolaw, but almost exclusively as a debt elimination strategy.

[37] Netolitzky (n 7) 814–15.
[38] Netolitzky (2018) (n 34).
[39] Netolitzky (2023) (n 34) III(C); Netolitzky (2018) (n 34) 430–34.
[40] Netolitzky (2023) (n 34) IV(C).

B. Freemen-on-the-Land

In contrast to the Detaxers, who were almost exclusively mercenary non-believers looking for direct economic advantage, the Freemen-on-the-Land movement had both ideological and functional aspects. In its mature form, the Freemen-on-the-Land movement[41] superficially appeared to be a cloud of leftist, Green, NeoHippy, anti-authority actors circling first one, then a second, guru. However, that first impression conceals the criminal activity underlying this population. The Freemen were primarily recruited via Canadian online and in-person marijuana advocacy, production and trafficking networks. Their chief objective was to engage in a broad range of unrestricted illegal activity ranging from drug offences to sex crimes against children and, secondarily, obtain government and social benefits without obligation. Freemen sought a form of institutionalised Eric Cartmanism: 'do as I please' and 'take what I want'. Once the Freemen surfaced, the Canadian public emphatically rejected these 'Freeloaders-on-the-Land'.

The Freeman movement was founded by street comedian Menard circa 2000. For the next decade Menard was the central Freeman theorist and authority. Initially Freemanism had a very different focus than its final form. Menard's early publications and websites describe how Menard fathered a child with a young runaway female, but then British Columbia Government children's services actors blocked Menard's access to the child and her mother. Menard then framed state authority through Strawman Theory, and instructed parents not register their children. However, over time, Menard's teachings shifted to nullifying state criminal and regulatory authority so as to ignore tickets, reject bills, use motor vehicles without registration and insurance, operate as vigilante 'peace officers', and employ notaries as super-judges to impose control and demands on others.

Freeman pseudolaw theory never matured past a thin and superficial adaptation of conventional pseudolaw. Instead, theory was secondary to anti-government and anti-establishment politics and rhetoric. The most sophisticated 'textbook' produced by Menard, *With Lawful Excuse*,[42] was nothing more than a graphic novel largely composed of clipart and letters from Menard to government and police actors. Menard's innovation was, instead, his use of episodic YouTube videos where Menard, as a talking head and whiteboard presenter, led his followers through a succession of pseudolaw revelations. These videos attracted much

[41] Reviewed in Netolitzky (2016) (n 4) 624–27; Netolitzky (2023) (n 45) 818–20; Netolitzky (2018) (n 34) 434–41. Certain published commentary on the Freeman phenomenon, particularly DC Hofmann, 'Breaking Free: A Socio-Historical Analysis of the Canadian Freeman-on-the-Land Movement' in J Littlewood, L Dawson and SK Thompson (eds), *Terrorism and Counterterrorism in Canada* (University of Toronto Press, 2020) 77 and Hodge (n 6), should be approached with caution given incorrect links to US influences, grouping together pseudolegally and socially distinct populations, and relying upon media and US non-governmental organisation reporting that was badly distorted by imagined but false parallels between US sovereign citizen and Canadian Freeman groups.

[42] RA Menard, *With Lawful Excuse* (Elizabeth Anne Elaine Society and Freddie Freepickle Productions, 2011).

attention in counter-culture and marijuana-advocacy circles, and that approach was copied by Menard's chief competitor, the more confrontational and threatening 'muscular Freemanist' Dean Clifford. Freemanism's rapid decline post-2010 was because, when tested, Freeman pseudolaw did not work. This was most vividly demonstrated when Menand and Clifford were themselves unable to 'get out of jail free' during criminal prosecutions.

A related factor is a highly influential anti-pseudolaw court decision released near the highpoint in Freeman activity. *Meads v Meads*,[43] the first comprehensive review and response to pseudolaw in Canada, attracted substantial public and media attention, and still remains a key authority that rebuts and denounces pseudolaw.[44] The Freeman community was simultaneously abruptly faced with a detailed systematic dismantling of their concepts, accumulating in-court failures, and a guru caste who offered no reasoned response.[45]

The Freeman rank and file communicated in website message forums and social media, chiefly Facebook. Interestingly, substantial independent debate and discussion occurred in these forums, including of in-court failures and criticism of Freeman gurus. Comparatively unrestricted information sharing probably helped precipitate Freemanism's collapse. By 2014, Freeman activity had essentially ceased, and the movement was, for all practical purposes, dead. Freemen bitterly accepted from experience and observation that the benefits promised by pseudolaw were not possible, at least not yet. The former members of the now defunct Freeman movement still hold the same social and political objectives, and wait for a proven mechanism to obtain their unrestricted criminal 'freeloader' lifestyle objective.

V. The Lull: 2015–20

Following the collapse of the two first-wave Canadian pseudolaw movements, new pseudolaw adherents and litigation practically disappeared in Canada. During this lull a series of new promoter/theorists emerged who framed their pseudolaw concepts in what resembled Freeman ideology and language, rather than foreign pseudolaw schema. These 'Freeman Echo'[46] theorists typically expanded on Menard's and Clifford's concepts with some new hook or revelation that fixed what had been (purportedly) missed or misunderstood by the original Freeman leadership. The Freeman Echo promoters targeted the now demoralised Freeman rank and file. While Freeman remnants were clearly interested, most adopted a 'wait and see' approach before adopting and applying Freeman Echo theories.

[43] *Meads* (n 8).
[44] Netolitzky (n 3).
[45] ibid 1192–98.
[46] Netolitzky (n 7) 821–28.

Certain Freeman Echo gurus operated less in a legal or litigation context, than a mystical/philosophical space. Wilfred Emonts, 'Marcus', of the Servant King website reframed the strawman duality as religious-based magic, with necromancy, and infant 'Baby-lonians'.[47] Similarly, 'rob in the pagé family', aka 'White Walking Feather', oriented his 'off-the-grid' lifestyle separate from government in spiritual and New-Age channels.[48]

The lull is also notable for a dramatic maturation in Freeman-style legal reasoning. As previously noted, Menard and Clifford were unsophisticated and legally inept. What becomes apparent is that the Freeman rank and file learned much about law, legislation and court jurisprudence while watching Freemanism implode. The remnant Freeman Echo litigants employed legal rather than political arguments, culminating in an impressive scheme developed by 'John Spirit' (a pseudonym), that combined passages from international human rights treaties with selected quotes from actual Supreme Court of Canada jurisprudence to claim strawman-based special status and immunities.[49] Former Detaxer Wally Dove then copied Spirit's scheme. A significant volume of litigation and appeals based on Spirit's scheme soon followed. To Spirit's credit, he ceased promoting his concepts and largely disappeared after his concepts were systematically dissected and rejected in *Pomerleau v Canada (Revenue Agency)*.[50]

The majority of new pseudolaw court-related activity during the lull flowed from a series of 'money for nothing' and debt elimination schemes promoted by Canadian gurus (Menard: Association of Canadian Consumer Purchasers; Clifford: Dean Clifford Debt Abatement), or imported from the United States (One People's Public Trust; Gold Shield Alliance), the United Kingdom (WeRe Bank; GetOutOfDebtFree.org), and Indonesia (SwissIndo Trust).[51] Within the Canadian pseudolaw ecosystem these schemes simply came and went in sequence, usually lasting only one to two years. Reported Canadian case law rebutted these claims, so most 'money for nothing' and debt elimination litigation was disposed of via summary processes. By this point, and with over a decade of experience, Canadian banks had become highly sophisticated in responding to and disposing of pseudolaw money-related litigation.

VI. The Second Wave of Modern Canadian Pseudolaw

The second wave of Canadian pseudolaw groups predates the COVID-19 pandemic, with two branches grounded in the Canadian 'Yellow Vest' economic

[47] ibid 824–26.
[48] ibid 826–27.
[49] Netolitzky (2023) (n 4) 822–23.
[50] *Pomerleau v Canada (Revenue Agency)* [2017] ABQB 123.
[51] Netolitzky (n 3) 1176–82.

protest and anti-regulatory resistance that was developing in the late 2010s. Second-wave movements have little connection to first-wave pseudolaw groups and ideas and, instead, involved entirely 'virgin' populations adopting pseudolaw. The second wave can be grouped into three categories: (A) alternative/replacement governments; (B) the Magna Carta Lawful Rebellion; and (C) Indigenous-styled pseudolaw groups.

A. Alternative/Replacement Governments

Within the second wave were at least seven pseudolaw-using alternative/replacement governments. These entities purported to be nation-states of some kind, though their conceptual basis was often nothing but self-declared authority. Some displaced Canada as a whole, others were more regional in focus, similar to micronations.[52]

The first and most substantial alternative/replacement government scheme has been labelled the New Constitutionalists.[53] Starting in 2017, New Constitutionalists resurrected the 90-year-old Social Credit theory that Canada had only existed between 1867 and 1931, and was terminated by the Statute of Westminster. According to New Constitutionalists, the Canadian provinces were now each separate nation states, but without any formal constitutional and government structure. Guided by a number of key figures with long-standing fringe and dissident political perspectives, committees organised to develop government structures for these new nations, such as The Republic of Alberta.

New Constitutionalism would probably not have drawn much attention, except that the Canadian Republics concept was attractive first to the Yellow Vest movement (2017–19), and then 'scamdemic' resistance protesters during the COVID-19 pandemic (2019 onward).[54] New Constitutionalism provided a basis to reject state authority and perceived oppressive and intrusive overreach. New Constitutionalist logos, slogans and website addresses frequently appeared on banners, signs and vehicles during public anti-quarantine and vaccination scamdemic protests and marches, particularly early in the COVID-19 pandemic. However, that was as far as New Constitutionalism developed. No litigation to enforce the new purported nations occurred and, instead, New Constitutionalist communities gradually fragmented amidst interpersonal conflict, and disinterest in the Republic-building project. By September 2022, the keystone New Constitutionalist website, 'unifythepeople.ca', was offline.

Unlike the long-standing alternative/replacement governments in the United States and Germany,[55] New Constitutionalism never evolved past a debating

[52] H Hobbs and G Williams, *Micronations and the Search for Sovereignty* (Cambridge University Press, 2021).

[53] Reviewed in Netolitzky (n 7) 976–81.

[54] ibid 977–78, 980.

[55] Netolitzky (n 2) 172–73; Netolitzky (n 7) 975–76.

society stage. New Constitutionalist politics were more diverse than cohesive. QAnon, militia, conservative, and 'alt-right' motifs were obvious, but also ideologically opposite objectives, such as a libertarian-style abolition of income tax, and even economic socialist objectives such as nationalisation of utilities and transport infrastructure.

New Constitutionalism clearly struck a chord with pandemic-sceptic and anti-mitigation protestors; signs and banners linked to New Constitutionalism were present at practically any such protest during this period. A substantial population was involved. While sometimes disruptive, no actually revolutionary or violent activity appears to have occurred. Thus, the main interaction between New Constitutionalists and Canadians was when law enforcement engaged to manage and monitor these protests. New Constitutionalism was never a threat to Canadian society and order. It is unlikely most Canadians even placed any meaning upon public endorsements of New Constitutionalism.

Other alternative/replacement governments were even more tenuous. Long standing political activist and crank Kevin Annett, aka Eagle Strong Voice, early in the COVID-19 pandemic resurrected his Freeman-era Republic of Kanata and began issuing proclamations and 'International Common Law Court of Justice' arrest warrants and judgments. Annett called on Canadians to form self-organised vigilante groupings – Common Law Assemblies – and then destroy 5G telecommunications facilities and vaccines. However, the Republic of Kanata was literally nothing more than Annett, personally, standing in front of a banner and recording videos, self-publishing court-like documents, and issuing press releases. At least four Common Law Assemblies were announced, but all disappeared within several months. The Republic of Kanata is best characterised as Annett engaged in vigorous but bizarre self-promotion. Annett has obtained substantial media and alternative culture attention for over a decade. That, apparently, is reason enough for Annett to continue his activities.

Additional pseudolaw alternative/replacement governments – the True North Guardians Alliance/Lakeshore Sovereign Assembly, Sovereign Republic of British Columbia, and Arbutus Nation State[56] – emerged early in the COVID-19 pandemic. Their chief activity was to issue documents, ID and other paperwork that purportedly put their followers outside government authority. No information suggests any of these groups retained significant followings or engaged in litigation. The Kingdom of Tayos micronation subsequently appeared in 2022,[57] though its King Regis Lucius I is facing criminal proceedings.

Yet more Canadian alternative/replacement governments may plausibly have temporarily surfaced during the COVID-19 pandemic. This concept obviously emerged on multiple occasions. None of these organisations matured into anything tangible and had no or little social or legal impact. In Canada there appears to be

[56] Reviewed in Netolitzky (n 7) 989–91.
[57] Sovereign State of Tayos: www.state-of-tayos.com.

little appetite for this kind of 'revolution from below' by 'We The People'. However, one specialised and exotic exception has survived: 'Queen' Romana Didulo's 'Kingdom of Canada', which is examined in section VII.C below.

B. Magna Carta Lawful Rebellion

The United Kingdom-sourced Magna Carta Lawful Rebellion (MCLR) is among the more unique Canadian pseudolaw movements.[58] The MCLR was invented by United Kingdom guru David Robinson in 2014, and, reduced to its conceptual core, claimed that some minor political theatrics in 2001 by 28 members of the United Kingdom House of Lords was, in fact, the binding invocation of the 1215 Magna Carta's supraconstitutional authority.[59] When Queen Elizabeth II did not withdraw the United Kingdom from the European Union, that ended valid government authority in the United Kingdom, and, apparently, the remainder of the Commonwealth. Based on that foundation, Robinson developed form documents that his followers were to use in sequence. The first swore fealty to Lord Craigmyle of Invernesshire. That step purportedly placed the pseudolaw adherent into the only authentic and valid lawful authority in the United Kingdom: the 28 Rebel Barons. The MCLR's scheme purportedly involved 1215 Magna Carta article 61, though that authority was not actually invoked by the 28 'new rebel' Lords in 2001.[60]

What followed was a variation on the 'Three/Five Letters'[61] scheme where a series of five documentary packages were sent to government and court targets, which purportedly would impose various outcomes, such as negating council (municipal) taxes, eliminating traffic tickets, validating unauthorised business activities, and so on. Failure to comply meant the targeted actor would be subject to 'The Gallows'.

The MCLR and Robinson were marginal and unsuccessful players in the United Kingdom pseudolaw ecosystem, until in 2019 an Alberta resident, Jacquie Robinson, aka 'Jacquie Phoenix',[62] began promoting MCLR theory online. Phoenix proved a wildly successful guru/acolyte; MCLR social media accumulated tens of thousands of adherents. A confused Lord Craigmyle reported receiving thousands of oaths of fealty. Then, on 10 November 2020, Robinson died. Phoenix immediately travelled to the United Kingdom, where she seized control of the MCLR infrastructure as an unchallenged inspired leader and genius.

[58] Netolitzky (n 17), see also Netolitzky (n 7) 992–94.
[59] Netolitzky (n 17) pt I(B); *AVI* (n 17) [63]–[71].
[60] Netolitzky (n 17) pt I(B).
[61] *Bank of Montreal v Rogozinsky*, 2014 ABQB 771 [55]–[73].
[62] The two Robinsons were not related. For clarity, this chapter refers to Jacquie Robinson by her pseudonym.

In 2021, Phoenix, now illegally in the United Kingdom, held numerous face-to-face 'Redress' meetings with her predominately female following in breach of COVID-19 pandemic regulations. These amounted to nothing, and after some notional public demonstrations, the MCLR imploded. Phoenix declared her followers had failed her and she was dying. By 2022, the MCLR was operationally dead, though Phoenix remains alive.

Phoenix had a smaller cohort of Canadian followers whose chief activity was to send MCLR paperwork to Canadian government and court actors. Phoenix directly participated in and guided these activities while she still was in Alberta. After her exit to the United Kingdom in 2020, MCLR activity in Canada withered. Very few MCLR documents were received after early 2021.

The MCLR in Canada never expanded much beyond irregular and threatening documents. Other than that, the MCLR simply did not interface or interact with Canadian governments and institutions. Almost no litigation and court activity resulted,[63] and the MCLR was almost unnoticed by the Canadian public and media. Rather, the MCLR operated in its own separate online community space.

Unusually, the MCLR under Phoenix was a predominately female movement. Both Richardson and Phoenix exercised strict control of group affiliation and communications, tolerating nothing other than absolute obedience and devout adulation of themselves. Most MCLR adherents were of low economic status and poorly educated, barely able to complete and deliver simple form documents. Why the MCLR met with such success is not easy to understand, except perhaps thanks to unusually sophisticated branding, and emerging at the right time to ride the crest of a social crisis.

C. Indigenous-Styled Pseudolaw Groups

Canada has a lengthy history of pseudolaw movements and promoters who claim to be Indigenous, and extraordinary legal status derives from that heritage,[64] though the basis of these claims is almost always anchored in Canadian case law and/or academic perspectives of a separate 'indigenous law' and 'indigenous governance' apparatus and authority. Many of these groups engage in simulated government-like activity, and purportedly provide Indigenous status and/or privileges for a fee. While some (eg, Anishinabe Nations of Turtle Island, Sovereign Squamish Government, Peoples of the Salmon) do appear to be led by First Nations people, the most legally active entities, the inter-related 'Kinakwii Private Sovereign Nation' 'Sovereign, Indigenous, Aboriginal' country, and

[63] *AVI* (n 7) is the chief exception.
[64] Reviewed in Netolitzky (2016) (n 4) 622, 628; Netolitzky (n 7) 994–99.

the 'Anishinabek Solutrean Metis Indigenous Nation' (ASMIN),[65] have been rejected and denounced by academics and courts as instances of 'raceshifting':[66] illegitimate claims of Indigenous and First Nations status. The Kinawkii and ASMIN explicitly sell Métis status memberships and promise special 'Sovereign' privileges.

None of these groups appears to have had significant uptake, with available information suggesting adherent populations of under 100. Indigenous-styled pseudolaw groups have not led to much identified court litigation, the exception being the Kinakwii and ASMIN, whose leadership figures Zane Viger Plouffe aka Grand Chief Wabiska Mukwa, and Glenn Patrick Bogue, aka Chief Justice and Attorney General Spirit Warrior, operate as unauthorised representatives and 'busybody' litigants in dozens of diverse legal actions Canada-wide. Bogue's activities are particularly problematic because Bogue is a trained lawyer who was suspended in 2020 by the Law Society of Ontario.[67] That made no difference to Bogue, who continues to act as a lawyer in court, claiming his 'Indigenous' status puts him outside professional regulation. Bogue claims 'Indigenous' means 'physically born in Canada', without requiring any historical or community links. Disturbingly, despite now over three years of Bogue's unauthorised practice of law, the Law Society of Ontario has taken no steps to deter or stop this rogue lawyer.

In Canada, nothing indicates that genuine Indigenous and First Nations groups have adopted pseudolaw. Instead, when Indigenous-styled pseudolaw is affiliated with First Nations persons, the usual pattern is those Indigenous individuals are dissidents or outsiders to their own communities.[68]

VII. Outliers

As the preceding review illustrates, in Canada pseudolaw has manifested in many different ways. That said, several groups diverge far enough from the mainstream to be classified as atypical and outliers. This chapter briefly describes and examines three such examples, but focuses on their unique aspects, since these outliers have previously been profiled in some detail, and usually parrot stereotypic pseudolaw memeplex arguments.

[65] 'Solutrean' here refers to the now rejected hypothesis that North America includes populations who immigrated from France 20,000 years ago. LG Straus, 'Solutrean Settlement of North America? A Review of Reality' (2017) 65 *American Antiquity* 219.

[66] D Leroux, *Distorted Descent: White Claims to Indigenous Identity* (University of Manitoba Press, 2019).

[67] Activities reviewed in Netolitzky (2018) (n 34) 472–82; Netolitzky (n 7) 997–98.

[68] For example, Netolitzky (2016) (n 4) 622, 628; *Little Shuswap Lake Indian Band v August-Sjodin*, 2016 BCSC 1214.

A. Church of the Ecumenical Redemption International

The Edmonton-based Church of the Ecumenical Redemption International (CERI) is Canada's oldest continually operating pseudolaw movement, founded circa 2001 and operated by 'minister' Edward Jay Robin Belanger.[69] CERI purports to espouse King James Bible literalist religious belief. CERI members denounce and ignore laws and contracts that intrude into the 'ministry of Christ'. Canadian courts have, however, consistently rejected these claims as baseless, and concluded CERI is basically a fake church of convenience for its followers and guru Belanger. Earlier, Belanger purported to have essentially the same status and immunities, but as a 'reformed druid', which no-one took seriously. CERI objectives parallel its Freeman competitors. Another Freeman-like aspect is Belanger's extensive criminal record, including marijuana-related offences.

Besides CERI's longevity, Belanger's project has a unique target market. Belanger does not direct his activities to the general public, but, instead, produces videos and communicates online to criticise and denounce the concepts of pseudolaw guru competitors. Belanger is therefore a kind of second-order parasite, attempting to intervene with persons who have already adopted pseudolaw, but encountered setbacks. Belanger then enters as a kind of 'fixer', with his purportedly superior religion-based pseudolaw knowledge. Belanger sometimes even travels to and lives with his new fellow 'ministers'. Naturally, that only aggravates unfavourable outcomes. As failures and setbacks accumulate, Belanger discards and denounces his 'faithless' former collaborators. This tight victim–host relationship pattern have now occurred for at least 14 years. Belanger and CERI are otherwise marginal, though very well-established agents, in Canada's pseudolaw ecosystem.

B. United Sovran Nations

Circa 2009 an unusual matriarchal marijuana-focused pseudolaw group emerged in North America, allegedly empowered by the 'Camel's Eye Treaty 408 AD'.[70] This group shortly thereafter fragmented into at least four competing branches that threatened each other with 'court orders' issued by their individual 'Tacit Supreme In Law Courts'. All but one of these parallel groups met with little to no success and ultimately withered away. However, the Calgary-based United Sovran Nations (USN) and several little-documented subordinate groups followed a much more dramatic trajectory.

[69] Reviewed in DJ Netolitzky, 'Jesus Built My Strawman: The Church of the Ecumenical Redemption International and "minister" Edward Jay Robin Belanger' (2023) 6 *International Journal of Coercion, Abuse, and Manipulation*, DOI: 10.54208/1000/0006/004.

[70] Netolitzky (2016) (n 4) 628–29; Netolitzky (2023) (n 4) 828–31.

The USN was headed by Mario Antonacci, who operated as Senior Chief Justice Andreas Pirelli. Comparatively little is known about Antonacci and the USN because, unlike practically all other Canadian pseudolaw groups, Antonacci and the USN maintained strict operational security and were practically invisible to outside observers and agencies. The USN developed a surprisingly elaborate structure of organisations and businesses that ranged from financial institutions, various subordinate 'embassies', construction and renovation businesses, and a vigilante police force, the Territorial Marshals, whose uniforms were sufficiently convincing that Territorial Marshals successfully entered at least one secured government location.

Unusually, USN members and subordinate organisations maintained detailed documentary records and were subject to extremely strict centralised supervision. The USN accumulated a very substantial pool of funds of unknown origin that were intended to purchase a multi-million-dollar Calgary-area ranch that the USN advertised would become a separate community, outside Canadian jurisdiction. The USN recruited in Canadian Freeman, Indigenous, counter-culture and United States sovereign citizen circles for persons to join this 'separate system'.

All this ended on 27 September 2013 when Antonacci was arrested in Calgary for absconding from 2009 criminal proceedings in Québec. USN's cadres then fled from the USN's headquarters, or 'Embassy', a rental home Antonacci and his core supporters had squatted in for years. While extensive USN records were seized, regulatory and criminal prosecutions against USN members were not pursued. The fate of the USN funds is unknown, but court records indicate violence among Antonacci and his former followers apparently related to that question.

Police and landlord actions that precipitated the USN's dispersal were broadly reported, along with the resumed criminal proceedings against Antonacci. Media mischaracterised this as 'Freeman' activity, while Antonacci's groups were, factually and pseudolegally, entirely different.

The USN is notable for defying the stereotype that pseudolaw groups are loosely focused, badly financed and easily evaluated. Our understanding of this organisation is impeded by the USN's post-2013 systematic recovery and destruction of online and documentary records. What is clear is Antonacci led a well-financed and disciplined group with diverse anti-authority backgrounds and came very close to establishing a physical localised community who placed themselves outside 'The System of Things', under their own purported law and order.

C. 'Queen' Romana Didulo and the 'Kingdom of Canada'

The final pseudolaw outlier is a movement centred on Romana Didulo, a 49-year-old Filipino woman who claimed in 2019 she was appointed Queen of the Kingdom of Canada by 'King Carlson' of the United States after Didulo in 2017 removed Communist Chinese military forces from a tunnel complex under

North America.[71] Didulo initially operated primarily in the QAnon online space. Much of her early activity was to issue 'Royal Decrees' that responded to QAnon and 'scamdemic' conspiracy narratives. Unexpectedly, Didulo attracted a large online following, possibly peaking with as many as 70,000 Telegram channel subscribers.[72]

Over time Didulo's claims became increasingly exotic, with Didulo self-identifying as a shape-shifting Arcturian extraterrestrial, possessing supernatural and/or super-science capabilities, and in control of both terrestrial military and special forces assets, and an interstellar space fleet. Didulo's Royal Decrees promise diverse benefits to followers, ranging from debt and mortgage elimination, free utilities and transit, and ending income tax, through to advanced supercomputer technologies, and 'med beds' that would cure any illness, regenerate limbs and restore youth.

Didulo also shifted from being primarily an online personality to touring across Canada in a convoy of recreational vehicles, accompanied by a uniformed entourage/guard. This 'mobile government' is funded by supporter donations, conducts regular video broadcasts to followers, and locally holds 'meet and greet' meetings with supporters where Didulo speaks and distributes 'loyalty money' and 'Sovereign' status documents. Originally, the pseudolaw aspect of Didulo's programme was comparatively minor, such as using 'money for nothing' promissory notes based on the United States One People's Public Trust, and claiming to be subject to 'Natural Law'. However, by 2023, Didulo increasingly directed her followers to investigate and understand core pseudolaw concepts, such as Strawman Theory and motor vehicle 'travelling' arguments.

Available data indicates Didulo's follower base is predominately older, low-income females, and plausibly still number in the thousands. Didulo directs her followers send her decrees and 'cease and desist' orders to government and institutional authorities, which naturally has no beneficial effect. Unfortunately, her followers' reliance on Didulo's decrees has led to foreclosures, evictions, utility disconnection and negative income tax consequences. The mobile government has currently holed up in a decommissioned school in a small Saskatchewan town which has been converted into a kind of ritual centre.

Any prediction as to the future of Didulo and her cult is simply a guess. Didulo has obtained much unfavourable media attention inside and outside Canada. The Canadian public is hostile. While Didulo herself and her inner circle do not appear to have engaged in any court litigation, escalating conflict with law enforcement and government suggests that Canadian courts will, at some point, have to directly respond to Didulo in a substantive manner. Unsurprisingly, early commentary is negative.[73]

[71] Netolitzky (n 7) 981–85; C Sarteschi, 'The Social Phenomenon of Romana Didulo: "Queen of Canada"' (2023) 6 *International Journal of Coercion, Abuse, and Manipulation*, DOI: 10.54208/1000/0006/002; C Celestini and A Amarasingam, 'Reviving the Violet Flame: The New Age conspiratorial journey of Canada's Queen Romana Didulo' (2023) *Studies in Religion* 1.

[72] Celestini and Amarasingam (n 71) 5 reports the level of related Telegram activity over time.

[73] For example, *Manulife Bank of Canada v Thomas* [2023] ABKB 564.

VIII. Pseudolaw in Canada – The Broad Landscape

Pseudolaw and its Canadian host communities have always been marginal actors, both socially and in volume. Canadians' responses to these ideas were and are overwhelmingly negative. That even includes the large early 2022 pandemic response 'Freedom Convoy' protests, which ought to have been the dry tinder upon which a pseudolaw flame could ignite. But it didn't. Even though at least four of the second-wave pseudolaw factions/promoters were present in Ottawa, each attempting to garner attention and followers, neither the author[74] nor the official inquiry into the Freedom Convoy[75] identified any significant role by pseudolaw activists and agents. Instead, the Freedom Convoy's leadership advanced eccentric and ill-informed but conventional legal demands.[76]

The only pseudolaw actor to become a significant figure in the Canadian pandemic mitigation resistance phenomenon, Detaxer guru and scholar David Kevin Lindsay, did not operate upon or primarily engage with his audience on a pseudolaw basis.[77] Lindsay's claims and allegations were instead based around the usual suite of marginal and distorted medical and scientific claims advanced in COVID-19-sceptic and scamdemic resistance circles.[78]

This outcome is not a surprise when the history of pseudolaw in Canada is examined as a whole.

First, the objectives of most pseudolaw movements and actors are incompatible with Canadian social and community norms. Canada is unlike the United States where sovereign citizens (radical conservative, libertarian constitutionalists) and Moors (black racial separatists) are, at a minimum, extensions of existing and recognised, if not legitimate, political spectrums and movements. Canadian pseudolaw actors have objectives such as evading income tax, cheating the public and state via a life of 'do as I please' and 'take what I want', and criminal activities ranging up into child sexual abuse and murder.[79] Canada also lacks the sacralised United States national tradition of populist and/or charismatic revolt and revolution, and, instead, most Canadians accept state institutions and authority.

Furthermore, many who seek to dramatically transform and reshape the Canadian order are able to do so without recourse to pseudolaw due to the expansive policy-related decision making of Canadian appellate courts in the

[74] Netolitzky (n 7) 1006–09.

[75] Public Order Emergency Commission, 'Report of the Public Inquiry Into the 2022 Public Order Emergency, Volume 2: Analysis (Part 1)' (February 2023) 87–88.

[76] Netolitzky (n 7) 1006–08.

[77] Netolitzky (2023) (n 4) 815–17.

[78] Common Law Education and Rights: www.clearbc.org.

[79] Netolitzky (n 2) 180–83.

post-Charter of Rights and Freedoms period.[80] For example, legitimate Canadian Indigenous communities have no need to escalate to the pseudolaw 'duel of laws' because of the broad success regular Canadian law and courts have provided in support of Indigenous and Treaty rights, and via the special 'honour of the Crown' state obligations.

The evolution and patterns of Canadian pseudolaw jurisprudence is another factor. Early case law between 2000 and 2010 responded to the more technically and legally sophisticated Detaxer population.[81] This tradition of sophisticated and legally responsive anti-pseudolaw case law is usually associated with the comprehensive *Meads v Meads*[82] review decision, but, factually, extends far beyond that. Canadian case law that responds to pseudolaw is not simply a legal response, but a social one as well, with written court decisions obviously designed to be accessible to the general public. These 'weaponised judgments' were intended to communicate with both pseudolaw populations and the general layperson population, and shape public dialogue and perceptions.[83] That strategy worked. Canadian and foreign pseudolaw gurus have provided no meaningful legal or logical response to Canadian jurisprudence.

A related factor is that law in Canada is accessible. Since 2001, the not-for-profit Canadian Legal Information Institute (CanLII),[84] funded by the Federation of Law Societies of Canada, has provided no-cost access to Canadian jurisprudence and legislation via what is now a state-of-the-art website and database that matches or is superior to commercial alternatives in almost every sense. CanLII has revolutionised access to legal materials and information in Canada. During the pre-Detaxer and first-wave periods, for-pay pseudolaw sources might provide a few photocopied cases or case excerpts. Freeman materials rarely referenced actual law at all, unsurprising given Menard and Clifford were essentially ignorant of actual Canadian or foreign jurisprudence. For example, Clifford did not understand the meaning of a headnote to *Meads v Meads*,[85] and Menard concluded the 'security of the person' language in section seven of the Canadian Charter of Rights and Freedoms meant the imaginary strawman 'birth bond' bank account.[86]

In the 2010s that shifted, and increasingly pseudolaw adherents conducted research via CanLII that was then used and shared. This self-education process

[80] This shift in function and authority is questioned by experienced judicial decision-makers, even by Supreme Court of Canada justices; for example, M Rowe, 'The Virtue of Judicial Restraint, or Who Guards the Guardians?' (2022) 55 *University of British Columbia Law Review* 311.

[81] Netolitzky (n 3) 1183–84.

[82] *Meads* (n 8).

[83] C McRoberts, 'Tinfoil Hats and Powdered Wigs: Thoughts on Pseudolaw' (2019) 58 *Washburn Law Journal* 637, 664–69; Netolitzky (n 3).

[84] Canadian Legal Information Institute: www.canlii.org.

[85] Netolitzky (n 3) 1198.

[86] Netolitzky (2016) (n 4) 626.

included review and discussion of Canada's sophisticated anti-pseudolaw jurisprudence. Interestingly, argument that published case law is wrong is uncommon. Appeals on that basis are very rare. Making law accessible to pseudolaw adherents appears to have had a positive effect. What is also clear is that ordinary laypersons are actively interested in and read Canada's 'weaponised judgments',[87] which plausibly subverts interest and pursuit of these ideas. Notably, second-wave pseudolaw groups in Canada are often remarkably anti-intellectual, and instead emerge from populist, New Age and conspiratorial populations. Put another way, these people do not read. Instead, they prefer Internet videos.

The populations and schemes described in this chapter are an incomplete review; there have been yet more small-sized and transient Canadian pseudolaw groups, as well as 'sole practitioner' pseudolaw gurus, such as John Ruis Dempsey, Christopher James Pritchard and Daniel Terry Lozinik.[88] The province of Québec is its own pseudolaw ecosystem, historically dominated by United States-style copycat schemes.[89] Truly 'bilingual' pseudolaw movements are the exception, with the early Detaxers and Didulo's Kingdom of Canada being the best examples.

Table 7.1 illustrates the complexity of Canada's pseudolaw ecosystem. Many groups have emerged and disappeared over the past 30 years.

Unsurprisingly, most of these groups have an anti-authority orientation, and sought escape from legal obligations and prohibitions. Interestingly, the two largest and most disciplined/controlled pseudolaw movements are led by women and are predominately composed of females.

A crude[90] appreciation of how pseudolaw has been employed in Canada can be obtained by examining reported Canadian court and tribunal decisions. Figure 7.1 shows the year-to-year volume of identified cases:

Figure 7.1 Annual volume of 1995–2023 Canadian court and tribunal reported decisions that involve pseudolaw (N=1,450)

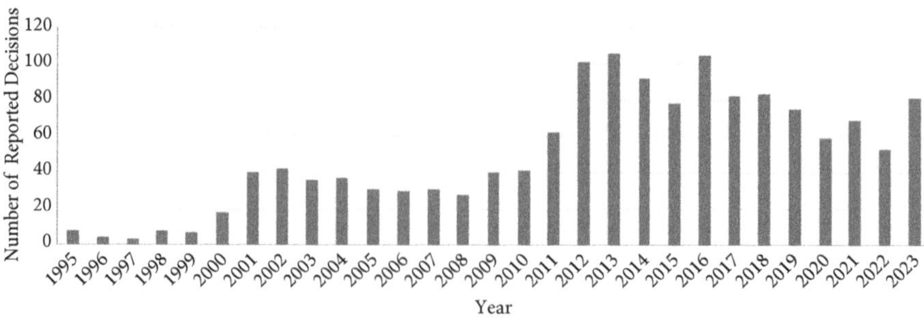

[87] For example, *Meads* (n 8); see Netolitzky (n 3) 1199–1201.
[88] Netolitzky (2016) (n 4) 627; Netolitzky (n 7) 999–1004.
[89] Netolitzky (2016) (n 4) 632–33.
[90] See Netolitzky (2023) (n 4) 809–11, for the limitations of this data type.

Table 7.1 Characteristics of certain Canadian pseudolaw movements and groups

			Orientation and Objectives					Community Structure & Social Controls		
Name	Years Operational & Current Status	Estimated Population	Political Orientation	Social Objectives	Legal Focus	Criminal Activity	Main Gender	Organised Around Gurus	Group Control & Discipline	Communication Censorship & Moderation
PreDetaxers	1950–2000 – dead	Hundreds	Libertarian, socially conservative	Christian, racist anti-banking theories	Income tax evasion	Yes, tax evasion	Male	Yes, but low – peer leader figures	None	None
Detaxers	2000–2011 – dead	Shifting from hundreds to low thousands	Diverse	Limited anti-authority	Income tax evasion	Yes, tax evasion	Male	Yes, changed from near peers to structured corporate-like organisations	None	None
Freemen-on-the-Land	2000–2014 – dead	High hundreds to low thousands	Reactionary anti-authority, governments & institutions	Do as you please, take what you want lifestyle	Get out of jail free, especially drug offences, impose vigilante & parasitic demands on state	Yes, drug offences, firearms, assault, sex crimes	Male	Yes, high, preacher/leader figures, use video & seminar-based instruction	Limited, gurus had no direct control	None, frequent internal dissent
New Constitutionalists	2017–2022 – dead	High hundreds to low thousands	Right-wing, counter-revolutionary, 'Yellow Vest' small government advocates	Populist, QAnon, 'law & order' conservative, xenophobic	Replace government, administration, & courts	No	Male	Yes, high, core revolutionary cadre/organisers	Limited, operated more as committees	None, but substantial intra-group politics

(continued)

Table 7.1 *(Continued)*

Name	Years Operational & Current Status	Estimated Population	Orientation and Objectives			Criminal Activity	Main Gender	Community Structure & Social Controls		
			Political Orientation	Social Objectives	Legal Focus			Organised Around Gurus	Group Control & Discipline	Communication Censorship & Moderation
Republic of Kanata	2012–present – notational	Minimal, one man show	Indigenous advocacy, anti-authority, scamdemic	A PR engine for an individual marginal dissident	Fake vigilante court orders & proceedings, news releases	No	Male	Yes, one keystone figure	N/A	N/A
Magna Carta Lawful Rebellion	2014–2022 – dead	Canada: high hundreds; UK: tens of thousands	Anti-authority, authoritarian, mass purge of government, courts, politicians	QAnon, conservative, xenophobic, economic social class conflict	Debt relief, municipal taxes, licencing	No	Female	Yes, extremely high, cultlike	Strong, dissidents expelled, targeted & ostracised	Yes, strict and extensive
Anishinabe Nations of Turtle Island	2002–2008 – dead	Under 100	Anti-authority	Evade government regulation	Evade income tax & government regulation	Yes, tax evasion, drug offenses, murder	Unclear	Yes, high, 'Sovereign King Kanee Kaneet'	Unknown	Unknown
Sovereign Squamish Government	2009–present – active	Under 100	Anti-authority & institutions	Evade government regulation & contractual obligations	Indigenous affiliation puts outside Canadian law	Yes, tax evasion	Unclear	Yes, high, 'Elder' figurehead, one directing mind	None identified	None
Peoples of the Salmon	2020–present – active	Under 100	Anti-authority & institutions, scamdemic	Evade government regulation & contractual obligations	Paid for Indigenous affiliation puts outside Canadian law, money for nothing	Unclear	Male	Yes, two 'Headsmen'	None	None

ASMIN/Kinawkii	2013–present – active	Hundreds	Anti-authority, fake claims to Indigenous status	Evade government regulation & criminal prohibitions	False claims Indigenous status places outside Canadian law	Yes, diverse	Male	Yes, high, several core 'First Nations Métis' leaders	None identified	Some communicaitions is 'for pay' only
Church of the Ecumenical Redemption International	2001–present – active but marginal	Under 25	Anti-authority, New Age, pro-drugs	Do as you please, take what you want lifestyle	Negate legal authority, escape criminal & debt consequences	Yes, mainly drug & vehicle offenses	Male	Yes, high, single core guru figure	Followers are used and discarded	Moderate, some social media message control, tight on home website
United Sovran Nations	2009–2013 – dead	Mid to high hundreds	Anti-authority, separatist, New Age	Separate utopian New Age Econik community outside state authority	Global rejection of all Canadian law & authorities	Yes, unlicenced business activities	Unclear	Yes, high, single core guru figure	Extreme & intrusive control over members & activities	Yes, practically invisible to outside, except inter-faction 'litigation'
Queen Didulo, Kingdom of Canada	2021–present – active	High thousands to tens of thousands	Anti-authority, authoritarian, conspirato-rial, mystical, scamdemic	QAnon, anti-scamdemic, debt & expense elimination	Discipline conspiratorial enemies, scam-demic, debt & expense rejection	Yes, but rarely implemented	Female	Yes, extreme, single core deity guru figure	Extremely strict among inner circle	Yes, strict and extensive

Figure 7.2 illustrates the proportion of the most common subjects of those reported decisions:

Figure 7.2 Proportion of the four most common litigation subject types in annual 1995–2023 Canadian court and tribunal reported decisions (N=1,450). 'Income tax' includes both Tax Court of Canada and tax-related criminal proceedings and appeals

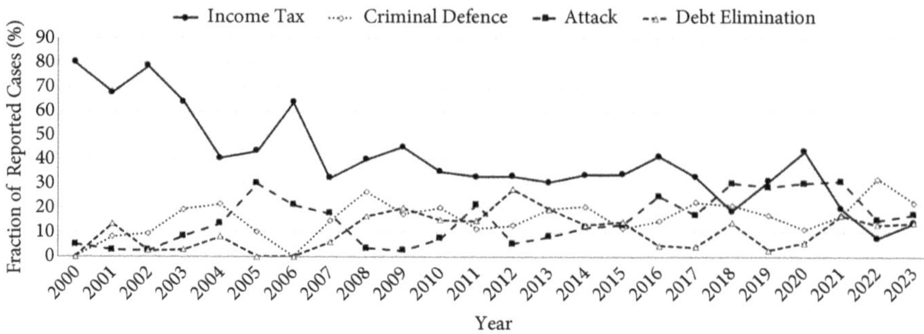

The shift away from income tax pseudolaw strategies is obvious, but somewhat deceptive. The last Detaxer schemes had ended by the early 2010s, so reported cases after that point relate to historic, pre-2012 pseudolaw activity moving through criminal and tax court processes. In contrast, the other categories of pseudolaw decisions are more contemporary to the reported court decision-making. Figure 7.3 separates out tax and non-tax annual decision volume:

Figure 7.3 1995–2023 Annual volume of tax and non-tax Canadian court and tribunal reported decisions that involve pseudolaw per year. 'Tax reported decisions' includes both Tax Court of Canada and tax-related criminal proceedings and appeals. Total reported decisions: N=1,450; non-tax reported decisions: N=940; tax reported decisions: N=510

Post-2012, the 'non-tax reported decision' bars are a better representation of actual current year-to-year pseudolaw decision volume, and, by implication, attempts to apply pseudolaw in an operational sense.

In Canada, pseudolaw users can be roughly divided into those: (1) committed to the conspiratorial narrative and political/philosophical orientation of pseudolaw; and (2) who simply use these strategies for a promised end result, such as Detaxer and debt elimination customers. Each population appears to operate in two largely separate ecosystems, with the first population organising online in marginal conspiratorial circles, but the second primarily relying on social and personal connections.[91]

Table 7.1 illustrates the 'degree of organisation' in Canadian pseudolaw phenomena varies greatly, but in almost every instance some kind of keystone or central figure is in play. That challenges the model that pseudolaw adherents in Canada are a cloud of unaffiliated 'salad bar' consumers. While outside the scope of this chapter, the issue of how much imagined 'unaffiliated' pseudolaw activity is occurring in Canada is complicated by factors such as the low incidence of truly novel schemes, the fact that old approaches are sometimes resurrected, even over decades, and the commonplace pattern that pseudolaw adherents switch gurus. Furthermore, very few observers see hundreds of pseudolaw documents and filings, and thus might detect larger patterns. Courts are unusually well positioned to do that.[92]

There is little reason to anticipate that pseudolaw activity will expand in Canada. The COVID-19 pandemic was a near ideal social and political environment for such an expansion. The most plausible scenario is a conservative, nostalgic, anti-crime, anti-immigration political/cultural movement analogous to the German Reichsbürgers, but there is no sign of pseudolaw being employed by persons with those political affiliations. What is almost certain is that claims of special legal rights and privileges affiliated with Indigenous status will become increasingly commonplace, given the special status broadly acknowledged in Canadian law and policy. Already claims about 'unceded Indigenous land' have appeared as boilerplate in pseudolaw documents,[93] not much different to ritualistic invocations of the Magna Carta. The United Nations Declaration on the Rights of Indigenous Peoples is a plausible supraconstitutional authority on which to declare rights.

Thus, pseudolaw will probably persist in Canada, but only in a marginal sense. Canada is already largely immunised against this disease of ideas.

[91] Netolitzky (2023) (n 34).
[92] Netolitzky (n 7) 974–75.
[93] For example, *Toronto Dominion Bank v Giercke* [2021] ABQB 262.

8

A Kind of Magic: Pseudolaw in Australia

GLEN CASH

I. Introduction

On 3 September 1783 a small group of men came together at Rue Jacob, Paris, in what was then the Hôtel d'York. It had been an unusual summer in Europe. A series of volcanic eruptions in Iceland, later known as the Laki eruption, spewed untold quantities of sulphur into the atmosphere. The resulting sulphuric fog settled like a pall over the northern hemisphere, producing one of the most severe winters on record in Europe and North America. One of the men attending the Hôtel d'York that day was Benjamin Franklin. He later recalled:

> During several of the summer months of the year 1783, when the effect of the sun's rays to heat the earth in these northern regions should have been greater, there existed a constant fog over all Europe, and a great part of North America. This fog was of a permanent nature; it was dry, and the rays of the sun seemed to have little effect towards dissipating it, as they easily do a moist fog, arising from water. They were indeed rendered so faint in passing through it, that when collected in the focus of a burning glass they would scarce kindle brown paper. Of course, their summer effect in heating the Earth was exceedingly diminished. Hence the surface was early frozen. Hence the first snows remained on it unmelted, and received continual additions. Hence the air was more chilled, and the winds more severely cold. Hence perhaps the winter of 1783–4 was more severe than any that had happened for many years.[1]

Widespread air pollution from the eruptions directly contributed to a mortality crisis in England and France. The number of people who died in England in the year 1783 was about 10,000 more than was normal for the time. It has been suggested the French experience was similar.[2] The following severe winters caused

[1] B Franklin, 'Meteorological imaginations and conjectures' in Literary and Philosophical Society of Manchester (ed), *Memoirs of the Literary and Philosophical Society of Manchester*, 1st series, Vol 2 (YW Eyres, 1785) 357, 359–60.

[2] J Grattan, R Rabartin, S Self and T Thordason, 'Volcanic air pollution and mortality in France 1783–1784' (2005) 337 *Comptes Rendus - Geoscience* 641.

crops to fail across Europe, including in France. It is quite probable that the direct and indirect increase in mortality from the Laki eruption devastated the working population of Europe and contributed to the French Revolution six years later.

But in the Latin Quarter in early September 1783, it was a different revolution that was on the minds of the men who gathered at the Hôtel d'York. These were representatives of the Kingdom of Great Britain and the nascent republic of the United States of America. They came together to sign the treaty to end the American Revolution and recognise the sovereignty of the United States. The Revolutionary War had been long and brutal. Its last battle, the Siege of Yorktown, was fought in the fall of 1781 and saw the surrender of Lord Cornwallis and the capture of his army.

At various times between 1776 and 1781 the United States came perilously close to bankruptcy.[3] To fund the war, the Continental Congress secured loans from European powers whose interests were hostile to the British. Between them, France, Spain and the Netherlands advanced loans that would today be valued in the tens, if not hundreds, of millions of dollars. In 1777, Benjamin Franklin personally negotiated the loan of 1,000,000 French livres, today worth something like USD 8–10 million.[4] The United States struggled to repay these debts after the war. At times it defaulted on payments, and it was not until the late eighteenth century when the loans were finally settled.

Franklin, of course, has come to be regarded as one of the great American heroes (despite being an unabashed British patriot for all but the last two decades of his life).[5] He helped draft the Declaration of Independence and, from 1776 to 1785, was the United States' ambassador to France. Franklin is the only person to have signed the Declaration of Independence in 1776, Treaty of Alliance with France in 1778, Treaty of Paris in 1783 and the United States Constitution in 1787. Among his many memorials is a reproduction of Franklin's likeness on the USD 100 bill. But before all this, when Franklin was in his 30s, he was appointed as the postmaster of Philadelphia. He reorganised the postal system in the north-east, which turned a profit for the first time. When the American Revolution began in 1775, the Continental Congress named Franklin as the first United States Postmaster-General.

What does any of this have to do with pseudolaw? What connection could there be between Benjamin Franklin, the American Revolution and the disparate, ever-changing ideas of a group of people who reject legal orthodoxy in favour of their own notions of 'natural' law?

[3] In early September 1781 an army of 4,000 French and 3,000 American soldiers marching to Yorktown refused to leave Maryland until paid in hard coin rather than worthless Continental paper money.

[4] S Bemis, 'Payment of the French Loans to the United States, 1777–1795' (1926) 23 *Current History* 824. Providing the current value of a European currency that has not been used since 1795 is difficult, and these figures represent rough estimates only.

[5] G Goodwin, *Benjamin Franklin in London: The British Life of America's Founding Father* (Yale University Press, 2016).

To find the answer to these questions we must jump forward in history to the end of the twentieth century and Russell Jay Gould, or, as he would style himself, :Russell-Jay: Gould.

Gould believes – or at least he claims to believe – that in July 1776 the United States was bankrupt. It was bankrupt because of a loan Benjamin Franklin had secured from France a year earlier, just after he had been named Postmaster-General.[6] In 1776, at the time of the Declaration of Independence, the creditors moved in and, according to Gould, a consortium of 'foreign elites' and bankers, led for some reason by King George III, took ownership of the United States and the office of Postmaster-General. This position obtained for centuries, with the real power in the United States resting with the 'true' Postmaster-General. It was a situation unnoticed by Presidents, politicians and the people. Then, in the late 1990s when Gould was researching bankruptcy law and the legal system (for reasons he does not disclose) he discovered this startling fact. Working with the now deceased David Wynn Miller (:David-Wynn: Miller), the pair unlocked the secrets of 'quantum grammar', a concept to which I will return. Armed with this novel linguistic tool, Gould was able to discover that the bankruptcy of the United States was finally to be enforced on 2 November 1999, coincidentally an 'off-year' election day. If nothing were done, the United States would once more become a colonial possession of the British Crown. In an even more remarkable twist, the shadowy cabal behind this enterprise had allowed the position of Postmaster-General to lapse. Gould seized his opportunity.

> Ninety days before the election I filed in as Postmaster-General with the bills of lading here with the United States Postal Office but I hand wrote it under here and you can see my ink under here and they put a label on this mail-slip – and labels are classified as tickets, and tickets are classified as stamps, and when I put my autograph across it I became the Postmaster-General of the United States Postal Service.[7]

Together with a filing in the United States Federal Courts pursuant to Title 4 of the United States Code,[8] and a quick visit to the Pentagon to negotiate a peace treaty, Gould became the 'sovereign king' of the United States, with plenary powers to authorise or dismiss governments, banks, the military and the courts.[9] This also had the happy consequence, or so Gould claims, that the tax laws of the United States do not apply to him, though he has not convinced any court of the

[6] There is no evidence of any such loan in 1775. The first loan seems to have been in 1777 and the earliest gift from France was on 10 June 1776 – Bemis (n 4) 826.

[7] Ramola D, 'The Restoration of the United States of America–Commander-in-Chief, Postmaster-General-of-the-World: Russell-Jay: Gould has the Title 4 Flag' The Everyday Concerned Citizen, blog post (30 August 2020), everydayconcerned.net/2020/08/30/the-restoration-of-the-united-states-of-america-commander-in-chief-postmaster-general-of-the-world-russell-jay-gould-has-the-title-4-flag.

[8] The US Code is the compendium of standing Federal Statutes in the United States. Title 4 deals with the flag, including its description and permitted use, the Great Seal of the United States, and designates Washington DC as the seat of the Federal Government.

[9] Ramola D (n 7).

correctness of this proposition. Gould maintains a YouTube channel with a healthy audience.[10]

Gould also seems to attract like-minded people from around the world who seek him out for 'authorisation' of documents in his position as Postmaster-General-of-the-World. His acolytes in Australia include ':Kym-Anthony: Sweet' and ':Glenn-Matthew:Linnett'. Both provide useful examples of typical pseudolaw documents, authorised by Gould and presented as evidence of a dual legal personality or, in Linnett's case, the 'capture' of the Australian flag.[11] Linnett's document is replete with reproductions of flags, fingerprints, dense syntax in the form of quantum grammar, and a marked-up copy of the Flags Act 1953 (Cth). The latter seems to be an attempt to 'decode' the words of the Act according to the rules of quantum grammar. It is a document weighed down with magical portent, a common theme in pseudolaw. Sweet, whose arguments I will discuss in more detail below, employed a similar document when facing charges (which were ultimately withdrawn by the prosecution) in the District Court at Maroochydore, Queensland. A written description of these documents does no justice to their appearance, as shown in Figure 8.1.

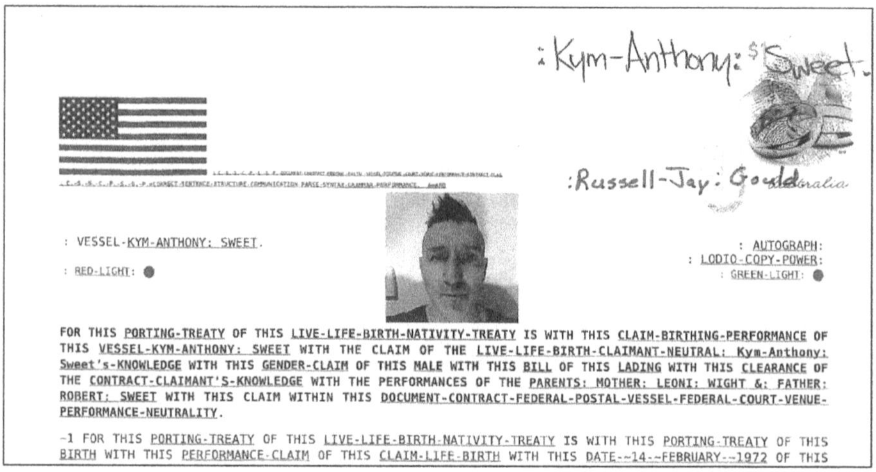
:Kym-Anthony: $Sweet.

:Russell-Jay: Gould

: VESSEL-KYM-ANTHONY: SWEET.

: RED-LIGHT:

: AUTOGRAPH:
: LODIO-COPY-POWER:
: GREEN-LIGHT:

FOR THIS PORTING-TREATY OF THIS LIVE-LIFE-BIRTH-NATIVITY-TREATY IS WITH THIS CLAIM-BIRTHING-PERFORMANCE OF THIS VESSEL-KYM-ANTHONY: SWEET WITH THE CLAIM OF THE LIVE-LIFE-BIRTH-CLAIMANT-NEUTRAL: Kym-Anthony: Sweet's-KNOWLEDGE WITH THIS GENDER-CLAIM OF THIS MALE WITH THIS BILL OF THIS LADING WITH THIS CLEARANCE OF THE CONTRACT-CLAIMANT'S-KNOWLEDGE WITH THE PERFORMANCES OF THE PARENTS: MOTHER: LEONI: WIGHT &: FATHER: ROBERT: SWEET WITH THIS CLAIM WITHIN THIS DOCUMENT-CONTRACT-FEDERAL-POSTAL-VESSEL-FEDERAL-COURT-VENUE-PERFORMANCE-NEUTRALITY.

-1 FOR THIS PORTING-TREATY OF THIS LIVE-LIFE-BIRTH-NATIVITY-TREATY IS WITH THIS PORTING-TREATY OF THIS BIRTH WITH THIS PERFORMANCE-CLAIM OF THIS CLAIM-LIFE-BIRTH WITH THIS DATE--14--FEBRUARY--1972 OF THIS

Figure 8.1 Excerpt from a document filed by the defendant in the matter of *R v Sweet* [2021] QDC 216

Despite the fervour with which Gould, Sweet, Linnett and others appear to hold to these views, they are yet to find favour in any legal system throughout the world.

[10] RJ Gould, ': Russell-Jay: Gould.' YouTube, www.youtube.com/channel/UC2FPVSe66WpLdfoiQem4FzA. Gould's most popular video has been viewed nearly 334,000 times.

[11] GM Linnett and RJ Gould, ': AUSTRALIAN-SOVEREIGN-FLAG-TREATY:' :Aumstead: (28 March 2019), www.fortheaumstead.com/wp-content/uploads/documents/for-the-australian-sovereign-flag-treaty.pdf.

It is tempting to dismiss proponents of pseudolaw as mere crackpots and annoyances. But there is a darker side to pseudolaw, one found in its origins in the United States in the late nineteenth and early twentieth centuries. The framework of pseudolaw can be traced to the same explicitly racist and antisemitic beliefs that underpin the white supremacist movement.[12] The imprint of these origins remains – some sub-movements express the antisemitic belief that 'foreign elites' and the 'Rothschild banking faction' control the world and are the enemies of sovereign citizens.[13]

The pseudolaw movement is also growing in line with a broader anti-government sentiment. There would be few people who have not seen images of so-called 'Freedom' rallies since the beginning of the COVID-19 pandemic in early 2020. In Australia, it was common at these rallies to see prominent displays of the Australian Red Ensign, a flag adopted by the pseudolaw movement. In keeping with the problematic origins of the movement, the flag of the Ustaše, a Croatian ultra-national fascist movement of the early twentieth century who were aligned with the Nazis in World War II, could also be seen.[14]

What has come to be called 'pseudolaw' has endured for decades. The idea that there exists an alternate legal universe has a small, but firm, foothold in some parts of modern society. Though the believers may be relatively few, they make up for it in the fervour of their belief.

Superficially, pseudolaw appears to be a grab bag of inconsistent ideas. That is true in part, but there is also a structure and consistency to the broader concepts. In particular there is a heavy emphasis on *form* and *ritual* to the point it resembles an attempt to invoke magic.

As courts in Australia – and across the world – confront a growing number of pseudolaw adherents, it is timely to consider what pseudolaw is, how it came to be, and to discuss some examples of the techniques employed by adherents.

II. The Origins of the Pseudolaw Movement

Many points in time could be selected when tracing the development of pseudolaw. I have selected three which together draw a straight line between racism

[12] L Zeskind, *Blood and Politics: The History of the White Nationalist Movement from the Margins to the Mainstream* (Palgrave Macmillan, 2009).

[13] 'Judge' Dale, *The Great American Adventure* (2014). Dale is a soi-disant retired United States federal judge who, among other things, expresses the view that, 'The Illuminati are hell bent upon making Bible Prophecy come true and are responsible for much of the Biblical like devastation that has been occurring around the Earth.'

[14] Z Crellin, 'From anti-vaxxers to "Sovereign Citizens": A who's who of the Convoy to Canberra protest' *The New Daily* (7 February 2022), www.thenewdaily.com.au/news/national/2022/02/07/canberra-protest-anti-vaxxers; J Roose, 'How "freedom rally" protesters and populist right-wing politics may play a role in the federal election' The Conversation (15 February 2022), www.theconversation.com/how-freedom-rally-protesters-and-populist-right-wing-politics-may-play-a-role-in-the-federal-election-176533.

and anti-government ideas and the modern presentation of pseudolaw. The first is the period following the American Civil War known as Reconstruction, during which time the 14th Amendment to the United States Constitution was adopted, and which saw the passage of the Posse Comitatus Act in 1878. The second is a time in the early 1970s when the notion of 'posse comitatus'[15] was revived and explicitly realigned with the racist Christian Identity movement. The third is the period from the late 1990s to the present which has seen an explosion in the dissemination and evolution of pseudolaw ideas.

A. Reconstruction

On 26 April 1865, just 12 days after John Wilkes Booth shot and killed President Abraham Lincoln, the 90,000-strong Army of Tennessee surrendered to Major General William Tecumseh Sherman in North Carolina. Within weeks, the rump of the Confederate Army had surrendered or been captured. The Civil War was over, and Reconstruction could begin. A critical component of the attempt at Reconstruction was the 14th Amendment, passed by Congress in the middle of 1866. Its first clause guaranteed citizenship to former slaves by promising:

> All persons born or naturalized in the United States, and subject to the jurisdiction thereof, are citizens of the United States and of the State wherein they reside. No State shall make or enforce any law which shall abridge the privileges or immunities of citizens of the United States; nor shall any State deprive any person of life, liberty, or property, without due process of law; nor deny to any person within its jurisdiction the equal protection of the laws.[16]

By late July 1868 sufficient states had ratified the amendment for it to pass into law. Ratification was a necessary pre-condition to admission to the Union. Some confederate states chafed but eventually relented. Still, there was a significant portion of the southern population who were not prepared to accept equal rights for African Americans. As resistance continued, the legal notion of '*posse comitatus*' was relied upon by the northern Radical Republicans to employ troops to enforce Reconstruction policies and to police organisations such as the Ku Klux Klan.

Posse comitatus has a long history that can be traced to the reign of Alfred the Great in ninth-century England.[17] Its use has waxed and waned in the United

[15] Literally 'power of the country'. *Posse comitatus* describes ad hoc militia groups deputised by a local authority, such as a sheriff, to assist in law enforcement. See S Young, H Hobbs and R Goldwasser, ch 6 in this volume.

[16] This provision has been at the heart of some of the most significant constitutional cases in United States history: *Brown v Board of Education of Topeka* 347 US 483 (1954) (desegregating schools and overruling the 'separate but equal' doctrine of *Plessy v Ferguson* 163 US 537 (1896)); *Roe v Wade* 410 US 113 (1973) (abortion rights); and *Obergefell v Hodges* 576 US 644 (2015) (same-sex marriage).

[17] D Kopel, 'The Posse Comitatus and the Office of Sherriff: Armed Citizens Summoned to the Aid of Law Enforcement' (2015) 104 *Journal of Criminal Law and Criminology* 761, 790.

States. There have undoubtedly been times in the history of the United States when posses carried out lynching and other unlawful killings. Immediately before the Civil War the use of posse comitatus to enforce the Fugitive Slave Act of 1850[18] in Northern States forced them to confront the reality of slavery and helped bring on the Civil War.[19] The reliance on Federal troops in the south during the Reconstruction period was a source of tension. Resistance from the Southern Democrats was such that in 1877 political necessity forced President Rutherford Hayes to withdraw Federal troops from the south. This was followed in 1878 by the Posse Comitatus Act, which prohibited the use of army troops as a *posse comitatus*.[20] The withdrawal of the military from the south and the effect of the Posse Comitatus Act significantly contributed to the failure of Reconstruction.[21]

Reconstruction's failure allowed racism to become embedded in the structure of Southern society. The result was lower levels of Black wealth and education in the South and the massive migration of Black people to the northern states in the decades that followed.[22] This structural racism and its effects continued into the Jim Crow era and the Civil Rights struggles of the 1950s and 1960s (and, it may be argued, continues today). The passage of the Civil Rights Act in 1964 was significant, but alone it was insufficient to remediate the racism of some white Americans. White supremacism flourished.

B. 'Christian Identity' and the 'Posse Comitatus'

In the 1970s some of these American white supremacists found a home in a new anti-government movement: Christian Identity. The movement evolved from a fringe belief that the inhabitants of the British Isles were the true descendants of the Jewish tribes exiled from the Kingdom of Israel in the eighth century. Once on American soil, this idea morphed into a virulent antisemitic ideology.[23] The Anti-Defamation League describes 'Christian Identity' as follows.

> Christian Identity is a religious ideology popular in extreme right-wing circles. Adherents believe that whites of European descent can be traced back to the 'Lost Tribes of Israel'. Many consider Jews to be the Satanic offspring of Eve and the Serpent,

[18] An act that required all escaped slaves, upon capture, be returned to the slaver.

[19] Kopel (n 17) 799–800.

[20] ibid 801.

[21] A Melkonian, 'The Posse Comitatus Act: its Reconstruction Era Roots and Link to Modern Racism' Sydney University Law Society, blog post (2 September 2020), www.suls.org.au/citations-blog/2020/8/28/the-posse-comitatus-act-its-reconstruction-era-roots-and-link-to-modern-racism. See also A Guelzo, *Reconstruction: A Concise History* (Oxford University Press, 2018) and D Byman, 'White Supremacy, Terrorism, and the Failure of Reconstruction in the United States' (2021) 46 *International Security* 53–103, 84–85.

[22] Byman (n 21) 101.

[23] *Anti-Defamation League*, 'Christian Identity' web page (5 April 2017), www.adl.org/resources/backgrounders/christian-identity.

> while non-whites are 'mud peoples' created before Adam and Eve. Its virulent racist and anti-Semitic beliefs are usually accompanied by extreme anti-government sentiments. Despite its small size, Christian Identity influences virtually all white supremacist and extreme anti-government movements. It has also informed criminal behavior ranging from hate crimes to acts of terrorism.[24]

The link between this Christian Identity movement and pseudolaw may be found in the early 1970s and the actions of William Potter Gale. Gale was a former army Lieutenant Colonel and some-time preacher who observed the tenets of Christian Identity. He was also fiercely anti-government. In 1971 he established a group he called the 'Posse Comitatus', reflecting Gale's idea that the Christian god was the source of all law and consequently the Federal Government had no authority over individuals. This 'Christian law' is the 'common law' or 'natural law' often cited by pseudolaw adherents. Immutable and unchanging, it is distinct from statute or 'judge-made' law.[25] The adoption of the name Posse Comitatus came from Gale's belief that local Sheriffs were obliged to defend the people from government tyranny. But beneath the surface of Posse Comitatus was the familiar antisemitic theory of corrupt Jewish bankers being the secret controllers of the world.[26]

Gale and others focused on 'delegitimizing the federal authority through arcane and dubious explanations of how citizens have been misled into subjecting themselves unnecessarily to federal authority'.[27] In the early 1970s, at a time of economic stress, the Posse Comitatus attracted, and borrowed ideas from, those who wished to avoid bankruptcy and foreclosure. It is no surprise that in 1987 Gale was convicted of tax offences and imprisoned. He died in jail in 1988 while his appeal was pending. Other so-called 'tax protestors' became integrated into the movement.

From this fertile soil, the modern pseudolaw movement emerged.

C. 'Organised Pseudolegal Commercial Arguments'

By the mid-1990s, billions of dollars of government subsidies for farming and agriculture in the United States had been slashed.[28] The United States had just been through a recession, and the 'Savings and Loan' crisis saw the collapse of more than 1,000 financial institutions.[29] It is unsurprising that the resulting

[24] ibid.

[25] D Bell, 'The Sovereign Citizen Movement: The Shifting Ideological Winds' MA Thesis, Naval Postgraduate School (2016) 23–24.

[26] JM Berger, 'Without Prejudice: What Sovereign Citizens Believe' paper, George Washington University Program on Extremism (2016).

[27] Bell (n 26) 7.

[28] M Porterfield, 'U.S. Farm Subsidies and the Expiration of the WTO's Peace Clause' (2006) 27 *University of Pennsylvania Journal of International Economic Law* 999, 1002–42.

[29] T Curry and L Shibut, 'The Cost of the Savings and Loan Crisis: Truth and Consequences' (2000) 13 *FDIC Banking Review* 26.

financial pressures ensured that interest in tax avoidance and other types of financial 'protest' remained high. At around the same time, the World Wide Web was becoming mainstream. Microsoft bundled a web browser with Windows 95. The google.com domain was registered in 1997 and by the end of 1998 had indexed tens of millions of web pages. The ability for humans to connect and communicate had taken a giant leap. As message boards and internet forums proliferated, so too did the capacity of protean pseudolawyers to publish and discover theories and treatises. The consequent increase in pseudolaw adherents meant that by the early 2000s, courts around the world were seeing an increase in litigants presenting pseudolaw theories.

As individual claims were dealt with on an ad hoc basis, there was little opportunity for a comprehensive analysis of the disparate theories presented by pseudolaw adherents. Appellate courts often dismissed the more spurious claims summarily. Then in 2012 a Canadian judge sitting at first instance heard a case management application in a divorce matter. The husband was representing himself. He was known in the proceeding as Dennis Larry Meads, but preferred to style himself as '::Dennis-Larry: Meads::'. The result of the application was an order that the matter be referred to case management, and a seminal 736-paragraph judgment responding to the collection of pseudolaw documents and arguments presented by Meads.[30] The decision in *Meads* is a rare example of a 'rock-star' decision. Each year between 2012 and 2019 it was among the top three most accessed decisions on CanLII.[31] In his decision, Associate Chief Justice John D Rooke considered, analysed and debunked a wide range of pseudolaw concepts. He also coined the phrase 'organised pseudolegal commercial arguments' (OPCA) to describe the array of arguments presented by pseudolaw adherents. At the time of its publication in September 2012, *Meads* represented a comprehensive survey of pseudolaw in Canada (and by extension much of the common law world).

In the years since, the analysis and understanding of pseudolaw has been profoundly influenced by *Meads*. It is the lens through which pseudolaw has been, and continues to be, examined. The adherents of pseudolaw have little interest in organisation, structure and taxonomy. It was not until *Meads* that there was an attempt to catalogue the key concepts of pseudolaw – which appear to be relatively unchanging[32] – and to provide a 'toolkit of examples and explanations for what has been encountered to date, and the responses that have (or have not) worked'.[33] *Meads* has been embraced by courts around the common law world and provided the vocabulary for academic analysis of the pseudolaw movement.[34]

The response of the pseudolaw movement to *Meads* has been considerably more muted. At best, some Canadian pseudolaw 'gurus' deny the validity of the

[30] *Meads v Meads* 2012 ABQB 571.
[31] DJ Netolitzky, 'After the Hammer: Six Years of *Meads v Meads*' (2019) 56 *Alberta Law Review* 1167.
[32] DJ Netolitzky, 'Organised Pseudolegal Commercial Arguments as magic and ceremony' (2018) 55 *Alberta Law Review* 1045, 1046.
[33] Netolitzky (n 31) 1205.
[34] ibid 1186–88.

decision without proffering any basis for this conclusion.[35] In Australia, pseudolaw adherents seem mostly unaware of the decision, at least until it is cited in a decision rejecting their claims. For judges and lawyers, the value of *Meads* lies not in the forlorn hope it will be read by, and discourage, potential pseudolawyers, but in its characterisation of common pseudolaw theories. The analysis in *Meads* remains of relevance, despite the tendency of pseudolaw to splinter as it expands.

D. Observations on the Splintering of Pseudolaw

We are now at the point when there truly are many branches to the tree that is pseudolaw. They include the 'Freemen on the Land' movement, found in Australia, Canada, New Zealand and parts of Europe, the 'Detaxers' of Canada and the 'Moorish Sovereign Citizens' of North America. This last group reflects an odd occurrence. Somewhere in the evolution of pseudolaw the racism and antisemitism inherent in the ideology was abandoned by some adherents.[36] The Moorish sovereign citizen movement is made up largely of African Americans who, it might be thought, would be surprised to learn the true origins of their belief system. There are some signs of comparable evolution in Australia, with suggestions of a pseudolaw 'infiltration' of the First Nations Sovereignty movement in Australia.[37] The Freeman movement is also something of an outlier. It is largely populated by a more left-leaning group whose motivation to resist the Government comes from the opposite end of the political spectrum to 'traditional' sovereign citizens.

From this many-branched tree we can infer that the pseudolaw ideology has wide appeal. Its tenets may be adopted even by those who would resist the more right-wing elements of the original ideology.

The rapid splintering and evolution of pseudolaw in the last 20 years should not be surprising. It has coincided with the explosion of instant communication fostered by the internet. An idea can be transmitted anywhere in the world. It can be replicated countless times on Facebook, Reddit, Discord, Snapchat, TikTok and so on. As this happens, a type of natural selection occurs. The original idea is added to, changed, or misunderstood. A new and slightly different idea emerges. Some gain currency and are themselves replicated. Other ideas wither and die. This process explains the existence of what Donald Netolitzky called 'the mature Pseudolaw Memeplex',[38] coopting a term coined by Richard Dawkins nearly

[35] ibid 1192.

[36] M Mallek, 'Uncommon Law: Understanding and Quantifying the Sovereign Citizen Movement' MA Thesis, Naval Postgraduate School (2016) 24–25.

[37] Toni Hassan, 'Who are the 'Original Sovereigns' who were camped out at Old Parliament House and what are their aims?' The Conversation (17 January 2022), www.theconversation.com/who-are-the-original-sovereigns-who-were-camped-out-at-old-parliament-house-and-what-are-their-aims-174694.

[38] DJ Netolitzky, 'A Pathogen Astride the Minds of Men: The Epidemiological History of Pseudolaw' conference Paper, CEFIR Symposium: Sovereign Citizens in Canada (3 May 2018).

50 years ago.[39] Netolitzky is a prolific author on the topic of pseudolaw whose background in microbiology was put to good use in his 2018 analysis of the development of pseudolaw.[40]

In his paper, Netolitzky identified the rapid expansion of pseudolaw since the invention of the 'Strawman' concept in the late 1990s. He treated the analysis as one would trace viral infection, investigating 'the transmission of the Pseudolaw Memeplex from the Sovereign Citizen community into different countries and populations. These ideas spread much like a disease, from host-to-host, accumulating adaptations that then facilitated new cycles of infection'.[41] Netolitzky noted that international experience suggested pseudolaw concepts were 'acceptable to a diverse and in many ways incompatible range of counterculture and marginal groups'.[42]

His paper only permitted a superficial consideration of the transmission of pseudolaw to Australia. Even then, Netolitzky drew attention to the merging of idiosyncratic local pseudolaw concepts with imported ideas. One such 'original' Australian idea was the claim that the Australian Constitution prohibited paper money propounded by Alan Skyring in the 1980s and 1990s. This claim, and Skyring's associated claim that Magna Carta 1215 prohibits the award of costs in litigation, have been comprehensively dismissed by Australian courts.[43] Skyring has been declared a vexatious litigant in the High Court of Australia and the Supreme Court of Queensland. The 'currency argument' appears to have become an evolutionary dead end – the most recent attempt to agitate the theory was in 2011.[44] Reliance upon Magna Carta is, however, evergreen, as will be discussed below.

One of Netolitzky's early observations of the Australian pseudolaw landscape may, with the benefit of hindsight, appear to be a little optimistic:

> Pseudolaw appears [to] have developed a firm presence in Australia and New Zealand, with a steady stream of reported decisions appearing in both jurisdictions. However, these concepts are apparently sequestered in a diverse collection of dissident groups and individuals. Currently, there is no basis to expect these ideas will expand outside this marginal host population base.[45]

[39] R Dawkins, *The Selfish Gene – 30th Anniversary Edition* (Oxford University Press, 2006) 322. Dawkins invented the term 'meme' in the context of his argument that in any system, slightly inaccurate self-replicating entities are almost limitless drivers of evolution. 'Meme' has now entered the lexicon and is defined by the Macquarie Dictionary online as 'a cultural element, as a custom, concept, etc., which is passed on through time and across cultures by communication or imitation'.

[40] Netolitzky (n 38).

[41] Netolitzky (n 38) 3.

[42] ibid 17.

[43] *Re: Skyring's Application (No 2)* (1985) 59 ALJR 561; *Re: Skyring* (1994) 68 ALJR 618; and *Skyring v ANZ Banking Group Limited* [1994] QCA 143 to select just three examples of Skyring's unsuccessful litigation.

[44] *Kosteska v Phillips; Kosteska v Commissioner of Police* [2011] QCA 266. It appears that Skyring was behind this litigation despite being a vexatious litigant.

[45] Netolitzky (n 38) 17.

More recent – if anecdotal – experience suggests that in the period since the outbreak of the COVID-19 pandemic there has been a marked increase in the number of pseudolaw adherents appearing as litigants. While a firm conclusion must await a proper analysis of court statistics, it would be surprising if the impression of many judicial officers of such an increase were disproven. There is also evidence to suggest evolution and adaptation in the Australian pseudolaw movement. I have mentioned indications it has seeped into the Indigenous Sovereignty Movement,[46] and there are signs of a conscious rejection of the label 'sovereign citizen' by some adherents – a change which may be attributed to the increasingly negative perceptions associated with the term. In this expanding and changing landscape the ability to recognise, and respond to, pseudolaw rests upon an appreciation of its history and common attributes.

With this in mind, the next section will examine some common pseudolaw beliefs and claims, and aspects of the culture and symbols embraced by its adherents.

III. The Culture of Pseudolaw – A Kind of Magic?

A distinction may be made between the culture of pseudolaw and its argumentation. The former includes the forms and rituals that go to identify the pseudolaw adherent as a member of a cultural subgroup. The latter is the claims or arguments presented by adherents in court. While the argumentation of pseudolaw is more immediately relevant to lawyers than its culture, the culture of pseudolaw informs its performance. It is helpful to consider both, beginning with aspects of pseudolaw culture.

A. The Rituals and Ceremony of Pseudolaw

Ritual and ceremony have long been at the heart of pseudolaw ideology: documents are marked with sigils and signs, the finger or thumb print being a particular favourite.[47] Written submissions bear the appearance of incantations. Statutes are parsed according to the 'rules' of quantum grammar to discover hidden meaning and codes. Crests and flags are never what they seem and, for the initiated, reveal telling indications of the secret powers that control the world. For some pseudolaw adherents the gold braids on the edges of flags adorning courts in the United States is an indication of admiralty jurisdiction, another favourite of the converted. There is an interest in postal operations that borders on an obsession. Many documents

[46] See n 37.
[47] For example, *R v Sweet* [2021] QDC 216, [5].

have affixed stamps which are then defaced with fingerprints or writings. The origin of this interest is obscure but may be traced back to the international Treaty of Bern in 1874 which established the Universal Postal Union.[48]

In *R v Sweet*,[49] mentioned above, the defendant in a criminal proceeding (which was ultimately withdrawn by the prosecution) identified themselves as ':Kym-Anthony: Sweet' or ':Kym-Anthony: of the House Sweet'. Sweet's filings in pre-trial proceedings included the document shown in Figure 8.1, which was seemingly addressed to the 'strawman duality' discussed below. Affixed to the top-right corner of the document was an Australian postage stamp,[50] overlaid with a finger or thumb print in blue ink. In the same proceeding Sweet also filed an extract of his birth certificate endorsed with a purported renunciation of the document, as well as a black-and-white photograph of the extract. The photograph (Figure 8.2) showed the extract beside a postage stamp and a 50c coin. The reverse of the 'original' extract (Figure 8.3) showed Sweet's intention to 'surrender' the document.

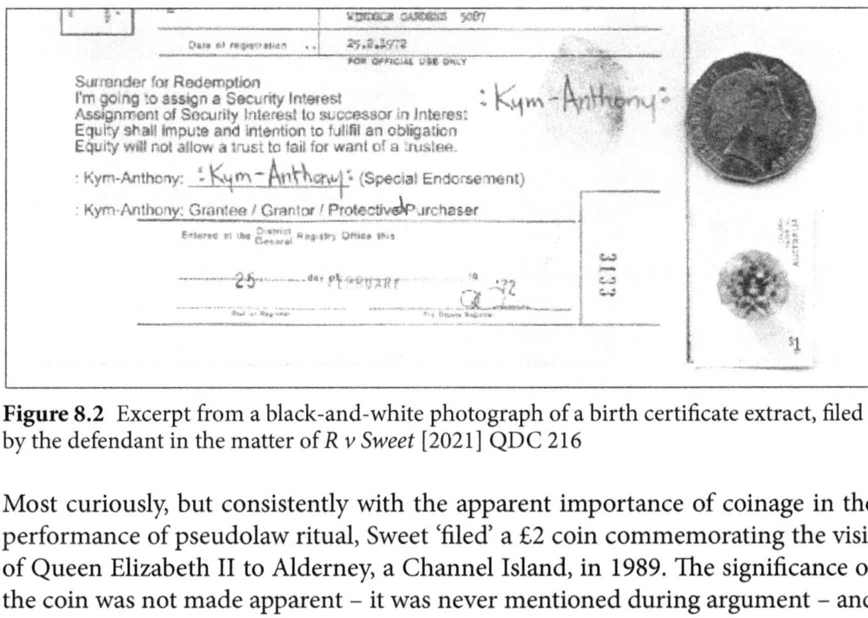

Figure 8.2 Excerpt from a black-and-white photograph of a birth certificate extract, filed by the defendant in the matter of *R v Sweet* [2021] QDC 216

Most curiously, but consistently with the apparent importance of coinage in the performance of pseudolaw ritual, Sweet 'filed' a £2 coin commemorating the visit of Queen Elizabeth II to Alderney, a Channel Island, in 1989. The significance of the coin was not made apparent – it was never mentioned during argument – and I suspect even Sweet could not explain its meaning. The combination of coins, stamps and fingerprints deployed by Sweet in a single case are illustrative of how deeply forms and rituals of this kind have become embedded in the pseudolaw movement.

[48] Netolitzky (n 32) 1058–59.
[49] *Sweet* (n 47).
[50] One depicting wedding bands from a February 2019 issue of a series called 'Moments to Treasure'.

Figure 8.3 Excerpt from the reverse of a birth certificate extract filed by the defendant in the matter of *R v Sweet* [2021] QDC 216

B. Flags and Symbols of Pseudolaw

There is considerable variety in how pseudolaw is expressed, and flags are as much the object of interest among pseudolawyers as coins and stamps. This interest has coalesced in recent years with the hijacking of the red ensign by right-wing extremists and 'freedom' groups in Canada and Australia. In Canada in the 2010s some far-right groups usurped the Canadian Red Ensign. This civil ensign had been the de facto national flag of Canada before the adoption of the Maple Leaf flag in 1965. It has been said that its use by Canadian extremists is intended to recall a time when Canada's population was mostly white and of European descent.[51] In turn this may have influenced the adoption of the red ensign as a symbol of pseudolawyers and 'sovereign citizens' in Australia.

The Australian red ensign is the product of a competition run by the Australian Government soon after federation. The brief was for the design of a blue ensign for naval and official purposes and a red ensign for use by the merchant navy and public. The now familiar design was selected as the winner of the competition.[52] There followed decades of confusion as to what flag was to be used. The Union

[51] G Hamilton, 'Former Canadian flag, the Red Ensign, gets new, darker life as far-right symbol' *National Post* (10 July 2017), www.nationalpost.com/news/canada/former-canadian-flag-the-red-ensign-gets-new-darker-life-as-far-right-symbol.

[52] The 'Commonwealth Star' in the lower-left canton was originally six-pointed. It was not until 1908 that a seven-point star was adopted to represent Australian territories.

Flag still had precedence over the Australian ensigns.[53] To further complicate matters, it was widely held that the blue ensign was reserved for official and government use. One result was the adoption of the red ensign as the flag of patriotic citizens, something reinforced during World War I: Australian forces fought as divisions of the British Army and, perhaps out of a desire to assert individual national identity, some Australian troops adopted the red ensign as a battle flag. This appeared to fix the red ensign as the flag of 'the people' rather than the Government.

It is of little surprise that it has, in recent times, been coopted as a symbol of the sovereign citizens and pseudolawyers. The first signs of the spread of this symbol into the pseudolaw population could be seen in anti-lockdown protests during the height of the COVID-19 pandemic. The red ensign was a familiar sight, and the correlation between those protesting government controls and those aligned with pseudolaw ideas was predictably extensive. For some the red ensign was both a symbol of protest and a means of identifying oneself as a patriot or true-Australian – someone who understood the truth of pseudolaw and the fallacy of government authority.[54] The power of flags as symbols is well understood,[55] and it is unsurprising that the red ensign has become perhaps the most well-known symbol associated with pseudolaw.

C. Quantum Grammar

A third and less well-known aspect of pseudolaw culture is the phenomena of quantum grammar. That it is less widespread than other aspects of the culture may be attributed to its impenetrable nature. Miller claimed to have discovered the mathematical interface between language and meaning during his many failed attempts to secure access to his children in the context of divorce proceedings.[56] By acquiring this inside knowledge Miller believed he could free himself from the consequences of his actions as judged by the orthodox legal system. The appearance of quantum grammar defies understanding. While Miller is now deceased, examples of his dialect can still be found online at his website.[57] Some examples

[53] It was not until 1953 and the passage of the Flag Act 1953 (Cth) that the precedence of the blue and red ensigns was put beyond doubt. An interesting aside is an error in the legislation, soon remedied, which had the Commonwealth star occupying three-eighths, or almost half, of the flag instead of the intended three-tenths.

[54] J McIntyre, 'What is the Australian merchant navy flag, the red ensign? And why do anti-government groups use it?' The Conversation (12 November 2021), www.theconversation.com/what-is-the-australian-merchant-navy-flag-the-red-ensign-and-why-do-anti-government-groups-use-it-170270.

[55] R Shanafelt, 'The nature of flag power' (2009) 27 *Politics and the Life Sciences* 13.

[56] K Stollznow, 'Syntax Error' The Skeptical Inquirer (2 February 2011), skepticalinquirer.org/exclusive/syntax-error.

[57] *:Judge: David-Wynn: Miller*: www.dwmlc.com.

also exist in Australia, such as the document of Glenn Linnett mentioned above. A small extract is enough to demonstrate the turbid nature of the dialect and explain why it has not been more widely adopted.

> ~**0** FOR THIS GLOBAL-POSTAL-PLOYMENT-SERVICE-TREATY OF THIS WITNESS, CLAIMANT, LIFE-BIRTH-CLAIMANT, VISITOR, NEUTRAL &: POSTMASTER: Glenn-Matthew: Linnett's- KNOWLEDGE &: WITNESS, CLAIMANT, LIFE-BIRTH-CLAIMANT, VISITOR, NEUTRAL, POSTMASTER, SOVEREIGN &: POSTMASTER-GENERAL OF OUR WORLD: Russell-Jay: Gould's- KNOWLEDGE **ARE** WITH THESE PERFORMANCES OF THIS SALVAGE &: TOW WITH THIS CARGOS: AUSTRALIA-NATIONAL-FLAG, AUSTRALIA-RED-FLAG &: AUSTRALIA-NAVAL-FLAG OF THIS C.-S.-S.-C.-P.-S.-G.-P.-FLAG-VESSELL

The document continues in the same incomprehensible manner for several pages. Sweet employed a very similar document (Figure 8.1) in an attempt to show that he was comprised of separate legal and human personalities. Whatever rules or logic lay behind quantum grammar were lost when Miller died. One Wisconsin judge wrote of Miller and his language:

> The hallmark of David Wynn Miller and his followers is their use of an English dialect they call 'In the Truth.' The dialect, invented by Miller, purports to be based on mathematics and is characterized by the abundant use of prepositional phrases, the absence of action verbs (except in gerund form) and the overuse of hyphens and colons. In addition, speakers of the dialect reject the use of pronouns, adjectives and adverbs.[58]

Miller visited Australia in the early 2010s, charging potential disciples thousands of dollars to attend seminars about quantum grammar.[59] He also appeared in the New South Wales Land and Environment Court, where his language arguments failed to persuade the Court.[60]

Quantum grammar is but one example of a pseudolaw belief claimed to operate as a 'get out of jail free card'. A common tenet is that if the right symbols are employed and the correct form of words is used, the pseudolawyer will expose orthodox legal theory as a sham and succeed in their cause. It is unsurprising then that pseudolaw has been likened to magic.[61]

For some pseudolawyers the use of quantum grammar is both a sign of the culture and a means of argumentation. The next section will address common arguments presented by pseudolaw adherents.

[58] *Krizan v Farm Credit Service of North-Central Wisconsin*, 12-CV-798-bbc (WD Wis, 6 December 2012); *Bohman v Taylor, Bean & Whitaker Mortgage Corp*, 12-CV-814-bbc (WD Wis, 6 December 2012); *Fretschel v M&I Bank FSB*, 12-CV-821-bbc (WD Wis, 6 December 2012); *Bix v Envoy Mortgage, Ltd*, 12-CV-822-bbc (WD Wis, 6 December 2012).

[59] N Wallace, '"Messiah-like figure" is doing own harvesting' *Sydney Morning Herald* (15 January 2011), www.smh.com.au/world/messiahlike-figure-is-doing-own-harvesting-20110114-19r9v.html.

[60] *Wollongong City Council v Dr Masood Falamaki* [2010] NSWLEC 66 [37].

[61] Netolitzky (n 32) 1049.

IV. The Argumentation of Pseudolaw

As much as the trappings of pseudolaw might vary, the ideas underpinning its theory are relatively static. Netolitzky has written that the Pseudolaw Memeplex has at its core six concepts:[62]

(1) Everything is a contract,
(2) Silence means acceptance or agreement,
(3) Legal action requires that there be an 'injured party',
(4) Government authority is defective or at least limited,
(5) The 'Strawman' duality, and
(6) Financial and banking conspiracy theories.

Most of these concepts are much the same wherever they are found in the world. The fourth – that government authority is defective – is adapted to suit local conditions and legal history. The Strawman duality is in some ways the apotheosis of pseudolegal theory and is perhaps the most encountered in the courts. As may be seen, each concept is based in conspiracy narratives and the belief that pseudolaw adherents know something the rest of society does not. It is useful to consider how these ideas are presented by pseudolaw adherents in the Australian context. Not all these concepts are relevant to the argumentation of pseudolaw in Australian litigation. To the extent that finance and banking conspiracies inform wrong-headed beliefs that the payment of tax is optional, or costs cannot be awarded in a civil claim, these claims have been thoroughly debunked in Australian courts.[63] A further examination of the cases at this point would not be helpful. With this in mind, the core concepts of pseudolaw may be collapsed into the four groups dealt with below.

A. 'Everything is a Contract' and 'Silence Means Consent'

These two concepts are linked. The first is derived from the idea that no state authority can be imposed on an individual without consent. That is, the 'social contract' is not given effect by some collective decision of society at, say, an election, but rather requires individual consent. It follows that it is possible for individuals to achieve immunity from the state by denying the existence of a 'contract' or by renouncing the agreement. Under this theory practically any state issued document (birth certificates, driver licence, etc) can be evidence of the contract. Pseudolaw adherents may go to great lengths to disavow or repudiate such documents.[64] Returning

[62] D Netolitzky, 'A Rebellion of Furious Paper: Pseudolaw as a Revolutionary Legal System' conference paper, CEFIR Symposium: Sovereign Citizens in Canada (3 May 2018).
[63] See nn 43–44.
[64] *Meads* (n 30) [395]–[396].

or surrendering a birth certificate is common.[65] This is done because otherwise the silence of the pseudolawyer in the face of government documents may be taken as their consent to the 'contract', an extension of the idea that silence equals consent.

There is a basis for belief in this second concept, but it is one that reflects a fundamental misunderstanding. *Black's Law Dictionary* is a favourite of the North American pseudolawyer. Dealing with the rules of pleading, an early edition set out the Latin maxim *qui non negat fatetur*, which roughly translates as 'Those who do not deny, admit'. Pseudolaw theory took this maxim and from it developed the notion that it is possible for contracts to be imposed or foisted upon individuals. The premise is flawed. The full passage in *Black's Law Dictionary* goes on 'He who does not deny, admits. A well-known rule of pleading.' It is clear this is not a statement of the law of contract. It is a rule of pleading that exists today.[66]

These two elements come together to explain some actions of pseudolaw adherents. One is the so-called 'fee schedule'. These are documents that might be given to a police officer during a traffic stop and which assert that by talking to the pseudolawyer the police officer enters a contract and is obligated to pay some exorbitant sum of money. Less commonly, such documents are given to judicial officers. They are obviously meaningless and may easily be disposed of with the application of conventional principles of contract law.

The claim that an individual must consent to the application of state authority is also obviously wrong, but it is more difficult to explain why that is so to a determined OPCA litigant. A courtroom is not a suitable place for a descent into political theory and ideas of collective consent. It is, I think, sufficient to note that it is accepted reality that as a society we collectively admit the authority of the state. A litigant who challenges that reality bears the burden of proving, in a manner decipherable to the court, why their claim should prevail. Absent such proof, the litigant will remain subject to the law. This has been the result in recent cases where litigants made such claims.[67]

One such matter in which a litigant argued they were not subject to the law illustrates the misplaced confidence and certainty pseudolaw imbues in some of its adherents. Stephen Woodhead was convicted of traffic offences in the magistrates court. The offences were relatively minor and could have been dealt with by the payment of a fine, had he not chosen to contest them in court. The commission of one offence was recorded on the dashcam of another motorist and the other was witnessed by two police officers. The evidence seemed strong. When a police officer attended at Woodhead's home to serve the offence notice, Woodhead was polite and articulate. He calmly explained to the police officer that he had been on a 'private journey' and would dispute the charges in court where, Woodhead said, he would be vindicated. Before the summary hearing, Woodhead wrote to

[65] As discussed above in relation to the matter of *R v Sweet* (n 47).

[66] See, for example, Uniform Civil Procedure Rules 1999 (Qld), r 166.

[67] See, for example, *Wells v Queensland Police Service* [2024] QDC 38 [8] and *Woodhead v Commissioner of Police* [2023] QDC 143 [11].

the registry. He would later argue this correspondence had the effect of creating a contract and estopping the prosecution. At the hearing Woodhead did not contest any of the alleged facts. When this claim of estoppel was dismissed by the magistrate, Woodhead pressed the Strawman argument and argued he was immune from the law as he did not consent to its operation. These claims were also rejected by the magistrate.

Woodhead then appealed his convictions to the District Court.[68] He conducted the appeal politely and with complete, if utterly misguided, confidence in the correctness of his claims. As usual for pseudolawyers, he was accompanied to court by a group of supporters. Woodhead showed an initial reluctance to make submissions from the bar table – it is a common belief that to do so amounts to a surrender to the jurisdiction of an otherwise illegitimate court. When he did, Woodhead was keen to point out that he was not a sovereign citizen. He maintained the Strawman and absence of consent arguments. There were the usual references to equity and trusts. One curiosity in the presentation of his case was that he repeated each statement three times, the last being 'for the record'. When asked, Woodhead was unable to explain the significance of this repetition, resembling as it did a prayer or a spell.

In dismissing Woodhead's appeal, I observed that:

> There exists in Queensland a recognised body of statute and common law. As a society we have developed techniques and processes for interrogating and developing that law. Those who wish to stand outside of that law and ignore long recognised processes must realise they bear the onus of rationally explaining why these almost universally accepted understandings are wrong. Until such time, the claims of such people will continue to be summarily dismissed.[69]

This is the simple yet undeniable reality that distinguishes 'pseudolaw' from 'the law'. The law, as we understand it, represents rules and norms that are generally accepted as being correct and binding on citizens. It is the product of centuries of incremental development and refinement and represents the orthodoxy in the true sense of the word. Our understanding of the law will sometimes change. But that change will be the result of the application of logic and reason, not the pursuit of wild and implausible – not to say ahistorical – tales.

B. Legal Action Requires that there be an 'Injured Party' and Financial Conspiracies

The 'no injured party' theory is one that derives from William Potter Gale's version of god-given common law. It is god's rule that one should not harm another or their

[68] *Woodhead* (n 67).
[69] ibid [11].

property. This 'rule' has been transmuted into a requirement for proof of harm to a person or property before the law can intervene. It follows (conveniently) that so-called victimless crimes – such as producing cannabis or driving without a licence – cannot be prosecuted. The theory may be seen as an extension of libertarianism. Whatever its merits as a political theory, it does not represent the law of Queensland or Australia, where parliament legislates to denote certain conduct as criminal or otherwise, and the executive and the courts enforce this legislation. So much has been confirmed in Australian courts many times.[70] While it appears this claim is sometimes deployed when pseudolaw adherents are stopped for some traffic infringement, I am unaware of any serious attempt to argue the point in litigation.

The same may be said of various fiscal conspiracy theories that are found overseas. They may underpin claims such as the currency argument, but do not seem to be deployed as free-standing arguments in Australian courts. An example is the conspiracy theory based on the modern economic practice by which banks might loan an amount greater than the money they hold as deposits. This is said to be creating money out of 'thin air', confirming that paper money is not real and creating no obligation in the borrower to repay this 'fake money'. Another idea relates to the Strawman. It is said that at birth, governments 'mortgage' the value of a person to secure funds. Once one knows this, and how to revoke the 'contract' evidenced by one's birth certificate, the arrangement can be voided and the person may claim the funds.[71] The attraction of the theory was pithily summarised by Rooke ACJ in *Meads*: 'These are the proverbial caves of hidden treasure. OPCA gurus who advance these concepts claim that, with the correct combination of documents, one can open a secret path to vast riches. One needs only know the spell!'[72] The application of this theory is more likely to be an issue for the Executive Government rather than the courts. I am unaware of any suits brought before Australian courts claiming money on this basis.

C. Government Authority is Defective

This is one area where pseudolaw theory shows significant regional variation. In the United States the lack of state authority is said to derive, variously, from the citizenship clause of the 14th Amendment,[73] or from the bankruptcy discussed earlier in this chapter. Moorish law adherents believe government illegitimacy stems from the *Moroccan American Treaty of Friendship of 1786* and the subsequent events of the First Barbary War. In Germany the Reichsbürger movement offers several different theories, including that the Third Reich did not surrender

[70] See, for example, *Hubner v Erbacher* [2004] QDC 345.
[71] *Meads* (n 30) [532]–[536].
[72] ibid [530].
[73] Netolitzky (n 62) 14.

at the end of World War II (they claim only the army surrendered) and that the Allied occupation which began in May 1945 never ended.[74] As we are concerned with Australian law there is no need to discuss how courts in these countries respond to the claims.

In Australia there have been three broad arguments to support the claim that government authority is illegitimate or deficient. The first, the 'currency argument', has been mentioned and must now be considered wholly discredited. Another argument centres on what is said to be the invalidity of constitutional legislation with the result that almost all state authority is without foundation. The argument has taken slightly different forms but reached its peak in *Sharples v Arnison*.[75] The argument was later summarised in these terms:

> The appellant's argument runs as follows. The *Australia Acts (Request) Act 1985* (Qld), an Act of the Queensland Parliament, which preceded the *Australia Act 1986* (UK) of the Parliament of the United Kingdom, was not preceded by a referendum. That was contrary to the requirements of s 53 of the *Queensland Constitution Act 1867* (Qld) which, because the Queensland Act anticipated alterations to the office of Governor, necessitated a precedent referendum.[76]

In *Sharples* McPherson JA demonstrated the many flaws in the argument. While others attempted to revive the argument in the decade that followed, it too appears to have gone the way of the 'currency argument'.[77]

Magna Carta is a different creature. Its historical and cultural significance is such that it still bobs up from time to time, usually in purported support of arguments that all litigation must be tried by juries or that it is unlawful to levy taxes. Of course, any invocation of Magna Carta must be met with the question, 'Which one?'[78] The 1215 settlement between King John and his barons that was repudiated within months? The revival of 1216 that was an attempt to garner support for John's infant heir? The charters of 1217 or 1225? Or the version confirmed by Edward I and which entered English, and subsequently Australian, statute books in 1297? It would be surprising if many of the people who attribute great significance to Magna Carta were aware of its history. It is enough for them to 'cherry-pick' apparently helpful sections, such as the famous chapter 39 (or 29 depending on the version):

> No freeman shall be taken or imprisoned, or disseised of his freehold, liberties or free customs, or be outlawed or exiled or in any other wise destroyed; nor will We pass upon him nor condemn him, but by lawful judgment of his peers or by the law of the land.

[74] Netolitzky (n 62) 15.

[75] [2001] QCA 518; [2002] 2 Qd R 444.

[76] *Clampett v Hill & Ors* [2007] QCA 394 [13].

[77] *Clampett v Hill & Ors* [2007] QCA 394; *Clampett v Wensley & Ors* [2009] QCA 277; *Lohe v Gunter* [2003] QSC 150.

[78] Maitland, the 'father of English legal history', wrote more than a century ago, 'It is never enough to refer to Magna Carta without saying which edition you mean.' FW Maitland, *The Constitutional History of England* (Cambridge University Press, 1908) 15.

As interesting as it may be, in the end, none of this matters. As was explained by Chesterman J in *Carnes v Essenberg*,[79] while Magna Carta was incorporated into Australian law, the Imperial Parliament and, consequently, Australian parliaments were empowered to amend or repeal its provisions. The result is that legislation that is inconsistent with any of Magna Carta's 'liberties' may be taken to have impliedly or expressly repealed them.[80] Whatever the Great Charter's historical significance,[81] it cannot be said to be a piece of functioning legislation that determines rights and obligations today.

D. The Strawman Duality

That leaves the ultimate expression of pseudolaw theory – the 'Strawman duality'. It is here that pseudolaw theory becomes its most magical. While there are some variations of detail, the essence of the Strawman duality remains as summarised by Netolitzky:

> 1. Physical humans are bound or linked to a non-physical legal person doppelganger: the 'Strawman'.
> 2. Government has inherent authority over the non-corporeal 'Strawman' doppelganger, but not a human being. The link between the physical and legal parts of the duality is a channel for government authority.
> 3. The government attaches the 'Strawman' to the physical human via a concealed contract that involves birth or identification documentation.
> 4. The 'Strawman' is identified by an all upper-case letter name (e.g. JOHN SMITH), and that is why government and legal documentation capitalizes names. Those materials do not actually refer to the associated human being.
> 5. Government authority can be negated by denying you are the 'Strawman', and/or by breaking the 'Strawman' contract.
> 6. A human is only subject to 'Common Law' once the 'Strawman' is removed.[82]

It can be seen how this theory builds on other pseudolaw concepts. The legal being is attached to one's corporeal being because of a contract. The contract is evidenced by documents such as a birth certificate. The authority of the state over an individual is limited and depends on the existence of this contract. Once the contract has been revoked, the state can no longer exercise authority over the individual. The

[79] [1999] QCA 33. A much earlier, if brief, decision to a similar effect is *Chia Gee v Martin* (1905) 3 CLR 649, 653.

[80] By reason of the Imperial Acts Application Act 1984 (Qld), there are only three clauses that remain in force in Queensland. One is clause 29. The others are clauses 1 and 9, which are concerned with the Church of England and the City of London.

[81] For just two analyses of the historical significance of Magna Carta see P Brand, 'Magna Carta and the Development of the Common Law' paper, High Court Public Lecture series (13 May 2015) and J Spigelman, 'Magna Carta in its Medieval Context' Address, Supreme Court of New South Wales (22 April 2015).

[82] Netolitzky (n 62) 15–16.

supernatural overtones of the theory are obvious. As Netolitzky recognised,[83] there are parallels with demonic possession and exorcism. The Strawman is an unwelcome intruder to be banished through the ceremonial revocation of, say, a birth certificate. This is achieved by marking a copy of the certificate with fingerprints, stamps or other marks. Ritual phrases are invoked and, perhaps, the recission is sealed by the offer of a coin.

The attraction of the Strawman idea is that it provides the solution to every problem a pseudolaw adherent may face. Any debt or liability stays with the Strawman, who is jettisoned by the real person. The real person need not be troubled by matters like taxation, or the inconvenience of licenses or permits, because the state has no authority over the real person. Similarly, the criminal law has no reach over them.

It would be very difficult to convince those who truly believe in these ideas that they are wrong, as are the conspiracy theories that provide their foundation. But conventional legal theory is enough to demonstrate why the law cannot countenance the existence of a human being without a legal personality. As much as the law might impose obligations upon a person, it also attaches to them rights. To be subject to the law is to have the benefit of the latter, while also being bound by the former.

Since as long ago as the eighteenth century, the common law set itself against the notion that there existed classes of human beings who were mere property and possessed no legal personality.[84] Neither the common nor statute law of Australia permits a human being to be considered property. Yet that would be the consequence of the Strawman duality. The result of the divorce of the legal and real persons would be a human being without rights. Someone who was no more than a chattel. Such an outcome could not be tolerated in modern society.

This was an argument presented by Sweet, as well as others.[85] Sweet's argument assumed the correctness of the Strawman duality. He then proceeded to rely upon documents to prove his repudiation of his 'legal' identity, rendering his 'personal' identity immune from prosecution. The documents included those already mentioned, such as the extract of his birth certificate, authenticated with red fingerprints and with the authority of Gould as Postmaster-General to show Sweet's rejection of the contract he claimed to have been imposed upon him at his birth. Sweet also filed a document titled 'Evidence-claim-of-live-life-certificate', expressed in terms consistent with the fictitious language of quantum grammar. To the extent that Sweet presented any argument in support of his claim to be immune from the law, it failed to address why a court should accept that his underlying assumption as to the existence of the Strawman duality was correct.

[83] Netolitzky (n 32) 1076.

[84] For example, *Somerset v Stewart* (1772) 98 ER 499, a decision in which Lord Mansfield ordered the discharge of a slave pursuant to a writ of *habeus corpus*, uttering (as he also did in *R v Wilkes* (1770) 4 Burr 2527 at 2561–62 [98 ER 327 at 346–47]) the phrase '*fiat justicia, ruat cœlum*, let justice be done whatever be the consequence'.

[85] Such as *Van den Hoorn v Ellis* [2010] QDC 451 and *Wells v Queensland Police Service* [2024] QDC 38.

V. Recent Developments in the Argumentation of Pseudolaw

There are signs of some recognition that old arguments based on the core concepts of pseudolaw are no longer tenable. Some recent attempts to adapt arguments are worth mention.

In the matter of *Woodhead*, there was an attempt to invoke the pseudolaw ideas that 'everything is a contract' and 'silence means consent' to argue that a failure to reject some offer of settlement in a letter amounted to estoppel. This argument was pure pseudolaw. A more recent case involved an attempt to combine accepted common law and pseudolaw in pursuit of a similar result.

In March 2022 a car registered to Amy Wells was photographed by a police camera while exceeding the speed limit. Wells was ultimately summonsed to appear in the magistrates court and the matter proceeded to a trial. After failing to persuade the magistrate that 'The Twelve Presumptions of [Roman] Court' required dismissal of the case, Wells was convicted and fined. There followed an appeal to the District Court.[86] One of Wells's arguments was that prior to the appeal hearing she made a 'Calderbank'[87] offer to settle the matter which, by operation of the 'postal acceptance rule',[88] was accepted by the respondent and compromised the proceeding. This melding of two recognised aspects of the common law – one concerning the effect of an offer to settle on the question of costs and one concerning communication of the acceptance of an offer for the purposes of contract law – and the pseudolaw ideas that 'everything is a contract' and 'silence means consent' may represent an interesting adaptation. Of course, the argument faced the insuperable difficulty that there is no scope to 'compromise' a criminal appeal of this kind and was rejected by the court.

Wells's grounds of appeal also included an assertion that she had been 'governed without … consent' and a repetition of claims based on the so-called 'Twelve Presumptions of Roman Law'. The originator of the latter idea seems to be Australian man Frank O'Collins, described online as a 'former Jesuit lawyer'[89] and whose YouTube videos present an incredible combination of confused linguistics, misunderstood history, mythology, religion, Freemasonry and conspiracy theories (such as the existence of the 'Illuminati').[90] O'Collins adopts the definition of a 'canon' as a 'fundamental principle' or 'a standard' or 'criterion' to argue that Roman or Vatican law is the only true and valid law of the world.

[86] *Wells v Queensland Police Service* [2024] QDC 38.

[87] *Calderbank v Calderbank* [1976] Fam 93, [1975] 3 All ER 333.

[88] *Henthorn v Fraser* [1892] 2 Ch 27, 33.

[89] J Harder, 'FRANK O'COLLINS LUCIFER THE ROMAN JESUIT ORIGINS & MEANING OF THE LIGHT BRINGER' BitChute (31 August 2023), www.bitchute.com/video/6NaZZ42JnJp9.

[90] A Barker, 'Frank O'Collins Explains Western Roman Law Parts 1 to 4' YouTube (23 June 2013), www.youtube.com/watch?v=zUDCagYFyhI.

The simple answer to Wells's claims is that our legal system is not governed by any form of Roman, Vatican or Canon law. The argument is just another iteration of the common pseudolaw view that there is a secret history of the world, an understanding of which grants an individual the power to escape the legal consequences of their actions.

Wells and O'Collins are indicators that dealing with pseudolaw is akin to the arcade game 'Whac-a-mole'. No matter how many times arguments based on the core principles of pseudolaw are debunked, they are repackaged and re-presented in a seemingly endless cycle.

VI. Conclusion – Where are We, How did We Get Here and Where are We Going?

The history and current expression of pseudolaw permits some conclusions to be drawn.

First, those attracted to pseudolaw fervently believe in forms, processes and rituals akin to magic as an effective method to achieve their aims in the face of what they perceive as a hostile legal system. Adherents believe, despite a conspicuous absence of prior success, that if these methods are properly deployed, they will win.

Secondly, the source of these forms and rituals is almost always some 'guru' who profits from selling these ideas.

Thirdly, the core ideas of pseudolaw are entrenched but the veneer is not static. There is a mutability to the way these core ideas are expressed. This produces an evolution that is almost organic. This may be seen in the rejection in recent times of the term 'sovereign citizen' by pseudolaw adherents who have realised the appellation is now freighted with negative connotations. This superficial evolution will continue, while the discredited core ideas will remain.

How did we get to this point? What is it that drives pseudolawyers to embrace alternative legal theories that have failed time and time again? Why keep rolling that boulder up the hill? Often the answer is the same. The persons attracted to pseudolaw are persons who feel they are disenfranchised or marginalised. They are in a position of relative disadvantage in society, and pseudolaw presents an opportunity to take control. Pseudolaw is the 'inside knowledge' that permits them to command a secret power. This can drive some litigants into a fervent, if not febrile, pursuit of what they perceive as 'justice'.

There is, I suspect, a substantial overlap between pseudolawyers and the category of litigants in person described as querulous or vexatious. The latter has been the subject of much investigation in recent years, especially through the lens of psychiatry. Dr Grant Lester describes the 'normal' complainant as one who believes they have experienced a loss but who maintains perspective and is able to evaluate the loss compared to the effort required to seek redress.[91] In contrast:

> The 'difficult' complainant also believes that they have experienced a loss. This complainant will generally attribute loss to external causes and become not only aggrieved but also, to varying degrees, indignant. This is because, cognitively, their egocentric view of the world centralises their own importance and devalues and dehumanises others. There are distinct themes of victimisation. Hence they feel angry, innocent of responsibility and a victim of an unjust act.[92]

It would surprise no one to learn that querulous litigants are largely male, middle-aged, and white – as it seems are pseudolawyers.[93] Dr Lester surmises that such persons can be primed to become vexatious. These people are aging. They face mortality and perhaps a sense of failing to accomplish goals. Add to this some insult or loss and the relentless pursuit of an idiosyncratic idea of justice becomes the way they seek to prove their worth as a person. The attraction of pseudolaw to a person in this position is obvious.

What about the future? In 2018 Donald Netolitzky wrote:

> The Pseudolaw Memeplex's function is to subvert state and institutional authority, so that sets the limit of where these ideas will encounter vulnerable potential hosts. So far, that has been the outskirts of society. Could that change? Perhaps. The Pseudolaw Memeplex is a tool of (pseudo)legal revolt. Would these ideas become more broadly acceptable if the public concludes government and its institutions are illegitimate? …
>
> This disease of ideas is obviously potent and adaptable … [A] new process is underway: hybridization. Formerly isolated regional pseudolaw strains are increasingly shared as a common language of pseudolaw permeates online communities. Will this intermingling provide new adaptive motifs, or solidify pseudolaw as a monolith, a third global system of law? Only time will tell.[94]

Since then, we have seen a global pandemic and with it increasing societal challenge to the legitimacy of government authority around the world. We have also seen the violent insurrection of 6 January 2021 when terrorists[95] attempted to overturn the results of the United States presidential election. The derision of government institutions and authority continues apace, sometimes fomented by those on the inside. Mobile telephones, the internet and social media allow ideas to be transmitted more rapidly than ever before. Conditions remain ripe for the infection of pseudolaw to spread. It would be naïve to think otherwise.

[91] G Lester, 'The Vexatious Litigant' (2005) 17 *Judicial Officers' Bulletin* 17, aija.org.au/wp-content/uploads/2017/10/Lester1.pdf.

[92] ibid.

[93] For understandable reasons there has been little demographic research in this area. An ADL special report in 2012 considered most 'sovereign citizens' to be middled-aged and the majority to be white men; see 'The Lawless Ones: The Resurgence of the Sovereign Citizen Movement', 2nd edn Anti-defamation League (2012), www.adl.org/sites/default/files/Lawless-Ones-2012-Edition-WEB-final.pdf. See also SG Smith, 'An analysis of the Sovereign Citizen Movement: Demographics and Trial Behaviors' graduate thesis, University of Arkansas, Fayetteville (2016) 31–33.

[94] Netolitzky (n 38) 18.

[95] As they would be properly described according to the definitions in the Criminal Code 1995 (Cth).

9

Asserting Sovereignty: An Empirical Analysis of Sovereign Citizen Litigation in Australian Courts

MARILYN McMAHON

I. Introduction

In 2023, Justice Solomon of the Supreme Court of Western Australia observed that the sovereign citizen movement

> has been gaining popularity and traction in Australia over the last few years … The growing prevalence of this class of beliefs and associated conduct is a matter of concern for the preservation of the authority of the court and the administration of justice.[1]

A brief review of recent sovereign citizen activity confirms this view. Linked to arson at Old Parliament House in Canberra,[2] occupations of public buildings while claiming sovereignty,[3] and social media posts objecting to preventative public health measures,[4] sovereign citizens have attracted increasing attention in Australia.

Behind the headlines and confrontational videos is a diverse range of legal issues. When restrictive public health measures operated during the pandemic, police reported an increased number of members of the community engaging in argumentative and combative exchanges, demanding that officers recognise them as a 'living person' and refusing to comply with requests to provide lawful

[1] *Yap v Matic (No.7)* [2023] WASC 55.

[2] M Ireland-Jones, 'Who Set Fire to Old Parliament House, and Why?' Aulich (27 January 2022), www.aulich.com.au/fire-old-parliament-house/.

[3] G Hutchinson, '"It'll certainly go into my library of anecdotes": WA Police Inspector chats about arresting secessionist occupiers at Old York Courthouse Museum' ABC Perth (5 June 2020), www.abc.net.au/radio/perth/programs/drive/old-york-courthouse-occupier-arrests/12327882.

[4] T Clarke, '"Sovereign Citizen" Stephen John Carreras Cops Fine for Refusing to Wear Mask' *The West Australian* (30 August 2021), www.thewest.com.au/news/court-justice/sovereign-citizen-stephen-john-carreras-cops-fine-for-refusing-to-wear-mask-ng-b881986481.

information because they were sovereign citizens.[5] Individuals identifying as sovereign citizens have been arrested for trespass, assault, making death threats against politicians,[6] weapons offences, and stalking and harassment. Not only are sovereign citizens involved in criminal matters[7] but they are now appearing in property,[8] family,[9] defamation[10] and taxation[11] cases in Australia. They have been identified as a 'potential terrorist threat' here and elsewhere.[12] These developments are unsurprising as sovereign citizens do not accept that most laws are binding on them; the concept of sovereignty that is integral to their narratives is that citizens cannot have their freedoms restricted by governments without their express consent.

Given their distinctive, hostile attitudes towards laws and justice systems, combined with their recent, heightened public profile in Australia, investigating how sovereign citizens interact with laws and legal systems is timely. Focusing on legal cases involving them seems appropriate. A senior Australian Federal Police officer recently observed that, unlike other extremists, sovereign citizens are relatively unconcerned about concealing their identities;[13] this contributes to their willingness to engage in litigation in open courts. Their high rates of self-representation in proceedings also ensures that their arguments are directly presented.[14] Accordingly, this chapter explores the jurisprudence of sovereign citizens by identifying and analysing a sample of Australian cases involving them.

It begins with a brief overview of the sovereign citizen movement in Australia, before undertaking an empirical analysis of reported cases in the decade from 2014 to 2023 in which sovereign citizen litigants asserted rights, raised objections or claimed defences in legal proceedings. Through this analysis, the chapter explores how sovereign citizens' rejection of the sovereignty of parliament and the

[5] In August 2021, the Chief Commissioner of Police for Victoria stated that police were witnessing an increasing trend for sovereign citizens to refuse to provide their names and addresses upon request by police. He noted that on at least three or four occasions in the previous week police had to 'smash the windows of cars' and pull out drivers so that they would provide the information to police: E Gillespie, 'The Rise of "Sovereign People" and Why They Argue Laws Don't Apply to Them' SBS (21 August 2021), www.sbs.com.au/news/the-feed/the-rise-of-sovereign-people-and-why-they-argue-laws-don-t-apply-to-them.

[6] In *State of New South Wales v Hardy* [2021] NSWSC 323 and *Hardy v State of New South Wales* [2021] NSWCA 338 reference is made to Hardy's conviction for offences related to making threats to politicians in New South Wales.

[7] See *Bradley v The Crown* [2020] QCA 252.

[8] See *Steepe v Commonwealth of Australia* [2021] NSWSC 348.

[9] *Beaumont & Timms (No 2)* [2018] FCCA 2889 [59]; *Locatelli and Smith* [2020] FCWA 198.

[10] *Application by John Wilson* [2016] NSWSC 1527.

[11] *Deputy Commissioner of Taxation v Truden* [2020] VCC 324.

[12] D Baldino and K Lucas, 'Anti-Government Rage: Understanding, Identifying and Responding to the Sovereign Citizen Movement in Australia' (2019) 14 *Journal of Policing, Intelligence and Counter Terrorism* 245–64.

[13] S Dametto, 'The Sovereign Citizen Movement in Australia' AFP Presentation and Report (2022), www.afp.gov.au/sites/default/files/2023-09/123-2023.pdf.

[14] JK Phillips, 'Not All *Pro Se* Litigants Are Created Equally: Examining the Need for New *Pro Se* Litigant Classifications Through the Lens of the Sovereign Citizen Movement' (2016) 29 *Georgetown Journal of Legal Ethics* 1221, 1222.

jurisdiction of the courts informed these proceedings. The conclusion then identifies how this use of the courts primarily as a political forum challenges traditional strategies for dealing with meritless cases.

II. Overview of Sovereign Citizen Narratives in Australia

Sovereign citizen narratives in Australia originated in the United States, where they have been linked to white supremacist, antisemitic and other right-wing organisations.[15] Those most prominently associated with these narratives are predominantly white, male and middle-aged or older.[16]

The few individuals who publicly assert and elaborate sovereign citizen narratives in Australia are relatively isolated; there is no large-scale, established political party[17] or organisation that represents their views, and there is no centralised, formal leadership. This type of 'leaderless resistance' is increasingly common,[18] and distinguishes sovereign citizens from traditional cults. Like several other contemporary populist movements, their narratives are also 'thin-centred';[19] that is, they address only part of the political agenda. There is some suggestion that Queensland and Western Australia are the main locations for their activities.[20]

[15] CE Loeser, 'From Paper Terrorists to Cop Killers: The Sovereign Citizen Threat' (2015) 93 *North Carolina Law Review*, 1106–39. See S Young, H Hobbs, and R Goldwasser, ch 6 in this volume.

[16] 'The Lawless Ones: The Resurgence of the Sovereign Citizen Movement', *Anti-Defamation League* Report, 2nd edn (2012) 11, www.adl.org/sites/default/files/documents/assets/pdf/combating-hate/Lawless-Ones-2012-Edition-WEB-final.pdf ('The Lawless Ones'); C Sarteschi, 'Sovereign Citizens: A Narrative Review with Implications of Violence Towards Law Enforcement' (2020) 60 *Aggression and Violent Behaviour* 101509.

[17] Sovereign citizens have occasionally established fringe political parties. For example, in 2020 the Original Sovereign Tribal Federation (an Indigenous sovereign citizen movement) signed a memorandum of understanding with Rod Culleton's Great Australian Party. R Baker, 'Alt-right Seeks Indigenous Help for Fight with "Illegal" Government' *The Sydney Morning Herald* (16 February 2021), www.smh.com.au/politics/federal/alt-right-seeks-indigenous-help-for-fight-with-illegal-government-20210212-p571w1.html. In the 2019 federal election Wayne Glew also was a candidate for the Senate in Western Australia as a representative of the Great Australian Party; he obtained 0.02 per cent of the vote. Australian Electoral Commission, 'First preferences by candidate' Tally Room 2019 Federal Election (14 June 2019), results.aec.gov.au/24310/Website/SenateStateFirstPrefs-24310-WA.htm.

[18] D Baldino, 'The International Blueprint for Anti-Government Extremism and the Rise of the Sovereign Citizen Movements' Australian Institute of International Affairs (18 February 2022), www.internationalaffairs.org.au/australianoutlook/the-international-blueprint-for-anti-government-extremism-and-the-rise-of-the-sovereign-citizen-movements.

[19] C Mudde, 'Populism Isn't Dead. Here Are Five Things You Need to Know About It' *The Guardian* (8 July 2017), www.theguardian.com/commentisfree/2017/jul/07/populism-dead-european-victories-centrists.

[20] M Elias, 'Robert Says Being a Sovereign Citizen is Like Having a "'Mind Virus'" The Feed (18 December 2022), www.sbs.com.au/news/the-feed/article/robert-says-being-a-sovereign-citizen-is-like-having-a-mind-virus-its-a-movement-the-pseudo-law-expert-knows-well/h9ftkonin.

Sovereign citizen narratives have been identified as a particular variant of 'pseudolaw': 'spurious concepts that sound like law, and which may use legal terminology, but that are otherwise unrelated to "true" or "conventional" law.'[21] Their core, linked narratives are:

- That each person has two personalities: a 'living' or natural personality that is largely unfettered by legal obligations or responsibilities and a legal (artificial) personality that is imposed on them, which they can revoke at will.
- The 'living or natural' personality is born with inalienable ('sovereign' or 'natural') rights that precede the state and cannot be taken away from them.
- Revoking their legal personality means that, unless they specifically consent to the common law or a statutory provision, or agree to enter into a contract with the Government or its agents, their liberty cannot be restricted.

The amorphous, often fuzzy nature of these narratives widens their appeal and allows followers to 'cherry-pick' aspects that appeal to them.[22] This allows for markedly different levels of engagement.[23]

The variability of engagement and the imprecision of sovereign citizen narratives makes it extremely difficult to assess the number of individuals in Australia who endorse these beliefs. One of the few estimates of those strongly committed to this ideology came from confidential information leaked from a report prepared by the New South Wales Police Counter Terrorism and Special Tactics Command in 2015. It identified about 300 sovereign citizens in that state and suggested the number was increasing.[24] Given that this estimate applied to a single state, was prior to the pandemic (when members of the community with libertarian objections to contemporary public health measures found some ideological affinity with aspects of their anti-government message) and focused on those extremists who most militantly endorsed sovereign citizen views, it is likely that it significantly underestimates the number of those who now endorse, to varying degrees, sovereign citizen narratives in Australia.

Accordingly, 'sovereign citizen' is best regarded as an umbrella term describing those associated with largely heterogeneous and amorphous narratives, united by a core hostility to government and the belief that laws do not apply to them without their consent or contractual agreement.[25]

[21] D Netolitzky and R Warman, 'Enjoy the Silence: Pseudolaw at the Supreme Court of Canada' (2020) 57 *Alberta Law Review* 715, 719.

[22] Consequently, the views that are linked to the movement are diverse. For instance, one faction has aligned with the Yellow Vest movement. See Crypto Cothesline, 'Mike Holt, Visionary of the Australian Yellow Vest Movement', Tune In (18 January 2019), www.tunein.com/podcasts/Technology-Podcasts/Crypto-Clotheslines-Podcast-p1148476/?topicId=128779551.

[23] See the Canadian case *Meads v Meads* 2012 ABQB 571 and *R v Sweet* [2021] QDC 216.

[24] Baldino and Lucas (n 12).

[25] It is likely that an observation about sovereign citizens in the United States is equally apposite for Australia; the Southern Poverty Law Center observed: 'Those who are attracted to this

The core political concept underpinning sovereign citizen narratives is sovereignty. While the concept of sovereignty is complex, it is essentially about 'the power and authority to govern'.[26] In relation to sovereignty internal to Australia and, more specifically, how power is distributed within the territorial boundary between government and individual citizens, much of the relevant Australian law has developed from cases involving claims by First Nations people. Sovereign citizens have controversially sought to form links with organisations promoting Indigenous land rights, however the claims for sovereignty are dissimilar. Sovereign citizen narratives are not grounded in collective claims of prior occupation of territory and unceded sovereignty,[27] nor do they constitute a traditional variety of micro-nationalism.[28] Instead, they are based on a claim of inherent, individual sovereignty; the individual is sovereign, not governments or even collections of citizens. As Josh Wilson, a self-identified sovereign citizen in New South Wales, stated: 'the word sovereign means the ultimate authority to make and impose laws. That applies to you. If you're a sovereign person, you make the laws for yourself'.[29]

This individualised concept of sovereignty conflicts with the notion of popular sovereignty in Australian constitutionalism whereby elected representatives exercise sovereign power on the people's behalf.[30] Additionally, a significant corollary of the view you that you 'make the laws for yourself' is that the protection of those laws is a personal responsibility. This drives sovereign citizens to litigate in Australian courts to protect their rights while simultaneously (and paradoxically) denying the validity of those courts.

subculture typically attend a seminar or two or visit one of the thousands of websites and online videos on the subject and choose how to act on what they have learned'. Southern Poverty Law Center, 'Sovereign Citizens Movement' www.splcenter.org/fighting-hate/extremist-files/ideology/sovereign-citizens-movement.

[26] S Brennan, B Gunn and G Williams, '"Sovereignty" and Is Relevance to Treaty-Making Between Indigenous Peoples and Australian Governments' (2004) 26 *Sydney Law Review* 307.

[27] See K Menzel, 'Whose Sovereignty is Really Being Fought For? What Happens When First Nations People Are Dragged into Extremist Protests' The Conversation (7 February 2022). However, occasionally claims for sovereignty will merge the two movements; see *Lacey v Earle* [2014] ACTSC 397 and the Original Tribal Federation.

[28] Sovereign citizens wish to avoid the limitations of government, not substitute their own form of government. One notable exception is Leonard Casley (aka Prince of the Hutt River Province) who, after three decades of claiming the micronation of Hutt River adopted sovereign citizen narratives. See H Hobbs and G Williams, *Micronations and the Search for Sovereignty* (Cambridge University Press, 2022).

[29] Sydney Criminal Lawyers, 'Sovereign Citizens: The Real Terrorist Threat?' (14 January 2016), www.sydneycriminallawyers.com.au/blog/sovereign-citizens-the-real-terrorist-threat.

[30] *Australian Capital Television Pty Ltd v Commonwealth of Australia* (1992) 177 CLR 106, 138 (Mason CJ). In *R v Buzzacott* [2004] ACTSC 89, Connolly J similarly observed that the 'ultimate source of … sovereignty is the consent of the people of Australia'. ibid [17]. Some prominent sovereign citizens have advocated for the abolition of general elections and their replacement by multiple referenda and polls ('Citizen Initiated Referendums') where voting occurs on specific issues. See Crypto Cothesline (n 22).

III. Empirical Analysis of Sovereign Citizen Cases in Australian Courts

Although there has been considerable contemporary discussion of sovereign citizens, there has been little systematic, empirical analysis of their use of the courts.[31] This lacuna is surprising. Their core narratives make it highly likely that they will fail to obey laws and be in conflict with law enforcement personnel. How sovereign citizens assert and seek to protect their perceived rights and deal with that conflict is a matter of real interest. Socio-legal research which empirically investigates their interactions with justice systems, particularly in relation to the highest point of conflict – adversarial proceedings in courts – can provide significant insights.

The current study is the first quantitative study of sovereign citizen cases in Australia and specifically investigates the variety of pseudolaw associated with them. It complements doctrinal analyses of their narratives[32] and contributes to the emerging international, empirical literature on pseudolaw litigation.[33]

A. Methodology of the Study

This section describes the methodology of the study, then presents the results. The findings are analysed, with key case narratives identified. The conclusion identifies how this litigation is used strategically by sovereign citizens to advance political goals.

To identify recent legal proceedings involving sovereign citizens and to distinguish them from other claims for sovereign status, initial searches of the AUSTLII database were conducted for the decade 2014 to 2023, using the terms 'sovereign citizen', 'citizen sovereign', 'sovcit', 'sov cit', as well as other distinctive terms frequently used by sovereign citizens: 'freeman on the land', 'straw man' and 'living man'/ 'living woman' and 'Affidavit of Truth'. This was supplemented by a search of Australian newspapers, using the same terms; a chain-referral ('snowball') method for both sources was useful in providing information that informed subsequent, further database searches. Websites advocating sovereign citizen views (such as

[31] Several studies have analysed the arguments made in court by sovereign citizens or described their behaviour in court, but have not provided a systematic, quantitative analysis of their litigation. See DJ Netolitzky, 'Lawyers and Court Representation of Organized Pseudolegal Commercial Argument [OPCA] Litigants in Canada' (2018) 51 *University of British Columbia Law Review* 419; C Sarteschi, *Sovereign Citizens* (Springer, 2020) 71–82.

[32] H Hobbs, S Young and J McIntyre, 'The Internationalisation of Pseudolaw: The Growth of Sovereign Citizen Arguments in Australia and Aotearoa New Zealand' (2024) 47 *University of New South Wales Law Journal* 309.

[33] See Netolitzky and Warman (n 21); DJ Netolitzky, 'Organized Pseudolegal Commercial Arguments in Canadian Inter-Partner Family Law Court Disputes' (2017) 54 *Alberta Law Review* 955.

Office of the Public Defender, Friends of West Stralia), were also searched and names of prominent members identified; these names were then included in a further round of AUSTLII searches.

Identified cases were then analysed for confirmation that a key participant – plaintiff, respondent, defendant, appellant or applicant (hereafter collectively referred to as a 'litigant') – was a sovereign citizen by ascertaining whether that person self-identified as a sovereign citizen, and/or used language or other distinctive indicia employed by sovereign citizens by, for example, referring to themself as a 'living person' and the government as a 'corporation', or demanding that their name be recorded in a sovereign citizen manner.[34]

Requiring an express or explicit link to the sovereign citizen narratives reflected a conservative approach in relation to the identification of cases. Additionally, restricting the search to *reported* cases meant that this analysis necessarily under-represents relevant cases, most particularly by excluding most summary cases.

A sample of 103 cases was identified in the period 2014–2023. These cases were analysed to determine the gender of the sovereign citizen litigant, the state or territory in which the case originated, the nature of the legal proceeding (civil or criminal), whether the sovereign citizen represented themself or had legal or other representation (eg McKenzie friend), the matters litigated and the outcome of the proceedings. As a preliminary matter, it must be noted that the legal issues raised by sovereign citizens were often difficult to determine. Courts not infrequently described their pleadings and oral arguments as making 'no sense at all'[35] and being 'embarrassing' or similar; that is, they contained inconsistent, confusing or irrelevant allegations and/or were 'unintelligible, ambiguous, or so imprecise in [their] identification of material factual allegations as to deprive the opposing party of proper notice of the real substance of the claim or defence'.[36]

Additionally, their arguments tended to be omnibus; while triggered by particular legal charges or issues, these litigants often responded with multiple challenges, most very briefly articulated. For example, when Gary Bonaccorsco challenged his liability to pay more than one million dollars in income tax: he argued that the proceedings were an abuse of process; challenged the Deputy Commissioner's standing as well as the existence of the legislative scheme under

[34] These cases were then compared with those on the comprehensive private website created by Robert Suby which lists Australian cases involving sovereign citizens. R Sudy, 'Freeman Delusion: The Organised Pseudolegal Commercial Argument in Australia', www.freemandelusion.com/index. The cases used in the present study are more limited than those on the website because of the requirement of an independent marker confirming that the litigant was a sovereign citizen. For example, a case *not* included in the current analysis, which is included in Suby's website, is *Covington & Covington* [2021] FamCAFC 52; nowhere in the judgment can either the applicant or respondent be identified as a sovereign citizen. Additionally, given that *Covington* was a pseudonym adopted by the court, it was impossible to conduct further cross-referencing to check whether the case involved a sovereign citizen.

[35] *Ross-James v Turnbull* [2017] QSC 275 [20], Davis J citing the statement of Fraser JA in *Re Ross James Bradley* [2017] QCA 66 [2].

[36] *Deputy Commissioner of Taxation v Bonaccorso (No 3)* [2016] NSWSC 1018 [14]–[18].

which the proceedings were pursued; claimed that the Court lacked jurisdiction to hear the matter; disputed the existence of Australia as a nation and the Constitution as a law under which the Federal Parliament could lawfully enact statutes; and asserted that certain statutes were not enacted in accordance with the requirements of the Australian Constitution.[37]

Despite these challenges, a thematic analysis of the cases broadly identified the most common, usually overlapping, arguments raised by sovereign citizens. However, due to the difficulties in accurately identifying cases in which sovereign citizens were litigants, taken in conjunction with their frequent failure to clearly identify legal causes of action and defences, the following analysis is best regarded as providing broad, suggestive insights into the sub-set of cases identified through the particular search strategy used, rather than a definitive identification and analysis of such cases.

B. Key Findings of the Study

Similar to the United States and Canada,[38] most cases involved males as sole litigants (n=78, 75 per cent of cases) or co-litigants with their female partners (n=13, 12.5 per cent). Females appeared as sole litigants in 13 cases (12.5 per cent).

Litigation peaked in 2014 when 27 cases were litigated. This was largely due to the activity of four high-profile individuals (Alan Skyring, Wayne Glew, Jan Roscott and Peter Paalvast) who repeatedly relitigated the same issue and/or were linked to cases involving different litigants but identical issues. The period from 2018 to 2020 was relatively quiescent (four to six cases per year), and was preceded and followed by greater activity (11–13 cases each year).

Figure 9.1 Sovereign citizen cases, 2014–23

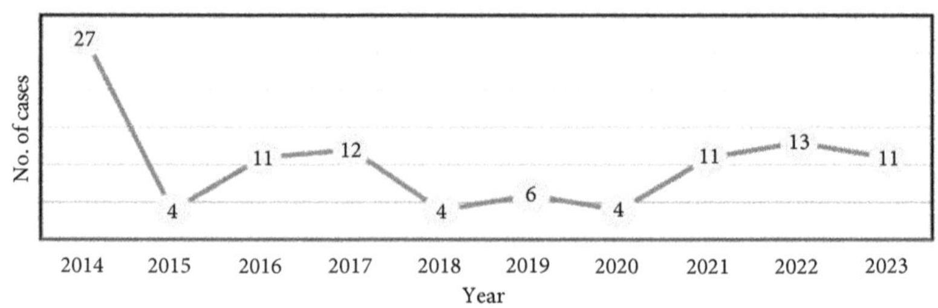

The cases predominantly originated in Queensland (33 per cent), New South Wales (30 per cent) and Western Australia (21 per cent), with a smaller number of cases in Victoria (13 per cent). There were very few cases reported in Tasmania

[37] *Deputy Commissioner of Taxation v Bonaccorso* [2016] NSWSC 595.

[38] Sarteschi notes the lack of female litigants in court proceedings in the United States involving sovereign citizens. Sarteschi (n 31) 76. Netolitzky made the same observation more broadly in relation to pseudolaw litigants in Canada. Netolitzky (n 33) 992.

(two per cent), the Australian Capital Territory and the Northern Territory (one per cent for each jurisdiction) and no case was reported from South Australia in this period. The high frequency of cases from New South Wales has not previously been identified, whereas it was expected for Queensland and Western Australia. The high number of cases in each of these jurisdictions was largely driven by particular, repeat litigants; for example, Sandi Matic appeared in eight cases in Western Australia, and Christopher Hardy was involved in eight cases in New South Wales.

Figure 9.2 Sovereign citizen cases by jurisdiction, 2014–23

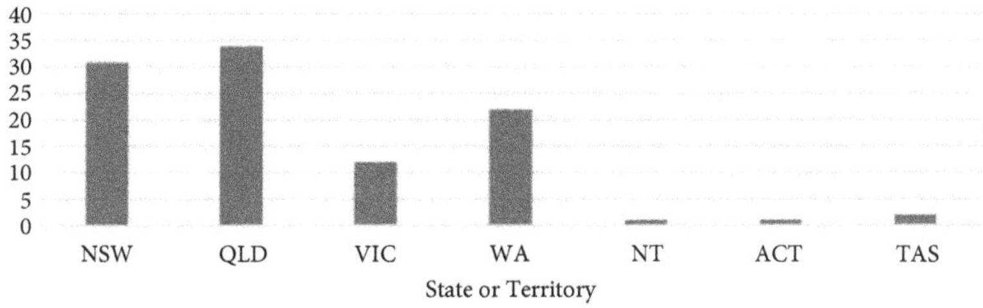

Seventy-seven (75 per cent) of the cases dealt with civil disputes, with the remaining 26 cases (25 per cent) involving criminal matters. The predominance of civil litigation by sovereign citizens has been noted elsewhere. Similar to Netolitzky's analysis of Canadian cases, the Australian civil cases rarely involved interpersonal disputes;[39] instead, litigants typically sought to defeat debts owed to bodies such as the Australian Taxation Office, local councils and authorities, banks and other financial institutions or challenged the decisions of local government. This focus is unsurprising, as sovereign citizen narratives primarily relate to relations with government and other institutions, rather than private individuals.

The criminal cases overwhelmingly related to driving and motor vehicle offences; 20 of the 26 cases involved charges for speeding, driving without a licence, failing to give way at an intersection, refusing a breath test or driving an unregistered motor vehicle, as well as related applications for bail and criminal appeals.[40] These matters also occasionally involved charges of obstructing or assaulting a police officer and three cases concerned offences involving the unlawful possession of drugs. The proceedings essentially arose from litigants' beliefs that they had an inalienable right to travel freely on the roads, or possess marijuana, without governmental interference.

A common strategy in several cases was to try to have notice of a constitutional matter given to the Attorneys-General of the Commonwealth and each State and Territory under section 78B of the Judiciary Act 1903 (Cth)[41] and to

[39] Netolitzky (n 33) 982, 993.
[40] See eg *Christie v Commissioner of Police* [2014] QDC 70; *Elliott v Commissioner of Police* [2014] QDC 161; *Lacey v Earle* [2014] ACTSC 397.
[41] See *Deputy Commissioner of Taxation v Bonaccorso* [2016] NSWSC 595 [26].

apply to the High Court for removal of whole or part of the proceedings under section 40 of that Act.[42] For instance, when Michelle Schafer challenged the authority of a local authority to prosecute her for a breach of a planning act she brought 12 unsuccessful applications on the matter to the High Court, each asserting that local government was invalid because it was not recognised in the Australian Constitution.[43] The applications were dismissed.[44] Other cases were similarly unsuccessful, with courts pointing out that section 78B did not operate when a party simply asserted that the circumstances in which it applies were present, but required a court to find that those circumstances appeared to be present.[45]

In relation to legal representation at trials and hearings, consistent with research from North America,[46] the majority of litigants (82 per cent) represented themselves. A further three per cent of cases involved a McKenzie friend or similar (often a fellow sovereign citizen);[47] only 15 per cent had legal representation. The small number of cases involving lawyers had a higher likelihood of a successful outcome; in seven of the 15 cases in which sovereign citizens had legal representation they obtained a beneficial outcome (a grant of bail, a state application for an Extended Supervision Order denied, successful appeals against conviction and costs awarded, a vexatious litigant allowed to commence legal proceedings). This can be compared to the low success rate when these litigants represented themselves or had a friend appear for them; only two of the 88 cases (two per cent) had a successful outcome, neither of which concerned the substantive matters involved in the cases.[48]

Two aspects of these findings regarding representation are noteworthy:

- Lawyers appeared in cases involving conventional legal issues: bail applications, opposing the making of an Extended Supervision Order or a Continuing Detention Order, an appeal against conviction, an application for costs and an application to commence legal proceedings by a sovereign citizen who had previously been declared a vexatious litigant. Thus, while being represented by a lawyer was associated with a higher success rate, lawyers appeared in more conventional proceedings that, by their nature, had a higher likelihood of success.
- Sovereign citizens did not succeed in a single case where they litigated a distinctively 'sovereign citizen' matter, such as their lack of consent to a

[42] See *Makascheff v Commonwealth Bank of Australia* [2017] NSWCA 126.

[43] *Schafer v Bacon* [2022] QDC 60.

[44] ibid [15].

[45] *Makascheff v Commonwealth Bank of Australia* [2017] NSWCA 126; *In the Matter of Glew* [2022] HCATrans 10.

[46] Phillips (n 14) 1230–31.

[47] See B Toy-Cronin, ch 14 of this volume.

[48] The cases involved two litigants seeking the permission of the court to have a friend who was not legally qualified represent them (*Makascheff v Commonwealth Bank of Australia* [2016] NSWSC 1108) and a successful appeal against sentence due to defects in the prosecution case on appeal (*Queensland Police Service v Messer* [2016] QDC 214).

particular law or the unilateral issuing of a conditional 'bill of exchange' to a creditor to extinguish a debt. These latter cases were frequently described as 'incoherent', 'meritless' or 'nonsensical' by courts.[49] They did not experience the 'filtering out' provided by lawyers and the lack of expert knowledge of the self-represented litigants, combined with their ideological commitment, were the likely reasons why judges rejected (and even had trouble understanding) the causes of action asserted, or defences claimed, by sovereign citizen litigants.

C. The Arguments Advanced by Sovereign Citizen Litigants

Sovereign citizens very rarely challenged the facts in cases in which they were involved. Procedurally, this meant that there were few challenges to the sufficiency of evidence tendered by an opposing party; instead, the challenges were to jurisdiction and/or the validity or interpretation of a statute. This approach was most clearly illustrated in a criminal case when a litigant sought to enter a plea of 'guilty to the facts' and distinguish this from a plea of guilty; the distinction was dismissed by the court as 'illusory'.[50]

As noted, sovereign citizens usually purported to identify some fundamental deficiency in relevant laws and/or legal processes. Appropriately analysing their arguments required the development of a suitable, qualitative classification framework. Prior analyses of their litigation,[51] including Christine Sarteschi's outline of 28 legal matters frequently raised in the US,[52] Netolitzky's identification of the key elements of the 'pseudolaw memeplex',[53] and Hobbs, Young and McIntyre's doctrinal review of Australian (and New Zealand) cases, provided the initial basis for the classification.[54] Those studies suggested that the most common arguments would relate to dual personality, lack of consent/contract and defects in the enactment of laws. Reading the current cases suggested that those categories could be further elaborated, that some arguments advanced in North America had not been made in Australia, and that other arguments had a distinctive domestic form.[55] The iterative process that was adopted resulted in nine key arguments being identified:

(i) Without consent or contractual agreement, laws were not binding (17 cases).
(ii) Debts could be extinguished by the debtor unilaterally issuing a creditor a conditional bill of exchange or promissory note (16 cases).

[49] See *Walter v Premier of Queensland* [2018] QSC 237 [14]; the statement of claim was 'incoherent'.
[50] *Pullen v O'Brien* [2014] QDC 92 [17].
[51] Netolitzky (n 31).
[52] Sarteschi (n 31) 9–29.
[53] DJ Netolitzky, 'A Pathogen Astride the Minds of Men: The Epidemiological History of Pseudolaw' CEFIR Symposium Sovereign Citizens in Canada, Montreal (3 May 2018), www.ssrn.com/abstract=3177472. Netolitzky (n 39) 963–64.
[54] Hobbs, Young and McIntyre (n 32).
[55] Australian variations in sovereign citizen arguments were noted by Netolitzky in relation to 'constitutional arguments to defeat government authority'. Netolitzky (n 53) 16.

(iii) Courts had no jurisdiction over them, and laws had no authority (15 cases).
(iv) Summary courts were not courts of competent jurisdiction because they did not comply with Chapter III of the Australian Constitution (11 cases).
(v) Laws did not apply because they had a dual personality, and their 'natural' or 'free' personality was not bound by laws (nine cases).
(vi) The power to judge could only be exercised by a jury (seven cases).
(vii) Defects in the law-making process made certain legislation invalid (seven cases).
(viii) Defects in the establishment of a court meant that it was invalid (seven cases).
(ix) The 'natural common law' invested citizens with rights that could not be overridden by other laws (six cases).

These claims were heavily interrelated and overlapping, but highlight the focus of the sovereign citizen arguments. Other arguments were raised in less than five cases each (eg local government was not constitutionally valid, paper money was not valid, the grant of an estate in fee simple precludes the exercise of legislative power in relation to the land, a declaration that a sovereign citizen was vexatious litigant); these infrequent claims are not further investigated. The most frequent claims are now explored.

i. Without Consent or Contractual Agreement, Laws were not Binding

Consent is a core sovereign citizen narrative and is grounded in the claim that individuals have dual personalities. The absence of consent was used to justify non-compliance with legal obligations and was expressly raised in 17 cases. Although this argument appeared in cases throughout the review period, the frequency increased after 2020, when objections to public health restrictions associated with the COVID-19 pandemic increased the public profile of sovereign citizen narratives about consent and objections to laws.

The litigants who advanced these arguments believed that they could unilaterally opt out of federal, state and territory legal systems, including the application of law and the jurisdiction and supervision of courts, by indicating that they did not consent to a law or legal process. This approach was exemplified in the statement by the sovereign citizen Maurice Cutts, who informed the court hearing his case, 'Without my consent, any Judicial decision is null and void and of no legal consequence.'[56]

In addition to indicating that they did not consent to a particular law, litigants sometimes argued a lack of privity of contract between them and a government or its agencies;[57] again, the consequence that was claimed was that they were

[56] *Deputy Commissioner of Taxation v Cutts (No 4)* [2019] FCCA 2866 [89].
[57] *Deputy Commissioner of Taxation v Bonaccorso (No 3)* [2016] NSWSC 1018 [13]; *Police v Gale* [2020] TASMC 11 [14]–[15].

not bound by relevant laws and processes. This argument very loosely generalised notions of freedom to contract, developed in commercial law, to the context of public law. For instance, when Yvette Reiman refused to comply with a lawful directive from a police officer, she asserted that she was refusing to enter into a 'contract'.[58] Similarly, Garry Bonacorsso denied liability for monies owed to the Australian Tax Office (ATO) by asserting that the ATO had, by assumed contract, changed him from a 'flesh and blood man' to a taxpayer and that this was 'a violation of contract law'.[59]

A further, unique, variant in the use of contract law occurred in cases where sovereign citizen litigants claimed that the party to whom they were opposed in litigation had, by acquiescence, accepted a contract initiated by the sovereign citizen and had thereby become liable to them for the payment of extravagant fees. For instance, when Julie Steepe objected to Royal Australian Air Force (RAAF) planes flying over her property she claimed more than 15 million dollars in damages based on her issuing a 'cease and desist' notice to the RAAF, accompanied by a schedule of fees for which it would be liable if the 'breaches' continued.[60] Similarly, after being dismissed from their jobs for failing to comply with vaccination requirements during the pandemic, two sovereign citizen litigants initiated a statutory demand for just over six million dollars from their former employer as compensation for loss of employment and breaches of their human rights. The litigants argued that providing a 'Schedule of fees' had initiated a 'contract' and the employer's failure to respond constituted acquiescence.[61]

Unsurprisingly, Australian courts gave short shrift to these arguments and unequivocally responded that they did not have any merit. Courts noted that sovereign citizens' 'contracts' typically did not satisfy essential legal elements and could not be imposed unilaterally.[62] Courts also informed litigants that all inhabitants of Australia are subject to the laws of the Commonwealth and of the states or territories in which they reside,[63] and those laws were not in any way subject to their acceptance, adoption, request, contract or consent.[64] Litigants were advised of the traditional position, stated by Mason CJ in relation to the laws of New South Wales:

> The legislature of New South Wales has power to make laws for the peace, welfare and good government of New South Wales in all cases whatsoever … The proposition that

[58] *Reiman v Commissioner of Police* [2021] QDC 242 [17].

[59] *Deputy Commissioner of Taxation v Bonaccorso (No 3)* [2016] NSWSC 1018 [13].

[60] *Steepe v Commonwealth of Australia* [2021] NSWSC 368.

[61] *Re Coles Supermarkets Australia Pty Ltd* [2022] VSC 438.

[62] *Steepe v Commonwealth of Australia* [2021] NSWSC 368; *Re Coles Supermarkets Australia Pty Ltd* [2022] VSC 438.

[63] Courts have mainly addressed this issue in cases where Indigenous Australians have asserted that sovereignty remained with them. For instance, see *Walker v State of NSW* (1994) 182 CLR 45 [48] (Mason J); *Deputy Commissioner of Taxation v Casley* [2017] WASC 16 [15].

[64] *R v Sweet* [2021] QDC 216 [6]–[7]; *Deputy Commissioner of Taxation v Cutts (No 4)* [2019] FCCA 2866 [126]–[130];*Cardinia Shire Council v Kraan* [2017] VMC 18 [46]–[47], [69]–[70].

> those laws could not apply to particular inhabitants or particular conduct occurring within the State must be rejected.[65]

In *Stefan v McLachlan*,[66] Dixon J further identified that the sovereign citizen individualised conception of consent was incompatible with the Australian system of government, where consent to laws followed from the election of parliamentarians to make laws for the peace, order and good governance of the state and their subsequent exercise of that legislative power.

ii. Debts could be Extinguished by the Debtor Unilaterally Issuing the Creditor a Conditional 'Bill of Exchange' or 'Promissory Note'

Adopting a strategy originally used in Canada,[67] Australian sovereign citizens sometimes sought to avoid liability for debts owed to the ATO, banks and other financial institutions, by turning statements of account into bills of exchange. This approach was adopted in 16 cases, all heard prior to 2018; an indebted party unilaterally presented to their creditor a bill of exchange or promissory note in which they promised to pay them a trivial sum (typically zero or a few dollars) and imposed conditions which, if not fulfilled, not only purportedly extinguished the debt under the Bills of Exchange Act 1909 (Cth), but also imposed penalty payments on the creditor.[68]

Australian courts repeatedly held that this strategy demonstrated a complete misunderstanding of a bill of exchange or constituted a cynical strategy to avoid a debt. They dismissed the strategy as 'hopeless and nonsense'.[69] As Jagot J observed in relation to a case where a sovereign citizen delivered to the ATO a non-negotiable promissory note to discharge his tax debt and then claimed that, because the promissory note was neither presented for payment by the ATO nor dishonoured, his debt was discharged:

> The notion that a person who owes the ATO money for non-payment of tax can transform the ATO's statement of account into a bill of exchange and then deliver the statement of account back to the ATO and, in so doing, discharge the person's own indebtedness for some nominal amount … and render the ATO liable to pay the original amount owed to the ATO plus interest and other charges is some form of fantasy.[70]

[65] *Walker v State of NSW* (1994) 182 CLR 45 [2] (Mason J).
[66] [2023] VSC 501 [26].
[67] *ACM Group Ltd v Jenner* [2014] QMC 7 [26]–[27].
[68] *Bertola v Australian and New Zealand Banking Corporation* [2014] FCA 609; *Atkinson v Commissioner of* Taxation [2014] FCA 1217; *Wilmink as Trustee for the Bangarra Trust v Westpac Banking Corporation* [2014] FCA 872; *ACM Group Ltd v Jenner* [2014] QMC 7; *Commonwealth Bank of Australia v Roskott* [2014] NSWSC 246. A related strategy is to purport to issue a commercial lien against a body to whom a debt is owed and then claim that the contract has been breached, discharging the debt. *Living Word Outreach Inc v Deputy Sheriff of Victoria* [2014] VSC 454.
[69] *Bertola v Australian and New Zealand Banking Corporation* [2014] FCA 609 [16].
[70] *Atkinson v Commissioner of* Taxation [2014] FCA 1217 [44]–[47].

iii. Courts had no Jurisdiction Over them, and Laws no Authority

A fundamental narrative of sovereign citizens was that laws did not apply to them and prosecuting bodies did not have the authority to bring cases, nor courts have the power to hear them. This blunt argument was expressly advanced in 15 cases. It was derived from an individualised conception of sovereignty and notions of dual personality,[71] and constituted a basic rejection of the sovereignty of Parliament[72] and the application of laws to a sovereign citizen's 'natural or living' personality. Put simply, these litigants argued that 'Courts have no jurisdiction over living women and men'[73] and that 'A judge without jurisdiction may be disobeyed with impunity'.[74]

This repudiation was frequently expressed by pejoratively designating the courts and law enforcement as 'corporations' to which sovereign citizens owed no obligations.[75] The notion that having the status of a corporation was somehow antithetical to having legitimate authority permeated sovereign citizen attitudes to law enforcement and government. This characterisation was associated with non-compliance with lawful directives, including a refusal to provide names and addresses to police and failing to pay taxes and rates (these matters are further addressed at point v).

However, these litigants exhibited a considerable amount of pragmatism (and ideological inconsistency) in their use of the courts. Judges noted that, while challenging the jurisdiction and validity of courts to hear matters in which they were appellants, they simultaneously sought enforceable orders and judgements from those courts.[76]

iv. Summary Courts were not Courts of Competent Jurisdiction

While sovereign citizens frequently challenged the authority of courts, in 11 cases, they specifically rejected the authority of summary courts. These litigants had appeared before summary courts and been convicted of criminal offences; they subsequently lodged appeals which challenged the validity of the court, typically on the basis that the courts were not courts of competent jurisdiction because they did not conform to Chapter III of the Australian Constitution. Appellate courts

[71] Leonard Casley also claimed that he was not bound by Australian laws and legal systems because he had seceded from the Commonwealth of Australia. *Deputy Commissioner of Taxation v Casley* [2017] WASC 161 [11]–[14]. Courts have readily dismissed this argument, pointing out that under cl 5 of the Commonwealth of Australia Constitution Act 1900 (Imp) inhabitants of Australia are subject to the laws of the Commonwealth and of the States or Territories in which they reside; also *Stefan v McLachlan* [2023] VSC 501 [39].

[72] *Stefan v McLachlan* [2023] VSC 501 [39].

[73] *Locatelli and Smith* [2020] FCWA 198 [2].

[74] This purported 'legal maxim' was cited by the sovereign citizen litigant in *Deputy Commissioner of Taxation v Bonaccorso (No 3)* [2016] NSWSC 1018 [13].

[75] *Police v Gale* [2020] TASMC 11 [14]–[15].

[76] See *Pullen v O'Brien* [2014] QDC 92 [12]; *Bradley v The Crown* [2020] QCA 252.

repeatedly dismissed this argument, finding that it evidenced 'a fundamental misunderstanding' of the power of the States to maintain their own courts.[77]

v. Laws did not Apply because they had a Dual Personality and their 'Natural' ('Living Man/Woman' Personality was not Bound by Laws

As previously noted, the narrative that a law did not apply to a sovereign citizen who did not consent to that law or enter into a relevant 'contract' with the government or its agents, is grounded in the notion of dual personalities.[78] In nine cases, all heard from 2016 onwards, sovereign citizens made this specific argument and adopted a dualistic approach that distinguished 'legal' ('corporate', 'strawman') and 'living' (natural, physical) personalities, with the former being able to be rejected at will, leaving the residual 'natural personality' beyond the reach of the law. For instance, the sovereign citizen Kym Sweet unsuccessfully advanced this argument when he claimed that drug charges against him should be dismissed because his 'real person' was not subject to the laws of Queensland.[79] Similarly, when denying liability for a tax debt, Garry Bonaccorso stated 'I am not a "legal entity" known as a "taxpayer" subject to income Tax Act of Australia'.[80]

But on what basis did these litigants believe they could repudiate their legal personality, with its attached obligations and duties? They claimed that the two personalities arose at birth and soon thereafter; the living person was born with inalienable rights, whereas the issuing of a birth certificate by government marked the beginning of the imposition of the corporate/legal personality. Subsequently, the living or natural person remained a free, unencumbered, agent, whereas the legal/corporate person was increasingly invested (without the express consent of the living person) with the legal obligations and duties of a citizen. Sovereign citizen litigants asserted that because they did not originally consent to the creation of their legal personality, they were free to withdraw their consent to this personality at any time; their residual personality was that of a living person, not subject to the laws of Australia, at any level of government.

Courts readily dismissed these arguments, describing them as 'legal nonsense'.[81] As Justice Solomon observed in *Yap v Matic*: 'as a matter of law, a living person is a legal person … In law, a person who is alive has status, legal status, as a person. They are one and the same thing. They are not two separate identities or entities'.[82]

[77] *Reiman v Commissioner of Police* [2021] QDC 242 [19]; *Pullen v O'Brien* [2014] QDC 92 [10(c)]–[11]; *ACM Group Limited v McClymont* [2014] FCCA 2581; *Pengelly v Serpentine Jarrahdale Shire* [2014] WASCA 5; *Cardinia Shire Council v Kraan* [2017] VMC 24 [25]. A similar, unsuccessful challenge was made to the validity of the Administrative Appeals Tribunal: *Girle and Secretary, Department of Social Services (Social services second review)* [2021] AATA 2579 [32]–[49].

[78] *R v Sweet* [2021] QDC 216 [4].

[79] ibid. Also see *Smadu v Stone* [2016] WASC 80; *Locatelli and Smith* [2020] FCWA 198 [7.1].

[80] *Deputy Commissioner of Taxation v Bonaccorso (No 3)* [2016] NSWSC 1018 [13]. Also see *Re Coles Supermarkets Australia Pty Ltd* [2022] VSC 438 [17].

[81] *In the Matter of Glew* [2022] HCATrans 101 [1].

[82] *Yap v Matic* [2022] WASC 181 [22], [61], [65]–[70].

The repudiation of a legal personality could, however, create significant confusion and procedural difficulties. For instance, Sandi Matic's claim that the party named in court documents was not him but 'a fictional person/trust with the same name' eventually contributed to him being convicted of contempt of court.[83]

vi. The Power to Judge could Only be Exercised by a Jury

Sovereign citizen litigants believed that trial by jury was an inalienable right and that the power to judge could only be exercised by a jury.[84] In seven cases, all heard prior to 2018, this meant that despite the statutory bases of decisions of magistrates,[85] litigants regarded decisions made by judges in trials or other hearings without a jury,[86] and orders made by judges alone (such as a sequestration order in the Federal Court or an order made on an interlocutory appeal in the Supreme Court) as void. Their claims essentially relied on Chapter 29 of Magna Carta and/or section 80 of the Constitution of Australia.

However, more than 100 years ago the High Court established that a law is not invalid simply because it is not in conformity with Magna Carta.[87] As well as pragmatically pointing out that juries did not exist at the time that Magna Carta was introduced, courts have reiterated the well-established principle that Magna Carta and the Bill of Rights (another document frequently relied upon by sovereign citizens)[88] do not have paramount force. As Justice McHugh observed in an earlier period in relation to another sovereign citizen claim:

> Magna Carta and the Bill of Rights are not documents binding on Australian legislatures in the way that the Constitution is binding on them. Any legislature acting within the powers allotted to it by the Constitution can legislate in disregard of Magna Carta and the Bill of Rights. At the highest, those two documents express a political ideal, but they do not legally bind the legislatures of this country or, for that matter, the United Kingdom. Nor do they limit the powers of the legislatures of Australia or the United Kingdom.[89]

Additionally, courts pointed out that section 80 of the Constitution did not have universal application in hearings, and did not apply to a minor civil claim[90] or driving offences[91] heard in summary courts, because it was only relevant to trials on indictment of offences against laws of the Commonwealth.[92]

[83] ibid [60].
[84] See *Deputy Commissioner of Taxation v Bonaccorso (No 3)* [2016] NSWSC 1018 [13].
[85] See *Jackson v Western Australia Police* [2014] WASC 72; *Stearman v Taylor* [2014] WASC 247; *Nibbs v Devonport City Council* [2015] TASSC 34 [45]–[46].
[86] See *Summerland Credit Union Ltd v Lamberton; Summerland Credit Union Ltd v Jonathan* [2014] NSWSC 547; *Deputy Commissioner of Taxation v Bonaccorso (No 3)* [2016] NSWSC 1018 [13].
[87] *Chia Gee v Martin* (1905) 3 CLR 649, 653.
[88] See, for example, *Living Word Outreach Inc v Deputy Sheriff of Victoria* [2014] VSC 454.
[89] *Essenberg v The Queen* B55/1999 [2000] HCATrans 386.
[90] *Nibbs v Devonport City Council* [2015] TASSC 34 [46].
[91] *Stearman v Taylor* [2014] WASC 247.
[92] *Cardinia Shire Council v Kraan* [2017] VMC 18 [33]–[35].

vii. Defects in the Law-making Process Rendered Legislation Invalid

In seven cases, sovereign citizen litigants asserted that some fundamental defect in the law-making process made legislation invalid. These cases typically involved detailed arguments about procedural matters that were claimed to have profound impact. For instance, the high-profile sovereign citizen Alan Skyring purported to identify a fundamental defect in the passing of the Australia Act 1986 (Cth). In a series of cases, he argued that the Australia Acts (Request) Act 1985 (Qld) was invalid because it unlawfully altered the office of Governor in contravention of the Commonwealth of Australia Constitution Act. The 1985 Act was the mechanism by which the Parliament of Queensland consented to the enactment by the Parliament of the United Kingdom of the Australia Act 1986 (UK) and of the Commonwealth of Australia of the Australia Act 1986 (Cth). Due to the claimed unconstitutionality of the 1985 Act, it and the subsequent Acts were said to be invalid. Skyring argued that this had the effect that all legislation passed in Queensland since 1987 (including the statutes under which actions had been brought against him) were therefore of no force and effect.[93] Courts repeatedly dismissed this argument, holding that there had been no alteration to the office of Governor and, even if the 1985 Act was invalid, it did not have the effect contended by the litigant.[94]

Similarly, it was argued that local governments did not have the power to levy rates because legislation which purportedly empowered them to do so had not been given proper Royal Assent,[95] or was unconstitutional because local government was not recognised as a tier of government in the Australian Constitution, or the power to tax was limited to the Commonwealth. Courts dismissed these arguments, noting that procedural requirements concerning Royal Assent had been satisfied,[96] that sovereign states are recognised in the Constitution and could legislate about local government,[97] and that while section 51(ii) of the Constitution enabled the Commonwealth Parliament to make laws with respect to taxation, a state government was not thereby precluded from making such laws, provided there was no inconsistency.

viii. Defects in the Establishment or Processes of a Court or an Office-holder Made Decisions Invalid

In seven cases, sovereign citizen litigants asserted that a defect in the establishment of a court, the appointment of an office-holder, or associated processes, made decisions and other outcomes invalid.

[93] *Skying v Cooper* [2014] QSC 103.
[94] ibid [3], citing *Skyring v Lohe (Crown Solicitor)* [2001] QSC 350 [19] and *Skyring* [2013] QSC 197.
[95] *Nibbs v Devonport City Council* [2015] TASSC 34 [19]–[29].
[96] ibid [13].
[97] ibid [6].

In relation to an office-holder, a bizarre action sought to have the then-Prime Minister declared a criminal because he had allegedly incorrectly sworn the oath of office.[98]

Concerning courts, the claim of fundamental defect was made in relation to summary courts,[99] superior courts[100] and tribunals.[101] The arguments were varied and included that a state court had no power to hear federal matters, judicial officers could not lawfully exercise jurisdiction and that prosecuting authorities lacked standing:

- *State courts had no power to hear federal matters:* sovereign citizen litigants argued that state courts had no power under the Australian Constitution to hear matters involving Commonwealth laws and legislation. This was frequently the basis on which they sought to issue section 78B notices under the Judiciary Act 1903 (Cth), seeking to have their cases transferred to the High Court of Australia, which was viewed as the necessary forum for federal cases. Courts repeatedly established that this argument evidenced 'a fundamental misunderstanding' of the power of the states to maintain their own courts and for those courts to be adopted by the Commonwealth for the enforcement of the laws of the Commonwealth.[102]
- *Judicial officers cannot lawfully exercise jurisdiction:* sovereign citizen litigants argued that a proceeding was invalid because a legal process concerning the appointment of judicial officers had not been adequately complied with. For instance, the appointments of magistrates were sometimes challenged on the basis that they had not properly sworn[103] or taken[104] the oath of office. The argument here is not that the conferral of jurisdiction was invalid; rather, the point was that these judicial officers could not exercise that jurisdiction. The objection was repeatedly addressed and dismissed.
- *The prosecuting authority was invalid:* sovereign citizens alleged defects in the appointment process for parties and prosecuting bodies and frequently designated those believed to be unlawfully exercising authority as 'corporations'. For instance, police were identified as a private corporation, leading sovereign citizen litigants to claim that they could not act as prosecuting authorities and/or could not enforce laws without the consent of the sovereign citizen.[105] Similarly, challenges to the authority of local councils to prosecute were based on the claimed invalidity of empowering legislation[106] and/or their failure to

[98] *Ross-James v Turnbull* [2017] QSC 275.
[99] See *Sorensen v Queensland Police Service* [2022] QDC 121.
[100] See *Wilson v Western Australia Police* [2014] WASCA 145.
[101] See *IEX (Guardianship)* [2022] VCAT 1000 [41].
[102] *Pullen v O'Brien* [2014] QDC 92 [12]; *Makascheff v Commonwealth Bank of Australia* [2017] NSWCA 126 [30].
[103] *Cardinia Shire Council v Kraan* [2017] 18 VMC [71]–[72].
[104] *Nibbs v Devonport City Council* [2015] TASSC 34.
[105] *Stefan v McLachlan* [2023] VSC 501 [39].
[106] See *Cardinia Shire Council v Kraan* [2017] VMC 24 [23]–[24], [26].

be specified in the Australian Constitution.[107] Related arguments were raised in relation to the power of the Commissioner and Deputy Commissioners of Taxation to initiate proceedings.[108] Courts dismissed these arguments, holding that the initiation or response to a case was with the relevant statutory authority to prosecute or litigate, a prosecution was not invalid because the body was also a corporation, and the authority to prosecute could be based in statute.[109]

ix. They Possess 'Natural Common Law' Rights that are Inalienable

Sovereign citizens did not reject *all* laws. In six cases, they asserted that the 'natural common law' invested them with rights that could not be limited by state or Commonwealth statutory provisions.[110] This was a relatively recent development, with all cases being heard after 2016.

The rights that were asserted included matters relating specifically to legal proceedings (such as the previously discussed right to trial by jury) as well as the quotidian, including a right to travel freely on public roads, with a consequent freedom from obligations to obey traffic laws, have a driving licence, register a motor vehicle, etc.[111] For example, Yvette Reiman challenged her convictions for driving offences and assaulting police on the basis, inter alia, that she was not subject to the statutory laws and jurisdiction of the State of Queensland because of her 'unalienable/inalienable indefeasible rights to life, liberty, freedom and property'.[112] More recent cases have asserted an 'inalienable right as an independent sovereign citizen to refuse … mandated and coerced medical injection'.[113]

Sovereign citizens' narratives about the 'natural common law' are very different to lawyers' understanding of the common law. They indiscriminately use the term to refer to a variety of legal documents (particularly Magna Carta)[114] and occasionally to arcane legislation (including the Statute of Monopolies),[115] and treaties (particularly the Universal Declaration of Human Rights). They also use

[107] *Nibbs v Devonport City Council* [2015] TASSC 34 [6]; *Schafer v Bacon* [2022] QDC 60.

[108] See *Deputy Commissioner of Taxation v Bonaccorso* [2016] NSWSC 595 [35]–[42]; *Deputy Commissioner of Taxation v Bonaccorso (No 3)* [2016] NSWSC 1018 [13].

[109] See *Deputy Commissioner of Taxation v Bonaccorso* [2016] NSWSC 595 [35]–[42].

[110] See *Cardinia Shire Council v Kraan* [2017] VMC 18 [38]–[39]; *Deputy Commissioner of Taxation v Bonaccorso (No 3)* [2016] NSWSC 1018 [13].

[111] Sovereign citizens distinguished 'driving' from 'travelling', claiming that their use of the roads was an exercise of the inalienable right to travel, was different to driving on those roads and that only 'driving' was regulated by legislation. Court unequivocally rejected this distinction: *Police v Gale* [2020] TASMC 11 [6]–[10].

[112] *Reiman v Commissioner of Police* [2021] QDC 242 [17].

[113] *Bakhash v State of Queensland (Department of Education)* [2022] QIRC 362 [9]. See M O'Sullivan, ch 3 of this volume.

[114] 'No free man shall be seized or imprisoned, or stripped of his rights or possessions, or outlawed or exiled, nor will we proceed with force against him except by the lawful judgement of his equals or by the law of the land (*common law*)'. Magna Carta (1215) 17 John, c 39 (emphasis added).

[115] *Pullen v O'Brien* [2014] QDC 92 [41]–[47].

the concept in more idiosyncratic ways, such as limiting the 'natural common law' to decisions of the High Court of Australia.[116] Although the natural common law was said also to invest sovereign citizens with duties, this appeared to be entirely theoretical and was not manifest in the cases.

Courts have repeatedly held that asserting the superiority of a 'natural common law' reflects fundamental misunderstandings about Australian law. Litigants who rely on a natural common law fail to acknowledge that the parliaments of Australia have authority to enact binding laws,[117] that these laws may repeal imperial law,[118] and that international human rights instruments must be given effect in domestic law if they are to operate within Australia.

x. *Issues that were not Raised*

Before leaving this analysis, it is appropriate to note three matters that were *absent* from the cases.

(1) *No historical and local uniformity in matters litigated:* There were notable differences in the arguments raised in these cases and those identified in previous litigation in Australia, as well as North America. Challenges to the validity of the banking and currency system in Australia – once a common topic of sovereign citizen litigation – did not appear in these recent cases.[119] Moreover, unlike their American counterparts, these Australian litigants generally were *not* concerned with the abandonment of the gold standard by the Federal Government in 1932,[120] nor did they frequently allege that secret Treasury accounts were established for every citizen which the Government used as collateral for international debt.[121] Additionally, only one of these cases reflected the 'paper terrorism' (ie inundating 'the court system with frivolous lawsuits seeking fictitious reparations from government administrators and officials, unfounded property liens that could tie up sales and destroy credit, and unsubstantiated ethics complaints intended to taint the reputation of lawyers and judges') that has been common in the United States.[122]

[116] *State of New South Wales v Gavin* [2022] NSWSC 84 [88].

[117] See *Nibbs v Devonport City Council* [2015] TASSC 34 [10].

[118] See *Pullen v O'Brien* [2014] QDC 92 [46].

[119] For instance, litigation about the validity of paper money, as occurred in earlier cases such as *Lohe v Gunter* [2003] QSC 150 [8]–[9] and *Gunter v Hollingworth* [2002] FCA 943, was not the subject of litigation in the current cases.

[120] Southern Poverty Law Center (n 25).

[121] See ibid; 'The Truth About Frivolous Tax Arguments' Internal Revenue Service (March 2022), www.irs.gov/privacy-disclosure/the-truth-about-frivolous-tax-arguments-section-i-d-to-e. In *Locatelli and Smith* [2020] WAFC 198 [9] the respondent claimed that a constructive '*Cesti Quie Vie Trust*' was held by the State in relation to her, that she was a beneficiary, and she sought to have the trust dissolved.

[122] M Colacci, 'Sovereign Citizens: A Cult Movement That Demands Legislative Resistance' (2015) 17 *Rutgers Journal of Law and Religion* 153, 156; 'The Lawless Ones' (n 16). In *Bradley v McDermott* [2017]

(2) *Mental health issues:* Although it was frequently observed that sovereign citizen litigants could be difficult to deal with and held obsessively to their views, none of the criminal cases raised the issue of fitness to stand trial or mental impairment as a defence or factor in sentencing. The issue of mental health was, however, raised in 10 matters where supervision orders of some type were sought against five sovereign citizens. In these cases, endorsement of sovereign citizen views (especially in relation to non-compliance with orders) was typically regarded as a risk factor to be taken into account when determining whether to make the order, rather than the basis of a mental disorder per se.[123] In a further case relating to an appeal against a compulsory treatment order for mental illness, adherence to a sovereign citizen narrative was regarded as just one of the many beliefs associated with the appellant's underlying diagnosis of schizophrenia. These findings are generally consistent with prior research that has found that 'published studies about the mental health of sovereign citizens have indicated that the majority are not psychotic nor unfit to stand trial'.[124]

(3) *Public health cases:* Despite the apparent increase in unlawful behaviour associated with sovereign citizen narratives during the pandemic, this was not reflected in the cases analysed. While a refusal to comply with public health directives, including the requirement to wear a mask in some circumstances or provide a reason for travel, led to considerable media coverage of sovereign citizens, only a very small number of cases involved disputes relating to vaccinations and public health directives. The surprising absence of these cases may be due to several factors. The charges associated with these matters are usually initially heard in summary courts and media reports suggest that even high-profile sovereign citizens frequently pled guilty;[125] consequently, these cases would not appear in the predominantly appellate level cases analysed in this study. Additionally, where sovereign citizens did unsuccessfully contest charges in summary courts and are appealing the decision, the backlog of cases in higher courts caused by the pandemic may mean that these cases are yet to be heard.

QCA 19 the plaintiff unsuccessfully brought an action (seemingly for perverting the course of justice) against a solicitor who had been employed by the firm acting for a local council that had succeeded in obtaining an order allowing it to enter the plaintiff's property to undertake works. An appeal was dismissed as disclosing no cause of action.

[123] See *State of New South Wales v Gavan* [2022] NSWSC 84.

[124] Sarteschi (n 31) 76.

[125] C Schelle, 'Eve Black: Infamous Covid-19 Breacher Pleads Guilty to Licence Charge' *The West Australian* (18 November 2021), www.thewest.com.au/news/eve-black-infamous-covid-19-breacher-pleads-guilty-to-licence-charge-c-4605541; H Neale, 'Rayne Crowe Pleads Guilty to Obstructed Police During Old Parliament House Blaze', *The Canberra Times* (23 August 2023), www.canberratimes.com.au/story/8319592/sovereign-citizen-obstructed-police-during-old-parliament-house-blaze; C Bates, 'Sovereign North Queensland Citizen Pleads Guilty to Two Charges in Ingham Magistrates Court' *Townsville Bulletin* (23 June 2022).

D. Semantic and Linguistic Strategies Used by Sovereign Citizens and their Legal Consequences

Before concluding the case analysis, it is appropriate to note the difficulties caused by the distinctive semantic and linguistic strategies used by sovereign citizens. Sovereign citizen narratives posited that any document that contained the person's name in all capital letters (such as a driver's licence) related only to the legal person, whereas their preferred language was characterised by the variable use of capitals and small case letters, as well as idiosyncratic punctuation (sometimes designated 'Quantum Language').[126]

These systematic irregularities are derived from their distinction between living and legal persons (with the name of the former often involving dashes and colons), the insistence that the name and surname begin with a capital letter followed by small letters, and the use of archaic constructions such as 'family/house of'. For instance, when Kym Sweet was charged with drug offences in Queensland, he designated himself as a living person with the name Kym-Anthony and distinguished this from the 'straw man' KYM ANTHONY SWEET identified in court documents.[127] Sovereign citizens also typically placed great emphasis on the 'signs of sovereignty and citizenship':[128] seals, appointments, declarations, flags and markers and frequently used red ink to append their thumbprint (rather than a signature) to documents,[129] believing that this signified their living (rather than legal) personality.[130] The use of Latin maxims and archaic jargon was also extremely common.[131]

These strategies actually formed the basis of an unsuccessful defence by a sovereign citizen (who asserted 'syntax fraud' because court documents were not in sovereign citizen language),[132] and caused problems in several cases. The use of multiple, slightly different names and the insistence that police and the judiciary used the 'correct' (living person) name when addressing litigants generated confusion and breaches of the law in routine matters, such as providing a name to police when lawfully requested to do so,[133] accepting notice of a hearing,[134]

[126] In 2011, the American Sovereign Citizen David Wynn Miller conducted a six-day course on 'Quantum Language' in 10 capital cities and regional centres in Australia. Participants paid $1,400. N Wallace, '"Messiah-Like Figure" is Doing His Own Harvesting' *Sydney Morning Herald* (15 January 2011).

[127] *R v Sweet* [2021] QDC 216 [2].

[128] 'The Sovereign Citizen Movement: Common Documentary Identifiers & Examples' Anti-Defamation League (2016), www.adl.org/sites/default/files/documents/assets/pdf/combating-hate/Sovereign-Citizen-Documentary-Identifiers.pdf.

[129] *Scordo v Commonwealth Bank of Australia* [2024] FCA 359 [69].

[130] See *R v Sweet* [2021] QDC 216 [5].

[131] See *Police v Gale* [2020] TASMC 11 [6].

[132] See *Trustee of the Property of Currey (A Bankrupt) & Anor v Currey & Anor* [2017] FCCA 2692.

[133] *Thammaruknon v Queensland Police Service* [2016] QDC 31 [27].

[134] In *NSW Land and Housing Corporation v George Katanasho* [2014] NSWCATCD 198 [4] the respondent returned a notice of hearing to the NSW Civil and Administrative Tribunal because it was

identifying oneself for a bail hearing and other matters.[135] This sometimes resulted in significant, adverse outcomes for litigants: the issuing of warrants to arrest for non-appearance in court in breach of bail when the individual was actually present in court but refusing to respond to the name on the bail order,[136] and a conviction for contempt of court when the litigant refused to recognise court communications that used capital letters in his name.[137]

Courts were unsympathetic to these matters, expressing frustration at the archaic jargon used by sovereign citizen litigants, describing their language as 'gobbledy gook'[138] and readily dismissing claims that legal proceedings were invalid because documents were not issued in the litigant's preferred ('natural') name.[139]

IV. Conclusion: Litigation as Political Performance

This empirical review of sovereign citizen cases in Australian courts identified that they typically involved a male litigant seeking to defeat a debt owed to a government body or financial institution, or challenging the authority of local government. Less frequently, they involved a denial of liability for criminal charges. There was some shift in the arguments advanced to support these claims. Before 2018, several litigants argued that a debt could be extinguished by the debtor unilaterally issuing the creditor a bill of exchange; no such cases appeared in more recent years. Instead, a lack of consent/contract and the express rejection of a corporate personality increased in frequency as the basis for denying liability. Lawyers only represented these litigants in a small proportion of cases, typically involving conventional legal matters. In cases where core sovereign citizen narratives were advanced, litigants represented themselves and were *always* unsuccessful.

A key question is why sovereign citizens persisted in litigating matters that had already been authoritatively decided, advancing idiosyncratic arguments that judges had trouble understanding and routinely condemned as nonsensical and a waste of the resources of the courts? The answer lies in sovereign citizens'

addressed to him with his full name in capital letters; he advised the Tribunal that 'All capital letters refer to either a corporation or a slave. In the above-mentioned address, no Corporation or slave reside here. So obviously the letter … is either addressed with a misspelling or sent to the wrong address'. ibid.

[135] See *Yap v Matic* [2022] WASC 181 [22].

[136] *Wilson v Western Australia Police* [2014] WASC 77 [3]. On appeal, Commissioner Sleight observed that it would have been preferable for the magistrate to have accepted the response by Wilson as sufficient indication that he was present in court.

[137] Sandi Matic refused to recognise court communications that used capital letters in his name; this eventually contributed to his multiple convictions for contempt of court. *Matic v Yap* [2022] WASC 181 [22].

[138] *Bertola v Australian and New Zealand Banking Corporation* [2014] FCA 609; *Deputy Commissioner of Taxation v Casley* [2017] WASC 161.

[139] See *Re Coles Supermarkets Australia Pty Ltd* [2022] VSC 438 [17]–[18].

use of the courts primarily as a strategic political site, rather than a venue for the resolution of disputes.

The weapon of choice for sovereign citizens was litigation. Adherents did not simply end up in court because they had broken the law, but chose the courts as the key public venue to play out their political views.[140] Their frequent appeals simply prolonged their use of the courts as a forum to express their views. Judges condemned this misuse of the courts. As the Western Australian Court of Appeal unanimously observed in relation to early litigation by the sovereign citizen Wayne Glew: 'The appellant has invoked the court's process and procedures for an illegitimate or collateral purpose, namely, as a platform for advancing his nonsensical theories.'[141]

As previously noted, this analysis of cases in which sovereign citizens challenged the sovereignty of Australian parliaments, the jurisdiction of courts, the validity of laws and the authority of law enforcement, did not identify a single case in which their substantive arguments were accepted. In their quest for autonomy, they asserted untenable propositions and repeatedly advanced unsuccessful arguments that had been authoritatively decided. Judges dismissed their arguments as frivolous, vexatious, futile and an abuse of process.[142] However, sovereign citizens were undeterred by their spectacular lack of success. In a Popperian sense, their beliefs were unfalsifiable.[143] Success would have confirmed the correctness of their views of the law; their failures confirmed its corruptness. In essence, their appearances in courts served the hermeneutic function of facilitating and elaborating their narratives with their lack of success confirming their hostile views of judges, lawyers and legal systems. More broadly, it reinforced their hostility towards experts and elites. Unwittingly, they also benefitted from their lack of success because if courts actually accepted their renunciation of legal personhood they would become 'human being[s] without rights … mere property'.[144]

Taken in conjunction with their frequently disruptive and hostile behaviour in court,[145] often in the presence of supporters, this analysis identifies that the

[140] Justice Bongiorno of the Supreme Court of Victoria made a similar observation in relation to criminal charges contested by a sovereign citizen: 'neither this Court, the County Court nor the Magistrates' Court is a political forum. If [the appellant] has a political point, whatever it is, it must be taken up with the legislature, not the Courts. It is not part of a Court's function to entertain political argument nor is it a Court's function to rule on the validity or otherwise of any political argument'. *Moyle v County Court of Victoria* [2006] VSC 87 [16]). Also see *Wilson v Hazistergos* [2008] NSWSC 230 [5].

[141] *Glew v White* [2012] WASCA 138 [11].

[142] See *Wilson v Police* [2014] WASCA 145 [14].

[143] Sovereign citizen narratives and litigation have much in common with conspiracy theories which, as Joseph Ucinski has noted, 'have unique epistemological properties which shield them from falsification'. J Ucinski, 'The Study of Conspiracy Theories' (2018) 3 *Argumenta* 233, 234.

[144] *R v Sweet* [2021] QDC 216 [6].

[145] See *Ross-James v Turnbull* [2017] QSC 275 [23]; *Elliott v Commissioner of Police* [2014] QDC 161 [23]. In Canada, Rooke ACJ similarly observed that Sovereign Citizens 'disrupt court operations and frustrate the legal rights of governments, corporations, and individuals'. *Meads v Meads* [2012] ABQB 571 [1].

primary function of this litigation was performative and political.[146] The key political/legal issue was sovereignty. The concept of sovereignty that was manifest in these cases was profoundly individualistic, demonstrating an approach to citizenship that was atomistic, pessimistic and dystopian. The litigation did not embody any notion of a social contract. This extraordinarily reductionist approach was succinctly captured in the statement of the sovereign citizen Ross-James: 'my natural body … is my own jurisdiction'.[147] Like many conservatives, these litigants also frequently valorised an idealised society devoid of political obligations or duties where the Bible, the monarch, a selective common law and an unfettered right to land prevailed.

The litigation reflected a profound hostility towards lawyers and judges and the bureaucratic apparatus that supported them. Paradoxically, the devaluation of legal officers and systems was combined with an aping and reproduction of those very roles and systems, reflected in an obsession with stamps, badges, Latin maxims and archaic jargon. These litigants mimicked the very things they condemned. Although some commentators have used the concept of anomie to analyse this behaviour,[148] the work of the German social theorist Max Scheler is more apposite. Scheler extended the concept of *ressentiment*, originally developed by Nietzsche, and used it to describe how social inequality could generate a deep sense of grievance, involving feelings of frustration and alienation, where the goal was to become (rather than overthrow or dismantle) a detested source of power and authority.[149] Sophie Kaldor's development of *ressentiment* in her work on extreme political movements has much relevance to these sovereign citizen litigants, as it explicates why established authorities are targeted rather than more vulnerable groups.[150]

How our courts should respond to this litigation is an obvious practical consideration. It is not simply the political nature of sovereign citizen litigation that is troublesome (all legal cases are to varying degrees political), but rather its legal futility and unreasonableness, leading to a waste of court resources. In *White Industries (QLD) Pty ltd v Flower and Hart*,[151] Goldberg J adverted to the notion of unreasonably initiating or continuing proceedings requiring something more than having no or little chance of success. His honour suggested that it also involved 'some deliberate or conscious decision taken by reference to circumstances

[146] Sometimes this was made explicit by Sovereign Citizens. See *Woods v Scipione* [2014] NSWSC 1100 [68].

[147] *Bradley v The Crown* [2020] QCA 252.

[148] EJH Abromeit, 'Sovereign Citizens: Losing the Game by Refusing to Play' *Iowa Journal of Gender, Race and Justice* (22 September 2023), jgrj.law.uiowa.edu/news/2023/09/sovereign-citizens-losing-game-refusing-play.

[149] M Scheler, *Ressentiment* (Marquette University Press, 1994).

[150] S Kaldor, *Far-Right Violent Extremism as a Failure of Status: A New Approach to Extremist Manifestos through the Lens of Ressentiment* (International Centre for Counter-Terrorism, 2021), www.icct.nl/sites/default/files/2022-12/Far-Right-Violent-Extremism-as-a-Failure-of-Status.pdf.

[151] *White Industries (QLD) Pty ltd v Flower and Hart* (1998) 156 ALR 169.

unrelated to prospects of success with either a recognition that there is no chance of success but an intention to use the proceedings for an ulterior purpose'.[152]

Courts have repeatedly identified that sovereign citizen litigation, undertaken for the purpose of using proceedings to advance political views, is unreasonable and a waste of court resources.[153] It is likely that sovereign citizens will continue to litigate as their narratives engage with new and emerging issues.[154] The shift in arguments raised in litigation during the past decade, with a contemporary emphasis on consent and contract, demonstrates fluidity in the narratives they adopt. Consequently, it is likely that they will continue to present problems for courts. This will make it necessary to re-examine the balancing of rightful access to justice by citizens against the politically motivated, inappropriate burdening of our legal systems with embarrassing cases. While courts have declared several sovereign citizens to be vexatious litigants,[155] individualistic solutions are inadequate because they fail to recognise the distinctive nature of sovereign citizen litigation.[156] Recent decades have been rightfully concerned with reforms to court procedures to promote access to justice; it is likely that an unintended consequence of those reforms has been to open courts to problematic litigation. It may be that the most significant contribution of sovereign citizen litigation to legal analysis is that it prompts consideration of the countervailing issue of how best to restrict access for cases that are hopeless and devoid of legal merit.

[152] ibid 236.

[153] The Judicial Commission of New South Wales notes about cases involving self-represented persons Sovereign Citizens: 'It may be much harder, and might take longer than usual, to get to the essence of what the case is about, particularly if the [self-represented person] is a Sovereign Citizen who may make nonsensical and voluminous submissions which generally have no foundation in Australian law. It may be time-consuming and frustrating to deal with the submissions of a Sovereign Citizen as they are turgid and illogical. Effective communication may be difficult as the Sovereign Citizen may claim not to recognise or go by the name on the court papers and/or may claim the law does apply to them.' Judicial Commission of New South Wales, *Equality Before the Law Bench Book*, s 10.2, www.judcom.nsw.gov.au/publications/benchbks/equality/section10.html#p10.2.

[154] For instance, a school for children of sovereign citizens and others opposed to vaccinations has been established in Sheffield, England. T Hume, 'Sovereign Citizens Are Trying to Set Up Their Own Anti-Vax Schools in the UK' Vice (10 October 2021), www.vice.com/en/article/bvz9n4/sovereign-citizens-are-trying-to-set-up-their-own-anti-vax-schools-in-the-uk.

[155] During the period under review, two sovereign citizens were declared vexatious litigants: *Attorney-General (WA) v Glew* [2014] WASC 100; *Bradley v The Queen* [2020] QCA 252.

[156] Phillips (n 14) 1222. Phillips outlined the distinctive form of sovereign citizen litigation in the United States and observed: 'Sovereign Citizen *pro se* litigants … fall outside of the realm of the typical "uninformed" non-attorney *pro se* litigant and should be considered a separate type of litigant supported by a wide range of like-minded active participants'. ibid.

10

'Germanite is a Rare Mineral': Sovereignism in Germany

ANNA LÖBBERT*

I. Introduction

In 2011, an appeal to a decision by a German tax office was heard in front of the Financial Court in Hamburg.[1] The tax office had altered the tax liability of a business in 2010 after an audit showed undeclared income in 2006, 2007 and 2008.[2] The owner appealed the decision, arguing that he was a member of the *Staatsvolk* (the people of a state) 'Germaniten' of the state 'Germanitien'. As such, the code of procedure for fiscal courts, the code of procedure, and tax law of the Federal Republic of Germany (FRG) should not apply to him as an 'extraterritorial' person, and he had no obligation to pay taxes to the 'company Federal Republic'. Moreover, he argued that the state Germanitien confers individual immunity onto its diplomats, of which he was one. The appellant explained that Germanitien had been founded by a certificate issued on 7 January 2010, and that its establishment had been announced to the United Nations on 25 March 2010.[3]

To bolster this argument, the appellant cited a range of existing legal instruments, including the Vienna Convention on Diplomatic Relations, United Nations Resolution 56/83, the 1997 European Convention on Nationality, Article 9 of the Weimar Constitution, the law issued by the American occupation forces in Germany, and the Basic Law, the contemporary German constitution of the Federal Republic of Germany (FRG). A list of alleged further flaws in the legal basis for the tax code and arguments against the competence of FRG courts to hear the case followed.

* This work was supported by the Economic and Social Research Council (grant number 2262026), the Lincoln College Kingsgate studentship and the Faculty of Law at the University of Oxford.

[1] Finanzgericht Hamburg (Finance Court Hamburg), 3 K 6/11, (2013) OpenJur 1660.

[2] Finanzgericht Hamburg (Finance Court Hamburg), 3 K 94/14, (2014) OpenJur 18349 [1].

[3] Finanzgericht Hamburg (n 1) [3].

Unsurprisingly, the Court held that German tax law did indeed apply, and no plausible reason for the opposite had been presented:

> [T]here is neither a nation of 'Germanites' nor a state of 'Germanitien'. A few signatures on a founding document so designated and a proclamation allegedly sent to the United Nations do not constitute a Staatsvolk and, in the absence of state territory and state authority exercised on it, certainly not a state …, quite apart from any international recognition … The term 'Germanite' rather refers to a rarely occurring mineral from the mineral class of sulphides and sulphosalts (Wikipedia).[4]

Further appeals to subsequent tax liabilities in 2010 and 2011, alongside a petition to dismiss the judge, were again rejected by the courts.[5]

The following year, a man sued the *Landratsamt* (a district-level administrative authority) for threatening to immobilise his car for failing to produce a valid insurance policy.[6] He argued that the insurance requirement under Article 2 of the Compulsory Insurance Act did not apply in the FRG. Moreover, he argued that according to Article 25 of the Basic Law, 'international agreements take precedent over any other laws'.[7] Therefore, as a minister and diplomat of the indigenous people and state Germanitien, even if the Compulsory Insurance Act was a valid law, it did not apply to him. The court dismissed these arguments, concluding that the state Germanitien is 'nonsensical' and 'a pure product of phantasy'.[8] The Compulsory Insurance Act regulates exemptions from the insurance obligation for certain owners. The idea that this German law stipulates that it is not valid in Germany would be 'just as nonsensical as his statements about the "State of Germanitien"'.[9]

In 2016, the social court in Potsdam decided on an 'urgent motion' it received in the mail.[10] The letter, addressed to the German foreign ministry, was copied to countless government institutions across Germany, and asked the state to register the 'Indigenous people Germaniten' in the state's list of Indigenous peoples.[11] The social court, as well as subsequently two higher-level courts, rejected the petition as inadmissible because it had an 'inadmissible content' and represented no legitimate interest to take legal action (*Rechtsschutzbedürfnis*).[12] The petitioner also

[4] ibid [30]–[31] (reference to '(Wikipedia)' in original).

[5] Finanzgericht Hamburg (n 2).

[6] Verwaltungsgericht Augsburg (Administrative Court Augsburg), 3 K 12.573, (2012) OpenJur 123492.

[7] ibid [9].

[8] ibid [18].

[9] ibid [20].

[10] Sozialgericht Potsdam (Social Court Potsdam), 0 S 16 SV 8/16 ER (2016) (unpublished decision).

[11] Judging by Germaniten online appearance and the wording used, they are most likely referring to the International Labour Organization Indigenous and Tribal Peoples Convention, 1989 (No 169), which recognises Indigenous populations' interest in political independence. However, Germany ratified the Convention only in 2021 and holds there are no such communities in Germany. No immediate benefits would be won by a recognition under this Convention. The recourse on the convention is best read as an attempt to generate legitimacy for their claims to self-determination.

[12] Landessozialgericht Berlin-Brandenburg (State Social Court Berlin-Brandenburg), 1 SV 1/16 B ER (2016); Bundessozialgericht (Federal Social Court) B 13 SF 9/17 S (2017).

argued that charging him court fees was 'incompatible with ius cogens/erga omnes' and 'unrealistic to an extent that one cannot, even with an incredible amount of humour and masochism, accept'.[13] The federal social court upheld the payment order, describing the argument as 'without any basis in valid law'[14] despite the 'recourse to terms that may sound impressive to a legal layman'.[15]

All the above cases reference a supposed Indigenous population in Germany who possess a separate state. The grand language of the petitions stands in stark contrast to the dismissive rejection they receive in court. Yet, similar arguments have been heard in courts across Germany, across all levels, and in many areas of law. Indeed, several recent unpublished cases that refer to a state Germanitien concern child support payments,[16] driving without a licence and attempting to run over police officers in a traffic stop,[17] and the issuing of hundreds of false medical documents in the context of the COVID-19 pandemic.[18]

News and intelligence reports indicate that there may be several hundred 'Germaniten' across Germany,[19] and additional followers in the Netherlands and Switzerland.[20] The same applicants keep returning to the courts with the same argument, asking for re-evaluations, making further petitions, and thereby increasing the costs of the administration of justice. Some of the above cases were proactively initiated, yet the petitioners did not show up when a hearing was scheduled. As the administrative court in Hamburg notes, the entire behaviour is paradoxical: the plaintiffs denied the existence of a German state yet were appealing to its courts.

This begs a deeper question: What are we to make of such a phenomenon?

[13] Landessozialgericht Berlin-Brandenburg (n 12) [3].

[14] Bundessozialgericht (n 12) [13].

[15] ibid [12].

[16] 'Ein sogenannter Germanit beschäftigt Juristen: Gericht mit Briefen „bombardiert"' ('A so-called Germanite keeps jurists busy: court "bombarded" with letters') *Westfälische Nachrichten* (24 January 2023), www.wn.de/muensterland/kreis-steinfurt/lengerich/germanit-beschaeftigt-gericht-briefe-reichsbuerger-2695269.

[17] P Wagner, 'Prozess in Rendsburg: Bewährungsstrafe für Frau vom "Indigenen Volk der Germaniten"' ('Trial in Rendsburg: suspended sentence for woman from the "Indigenous Germanite People"') *Kieler Nachrichten* (28 February 2024) www.kn-online.de/lokales/rendsburg-eckernfoerde/prozess-in-rendsburg-bewaehrungsstrafe-fuer-frau-vom-indigenen-volk-der-germaniten-BJBCGQ-V34EOMKANFM34L54HDKY.html.

[18] A Röpke, 'Mit „Uschi" und „Uta" raus aus dem System' ('Get out of the system with "Uschi" and "Uta"') *Endstation Rechts* (24 August 2022) www.endstation-rechts.de/news/mit-uschi-und-uta-raus-aus-dem-system.

[19] G Mueller, 'Sie stehen unter Beobachtung des Verfassungsschutzes: "Indigene Germaniten" bauen Seiffener Hotel zu Schulungszentrum um' ('They are under surveillance by the Office for the Protection of the Constitution: "Indigenous Germanites" are converting the Seiffen hotel into a training centre') *Freie Presse* (6 October 2023) www.freiepresse.de/erzgebirge/marienberg/sie-stehen-unter-beobachtung-des-verfassungsschutzes-indigene-germaniten-bauen-seiffener-hotel-zu-schulungszentrum-um-artikel13078365.

[20] T Soliva, 'Vollstreckungsmassnahmen nach SchKG gegen angebliche Angehörige eines indigenen Volkes' ('Enforcement measures under SchKG against alleged members of an indigenous people') *Medienmitteilung des Thurgauer Obergerichts* (5 April 2023), obergericht.tg.ch/hauptrubrik-1/medienmitteilungen/detailseite-medienmitteilungen.html/7410/news/63219/newsarchive/1.

Far from being an isolated incident, the Germanites are part of a larger milieu that inundates state authorities with unusual claims, petitions and complaints. Because these are based on the assumption of defunct sovereignty, I follow Jan Rathje[21] and use the shorthand 'conspiratorial sovereignism' to describe this phenomenon. In this chapter, I argue that a qualitative reading of court verdicts can help make sense of what sovereignists are doing. I begin by situating the phenomenon in context and then outline my methodology. I discuss some key elements of sovereignism as it is described in the court verdicts, arguing that sovereignist law is used to reframe situations, the self, and the world.

II. A (Very) Short History of Sovereignism in Germany

After World War II, plans to re-establish the German Reich (Empire) were fostered across the political spectrum. Between the Allied occupation and the declaration of two separate German states (the Federal Republic of Germany (FRG) and the German Democratic Republic (GDR)), and various discontinuities of German territory caused by the war and military defeat, where exactly a German state was and should be, and what it should look like, remained, for a time, controversial. This is mirrored in a somewhat confused early legal doctrine of FRG statehood, which was first committed to the political vision of a unified Germany and only secondly to legal coherence.[22]

While the largest part of the population, and the centre parties, successively adjusted their political vision with the changing political reality after the war, the extreme right in Germany to this day remains tethered to a vision of a Reich that must be reclaimed against the perceived onslaught of liberalism.[23] As early as 1975, conspiratorial legal reasoning took hold in the German far right as one of several strategies for recreating the Reich. Starting from the assumption that the FRG was de jure not a state, Manfred Roeder reached out to the imprisoned Karl Dönitz, Hitler's designated successor as head of the Third Reich. When Dönitz declared that he did not consider himself head of the German state, Roeder concluded that the position was up for grabs. His followers voted him

[21] J Rathje, 'For Reich and Volksgemeinschaft – Against the World Conspiracy: Antisemitism and Sovereignism in the Federal Republic of Germany Since 1945' (2021) 5 *Antisemitism Studies* 100.

[22] C Caspar and R Neubauer, 'Durchs wilde Absurdistan – oder: Wie "Reichsbürger" den Fortbestand des Deutschen Reiches beweisen wollen' [2012] *Landes- und Kommunalverwaltung* 529; F Günther, '"Die Uhr noch einmal zurückdrehen": Die Reichsbürgerbewegung und die rechtlichen Narrative zum Fortleben des Deutschen Reiches nach 1945' in C Schönberger and S Schönberger (eds), *Die Reichsbürger. Verfassungsfeinde zwischen Staatsverweigerung und Verschwörungstheorie* (Campus Verlag, 2020) 71.

[23] D Begrich and A Speit, '„Heiliges Deutsches Reich". Reichsidee Und Reichsideologie der extremen Rechten' in A Speit (ed), *Reichsbürger. Die unterschätzte Gefahr* (Christopher Links Verlag GmbH, 2017) 22.

in as *Reichsverweser* (administrator of the Reich) and began creating their own 'government' institutions.[24]

Ten years later, former railway employee Wolfgang Ebel[25] declared he had been entrusted by the Allied Powers to restore the German Reich. Like Roeder, Ebel sought to build a counter-government that would replace a not-truly-sovereign FRG. Many would follow their examples in the coming decades, as dozens of counter-governments began to spring up across Germany. In both far-right and sovereignist milieus, the Reich functions as an imagined space of mythical retreat and a glorious future. In conspiratorial groups, this is complemented with a legal-practical claim: that in the face of a factual de jure continued existence of the Reich, its laws should rule supreme, and that by such laws, governing bodies alternative to the FRG could be legally and legitimately called into being *not qua revolution or popular consent, but qua law.*

Since then, groups and arguments have proliferated. Today, the Reich no longer takes centre stage in all of them.[26] Some, instead, focus on international conventions on self-determination or natural law ideas, sometimes couched in religious, and sometimes in a common law language. Some, like the Germanites, aspire to an alternative collective sovereignty or declare themselves sovereign individually, declaring their property their state territory. Others argue that the FRG is a company, all law commercial, and relationships to the state based on contract. The organisational structure of this milieu is loose, and most members engage with various, mutually contradictory, groups. The exchange of ideas with similar groups in other countries has become increasingly visible over the last two decades, shaping legal ideas and practices.[27] While more visible libertarian, spiritual and escapist undercurrents among German sovereignists exist today, the arguments and networks in this milieu remain firmly rooted in the extreme right.[28]

Notwithstanding amorphous organisation and varied arguments, there is something distinctive about these groups.

People who engage with these ideas argue that Germany is not a state. They believe that what we think of as state institutions – constitution, courts, governments – are just scams. The law is, in fact, a cunning system that makes you

[24] For more on Roeder, see Begrich and Speit (n 23); J Rathje, *Reichsbürger, Selbstverwalter und Souveränisten. Vom Wahn des bedrohten Deutschen* (Unrast Verlag, 2017).

[25] For details on Ebel, see C Schönberger, 'Geschichten vom Reich, Geschichten vom Recht: Der Fortbestand des deutschen Reiches als rechtliche Imagination' in C Schönberger and S Schönberger (eds), *Die Reichsbürger. Verfassungsfeinde zwischen Staatsverweigerung und Verschwörungstheorie* (Campus Verlag, 2020) 37.

[26] M Hüllen and H Homburg, '„Reichsbürger" zwischen zielgerichtetem Rechtsextremismus, Gewalt und Staatsverdrossenheit' in D Wilking (ed), *'Reichsbürger'. Ein Handbuch* (demos Brandenburgisches Institut für Gemeinwesenberatung, 3rd edn, 2018); Rathje (n 24).

[27] Hüllen and Homburg (n 26); H Berlekamp, 'Die Reichsbürger, ein internationales Phänomen. Personen und Strukturen in Österreich und der Schweiz, Kanada und den USA, Australien und Neuseeland' in A Speit (ed), *Reichsbürger. Die unterschätzte Gefahr*, vol 10184 (Christopher Links Verlag GmbH, 2017) 179.

[28] Rathje (n 21).

believe you have rights, but in truth exists to extract wealth from an unsuspecting population in the form of taxes and fines. The law works like a smokescreen: it hides the conspiracy and makes us willingly submit to our exploitation. And the law is also the tool that allowed the conspirators to take control through some legal change that ostensibly says one thing but means another. To explain who profits from this elaborate plot, they employ conspiratorial, often antisemitic narratives. As a consequence, sovereignists believe that they do not need to follow state law, and they establish their own counter-institutions. People in these groups are constantly in conflict with state authorities due to their belief that state law should not apply to them.

These assumptions are shared by groups elsewhere, whose unconventional legal arguments have often been dubbed 'pseudolaw'.[29] The German sovereignists form part of this larger international phenomenon, constructing and exchanging structurally similar arguments about the state and individual rights and obligations: readers familiar with arguments advanced in other countries may recognise the arguments I use to illustrate my analysis.

III. The Empirical Analysis of German Sovereignism

Like Stephen Young, Harry Hobbs and Joe McIntyre, I was baffled by the central and paradoxical role of law in these groups. It is the attraction of law for these groups that my doctoral research investigates, observing court hearings, speaking to sovereignists and legal professionals, as well as online research. As part of this research, I looked to published court decisions for answers.

Others[30] have skilfully described the legal errors that German sovereignists commit. Some studies internationally have grouped cases with sovereignists by litigation goals or developed typologies of sovereignist arguments.[31] These studies informed my analysis. However, in this study, my main focus is to better understand what drives the paradoxical use of law. I therefore ask: Can a close reading of published court cases tell us more about what sovereignists may be trying to achieve with their legal arguments? Attention to more subtle clues contained in interaction patterns and wording may reveal something about sovereignists'

[29] DJ Netolitzky, 'A Rebellion of Furious Paper: Pseudolaw as a Revolutionary Legal System' (2018); S Young, H Hobbs and J McIntyre, 'The Growth of Pseudolaw and Sovereign Citizens in Aotearoa New Zealand Courts' (2023) 47 *New Zealand Law Journal* 6; C McRoberts, 'Tinfoil Hats and Powdered Wigs: Thoughts on Pseudolaw' (2019) 58 *Washburn Law Journal* 637.

[30] Caspar and Neubauer (n 22); M Vorbaum, '„Reichsbürger" und Strafrecht' (2017) 10 *Juristische Rundschau* 503.

[31] Netolitzky (n 30); S Barrows, 'Sovereigns, Freemen, and Desperate Souls: Towards a Rigorous Understanding of Pseudolitigation Tactics in United States Courts' (2021) 62 *Boston College Law Review* 905; Young, Hobbs and McIntyre (n 30); B Slater, 'Sovereign Citizen Movement: An Empirical Study on the Rise in Activity, Explanations of Growth, and Policy Prescriptions' Master's Thesis, Naval Postgraduate University (2016).

intentions beyond winning whatever is at stake in the decision. In this section, I outline my methodology and dataset, before moving on to the qualitative analysis in the next section.

In this chapter, I focus primarily on a qualitative analysis of a dataset of 253 court verdicts published by 2020. Sovereignist cases are challenging to identify in online databases. Many verdicts do not explicitly mention sovereignist beliefs, as they are considered irrelevant to the legal matter at hand.[32] Cases discuss a multitude of issues. And sovereignist arguments take countless different shapes. A legal professional I interviewed for my doctoral dissertation shared with me a list of published cases he had compiled in years of legal practice. I snowballed further cases based on mentioned verdicts and, to a limited extent, keyword searches (ie 'Reichsbürger' but also laws typically used by sovereignists, such as Article 146 of the Basic Law).

Once I identified the cases, I read them against a range of criteria. I used Nvivo to categorise cases according to legal classifications and demographic information. I then coded the decision text based on an open coding system.[33] I started with a list of codes developed from my familiarity with existing research and the milieu. This coding system was amended throughout the coding process, adding codes as required to keep track of unexpected findings.

Overall, I categorised and coded:

- demographic information (age, sex, occupation, family and biographic information);
- case facts (area of law, type of case, date, court);
- interaction patterns (ie case history, records of interaction predating case at hand, previous convictions, case outcomes); and, most interestingly,
- elements of sovereignist law (ie arguments, behaviours, rhetoric, authorities, emotions).

In the following, I briefly explain the findings about demographics, case facts and interaction patterns before discussing the elements of sovereignist law.

A. Demographic Information

Sovereignists involved in these cases come from a wide range of economic and educational backgrounds. Biographical information is not always stated in verdicts, but available information indicates white-collar workers, civil servants, self-employed, working-class and unemployed people can find sovereignism attractive.

[32] In my doctoral research I saw case files of sovereignists that had no mention of their arguments in the verdict text, leading me to assume more cases than identified exist. Such cases I saw were unpublished. For consistency, I have excluded unpublished cases from this analysis.

[33] J Gläser and G Laudel, *Experteninterviews und qualitative Inhaltsanalyse* 4th edn (VS Verlag für Sozialwissenschaften, 2010) 198.

Most decisions withhold age for anonymisation, but where it is mentioned, it is predominantly above 50. Most sovereignists are male, though there are several cases with female plaintiffs and in a few, a married couple or family acts together. This conforms to what is known about the milieu from police statistics.[34]

B. Case Facts

The earliest case in the resulting dataset was decided in 2002. I am aware of earlier cases, but these are not available in online databases. Until 2011, the number of cases per year is under five, until 2015 under 10. In 2017, 2018 and 2019, the yearly number of cases was around 50, and in 2020, 25. This fluctuation may be indicative of changes in litigation but is likely also indicative of a form of detection bias. In 2016, a police officer was fatally shot when attempting to remove weapons from a sovereignist whose permit had been revoked. This incident increased awareness of this phenomenon and likely prompted the publishing of more cases. The drop in published cases in 2020 is likely due to reduced operational capacity of courts during the pandemic.

In my dataset, of 168 cases heard in low-level courts, only three cases were heard in courts of 'ordinary justice', but 141 were in low-level administrative courts. Nine cases were heard on a federal level, one in the highest instance in the court system, the *Bundesverfassungsgericht*. The rest were heard in the mid-level courts. Put differently, over 200 cases were heard in administrative courts, 20 each in social and financial courts, and eight in ordinary justice. In analysing the dataset, I initially categorised cases according to their respective areas of law and specific topics ('case sets'). However, I subsequently grouped them based on common themes or patterns that transcended their legal classifications ('case groups'). This revealed a strong pooling in certain areas.

The largest case group contains 170 cases in administrative law. These cases happen as a result of someone attempting to realise sovereignist law: engaging in legal practices they believe remove them from the authority of the FRG, such as returning ID cards or failing to pay minor fees and fines by arguing that the FRG law is not valid or applicable. Where the law requires reassurance that a person will follow legally proscribed behaviour, these 'on the record' behaviours become a red flag. To authorities, they indicate that a person does not only hold some immaterial or abstract belief that the FRG is not a state (protected by fundamental rights), but is also willing to act on that belief. In court decisions, how closely sovereignist beliefs can be linked to future (un-)reliability is generally measured through the behaviours they have exhibited towards authorities in the past and in the course of the case in question. This makes them easy to identify in databases, partially explaining their prevalence in the dataset.

[34] JG Keil, 'Zur Abgrenzung des Milieus der „Reichsbürger" – Pathologisierung des Politischen und Politisierung des Pathologischen' (2021) 15 *Forensische Psychiatrie, Psychologie, Kriminologie* 255.

Almost half of all cases in the entire dataset pertain to weapons law. Most of them occurred after the 2016 murder of a police officer caused a spike in permit removals and related appeals.[35] I grouped these cases with over 20 similar cases relating to permits such as work safety checks for nuclear sites, air traffic as well as driving licences. These cases typically involve sovereignists appealing a decision by state authorities to withdraw or not renew permissions. I also added almost 30 cases on disciplinary measures – removal from office, a demotion, or removal of state pensions – against sovereignist state employees, to this group. In addition to public safety concerns, these cases discuss public faith in state institutions and civil servants' obligation to uphold the constitutional order.

The second largest group of case sets concerns cases that are about claiming some sort of financial benefit. Several cases concern sovereignist attempts to not pay contributions to social insurance and taxes, while others attempt to claim higher benefits. Cases in social benefit law are the third largest subset with over 25 cases, followed by tax law with over 20 cases. Several researchers in other countries have pointed to the prominent role of tax protest and rejection for sovereignists. This is only to a limited extent mirrored in this dataset: it is the fourth largest subset, but only after weapons, disciplinary, and social welfare law.

A third notable group, though just over 10 cases, concerns nationality law. German sovereignists are almost exclusively German nationals, born and raised in Germany, and their nationality is not in question by anyone but themselves. Yet, they petition courts to certify a particular formulation of their German identity, such as by reference to outdated legislation of the German Reich. This is noteworthy, and I will return to this in the qualitative analysis.

C. Interaction Patterns

Regarding interaction patterns, published verdicts often contain some information on prior convictions, prior appearances before courts, and prior confrontational interactions with the state in general. Where this information is provided, it indicates that many have no criminal history. But on the other hand, many sovereignists repeatedly clash with state institutions in their rejection of state authority and in diverse areas of life. Many published cases from higher instances record a previous march through the institutions and list other conflicts with state institutions the same person had been involved in. They indicate, like the cases with the Germaniten, that people are not deterred from using sovereignist arguments if they have previously lost court cases.

According to the verdicts, not a single case was decided because the court was convinced by sovereignist (as opposed to conventional) arguments. In rare

[35] C Janz and A Speit, '„Wir sind im Krieg". Waffen innerhalb der Szene' in A Speit (ed), *Reichsbürger. Die unterschätzte Gefahr* (Christopher Links Verlag GmbH, 2017) 115.

instances, courts decide in favour of sovereignists or at least not entirely to their detriment. This is usually because the nature of the evidence presented does not allow for the state action under consideration (ie the removal of a permit, a disciplinary measure, or a policing measure) or because of an earlier error committed by state institutions (ie procedural mistakes).

D. Situating the Dataset in Context

Interviews with judges, prosecutors and sovereignists, as well as observation of sovereignist online communities, suggest that most interactions sovereignists have with the legal system occur in lower-level courts and involve contesting small and mundane matters: not stopping at a traffic stop, objecting to the requirement to purchase a TV licence, refusing to show ID, refusing the census, altering licence plates and improper insurance. Another type of case I came across frequently in fieldwork concerned minor criminal charges, such as cases for insult or for resisting arrest. Both aspects are mirrored in the case history and biographical data that verdicts sometimes contain. Yet only very few published verdicts concern these topics.

In the German civil law system, comparatively few court verdicts are published in general. Studies on datasets from the 1990s have estimated the publication ratio at an average of under one per cent of all cases, with almost no first-instance decisions published.[36] Published cases are typically those deemed relevant for legal discourse and public interest. However, in cases involving sovereignists, this is often deemed not to be the case. This skews my dataset towards certain types of cases, further explaining the extreme pooling in the first dataset, which evaluates state sanctions.

However, the published verdicts cover a wide range of topics and contain a wealth of information on case history and on sovereignist arguments. Most importantly, the arguments, rhetorical devices and interaction patterns are strikingly similar across all areas of law and all levels of the justice system. This indicates that to understand the attitudes of sovereignists to the law, a close qualitative reading of such recurrent elements is a more fruitful way of analysing published verdicts. It is this task I turn to in the next section.

IV. Common Elements of Sovereignist Law

The qualitative coding of the sovereignist cases revealed recurrent themes that can be found in the rhetorical devices, arguments and interaction patterns the

[36] M Stock and WG Stock, 'Digitale Rechts- und Wirtschaftsinformationen bei LexisNexis' (2005) 82 *JurPC*, DOI 10.7328/jurpcd/200520781.

decisions depict. I will introduce each theme with examples from my dataset and examine what it reveals about sovereignism, drawing on existing literature in the field to situate my analysis. The themes indicate answers to a set of questions about what sovereignists may be trying to achieve. First, I examine what the analysis reveals about the effect sovereignists hope their arguments will have on interactions with state institutions. Second, I discuss why sovereignist arguments are attractive even though they are costly. Third, I ask why sovereignists seek out the legal system in the first place if they reject the authority of the state. Fourth, I examine what is so attractive about framing arguments legally. I close with a fifth section that summarises the previous sections as indicating that sovereignism allows people to reframe their identity and world. Of course, the answers to the questions I raised are multifactorial. Here, I only indicate some answers based on the most prevalent characteristics revealed in the coding process.

A. Sovereignists Attempt to Define the Rules of Engagement

In this section, I examine what the decisions reveal about how sovereignists hope their arguments will affect the court case at hand. The coding revealed that sovereignists attempt to set the rules of engagement by using rhetorical devices that aim to control the structure and content of the court proceedings by setting timelines, reversing the burden of evidence, and reversing the overall capacity to decide on rules. Often, these arguments do not directly counter, but rather sidestep the requirements placed on them by authorities.

In his analysis of the milieu's age profile, Jan-Gerrit Keil, a psychologist with German criminal police, highlights how many sovereignists seem to turn to this thinking after a 'biographical break' – a crisis such as the loss of job, a family break-up, or decline in health. He interprets their turn to sovereignism as an attempt to make sense of their experience or reorder their life.[37] A similar motivation appears to exist among US sovereignists. As Robert Black highlights, law 'purports to be not only a history that explains, but also [a] technique which controls'.[38] This desire for control shines through the behaviour and language of sovereignists cited in the judgments.

Sovereignists often[39] submit statements such as 'You have silently refrained from raising legal obstacles, therefore, what I have written applies'.[40] The writer

[37] JG Keil, '„Reichsbürger" und Selbstverwalter – (k)ein Problem der Jugend?' (2018) 2 *Zeitschrift für Jugendkriminalrecht und Jugendhilfe* 126.

[38] RC Black '"Constitutionalism": The White Man's Ghost Dance' (1998) 31 *John Marshall Law Review* 513, 514.

[39] Netolitzky (n 29).

[40] Verwaltungsgericht Ansbach (Administrative Court Ansbach), AN 13b D 19.01044, (2020) rewis.

explains that because his declaration remained without contradiction, it is now an enforceable agreement. In the German context, this argument is often used to determine the timeline of cases. Sovereignists hope to create cut-off points, after which they no longer have to engage with authorities. The language and style of such letters imitate the way that authorities communicate deadlines for appeals and complaints.

In one tax case, a sovereignist responds to a request for information by threatening to sue the tax office clerk with the German Reich and inform the occupation powers. This could only be averted if the authorities can 'show with evidence that they rely on a valid legal basis'.[41] Confronted with a request to justify why he does not need to pay taxes, he instead asks that the court justify the legal basis of its requests. Sovereignists regularly declare that they would like to comply with the court if only it can produce a specific type of evidence for the legitimacy of their action within a set timeframe. They may ask for proof of the existence of the FRG, a valid foundation document of the federal state they live in, a certain form of signature, or an oath of office. All these examples attempt to place the burden of evidence on state institutions. Such arguments play and expand on existing ideas about bureaucratic institutions' obligation to act in legally proscribed, documented and transparent ways. The sort of proof that sovereignists request is usually impossible to meet because it does not exist or is not legally required. Yet, such arguments draw on the common idea that in a democracy, a state under the rule of law, the bureaucracy should be accountable to citizens and able to explain their authority and reasoning. They are intended as a challenge to the courts: 'Prove me wrong if you can'.

Regularly, sovereignists reject entire legal codes or the basis of the legal order itself. By undermining the legal basis, sovereignists attempt to outright dismiss and immediately end cases. They argue that the FRG is not truly sovereign and lacks the legal and moral authority to command the coercive power we associate with the state. Often, they say this power lies with some other authority, such as the German Reich. But sometimes, German sovereignists use a more fundamental argument. In a 2014 submission to a social benefits office 'rejecting' an order to supplement a parent's upkeep, a sovereignist writes:

> Your above-mentioned demands are ultimately based on the Basic Law. Neither my ancestors nor I have legitimized the Basic Law or the laws based on it … Furthermore, the Basic Law is obviously illegal according to its own provisions anyway and the laws etc. based on it are null and void.[42]

According to this argument, because neither he, nor his ancestors, personally ratified the Constitution, it cannot be valid. The idea that all law is based on

[41] Finanzgericht Berlin-Brandenburg (Finance Court Berlin-Brandenburg), 4 K 1739/04, (2012) OpenJur 2419.

[42] Oberverwaltungsgericht des Landes Sachsen-Anhalt (Higher Administrative Court of the State of Saxony-Anhalt), 10 L 9/17, (2018) OpenJur 8708.

contract has been identified as a core principle in pseudolaw internationally.[43] It is mirrored in the insistence that Germany is a 'company' I noted in the introduction. In emphasising consent, this argument rejects the state's authority to define basic rules for social and political life regardless of individual consent.

My analysis of the cases confirms existing literature on sovereignism, suggesting that law is attractive to such marginal actors because they hope to usurp this control and hijack the authority associated with law. This suggests that law is an attractive vehicle for conspiracy narratives because it seemingly 'offers the possibility of mastery over the conditions of one's life that is rarely possible in contemporary mass society'.[44] This desire here expresses itself in attempts to control the conditions of interactions with state authorities.

B. Why Persist in Using Legal Argument that has been Rejected? Improving Self-perception

As I noted when discussing interaction patterns, case outcomes are rarely favourable to sovereignists. What makes people persist in using these arguments even when they have been previously rejected? Most cases originate in a reaction to quite mundane and individual issues. However, relying on sovereignism allows them to present their dispute as something much more dynamic: by situating them in a larger argument about German sovereignty, they obtain a new significance as the fight of an oppressed minority against an unlawful state.

One illustration of this form of argumentation arises in the tendency to frame disputes as being derived from unresolved issues regarding the military occupation of Germany. These modern arguments are an evolution of early sovereignist arguments that contemporary German state institutions are, in fact, organs of ongoing military occupation. According to this theory, the military occupation of Germany after WWII was never disbanded and was instead slowly hidden from plain sight.[45] The contemporary version argues that as Germany remains

[43] This position raises some interesting issues about how legal legitimacy is perceived. This has been discussed by others. W Huhn, 'Political Alienation in America and the Legal Premises of the Patriot Movement' (1999) 34 *Gonzaga Law Review* 417; DL Levin and MW Mitchell, 'A Law unto Themselves: The Ideology of the Common Law Court Movement' (1999) 44 *South Dakota Law Review* 9; F Walter and A Kretschmann, 'Recht als Imagination und Symbol' in C Schönberger and S Schönberger (eds), *Die Reichsbürger. Verfassungsfeinde zwischen Staatsverweigerung und Verschwörungstheorie* (Campus Verlag, 2020) 127; S Schönberger, 'Das imaginäre des Rechts: Wer ist hier eigentlich verrückt?' in C Schönberger and S Schönberger (eds), *Die Reichsbürger. Verfassungsfeinde zwischen Staatsverweigerung und Verschwörungstheorie* (Campus Verlag, 2020) 1.

[44] AP Harris, 'Vultures in Eagles' Clothing: Conspiracy and Racial Fantasy in Populist Legal Thought' (2005) 10 *Michigan Journal of Race and Law* 269, 272.

[45] This idea is used to explain the visibly existing administrative, executive and legal institutions of the FRG. It fits into various broader narratives about what happened to German sovereignty, such as that Germany had not been sovereign since the emperor abdicated in 1918, or that the German Basic Law was invalidated when the reunification treaties were signed.

occupied, it is the Hague Convention that provides the substantive law to apply to its territory. The Hague Convention is a series of multilateral treaties establishing the laws of war by defining the rules belligerents must follow during hostilities and occupation. It holds great sway in sovereigntist circles and seems particularly attractive to people who face seizure of assets, arguing that this is 'pillaging'.[46] In front of the social courts, at least 10 cases discuss whether the Hague Convention is applicable to social benefits. The LSG München sums up such a claim as follows:

> According to Art. 7 The Hague Convention, which in her [the claimant, AL] opinion applies, the government in whose power the prisoners of war are held must provide for their upkeep. … According to Article 120 of the Basic Law, the federal government had to bear the expenses incurred by the occupation. As a prisoner of war, she had to be treated like a soldier in the Bundeswehr and was entitled to maintenance in accordance with A2 pay grade, level I.[47]

This argument is ostensibly about pensions. It is obviously an unusual way of attempting to claim benefits and one that will be immediately rejected by any authority it is presented to. What seems to make this argument so powerful, such that sovereignists repeatedly persist in their claim through the courts and in appeals, is the reframing of social roles it offers. This framing emphasises the right of the plaintiff as a sufferer of injustice, a different position to that of a supplicant. It is that reframed position which entitles them to higher payments, which they feel comfortable asking for precisely because they are not looking for charity.

This framing has multiple unintended effects. Claimants might be entitled to benefits under contemporary German law. However, courts find that state institutions have no obligation to decide on such a petition because German law does not provide for payment under the Hague Convention.[48] The LSG Niedersachsen-Bremen[49] confirms a lower court's stance that according to the plaintiff's logic, the occupying power would be the United Kingdom and Northern Ireland and that he would be free to assert his claims there. Almost all decisions note the contradictory stance of appealing to the courts of a supposedly non-existent state indicates the petition is abusive of law and does not require evaluation. While sovereignists file petitions based on the Hague Convention, they may miss deadlines for applications, appeals and complaints in their FRG benefits procedures.[50]

[46] Verwaltungsgericht Ansbach (Administrative Court Ansbach), AN 5 K 12.01332, (2013) OpenJur 5032.

[47] Bayerisches Landesozialgericht (Bavarian State Social Court), L 1 SV 8/17 B ER, (2020) OpenJur 60619.

[48] Sozialgericht Düsseldorf (Social Court Düsseldorf), S 28 SO 683/13, (2015) OpenJur 21879.

[49] Landessozialgericht Niedersachsen-Bremen (State Social Court Lower Saxony-Bremen), L 8 SO 31/14 B ER, (2015) OpenJur 1436.

[50] Landessozialgericht Sachsen-Anhalt (State Social Court Lower Saxony-Anhalt), L 8 SO 24/15 B ER, (2020) OpenJur 26658.

Despite the legal arguments remaining ineffective and even counterproductive, these cases indicate that sovereignism is partially about proactively claiming things for oneself that are both monetary and symbolic. It symbolically alters the roles: from a plaintiff facing a benefactor to a victim claiming compensation from the perpetrator. Their individual struggle is placed within a historical trajectory which bestows a grander meaning.

C. Why do Sovereignists Seek Out the Legal System if they Reject its Authority? Courts Know about True Law

In this section, I ask why sovereignists seek out the legal system in the first place if they reject the authority of the state? I argue that sovereignists assume that at least some state officials are aware of and bound by law as understood by sovereignists. This results in strategic litigation behaviour.

As I indicated before, one subset of cases sovereignists bring to the courts concerns nationality law. The cases in this subset are not immediate reactions to government actions. Rather, they are motions or claims proactively brought before the courts in an attempt to have the courts certify alternative concepts of citizenship and belonging.

These proactive filings are often part of a multitiered strategy by sovereignists to remove themselves from the jurisdiction of the FRG: while other conflicts are not part of the case at hand, the same person is likely involved in other cases in front of the courts. By attempting to have an argument or technique of right-claiming assessed, sovereignists anticipate an institutional trickle-down effect, where other courts and state offices would then have to recognise their claim. The nationality cases, just like the example of the Germanites in the introduction, show that sovereignists share arguments and legal templates that make their way into numerous cases in different courts, on different topics, and at different times. It seems, sovereignist actors are trying to produce a shift in legal paradigm. A webpage connected to the Germanites, illustrated with the slogan 'We clear the path!', shares an instruction booklet in a section titled 'Help to self-help for laypeople/nonlawyers'.[51]

Some sovereignists calculate the risk that using these templates implies and state their willingness to 'sacrifice' themselves.[52] Being convinced of their truth and situating their individual struggle as part of a larger struggle for true law and freedom makes this risk worthwhile.[53]

[51] *Justiz-Opfer-Hilfe Deutschland*, www.joh-nrw.com/blog/selbsthilfe-fuer-nichtjuristen.

[52] Landgericht Rottweil (Regional Court Rottweil), 11 Strafkammer 11 Ns 20 Js 1338/14, (2016) juris.

[53] Bayerischer Verwaltungsgerichtshof (Bavarian Administrative Court), VGH 10 ZB 19.2459, (2020) OpenJur 49793. This case discusses a sort of sovereignist vigilante group. A few such groups have existed. Because they often engage in violence and are seen as obviously threatening to the state's monopoly of violence, they are met with more severe and swift repercussions than other activities by the milieu.

Sovereignists seem to believe that judges will ultimately understand and agree with their arguments. For example, one court decision quotes a sovereignist declaring in a prior interaction with a town hall official that the civil servant, 'as an official of the city of … would know exactly that the defendant was right with his statements'.[54]

Sovereignists often declare that only a document that is hand-signed in a specific way is valid and that judges are trying to avoid responsibility for colluding with the conspiracy by creating invalid documents through invalid signatures.[55] This way, judges could pretend that the people in front of the court chose to comply with the verdicts – that are formally invalid – out of their own free will. As I outlined above, sovereignists believe that the courts can act only if those before it willingly submit to it. Therefore, sovereignists continuously point out what they identify as legal errors. They assume they are demonstrating a superior understanding of the hidden rules, making it impossible for the judges to uphold their 'charade'. This is often coupled with threats of consequences, that judges could no longer hide by claiming they had not been made aware.

In this way, sovereignists often assert they know that the courts recognise true law to pre-empt shared understanding and assert dominance. Sovereignists engage with legal processes and conventional legal sources because they are hoping to force a recognition of their stance in the state's language and institutions. They seek out state institutions proactively, acting strategically rather than aiming at an immediate benefit to produce shifts in legal paradigms.

D. What is Attractive about Legal Framing? Conformist Rebellion

As I argued in the history section, many arguments are embedded in far-right narratives. Closely reading sovereignist submissions to court, the political intentions of their arguments shine through. If their goals are political, why are they using legal arguments? As Netolitzky has pointed out, sovereignists are 'a kind of anti-state rebel, but one who believes revolution can be achieved by superior law, rather than force or democratic choice'.[56] Do the verdicts contain indications of why such a 'lawful rebellion', as some English language groups self-describe their behaviour,[57] is attractive?

[54] Verwaltungsgericht Ansbach (Administrative Court Ansbach), An 13b D 19.00958, (2020) OpenJur 50002 [42].

[55] Verwaltungsgericht Ansbach (Administrative Court Ansbach), 13b D 18.00529, (2019) BeckRS 29392; Finanzgericht Münster (Finance Court Münster), 1 K 3123/14 F, (2015) OpenJur 15457; Finanzgericht Berlin-Brandenburg (Finance Court Berlin-Brandenburg), 6 K 6106/15, (2015) OpenJur 41563.

[56] Netolitzky (n 29) 9.

[57] DJ Netolitzky, 'Ten Seconds to Implosion: The Magna Carta Lawful Rebellion' (2023) 6 *International Journal of Coercion, Abuse, and Manipulation*, DOI: 10.54208/1000/0006/003.

In 2019, the administrative court in Düsseldorf confirmed the legality of disciplinary measures against a police superintendent.[58] In 2016, the superintendent sent his passport to his council with a petition to remove his registration as 'German' and instead register him as a citizen of the 'Kingdom of Prussia'. In his petition, he explains that the FRG is only a *Scheinstaat*, a pseudo-state, the citizenship category 'German' a national-socialist category that would deprive him of his human rights, and that the true shape of the German state was that of the 1871 Reich. To bolster his argument, he quotes extensively from legal dictionaries and furnishes his assertions with long lists of articles of law. In a written submission to the appeals court in 2019 he wrote:

> From now on, I reserve the right to file charges in accordance with §186, 187 StGB against anyone who continues to refer to me or judges me as a 'Reichsbürger', as belonging to the 'Reichsbürger', as being 'close to the ideology of Reichsbürger' (in the sense of confused, radicalized, political persons or 'fringe groups'), or as 'rejecting the legal system'! All my actions, written statements and justifications are based on the existing legal system! Conclusions and logical consequences resulted from a conscientious (i.e. without influencing a conviction, opinion or attitude), purely factual and as objective as possible examination of the subject matter! Since my entire argumentation is based on logic, the accusation of 'adhering' to an ideology (i.e. the opposite of logic) is completely unfounded!

The police superintendent describes himself as someone concerned for and with the law. He achieves this by drawing on formalism. He does not alter or defend his substantive stance, but rather vindicates it by emphasising the validity and neutrality of the means with which he reached it. He uses legal language as a technocratic, apolitical justification for radical political opinions, aiming at a total overthrow of state and society. Ultimately, most of his statements contained in the verdict express his desire to recreate the monarchical order of 1871 and are directed against what he perceives as a dilution of Germanness through European integration. He ends his statement with the words:

> Quod ultimum verbum: In my responsibility before God and my ancestors, I refer in my actions to Art. 20.4 of the Basic Law and conclude with the "word" (dogma) of a high personality: 'When right becomes wrong, resistance becomes a duty, but obedience becomes a crime'.

The quoted law defines the citizen's right to resist anyone attempting to overthrow the constitutional order. Here again, drawing on law, he is affirming his assessment that the FRG is an unjust, undemocratic state against which citizens have the right and even duty to resist. Despite the multiple pages of his submissions that the court quotes in the verdict, there is no substantive argument presented for this position. The 'crimes against humanity' he accuses the FRG of are defined in

[58] Verwaltungsgericht Düsseldorf (Administrative Court Düsseldorf), 35 K 3745/19.O, (2019) OpenJur 34466.

terms of improper wording of bureaucratic categories. Both the arguments and the language used by this claimant are extremely common in my dataset.

The rhetoric of sovereignists often displays the Manichean thinking characteristic of conspiracy theorising,[59] using language that attempts to generate moral outrage. Sovereignists time and again threaten public servants by claiming they are personally liable, and their behaviour punishable with severe fines or even death. This extreme sentiment is both justified and almost softened with the assertion that this is merely a legal assessment. In response to being asked to fill out a tax questionnaire, a sovereignist argues the questionnaire would be without legal basis,

> as the Weimar constitution is still the law in force. From a purely legal point of view, by sending the questionnaire, the defendant [the tax authority] was therefore committing usurpation of office, treason and high treason, which is still punishable by death.[60]

These examples indicate that sovereignism allows people to defend actions and beliefs that are far outside of what is commonly thought of as acceptable, by appealing to legal authorisation. It protects their self-image as a moral person and law-abiding citizen. And it justifies their political beliefs as though they are not making any choices or judgements at all – it is just an inevitable, technocratic, fact.

In his study of European bureaucracy, Michael Herzfeld suggests that citizens' attempts to appropriate state-legal discourses to question the legitimacy of the very same discourse can be read as an attempt 'to play the state at its own game'.[61] Adopting this metaphor, sovereignist legal arguments are telling state institutions: 'I understand your game, you are cheating, and I will not be playing'. Instead of being stuck in a game, sovereignists take the bird's eye view of the labyrinth of bureaucratic process and reject being forced to play by the 'wrong' rules, because they have discovered the true rule book that the cheating players have tried to hide. This move must be recognised by other players, embodied by the judge, police, insurance provider, etc, *because it follows the rules*.

Despite the diversity of rules followed within the milieu and the high degree of personalisation, leading to a heterogenous appearance of the phenomenon, sovereignism only makes sense if we read it as an attempt at superior, not rule-breaking or rule-rejecting, behaviour. The capacity of law to frame rebellious behaviour as essentially conformist, legally and socially compliant, appears to be very attractive.

[59] Rathje (n 24) 42; A Pfahl-Traughber, '„Bausteine" einer Theorie über „Verschwörungstheorien". Definitionen, Erscheinungsformen, Funktionen und Ursachen' in H Reinalter (ed), *Verschwörungstheorien. Theorie, Geschichte, Wirkung* (Studien Verlag, 2002) 30.

[60] Oberverwaltungsgericht des Landes Sachsen-Anhalt (n 42).

[61] M Herzfeld, *The Social Production of Indifference: Exploring the Symbolic Roots of Western Bureaucracy (1992)* (University of Chicago Press, 1993) 145.

E. Summary: Reframing Self and World Through Law

In this last section, I argue that sovereignists use law creatively to assert their humanity in the face of a bureaucracy they experience as depersonalising. They use law to symbolically place themselves into a new context of meaning.

Many interactions of sovereign citizens with courts revolve around the construction and assertion of identity. Sovereignists' submissions to court are often extremely abstract, discussing the state of law and sovereignty, and world history, moving back through the centuries and up through ever more abstract levels of politics. Yet, sovereignist letters I saw in my fieldwork were often curiously personalised. They were written in coloured inks that change over the course of a letter and in the course of a case. Some were entirely handwritten. Others contained DNA samples, red thumbprints, footprints, coloured borders, coats of arms, individual signatures on every page, and ancestry records.

This personalisation is mirrored in the court verdicts, too. One plaintiff interjects in a long list of arguments: 'I don't want to keep from you that I am a German national according to Art 4 para 1 RuStag (1913). I would thus ask you to stop treating me like a slave, with whom you can do as you please.'[62] The administrative court in Munich quotes a plaintiff's declaration concerning the withdrawal of a weapons permit:

> He, the person …, was in full possession of his physical and mental powers, a man and from the house and family … He was born a free man in … in the former Kingdom of Bavaria. Rooted exclusively in natural law, it was his express will as a living, animated and free human being, who had not been lost at sea or anywhere else, to no longer conform to the legal cataloguing and registration of 'BRiD' personnel. He distances himself from the past and future from the beautiful appearance that has made him a slave, lawless and outlawed stateless person with the citizenship 'German' assigned to him by the state fiction 'BRiD' and claims for himself – thanks to his second citizenship of the Kingdom of Bavaria inherited through the jus sanguis – a BEING on the level of a free person in the legal status of January 1, 1896, subject to the Reich. Connected with the act of creation for the restoration of freedom, legal capacity and humanity is, with immediate effect, the non-entitlement and non-liability of the state-created fiction of the 'legal person'; with immediate effect, he bears the surname … from the house and the family … and live in freedom and sovereignty – which is to say: obliged only to God and himself.[63]

Sovereignist discourse, as observed through these verdicts, describes a juxtaposition. On one side, when articulating how they imagine the Federal Republic frames them, they use terms like thing, object, slave, legal person, personnel, lost at sea, lawless, outlawed and rightless. On the opposing side, when defining how they understand their own identity, they use terms like alive, soulful, spirited, full capacity, rights, of the family, ancestry, freedom and sovereignty, and natural

[62] See (n 55); also Oberverwaltungsgericht Thüringen (Higher Administrative Court Thuringia), 2 EO 887/16, (2017) OpenJur 1655.

[63] Verwaltungsgericht München (Administrative Court Munich), 7 K 17.750, (2020) OpenJur 55879.

person. This identity is seen to be protected by natural law, God or the German Reich and its states.

A dominant trend in critical legal studies and legal anthropology focuses on the oppressive capacities of law, discussing how law masks and upholds inequalities. This literature often thinks of legal categories as flattening the world, drawing experiences, people and histories into a world of paper and neat categories; cramming complex characteristics and trajectories into boxes that must fit countless other (not so) alike cases.[64] In a way, sovereignists appear to critique this flattening when they reject legally defined personhood and replace it with a more profound, spiritually charged identity as 'a spirited being' 'a man of the family', and not a 'Mr. so-and-so'.

But this indicates that legal categories can also be used creatively to humanise. As Mayur Suresh highlights in his study of terror trials in India,[65] his interlocutors learned to speak and use law as a way of inhabiting the world and striving to create a future for themselves. They made creative use of the law which exceeded its intended purposes. Sovereignists also use law in an imaginative way:[66] their use of legal language exhibits an existential search for a fuller meaning, redefining central elements such as naming conventions and concepts such as human, person, and nationality.

Thomas Schmidt-Lux has exploratively explained sovereignism as a form of symbolic emigration. A concept originating in religious studies, it describes how converts symbolically place themselves in contrast to their prior context of life by converting.[67] It allows them to replace their existing context with a more satisfying concept of meaning and belonging. Sovereignists are doing the same when confronted with legal problems or a crisis of meaning, they symbolically place themselves in a new context by assuming this new identity as, say, 'Prussian'.

V. Concluding Thoughts

Sovereignists often worsen their situation by attempting to practise sovereignist law. Unlike what sovereignist blogs advertise – presenting the right argument and walking out of court happy and unbothered – the vast majority of case outcomes are to sovereignists' detriment. No court decision I know was positively influenced by sovereignist arguments.

[64] A Barros, 'Water Justice, Mining, and the Fetish Form of Law in the Atacama Desert' in S Brunnegger and KA Faulk (eds), *A Sense of Justice: Legal Knowledge and Lived Experience in Latin America* (Stanford University Press, 2016), doi.org/10.1515/9780804799119-010; B Latour, *The Making of Law : An Ethnography of the Conseil d'Etat* (Polity, 2010).

[65] MR Suresh, *Terror Trials: Life and Law in Delhi's Courts* (Fordham University Press, 2023).

[66] Walter and Kretschmann (n 44).

[67] T Schmidt-Lux, 'Reichsbürgerschaft als symbolische Emigration' in C Schönberger and S Schönberger (eds), *Die Reichsbürger. Verfassungsfeinde zwischen Staatsverweigerung und Verschwörungstheorie* (Campus Verlag, 2020) 101.

The cases I highlighted in this chapter reveal that people follow sovereignist law at high personal costs, sometimes implying the loss of livelihood when licences are revoked and jobs are lost. But sovereignism causes users to incur costs in multiple other ways: encouraging hopeless appeals and complaints; dragging out cases; missing legally relevant deadlines for appeals and complaints by filing papers that do not fulfil legal requirements; and encouraging a confrontational stance that can result in additional charges for disrespectful, insulting or threatening behaviour.

Many courts have rejected sovereignist claims as abusive of law because of the paradoxical nature of the stance overall. Without a state codifying rights and backing them with institutions that can be called upon to enforce them, appealing to a court is nonsensical.[68]

Despite the seeming ineffectiveness of sovereignist law, analysing the context of cases in which they use it and the outcomes they seek reveals that sovereignists desire certain benefits and reject the intervention of more powerful actors in their lives. Sovereignism promises control and provides rhetorical devices intended to reverse power dynamics. The opportunistic element of the use of law in these movements has often been highlighted in the literature.[69]

But opportunism in itself does not explain what makes sovereignism attractive. Looking at the interaction patterns of sovereignists with courts, it becomes clear that a rejection of sovereignist law by courts, and even enforcement thereof, does not necessarily change sovereignists' behaviour. Yet, their activities and arguments in front of the court are not signs of a simple disregard for the law or intentional law-breaking. Rather, sovereignists are attempting to challenge and outperform state law according to their understanding of its rules.

Beyond being a practical tool, sovereignism transcends into a worldview, shaping how individuals perceive the world and themselves. Sovereignists retell recent German history by reinterpreting developments in the legal system as a story of the establishment of foreign oppression. In this story, the individual can be both a victim – someone wronged – and a hero seeing the truth and fighting against evil.

Time and again, sovereignists emphasise the legality and morality of their actions grounding their behaviour in a perceived adherence to true law and their mission to restore sovereignty. Legal framing works to shift attention away from the more political question of content – what sort of behaviour is acceptable or what sort of social order is desired – towards the means by which they are legitimised. As ethnographic research on how people contest legal orders reminds us: 'when people turn towards legal norms to express their hopes and strive for their

[68] Verwaltungsgericht Köln (Administrative Court Cologne) 25 L 2773/17, (2017) juris.

[69] C Caspar and R Neubauer, 'Reichsbürger contra öffentliche Verwaltung. Erfahrungen und Argumentationen in der praktischen Auseinandersetzung' in A Speit (ed), *Reichsbürger. Die unterschätzte Gefahr* (Christopher Links Verlag GmbH, 2017).

future, they interpret norms in the light of these aspirations rather than simply in terms of existing normative orders'.[70] This is the case here, too.

The way the law is reinterpreted in these groups appears to be guided by both personal and political hopes and problems, mirroring the often-observed link between conspiracy beliefs and a desire for control, identity and belonging. Rathje has argued that 'The legal practical aspect is just the surface: hidden in it is the accusation of conspiracy'.[71] This accusation guides what people think the law is, how it should be approached and why their interactions with it remain unsuccessful.[72]

To understand the way sovereignists interact with law, we need to look beyond the legal content of arguments, and the immediate content of court cases. The alignment of self-perception, hopes and fears is crucial to understanding the persistence of sovereignism: Conspiratorial legal argument allows people to see the world as they hope (or fear) it is, and to 'lawfully' act on that understanding.

[70] J Eckert et al, 'Law's Travels and Transformations' in J Eckert et al (eds), *Law against the state. Ethnographic forays into law's transformations* (Cambridge University Press, 2012) 1.

[71] Rathje (n 24) 32.

[72] How sovereignists experience and make sense of the factual rejection of their arguments is an interesting and complex question. I attempt to more fully answer this question based on conversations with sovereignists in my dissertation.

PART III

Emerging Areas and Issues Involving Pseudolaw

11

American State Nationals: The Next Iteration of the Sovereign Citizen Movement

CHRISTINE M SARTESCHI

I. Introduction

Sovereign citizens are a loose group of individuals who deny the legitimacy of their respective governments. The movement has been present in the United States, in various forms, since the 1950s and it continues to evolve.[1] Modern technology, namely alternative social media platforms such as Telegram, has enabled the global dissemination of the movement's ideology. At least 31 countries have documented instances of sovereign citizen-like, anti-government activity.[2] There is no one agreed-upon definition, or official checklist to classify an individual as a sovereign citizen. This chapter will concentrate on the sovereign citizen movement in the United States and will consider 'sovereign citizens' as those who deny the legitimacy of the United States Government, reject their citizenship status, and believe themselves to be immune from federal, state and local laws.[3] This is a broad definition that focuses on the adherent's core belief that the American

[1] C Sarteschi, *Sovereign Citizens: A Psychological and Criminological Analysis* (Springer, 2020). For more information on a few, see S Young, H Hobbs, and R Goldwasser, ch 5 in this volume; Netolitzky, ch 7 in this volume; Cash, ch8 in this volume; Löbbert, ch 10 in this volume.

[2] The original list appears in C Sarteschi, 'This Law Doesn't Apply to Me: The Spread of the Sovereign Citizen Movement Around the World', International Center for the Study of Violent Extremism (19 April 2022), www.icsve.org/this-law-doesnt-apply-to-me. Additional countries have been added since the 26 listed in this 2022 original list: Czech Republic, Hungary, Israel, Latvia and Poland. The complete list is: Australia, Austria, Belgium, Canada, Czech Republic, England, Estonia, Germany, Greece, Hungary, Ireland, Israel, Italy, Jamaica, Latvia, Lithuania, Netherlands, New Zealand, Norway, Philippines, Poland, Republic of Ireland, Russia, Scotland, Singapore, Slovakia, South Africa, Spain, Sweden, Switzerland and Wales.

[3] US Department of Homeland Security, 'Domestic Violent Extremists Pose Increase Threat to Government Officials and Law Enforcement' Office of Intelligence and Analysis (2014); Federal Bureau of Investigation, 'Black Identity Extremists Likely Motivated to Target Law-Enforcement Officers' Counterterrorism Division (2017); Sarteschi (n 1).

Government is illegitimate.[4] Under this definition, the self-identifying labels of adherents are irrelevant: those who deny the label of sovereign citizen are considered such if they behave in ways consistent with the aforementioned core beliefs. Individuals who refer to themselves using other terms – including, but not limited to: state nationals, American state nationals, private man or woman, Moor, living man, living woman, a flesh-and-blood person, a natural person, or other similar variations – upon thorough examination, fit the working definition. By adopting a broad definition, such distinctions are subsumed in the overarching concept.

Some researchers make a distinction between sovereign citizens and other pseudolaw adherents. Donald Netolitzky, for instance, argues that sovereign citizens in the United States tend to be politically right-wing, whereas the Canadian 'Freeman-on-the-land' pseudolaw adherents are more left-leaning.[5] Though sovereign citizens are broadly categorised as being far-right, it should be noted that sovereign citizen ideology itself tends to be apolitical.

Research attempting to determine the actual number of sovereign citizens in the United States and the world is lacking. A frequently cited metric from the Southern Poverty Law Center (SPLC) indicates that there are approximately 300,000 sovereign citizens in the United States, but as of 2023, that figure has been removed from their website. Researchers have noted flaws in calculating these figures, and SPLC acknowledges the difficulties inherent in quantifying a leaderless movement.[6] Netolitzky notes the 300,000 figure was used as a basis to quantify Canadian pseudolaw activity (to be approximately one-tenth of what it is in the United States) which he believes has no basis in fact.[7] To the best of this author's knowledge, no government agency specifically tracks the sovereign citizen movement and regularly reports on its findings. Lack of reporting and unreliable data complicate efforts in effectively addressing the movement. Systematic tracking, at minimum, is a critical necessity.

The spread of the sovereign citizen movement has witnessed the emergence of a new trend. It is increasingly common for extremists to adopt a multitude of diverse ideologies. This trend has several names including fringe fluidity, salad bar extremism and compositive violent extremism (CoVE).[8] It involves the mixing of

[4] Sarteschi (n 1).

[5] DJ Netolitzky, 'The Perfect Weed For This Spoiling Soil: The Ideology, Orientation, Organization, Cohesion, Social Control, and Deleterious Effects of Pseudo-Law Social Contracts' (2023) 6 *International Journal of Coercion, Abuse, and Manipulation* 1. doi: 10.5408/1000/0006/001.

[6] 'Sovereign Citizens Movement' Southern Poverty Law Center (2014), www.splcenter.org/fighting-hate/extremist-files/ideology/sovereign-citizens-movement; M Mallek, 'Uncommon Law: Understanding and Quantifying the Sovereign Citizen Movement' Masters of Art, Naval Postgraduate School (2016).

[7] DJ Netolitzky, 'The Dead Sleep Quiet: History of the Organized Pseudolegal Commercial Argument Phenomenon in Canada- Part II' (2023) 60 *Alberta Law Review* 795.

[8] D Gartenstein-Ross et al, 'Composite Violent Extremism: A Radicalization Pattern Changing the Face of Terrorism' Lawfare (22 November 2022), www.lawfaremedia.org/article/composite-violent-extremism-radicalization-pattern-changing-face-terrorism; United States Senate Committee on Appropriations, 'A Review of the President's Fiscal Year 2023 Funding Request for The Federal Bureau of Investigations'

multiple ideologies, choosing elements of a variety of seemingly disparate ideas with the possibility of switching to others over time.[9] Commonly, sovereign citizens tend to intermix ideologies with anti-vaccination, QAnon and conspirituality or New Age movements.[10] This intermixing phenomenon has likely promoted the dissemination of sovereign citizen ideology in ways that are not yet understood or adequately documented.[11]

A factor that contributes to the difficulty of monitoring the sovereign citizen movement is its decentralised nature. The movement lacks a formal leadership structure. There is no official sovereign citizen central authority, certification-board, or established membership standards. Although individuals involved in the movement hold similar ideas they tend to act independently, often creating their own set of tactics and strategies. Many learn about sovereign citizen ideas via internet message boards, forums and websites where they are sold information by those who claim to have specialised knowledge, which they are willing to sell, to show the buyer how to achieve freedom from the reach of government. These same places, which are intended as commerce sites, offer communication, companionship and the ability to share one's ideas with like-minded peers.

This chapter will provide an insight into the US experience of pseudolaw by focusing on a particular emergent sect of pseudolaw – the American State Nationals (ASNs). While the sovereign citizen movement is predominantly characterised by its lack of central leadership, there are exceptions. Leaders can and do emerge in digital spaces. Notably, ASNs, under the leadership of Bobby Lawrence and David Straight, are currently popular in the United States. This is evident through the increasing police body cam footage, found on YouTube, of individuals claiming to be ASNs, in court records of individuals identifying as ASNs, and the group's expanding social media presence. Despite these developments, very little is known about the group and its tactics.

The primary objective of this research is to explore the ASN movement in greater depth. Increasingly, it appears as though their techniques, language and strategies have become more dominant among modern-day sovereign citizens. This chapter will provide a comprehensive examination of the ASN evolution, its behaviour and ideology, and a general description of their methodology. In doing

(25 May 2022), www.appropriations.senate.gov/hearings/a-review-of-the-presidents-fiscal-year-2023-funding-request-for-the-federal-bureau-of-investigation; A Meleagrou-Hitchens and M Ayad, 'The Age Of Incoherence? Understanding Mixed and Unclear Ideology Extremism' National Counterterrorism Innovation Technology in Education (June 2023).

[9] Meleagrou-Hitchens and Ayad (n 8).

[10] C Sarteschi, 'Sovereign Citizens and QAnon: The Increasing Overlaps with A Focus on Child Protective Service (CPS) Cases' (2023) 6 *International Journal of Coercion, Abuse and Manipulation* 1, doi:10.54208/1000/0006/006; C Sarteschi, 'The Social Phenomenon of Romana Didulo: "Queen of Canada"' (2023) 6 *International Journal of Coercion, Abuse and Manipulation* 1, doi:10.54208/1000/0006/002.

[11] Sarteschi (n 2); Meleagrou-Hitchens and Ayad (n 8); S Varda, 'Statement for the Record: Submitted to the House Select Committee to Investigate the January 6 Attack on United States Capitol' United States House Select Committee to Investigate the January 6 Attack (7 April 2022).

so, this chapter also highlights the need for a broad and comprehensive societal response to the evolving sovereign citizen movement.

II. A US Pseudolaw Case Study: American State Nationals

ASNs are unique in the sense that most sovereign citizens do not typically function collectively. Organisationally, the narrative framework centres around three main themes: a leadership driven movement, core ideologies and mercenary enterprise. Through this case study approach, this section highlights the nature of how the group evolved and functions.

A. ASN Movement Overview

The ASN movement is a recent form of pseudolaw that emerged in 2021. Limited information exists regarding the circumstances and motivation that led to its development. The group appears to have exclusively formed online, where the majority of its activities are concentrated. The group's leaders, Mr Lawrence and Mr Straight, maintain multiple popular Telegram channels which serve as their primary means of connecting with followers. Mr Lawrence's main Telegram channel was created in January 2021, and it has grown to approximately 40,000 members. Mr Straight created his Telegram channel in March 2022 and now has approximately 43,000 members. Unlike Mr Lawrence, it is worth noting that Mr Straight does not personally moderate his Telegram channel and has delegated that task to another individual.

ASN concepts are variations of the ideology ascribed to by sovereign citizens. Like other sovereign citizens, ASNs are a group of like-minded individuals attempting to liberate themselves from what they perceive to be government 'tyranny'. ASNs are attempting to 'restore our Constitutional Republic' in a 'bloodshed-free way'. ASNs believe (as do other sovereign citizens) that the 14th Amendment of the Constitution took away one's freedom 'under the natural law of God'.[12] From the ASN perspective, when our mothers signed our birth certificates, they inadvertently or unintentionally created a 'contract' with the Federal Government.[13] These contracts effectively enslaved us to the Government.[14] To correct this lifelong enslavement, one must remove one's self from all contracts,

[12] J Sharlet, *The Undertow Scenes from a Slow Civil War* (WW Norton & Company, 2023) 179.

[13] Sarteschi, 'Sovereign Citizens and QAnon' (n 10).

[14] ibid; C Kalinowski IV, 'A Legal Response to the Sovereign Citizen Movement' (2019) 80 *Montana Law Review* 153, 154; 'Sovereign Citizens: A Growing Anti-Government Movement' Anti-Defamation League (1 September 2016), www.adl.org/resources/backgrounder/sovereign-citizen-movement.

and thus achieve the goal of living 'in the private'. To live 'in the private' is to have successfully removed oneself from all 'commercial' contracts by having cancelled or rescinded those contracts. Ways to achieve those goals, the necessary techniques, methodologies and procedures, can conveniently be purchased on ASN websites.

Much of the interaction on the Telegram ASN message boards involves discussions and interpretations of ASN concepts. Debate is common as adherents grasp or construe ASN theories in varying ways. New tactics are frequently announced, further complicating the clarity of which specific tactic one should be adhering to at any given time, and it is common for adherents to express confusion. The leaders openly acknowledge that they are improvising and characterise it as evidence of their commitment to the movement. Their constant revision in methodology is more likely the result of the ineffectiveness and failure of their current teachings. Of course, the new and improved techniques are also for sale on their websites.

B. A Leadership Driven Movement

As outlined above, the ASN movement is distinguished from many other sovereign citizen movements by the significant role individual leaders play in its development and promulgation. Followers commonly defer to the group's leaders as they trust their expertise and explanations of ASN concepts. Even when the group's leaders change course and correct previously stated positions and tactics, followers remain loyal, continuing to look to their leaders for direction and guidance.

Very little is known about either Mr Straight or Mr Lawrence. Before pivoting to the movement, Mr Lawrence attempted to run for the United States Senate in 2018 on the Republican ticket, but withdrew before the election.[15] No other documented instances can be found of Mr Lawrence attempting to run for political office.

Mr Straight is a popular figure in the conspiracy theory community, yet his personal history remains a mystery. He makes fantastical claims for which he provides no evidence. For instance, he claims to have worked through the United States Judge Advocate General's (JAG) Corps and for various high-level law enforcement agencies, including the Secret Service, Texas Rangers and Navy Seals, among others.[16] He maintains that he worked for Donald Trump on a presidential task force whose mission was to prevent child sex trafficking,[17] leading to the unsubstantiated claim of 15,000 child sex traffickers having been arrested.[18] He also said that he has personally contributed to over 800 legal victories using sovereign citizen methodology,[19] but does not offer evidence for this or any other claim.

[15] Sarteschi, 'Sovereign Citizens and QAnon' (n 10).
[16] ibid.
[17] ibid.
[18] ibid.
[19] ibid.

Less prominent figures exist in the ASN movement. Bonnie Straight, Mr Straight's spouse, was also once considered a leader of the movement. This appears to have ended in 2023, when she was convicted for a probation violation and sentenced to five years' incarceration.[20] At the time of writing she remains incarcerated and efforts are underway by ASNs to advocate for her freedom. The published advocacy plan includes requests to Supreme Court Justice Samuel Alito, Texas Governor Greg Abbott, and Texas Attorney General Ken Paxton. ASNs are requesting a 'full pardon and blanket immunity' for Mrs Straight. In a letter posted on Telegram, ASNs are encouraged to send the following letter. It reads, in part:

> There is simply no reason for the FOR PRIVATE PROFIT CORPORATIONS TO pursue, kidnap and unlawfully incarcerate a woman who has NOT harmed a living soul and pursuant to the Clearfield Doctrine, her imprisonment is HUMAN TRAFFICING and as such Ultra Vires to everything that the State of Texas is obligated for under its statutes and that of United States Code particularly Title 18 USC 242 and 241. If either of you stand for the principles on which our great nation was founded as set forth in the Declaration of Independence, that being: Life Liberty and the Pursuit of Happiness, you will remedy this grave miscarriage of justice in the name FUNDAMENTAL FAIRNESS and immediately give Bonnie Ruth Allen Straight, held as THOMAS, BONNIE ALLEN a pardon and blanket immunity to end this needless act of what is clearly human trafficking.

In late 2023, a major shift transpired among ASN leadership. The collaboration between Mr Lawrence and Mr Straight has seemingly ended, likely influenced by the legal problems of Mr and Mrs Straight. Presently, Mrs Straight remains in prison and Mr Straight's whereabouts are unknown, although he recently began posting videos introducing new ideas and tactics he plans to discuss at his upcoming seminars. Both leaders are now teaching differing approaches. Mr Lawrence has portrayed the legal challenges faced by the Straights as a catalyst for propelling the movement in a new direction, one in which they can alter their methodology to be more effective.

The splintering of the group suggests that leadership driven models, at least among sovereign citizens, are unsustainable. Power struggles, disagreements over ideology, the constant changing of tactics and methods without logic or explanation, and personal grievances among members likely contributed to internal divisions within the group. Followers can easily become confused and angry about who or what methods to follow. Considering that sovereign citizen tactics are fundamentally ineffective, fragmentation and in-fighting seem an inevitability.

C. Core Ideology: Freedom under Attack

Mr Lawrence's first Telegram post provides insight into ASN ideology. He included a warning about 'the greatest crime in political history'.[21] Many of his posts are

[20] ibid.

[21] B Lawrence, 'You Have Witnessed the Greatest Crime in Political History' Telegram (20 January 2021), www.t.me/c/1326817170/35.

based on the premise that freedom and liberty 'are under constant assault' and that a 'remedy' is needed. Mr Lawrence believes that 'we must go back to the beginning, 1776' and look to the 'Declaration of Independence and the Constitution' to understand 'our God-given rights' to 'restore our Republic'.[22] His published ideology includes his admiration of founding fathers John Adams and George Washington, his unique interpretations of their words, along with biblical quotes that he contends support his interpretation of founding documents such as the United States Constitution, and other law. The goal, he explained, is to 'become free to take your proper dominion over government. Once we are free, we can then use our founding documents to correct the errors of our out-of-control government'.[23]

ASNs frequently emphasise that they are different from sovereign citizens. Some argue that ASNs and sovereign citizens are being lumped together unfairly by the 'deep state' [who] is 'doing whatever they can to stifle the movement on technicalities'.[24] Others believe that the Central Intelligence Agency (CIA) created the notion of a sovereign citizen to harm the movement, despite no evidence for their claims. Nevertheless, their foundational ideas are consistent with those in the sovereign citizen movement. For instance, Mr Lawrence argues:

> You are not free. You are a vessel to the corporations of government. You must learn how deeply the corporate interests have become in YOUR government. You are not a party to the founding documents. You give tacit agreement to the corporations bylaws every time you sign one of their unconstitutional documents. You made slaves of your children when you signed them over as a vessel to the government with a birth certificate. They (government) take their soul (the soul print) and then they (your children) are a vessel, a purser of a ship. Dig deep to find the truth. You can correct your status from a citizen to a living soul.[25]

The idea that the United States is a corporation is consistent with sovereign citizen ideology.[26] Relatedly, the idea that certain documents, including birth certificates, constitute a 'tacit agreement' with the United States 'corporation', and that you are an artificial person or vessel, is also in line with what sovereign citizens commonly espouse and is essential to their core beliefs.[27] These ideas are consistent with the broader definition of sovereign citizens as individuals who deny the legitimacy of their respective governments.

i. Religious Element

Unlike the broader, documented sovereign citizen movement, ASNs incorporate Christian-oriented religious beliefs that form the foundation of their philosophy.

[22] B Lawrence, 'From Where Does the U.S. Constitution Derive its Power?' Telegram (16 October 2021), www.t.me/c/1326817170/941.

[23] ibid.

[24] Unknown Author, 'I Am Only Sharing' Telegram (original on file with the author).

[25] B Lawrence, 'For Those Who Ask Me to be Direct' Telegram (23 February 2021), www.t.me/c/1326817170/388.

[26] Kalinowski IV (n 14).

[27] ibid.

This is true of both the group's leaders and its adherents. For instance, Mr Straight's most popular and most referenced teachings are his eight-part 'Out of Babylon' training series. In an advertising video about the seminar, linking followers to a thumb drive for purchase, Mr Straight cites a portion of *Revelation 18:4*: 'And I heard another voice from heaven, saying, Come out of her, my people, that ye be not partakers of her sins, and that ye receive not of her plagues'.[28] The ad goes on to say 'Come out of Babylon. Leave the corporate construct designed to enslave you. Become a state national.'[29] His teachings commonly intertwine religious concepts alongside mentions of the 'deep state' and the 'cabal', two common references to QAnon. Relatedly, Mr Straight contends that child protective services (CPS) are a cover for child sex traffickers, a clear QAnon reference.[30]

Similarly to Mr Straight, Mr Lawrence utilises pseudo-religion, but he takes a giant leap forward by asserting that he has a direct link to God. Interestingly, a significant portion of his teachings are attributed to 'divine guidance'. He characterises his teachings as 'downloads' from his creator. Because they are downloads, as opposed to something coming directly from him, he struggles to recall his teachings and relies on replays of his videos or the memories of those in the audience.

Mr Lawrence commonly references the three dominions of land, air, and water ('LAW'). These, he explains, come directly from a biblical verse:

> And God said, 'Let us make man in our image, after our likeness: and let them have dominion over the fish of the sea, and over the foul of the air, and over the cattle, and over all the earth, and over every creeping thing that creepeth upon the earth'.[31]

Mr Lawrence has interpreted this biblical verse as having particular meaning for the ASN movement. In his view, land specifically relates to what you own; superior title of one's property. Air stands for trust and wills; something that benefits another person. Water relates to admiralty and commerce law which is anything involving contracts and public business dealings.

Mr Lawrence explains that the rebuilding of God's WAL is LAW spelled backward. He argues that:

> We are born out of the water in our mother's womb; we take our first breath of god's air, we learn to walk on the land as free people. God's words created a WAL and I believe this is his order of life we are to follow. A WAL created between his creation and the fallen one, Satan.[32]

He goes on to say:

> As Satan mirrors Yahweh, Satan created a mirror of WAL and created LAW. The servant of Satan atturned (sic) people away from God's order and enslaves us with man's LAW,

[28] *The Bible* (King James Version), Revelation 18:4.

[29] D Straight, 'Come Out of Her' Telegram (31 May 2022), www.t.me/DavidLesterStraightChatroom/17481.

[30] Sarteschi, 'Sovereign Citizens and QAnon' (n 10).

[31] *The Bible* (King James Version) Genesis 1:26.

[32] B Lawrence, 'Restoring God's Order of Law' Telegram (10 August 2022), www.t.me/c/1326817170/4120.

> Land, Air and Water. They have taken our land held in allodium and pledged it to the moneychangers of debt … God have given his People freewill and we have the ability to exit LAW and restore God's WAL.[33]

Mr Lawrence contends that he is involved in spiritual warfare. He is fighting a battle that is taking a mental and physical toll on him personally. He is being attacked by evil spirits. As evidence of this, he recently discussed on a live stream, having had a spiritual attack during one of his in-person seminars. An adherent described what he witnessed (and experienced) during Mr Lawrence's spiritual attack:

> I was setting front row near the speakers. Within 3 hours of the day I was dizzy; nauseated and my head felt out of equilibrium like I had water in my ears. Yesterday Bobby had such severe headaches he suffered greatly and kept teaching like the trooper he was … Those of us there saw and felt the spiritual warfare going on … Bobby; under attack yesterday; taught his heart out and kept going while physically suffering; today Kiki stayed strong teaching and I felt what was attacking her and had to go outside and just breathe. This event was a serious threat to the darkness …! I just wanted to share with you all how very real the attack was this event. I've been to so many events I don't know how many; but have never seen or experienced what happened at this event. As we all learn and get close to our true private freedom; the threat becomes very real … They are the tip of a very bloody arrow.[34]

The assertion of these attacks is meant to serve as evidence of evil spirits trying to stop the 'good' Mr Lawrence and his 'good' works. However, it must be noted these 'evil' spirits are apparently rather weak and can only muster a headache or two. Are all headaches the work of evil spirits? Should we be treating them with aspirin, Ibuprofen, Tylenol, etc, or psychic intervention? Mr Lawrence asserts that he struggles to reveal the truth to the world. Both he and his followers consider him a sacrificial martyr of sorts, having to endure the occasional headache. He must continue his work, even with a headache and this makes him a martyr. Would it be fair to say that millions of people go to work with a headache every day? Should we think of them as martyrs? Do we believe that Mr Lawrence, should he quit his 'good' work, would never again get another headache? In our world are headaches rare or extremely common?

Mr Lawrence and his followers would have us believe that he is someone who willingly endures adversity to expose a truth that the deep state and the cabal are determined to keep hidden. Followers also see this spiritual attack as evidence of Mr Lawrence's deep commitment to the movement and they offer us the evidence of the headache. Increasingly, adherents are reporting that they too are experiencing similar spiritual attacks. Integrating religious and spiritual concepts into their narratives may serve to unite followers and give them the impression they are fighting a battle much larger than themselves.

[33] ibid.
[34] Iowafreedomcoach, 'Let Me Share With You All' Telegram (14 October 2023), www.t.me/c/1245253765/267008.

ii. ASN Attitudes Toward Law Enforcement

ASNs also make a distinction between police officers and peace officers. They regard police officers as 'policy enforcement officers' and see their role as simply enforcing statutes which are comprised of legal terms, and conditions of contracts that have penalties articulated by the artificial government corporation. 'Policy enforcement officers', in their view, have no jurisdiction over a 'sovereign being' unless that individual explicitly gives their consent.

ASNs believe that peace officers uphold the common law. Their job is to protect and keep the peace. Peace officers are seen as being more honourable than 'policy enforcement officers' and will supposedly only intervene when there is a victim of a crime. To the ASN, if there is no victim, there is no crime. 'No victim no crime' is a commonly held mantra used by those in the sovereign citizen movement.[35]

It is common for ASNs to want to educate 'policy enforcement officers' on their role in the community and how they believe they should be interacting with ASNs. They contend that 'policy enforcement officers' have simply not been properly educated about the interpretation of the law as ASNs understand it. To address this lack of knowledge, many ASNs contact or visit their local police chief to explain their understanding of the law, specifically their 'right to travel'. ASNs contend that if they are not involved in commerce then no driver's licence or vehicle registration is necessary. Their vehicle is considered 'private property' and therefore not something that can be regulated by police officers or 'policy enforcers'.

iii. Secrecy

ASN leaders have stated they deliberately withhold certain information from both adherents and the public. They believe that some information is too risky to share. They worry that some adherents may use the tactics inappropriately, potentially resulting in legal troubles. They contend that adherents may not have dedicated enough study time and mastered all the many required steps involved in their process. They have also cautioned that the information they are sharing has the potential to upset the deep state or the cabal.

The secrecy element of the movement serves as a convenient excuse when adherents request evidence as to the effectiveness of the purchased ASN tactics. ASN adherents and supporters rationalise, in the Freudian sense, the failure of their learned, often paid-for, tactics. For instance, one adherent explained that successful ASN cases are sealed by the court. Put simply, they work but the court hides their success from the public. Their success is held in secret, sealed court documents. He explained that he:

> [R]ecently listened to a discussion talking about status and winning court cases. The guy pointed out he had seen cases where the person absolutely ruled the courtroom,

[35] Sarteschi (n 1).

> but was prosecuted anyway … even with the judge admitting such in private chambers discussion. The REASON why they convicted him ANYWAY … Was exclusively because they could not allow those kinds of victories to existing case law for people to study. The REMEDY … was having the case sealed. Once that happened they were allowed to win.[36]

In another instance, when an adherent asked why it was difficult to ascertain public information about Mr Straight, Mr Lawrence responded that the follower should use proper 'discernment'. He also indicated that the lack of information (about Mr Straight) was intentional to avoid alerting the cabal. In response to the inquiry about Mr Straight, Mr Lawrence wrote: 'If one is a former military special operator, a former Secret Service agent in his high level security clearance, wouldn't it hold true that it might be hard to find any public information on them? … The goal is to become invisible to the cabal'.[37] The 'cabal' is a reference to the QAnon conspiracy theory suggesting that powerful elites control the world and use that power to secretly abuse children.[38]

The secrecy element provides a convenient cover story for the lack of successes of the group. Leaders never have to face scrutiny regarding their ineffective methods, which allows them to maintain a more favourable image. Studies also show that for some, there is a certain pleasure in possessing supposed secret knowledge available to only a special select few.[39]

D. A Mercenary Enterprise

Some adherents are drawn to the sovereign citizen movement after experiencing financial distress, making them vulnerable to exploitation.[40] Likewise, ASN gurus charge fees for their supposed secret knowledge. On the rare occasion when adherents complain about being charged, others will defend both Straight and Lawrence, claiming that they are doing the work of the Lord, revealing hidden truths and restoring their loss of freedom. The following section details the nature of the services offered by ASNs and their close associates.

i. Costly Seminars

The ASN Telegram channels serve to educate followers about techniques necessary to remove themselves from the 'tyranny' and 'dominion' of government. Though

[36] M Anthony, 'Something Worth Considering' Telegram (19 August 2023), www.t.me/c/1245253765/259582.

[37] B Lawrence, 'Use Discernment' Telegram (15 January 2022), www.t.me/c/1326817170/1120.

[38] A Amarasingam and M-André Argentino, 'The QAnon Conspiracy Theory: A Security Threat in the Making?' (2020) 13 *CTC Sentinel* 37.

[39] D Muron, 'Cults, Conspiracies, and Fantasy Knowledge' Advance Online (2023) *Episteme* 1.

[40] JM Berger, 'Without Prejudice: What Sovereign Citizens Believe' George Washington University Program on Extremism (June 2016).

the ASN leaders have separate Telegram channels, they share many of the same ideas about achieving the goal of freedom. In-person seminars are commonly advertised. These events occur across the United States and on occasion, in Canada. The price per person has been USD 150 (in the form of a donation or a gift), and the duration of the sessions can last several hours or longer on weekends.

Though it is rare for Mr Lawrence and Mr Straight to make joint appearances, they have done so for weekend-long conferences. These lengthier conferences include various other speakers and are costly (USD 1,300 per person) relative to the day-long seminars (USD 150). Seminar speakers at the lengthier conferences have created specific strategies they wish to teach others. Presumably, their tactics are endorsed by Mr Lawrence and Mr Straight.

The in-person seminars are attended by a subset of particularly enthusiastic followers who participate in these physical gatherings. Both Mr Lawrence and Mr Straight have hosted these seminars, as have their spouses and close associates. On occasion, these seminars are hosted online and posted on websites such as Rumble. Rumble is an alternative social media video website whose user base identifies mostly as Republican.[41] Despite some of their material being available on Rumble, ASN leaders commonly express their desire to maintain their secrets and limit the recording of seminars.

In advertising the first seminar in March 2021, Mr Lawrence explains:

> Right now we cannot do anything to stop an out-of-control elected servant. We do not have the proper status. We do not have an established assembly process at the county level. We the people at large do not understand how much control and power we have that was given to us in our founding documents. Until we learn what our proper status needs to be, which is an American State national, a living soul, a su Juris, we can do nothing about it. We have to learn what I've posted in the channel. And then take steps to become free men and women. We must correct our status. We must take control of the three dominions of law, the air, the land, the water. Then we must get our personal affairs in order and secure our Superior titles to everything we own. Then we can go about the task of restoring our Republic and fixing a broken out of control government. That is the singular goal of what I post.[42]

'Proper status' relates to the espoused ASN idea that one needs to 'correct' their status to be free from government reach. ASNs believe that one could either live 'in the public' or 'in the private'. ASNs also warn that sometimes people inadvertently mix the private and the public, which can be disastrous. ASN philosophy suggests that most people unknowingly live 'in the public' thereby allowing government to control their lives. They are servants to the 'corporation' and are obliged to adhere to its laws.

A related philosophy commonly espoused by ASNs is that one should not 'act like a king until you are a king'. Essentially, one cannot 'stand' on their rights

[41] S Ghosh and G Stocking, 'Key Facts About Rumble' Pew Research Center (21 December 2022), www.pewresearch.org/short-reads/2022/12/21/key-facts-about-rumble.

[42] B Lawrence, 'Right Now We Cannot Do Anything' Telegram (3 March 2021), www.t.me/c/1326817170/415.

until they have properly removed themselves from all 'corporate' constructs. The process to do so, the leaders explain, is a long, arduous journey that requires an intense level of study and devotion. The mechanisms to free oneself are hidden by the evil cabal who steadfastly attempt to prevent one's escape from the 'matrix'. Comprehending these difficult concepts, Mr Lawrence often reiterates, is the 'key to standing'.[43] He commonly warns that too many adherents attempt to utilise the tactics (ie 'stand') without the proper knowledge. In sum, those who fail to utilise their tactics successfully are doing it wrong. Why do it wrong, when you can simply purchase the knowledge to do it correctly, right here on their websites or by paying to attend a seminar?

Mr Lawrence will often post testimonials by adherents who tried to use a tactic unsuccessfully. These posts are designed to encourage others to keep studying. For instance, the following adherent admits to a mistake and vows to start again 'with more focus':

> I too in the beginning did AV[O]R process and I thought that it was good … but one day as I was heading to David Straight's level 1 seminar … I got pulled over for speeding and I tried to exercise my state national rights … I even pulled out my brand new Credentials card … and I kept telling them that I am not under their Jurisdiction … well they arrested me and charged me with a felony for forgery of the US seal on AVR's credentials card … that is how I found out that cards with pics and papers with words mean nothing to these Corporate Gestapo policy enforcement agents … we must Know whom we are and we must belligerently defend our God given sovereign rights with our standing … needless to say … afterwards I hit the books and started study Bobby and David's Process … and especially learning the meaning of Juris-diction and how to take dominion over three jurisdictions … and more importantly how to defend them … yes we use their own corporate codes, statutes and policies against them … sometimes painful lessons is exactly what we need to get our act together … there is no quick solution … we must learn, understand and undo everything we unknowingly have done thus far that gave away our sovereignty … and thanks to these guys here on this channel who are very skilled … I began the process all over again but this time with more focus.[44]

ASNs regard themselves as 'unincorporated persons' who are immune from prosecution by the United States Government. They do not believe they are subject to 'public' courts, nor can they be arrested by 'public' law enforcement officers.[45] Those who live 'in the private' have unshackled themselves from the government 'corporation'. They are outside and above all laws and maintain their inalienable, God-given rights. They are 'entitled to carry on their private business in their own way'.[46] They are free from all investigation and rights can only be taken from them by 'due process of law'.[47] Those who live 'in the private' are accountable to common law and only when they cause harm to 'any living soul'.[48]

[43] Lawrence (n 22).
[44] 'I Too in the Beginning' Telegram (3 July 2022), www.t.me/c/1326817170/1723.
[45] Living In The Private, 'In The Private' (2023), www.livingintheprivate.blogspot.com/p/home.html.
[46] Lawrence (n 37).
[47] ibid.
[48] ibid.

More recently, 'freedom coaches' have emerged in the ASN movement with the goal of having one designated for all 50 states. A 'freedom coach' is someone with enhanced knowledge of the ASN tactics and strategies. For their seminars, freedom coaches 'require' a USD 150 donation. That amount may increase if the seminar lasts more than one day. Examples of common seminar topics by 'freedom coaches' include: 'Claiming your name', 'status change', 'living as a free man or woman', and 'evolved steps to freedom', among others.

ii. Tactics and Sales

ASN adherents are directed to complete and publicly document (via the Recorder of Deeds, notary, courts and/or the Secretary of State) an expensive array of paperwork that their leaders assert is necessary to become an ASN. The tactics can change, and new ones are added on a fairly regular basis, which creates confusion and frustration among supporters. Many of their tactics involve the promotion of services of third-party sellers, friends, or business associates. Below is a description of their processes, and their associated descriptions.

- *Getting Started*: To begin the process of becoming an ASN, followers purchase paperwork sold via ASN websites associated with Mr Lawrence and Mr Straight. This paperwork is filled out by adherents and is presented to the Recorder of Deeds of one's respective state, with the intention of publicly recording it. There are three levels, and each level contains multiple steps.
- *Level I* is referred to as 'status correction' and the paperwork associated with it is called the 'freedom bundle'. The 'freedom bundle' contains the following paperwork: affidavit of truth, accessory oath, repudiation and revocation of citizenship, deed of reconveyance, certified proof of service, notice of acceptance of default certified judgment of unrebutted affidavit, patent of nativity or declaration of status. These materials are filled out by adherents (though most of the information contained therein is auto generated). It is often notarised, taken to the local Recorder of Deeds and or mailed to the Secretary of State. These are the first steps in the process of becoming an ASN.[49]

  An important additional step in the level I status correction process, is the acquisition of a United States passport. Mr Lawrence first introduced the concept of acquiring a passport in March 2021. Followers are instructed to apply for and receive a 'noncitizen national passport'.[50] They believe that this passport certifies them as a noncitizen of the United States thereby removing them from their 'corporate' citizenship. It also supposedly provides them limited diplomatic immunity, the freedom to never be detained nor

[49] See American Nationals, 'Welcome to American Nationals!', www.app.statenational.us/university.
[50] Sarteschi, 'Sovereign Citizens and QAnon' (n 10).

interrogated by law enforcement, and the privilege of being able to carry a concealed firearm in all 50 states.[51]

These claimed special privileges by ASNs were a major issue in the officer-involved shooting of Chase Allen. Mr Allen, a self-declared ASN, was pulled over by Utah police in March 2023 for having an illegal licence plate.[52] When asked for his ID, Allen argued with police, stating that they lacked the authority to stop him based on his belief that he was on a special 'do not detain' list.[53] He eventually produced his passport as a form of ID. Following continued arguments with police, they ordered him to exit the vehicle and he declined. Upon attempting to remove him from the vehicle, the officers suspected he was reaching for his firearm, and he was shot and killed. An investigation cleared the police of any wrongdoing.[54]

ASNs theorise that because they are 'travelling' (not driving), a passport is a logical necessity as one needs a passport to travel. During traffic stops like the one involving Mr Allen, it is common for ASNs to offer their passport to law enforcement when asked for a driver's licence. Like other sovereign citizens, the 'right to travel' is a commonly held belief among ASNs.[55] Despite believing they have a 'right to travel', 'every court to confront it (the right-to-travel theory) has held that it lacks a true basis in law and is patently frivolous'.[56]

An emerging trend, involving passports, is their presentation, by ASNs, to arms dealers (as a form of identification) when attempting to buy a firearm (which they prefer to call 'arms' as opposed to 'firearms' which they consider a 'corporate' term). Because ASNs believe they must break all contracts (which includes a driver's licence), most no longer have this form of identification or wish not to use it. Thus far, adherents have indicated that trying to use a passport, in place of their driver's licence, has not been successful.

- *Level II* was used to alert the Internal Revenue Service (IRS) and one's employer, via specific paperwork, that taxes are no longer to be taken out of their pay checks. However, elements of this tactic have recently been temporarily discontinued as ASN leaders have stated that it has caused legal troubles for followers. Adherents are instead instructed to register their names as trademarks, create a 'Familia GodTrust and property list' (to be kept private), acquire a land patent (ie, the superior title of your land), and fill out the 'affidavit and assertory oath of acceptance of trusteeship' and 'notice of existence of trust'.[57]

[51] ibid.

[52] ibid.

[53] ibid.

[54] S Lewis, 'Farmington Officers Cleared by Davis Co. Attorney in Fatal Shooting of Chase Allen' ABC4News (13 September 2023), www.abc4.com/news/wasatch-front/farmington-officers-cleared-by-davis-co-attorney-in-fatal-shooting-of-chase-allen.

[55] Sarteschi (n 1).

[56] *Andreaccio v Weaver* [2023] US Dist 144136 (Dorsey J).

[57] Living In The Private (n 45).

- *Level III* is only for those who have successfully 'corrected' their status. This means having successfully completed levels I and II. Level III involves filling out and filing the following materials: the cancelation of voter registration, rescinding one's marriage certificate, a 'petition to an annul state from marriage' (and in its place, physically recording your marriage in the family Bible with a new form provided in the freedom bundle), and the 'affidavit rescinding the signature from birth certificates'.[58] The newest tactic recently added involves acquiring one's certificate of live birth (also known as report of live birth in some states) (not to be confused with a birth certificate which is a separate document). It is common for adherents to confuse the two.

None of the aforementioned processes or tactics have any merit. A recent investigation, by the Arizona Center for Investigative Reporting, revealed that Pima County, Arizona has been inundated with such filings from ASNs across the country. Pima County has likely been targeted by the ASN community because information shared by adherents on Telegram suggests that the Pima County recorder's office is seen as willing to process their pseudo-legal paperwork. However, as noted by the Pima County recorder:

> [A]ccepting a document does not make it legal … But rather ensures it is available to the public in perpetuity. You can come in here and record your grandmother's chocolate chip cookie recipe if you wanted, and it would not make it a legal document, but it would make it a public document.[59]

ASN leaders are also teaching their followers that acquiring their vehicle's Manufacturer's Certification of Origin (MCO) and Certificate of Title circumvents and supersedes the need for proper vehicle registration of their automobiles. According to the American Association of Motor Vehicle Administrators (AAMVA), an MCO is the original ownership document for a vehicle.[60] These documents are provided by the manufacturer to the new car dealer and contain specific information about the vehicle including the year, the make, and the Vehicle Identification Number.[61] When a vehicle is sold, the document is surrendered for the issuance of a jurisdiction title.[62]

ASNs are attempting the following process related to MCOs: because they believe that they, 'the traveller', 'records' (on the public record) these two documents, once recorded, these are 'are merged into one'. They then become the 'Superior Title held in-trust' which gives them an 'undisputable private automobile'

[58] ibid.

[59] S Simonelli and B Derr, '"Sovereign Citizen" Filings Flood Pima County, Parallel National Resurgence of Controversial Movement' Arizona Center For Investigative Reporting (11 September 2023), www.azcir.org/news/2023/09/11/sovereign-citizen-paperwork-pima-county/.

[60] American Association of Motor Vehicle Administrators, 'Manufacturer's Certification of Origin' (2023), www.aamva.org/topics/manufacturer-s-certification-of-origin#?wst=4a3b89462cc2cff2cbe0c7accde57421.

[61] ibid.

[62] ibid.

and supposedly makes their vehicle privately owned.[63] ASNs subsequently affix private licence plates onto their vehicles which they falsely believe (when checked by a 'policy officer') will indicate their private superior title status, thus preventing legal troubles. Conveniently, ASN leaders advertise the services of the 'MCO guys' who assist adherents in acquiring their MCO's for approximately USD 700. There is no proof that this tactic has succeeded, even once. According to the National Conference of State Legislators, every state requires motor vehicles to be registered and titled with the state's transportation agency or their respective department of motor vehicles.[64] The idea that the MCO process described by ASNs can supersede or circumvent state vehicle registration laws is baseless. However, though not successful, it remains expensive.

It should also be noted that some ASN adherents have complained that they paid the 'MCO guys' for services never provided and have been unable to recoup their money. According to ASN group members, one of the 'MCO guys' is named Anthony Budreau from Texas who is in trouble with the law. A man of this same name and location was found in court records to have been convicted in 2019 of piloting an aircraft without a valid pilot certificate.[65] He was sentenced to five years' probation and six months' home detention.[66] Court records indicate that he was arrested again in August 2023 for violating his probation and remanded to federal custody for six months. Mr Budreau has filed a petition in federal court directed towards Texas officials identifying himself as a 'living Texian, American State national man', and 'a non-employee of the UNITED STATES Corporation, non-14th Amendment Citizen'.[67] In the petition, he accuses the state of Texas of 'patterns and practices of fraud, and deceptive trade practices, and child trafficking and genocide'.

iii. 'Minor Estate'

The 'minor estate', also known as the 'higher quantum estate' and the Cestui Que Vie (CQV) trust are variations of the Redemption Scheme, the long-running sovereign citizen notion that hidden government accounts exist for everyone and its money can be used to satisfy one's debts.[68] Sovereign citizens believe that secret government accounts exist and contain as much as USD 20 million per person.[69]

[63] B Lawrence, 'As One of We The People' Telegram (2 March 2023), www.t.me/c/1326817170/3195.

[64] 'Vehicle Registration Fees By State' National Conference of State Legislators (2020), www.ncsl.org/transportation/vehicle-registration-fees-by-state.

[65] 'Investigations' US Department of Transportation, Office of Inspector General (28 October 2019), www.oig.dot.gov/library-item/37559.

[66] ibid.

[67] ibid.

[68] Kalinowski IV (n 14); Anti-Defamation League (n 14); DJ Netolitzky, 'A Rebellion of Furious Paper: Pseudolaw as a Revolutionary System' Conference Paper, Sovereign Citizens in Canada Symposium, Centre d'expertise et de formation sur les intégrismes religieux et la radicalisation (3 May 2018).

[69] Kalinowski IV (n 14); Anti-Defamation League (n 14).

The 'redemption theory' was popularised by Roger Elvick, who told victims as part of an illegal scheme that they had been mortgaged at birth and that (for a fee) he would redeem their mortgages for them. He was subsequently tried and convicted on multiple pseudolegal schemes.[70]

Caesar Kalinowski IV has detailed the intricate procedure used by some sovereign citizens to attempt to unlock their secret accounts.[71] It involves the submission of worthless Uniform Commercial Code (UCC) filings to the state and the Secretary of the Treasury. Many sovereign citizens continue to try the UCC method,[72] but ASN adherents have devised their own strategy for acquiring their 'minor estate', avoiding the aforementioned UCC-based process due to legal concerns.

While ASNs claim to have developed new methods to acquire their 'minor estates', they are reluctant to reveal them publicly. As best discerned, the ASN guidelines for claiming the 'minor estate' are as follows:

- one must be 'totally withdrawn from the system' (ie, living fully 'in the private') before it can be acquired;
- one must go through probate court to acquire the money; special judges are utilised for this process;
- it takes approximately two to two and a half years of dedicated study to learn the steps; and
- one must own land (though how much is unclear).

Because of the highly confidential nature of how one can supposedly acquire the 'minor estate' within the ASN community, questions regarding its legitimacy are commonly raised. When followers seek proof of the 'minor estate's' existence, they are told that all successful claimants have signed non-disclosure agreements (NDAs).[73] Supposedly, if they were to admit to it, they would lose it. For instance, one adherent wrote: 'The NDA you sign agree to not tell anyone that you have claimed your CQV, or gets taken away'. Another adherent writes that 'essentially anyone that [has acquired their minor estate] cannot talk about it and therefore cannot respond [about it] publicly'.[74] Thus, followers are asked to believe, without evidence, that the 'minor estate' exists and that they too can acquire their secret money by filling out specific paperwork sold to them by ASN leaders. NDAs provide a convenient justification for the lack of evidence involving 'minor estates'.

[70] 'His "Straw Man'+" Free, A Scammer Finds The Rest of Him Isn't' Southern Poverty Law Center (27 July 2005), www.splcenter.org/fighting-hate/intelligence-report/2005/his-straw-man-free-scammer-finds-rest-him-isnt.

[71] Kalinowski IV (n 14); Anti-Defamation League (n 14).

[72] P Crusco, 'Sovereign Foreclosures and the UCC-1 Bogus Lien Scam' *New York Law Journal* (26 August 2016), www.law.com/newyorklawjournal/2019/08/26/sovereign-foreclosures-and-the-ucc-1-bogus-lien-scam.

[73] B Barnes, 'People Who Claim Their Minor Estate' Telegram (9 March 2023) www.t.me/DavidLesterStraightChatroom/143188.

[74] Klaus, 'I Don't Mean to Contradict Moonwingate' Telegram (14 August 2023), www.t.me/DavidLesterStraightChatroom/186681.

A contention exists among ASN group members that Mr Straight is one of the only people to have successfully claimed his 'minor estate', or the 'higher quantum estate', or the CQV trust. The belief among adherents is that Mr Straight supposedly asked for and receives USD 15,000 per month from his 'minor estate' fund. Mr Lawrence has claimed that he has spent two and a half years attempting to acquire his minor estate and as of June 2023, the 'finish line is in site [sic] … This will be the next journey for me to accomplish and with many many of you we will restore God's order'.[75] There is no evidence that Mr Straight or Mr Lawrence has achieved access to their supposed secret accounts or that such accounts exist. Nevertheless, it is a very appealing idea. The idea that you have millions of dollars, just waiting for you, and all you have to do is figure out how to fill out the withdrawal slip. Well, that is very appealing indeed. To ASN devotees, it is most certainly worth spending a few thousand to get back millions.

iv. Services for Sale

To attempt to remove themselves from the reach of government, ASN leaders have developed a set of profit-making services. These materials can be purchased on multiple websites and are frequently advertised through the Telegram group. ASN leaders sell products and services and also promote the services of others in the movement. A sample of products and services for sale (not an exhaustive list) is detailed below.

- *Sovereign Street Foundation*:[76] This is an organisation that assists people attempting to become ASNs. Services offered include one-on-one consulting at USD 150 a session, trust and wills (that range in price from USD 500–1,500), sessions for 'naturalized citizens' wanting to be ASNs (three sessions for USD 400) and help for those attempting to fill out the 'freedom bundle' (three sessions for USD 400), and assistance for those attempting to move their business 'into the private' via establishing a Private Membership Association (PMA).
- *State National Community*:[77] This website includes information about the basics of becoming a state national along with ads to purchase other related materials. These include: Auto-Generated Freedom Bundle (USD 175), Auto-Generated Affidavit of Repudiation (USD 50), Auto-Generated All Recording Papers (without Affidavit of Repudiation) (USD 150); the purchase of multiple recorded seminars that range in price between USD 80 and USD 300; decals, T-shirts, magnets, stickers that say 'I am NOT a sovereign citizen', keychains, pens, books by Ron Gibson about land patents and private property tax information, hoodies, jackets, hats, civil peace flags, automobile plates, golf cart and ATV plates, pins, and iron on patches.

[75] B Lawrence, 'Super Stoked About the Gettysburg Seminar' Telegram (9 June 2023), www.t.me/c/1245253765/247469.

[76] 'Services' Sovereign Street Foundation, www.sovereignstreetfoundation.org.

[77] American Nationals (n 49).

- *State National Store*:[78] A website selling ASN merchandise including magnets, stickers, calendars, books, flags, clothing, seminars (beginning at USD 70), and thumb drives (USD 80);
- *BirthRight the movie website*:[79] A donation-collecting website for the ASN film in development. At the time of this writing, USD 170,000 has been raised with the goal of USD 250,000. The purpose of the film is to 'awaken the masses to the fraud and corruption of our past and the unknowing delivery of our children into the commercial hand of the STATES INC'.[80] The film is directed by two filmmakers who are said to be Emmy-nominated and award-winning. It will feature Ann Vandersteel, Bobby Lawrence, David Straight and Ron Gibson, among others. Relatedly, during the Christmas season, an ASN from Wyoming Sunset Boutique partnered with Birthright to offer to sell Christmas ornaments and to donate 100 per cent of the proceeds towards the film.[81]
- *AORhelp.com*:[82] A website selling ASN products including the 'freedom bundle' (USD 400), a product that includes all the paperwork needed to 'claim American state national status', the American Sovereign book (USD 100) that 'teaches you how to live free from government regulation', ASN clothing, gift sets, and David Straight's training binder (USD 199), which includes over 555 pages that David uses to teach his seminars, among other related materials.
- *Straightevents.com*:[83] This website sells many of the same products mentioned above. Additional services include links to other websites that advertise 'StraightPMA' (USD 2,500), which will assist with setting up a business in a PMA. PMAs are advertised as a mechanism to protect one's business, to move it 'into the private' supposedly free of government intervention and legal liabilities.[84]
- *DavidStraightsilver.com*:[85] A site that allows one to purchase 'dealer direct pricing on gold & silver', and explanations as to how to rollover your IRA or 401K to gold or silver or 'bypass the banking system altogether'.
- *Asntrt.com*:[86] A website from which one can purchase approximately nine square feet (3'× 3') of land in Texas (USD 387), which ASN leaders claim is mandatory for anyone wanting to claim their 'minor estate'; Purchase of this Texas property, may be suitable for those who desire only to stand, but would

[78] American Nationals, 'Store', www.statenational.store.
[79] Birth Right, 'Born Free, Live Free', www.birthrightthemovie.com.
[80] ibid.
[81] B Lawrence, 'Fun News!!' Telegram (9 December 2023), www.t.me/c/1326817170/4577.
[82] Affidavit of Repudiation, 'Repudiation and Revocation of Citizenship' www.AORhelp.com.
[83] D Straight, Straight Events, www.straightevents.com.
[84] Sarteschi (n 1).
[85] D Straight, 'Welcome to the Wealth Strategies Presentation' David Straight's Patriot Silver Team, www.davidstraightsilver.com.
[86] American State Nationals of the Republic of Texas, PMA, 'Own Your Own Land Under Land Patent' www.asntrt.com.

prove impractical for those wishing to lie down. PMAs can also be purchased at this site.

- *ASNclothing.com*:[87] A website selling ASN merchandise.
- *Invitation 2 Freedom*: Described as their new sister community, this service provides information regarding 'having a life of freedom as nature and nature's God intended'. For five dollars annually, individuals will have access to a community of like-minded individuals and a three-part presentation addressing the 'Foundational Papers, Your Standing In Law' and trusts.[88]
- *Freeman Bot*:[89] A monthly subscription of USD 29.99 gives access to an artificial intelligence (AI) tool that is trained exclusively on 'God's law, Maxim's of law, freedom, patriotism and the US Constitution'. This project is being used by David Straight to 'have a mastermind on the platform'. It was a sales pitch coupled with asking for donations for his wife who he claims has, in essence, sacrificed herself for the movement, which is why she is in prison. He tells followers: 'If they can silence Bonnie, imagine the fate awaiting us in the shadows'.
- *Foreclosure Fraud Educational Protection Kit*: Purports to help people who are facing foreclosure.[90]

ASN methodology doubtlessly financially benefits the movement's leaders and their partners, but there appears to be absolutely no benefit to its purchasers. Perhaps the only benefit is a placebo-like effect, which keeps alive their dreams of untold wealth and provides hope for achieving their goal: the circumvention of all government laws. At the time of writing, certain vendors endorsed and platformed by Mr Lawrence, and whose methods were heavily promoted to followers, have failed to deliver their promised services. Some followers have lost a considerable amount of money, particularly those who purchased services from the 'MCO guys', among others. As a result, Mr Lawrence advised his followers to temporarily halt all filing and recording while he 'sorts out the new knowledge' he has learned.

In February 2024, Mr Lawrence announced that he is 'closing shop' and will no longer be selling merchandise or offering seminars. He plans to move fully 'in the private' and have no public presence. Adherents are eagerly awaiting his supposed final, more costly seminars, where he promises new information will be shared about how to acquire one's minor estate (AKA the quantum estate). Only those who attend the final seminars will be privy to a new special private Telegram channel being created. Without efforts to combat this type of movement, they will endure, and others will arise.

[87] American State Nationals Clothing, 'Welcome to ASN Clothing!' www.asnclothing.com.

[88] Cat Von W, 'Introducing Out NEW sister CommUNITY' Telegram (13 November 2023), www.t.me/DavidLesterStraightChatroom/202488; i2F community, 'Reigniting the American Spirit' www.invitation2freedom.com.

[89] Freeman Bot, 'Your Freedom is At Risk!' www.freemanbot.com.

[90] Stop Foreclosure Fraud, 'Educational Kit' www.stopforeclosurefraud.com/educational-kit.

III. Conclusion

A review of all available evidence finds none supporting any ASN assertion as achieving the result they claim to deliver. However, there is overwhelming, incontrovertible evidence that ASN adherents are consistently and quickly separated from their money. Many are quite willing to pay thousands for the 'treasure map' that shows the path to untold millions. WC Fields (as Larson W Whipsnade) is quite famous for remarking 'You can't cheat an honest man …'.[91] What is logically consistent, and the true meaning of the quotation, is 'you can only cheat a dishonest man'. Con men or confidence men are criminals who flourish by identifying dishonest individuals who seek to prosper, to escape the laws of their countries, to beat the system and in some way gain something that they do not deserve and have not earned. We are a nation of laws, some of which we may not like or agree with, but the 'honest man' obeys them nonetheless. Does the 'honest man' reject the law? Does the honest man, choose to stand outside the law? Should those who choose to stand outside the law, be labelled and thought of as anything other than 'outlaws?' Should the shorthand description of the ASN movement be 'con men exploiting the gullibility of those who are seeking to live outside the law, to acquire the treasure map to unearned wealth and the freedom to supersede all law?' PT Barnum is attributed with giving us the following admonition 'there is a sucker born every minute'.[92] Can we successfully argue the opposing position?

This chapter offered a comprehensive overview of the ASN movement, an anti-government group that blends conspiracy theories and religious beliefs. ASNs actively work to subvert the laws of society and propagate profit-oriented schemes. Like other sovereign citizen/pseudolaw groups, the ASN ideology has no factual basis. Courts, both in the United States and internationally, have consistently found that their ideas are frivolous, devoid of merit, and have no conceivable validity in law. We must do more to prevent the dissemination and promotion of these baseless ideologies.

[91] *You Can't Cheat an Honest Man* (Universal Pictures, 1939).
[92] AH Saxon, *P.T. Barnum: The Legend and the Man* (Columbia University Press, 1989) 335–36.

12

Traffic Matters and Pseudolaw: The Big Shakedown

DAVID HEILPERN

I. Introduction

I was a New South Wales (NSW) magistrate for 22 years, and before that a practising lawyer. In 1992 a long-term client of mine named Denis Walker was charged with a serious firearm offence. He argued that, as a consequence of the *Mabo* decision,[1] Aboriginal people were not bound by the assault laws of NSW. He lost at every step, all the way to the High Court.[2] This sparked my interest in issues of sovereignty, and as a magistrate I was regularly challenged by pseudolaw adherents.

There was a noticeable feature of those who appeared in the Local Court, and those who regularly feature in social media posts and videos advocating pseudolaw: the interaction with traffic laws. Traffic law in Australia is complex, with seven jurisdictions, each with their own schemes and structures. It is largely ignored in academia, and not covered except in the most perfunctory manner in law schools. Yet for most citizens, it is their primary contact with the criminal justice system. Offending ordinarily results in a fine and loss of demerit points. However, non-payment of fines also leads to loss of licence.[3] Driving once disqualified by courts or suspended by authorities is a serious offence, with rapidly escalating penalties up to imprisonment.

It is understandable that people may wish to avoid these consequences. The simplest way is to not break the road rules. Others purchase kits or subscriptions from the pseudolegal websites considered below. For numerous drivers this seems to be the start of their pseudolaw interest. This phenomenon appears to be uniquely Australian – in the United States, the movement is rooted in tax law,[4] and in Canada, family and constitutional law.[5]

[1] *Mabo v Queensland (No 2)* (1991) 175 CLR 1.

[2] *Walker v The State of New South Wales* (1994) 182 CLR 45.

[3] See, for example, Fines Act 1996 (NSW), s 66.

[4] C Kalinowski IV, 'A Legal Response to the Sovereign Citizen Movement' (2019) 80 *Montana Law Review* 153, 154.

[5] D Netolitzky and R Warman, 'Enjoy the Silence: Pseudolaw at the Supreme Court of Canada' (2020) 57 *Alberta Law Review* 715, 717.

In Australia, focusing on traffic laws is crucial in debunking the pseudolaw message because it is the chosen legal issue for so many pseudolaw adherents, and the consequences can ultimately lead to imprisonment. As a result of my experiences as a magistrate, I have a tragically magisterial and encyclopaedic knowledge of traffic law, and have seen every pseudolaw argument raised and lost, as well as closely observing interstate and international developments. I am now Dean of Law at Southern Cross University, and still practise law around Australia.

This chapter is structured around two sets of falsehoods that infect this area – pseudolegal and pseudofactual. The consideration is focused on refuting falsehoods on two key traffic law websites, and briefly considers the role of government in regulating these businesses. A key issue is the extent to which these websites encourage readers to be dishonest with police, courts and government agencies.

II. Examining Two Sources of Pseudolegal Traffic Nonsense

The purpose of this chapter is to identify, analyse and debunk some of the principal claims being made by pseudolaw adherents in Australia in their advice on interactions with traffic law. This requires, firstly, the identification and articulation of those claims, and secondly, critical analysis against existing law. The two most prominent sites are Aussie Speeding Fines (ASF)[6] and Lawfulme[7] – both for-profit websites with a paywall for key information. These websites were regularly quoted in my courts, and dominate the market. They are subscription or single-purchase and are available to the general public.

ASF sells an ebook, CDs and has a membership and ongoing service. For the purpose of this study, I purchased digital access to the website and the book titled *Digital Speeding Fines – What you REALLY need to Know*. There are other more expensive options, including an Advanced Membership subscription. The website is protected from printing or copying, and the only way to save the material is by screenshot. Mike Palmer, a founder, writer and spokesperson for ASF has recently had his own brushes with the law;[8] unsurprisingly these do not rate a mention anywhere on the website.

ASF claims to help the purchaser 'beat traffic' matters including speeding and parking fines. The website has hundreds of 'testimonials' from unverified and barely identified subscribers on the website – all claiming success.

[6] ASF: aussiespeedingfines.com.

[7] Living Free Movement: www.livingfreemovement.org/me-platforms/LawfulMe.

[8] Mr Palmer was ordered by McNamara J in *Deputy Commissioner of Taxation v Palmer (No 2)* [2022] VCC 2001 to pay the ATO in excess of $2.2 million for accrued taxes unpaid over the last decade.

The first hurdle in considering the material is the Legal Notice that appears only after paying the subscription joining fee. It demands that: 'You will read the document by yourself, and not share any information with anyone other than your legal representative.'[9] It further requires that the subscriber agrees 'not to use any information against the authors', and that no content will be posted or published anywhere. If you do not agree, then you are directed to immediately shut down the browser and go no further. There is no offer of a refund. Any breach of this 'agreement' will result, the reader is informed, in a '$1million fine'. There are also copious repetitive disclaimers purporting that nothing in the document is legal advice, and that they do not suggest readers do anything illegal.

Nevertheless, I shall press on. First, the condition is unilaterally imposed post-purchase, and is unenforceable. Second, the 'fine' has no basis in law. Third, there are a range of defences available should action be taken – not least the public interest in protecting consumers from shysters. Finally, the site clearly does give legal advice and suggests criminal conduct.

LawfulMe is a paid subscription service which includes video, role play and written information on traffic matters, and is part of a conglomerate of self-help sites run by Tom Barnett. This analysis focuses on a video presentation titled 'Handling a speeding fine on LawfulMe',[10] which, at the time of writing, was not paywalled. One of the principal participants in the video was recently convicted of a criminal offence in Queensland after pleading guilty to illegal fundraising.[11] For the purpose of this research, I also attended an information session from a related group which bases its pseudolaw material on the ASF books and the publications of Tom Barnett.

The challenge in analysing each site is determining a limit in refuting the head-swimming avalanche of supposed statements of law. Each of the authors and presenters makes so many overlapping and erroneous claims that many volumes could be written in response. For example, both sources are replete with the stock-standard pseudolaw arguments such as:

- governments are private corporations and have no power to make or enforce laws;
- without agreement by the person charged, the law does not apply;
- the laws are 'not enacted in the Queen's name';

[9] ASF (n 6).

[10] T Barnett, 'Handling a Speeding Fine on LawfulMe' TomBarnettTV (18 July 2022), tombarnett.tv/2022/07/18/handling-a-speeding-fine-on-LawfulMe.

[11] Queensland Government, 'Not so "Helpful Hands" Lands Fake Charity in Court' Media Statement (28 August 2023), www.qld.gov.au/law/laws-regulated-industries-and-accountability/queensland-laws-and-regulations/fair-trading-services-programs-and-resources/fair-trading-latest-news/media-statements/2023/not-so-helpful-hands-lands-fake-charity-in-court.

- there must be a victim for there to be a crime, and as there is no injured party, there is no crime;
- your name, unless capitalised, is not your name – 'YOU are actually not your name, and they are taking your NAME to court not you'.

Fortunately, others have systematically and cogently dealt with the key fundamental contentions in pseudolaw.[12] Accordingly, I focus here on traffic law and court tactics where a gap in the academic and published material is apparent.

One of the challenges in responding is that the mishmash of pseudolaw is not akin to a disprovable physical reality – for example, that the earth is flat. That is because law is, at its heart, a human construct. The only reality check is the acceptance or otherwise by the courts – and none of this gobbledygook has ever been adopted in any court in Australia.

III. Pseudolegal Falsehoods

Pseudolegal falsehoods are misstatements of the law. Psuedofactual falsehoods seek to present facts to the court which are demonstrably wrong or simply lies. For each falsehood, the methodology adopted is to articulate the claim and demonstrate its wrongness. The purpose is to show that those who adopt such falsehoods and seek to deploy them are doomed to fail in their ultimate aim.

Section A below focuses on examining the principal pseudolegal falsehoods that arise in the context of Australian traffic law. Section B then examines the equivalent pseudofactual falsehoods. The claims are drawn from the two pseudolaw sites identified above.

A. The Road Rules are not Law

The authors introduced above contend that the road rules in various states are guidelines only and have no legal authority. They conclude: 'What they don't tell you is that these rules are NOT law, they are simply Guidelines to help traffic flow.'[13] This is, they argue, partly because there has been no authorised delegation and the use of the words 'enabled' and 'as if' in the publication of road rules actually means that the rules are 'disabled' and not legally binding. Further, they state that the regulatory authorities are private corporations with no

[12] R Sudy, 'The Organised Pseudolegal Commercial Argument in Australia' Freeman Delusion (9 October 2023), www.freemandelusion.com. See also H Hobbs, S Young and J McIntyre, 'The Internationalisation of Pseudolaw: The Growth of Sovereign Citizen Arguments in Australia and Aotearoa New Zealand' (2023) 47 *University of New South Wales Law Journal* 309.

[13] ASF (n 6).

power or legitimacy: 'That's right, a company, VicRoads/NSW RTA/Queensland Transport etc are simply privately owned companies that have a contract with the Government to provide certain services for them.'[14]

I have traced the legislative pathway for each jurisdiction in Australia and confirmed that in each case the road rules are legitimate, enforceable delegated legislation.[15] The authors are simply wrong – the delegations are in place, the road rules are enforceable, the state and territory authorities and police forces are not corporations, and members of the public do not have to agree with the laws for them to be binding. Road rules are not 'guidelines', they are enforceable criminal provisions.

That delegated legislation is unenforceable is classic pseudolaw fare in Australia and internationally. In the United States in particular, the tax laws are frequently challenged, typically claiming that the relevant law is invalidly enacted or defective because of the Magna Carta, or the status or payment of the monarch,[16] or that delegated legislation only applies to 'government actors'.[17]

B. The 'Three Letters'

The authors of ASF advise their readers to send three letters – a Notice of Objection, a Clarification, and a Private Settlement Agreement. The Notice of Objection is over 1,000 words long and raises at least 12 points of pseudolaw. The Notice of Settlement, which they also recommend, is placed as an advertisement in a newspaper and reads in part:

> Let this serve as constructive notice that the matter between Senior Iva Radar, VICTORIA POLICE and John Smith of 10 Smith Street, Smithville VIC 3333, has been settled and closed by the private agreement of the parties. Copies of Private Settlement Agreement and related documents are attached in support. Interference in this private contract by any third party would constitute an unwelcome and unlawful trespass and a violation of any oath of office that such third party may be bound to uphold.
>
> Notice to the principal is notice to the agent. Notice to the agent is notice to the principal.[18]

The authors of ASF claim in the book that 'these letters will work in most cases'.[19] Even if they do not, the authors contend that they will give you a 'tremendous advantage' if the matter goes to court. That is untrue. In fact, I would contend that they have never worked. Such letters are commonplace in the Local Court in NSW

[14] ibid.
[15] See, for example, in NSW: Road Rules 2014 (NSW) are authorised by the Road Transport Act 2013 (NSW), ss 23–24.
[16] Hobbs, Young and McIntyre (n 12).
[17] Netolitzky and Warman (n 5) 733.
[18] ASF (n 6).
[19] ibid.

and are complete legal gobbledegook. In my experience, they are placed on file and ignored. None of these letters will assist a defendant in any way.

C. Taking the Matter to Court, You cannot Lose

The authors of ASF claim that right up until the date of the court case, you can withdraw your objection and just pay the original fine:

> But there will be NO extra costs to pay, and you still get the same points on your licence … you can have a number of adjournments and drag the case out for a year or so and then say at the last minute you withdraw your objection, and you still only have to pay the original fine. Again, this is your Constitutional and common law right.[20]

The basis of this is said to be Article 15 of the International Covenant on Civil and Political Rights:

> No one shall be held guilty of any criminal offence on account of any act or omission which did not constitute a criminal offence, under national or international law, at the time when it was committed. Nor shall a heavier penalty be imposed than the one that was applicable at the time when the criminal offence was committed. If, subsequent to the commission of the offence, provision is made by law for the imposition of the lighter penalty, the offender shall benefit thereby.[21]

Similarly, the panellists in the LawfulMe video suggest taking matters to court to fight them without consideration that the penalty may increase. Tom Barnett says: 'but you know from anyone who hasn't been to court, for a matter that's not very, there's not a lot at stake to it, this is a good way to wet your feet'.[22] However, the correct legal position is that by taking a matter to court the penalty can be significantly greater than the amount of the ticket fine.

I will give the example of NSW in a case where I was the initial magistrate. A Mr Cameron engaged a contractor to prune a tree blocking his sea view, and the tree was on council land. He was given a AUD $600 ticket by the council. He elected to take the matter to court and then pleaded guilty. I fined him AUD $10,000. Plus, he had to pay the legal costs of the council which were many thousands of dollars. He then unsuccessfully appealed.[23]

When you go to court for a traffic offence which started as a ticket, a whole different penalty regime applies. You may have to pay a far greater fine than the ticket and pay the legal costs of the prosecutor. Not only that, but the court in most jurisdictions also has the power to disqualify you from driving in addition to

[20] ibid.

[21] International Covenant on Civil and Political Rights, opened for signature 16 December 1966, 2200 UNTS 21 (entered into force 23 March 1976).

[22] LawfulMe (n 7) 0:42:43.

[23] *Cameron v Eurobodalla Shire Council* [2006] NSWLEC 47.

any fine. I exercised that discretion often with pseudolaw adherents, because they clearly were not going to obey the law in future.

This occurred in *Rossiter v Adelaide City Council*.[24] In that case Mr Rossiter challenged a parking fine and was convicted. He appealed to the Supreme Court and ran all the usual pseudolaw arguments. The court concluded:

> It is regrettable that the appellant has advocated the various pseudo legal arguments underpinning this appeal. If he has acted on the advice of others, he is well advised to stop doing so. His decision to defend has resulted in a trivial parking fine escalating to a financial burden exceeding $20,000. He also had to pay the costs of the prosecution.[25]

An unwitting pseudolaw adherent is likely to leave court with a significantly greater penalty than if they just paid the fine.

D. The Absence of Juries at Local/Magistrates Court

The insistence on a right to trial by jury is common in pseudolaw contentions in common law countries.[26] The authors of ASF make the same argument. They contend that a person can only be tried by a judge and jury, or with two magistrates on the bench, 'otherwise, the court is invalid and unlawful'.[27]

This is your right, they suggest, under Chapter III of the Australian Constitution. This is supported by reference to *Forge v ASIC*,[28] which is liberally quoted. Yet the passages quoted are not part of the findings of the court at all. The quotes are from paragraph [245] of the judgment, which set out the appellant's arguments. The court specifically 'reached no conclusion as to their correctness'.[29] There is no right to a jury, or to two magistrates as the authority quoted for that proposition is completely erroneous.

In any event, this has been repeatedly determined by Supreme Courts throughout Australia to be utterly without merit. For example, in *Moran v Police*,[30] the South Australian Supreme Court found:

> The appellant's first contention was that the court comprised of a single magistrate had no jurisdiction to hear the matter. This complaint is without substance. A breach of the *Australian Road Rules* is a summary offence and therefore hearing by a magistrate was appropriate.[31]

[24] *Rossiter v Adelaide City Council* [2020] SASC 61.
[25] ibid [52].
[26] See, for example, in *Canada Meads v Meads*, 2012 ABQB 571 [566]; E Haynie, 'Populism, Free Speech, and the Rule of Law: The Fully Informed Jury Movement and its Implications' (1997) 88 *The Journal of Criminal Law and Criminology* 343.
[27] ASF (n 6).
[28] *Forge v ASIC* (2006) 228 CLR 45 [246].
[29] ibid.
[30] *Moran v Police* [2010] SASC 269.
[31] ibid [12].

E. Legislative Quagmire on Fines

The authors contend that because of section 8(12) of the Imperial Acts Application Acts, in all states a person cannot be fined or have demerit points without a conviction first being imposed, rendering the tickets for speeding or other offences invalid. Not only that, but no fine above AUD 20 can be imposed due to sections 9, 11, 16 and 22 of the Currency Act 1965 (Cth), and section 115 of the Australian Constitution itself prohibits a state from enforcing a debt as a result of a fine. This latter conclusion is explained on the basis that we no longer have any 'gold backed currency'.[32]

Each of these arguments has been dismissed as misconceived (at best) in every Australian jurisdiction.[33] Interestingly, this argument mimics submissions made in Canada and the United States regarding currency and gold.[34]

F. Responding to Mail

Littered throughout the ASF material are comments that the laws cannot apply unless you accept them. So, if you receive a letter in the mail, including a ticket or reminder, you simply mark it 'return to sender', 'and then there is nothing that they can do, because you have the right not to accept it'.[35] Further advice suggests that if they 'EVER send you a fine again, you can have them charged with harassment, extortion and/or mail fraud under the Telecommunications Act which would be a Federal offence'.[36] It is contended that if the authorities do eventually take you to court despite returning all their mail, then 'you have a great case'.

This argument is a derivation of the strawman contention that the criminal law is a form of contract, and that if you do not accept the contract then the law does not apply to you. Some even argue that the Constitution itself is a contract.[37] In LawfulMe, Tom Barnett states that one way of dealing with the speeding fine is to 'question the validity of the offer in the first place, which is what we are talking about, if it was a different type or a different form or different circumstances we might be looking at a conditional acceptance process'.[38]

[32] ASF (n 6).

[33] See, eg *Pullen v O'Brien* [2014] QDC 92; *Skyring v Commissioner of Taxation* [2007] FCA 1526 [4].

[34] See, eg, *Meads* (n 26) [227]; Federal Bureau of Investigation (Domestic Terrorism Unit), 'Sovereign Citizens: An Introduction for Law Enforcement' (November 2010) 6, info.publicintelligence.net/FBI-SovereignCitizens.pdf.

[35] ASF (n 6).

[36] ibid.

[37] *Shar v Attorney General* [2004] WASC 144 [11]–[12].

[38] LawfulMe (n 7) at 0:42:39.

In reality, legislation in each jurisdiction in Australia contains deeming provisions relating to the service of mail by post.[39] Returning the notice would not assist a defendant at all. So, leaving aside the classic sovereign citizen argument about consent, posting the notice, and more recently even emailing it, is sufficient service. This further begs the question – who would actually do the charging under the Telecommunications Act 1997 (Cth) for any further communications?

G. Revocation or Annulment

All around Australia people are convicted in their absence, provided they are served with process.[40]

According to the authors of ASF, if convicted in your absence you can rely on annotation 206 of the UK's Australian Constitution Act 1900: 'No man can be legally bound by a judgment given behind his back without him having had an opportunity to be heard.'[41]

First, this is not a quote from the Constitution at all – it is from a constitutional law textbook authored by John Quick and Robert Garran.[42] Second, if you have been given a ticket, or served with a court attendance notice or infringement, then you have indeed had the opportunity to be heard. You have simply chosen not to exercise it.

H. Measurements

In ASF it is claimed that speeding detection devices are inconsistent with section 10 of the National Measurement Act 1960 (Cth). Section 10 provides that measurements should be ascertained in accordance with appropriate standards of measurement or certified measuring instruments. ASF contends that: 'Speed cameras, Lasers and radar devices do NOT comply with s 10 … and therefore their readings cannot legally be used to prove anything in a court of law.' Thus, it is argued, 'All speeding detection devices currently being used in Australia are being used ILLEGALY.'[43] Furthermore, it is claimed that any statutory presumptions on speed, where the court must accept a technological reading, are invalid. This is

[39] See, for example, Road Transport (General) Regulations 2021 (NSW), ss 153–158, which provide for postal service of all licencing and registration matters. Court attendance notices may be served by post or email, as per Local Court Rules 2009 (NSW), r 5.9.

[40] See, for example, Criminal Procedure Act 1986 (NSW), s 196.

[41] ASF (n 6).

[42] J Quick and R Garran, *The Annotated Constitution of the Australian Commonwealth*, revd edn (LexisNexis Butterworths, 2015).

[43] ASF (n 6).

because speeding is not a criminal offence,[44] amongst other reasons. A similar argument is made on LawfulMe by Tom Barnett:

> The photo you can see that it is clearly actually going up a hill, slight hill, now in the legislation of every state it clearly provides that in the measurement of any distance in regards to use of any act, so your road traffic act of the state, that the distance must be measured in a straight line and on a horizontal plane, so it cannot be on a hill, it has to be a flat road. So, the measurement itself cannot be used for the purposes of an act, the road safety act, or the traffic act of your state. So once again people, when they get these particular fines, you have got to check that there is no hill involved, and that the measurement is in a straight line.[45]

Again, this contention has been dismissed unceremoniously by the courts repeatedly. A clear example is a 2010 case, where the Supreme Court of South Australia found that:

> Section 10 of the Act operates only when it is necessary to ascertain whether or not a measurement of a physical quantity has been made in the terms of Australian legal units of measurement. It does not in its terms set out a method of determining whether an Australian legal unit has been measured correctly in a particular instance.[46]

I. The Slope

Closely related to the measurement falsehood (section H above) is the contention that a driver cannot be convicted of speeding if travelling on a slope. In the video presentation, Darren D says that a fine can be challenged in court because the interpretation acts in each state provide that distance must be measured on the horizontal plane and in a straight line. Because there is a slope, and the camera is at an angle, then it is not measured lawfully:

> Well it really comes down to, that it appears from the photo the device has been set up on an incline, and therefore it doesn't, the distance that has been measured can't be used for the purpose of an act. So, it is as simple as that … I have a friend who ah, in the last 18 months he has had three different speeding fines and they have all been on hills, and he's used that early defence that we mentioned and he has been successful all three times.[47]

On the video, there is a screenshot of the Commonwealth Acts Interpretation Act 1991: 'Section 35 – In the measurement of any distance for the purposes of any Act, that distance shall be measured in a straight line on a horizontal plane.' The video notes that although this is the Commonwealth provision and that each of

[44] ibid.
[45] LawfulMe (n 7) at 0:47:21.
[46] *Moran v Police* (2010) SASC 269 [15]; see also *Pearce v Dennis* [1997] QCA 239.
[47] LawfulMe (n 7).

the states have their own Interpretation Act, if there is an inconsistency, then the Commonwealth Act overrides the state.

First, I suggest there is no such trifecta of successful cases. If this was accurate, it would be front-page news in the national media, because it would apply nationwide and call into question every speeding fine issued on other than flat ground.

Second, the Commonwealth Acts Interpretation Act 1901 (Cth) does not override the state acts. The Constitution is explicit in section 109 that Commonwealth acts only prevail over state acts where there is an inconsistency. There is no inconsistency – the Commonwealth act is a guide to interpreting Commonwealth acts. The Queensland Act determines the interpretation of Queensland legislation. Here is the Queensland legislation:

> ***Measurement of distance***
>
> In applying an Act, distance is to be measured along the shortest road ordinarily used for travelling unless there is a contrary intention that distance is to be measured in a straight line on a horizontal plane or in another way.[48]

So, the acts are different, and the Queensland provision of 'in another way' prevails – obviously not prohibiting measurement of a speed camera on a slightly sloping road.

Third, and most tellingly, all the interpretation acts have a proviso – in the Queensland legislation it is section 4: 'The application of this Act may be displaced, wholly or partly, by a contrary intention appearing in any Act.'[49]

Clearly, there is a contrary intention by the speeding provisions in the traffic legislation which refers to any public road. They are not limited to speed detection on a dead flat road. So, for these reasons, this argument is destined to fail.

J. The Power of Local Government to Issue Fines

The ASF ebook claims that there is no power for local governments to issue fines because the constitution does not mention local governments: 'Then Local Government does not have any lawful power – Simple!'[50] This is demonstrably false. There is no obstacle in the Constitution to prevent state parliaments from legislating to create, empower and regulate local government. All states have done so. In Victoria, for example, the Constitution explicitly grants Parliament the power to make laws for and in relation to local government.[51]

[48] Acts Interpretation Act 1954 (Qld), s 37.
[49] Acts Interpretation Act 1954 (Qld), s 4.
[50] ASF (n 6).
[51] Constitution Act 1975 (Vic), s 74B.

K. Parking Fines

The ASF ebook contends that parking fines are largely invalid on several grounds. There is apparently no right to charge anyone for parking except commercial vehicles because of section 92 of the Australian Constitution (the annotated version by Quick and Garran).[52] Further, all roads are 'fee simple' so you cannot be charged for parking on them, and, in any case, parking meters do not comply with section 10 of the National Measurements Act. Finally, Article 1 of the International Covenant on Civil and Political Rights (ICCPR), protects parkers, while local authorities are 'just companies that have no right to issue fines at all'.[53]

Section 92 of the Australian Constitution relates to free trade between the states, and is silent on the topic of parking fines. The term 'fee simple' does not mean that any person can use any road for free. It is a property law term relating to absolute ownership of land. Section 10 of the National Measurements Act does not apply, as discussed above. Article 1 of the ICCPR, which provides that 'all peoples have the right to self-determination' has nothing at all to say about parking tickets, surprisingly. Local councils are not companies and the legislation in each jurisdiction specifically states this. For example, section 220 of the Local Government Act 1993 (NSW) reads:

> *220 Legal status of a council*
>
> (1) A council is a body politic of the State with perpetual succession and the legal capacity and powers of an individual, both in and outside the State.
>
> (2) A council is not a body corporate (including a corporation).

The thought that this hotchpotch of pseudolegal falsehoods could enable an adherent to lawfully park wherever and whenever they choose is perhaps the ultimate example of wishful thinking. I park, therefore it is legal.

L. Demerit Points

The authors suggest that if you delay your case for 12 months, then 'even if you pay your fine at the last minute your (demerit) points are only valid for half the time'.[54] This is simply untrue in most jurisdictions. The points are calculated from the time you pay the fine, or when the court convicts. It is fallacious to state that delaying the court date means that you only lose points for half the time.

M. Speed Cameras

In ASF, it is suggested that a photo from a speed camera cannot be used as evidence against a driver because 'these agencies cannot prove that a photo has not been

[52] ASF (n 6); Quick and Garran (n 42).
[53] ASF (n 6).
[54] ibid.

altered and therefore by law is inadmissible as evidence'.[55] This is demonstrably false because each state and territory has laws which create presumptions that the photo as tendered is proof of its contents and accuracy unless proven otherwise.[56]

This is also dealt with at length in the LawfulMe video, where it is argued that because the prosecution must prove its case beyond a reasonable doubt, issues such as challenging the calibration of the camera, the implications of another vehicle in the picture, the existence of power lines and other potential interferences will lead to an acquittal. Darren Dixon states:

> Yeah, quite often all you have to do is raise reasonable doubt, in the court, that the device was working accurately, you don't have to prove it 100%, it just must be beyond a reasonable doubt, so if you actually work out and in most of the manuals they have the, or they show the way you can actually work out the degree of errors, and there are many sites online that show this as well. So when you raise that reasonable doubt in the court, all you have to show is that that device, because of the way it was set up, and the angles, and you can actually work out how much, or how inaccurate the device was in relation to the amount of kilometres they're alleging you were going.[57]

It is true that in criminal cases, the prosecution bears the burden of proving each element of the offence beyond a reasonable doubt. However, this discourse fails to consider that parliaments have been aware for decades of the debacle that would occur in magistrates courts if the prosecution had to prove these issues every time. So, they have made it easier for the prosecution and enacted evidentiary provisions that mean that the prosecution does not have to prove certain matters.

In Queensland, for example, when the prosecution tenders the photo to the court it is evidence of everything contained on the photo, including speed and the accuracy of the device.[58] If a defendant turns up to court anywhere in Australia and tries to run these arguments, the magistrate will look at them with tired old eyes and just say: 'The photograph is evidence of everything stated on it, and depicted by it'. End of case.

N. Criminal Records

The ASF ebook states that even if the offence is found proven, the prosecution cannot rely on your prior record.[59] This is said to be because of the 'Road Safety Act section 90(4)' and the 'Geneva Convention on Driving'.

As to the former, this is a reference to the Road Safety Act 1986 in Victoria. The provision means that a record cannot be relied upon unless it was served on you prior to the hearing. Any objection by the defence can be remedied by the court by an adjournment.

[55] ibid.
[56] See, eg, Road Transport Act 2013 (NSW), s 137.
[57] LawfulMe (n 7) at 0:48:22.
[58] Transport Operations (Road Use Management) Act 1995 (Qld), s 120.
[59] ASF (n 6).

There is no Geneva Convention on Driving. There is a Geneva Convention on Road Traffic 1949.[60] Australia is a signatory; however, it has not been legislated in any jurisdiction and thus the provisions have no relevance to our legal system and our drivers are subject to our own road rules.

O. The 'Cosine Effect'

In the LawfulMe video, approximately 40 minutes is taken up with proposing that a speeding fine can be beaten by arguing the cosine effect. Here is just a sample:

> There is also certain things that the detection device must meet, and there is an amount of error that happens when there is angles involved when taking speed measurements, and that is known as the cosine effect, and from the legal standpoint, the measurement that, the inaccuracy of the measurement that is effected by the cosine effect is always in favour of the motorist, because the effect of that actual angle change reduces the measurement of the speed, so the greater that angle, the greater the reduction in the speed of the vehicle compared to the actual projected speed that has been detected ...[61]

This argument was run before me many times as a magistrate, probably because it features on so many pseudolaw websites. The problem for defendants is that the cosine effect *always* favours the driver by recording a lower speed than if the camera was directly in front. This is the case whether it is a fixed or mobile speed measuring device. So, even though the speed detected may be slightly out because of the angle, every expert who gave evidence in my court concluded that this meant the measuring device underestimated the actual speed of the vehicle because of the angle. The full Queensland Court of Appeal, for example, has specifically found that the cosine effect does not impact on the accuracy of the speed detection device.[62]

Further, every state has a manual available for speed cameras which debunks the cosine defence myth. Here is the key paragraph from the NSW manual:

> By application of the above formula it will be seen that relative velocity decreases as the angle increases. In short, the larger the angle the greater the error. It must be realised at this stage that the error is always to the advantage of the motorist.[63]

So, in short, despite the insistence of the participants in the video, this defence is destined to fail.

However, this falsehood, and others described in this chapter, raise the interesting and lightly researched connection between pseudolaw, and pseudoscience.

[60] Geneva Convention on Road Traffic 1949, opened for signature 19 September 1949, UNTS 125 (entered into force 26 March 1952).

[61] LawfulMe (n 7) at 0:22:29.

[62] *Osgood v Queensland Police Service* (2010) QCA 242 [43].

[63] NSW Police Service 'Highway Patrol Education Course – Silver Eagle II Operation Manual' NSW Police Service (2013) 37, www.police.nsw.gov.au/__data/assets/pdf_file/0006/291516/Silver_Eagle_II_Operation_Manual_06_2013.pdf.

So far, publication is limited to non-academic journals; however, it is an area ripe for discussion, particularly the connection between the anti-vaccination/masks/lockdown movement and pseudolaw adherents. Writing in 2016, Colin McRoberts noted:

> Pseudolaw resembles pseudoscience in both its methods and applications. Believers are typically intelligent and motivated, and capable of constructing complex edifices that sound superficially credible. A talented snake-oil salesman pitches miracle cures based on things such as DNA and nutraceuticals; likewise, pseudolegal gurus deal in tax relief or other schemes based on similarly serious-sounding concepts such as jurisdiction and legal personhood. Either way, believers feel more in control over forces that otherwise make them feel powerless – illness or the US Internal Revenue Service (IRS), for example.[64]

IV. Pseudofactual Falsehoods

It is not only pseudolaw that is promoted. The authors of ASF directly encourage readers to present known lies to regulatory authorities and courts. For obvious reasons, this is likely to be counterproductive for those making such representations.

When pulled over, no matter whether you were speeding or not, the advice is to firstly and firmly say 'I was not speeding' and if asked what speed you were doing, merely repeat the statement 'I was not speeding'.

> OK, so what do you say and not say? Firstly, in the words of that excellent TV show, the X Files – 'deny everything!' If they officer says they are pulling you over for speeding just simply say 'But I wasn't speeding'.[65]

But what if you were speeding? This advice is just plainly wrong, as any defence lawyer will tell you. First, if you end up pleading guilty or are found guilty, your denial of speeding will count against you on penalty.[66] Second, lying to the police is a criminal offence in some circumstances. Third, given in most cases your speed has been recorded on a device, your denial will be recorded by a body-worn camera, the police will know you are lying, and may well then be suspicious and investigate other crimes. The best advice in such circumstances is to say nothing beyond the statutory requirements of name, address and provision of licence.

Later in the book the authors recommend that you lie about your knowledge as to who was driving the vehicle if you get a ticket. They suggest that instead of nominating an alternate driver, a defendant should simply respond by saying that

[64] C McRoberts 'Here Comes Pseudolaw, a Weird Little Cousin of Pseudoscience' Aeon (21 March 2016), www.aeon.co/ideas/here-comes-pseudolaw-a-weird-little-cousin-of-pseudoscience.

[65] ASF (n 6).

[66] Generally, the earlier the admission, the greater the sentencing discount: see *Siganto v The Queen* (1998) 14 CLR 656.

you do not know who the driver was, because 'you had a number of friends staying and they all knew where the keys were'.[67] There is even a statutory declaration to that effect, ready for the reader to fill in:

> As per my previous correspondence to you, I was not the driver of ABC-123 on the 1/5/2008. We had 3 people staying with us from interstate: Jane Smith from 3 Smith Street, Smithville, QLD & 2 of her friends – Fred and Bob – I do not know their exact address but believe they also reside in Queensland.
>
> They took the car out on that day and I do not know which one of them was driving at the time. I have asked Jane who was driving on that particular day but, as they were staying with us for 2 weeks and shared the driving over that period, she cannot tell for sure who the actual driver was at the time.
>
> All I know is that it was not me, as I was at work and had driven our other vehicle ABC-321.[68]

If you do this, the authors claim, then 'they will have no option but to let it go'. The copious number of pretended disclaimers are masking an incitement to commit a serious crime. Completing a false statutory declaration is an imprisonable offence in every Australian jurisdiction,[69] as is seeking a benefit by deception.

If you get a speed camera offence:

> It is very easy to ring the agency who issued it and get an extension over the phone for a month by saying that you have been away for a month and only just got back and need time to find out who the driver is.[70]

All communications with these authorities and courts are recorded, and this lie will soon be exposed. Further, if the defendant ends up giving evidence and is questioned about this statement, things will only go from bad to worse. The suggested tactic is dangerous and wrong.

Chapter 5 of the book is titled 'How to legitimately adjourn your case for a long time'. One tactic is described as follows:

> All you need to do is ring the court a day or two before it is listed and explain that your barrister is on holidays and you can't get hold of him … it is a good idea to mention a barrister, even though you will be representing yourself.[71]

It is not legitimate to lie to the court – especially a sexist lie. A record of this will be kept on the court file. A keen-eyed magistrate will ask you who the barrister is and check. I know I regularly did.

Further adjournments can be obtained, it is suggested, by utilising the following falsehoods:

[67] ASF (n 6).
[68] ibid.
[69] See, for example, Crimes Act 1900 (NSW), s 307C.
[70] ASF (n 6).
[71] ibid.

- At the mention to set a date for the hearing, 'If they say July for example, you can say you know you will be travelling in July, but you are not sure when'.
- '[Y]ou can accept the date and then go home and find out you have something on that date – because you are new to all of this, and you didn't bring your diary to court.'
- On the day of hearing you can get a further adjournment by saying 'you are seeking clarification from your legal adviser on points of law … (or) that you have a relevant certificate coming from a mechanic … Explain that there was a death or illness in your family and as you are preparing the case yourself you need a clear head to be able to effectively represent yourself – they LOVE this one! … whatever it is make it seem half believable'.[72]

If you are convicted, further concoctions are suggested:

- If asked questions about your prior record on sentencing: 'all you have to do is say I don't know I don't have any recollection'.
- If you are about to lose your licence, then 'find someone in another state who will say that you live with them'. Then go to your local licensing agency 'and say you have misplaced your licence and need another copy'.[73]

This advice is no less than an incitement to commit crime which is likely to lead readers and adopters into serious legal strife.

These falsehoods are another typical characteristic not only of the pseudolaw adherent, but particularly of the pseudolaw for-profit promoter. The Southern Poverty Law Center in the United States maintains a Sovereign Citizens watch website, which documents the extent of fraud, dishonesty and violence inherent in the promotors and leaders of the movement.[74]

V. Where are the Regulatory Authorities?

This chapter does not provide a full analysis of the regulatory powers available to various arms of government to shut down these sources. However, it is clear from the analysis above that people who pay for this advice are being sold a pup.

There is no legal impediment to bush-lawyers spouting their opinions on what the law ought to be, nor even erroneous views of what the law actually is. However, if members of the public are, as consumers, paying for information which is simply false or suggesting criminal conduct then there are legal remedies available to authorities.

[72] ibid.
[73] ibid.
[74] Southern Poverty Law Center, 'Sovereign Citizens Movement', www.splcenter.org/fighting-hate/extremist-files/ideology/sovereign-citizens-movement.

I have considered whether the authors of the two sources considered above are engaging in 'legal practice'[75] and are thus prohibited under the various uniform practice laws in Australia. However, obviously, it is not legal practice to write nonsense books or state erroneous views about the law, even if they charge for the privilege. The sole test is whether they are engaged in legal practice. This term is not defined, and the courts have preferred a narrow definition which probably excludes the sort of mischief in these sources.[76]

Under Australian Consumer Laws,[77] federal, state and territory authorities have the power to seek injunctive relief and prosecute businesses that make false and misleading claims. The claims made by both these sources certainly are false and misleading. To take money from people and then suggest that by following the set advice they can win traffic matters in court is clearly within the definition of false and misleading conduct.[78]

Further, in the case of ASF, they are arguably engaging in criminal conduct by inciting, aiding and abetting consumers to make false statements to police and the courts. In some cases, they are encouraging and even drafting false statutory declarations. It beggars belief that they have not been prosecuted for these publications.

In the introduction, I stated the likelihood that for most pseudolaw adherents in Australia, their first exposure to sovereign citizen concepts are via websites such as these. Whilst some take the matters no further, pseudolaw adherents are a mixed bunch with a pointy end of violence. Apart from the well-known connections with the Train offenders which resulted in the deaths of two police and one civilian in Queensland in 2022,[79] there have been two other siege deaths with sovereign citizen overtones in New South Wales in recent times. The first was the death of Krista Kach in Newcastle, where the audio shows repeated classic pseudolaw claims.[80] The second is a suicide following shots at police and a siege in Lithgow with a long-term established sovereign citizen activist.[81]

[75] S Mark, 'What is Legal Work? – A Regulator's View' (2005) Conference Paper, Legal Services Commission, LAWASIADownUnder (20 March 2005).

[76] See, for example, *Legal Services Commissioner v Walter* [2011] QSC 132.

[77] Competition and Consumer Act 2010 (Cth), Sch 2 (Australian Consumer Law), ss 18(1), 29, 33, 224.

[78] *Australian Competition and Consumer Commission v Samsung Electronics Australia Pty Ltd* [2022] FCA 875.

[79] N Bucci and B Smee, 'Wieambilla Shooting: As More is Revealed about the Wieambilla Shooters, some Question why Gareth Train was not on Authorities Radar' *Guardian Australia* (17 December 2022), www.theguardian.com/australia-news/2022/dec/17/as-more-is-revealed-about-the-wieambilla-shooters-some-question-why-gareth-train-was-not-on-authorities-radar.

[80] H Alexander, 'Daughter Begged for Medical Care before Mother was Tasered and Died' *Sydney Morning Herald* (18 September 2023), www.smh.com.au/national/nsw/daughter-begged-for-medical-care-before-mother-was-tasered-and-died-20230917-p5e5bt.html.

[81] P Duffin, 'Man who Shot Himself in Siege Linked to Sovereign Citizen Movement, Police Suspect' *Sydney Morning Herald* (17 July 2023), www.smh.com.au/national/nsw/man-dead-after-shooting-at-police-in-siege-20230717-p5dotr.html.

There is clearly a road to travel between dodging traffic fines to these shocking acts of violence, but this analysis does support an argument that reasonable steps should be taken to curtail the traffic offence-related for-profit sovereign citizen movement.

VI. Conclusion

The profit-making arms of the pseudolaw movement prey on vulnerable members of the community, encouraging them to commit offences that can only land them in greater trouble with the law. Further, allowing them to continue to sell their illegal advice encourages more people into the movement. It may start with a parking fine, but it can, and regularly does, escalate. The authorities have been remiss in not shutting these websites down.

The advice of both the sources utilised for this chapter is utterly without foundation in law. Whether it be the cosine effect or service of documents, the conclusions presented by the websites and in ebooks have not been accepted by any court in Australia.

Hopefully, this chapter will serve two purposes. First, it will spur the regulatory and enforcement authorities to shut down these websites. Second, it will provide a resource for courts, prosecutors, lawyers and laypeople seeking to dispel the tsunami of falsehoods being promoted.

13

The 'First Nation Medical Board': A Case Study of Pseudolegal Parasitisation of Legitimate Indigenous Sovereignty

COLIN McROBERTS

I. Introduction

Pseudolaw is the substitution of false legal authority for legitimate but less convenient realities. It appeals to those who feel that regulatory oversight is an intolerable intrusion but cannot find an effective alternative. Pseudolaw fails when tested against real legal rules, but sometimes those tests are slow in coming – particularly when regulators prioritise other issues. Pseudolegal operations can therefore sometimes bumble along for years, appearing successful on the surface while doing terrible harm and heading for an inevitable failure.

This chapter presents a case study of an ongoing example, in which a pseudolegal enterprise in the United States is attempting to parasitise the sovereignty of a legitimate Indigenous tribe. The business, the First Nation Medical Board (FNMB), claims the tribe has authorised it to sell medical licences to non-members. These licences supposedly allow their bearer to practise medicine – even prescribe controlled substances – anywhere in the country. A significant number of these licensees have a history of regulatory problems, from serious felony convictions to stripped licences, so the promise is appealing. But the tribe has not authorised this scheme, does not have the power to license extraterritorial medical services delivered by and for non-members, and has never sought to do so. The firm is simply exploiting the tribe's name and status.

This case study is significant as an illustration of how pseudolegal actors escape detection and regulation. Some of those tactics are common in pseudolaw, such as targeting victims who are reluctant to trust and bring complaints to mainstream regulators – here, the alternative medical community. Others are more particular to this context. The operation relies on a misconception of Indigenous sovereignty, a subject that many North American authorities understand poorly and is in a state of flux in the United States in particular. Regulators may have been unduly reluctant to press on the firm's claim to sovereign authority if they felt uncertain about whether there was any possible merit to it. That suggests that Indigenous nations are uniquely vulnerable to pseudolegal exploitation, both because their sovereignty offers exactly the sort of alternative legal regime that pseudolegal actors want and because even an illegitimate claim to exercise that sovereignty may discourage scrutiny.[1]

This scheme also showcases the tremendous and varied harm pseudolaw can do, even when it seems too absurd to take seriously. This business makes money by helping alternative medicine providers market their services to unwitting patients. Since those providers may be incompetent – and indeed some have previously been sanctioned in their fields for serious lapses in competence and ethics – it puts those patients at extreme and unnecessary risk. The firm also claims to follow a pseudolegal tax strategy that very likely constitutes fraud, and may be helping its customers and members do the same. Beyond all these harms, at the very core of its business is a bogus claim to Indigenous sovereignty, and to an Indigenous identity that is not authentic to the company or its public affiliates. Such false claims are uniquely harmful and worthy of both study and censure.[2]

This case study grew from comments made by Dr Pierre Kory, an American physician who gained notoriety promoting a deworming agent as a 'miracle drug' to treat COVID-19.[3] In 2023, he gave public remarks at an anti-vaccine conference acknowledging that the backlash against his controversial campaign was putting his medical credentials in some jeopardy. He announced a solution: an Indigenous tribe would shield him with their sovereignty:

> I moved my practice under the jurisdiction restriction of the First Nations [*sic*] Medical Board, and what that relies on, it's actually first created by the Crow Indian Tribe and it's based on a federal statute which protects tribal practitioners, so I became a registered tribal practitioner … Any patient that sees me, all they have to do is join the tribe and so once you're a tribal member and you see me, that physician patient relationship is now protected. The states have no more jurisdiction over me.[4]

Dr Kory put his plan into action. As of the time of writing, his clinic advertises that it is 'a proud member of the First Nation Medical Board of the Crow Nation'.[5]

[1] For examples of pseudolegal operations claiming sovereign status through false claims of Indigeneity, see, for example, DJ Netolitzky, 'New Hosts for an Old Disease: History of the Organized Pseudolegal Commercial Argument Phenomenon in Canada – Part III' (2023) 60 *Alberta Law Review* 971, 994–99.

[2] ibid 996; D Leroux, *Distorted Descent: White Claims to Indigenous Identity* (University of Manitoba Press, 2019).

[3] See A Christiansen-Bullers, 'Ivermectin Shown Ineffective in Treating COVID-19, According to Multi-Site Study Including KU Medical Center' Kanas University Medical Centre (1 December 2022), www.kumc.edu/about/news/news-archive/jama-ivermectin-study.html.

[4] P Kory, 'From Big Pharma to Real Health' Better Way Conference, Bath, UK (2 June 2023).

[5] P Kory, 'Leading Edge Clinic', www.drpierrekory.com.

The theory is simple. The FNMB claims that the Crow Tribe, a sovereign Indigenous polity, 'has stepped forward to exercise its jurisdiction over the practice of indigenous medicine'.[6] In doing so, it supposedly 'provides sovereign immune protection for physicians and others who become licensed as tribal providers'.[7] In exchange for this supposed shield against state regulators, the licensees pay an upfront fee and a percentage of their gross revenue. The business model as described, therefore, is selling the Crow Tribe's sovereignty in order to gain immunity from state regulators.

The theory is flawed. While the Crow Tribe is a legitimate and ancient entity with recognised sovereign status, it did not create the FNMB and does not stand behind it. Until recently, the tribal Government was apparently unaware of its existence. The Tribe does not regulate healthcare provided by and to non-members who are outside its territory or claim the power to do so. It has never authorised the FNMB to do so on its behalf. It exercises no oversight over the FNMB, its customers or its patients. And it does not appear to be a financial beneficiary of the scheme.[8] The FNMB, in turn, has no actual power to act on the Crow Tribe's behalf and neither it nor its customers can grant anyone membership in the tribe.

This chapter describes what is currently known about the FNMB, its backers, its operations and the harm it may do. Because it is an ongoing enterprise that has yet to be exposed to significant scrutiny, much is still unknown. But its operations to date are a useful case study in the intersection of pseudolaw and Indigenous sovereignty.

II. The Organisation and Practices of the First Nation Medical Board

This part describes the FNMB itself, the services it provides for its customers, and a few of the individuals associated with it. It also describes and debunks the FNMB's claimed relationship with the Crow Nation. This analysis draws from publicly available information and a short, personal interview with one of the FNMB's operators.[9]

[6] FNMB, 'Crow Nation Defines "Indigenous Medicine"' (2020), www.firstnationmedicalboard.com/crown-nation-article-2-08-19.

[7] ibid.

[8] The Crow Tribe has not made any official statements about this matter. In a personal interview, an employee of the Tribal Government denied any ongoing involvement between the Crow Tribe and the FNMB, specifically including any form of regulatory oversight. Citing familiarity with Tribal revenue streams, they denied any significant participation in revenue sharing or other financial arrangements with the FNMB. Interview with Employee of Crow Tribal Government (26 July 2023).

[9] B Zvenia, described in more detail below, spoke to me briefly during the preparation of this report. He cut off further contact after being asked for documentation of the FNMB's authorisation to act on behalf of the Crow Tribe or to support his other claims. Interview with Benjamin Zvenia (9 June 2023).

A. Structure and Services

The FNMB is a private, non-governmental organisation that claims the authority to sell medical licences to healthcare practitioners.[10] It claims to be 'an organized board with members consisting of tribal practitioners, physicians (MDs and DOs), a tribal member, and a layperson'.[11] It does not name any.

In reality, the FNMB appears to be an alter ego of an 'alternative medicine' clinic called the Turtle Healing Band Clinic (THB), which the FNMB claims is one of its aliases.[12] They share the same contact information and a Nevada street address, roughly 1,000 miles away from the territorial jurisdiction of the Crow Nation.[13]

The FNMB sells a small assortment of 'licenses'.[14] There are very few details offered to differentiate between them, other than the label and the cost. The tiers may simply be a form of price discrimination, a common sales strategy.

Table 13.1 KCM: Licences sold by the FNMB

Licence	**Undiscounted annual price (USD)**
Certified tribal practitioner	$450
Certified tribal healer	$350
Certified tribal technician	$250
Traditional tribal healer	$150

Every licensee also pays for a 'background' check and pledges five per cent of their gross receipts to the FNMB as a 'tribal donation fee'. Since the FNMB has licensed providers with significant criminal and regulatory records, as described below, it seems unlikely that any background checks are being done. Nor does the FNMB provide any evidence that it has ever contributed any of the 'tribal donation fee' to any tribe.[15]

The FNMB describes its purpose as providing 'licensure where no Board exists for [Indigenous medicine] regulation'.[16] It also suggests its products provide

[10] FNMB, 'The First Nation Medical Board – Medical Licensing for Providers' (2020), www.firstnationmedicalboard.com.

[11] FNMB, 'FNMB Summary – First Nation Medical Board' (2020), www.firstnationmedicalboard.com/about/fnmb-summary.

[12] ibid.

[13] See, for example, THBC, 'Contact Us – Make Appointment' (2020), www.turtlehealingbandclinic.com/contact; FNMB, 'Contact Us' (2020), www.firstnationmedicalboard.com/about/contact-us.

[14] FNMB, 'Professional Applications' (2020), www.firstnationmedicalboard.com/professional-applications.

[15] Zvenia insisted in a personal email that these donations occur but refused to provide documentation. As described below, Zvenia has been disbarred at least twice and convicted of at least one felony; his unsupported claims are suspect. See section II.C.i above.

[16] FNMB, 'Medical Licensing for Providers of Medical Alternatives and Public Memberships for Patients Seeking for Health Optimization and Wellness' (2020), www.firstnationmedicalboard.com.

'dual licensure' for homeopaths in Nevada and Arizona, states that already offer formal homeopathy licences.[17] The most charitable reading of this is that the FNMB offers private, opt-in oversight where a formal, government licence is unavailable and unnecessary or already in hand. But, in practice, the FNMB and its licensees claim that 'Indigenous medicine', a largely undefined term, covers far more than this narrow safe harbour. One of the FNMB's representatives claimed in a short interview that its licences cover 'primary care', which he was unable to define other than being something less than 'brain surgery'.[18] Its licensees have repeatedly claimed that the FNMB's products act as a substitute for medical licences, including for medical doctors prescribing medication without a state licence.[19]

B. Claims to Indigenous Sovereignty

According to the FNMB, in 'July 2018, the Crow Nation's Tribal Chairman signed a Resolution recognizing FNMB as its official healthcare agency for the practice of indigenous medicine'.[20] Despite repeated requests, no copy of any such resolution has been produced. An employee of the tribal Government was unable to identify any such proclamation.[21] Even if such a resolution did exist, it would not authorise the FNMB to sell medical licences; the Crow Nation does not have the power to regulate healthcare practices by and for non-members outside its territorial jurisdiction.

The Apsáalooke Nation, commonly referred to as the Crow Nation and Crow Tribe, is a legitimate, sovereign Indigenous nation. Following a period of colonisation and violent expropriation, today the United States of America recognises the Crow Tribe and its jurisdiction over a reservation located in the state of Montana.[22] Its sovereignty is not in doubt. The United States and the European colonial powers that preceded it have consistently acknowledged – in principle, if not always in deed – that distinct Indigenous communities are 'qualified to exercise powers of self-government, not by virtue of any delegation of powers, but rather by reason of their original tribal sovereignty'.[23] That sovereignty is 'limited, but not abolished, by their inclusion within the territorial bounds of the United States', and it grants them a recognised right 'to govern their members and territories'.[24]

[17] ibid.
[18] Zvenia interview (n 9).
[19] See section III.A.
[20] FNMB, 'Indian Sovereign Immunity' (2020) www.firstnationmedicalboard.com/indian-sovereign-immunity.
[21] Interview with Employee of Crow Tribal Government (n 8). The employee requested anonymity.
[22] See for example, the Fort Laramie Treaty (1851); Treaty of Fort Laramie (1868).
[23] F Cohen and N Jessup Newton, *Cohen's Handbook of Federal Indian Law* (LexisNexis, 2012), § 4.01[1][a] (citing *United States v Wheeler*, 435 US 313, 322–23 (1978)).
[24] ibid.

As understood by the law of the United States, the power of sovereign Indigenous tribes is greatest in matters of self-government. Tribal governments have 'plenary and exclusive power over their members and their territory', though it can be limited by the federal government.[25] As the relationship of a regulation to a tribe's people and territory attenuates, the tribe's power diminishes rapidly. Thus, tribes generally only have power over non-members when those people are on tribal land or interacting with members of the tribe. The overall trend for nearly 50 years has been greater federal limits on tribes' power over non-members.[26]

In one case concerning the Crow Tribe, the Supreme Court held that the tribe lacked authority to regulate activity by non-Indians on land that fell within the reservation boundaries but was owned by non-Indians. In that case the Court held: 'Exercise of tribal power beyond what is necessary to protect tribal self-government or to control internal relations is inconsistent with the dependent status of the tribes, and so cannot survive without express congressional delegation.'[27] The Court did contemplate tribes regulating non-members 'who enter consensual relationships with the tribe or its members, through commercial dealing, contracts, leases, or other arrangements'.[28] But even here, the Court observed 'the general proposition that the inherent sovereign powers of an Indian tribe do not extend to the activities of non-members of the tribe', and that, as such, tribes would only have regulatory power 'over non-Indians *on their reservations*'.[29] The FNMB itself is located on the other side of the United States: in Las Vegas, Nevada.[30]

The Crow Nation therefore lacks the power to authorise the FNMB to licence non-member healthcare providers treating non-members outside of its territory. Nor has it attempted to do so. An employee of the tribal government flatly confirmed that the FNMB has never been an authorised tribal agency.[31]

In addition to trying to sell the benefits of the Crow Tribe's sovereignty, the FNMB heavily implies that its customers become members of the tribe itself. It tells its customers that it is an agency of the Crow Tribe, then sells them certifications as a 'Tribal Healer' or 'Tribal Practitioner'.[32] Some of the FNMB's customers similarly make indirect claims; one tells patients that they must pay a USD 35 fee to become a 'member' of the FNMB (which poses as a tribal agency).[33] Dr Kory was blunter, simply telling his audience that his patients 'join the tribe' and become 'a tribal member'.

[25] ibid § 4.01[1][b]; see also *United States v Mazurie*, 419 US 544, 557 (1975) ('Indian tribes are unique aggregations possessing attributes of sovereignty over both their members and their territory').

[26] Cohen and Newton (n 23) § 4.01[2][f].

[27] *Montana v United States*, 450 US 544, 545–46 (1981).

[28] ibid 565.

[29] ibid (emphasis added).

[30] FNMB, 'Contact Us' (2020), www.firstnationmedicalboard.com/about/contact-us.

[31] Interview with Employee of Crow Tribal Government (n 8).

[32] FNMB, 'Indian Sovereign Immunity' (2020), www.firstnationmedicalboard.com/indian-sovereign-immunity.

[33] My Go To Doc, 'Get Rx – Main Form' (2022), www.mygotodoc.com/get-rx.

These claims are false and disrespectful of the Tribe and its people. The Tribe controls its own enrolment. It is not for sale; the Tribe limits membership to people who have a minimum of 'one-quarter Crow Indian Blood'.[34] The FNMB is parasitising the Crow Tribe by selling claims to Indigeneity and even tribal affiliation. It cannot deliver on these promises, but it benefits from these claims by using them as a marketing tool. Its customers and affiliates value the ability to claim tribal affiliation, just as they value the claim to immunity from state licensing requirements.

C. Organisers and Affiliates of the FNMB

The individuals behind the FNMB and using its licences are the best guide to its background, impact and character. Despite calling itself a 'board', the FNMB does not publish the names of its board members. It is not clear whether there are any. Nor is there a directory or any other public guide to the number or nature of its licensees. But a few individuals are clearly associated with the FNMB at a high level, such as the pseudolawyer who briefly acted as a spokesman for it and the members of the clinic it claims as an alter ego. This section describes their background, with particular attention to the serious misconduct and sanctions that appear with remarkable consistency in each case.

i. Benjamin Zvenia

Zvenia is a man of many titles, although few of them appear to be legitimate. For example, he appears to be the same person listed as 'plenipotentiary ambassador' and 'General–Colonel Marquis Dr. Benjamin Zvenia, Commander of American-Russian Brigade of American Legion of the National Guard of Holy Russia' on the website of a theocratic, imperial, and fake Russian government.[35] Less amusingly, he has also described himself as 'an attorney' in a personal conversation, and he implies (without explicitly stating) that he is licensed to practise law.[36] He currently holds himself out as a 'tribal judge' for Paiute and Apache tribes.[37]

[34] Crow Tribal Constitution, Montana Indian Law (16 April 2002) Art III, § 1, www.indianlaw.mt.gov/_docs/crow/constitution/2002_constitution.pdf.

[35] Holy Russia, 'News of Holy Russia 24.02.2014: Plenipotentiary Ambassadors of the State Holy Russia Are Appointed' (24 February 2014), www.holyrussia.com/en/content/76.htm. Extravagant claims like this are relatively common in pseudolaw. For example, David-Wynn Miller claimed to be the King of Hawaii, and Winston Shrout described himself as 'the Earth delegate to an "interdimensional Galactic Round Table"'. C McRoberts, 'Tinfoil Hats and Powdered Wigs: Thoughts on Pseudolaw' (2019) 58 *Washburn Law Journal* 637, 639–40.

[36] Interview with Zvenia (n 9). See for example, 'Dr. Benjamin Zvenia, Esq', www.linkedin.com/in/dr-benjamin-zvenia-esq-11759312 (where Zvenia describes himself as 'Esq.' and a 'senior partner' in a 'law firm'").

[37] Interview with Zvenia (n 9). These claims are uncorroborated but potentially true. Zvenia has infiltrated tribal legal systems in the past by misrepresenting his credentials, leading to the disbarments discussed below.

Zvenia does not have a law licence. He does have at least one felony conviction. In 1994, a Nevada state court sentenced him to six years in prison for practicing medicine without a licence.[38] He apparently also has one or more convictions relating to fraudulently obtaining a loan and using an altered military identification card.[39] Nevertheless, he found his way onto a list of non-attorney arbiters approved by the Nevada Supreme Court – until the state found 'serious questions as to his character for honesty and truthfulness concerning his professional background and/or status'.[40] It struck him from the roster but seems to have done nothing to prevent Zvenia from continuing his deceptions in other jurisdictions.

Zvenia continued to represent clients before tribal courts and various federal agencies. In 2000, the Duckwater Shoshone Tribal Court uncovered his deception and disbarred him.[41] Their investigation found that he had failed to complete enrolment at his supposed law school, and that he was not – as claimed – licensed to practise law by the Federated States of Micronesia.[42] In 2017, the United States Department of the Interior's Board of Indian Appeals (BIA) recorded a party's complaints that Zvenia, acting as their representative, had 'misrepresented himself to be a licensed attorney in Federal practice' and prejudiced their case.[43] Like Nevada, though, the BIA tribunal seems to have declined to take any action to restrain Zvenia. In 2019, the Muscogee (Creek) Nation was more proactive, disbarring him after finding that he had falsely held himself out as a member of the Bar Association of the District of Columbia.[44]

For almost 30 years, courts have been publicly sanctioning Zvenia for dishonest and fraudulent conduct. They have also been largely overlooking that conduct, taking the minimum action necessary to protect the immediate proceedings. His fraudulent claims were therefore largely successful in a way, as the money he made and damage he caused through them was rarely addressed. It is perhaps no surprise that, at the time of writing, he still openly holds himself out as a legal representative for hire via his online firm, The Law Office of Zvenia & Associates.[45] The firm

[38] Judgment of Conviction (Plea), *Nevada v Zvenia*, C99837 (Clark County District Court, 14 July 1994) (on file with author).

[39] *In the Matter of the Continued Admission of Benjamin P Zvenia, 001-00* (Duckwater Shoshone Tribal Court, 26 July 2000) (on file with author).

[40] 'Recommendation and Report Pursuant to Order of Referral Re: Benjamin Zvenia, State Bar of Nevada, In the Matter of the Development of Alternatives to Traditional Litigation for Resolving Legal Disputes' (Nevada, 29 September 1998) (on file with author).

[41] *Zvenia* (n 39).

[42] ibid.

[43] *Muskogee County Indian Credit Association v Acting Eastern Oklahoma Regional Director, Bureau of Indian Affairs*, Interior Board of Indian Appeals (2 June 2017) 64 IBIA 182, www.oha.doi.gov/IBIA/Ibiadecisions/64ibia/64ibia182.pdf. Note that federal agencies and other tribunals may permit non-lawyers to represent clients under limited circumstances; whether Zvenia engaged in the unauthorised practice of law is beyond the scope of this report.

[44] *In re: The Matter of the Continued Admission to the Muscogee (Creek) Nation Nar Association by Benjamin P Zvenia* (2019) Administrative Order 2019-01 (14 March 2019) 4, www.creeksupremecourt.com/wp-content/uploads/Administrative-Order-2019-01-In-re-Benjamin-Zvenia.pdf.

[45] The Law Office of Zvenia and Associates (2022), www.myfedlawyer.com.

claims to employ 'lawyers & advocates', and while it admits they are not licensed in Nevada, it claims extensive experience representing clients in a wide variety of tribunals.[46] It does not disclose how much of that experience was its principal's own disbarment proceedings.

As many pseudolegal entrepreneurs do, Zvenia appears to have learned that confidently declaring himself to be a legal authority is a viable business strategy no matter how many legitimate authorities refute his claims.

Zvenia's niche in the pseudolaw economy seems to be exploiting Indigenous systems, such as attaching himself to tribal court systems. The most appalling example of this, prior to the FNMB, is the brief life and well-documented death of O'NA HealthCare. O'NA was a malformed insurance firm with strong similarities to the FNMB. The State of Maine's Department of Professional and Financial Regulation terminated it in 2019.[47] While many pseudolegal schemes go unreported, making it difficult to track them over time, Maine's laudable work documenting the O'NA scheme adds a great deal of background to this example.[48]

The Superintendent of the Maine Bureau of Insurance avoided the term 'fraud' in his order dissolving and sanctioning O'NA, but explained in detail how it lied to customers about its services and drastically overcharged them for illusory benefits.[49] He found O'NA liable for multiple violations, including offering unauthorised insurance, failure to respond and false advertising.[50] Zvenia, along with several other individual respondents, was jointly and severally liable for nearly USD 500,000 in fines.[51] The Bureau also assessed almost USD 50,000 in penalties against Zvenia personally.[52]

Like the FNMB, O'NA had its feet in a pseudolegal claim to Indigenous sovereignty. Its theory was that because it was 'comfortably nestled under a Native American tribal corporate umbrella, we are protected by many of the rights and privileges that Native American Indians enjoy today'.[53] O'NA even issued 'Tribal Membership ID' credentials; the order does not go into details, but suggests that these were promoted as a way to make 'O'NA's customers eligible for rights and privileges that by federal law are available only to "Indians" and their spouses and children'.[54] These claims to Indigenous sovereignty and identity were false.

[46] ibid.

[47] *In re: Active Management Services, LLC, d/b/a O'NA HealthCare, et al* [2019] State of Maine, Department of Professional and Financial Regulation, Bureau of Insurance INS-19-202.

[48] For an illustration of this work in documenting particular schemes, see D Heilpern, ch 12 in this volume.

[49] *In re: O'NA HealthCare* (n 47) 1–17.

[50] ibid 18–19.

[51] ibid 19.

[52] ibid 20–21. The order required O'NA and the individual respondents to pay more modest restitution and penalties, with additional, contingent penalties to be imposed if they failed to do so. ibid 19, 26. The sums reported here reflect those contingent penalties, as Bureau reports that neither O'NA nor Zvenia have paid the amounts owed.

[53] ibid.

[54] ibid.

The firm claimed a complex relationship with a Cherokee tribe, but the elders of that nation refuted that connection and stated that the 'whole thing was the brainchild of a tribal attorney named Ben Zvenia'.[55] O'NA and Zvenia also claimed a relationship with the Hoopa Valley Tribe, but it, too, disputed it: 'Zvenia has a history of using the Hoopa Valley Tribe's name. However, he has no connection to the actual Tribe. He has incorporated an organization under Hoopa's laws [but] this does not provide him or that organization with the ability to use the Tribe's name or its sovereign immunity in any way'.[56] Based on the evidence at hand, the Bureau concluded, 'It does not appear from the record that any Native Americans have been involved at any time in the establishment, management, or operation of O'NA'.[57]

The striking similarities between O'NA and the FNMB suggest an evolving strategy. As an undercapitalised and mismanaged insurer, O'NA was doomed to failure – at some point, it was going to let its customers down and attract regulatory attention. Zvenia's current operation may benefit from the lessons learned from that experience. The FNMB operates through a web of healthcare providers, with relatively little direct exposure to consumers. Those providers also seem to use the FNMB as a tactic to divert customer complaints about their services away from legitimate regulators.

In the absence of serious scrutiny, therefore, the FNMB may be a more stable scheme, enabling Zvenia and his associates to operate undisturbed for much longer.

ii. The Turtle Healing Band

The exact relationship between the THB and the FNMB is impossible to determine from the outside, but they are closely related, if not identical. As noted above, the FNMB shares a street address with the THB Clinic (THBC).[58] The FNMB publishes a 'Credo' on its website that refers to 'our THB members/patients'.[59] Most explicitly, it identifies the THB as a 'd/b/a' for the FNMB itself.[60] The THB's individual practitioners may or may not be involved in the operation of the FNMB itself, but each appears to carry an FNMB licence. Their practice turns the FNMB's jurisprudential notions into praxis. 'Active communities help translate theories into actions', and the visible application of pseudolegal notions is a strong driver in the spread of pseudolaw.[61]

[55] ibid 4–5.
[56] ibid 12.
[57] ibid 5.
[58] See THBC, 'Contact Us – Make Appointment', www.turtlehealingbandclinic.com/contact; FNMB, 'Contact Us', www.firstnationmedicalboard.com/about/contact-us.
[59] FNMB, 'FNMB Credo' (2020), www.firstnationmedicalboard.com/fnmb/fnmb-credo.
[60] FNMB (n 11).
[61] McRoberts (n 35) 657.

The THB also helps illustrate a link between pseudolaw and pseudoscience.[62] The Clinic uses its pseudolegal credentials to help sell intensely pseudoscientific quackery. For example, it advertises a 'photon sound beam' that kills germs, heals broken bones and relieves pain by blasting patients with musical plasma.[63] They also promote 'Spooky DNA Biofeedback', which allegedly 'extracts information electrical [*sic*] from the body's DNA … and then inverts abnormal frequencies to neutralize and eliminate them' through quantum mechanics.[64] This garbling of basic scientific concepts is strikingly similar to the FNMB's misuse of the law.

The practitioners offering such treatments are predictably unconventional. Their disregard for convention may help explain their rich histories of criminal and regulatory violations. The following descriptions outline their background and suggest the standard of care one might expect from FNMB affiliates, as a proxy for understanding the damage the FNMB does by lending pseudolegal support to practices such as these.

a. Daniel Royal, DO, JD, CTP

Royal is the first provider the THB lists. He carries an FNMB 'Certified Tribal Practitioner' licence, as well as legitimate licences as an osteopath and attorney.[65] Those latter licences subjected him to legitimate regulation, and in 2014 the Nevada State Board of Osteopathic Medicine filed a complaint against him alleging 'that the practices of Dr. Royal were below the standard of care' for pain management and pain medicine.[66]

The regulators alleged a long list of violations on the general theme of inappropriately prescribing and supervising the use of opioids, including

> inadequate patient histories; inadequate diagnostics; questionable diagnoses; inadequate or no treatment plans; inadequate or no assessment of the treatment provided; inappropriate prescribing of opioids, sometimes to opiate-naïve patients or in such doses as to present or create risks of serious harm to the patients; inadequate consideration of treatment options besides high-dose opioids; inadequate or no monitoring of the drugs being used by patients; [and] failure to obtain reports from the Nevada Prescription Controlled Substance Abuse Prevention Task Force database when legally required or appropriate.[67]

[62] While the intersection is beyond the scope of this chapter, the two often go hand-in-hand. See, for example, C Sarteschi, 'The Social Phenomenon of Romana Didulo: "Queen of Canada"' (2023) 6 *International Journal of Coercion, Abuse, and Manipulation* 27.

[63] THBC, 'Photon Sound Beam' (2020) www.turtlehealingbandclinic.com/services/photon-sound-beam.

[64] THBC, 'DNA Biofeedback' (2020), www.turtlehealingbandclinic.com/services/dna-biofeedback.

[65] THBC, 'Daniel Royal, DO, JD, CTP – Certified Tribal Practitioner' (2020), www.turtlehealingbandclinic.com/providers/daniel-royal.

[66] *Complaint for Disciplinary Action, In The Matter of: Daniel Royal* (2014) Nevada State Board of Osteopathic Medicine (3 September 2014), www.app02.k3systems.com/Licensing/uploads/disciplinary/1/Disciplinary_Complaint_352_Royal-20140903.pdf.

[67] ibid 2–3.

The complaint specifically asserted that these failures 'may have contributed to the death' of a patient who died of 'opioid toxicity, which consisted of a combination of heroin and the opioids prescribed by Dr. Royal and [his clinic]'.[68] He settled with the state board, agreeing to pay USD 18,000 and a two-year restriction on his ability to prescribe controlled substances.[69]

b. Robert Boer, CTH

Another THB provider, Robert Boer, was at one point a licensed physician's assistant in Illinois. The Illinois Department of Financial and Professional Regulation reports that in 2014 it put his licences as a chiropractor and physician's assistant on probation and suspended his controlled substance licence, due to violations including a 'failure to properly evaluate and prescribe medications, including controlled substances'.[70] In 2015, the state suspended his licences indefinitely.[71] He now claims to be a 'Certified Tribal Healer', another FNMB licence.[72]

c. Bill Bhogal, PhD, CTT

The third provider listed on the THBC's website is 'Bill Bhogal', who apparently has used several different names.[73] In 2014, the Federal Government charged him with trafficking counterfeit Viagra.[74] He pled guilty and was sentenced to three years of probation and a large fine.[75] Today, he describes himself as a 'Certified Tribal Technician', yet another FNMB licence.[76]

[68] ibid 3.

[69] *Settlement Agreement and Order, In The Matter of: Daniel Royal* (2015) Nevada State Board of Osteopathic Medicine (15 April 2015), www.app02.k3systems.com/Licensing/uploads/disciplinary/1/Disciplinary_SettlementAgreement_371_Royal-20150415.pdf. This triggered reciprocal sanctions from the state of Wisconsin, where Royal was also licensed. *In the Matter of Disciplinary Proceedings Against Daniel F Royal*, State of Wisconsin Medical Examining Board (16 December 2015), www.online.drl.wi.gov/decisions/2015/ORDER0004433-00012149.pdf.

[70] Illinois Department of Financial and Professional Regulation, 'Illinois Department of Financial and Professional Regulation News' (November 2014), www.idfpr.illinois.gov/content/dam/soi/en/web/idfpr/forms/discpln/2014-11enf.pdf.

[71] Illinois Department of Financial and Professional Regulation, 'Illinois Department of Financial and Professional Regulation News' 2015), www.idfpr.illinois.gov/content/dam/soi/en/web/idfpr/forms/discpln/2015-06enf.pdf. Robert Boer's LinkedIn profile confirms this is the same individual, listing both his time at the THBC and the Illinois clinic named in the disciplinary action (where he states he is 'currently not active in patient care'): www.linkedin.com/in/robertboer5healthcare. See also E Schelkoppf, 'North Aurora Chiropractor Placed on Probation' Shaw Local (31 December 2014), www.shawlocal.com/2014/12/31/north-aurora-chiropractor-placed-on-probation/ar1gfpo.

[72] See Robert Boer's LinkedIn profile (n 71), where he claims to be a 'Tribal Provider at Turtle Healing Band Clinic Las Vegas at Turtle Healing Band Clinic'.

[73] THBC, 'Bill Bhogal, PHD, CTT – Certified Tribal Technician, THBC' (2020), www.turtlehealingbandclinic.com/providers/bill-bhogal; D Gentry, 'Latest Path to Fountain of Youth Leads to Convicted Felon' Nevada Current (22 June 2018), www.nevadacurrent.com/2018/06/22/latest-path-to-fountain-of-youth-leads-to-convicted-felon.

[74] Indictment, *United States v Bhogal*, No 14-cr-00374-JFB (EDNY 2 July 2014).

[75] Order of Forfeiture, *United States v Bhogal*, No 14-cr-00374-JFB (EDNY 14 March 2016).

[76] THBC (n 73).

d. Lucinda Mallory, ND, CTH / Lucinda Messer

This person may no longer be with the Clinic, as it seems to have selectively removed her from portions of the website. Nevertheless, 'Dr' Lucinda Mallory was evidently affiliated with the practice at one point, and she is still listed on the site.[77] It credits her with the same FNMB 'Certified Tribal Healer' licence that Boer carries.[78]

Like the other THB providers, Mallory has a documented history that calls into question whether the FNMB performs any sort of background check or simply sells licences over the barrelhead. Mallory has also used the name Lucinda Messer.[79] The Washington State Board of Naturopathy suspended a naturopath by that name in 2016, upon extensive findings of misconduct.[80] The Board alleged that Messer issued multiple prescriptions she was not authorised to give, used invalid credentials to issue prescriptions, and overprescribed controlled substances, among other violations.[81]

The most serious charges stemmed from her attempts to treat dangerous, advanced tumours with coffee enemas and a toxic plant extract.[82] According to the Board, Messer 'inappropriately misled and isolated' her patients, taking one on as a live-in worker at her clinic as a form of payment.[83] The Board also accused her of failing to obtain 'adequate informed consent regarding these unproven treatment protocols'.[84] After a patient died, the Board found that their 'signature on the informed consent form was forged and Respondent misrepresented facts contained in [their] record to help insulate herself from any repercussions arising from [their] death'.[85]

[77] THBC, 'Our Providers Alternative Medicine' (2020), www.turtlehealingbandclinic.com/providers, listing 'Dr. Lucinda Mallory, ND, CTH' as a provider; An archived version of her profile is available at www.web.archive.org/web/20201124225347/https://www.turtlehealingbandclinic.com/providers/lucinda-mallory.

[78] 'Lucinda Mallory' LinkedIn, www.linkedin.com/in/lucinda-mallory-9a1aa129.

[79] This is apparent in her YouTube channel, which identifies the content creator as both 'Lucinda Mallory' and 'Lucinda Messer': www.youtube.com/channel/UCw3piD2nOw0fbPPtJ4doKyQ?app=desktop&feature=applinks. See also L Mallory, 'Vitamin D3 May Very Well Be a Strong Alternative Treatment for Covid-19' Longevity Health (29 March 2020), www.longevityhealth.life/post/vitamin-d3-may-very-well-be-a-strong-alternative-treatment-for-covid-19. It identifies Mallory as the author of a book titled *Powerful Medicine: Vitamin D: Shedding Light on a Worldwide Health Crisis*; it also shows the book cover, which credits Lucinda Messer as the author. Similarly, her profile on the THBC website (n 77) identifies Mallory as the author of *Powerful Medicine*.

[80] *Findings of Fact, Conclusions of Law and Final Order, In the Matter of Lucinda Y Messer*, State of Washington, Department of Health, Board of Naturopathy, No M2014-1078 (22 January 2016) (on file with author).

[81] ibid. See also S Barrett, 'Naturopathic "Cancer Specialist" Has License Suspended' Quackwatch (27 August 2016), www.quackwatch.org/cases/board/nat/messer/order_2016.

[82] ibid. Messer allegedly also used a 'Rife machine', the same sort of quackery the THBC advertises today. See n 64.

[83] ibid 2–3.

[84] ibid 2–3.

[85] ibid 4.

Unsurprisingly, the Board sanctioned Messer, suspending her naturopathy licence for five years.[86] But just one year later, in 2017, it was forced to act again after evidence emerged suggesting that she was continuing to treat cancer patients.[87] This time it permanently revoked her licence, finding that she 'cannot be rehabilitated, nor can she regain the ability to practise with reasonable skill and safety … it is necessary to revoke [Messer's] credential to protect the health, welfare and safety of the public'.[88]

Despite the detailed, documented wrongdoing found by the Board, the FNMB apparently licensed her in February 2018. Writing in the comments on a blog post about how physicians can maintain a career after losing their licences, she commented as 'Lucinda Mallory':

> I am a Naturopathic physician who lost her license in Washington state for using apricot kernels to help cancer patients! I had no extra money to fight those rat bastards!!
>
> I have the most wonderful site for all of you to check out;
>
> This is a legitimate/Sovereign medical board that you can belong to so that you can start practicing once again:
>
> I can practice in most states now with this sovereign license.
>
> I hope this helps most all of you!!
>
> I am also happy to train you at a small charge to get you up to speed on Natural medicines, if need be …[89]

It is impossible to determine how many patients Messer has been able to access using her FNMB credential. The THBC claimed her as a provider at one point, and she now claims to be a 'CTP' at an 'Indigenous Medicine Longevity Institute' in Nevada.[90] 'CTP' is likely a Certified Tribal Practitioner licence, the most expensive FNMB product.[91] If so, it indicates she found good cause to keep and even upgrade her FNMB credential. If so, the FNMB's supposed background checks were evidently no obstacle.

D. Key Observations on FNMB and THB

The people associated with the FNMB and its alter ego operate in obscurity, as is typical in pseudolegal enterprises. The FNMB is not quick to advertise the names

[86] ibid.

[87] C Willmsen, 'Despite Suspended License, Kirkland Naturopath May Have Continued Treating Cancer Patients' *The Seattle Times* (29 May 2017), www.seattletimes.com/seattle-news/health/despite-suspended-license-kirkland-naturopath-may-have-continued-practicing.

[88] ibid 3.

[89] Digital Nomad Physicians, 'Your Medical License Is Revoked – Now What?' (29 April 2018), www.digitalnomadphysician.com/medical-license-revoked.

[90] 'Lucinda Mallory' LinkedIn (n 78).

[91] See FNMB (n 14).

and locations of its members and customers, likely due to concerns about real regulators discovering what is being done under FNMB licences. Some of their licensees, after all, still belong to professions with real oversight, such as the osteopathy board that sanctioned Royal. The others remain subject to the intervention of state authorities, no matter what claims the FNMB makes about sovereignty. But the THB's close connection to the FNMB makes its practitioners more apparent than other customers (a few of which are discussed below). They are a useful lens for seeing what the FNMB really is, who it appeals to, and what it does.

Zvenia and the THB practitioners have incredibly rich histories of misconduct and dishonesty. In each of the cases outlined above, real regulators had to step in to prevent serious harm to patients and clients (or intervene where such harm had already happened). The rules those regulators enforce and the records of their decisions are detailed and public, because those regulators act transparently and in the public interest. The FNMB has no visible set of rules and there is no indication that it has ever responded to any misconduct by its licensees. Pseudolaw is 'replacement law', meant to supplant legitimate regulations.[92] But the goal is not to replace existing rules with equally effective ones; they would be equally intrusive. The FNMB sells the mere appearance of regulation; a vague suggestion that rules exist and are being enforced, but without inconveniencing its customers by actually implementing or enforcing real standards.

There is no way to tell how much regulatory attention these people may have diverted by sheltering under fraudulent claims to Indigenous sovereignty. Since they were each last sanctioned for their various misadventures, each of the people described above has been associated with what appears to be a seriously fraudulent enterprise. The FNMB also seems to be engaged in tax evasion, based on comments made by Zvenia and described below. Zvenia himself has been avoiding paying the fines assessed in the wake of the O'NA debacle, according to comments from the Maine regulator. However they have done it – and likely not even they know themselves – they have successfully flown under the radar. Likely this is at least partly due to their pretence to a false Indigenous identity. Indigenous sovereignty is not a subject most lawyers study in the United States, much less medical or insurance regulators. Investigators may see it as a thorny issue not worth engaging, particularly when it covers what may appear to be petty misconduct rather than serious malfeasance.

In that regard, the THB's reliance on snake oil such as 'Spooky DNA Biofeedback' may help these individuals. First, it means that they can make their pseudolegal (and likely fraudulent) claims to an insular audience that self-selects for credulity. Customers paying money to have their broken bones healed with 'photon sound beams' are not likely to be very sceptical of their gurus' *bona fides*. Nor are they likely to file complaints about their healers with the authorities who

[92] DJ Netolitzky, 'Lawyers and Court Representation of Organized Pseudolegal Commercial Argument [OPCA] Litigants in Canada' (2018) 51 *University of British Columbia Law Review* 419, 421.

represent the mainstream medicine they are trying to avoid. This may insulate the licensees from the kind of scrutiny that would defeat their pseudolegal claims. Second, the sheer silliness of those claims and the products and services these licensees sell may also be a shield. Many pseudolegal entrepreneurs avoid regulation or prosecution for many years despite blatantly selling obviously fraudulent tax evasion and other schemes. The bizarre nature of the beliefs that run along with the pseudolegal schemes may act as cover by making the gurus' claim seem to be beneath the notice of serious regulators. What agent, board or prosecutor wants to spend their career investigating 'quantum legal grammar' or sixth-dimensional fairy collaborators?[93] Similarly, regulators may simply be unwilling to peer too closely at the licences of people selling such transparent snake oil, as long as it is not directly poisonous.

But sometimes the snake oil is poisonous.[94] The THB's members stand on a long history of serious misconduct, much of which endangered patients. And while Zvenia's posturing as the 'Commander of American-Russian Brigade of American Legion of the National Guard of Holy Russia' is merely silly, his pretence to being a licensed lawyer and authorised representative of a tribal government is much more serious. The next part explores some of the surprisingly varied and quite serious damage that pseudolaw does by looking more closely at the impacts of the FNMB and its affiliates.

III. Potential Damage Caused by the FNMB

The FNMB has the potential to do a vast amount of harm to an extremely broad set of victims. Given the company's relatively low profile, it is impossible to confirm how much of that potential has been realised, but some of it – such as the grave insult to the dignity of the Crow Tribe – is inarguable.

The FNMB very likely does harm in at least three ways: helping sell medical services in a way that the law would otherwise limit; refusing to pay taxes; and insulting the dignity and sovereignty of the Crow Nation. Each is an outgrowth of the FNMB's illegitimate claims to sovereignty. If the FNMB were not making false claims to be an active Crow agency, it would have a vastly diminished capacity to do harm in these ways.

A. Enabling Unregulated Medical Services

One of the most obvious dangers of pseudolegal licensing schemes is simply that, as the ugly history of the THBC's providers illustrates, legitimate governments

[93] McRoberts (n 35) 638–41.

[94] The charges against Mallory even stemmed in part from her use of the toxin laetrile.

license healthcare providers for a reason. We only know about the lapses of the THBC's practitioners because various regulators, including a smattering of state boards and the Department of Justice, detected, investigated, documented and punished them. There is no indication that the FNMB is capable of any of these steps.

Insofar as its licensees practice under the supervision of appropriate and legitimate regulators, that may limit the harm the FNMB can do. For example, as a licensed osteopath, Royal is still subject to the oversight of a board that has already demonstrated some ability to hold him to minimal professional standards. But there is evidence that the FNMB's customers buy its licenses as a shield against such regulations.

i. Diverting Patient Complaints

Only about half of the states require licences for people holding themselves out as 'naturopathic doctors'.[95] A businessperson providing services under a bogus FNMB certificate could nevertheless advertise themselves as licensed and therefore held to a higher standard of practice than is actually the case. Or, in states that do require a licence, they could try to classify their services as falling outside its remit. One possible example is Dr Erica Zelfand, a naturopath (not a medical doctor) in Oregon. Dr Zelfand does carry a state naturopathy licence. But, as she informs her patients, 'her work in consultations is done independently of that licensure. Dr. Zelfand is also licensed by the First Nation Medical Board as a Certified Tribal Practitioner'.[96] Her marketing materials admit that she 'may discuss therapies with you that are not legal in your area', and disclaims her own responsibility for doing so.[97]

Dr Zelfand illustrates a relatively subtle harm the FNMB may do. She holds it up as a shield to divert patient complaints, urging her customers to contact the FNMB instead of her state's regulators in the event of a dispute:

> Much of the spiritually-focused work that Dr. Zelfand advises on and performs is done outside the jurisdiction and authority of federal, state, county, and city agencies and authorities. For any and all complaints in this regard, please contact the First Nations Medical Board.[98]

While she may have various reasons for funnelling patient complaints to the FNMB, clearly her state's regulators are far more likely to be sceptical of a provider

[95] Association of Accredited Naturopathic Medical Colleges, 'Naturopathic Doctor Licensure | List of States and Provinces' (2023), www.aanmc.org/licensure.

[96] E Zelfand, 'The Fine Print for Patients': www.ericazelfand.com/clinic-policies-and-procedures-for-patients.

[97] ibid.

[98] ibid. Zelfand does not specify what services she offers that may be illegal in her patients' jurisdictions. She does offer personal consultations regarding 'psychedelic-assisted healing', referring specifically to controlled substances that are illegal in many states: 'Psychedelic-Assisted Healing & Harm Reduction: Getting the Most out of Every Journey', www.ericazelfand.com/psychedelic-harm-reduction.

whose business model anticipates selling illegal services. The FNMB advertises its use in intercepting complaints as one of the benefits of its services.[99] This is a classic characteristic of pseudolaw as a form of 'replacement law'.[100] The practitioner seems to be using it to swap out an arm's-length regulator for a much more compliant substitute.

Another possible harm is that the FNMB may enable its licensees to access patients they could not otherwise reach. Dr Kory, whose comments helped expose the FNMB, showed the plainest and most serious way this could work. Facing the possible loss of his licence due to complaints stemming from his irresponsible advocacy of a deworming agent as a 'miracle drug' against COVID-19, Dr Kory pointed directly to the FNMB as a solution: 'The states have no more jurisdiction over me.'[101] His remarks contemplate treating patients as a medical doctor in states where he is unlicensed, even in the event his licence was stripped from him for misconduct. Nor is he alone in seeing this use of the FNMB's pseudolegal licenses, as Mallory preceded him by directly recommending the FNMB as an out for disgraced doctors.[102]

At the time of writing there is no available evidence that Dr Kory, Mallory, or any other FNMB licensee, has delivered healthcare in jurisdictions or circumstances where they are lawfully prohibited from doing so. Nor would we expect to see such evidence, given the private nature of their businesses. But FNMB licensees publicly walk very close to that line.

ii. Offering Unlicensed Medical Care

One example of FNMB licensees using pseudolaw to push the limits of lawful licensure is Syed Haider, a medical doctor licensed in Texas who may be based in either Puerto Rico or Virginia.[103] He markets his medical services online at mygotodoc.com, where he advertises 'general telehealth services' including antibiotics, supplies 'of your regularly prescribed Rx', pharmaceuticals to treat erectile dysfunction, and 'protocols' to treat COVID-19, 'vax injury', influenza and a variety of other conditions.[104] His marketing is not limited to his own website; he has featured prominently on very widely distributed platforms such

[99] For example, the FNMB states on its website that 'Complaints against providers will be handled by FNMB and/or Tribal Court; Records will be the property of the [FNMB] and are kept completely private': FNMB (n 11).

[100] Netolitzky (n 92) 421.

[101] Kory (n 4).

[102] Digital Nomad Physicians (n 89).

[103] Haider's LinkedIn profile associates him with 'Ivy Rock Health, LLC' and claims he is located in Virginia: www.linkedin.com/in/syed-haider-2a5b3329. Arizona lists an expired medical licence for a Syed Hussain Haider also associated with that entity. A current Texas licence under the same name, with a matching educational history, puts his current primary practice address in Puerto Rico. Texas Medical Board, 'Physician License, Syed Hussain Haider, MD' on file with author).

[104] My Go To Doc, 'Services: Your Problems/Our Solutions' (2022), mygotodoc.com/solutions.

as the Alex Jones Show, marketing himself to an audience of conspiracy theorists and extremists.[105]

Dr Haider holds himself out as able to write prescriptions, a regulated activity normally subject to the control of state governments. In fact, his own FAQ states that online prescriptions are legal when the patient is 'currently physically present in a state the physician has a license in'.[106] But his website tells visitors that if Dr Haider is not licensed in their state, they can simply become an FNMB member:

> Dr Haider is board certified in Internal Medicine and licensed in a number of states via their respective state medical boards which is the usual method of physician licensure, but he also has a nationwide practice license via a non traditional avenue called the First Nations Medical Board (FNMB), which is an American Indian tribal medical board protected by long standing US treaties.
>
> Many physicians who have experienced backlash from state medical boards, including censorship and loss of licensure due to off-label prescribing and COVID related care are now migrating to this alternative censorship free medical system.
>
> The FNMB option allows Dr Haider to protect his ability to practice medicine in any state even if his state license(s) were to be unfairly revoked and it also allows him to practice in states with smaller populations where he has not obtained a traditional state medical board license. To see Dr Haider under the purview of the FNMB you must become of a member of the board which costs $35 for 1 person, or $50 for families. The membership lasts 1 year and can be renewed upon request.[107]

Joining the FNMB through Dr. Haider's site seems to require joining the THB, pursuant to an onerous agreement. While it is hidden behind an automated form, search indexing suggests it has identical language to a form used by another alternative healing provider and affiliate of the FNMB and THB.[108] Patients agree to a long list of objectionable and/or pseudolegal terms:

- THB is outside the jurisdiction and authority of federal, state, county, and city agencies and authorities for any and all complaints or grievances against FNMB, FNMB licensees, FNMB staff, Turtle Healing Band Clinics ('THBC'), and THBC staff;
- THB member records are the private property of THBC licensed facilities and are kept confidential;
- I am here solely on my behalf (and that of my family) and not as an agent or representative for any Federal, State, County, or City Agencies. Further, I/we neither represent any Board (e.g., medical, zoning, etc.) or Licensing Agency (e.g., government, healthcare, etc.) nor am I on a mission of entrapment or investigation on behalf of these or any other agencies, either on this or any subsequent visit(s);
- I/We agree to hold the tribal practitioners, healers, technicians, staff, and other THB members harmless from unintentional liability resulting from my/our indigenous

[105] 'The Alex Jones Show' Vimeo (4 January 2022), www.vimeo.com/685435423.
[106] My Go To Doc, 'Frequently Asked Questions' (2022), www.mygotodoc.com/faq.
[107] My Go To Doc (n 33).
[108] Healing From The Root, 'Membership', www.healingfromtheroot.org/membership.html.

healthcare, except for harm that results from criminal misconduct or gross negligence as determined by FNMB and/or defined by Crow Tribal Court;
- I/We agree to submit to the jurisdiction of FNMB for the referral of any and all complaints against TPs to FNMB for dispute resolution. Further, I/We agree to submit any civil complaints against TPs to Crow Tribal Court for dispute resolution.[109]

It is unclear how many providers use this form, or a version of it, to enrol patients in the THB or FNMB. As Dr Zelfand's practice shows, even when paperwork is different or absent, the FNMB can be used to route patient complaints away from entities empowered and motivated to act on them. This extremely aggressive agreement shows how some FNMB customers hope to make the organisation a more effective weapon against oversight. Its focus on 'entrapment' also demonstrates a clear awareness of the implicitly hostile relationship between the FNMB and legitimate regulators, suggesting these providers are under no illusions about the laxity of FNMB's alleged oversight.

iii. Purporting to Authorise Medical Research on Human Subjects

The FNMB's potential impact on real patients goes beyond selling prescriptions and hijacking complaints. It claims to offer an 'Indigenous Medicine Institutional Review Board (IMIRB)', which it claims 'is necessary to approve, modify, or reject research' in Indigenous medicine.[110] The IMIRB supposedly consists of 'tribal practitioners, physicians (MDs and DOs), a tribal member, and a layperson'. The FNMB does have access to laypeople and physicians; its 'tribal practitioners' are self-declared, though, and it is unclear whether anyone working with the firm is a member of any tribe.[111] Its objectives include assuring the 'safety and efficacy of diagnostic devices, substances, and other modalities'.[112]

Alarmingly, the THB claims to be experimenting with invasive medical procedures under the auspices of the IMIRB.[113] It claims to have created a 'Dendritic Cell Vaccine Protocol', explicitly in conjunction with the IMIRB, which it says was '100% successful in helping its patients/subjects obtain IgG antibodies to

[109] ibid. While mygotodoc.com does not make this form publicly accessible, searching each of these cited terms using Google indexing reveals that the form – or a document containing the same provisions – is part of the enrolment process there. Note that despite the form's invocation of the Crow Tribal Court, there is no indication that tribunal has, has sought to exercise, or intends to exercise jurisdiction over such disputes. If it does not take jurisdiction, this agreement purports to leave the FNMB as the sole arbiter of disputes against its licensees.

[110] FNMB, 'Indigenous Medicine Institutional Review Board' (2020) www.firstnationmedicalboard.com/imirb.

[111] Zvenia does claim to be a member of a tribe. Assessing the accuracy of that claim is beyond the scope of this report. The Maine Bureau of Insurance concluded, in a section addressing Zvenia's role in running O'NA, that it did not 'appear from the record that any Native Americans have been involved at any time in the establishment, management, or operation' of that entity. *In re: O'NA HealthCare* (n 47) 5.

[112] FNMB (n 110).

[113] FNMB, 'An Oral Vaccine for COVID? (2020), www.firstnationmedicalboard.com/an-oral-vaccine-for-covid.

SARS-COV-2'.[114] In particular, the THB advertises that patients taking their 'vaccine' could be considered '"recovered" from "COVID-19" and … technically exempt from any vaccination requirements'.[115]

On the basis of this dubious success, the Clinic is soliciting donations to purchase equipment to manufacture its 'vaccine'. Donations are requested directly to the THB, which claims to be 'an IRC 7871 non-profit foundation'. The IMIRB and FNMB make the same, possibly fraudulent, claim.

B. Potential Tax Fraud

Possibly the single most common expectation of a pseudolegal organisation is that it acts, at least in theory, as a shield against taxation.[116] The FNMB is no exception. The FNMB claims to be tax-exempt both because it is 'preferably affiliated with a 7871-non-profit entity established as part of a Tribal Banded Health Care Program and as such is a non-profit organization', and because it is 'an IRS 7871 non-profit entity' itself.[117] Its IMIRB also claims to be 'affiliated with a IRS 7871 non-profit entity'.[118] The THBC also claims to be 'an IRC 7871 non-profit foundation'.[119] These entities directly and indirectly solicit donations using the promise of tax exemptions.

The FNMB and its affiliates are presumably referring to 26 USC § 7871, which allows Indian tribal governments to be treated as state governments and for donations to such governments to be deducted from federal taxes.[120] It does not create non-profit entities, and does not apply to the FNMB or THB, which are not tribal governments. The FNMB does make vague claims to be operating on behalf of a tribal government, but § 7871 only applies to

> a subdivision of an Indian tribal government … if (and only if) the Secretary [of the Treasury] determines (after consultation with the Secretary of the Interior) that such subdivision has been delegated the right to exercise one or more of the substantial governmental functions of the Indian tribal government.[121]

No such delegation or determination is in evidence. Finally, even if § 7871 did apply, it would be limited to contributions 'made for exclusively public purposes'.[122]

[114] ibid. Antibodies are also detectable for more than a year after COVID infection, suggesting another reason why they might be prevalent in the patients of an alternative medical clinic in 2021.

[115] Dr Daniel F Royal JD DO, CTP, 'DCV PROTOCOL 100% SUCCESSFUL!' Turtle Healing Band Clinic (21 January 2021), turtlehealingbandclinic.com/687-2.

[116] See, for example, DJ Netolitzky, 'Organized Pseudolegal Commercial Arguments as Magic and Ceremony' (2018) 55 *Alberta Law Review* 1045, 1048, listing tax evasion as the first of several goals pseudolegal arguments tend to have.

[117] FNMB (n 11).

[118] FNMB, 'IMIRB Clinical Study' (2020), firstnationmedicalboard.com/imirb/imirb-clinical-study.

[119] FNMB (n 113).

[120] 26 USC § 7871(a)(1).

[121] 26 USC § 7871(d).

[122] See 26 USC §§ 170(c)(1), 7871(a).

Purchasing a bogus medical licence from the FNMB would not satisfy this requirement.

If the FNMB is relying on such pseudolegal theories, as O'NA apparently did, it may be tax fraud.[123] There is no way to determine how much money is at issue. The FNMB sells relatively inexpensive products to a relatively small customer base. Its most expensive licence costs USD 450, and while its user base is not public, it cannot be very large. But at least some of those users are successful practitioners with active practices and aggressive marketing, and the FNMB charges 'a tribal donation fee of five percent (5%) on gross receipts for all goods and services'.[124] Given the size and sophistication of operations like Dr Haider's, this could be a significant amount – assuming that the FNMB's customers pay the promised tithe, and that it relies on its own bogus tax theories. Beyond the FNMB itself and its customers, there is likely no way to estimate how many patients and donors have taken illegal tax deductions in reliance on its absurd § 7871 arguments.

C. Insults to the Dignity and Reputation of Indigenous Communities

Pseudolegal enterprises often ape the form and function of legitimate institutions, covering themselves in stolen dignity. 'Queen' Romana Didulo, for example, travels the Canadian countryside draped in flags and seals, dispensing currency and leaving a trail of disgusted locals and evicted followers in her wake.[125] Her fraud does not dishonour the legitimate Canadian Government, because she has nothing to do with it. Similarly, the Crow Nation is hardly responsible for the FNMB's parasitisation. But the theft of the Nation's identity is nevertheless a deep and injurious insult precisely because so many of the FNMB's customers seem to have nothing to do with the people whose identity they are arrogating to themselves. The FNMB is selling a tool its largely white customers can use to claim a vague and false Indigenous identity; experts have called this practice 'self-Indigenization' or 'race shifting' and identified it as a powerful factor in the erasure of Indigenous peoples.[126]

The FNMB does not just sell its customers an excuse to call themselves 'Tribal'. It specifically appeals to disreputable customers whose claimed association with

[123] Whether the FNMB is committing tax fraud is beyond the scope of this chapter.

[124] FNMB (n 14).

[125] See, for example, M Wendling, 'A QAnon "Queen" and the Canada Town That Wants Her Gone' BBC News (27 September 2023), www.bbc.com/news/world-us-canada-66930536.

[126] See, for example, K TallBear, 'Indigenous Genocide and Reanimation, Settler Apocalypse and Hope' (2023) 10 *Aboriginal Policy Studies* 93, 93–94, which describes 'self-Indigenization' as 'a significant contributor in the 21st century to the project of Indigenous elimination and concomitant settler thriving upon the spoils of Indigenous death'. D Leroux, 'State Recognition and the Dangers of Race Shifting' (2023) 46 *American Indian Culture and Research Journal* 55 argues that illegitimate attempts to

Indigenous peoples – however false – has the potential to do reputational harm to them. Lucinda Messer, discussed above, is an example of such harm. A state naturopathy board investigated her twice, ultimately finding that she 'cannot be rehabilitated, nor can she regain the ability to practice with reasonable skill and safety'.[127] It revoked her state licence 'to protect the health, welfare and safety of the public', suggesting the board found that she was a serious danger to her patients.[128] The FNMB nevertheless sold her a brand new licence, empowering her to treat and endanger patients. And they put the Crow Tribe's name on that decision, crediting them with the ultimate oversight of her practice and responsibility for regulating her. FNMB licensees like her use the tribe's name to market themselves, trading on its legitimacy without actually submitting to any meaningful oversight by it.

Similarly, the FNMB is clearly designed at least in part to be a shield protecting its licensees from customer complaints. The forms and disclaimers used by Dr Zelfand, Dr Haider, the THBC and others show how the FNMB's licensees see it as a mechanism for routing patients away from legitimate regulators, who can act on their complaints, to the FNMB, which has no actual authority or demonstrated interest in exercise care and oversight. And in the absence of real authority, the FNMB justifies this dodge by pointing – again – at the Crow. It tells patients that the Crow is responsible for regulating the providers they want to complain about, and that Crow courts are the ultimate venue for them. But it is hardly likely that a Crow court would have, or want, jurisdiction over a patient dispute where no party has any connection to the tribe.

Some of the potential damage is even more subtle. The Crow Tribe provides legitimate medical services, through a hospital, clinic and other outlets. As those service providers engage the public, advocate for public health measures, negotiate and lobby for funding, and do all the other legitimate work set before them, they operate in an environment where their reputation is material to their ability to deliver critical services. The reputation and offences of its roster of felons and disgraced, self-proclaimed healers can only act against the interests of the tribe's legitimate healthcare providers. And the very extent of Indigenous sovereignty in the United States is in some flux; federal courts are still debating the balance of power between states and tribes, the interpretation of crucial treaties, and other questions that inform the extent of that sovereignty.[129] The perception that tribes sell their sovereignty to empower outfits like the FNMB could tar that debate in the minds of the public and the judiciary, even though it is false.

obtain government recognition as Indigenous are 'a form of settler governmentality that in fact claims and erases actual Indigenous Peoples'.

[127] *Messer* (n 80).

[128] ibid.

[129] See for example, *Arizona v Navajo Nation*, 599 US ___ (2023); *United States v Cooley*, 593 US ___ (2021), *McGirt v Oklahoma*, 591 US ___ (2020); *Oklahoma v Castro-Huerta*, 597 US (2022).

Finally, as discussed above, the FNMB and its affiliates shamelessly attempt to sell bogus claims to an Indigenous identity that is not theirs to offer. Dr Kory – a nationally famous figure, but not a member of the Crow Nation – nakedly told a rapturous audience that they could 'join the tribe', and become a 'tribal member'.[130] The suggestion that membership would be available to paying customers is shameless and shocking. The tribe is responsible for claiming its own members and does so through the rules it set forth in its own constitution.[131] Membership is not for sale.

IV. Conclusions

This chapter has presented a case study of one pseudolegal enterprise out of the many operating in obscurity around the world. It shows how difficult it can be to unpack and analyse such schemes. Each is different from the next in subtle and substantial ways, and it takes significant time and effort to untangle them.[132] Regulators with scarce resources may fail to interdict these schemes promptly, whether because they focus on more prominent targets or ones that do more obvious damage.

That reluctance to scrutinise opaque pseudolegal schemes is a particular benefit to the FNMB, due to its parasitism of Indigenous sovereignty. Lawyers and other regulators in the United States are typically quite unfamiliar with the limits of legitimate tribal sovereignty and may see it as a politically or culturally sensitive topic. That could discourage them from pressing on claims like those of the FNMB, despite how quickly its theories fall apart under scrutiny. If the FNMB's assault on tribal dignity and Indigenous identity perversely becomes a shield against oversight, it would hardly be surprising to see pseudolegal entrepreneurs replicating its model. After all, that has already happened; the FNMB seems to be a careful evolution of the earlier attempt to monetise other people's sovereignty through the O'NA scheme.

Two things should change to reduce the run time of such pseudolegal schemes. Regulators and even bystanders must be more focused on pseudolaw generally to help interdict schemes like this. As has been discussed elsewhere, a greater understanding of pseudolaw is likely to be one of the best antidotes to it in the long run.[133] A firm promising its customers immunity to regulations and taxes or creating an alternative licensing system should be an immediate red flag, and if regulators were more sensitive to such signals, they could take action more

[130] Kory (n 4).

[131] Crow Constitution (n 34) Art III, § 1.

[132] See also the significant work done by the State of Maine's Department of Professional and Financial Regulation in thoroughly describing the O'NA scheme above (n 47).

[133] See, for example, McRoberts (n 35) 659–63.

quickly. Here, regulators would have been more likely to pierce the defensive use of sovereignty had they approached the FNMB with the scepticism due a pseudolaw scheme. Even the tribe itself could have prioritised this issue and hobbled the FNMB by publicly disavowing it (although its failure to do so at the time of writing likely simply reflects how distant the FNMB is from the tribe's actual reality). Most importantly for such schemes generally, a greater public awareness of pseudolaw might make patients and clients more reluctant to trust firms like this, making them less profitable and less attractive to entrepreneurial schemers.

Second, regulators and other officials should be concerned with Indigeneity generally and the seriousness of attacks on Indigenous identity in particular. Indigenous sovereignty is incredibly valuable, for all that it is not for sale (despite the FNMB's best efforts). Pseudolegal schemes will continue to try to exploit it, because they can use it to claim exactly what they most want: immunity from laws they don't like. But Indigenous sovereignty does not actually cover the schemers, so it can only work where regulators fail to realise that such exploitation is serious and wrongful, or simply fail to prevent it.

These concerns are not unique to the United States. Pseudolaw and Indigenous sovereignty exist globally, and they are likely to intersect more commonly going forward. As they do, scholars, regulators and bystanders around the world must be focused on these collisions to minimize the harm that pseudolaw does in their communities of interest.

14

Pseudolaw Advocates: Managing Advocates who Advance Pseudolaw Arguments

BRIDGETTE TOY-CRONIN*

I. Introduction

While most litigants pursuing pseudolaw arguments appear unrepresented, some appear with assistance or representation.[1] What should the court's response be to those litigants who have assistants or representatives helping them advance a pseudolaw argument? A judicial officer faced with this question will be considering duties to the fair and efficient administration of justice in their courtroom. This chapter considers the difficult decision a judicial officer must make when faced with what I refer to as a 'pseudolaw advocate', a non-litigant who assists a litigant advance a pseudolaw argument.

Pseudolaw advocates may fulfil a number of different roles, including – in rare cases – the role of lawyers. Donald Netolitzky, reviewing Canadian pseudolaw cases with representation, identified four Canadian lawyers who 'abused the courts by arguing vexatious OPCA [Organised Pseudo-Legal Commercial Argument] concepts on behalf of their clients'.[2] More commonly, pseudolaw advocates are non-lawyers, who are involved in litigation by acting in lay advocacy roles available in courts. Fuelled by the high price of private lawyer services and the very

* Supported by the Marsden Fund Council from the Government funding, administered by the Royal Society of New Zealand. My thanks to the editors of this collection for their helpful suggestions and further case examples for this chapter. Thank you also to Rose Siebuhr for her research assistance.

[1] For discussion of pseudolaw arguments in general, see part one of this volume. Pseudolaw is also referred to by various authors cited in this chapter as Organised Pseudo-Legal Commercial Argument (OPCA).

[2] DJ Netolitzky, 'Lawyers and Court Representation of Organized Pseudolegal Commercial Argument (OPCA) Litigants in Canada' (2018) 51 *University of British Columbia Law Review* 419, 460. A more recent example of a lawyer advancing a pseudolaw argument, although as a self-represented litigant and on behalf of his company, can be found in *Bluerobin Inc v Kilian* (2023) ONSC 3391.

limited availability of legal aid and other free legal assistance, non-lawyers may be allowed to provide assistance to those accessing the legal system.[3]

The most well known of these non-lawyer assistants are McKenzie friends,[4] who are permitted in many common law courts.[5] The purpose of a McKenzie friend is to assist the litigant, to provide advice and support, but not to speak on behalf of the litigant except in special circumstances.

Pseudolaw advocates may also be fulfilling other lay assistant roles specific to the jurisdiction. For example, New Zealand allows laypeople to operate as employment advocates in the employment jurisdiction.[6] An employment advocate is a completely unregulated role and anyone can give themselves titles such as 'employment law expert' and undertake the role otherwise reserved to a lawyer, including in-court advocacy.[7]

The people acting as pseudolaw advocates may have varying loyalties to the ideas underpinning pseudolaw, ranging from casual adherents to fully fledged gurus. Gurus are the leaders and teachers of the pseudolaw movements who package and sell the ideas underpinning the pseudolaw ideology being promoted,[8] and who may act as "Typhoid Marys' who spread the pseudolaw "disease of ideas" into new populations'.[9]

The question I consider in this chapter is, what should the court's response be to the presence of a pseudolaw advocate? As I live in Aotearoa New Zealand, I draw primarily on examples from that jurisdiction, but I have also looked across the common law world for instances where pseudolaw advocates have been involved in litigation. The sources drawn on are case law, along with some case descriptions in Reddit threads,[10] which provide examples of pseudolaw advocates participating

[3] Independent Review Panel, *Regulating Lawyers in Aotearoa New Zealand Te Pae Whiritahi i te Korowai Rato Ture o Aotearoa* (New Zealand Law Society, March 2023) 110–15, www.lawsociety.org.nz/assets/Independent-Review/IR-Report-Received/Regulation-of-lawyers-final-report-for-submission.pdf; R Sandefur, 'Legal Advice from Non-Lawyers: Consumer Demand, Provider Quality, and Public Harms' (2020) XVI *Stanford Journal of Civil Rights and Civil Liberties* 282.

[4] The term originates from the English case *McKenzie v McKenzie* [1970] 3 All ER 1034.

[5] C Cameron and E Kelly, 'Litigants in Person in Civil Proceedings: Part I' (2002) 32 *Hong Kong Law Journal* 325, explaining they are permitted in England and Hong Kong, but not encouraged in Australia; Ulster University, 'Litigants in person in Northern Ireland: Barriers to Legal Participation Belfast' discusses McKenzie friends in Northern Ireland; M Downs and R D'Silva, 'McKenzie Friends and Counsel Assisting' (2022) *New Zealand Law Review* 149 on the New Zealand position.

[6] Employment Relations Act 2000, s 236, Schs 2 and 3, cl 2.

[7] For discussion of employment advocate advertising practices including titles used, see L Choe, 'How many "clicks" does it take?: Finding price information on New Zealand lawyers' websites' (2021) 52 *Victoria University of Wellington Law Review* 487. See also *CultureSafe NZ Ltd v Employment Relations Authority* [2022] ERNZ 556 [20], noting representatives 'are not required by the Act to be competent or ethical'.

[8] Netolitzky (n 2) 420.

[9] *AVI v MHVB* 2020 Court of Queen's Bench of Alberta 790 per Graesser J. The Alberta Court has also called the gurus a form of "' evil counsellor" – those who use their position to advise others to engage in fraud' who Dante placed 'into the inner canyons of the eighth circle of hell'. G Sammon, 'Organised Pseudo-Legal Commercial Argument Litigation: Challenges for the Administration of Justice in Ireland' (2015) 38 *Dublin University Law Review* 85, 100 quoting *Meads v Meads* 2012 ABQB 571 (ACJ Rooke).

[10] N Proferes et al, 'Studying Reddit: A Systematic Overview of Disciplines, Approaches, Methods, and Ethics' (2021) 7 *Social Media + Society* for discussion of the use of Reddit as a data source.

in litigation. This is not a systematic review to consider all cases and forms of pseudolaw advocates. Nor does it attempt to say anything about the frequency or likelihood of pseudolaw advocates assisting in litigation. Rather, it looks for case examples to explore and discuss the appropriate response to pseudolaw advocates seeking access to the courts.

I have also drawn on comparisons with the cases generated by the Fathers' Rights movement of the late twentieth and early twenty-first century.[11] Like the pseudolaw movement, leaders of the Fathers' Rights movement would sometimes appear as advocates, or help prepare documents, to put the ideas of the movement before the court. Also like the pseudolaw movement, although in a less extreme form, they were critical of the courts and expressed antipathy towards lawyers, reflective of larger populist suspicion of knowledge elites.[12] That movement therefore provides a useful point of comparison.

I begin in section II by exploring the tensions that underlie the decision about whether or not to permit a pseudolaw advocate, concluding that the courts should be ready and willing to exclude pseudolaw advocates from court. This differs from the Fathers' Rights movement where judges developed a line of precedent with a strong presumption in favour of allowing the litigant to have the support person of their choice.[13] I argue that the pseudolaw movement presents special challenges that mean that the court should be much more willing to exclude them. The goals of this approach are to enable space for the court to engage with the litigant, to protect the administration of justice and rule of law, and to avoid the court being used to stage a performative display to encourage more pseudolaw followers. In section III, I consider the powers and mechanisms available to the court for excluding pseudolaw advocates, before making some brief suggestions about wider reforms in section IV.

II. Pseudolaw's Challenge to the Courts

Court processes are primarily designed for represented litigants as legal representation is a fundamental assumption of the adversary system: 'The adversary system

[11] For a general background of the Fathers' Rights movement see A Jordan, *The New Politics of Fatherhood: Men's Movements and Masculinities* (Palgrave Macmillan, 2019) ch 6.

[12] H Rhoades, 'Yearning for law: Fathers' Groups and Family Law Reform in Australia' in R Collier et al (eds), *Fathers' Rights Activism and Law Reform in Comparative Perspective* (Bloomsbury Publishing Plc, 2006).cited in A Melville, '"Giving hope to fathers": discursive constructions of families and family law by McKenzie Friends associated with Fathers' Rights Groups' (2017) *International Journal of Law, Policy and the Family* 1.

[13] President of the Family Division, 'Guidance from the President's Office – McKenzie Friends England and Wales', www.judiciary.uk/wp-content/uploads/2022/07/pfd-guidance-mckenzie-friends.pdf. This guidance states: 'A litigant in person wishing to have the help of a MF [McKenzie Friend] should be allowed to do so unless the judge is satisfied that fairness and the interests of justice do not so require. The presumption in favour of permitting a MF is a strong one.' The court therefore has discretion, but the presumption is strongly in favour.

in its pure form assumes that each side will be represented equally'.[14] Litigants attending court without legal representation, therefore, present a disruption to this ideal. This in turn places the judicial role under strain, as the judge must be both an impartial arbiter and potentially assist or protect the unrepresented party.[15] To avoid this strain on the judicial role, a range of solutions have been suggested.[16] More legal representation is the most obvious, but as state funding for lawyers is reduced and the price of private representation climbs, other solutions are needed. One of these has been to allow non-lawyer assistants to support litigants. This relieves some of the strain on the judge and, while it might not amount to equality of arms, it reassures the court that the litigant has some support. Importantly, it also may – and often does – help with the administration of justice. A non-lawyer assistant who has previous in-court experience can guide the litigant on procedure, as well as provide social support. In general, therefore, the courts have been protective of the litigant's access to some form of litigation assistance.

Two related difficulties arise where these assistants have a second role – that of a leader of a movement such as land rights or fathers' rights. First, that the leader might use the litigant as a vehicle for their own cause, rather than help the litigant present the best argument for that litigant. Second, that the leader's engagement in political activity or protest out of court, particularly if that activity critiqued the court, might make them unsuitable assistants. Non-lawyer assistants have, however, been drawn from Fathers' Rights and other movements and have been able to provide the support the litigant needed without the movement's interests overshadowing the litigant's needs.

This previous experience with movement leaders suggests that pseudolaw advocates may be able to assist the litigant in putting forward a valid claim even if framed in pseudolaw terms. As Rooke AJ said in *Meads*, 'To be explicit, however, these indicia [of a pseudolaw claim] do not *prove* a claim or action is invalid, or that a litigant is vexatious'.[17] Furthermore, excluding a pseudolaw advocate might create a sense of alienation from court, fuelling the sense of disenfranchisement and alienation from society that perhaps drives the pseudolaw movement. As Kate Leader explains in chapter five of this volume, litigants faced with the mystification of the court process may turn to conspiracy theory to explain their struggle with successfully accessing the courts.[18] If pseudolaw adherents are refused entry to the courts, this will only further undermine the legitimacy of the courts. Might it

[14] M Cappelletti and B Garth, 'A Comparative Conclusion' in M Cappelletti (ed), *International Encyclopedia of Comparative Law* (Mohr Siebeck and Martinus Nijhoff Publishers, 1987) vol Civil Procedure XVI, 6-436, 644–48. For an oft-quoted passage about court design being for lawyers rather than litigants, see HMSO, 'Access to Justice: Interim Report to the Lord Chancellor on the Civil Justice System in England and Wales' [17.2].

[15] R Moorhead, 'The Passive Arbiter: Litigants in Person and the Challenge to Neutrality' (2007) 17 *Social and Legal Studies* 405.

[16] D Rhode, 'Whatever Happened to Access to Justice?' (2008) 42 *Loyola of Los Angeles Law Review* 869.

[17] *Meads v Meads* (n 9).

[18] K Leader, ch 5 in this volume.

not, therefore, be better to allow them to vent their position in court than to keep them out?

While these nagging concerns are understandable, and each case must be considered on its own merits, I argue that judicial officers should be ready and willing to exclude pseudolaw advocates – preferring to hear from litigants without their influence – because of the distinct aspects of the pseudolaw movement which pose a risk to litigants, the administration of justice and the rule of law.

A. Exploitation of Vulnerable Litigants

The first concern is that pseudolaw advocates might exploit the litigant's vulnerability and use them as a puppet for their political ends. There is a real possibility that pseudolaw litigants are vulnerable people who have fallen prey to a pseudolaw advocate in their search for assistance with a legal matter. As Netolitzky notes: 'pseudolaw injures its users. Some OPCA litigants are essentially victims drawn from a population that seems highly vulnerable to "snake oil", be it political, religious, health, or pseudolaw'.[19]

The clients of United States' guru Rick Martin might exemplify this group of litigants. Martin was prosecuted for the unlawful practice of law in Florida, for advertising to and representing parents whose children were being taken from them by state authorities.[20] Parents trying to regain custody of children will likely be a very vulnerable group, with issues such as poverty and addiction underlying the reasons for the children being uplifted and placed in state care. Out of hope and desperation, they may be open to a guru helping them advance pseudolaw arguments to get their children back. These litigants may have a genuine claim but have been duped into making a pseudolaw argument. Only by removing the pseudolaw advocate does the court have any opportunity to engage with the possibility that there is a genuine legal issue.

The concern that the assistant or representative might be manipulating the litigant – to the detriment of the litigant's interests – appeared in applications for Fathers' Rights adherents to appear as McKenzie friends. In an English case, a Dr Pelling had applied to be a McKenzie friend in a family law matter, but 'at times has difficulty in divorcing his campaigning role as Chairman of the [Fathers' Rights] pressure group to which he belongs from that as an assistant of litigants in person'.[21] In discussing whether he should be permitted, Lord Woolf said that if

[19] Netolitzky (n 2) 487.

[20] J Lambe, 'Larry Nassar's Judge Orders Arrest of Fake "Constitutional Lawyer" Who Tries to Represent "Client" Who Violated COVID Restrictions' Law & Crime (20 March 2021), lawandcrime.com/crazy/larry-nassars-judge-orders-arrest-of-fake-constitutional-lawyer-who-tries-to-represent-client-who-violated-covid-restrictions-watch. For another example, see B Morlin, 'Sovereign Citizen Faces Unlawful Practice of Law Charge in Florida' SPLC (16 June 2017), www.splcenter.org/hatewatch/2017/06/16/sovereign-citizen-faces-unlawful-practice-law-charge-florida.

[21] *R v Bow County Court Ex Parte Pelling (No 1)* [1999] 4 All ER 751.

the McKenzie friend was indirectly running the case, 'using the litigant in person in the manner in which a puppet master uses a puppet' then this would provide a 'firm foundation for a judge not wishing him to be present as "McKenzie Friend"'.[22] Similarly, in *BHR v Tauranga Family Court*, the judge referenced the Family Court's concern to be 'mindful of the need not to allow, or appear to allow, an opportunity for a proposed McKenzie friend to advance his or her own political or personal agenda through another's Family Court case'.[23]

The court cannot easily determine if the litigant is the pseudolaw advocate's puppet or tool for advancing a political agenda. This is true both of the Fathers' Rights movement and the pseudolaw movement. Litigants may be fully immersed in a movement and so committed to its ideology that they cannot express an argument without using the movement's framework. In the case of pseudolaw, the litigant may even have created the incident that has brought them before the court through pseudolaw ideology, for example a refusal to comply with police at traffic stops, and consequent arrests.

There is, however, an important difference between the Fathers' Rights movement and the pseudolaw movement. In the Fathers' Rights movement litigants had a particular framework: accusing the court of bias and pursuing an appeal to formal equality.[24] These are both socially acceptable discourses that had success in changing court and public policy, and engaged with the court on its own terms.[25] In contrast, the pseudolaw movement requires adherents to disclaim the court's authority and disrupt its procedure (discussed further below). This means the litigant will need to let go of the pseudolaw framing to be able to engage successfully with the court. With the pseudolaw advocate present, the court cannot know if the argument is the litigant's, or the litigant is a puppet.

While a judicial officer should have no expectation that a litigant will let go of the pseudolaw framing, there is always the possibility they will. A high-profile example of this happening is the case involving Robert Sudy, who was 'firmly convinced of several pseudolaw "common law" arguments', before a New South Wales Magistrate 'patiently took the time to comprehensively reject all the arguments'.[26] Netolitzky also suggests that talking to vulnerable litigants and showing that their guru failed in other arguments may help the litigant to be open to other lines of argument or other representation.[27]

[22] ibid [17] per Lord Woolf.

[23] *BHR v Family Court at Tauranga* (21 October 2011) HC Tauranga CIV-2011-470-505 [18].

[24] M Kaye and J Tolmie, 'Fathers' Rights Groups in Australia and their Engagement with Issues in Family Law' (1998) *Australian Journal of Family Law* 1; D Dinner, 'The Divorce Bargain: The Fathers' Rights Movement and Family Inequalities' (2016) 102 *Virginia Law Review* 79.

[25] For a discussion of how the Fathers' Rights movement changed policy, see V Amyot, 'Batman's Battle of Ideas: The Fathers' Rights Movement in Canada' (2010) 29 *Canadian Family Law Quarterly*.

[26] RR Sudy, 'Freeman Delusion: The Organised Pseudolegal Commercial Argument in Australia', freemandelusion.com.

[27] Netolitzky (n 2). Note that to be able to show a litigant that their guru has failed in other arguments, the court needs a comprehensive and accessible database tracking the activities of pseudolaw advocates.

Removing the pseudolaw advocate also provides the court with the opportunity to check that the litigant understands the pseudolaw advocate's qualifications, or lack thereof. Pseudolaw advocates may use a range of names that are not protected by statute in various jurisdictions such as 'lawyer' in England or 'legal expert' in New Zealand.[28] It is only through removing the influence of the pseudolaw advocate that the judge has the ability to engage with the litigant to raise these issues, to ensure that the arguments being put forward are the litigants' arguments.

B. Separating the Protest and the Assistant Role

The second related concern is whether the movement leader can put their political role down and perform the role of the assistant according to its requirements, which might include not speaking, and maintaining confidentiality. The courts wrestled with this issue in applications for Fathers' Rights movement leaders to perform the role of McKenzie friends. In general, the courts considered the two roles could be separated and that critique of the courts in protest was no barrier. For example, a McKenzie friend in a Family Court proceeding was allowed to serve, as long as he maintained confidentiality, even though 'He was critical of the Court process and officers of the Court as a result of his own experience in those proceedings' and 'He is critical of the process to date in this proceeding'.[29] Similarly, a leader of the movement who had protested outside of court – and had likened the Family Court to the Third Reich in that protest – was permitted to serve as a McKenzie friend.[30] The McKenzie friend said he could distinguish between his two roles (as protester and as McKenzie friend), and the judge concluded there was no reason to disbelieve him:

> I need to make it clear that just because the proposed McKenzie Friend is critical of the Family Court processes, or indeed its Judges or officers, he is not to be barred as a McKenzie Friend for that reason alone. … there should, on the face of it, be no objection to the appointment provided that confidentiality is maintained and the limits of the role are strictly observed.[31]

[28] For a discussion of the regulatory framework in England, see L Webley, 'When is a Family Lawyer a Lawyer?' in M Maclean, J Eekelaar and B Bastard (eds), *Delivering Family Justice in the 21st Century* (Bloomsbury Publishing Plc, 2017) 305. For a discussion of the New Zealand regulatory framework, see S Mize, 'New Zealand: Finding the Balance between Self-Regulation and Government Oversight' in A Boon (ed), *International Perspectives on the Regulation of Lawyers* (Hart Publishing, 2017) 115. In the USA, the Anti-Defamation League notes, 'Gurus may refer to themselves by a variety of terms (such as "constitutional scholar," "private attorney general," etc.; the list is endless), often claiming to be some sort of legal or constitutional expert … Some will offer their services as "legal consultants," …': 'The Lawless Ones: The Resurgence of the Sovereign Citizen Movement', 2nd edn (2012) 6, www.adl.org/sites/default/files/documents/assets/pdf/combating-hate/Lawless-Ones-2012-Edition-WEB-final.pdf.

[29] *C v M* (1995) 13 FRNZ 705, 709.

[30] *T v L* FAMC Hastings FAM-2004-020-64, 4 October 2006.

[31] ibid [8].

The Fathers' Rights movement tended towards deferring to the litigant's choice of assistant, as long as key obligations such as confidentiality were not violated.[32]

This tends to suggest that membership in the pseudolaw movement should not affect a pseudolaw advocate's ability to perform the role of assistant. Indeed, in a case that involved a sovereign citizenship argument, *R v MacKinnon*,[33] a McKenzie friend was permitted to serve and did put his beliefs to one side to support the litigant effectively. In that case the defendant had been charged with drug offences, and on the morning of trial, argued the court did not have jurisdiction as he was a sovereign citizen. The court allowed the McKenzie friend, who shared the defendant's beliefs, to assist the defendant. While the McKenzie friend initially disputed the court's jurisdiction on the basis that the defendant was a sovereign citizen, the McKenzie friend conceded that argument when met with resistance from the Court, saying: 'To us you have no jurisdiction … But you leave no room for us to move, Your Honour, so that we must, as a circumstance, proceed down the line as dictated by statute."[34]

The McKenzie friend was allowed to represent the defendant, to cross-examine and, ultimately, his conduct was not problematic.[35] Notably, however, the form of sovereign citizenship in *R v MacKinnon* was an argument that as an indigenous Māori person he recognised the sovereignty of the United Tribes of Aotearoa, not the New Zealand Government.[36] This is not a pseudolaw argument in the sense that, while it has been rejected it may have some legal basis (albeit a very unlikely one to succeed), and it did not rely on a complex web of ideas that have no foundation in law, characteristic of pseudolaw.[37]

In contrast, pseudolaw advocates are very unlikely to be able to put their beliefs to one side and engage with the court on its own terms. The attraction of pseudolaw is that it 'allows adherents to simultaneously disregard existing legal norms and disempower state actors, while retaining a self-conception of lawfulness and righteousness'.[38] Its internal logic leaves little room for compromise. Furthermore,

[32] A New Zealand example is *BHR v Family Court at Tauranga* (n 3) [23]. The English courts have also taken this position; see (n 13).

[33] *R v McKinnon* (4 May 2005) [2005] NZCA 240/04.

[34] ibid [14].

[35] ibid [24].

[36] This is an argument frequently raised by Māori defendants in New Zealand criminal courts. For a discussion of this, including its blurring with pseudolaw, see F Te Aho and J Tolmie, 'Māori Rejections of the State's Criminal Jurisdiction over Māori in Aotearoa New Zealand's Courts' (2023) 30 *New Zealand Universities Law Review* 409.

[37] This Northern American idea of sovereign citizenship has appeared in New Zealand courts more recently; for example, *Warahi v Chief Executive of the Department of Corrections* [2022] NZCA 105 [9], where the Court of Appeal observed that this 'ideology that first emerged in the United States in the 1970s. [The] core belief, for present purposes, is that [Sovereign Citizens are] not subject to the jurisdiction of the State (including legislation enacted by Parliament or decisions made by the courts). This belief is based (at least in part) on the dual persona theory – the proposition that individuals have two personas, one of flesh and blood and the other a separate legal or "corporate" personality that is subject to the jurisdiction of the State.'

[38] H Hobbs, S Young and J McIntyre, 'The Internationalisation of Pseudolaw: The Growth of Sovereign Citizen Arguments in Australia and New Zealand' (2024) 47 *University of New South Wales Law Journal* 309.

people appearing as advocates (rather than litigants) are likely to be very invested in the movement. The dataset created of Canadian cases by Netolitzky (which he appropriately acknowledged had a range of limitations), showed that 69 per cent of the pseudolaw litigants who were supported in court by a non-lawyer representative, were known pseudolaw gurus.[39] Pseudolaw gurus are much less likely than other movement leaders to be able to separate out their roles and provide constructive assistance to the litigant.

C. Disruptive Behaviour

A particular feature of pseudolaw advocacy that makes constructive engagement unlikely is the typical ways in which pseudolaw proponents behave in court, including: making demands that the judge prove their appointment or make certain oaths; trying to impose a fee schedule on the court and other litigants; and refusing to identify themselves by their legal name.[40] Such behaviour disrupts hearings, creates confusion and delay, and undermines the administration of justice.

This is quite distinct from the Fathers' Rights movement, which though expressing the view that the courts were biased against the interests of fathers, engaged with its procedures. While publicly framed as a critique of the courts, the Fathers' Rights movement has been described, in reality, as being a backlash movement against feminism.[41] In contrast, pseudolaw is a much broader backlash which cuts at the heart of the courts. It points its adherents towards radical individualism and freeing themselves from our shared system of governance and dispute resolution systems.

D. Risk to the Rule of Law

Pseudolaw advocates also present a particular threat to the rule of law. At the heart of pseudolaw is a distrust of government and an attempt by pseudolaw adherents and advocates to distance themselves from its authority.[42] This is in distinct contrast to the Fathers' Rights movement which, while engaging in critique of the courts, accepted their authority and presented arguments the court could engage with. Some pseudolaw advocates even go so far as to be explicit in undermining the rule of law. For example, in *AVI v MHVB* the judge noted that 'the client and McKenzie Friend "claim they are above the law"', clearly violating the central tenet

[39] Netolitzky (n 2) 429.
[40] *Meads v Meads* (n 9) [242]–[263].
[41] A Jordan, 'Masculinizing Care? Gender, Ethics of Care, and Fathers' Rights Groups' (2018) 23 *Men and Masculinities* 20; Amyot (n 25).
[42] C Kalinowski IV , 'A Legal Response to the Sovereign Citizen Movement' (2019) 80 *Montana Law Review* 153, 156.

of rule of law that everyone is bound by the law.[43] More commonly pseudolaw advocates profess a surface commitment to rule of law. As Hobbs, McIntyre and Young observe, 'In a sense, believers possess an almost endearing commitment to legality and the rule of law.'[44] They cite Chief Justice Peter Quinlan's observation:

> [T]he sovereign citizen almost always has a fervent belief in the importance of the 'rule of law' as they see it. Indeed, the sovereign citizen is deeply committed to the rule of law. It is simply that the 'law' for them happens to be the idiosyncratic subjective opinion that they hold.[45]

While it may appear that they believe in the rule of law, they only believe in it as far as *it excuses them from legal obligations*. Rule of law as a general principle, and its underlying *telos* of freedom from arbitrary power and domination[46] is used as a means to free adherents from our shared rule of law society, into an alternate space of radical individualism. Once excused – if we accept the internal logic of the pseudolaw realm – the alternate legal universe they enter does not possess the characteristics of a rule of law society. For example, it has limited or no means for resolving disputes, which is a minimum condition of a rule of law society.[47] Pseudolaw proponents are therefore making anti-rule of law arguments dressed up in legal clothes.

It is within the rights of a litigant to put forward such an argument (as long as they do not stray into contempt or otherwise violate the order of the court), but the court does not need to permit an advocate to do it on their behalf. It would certainly violate lawyers' responsibilities, as they owe duties to both the administration of justice and the rule of law. It is less clear that it would violate any rules for non-lawyers who, as discussed, are seen primarily in terms of assisting the litigant rather than owing duties to the court. But, as the court observed in *Pelling*, there is no right to a lay assistant and the court can consider the integrity of its own process in deciding whether to permit one.[48]

[43] *AVI v MHVB* [2020] ABQB 790 [24], per Graesser J. For the idea that everyone is bound by the law as a central tenet of rule of law, see T Bingham, *The Rule of Law* (Penguin, 2011).

[44] Hobbs, Young and McIntyre (n 38).

[45] ibid.

[46] M Krygier, 'Four Puzzles about the Rule of Law: Why? What? Where? And Who Cares?' in J Fleming (ed), *Getting to the Rule of Law* (New York University Press, 2011) 64–104; S Hui Kim, 'Reimagining the Lawyer's Duty to Uphold the Rule of Law' (2023) 3 *University of Illinois Law Review* 781.

[47] Bingham (n 43). At particular points in the pseudolaw movement, dispute resolution fora have been developed. For example, in the United States the common law movement has developed 'grand juries' and in New Zealand an adherent has developed a 'common law court' with three cases listed on the website. What is notable about both bodies is that they are not designed to resolve disputes between members, ie to provide an alternative rule of law system, but as a means to remove or attack people holding office in our society. See Anti-Defamation League 'Sovereign Citizens Create Vigilante "Grand Juries" in Latest Attempt to Flout the Law' Press release (20 February 2014), www.adl.org/resources/press-release/adl-sovereign-citizens-create-vigilante-grand-juries-latest-attempt-flout; Alexander: of the family Knox, 'New Zealand Common Law Court of Justice', nzcommonlawcourt.org/cases.

[48] *R v Bow County Court Ex Parte Pelling (No 1)* (n 21). See also in New Zealand, a clear statement that the McKenzie friend is allowable only at the court's discretion: *C v M* (1995) 13 FRNZ 705.

E. Use of Court for Collateral Purposes

A particular risk to the court in having a pseudolaw advocate present is that they may use it as an opportunity to promote pseudolaw to a broader audience. The courtroom gives the opportunity for the pseudolaw advocate to perform to an audience of followers, including those in the public gallery and, through social media, to a larger audience online.

An example of this is the appearance of guru Derek Balogh in a South Australian court.[49] Balogh sat next to the litigant as a support person, with about 10 followers in the public gallery, one of whom seems to have recorded and then posted a video. The litigant asked the judge to recuse herself and then Balogh suddenly stood and yelled a string of statements at the judge such as 'you are now charged, you are under arrest'. The judge adjourned the court, which Balogh reframed as the judge 'has left the ship'. In the ensuing standoff, the sheriffs and security guards asked the group to leave the court and Balogh continued his tirade before eventually leaving. During this exchange, his supporters burst into a round of supportive applause, celebrating Balogh's 'success'.

Balogh's behaviour in court recalls Daniel Newman's analysis of legal aid lawyers using 'pyrotechnics' in court, such as 'over-the-top speeches in cases that he deemed did not have a chance', made with 'verbose and florid language'.[50] These displays, while doing nothing for the client's case and indeed, reducing the likelihood of success, impressed the lay clients, who admired his passion and supposed ability to 'tear the police apart'.[51] Newman draws on Erving Goffman's dramaturgical analysis of impression management to consider the purpose of these displays, which do not help, or may even harm, the client's case.[52] Newman explains that a display of pyrotechnics is a form of social performance where

> the actor puts on a show, forever with the audience in mind. Each performance is tailored to ensure that the particular target is left with an impression consistent with the desired goal of the actor. So it was that the lawyer performed for the client; they are effectively playing to the gallery … Pyrotechnics may have been superficial, but they seemed to exert a considerable sway on clients.[53]

Applied to the displays of pseudolaw advocates, the purpose of the submissions to the court are not for the client's benefit in the legal sense, but are a performance to the gathered supporters (online and in court, and including the client). This

[49] A recording with commentary is available at Van Balion, 'Sovereign Citizen Tries to Arrest a Supreme Court Judge & Take over the Court with his Supporters' YouTube (11 August 2023), www.youtube.com/watch?v=H9Q1YnWXjmA; a commentary by a person attending is available at Vaxatious Litigant (@ExposingNV) (9 August 2023), threadreaderapp.com/thread/1689145813409382401.html. The description in this paragraph is derived from these sources.

[50] D Newman, *Legal Aid Lawyers and the Quest for Justice* (Hart Publishing, 2013) 134–35.

[51] ibid 135.

[52] ibid 136. See also K Leader, ch 5 in this collection, for further analysis of how theatre and performance studies can aid an understanding of court behaviour.

[53] ibid 136.

may be to increase their business, as gurus sell their services. The court appearance is not for the litigant's legal benefit, but for the collateral benefit of providing a 'stage' on which the pseudolaw advocate can perform their ideology and build their following. This does not seem to have been a feature of the Fathers' Rights movement, where I have found no suggestion that the advocates engaged in this kind of performative role in court.

The risks that pseudolaw advocates present to the administration of justice, the rule of law and the individual litigants, are sufficient to refute the 'strong presumption' that litigants should have their choice of litigation support. While it is possible that some pseudolaw advocates could help and support litigants, the characteristics of pseudolaw, its commercialisation and the behaviour of proponents in court which can be amplified and spread through social media, all suggest that pseudolaw advocates present a new and distinct challenge for the courts, requiring a new response. The court has always had the discretion to exclude them and, in the case of pseudolaw advocates, it should do so readily.[54] The question then is, what powers does the court have to do this?

III. Powers to Exclude Pseudolaw Advocates

Depending on the jurisdiction, different powers will be available but could involve excluding the advocate at the time of filing, use of inherent jurisdiction or use of specific rules. I consider each in turn.

A. Excluded at Filing

Advocates – lawyers and non-lawyers alike – perform much of their work before a case reaches hearing. For example, a study of McKenzie friends in England found that though their original purpose was in-court support, McKenzie friends performed a lot of work outside court, including advising clients and preparing documents.[55]

[54] Note that courts should be careful to consider each case on its own merits. In New Zealand, a family court developed a policy that litigants with extant litigation before the court should not be permitted to act as McKenzie friends. The court had developed the policy in response to Fathers' Rights movement members acting as McKenzie friends. They wanted to avoid confusion between cases and were 'also mindful of the need not to allow, or appear to allow, an opportunity for a proposed McKenzie friend to advance his or her own political or personal agenda through another's Family Court case'. A proposed McKenzie friend brought a successful judicial review against his exclusion from acting as McKenzie friend because the court had followed this policy, rather than starting with the presumption the McKenzie friend should be permitted and then considered the case on its merits: *BHR v Family Court at Tauranga* (n 23).

[55] For a discussion of the range of work McKenzie friends engage in and highlighting much of this is out of court, see L Smith, E Hitchings and M Sefton, 'A study of fee-charging McKenzie Friends and their work in private family law cases' Cardiff University and University of Bristol (June 2017),

A pseudolaw advocate performing this out-of-court role might explain what occurred in the England and Wales High Court case of *Gloria Lewis v 'The West Brom'*.[56] In this case, Master Thornett struck out seven seemingly unconnected claims that had 'curious similarity', leading the Master to be satisfied that 'there must be an unidentified guiding hand or hands behind them',[57] it being 'beyond any conceivable possibility that all of them coincidentally have been independently drafted yet share the same legal and factual oddities'.[58] The oddities included many of the pseudolaw hallmarks such as being 'variously festooned with fingerprints (in what one hopes is just red ink), seals and sigils'.[59]

This case highlights the possibility of preventing the involvement of pseudolaw advocates *before* they enter the court.[60] If registry offices know which hallmarks to look for, and to reject documents 'variously festooned', this avoids harm to litigants spending money on pseudolaw advocates and forecloses the opportunity to use the court as a performative space. Some courts have taken this robust approach. For example, the Newfoundland and Labrador Court of Appeal found that employing pseudolaw arguments indicates that the litigant is in court for an ulterior purpose, and therefore taking steps to interdict and terminate litigation are justified.[61] In Australia, the High Court refused to file a writ purporting to argue the Voice Referendum, a constitutional referendum held in 2023, was 'constitutionally invalid'.[62]

Taking these pre-emptive steps does require resourcing the registry officers to undertake this role, including providing clear guidelines. Few courts are likely to have the equivalent of the Alberta King's Bench which funds a specific position of 'complex litigant management counsel'.[63] However, such resourcing can help the courts to build the capacity to intercept pseudolaw litigation early, including keeping a list of active pseudolaw gurus so the court knows to reject applications for status as McKenzie friend if a guru applies.[64]

https://orca.cardiff.ac.uk/id/eprint/101919/1/A%20study%20of%20fee-charging%20McKenzie%20Friends.pdf.

[56] [2023] EWHC 1361 (KB).

[57] *Gloria Lewis v 'The West Brom'* [2023] EWHC 1361 (KB) [1].

[58] ibid [6].

[59] ibid [18.2]. For a description of pseudolaw characteristics, see *Meads v Meads* (n 9) 41.

[60] Various court rules may empower the court to do this. See, for example, High Court Rules (Australia), r 6.07; High Court Rules (New Zealand), rr 5.2 (non-complying documents) and 5.35A (Registrar may refer plainly abusive proceedings to Judge before service).

[61] Netolitzky (n 2) 422.

[62] K Atkinson, 'Unconstitutional voice claim is pure "nonsense"' AAP Fact Checker, www.aap.com.au/factcheck/unconstitutional-voice-claim-is-pure-nonsense.

[63] Donald Netolitzky, cited in this chapter, currently holds this position.

[64] Notably though, the pseudolaw adherents may still use the refusal to file as evidence of their success. In the High Court case regarding the Voice Referendum referred to above, the applicant posted on social media: 'High Court victory!! The 2023 Referendum is unconstitutional. … Once the constitutionality of the law underpinning the Referendum is/was challenged it needed to be affirmed by the High Court and by the Court declining to rule we won by default': Atkinson (n 62). Intervening early might protect the court but the court should have no illusion it will diminish the movement.

It has been suggested that another early intervention strategy would be to regulate pseudolaw advocates, although with the acknowledgment that 'the elements of such a sanction are difficult to imagine, and its enforceability may be problematic'.[65] It might be possible to introduce a pre-approval process for non-lawyer advocates seeking to assist or represent a litigant. This is the case in the New Zealand Family Court, where lay assistants must apply for approval in advance, although the focus is on ensuring the lay assistant understands the various confidentiality requirements and the nature of the role.[66] A similar process could be adopted to pre-screen all lay assistants, to identify pseudolaw advocates before the court appearance.

B. Excluding McKenzie Friends and Other Support Roles

Where the pseudolaw advocate appears in court, the court is likely to have powers to terminate their involvement if they are disruptive.[67] In England, the judge can exclude the McKenzie friend if their behaviour is 'inimical to the judge conducting the litigation in the manner which he or she considers is the most satisfactory way in which to do justice'.[68] This is also the position in New Zealand, where there is no right to a McKenzie friend, and the court can use its inherent jurisdiction to exclude a proposed support person if they would obstruct the efficient administration of justice.[69] As both the content and conduct of pseudolaw proceedings undermine the administration of justice, the McKenzie friend or other support person can be excluded using these powers.

Indeed, this has been the approach of some courts. For example, in England a support person appeared with the defendant in a tax evasion matter and announced to the judge, 'I will be acting as a McKenzie friend today'.[70] The Judge asked for the McKenzie friend's name and the McKenzie friend replied, 'I do not have a name, but have a calling and am commonly referred to as Hugh Jones'. When the Judge called him 'Mr Jones', the support person refused to respond to that name saying, 'that is not my title. I do not have a name'. After several attempts the Judge said: 'Okay look, for me to determine whether or not you are suitable to be a McKenzie Friend I first need to know who you are. Are you refusing to tell me who you

[65] Garret Sammon notes that in Ireland (writing in 2015) there were no clear rules about when a 'judge may direct that a McKenzie friend no longer participate in proceedings', but the situation is clearer in other jurisdictions: Sammon (n 9) 101.

[66] Courts of New Zealand 'Apply for a Lay Assistant, www.justice.govt.nz/family/family-court/about-the-family-court/people-and-roles-of-the-family-court/apply-for-a-lay-assistant.

[67] Sammon (n 9) 99.

[68] *R v Leicester City Justices, ex parte Barrow* [1991] 2 QB 260.

[69] Downs and D'Silva (n 5) 157–58.

[70] [Deleted account] Reddit (28 March 2019) 'I'm a magistrate in the UK and just had my first run-in with Freemen of the Land …', www.reddit.com/r/amibeingdetained/comments/b65e7m/im_a_magistrate_in_the_uk_and_just_had_my_first. The description in this paragraph, including the quotes, are drawn from this thread.

are?'. When the support person again stated, 'I do not have a name' and the Judge responded, 'Okay on that basis I reject your application to be a McKenzie Friend and order you to leave the court'. The non-lawyer was then removed from Court. This avoided the pseudolaw advocate continuing to have a presence in court, although they could still have launched into a tirade in the way Balogh did, having been given entrance. However, staying clearly in control of the courtroom – and ejecting a pseudolaw advocate rather than adjourning court – gives less scope for the pseudolaw advocate to frame their appearance as a 'success'.

C. Excluding Pseudolaw Advocates with Rights of Audience

Courts' powers may also extend to removing advocates with rights of audience. Courts have inherent jurisdiction to control the conduct of the proceedings before them.[71] This has been interpreted in some jurisdictions as including the power to remove advocates (lawyer or non-lawyer) who have rights of audience, a power that sits separately from the disciplinary regime that a body may have over a lawyer for the same conduct.[72] As explained by the New Zealand Supreme Court, all New Zealand courts 'have inherent powers and they include all, but only, such powers as are necessary to enable a Court to act effectively and uphold the administration of justice within its jurisdiction'.[73] This can include, in the relevant factual situation, the power to debar counsel or a non-lawyer advocate with rights of audience, from representing a party in a particular case:

> Removal will usually be ordered where counsel will not be able to comply with his or her duties to the Court: where there is a conflict of interest, or where there is a real risk that a client will not be represented with objectivity. The threshold for removal is a high one, requiring something extraordinary. The Court should guard against allowing removal applications to be used as a tactical weapon to disadvantage the opposing party.[74]

This power was discussed in the context of an Employment Court case where there was an employment advocate representing the employee and a lawyer representing the employer. In this case the argument was about removal of the lawyer, but the Employment Court noted the power must also apply to lay representatives who have rights of audience.[75]

[71] For English law see *Halsbury's Laws of England*, vol 11, 5th edn (Lexis, 2020) [23]; For Australian law see *Halsbury's Laws of Australia*, Vol 20 (LexisNexis, at February 2024) [325-10]; for New Zealand, see JC Corry, *Laws of New Zealand Civil Procedure: High Court* (LexisNexis, at February 2024) [47].

[72] In New Zealand see *Black v Taylor* ([1993]) [1993] 3 NZLR 403.

[73] *H v Employment Relations Authority* [2022] NZEmpC 87; BC202261338 citing *Siemer v Solicitor-General* [2013] NZSC 68, [2013] 3 NZLR 441.

[74] *Accent Management Ltd v Commissioner of Inland Revenue* [2013] NZCA 155, [2013] 3 NZLR 374 [32]–[35].

[75] *H v Employment Relations Authority* [2022] NZEmpC 87, [38]: 'I consider that the inherent powers must also be available to regulate the conduct of agents or representatives who act for employers and employees but are not admitted to practice as lawyers.'

Similarly, Netolizky cited Canadian authority for the Court's ability to deny access to 'rogue lay representative[s]' and suggested that since courts have a jurisdiction to supervise lawyer conduct that is parallel but separate from disciplinary proceedings, a court could intervene to remove a lawyer.[76] Given the risks to the court and to the litigant of having a pseudolaw advocate appearing or assisting in a case, I suggest that the threshold of 'something extraordinary' is met when a pseudolaw argument is advanced.

D. Using Other Procedures

Courts have various other powers that they can use to exclude pseudolaw advocates. Most commonly, courts have powers to hold people in contempt. This can be a suitable response if the pseudolaw advocate behaves in a way that justifies the exercise of this power. The judicial officer needs to be clear which power is being exercised: the supervisory power over representatives or the jurisdiction to punish contempt.[77] The jurisdiction to punish contempt, like the supervisory power, originates from the inherent jurisdiction to promote fair and expeditious administration of justice.[78] The contempt jurisdiction may reside in the inherent jurisdiction or may be partially or fully codified.[79] In New Zealand it is now codified in the Contempt of Court Act 2019 (NZ), with section 10 providing the power for a judicial officer to cite disruptive behaviour.

There may be other rules of specific ambit that can be used to control the presence of pseudolaw advocates. For example, in New Zealand, there is a rule that a company must be represented by counsel, although the court may exercise its discretion to allow an officer or agent to represent the company.[80] In a New Zealand High Court case, the Court refused to exercise its discretion to allow a director to represent a company, even though the company could not afford legal assistance, because the director was 'steeped in sovereign citizen theory'.[81] The judge commented that sovereign citizen theory was 'unhelpful to the company's interests in advancing a simple claim for breach of contract',[82] there was a 'real risk that the proceeding will not be pursued in a way that is in the best interests of the company', and 'an adverse costs award could prejudice both the plaintiff and its existing creditors, and might create an undue burden for the defendant'.[83] The

[76] Netolitzky (n 2) 484.

[77] *Weston v CCC Administrator* [1977] 1 QB 32, which discusses the confusion of the lower court judge between contempt of court and the inherent powers of the court to supervise counsel.

[78] *Johnson v Grant*1923 SC 789 (Scotland Court of Session); *Solicitor-General v Radio Avon Ltd and Another* [1978] 1 NZLR 225.

[79] For a survey of reform in other common law jurisdictions, see New Zealand Law Commission, 'Reforming the Law of Contempt of Court: A Modern Statute' 2017 R140 [1.71]–[1.74].

[80] *Re G J Mannix Ltd* [1984] 1 NZLR 309 (CA) at 311 and 314. An example of where the discretion will be exercised is where it would be burdensome to insist on counsel.

[81] *Republic Arms Ltd v Corporation (t/as New Zealand Police) (No 2)* [2022] NZHC 3185 [3]–[4].

[82] ibid [3]–[4].

[83] ibid [8].

judge stayed the proceedings, rather than striking them out, so that if the company instructed counsel and amended its claim, the stay could be reconsidered.[84] Specific rules such as this can therefore provide another basis for excluding pseudolaw advocates.

The court may also be able to exercise statutory or inherent powers to depart from the general principle of open justice and move the hearing into chambers.[85] This will not necessarily address the issue of a pseudolaw advocate but could minimise the performative aspect of the pseudolaw advocate's appearance by removing any supporters. While disruption to the proceedings which undermines the administration of justice will usually be a justification for removing members of the public from the hearing, it comes with some risks to public confidence. As Holland J observed in a New Zealand case, 'The more the Court operates with some veil of secrecy over its activities the less confidence there can be in the administration of justice'.[86] Given that prominent pseudolaw beliefs are organised around distrust in government and its institutions, hearing proceedings in chambers may only provide further 'evidence' to feed the movement.

IV. Further Controls, Outside of the Court

This chapter is focused on what courts themselves can do, rather than considering broader questions about social or regulatory change, but it is important to note that some of the answers lie beyond the court's control. The pseudolaw movement and the role of advocates within it points to the need for adequate regulation. In New Zealand it could strengthen the call for the regulation, even if at a light touch, of non-lawyer advocates with rights of audience in the employment jurisdiction.[87] In jurisdictions without a clear statement on when a support person or McKenzie friend can be excluded, the pseudolaw movement should create some urgency in creating this clarity.

The pseudolaw movement provides yet another justification for investing in legal assistance for vulnerable people. As discussed, some of the litigants who turn towards pseudolaw advocates are vulnerable, and pseudolaw advocates may

[84] ibid [9].

[85] *Daubney v Cooper* (1829) 10 B & C 237, 240 where interrupting the proceedings was stated as an exception to the general principle that anyone can attend a hearing: 'we are all of opinion, that it is one of the essential qualities of a Court of Justice that its proceedings should be public, and that all parties who may be desirous of hearing what is going on, if there be room in the place for that purpose, – provided they do not interrupt the proceedings, and provided there is no specific reason why they should be removed, – have a right to be present for the purpose of hearing what is going on.'

[86] *Re Wilson Neill Ltd* (1994) 7 NZCLC 260,617(HC) at 260, 617.

[87] A Williams, '"I was like, do you know how to do your job?" – Call to rein in rogue employment advocates' Radio New Zealand, www.rnz.co.nz/news/national/469512/i-was-like-do-you-know-how-to-do-your-job-call-to-rein-in-rogue-employment-advocates; J Bell, 'Government looks into regulating employment advocates' Newsroom, newsroom.co.nz/2022/04/11/calls-for-govt-regulation-of-employment-advocacy-sector.

be filling a void created by the absence of accessible legal assistance. Sammon suggests that providing a service like the Personal Support Unit in England might avoid having people 'tempted, by desperation or other reasons, to pursue OPCA litigation are dissuaded by the availability of another option'.[88] This lack of available advice and the alienation that people obviously feel from the law, 'should be seen as an invitation to the legal profession, and policy-makers, to engage with the criticisms this form of litigation [pseudolaw litigation] makes of the legal system'.[89]

V. Conclusion

Pseudolaw advocates are a sufficiently disruptive force that courts should be ready and willing to exclude them. This is both for the protection of the litigant (who is the party with the right to appear) and for the protection of the administration of justice and the rule of law. The court has a range of powers to prevent pseudolaw advocates assisting or appearing in cases, or to remove them if they become disruptive.

The court cannot prevent pseudolaw advocates from participating in litigation behind the scenes. Social media provides gurus with plenty of opportunities to coach litigants to self-represent with pseudolaw arguments, for example, Balogh runs a mock trial training programme.[90] It can use its powers to minimise their involvement and in doing so, the court is protected from being used for the collateral purpose of encouraging new adherents or strengthening the loyalty of the converted. Importantly, it also protects litigants, as it allows the court to engage directly with them. Pseudolaw litigants are unlikely to change their views, but the court will have provided a genuine opportunity for them to access justice away from the influence of a pseudolaw advocate.

[88] Sammon (n 9) 97–98.

[89] ibid 101.

[90] See, eg: Vaxatious Litigant (@ExposingNV), 'Derek Balogh running "Out of Court – Mock-Trials"' (28 May 2023).

15

The Paradox of Pseudolaw and Sovereign Citizen Ideology: Vulnerability, Malevolence and Disengagement

JOSH ROOSE*

I. Introduction

In the aftermath of the COVID-19 pandemic, sovereign citizen movements globally have evolved. Some have remained heavily isolationist, rejecting outside influences, whilst others have grown, cloaking themselves in the inclusivist rhetoric of the anti-COVID-19 lockdown 'freedom' movements and convoys that swept the Western world in response to public health-driven 'stay at home' orders and vaccine mandates. Some amongst these, particularly in Australia, have started working toward a 'revolution' grounded in pseudolegal concepts to replace the Government, starting with local councils, and demonstrated ideological convergences with other movements, including the far right, developing into larger social movements. This has significant implications for both security and social policy, including access to the legal system.

This chapter, which adopts an interdisciplinary socio-legal approach, is focused on developments in Australia in the aftermath of the COVID-19 pandemic. It aims to understand why people appear to be increasingly attracted to pseudolaw and sovereign citizen movements, to assess its potential for violence and to outline what steps can be taken by policy-makers to address its rise. It commences by examining core elements of sovereign citizen beliefs and the recent history and make-up of the movement in Australia, before exploring, in depth and across social scientific and legal theories, why Australians might be drawn to these conspiratorial ideas. It then explores the ideological evolution of the movement in the Australian context, and the extent to which these developments signal a greater

* Deakin University, Australia.

potential for violence, before discussing the intersection of vulnerability and malevolence, and the need for disengagement strategies to focus on the former.

The chapter makes two modest intellectual contributions to the literature on sovereign citizens. The first is the concept of the 'paradox of pseudolaw'. The paradox is this: those drawn to pseudolaw reject the Constitution, government and societal norms. They make claims to power and indeed, sovereignty, that is, 'supreme power or authority'. They pursue these claims vigorously and at times skillfully, using a variety of advocacy tactics ranging from letter-writing, protest and arguing, to concerted campaigns of 'paper terrorism'. Yet, many grassroots practitioners of pseudolaw are, despite their self-assured assertion of sovereignty, amongst the most powerless and vulnerable members of society. This may be for socio-economic reasons, though it may also speak to emotional or psychological vulnerability based on individual circumstance, often in strong contrast to those grifters selling pseudolegal solutions. This casts a light on the shadow of the Australian legal system and those who live within it; those who believe their only solution is to follow an alternative paradigm and who are consequently most open to exploitation.

The second contribution is the exploration of sovereign citizen beliefs as 'ideology'. In so doing, I draw upon political scientific theories of ideology to distinguish between 'thin' conspiratorial and grievance-fueled participation that may occasionally lead to individual confrontations with authorities, and 'thicker', ideologically motivated participation fused with more comprehensive political belief systems including far-right extremism that could lead to group confrontation and violence with authorities. I ground this in an exploration of several Australian movements and note the concerning development toward a thicker sovereign citizen ideology amongst at least one Australian sovereign citizen group, the My Place movement.

II. Core Elements of Sovereign Citizen Beliefs and the Role of Pseudolaw

The name 'sovereign citizen' is considered an 'umbrella term'.[1] Sovereign citizens may be understood as a 'loosely affiliated group of individuals' whose primary belief is the 'illegitimacy of the Government'.[2] They do not recognise federal, state or local laws, policies or governmental regulations.[3] Sovereign citizen beliefs are, due to their conspiratorial basis, complex and often difficult to unravel. Because

[1] D Baldino, and K Lucas, 'Anti-Government Rage: Understanding the Sovereign Citizen Movement in Australia' (2019) 14 *Journal of Policing, Intelligence and Counter-Terrorism* 245; C Kalinowski IV, 'A Legal Response to the Sovereign Citizen Movement' (2019) 80 *Montana Law Review* 153.

[2] C Sarteschi, *Sovereign Citizens: A Psychological and Criminological Analysis* (Springer, 2020).

[3] Federal Bureau of Investigations, 'Sovereign Citizens: An Introduction for Law Enforcement' (2010), info.publicintelligence.net/FBI-SovereignCitizens.pdf.

there is no centralised leadership or cohesive text,[4] some aspects of belief and practices evolve based on local context whilst others remain consistent across international borders.

To understand local beliefs, it is necessary to understand the basis of these in the United States.[5] Sovereign citizens believe that the current de facto form of government in the US commenced in the nineteenth century through usurping the de jure natural law government.[6] Sovereign Citizens believe, in the US context, that the 14th Amendment of the Constitution created a second tier of citizenship that 'enslaved', or created a contract with, the population under a federal corporation.[7] Further, there is a belief that the United States became bankrupt in 1933, with the Government borrowing against the future earnings of its citizens to keep its currency afloat.

Many sovereign citizens believe that the American (and Australian) Governments and common law were secretly replaced. The body of common law underpinning their nation's justice system, including Magna Carta (a British charter of civil liberties dating to 1215) and the 1688 Bill of Rights (UK), remains in place but is obscured. Sovereign citizens believe that the Government controls its citizens by creating a legal identity for everyone at birth: the 'Strawman'. This is the name on an individual's birth certificate and government-issued documents. This relates to other official documents and is a corporate entity or 'shell' to which all interactions with government can be directed. Sovereign citizens consider themselves 'flesh and blood'. They may not even refer to themselves as 'sovereign citizens' but may well use other terms such as 'free man' or 'free woman'.[8]

Sovereign citizens believe they can break free of the 'contract' with Government. This is ably articulated by His Honour Glen Cash KC of the District Court in Queensland:

> The legal being is attached to one's corporeal being as a result of a contract. The contract is evidenced by documents such as a birth certificate. The authority of the state over an individual is limited and depends on the existence of this contract. Once the contract has been revoked, the state can no longer exercise authority over the individual.[9]

A leading authority on sovereign citizens in the United States, Christine Sarteschi, states that the most important belief, which underlies others, is in the illegitimacy of the Government:

> They believe that the government is run in secrecy and well aware of its own illegitimacy. It is the secrecy of the government that allows it to impose its power upon the

[4] Kalinowski IV (n 1) 155; S Young, H Hobbs and J McIntyre, 'The Growth of Pseudolaw and Sovereign Citizens in Aotearoa New Zealand Courts' (2023) *New Zealand Law Journal* 6, 6–10.

[5] See Young, Hobbs and Goldwasswer, ch 6 in this volume.

[6] Kalinowski IV (n 1).

[7] CE Loeser, 'From Paper Terrorists to Cop Killers: The Sovereign Citizen Threat' (2014) 94 *North Carolina Law Review* 1123.

[8] See Young, Hobbs and Goldwasswer, ch 6, and Sarteschi, ch 11, both in this volume.

[9] G Cash, 'A Kind of Magic: The Origins and Culture of 'Pseudolaw' (2022) Paper delivered to the Queensland Magistrates Court State Conference (26 May 2022); also Cash, ch 8 in this volume.

> people. Once an individual can pierce through this veil of secrecy, then the individual is immune of the power of the government … the sovereign citizen no longer has to pay taxes, obtain a driver's license, register their vehicle, obey laws or follow the commands of police officers"[10]

These anti-government perspectives have maintained strong consistency since the early days of these movements.

Experts discussing sovereign citizen practices usually note the use of pseudolaw. Pseudolaw may be understood as a collection of 'legal-sounding, but false rules that purport to be law and replace conventional law … Pseudolaw is usually associated with a conspiratorial narrative or explanation for why pseudolaw is true but suppressed, a secret law known only to a few'.[11] Young, Hobbs and McIntyre claim that pseudolaw is 'a phenomenon where the form but not the substance of legal argumentation is used to advance a party's position'.[12]

Pseudolegal arguments are cloaked in legal jargon, structures and common law maxims, giving them a superficial appearance of legal argument. They very often use what the Southern Poverty Law Centre refers to as 'negative averment': an argumentative form that involves 'twisting all statements into the form of a question in order to shift the burden of proof to the opponent'.[13] However, they 'lack the substantive engagement with the core norms, principals and methods of legal reasoning',[14] and have been roundly criticised and rejected by the courts when they are brought before them. They have been described variously as 'gibberish',[15] 'incomprehensible',[16] 'ludicrous',[17] 'nonsensical'[18] and 'vexatious'.[19]

A. The Origins of Sovereign Citizens in Anti-government Extremism

The Sovereign Citizen movement has its roots in the anti-government extremist groups that emerged in the United States from the 1960s onwards. Sovereign citizen

[10] Sarteschi (n 2).

[11] D Netolitzky, 'A Revolting Itch: Pseudolaw as a Social Adjuvant' (2021) 22 *Politics, Religion & Ideology* 164.

[12] Young, Hobbs and McIntyre (n 4) 6. See also H Hobbs, S Young and J McIntyre, 'The Internationalisation of Pseudolaw: The Growth of Sovereign Citizen Arguments in Australia and Aotearoa New Zealand' (2024) 47 *University of New South Wales Law Journal* 309.

[13] Southern Poverty Law Centre, 'The Sovereign Citizens: A Dictionary of The Peculiar' (2010), www.splcenter.org/fighting-hate/intelligence-report/2010/sovereigns-dictionary-peculiar.

[14] Young, Hobbs and McIntyre (n 4) 7.

[15] *Deputy Commissioner of Taxation v Casley* [2017] WASC 161 [15].

[16] *Frank Jasper Pty Ltd v Glew [No 3]* [2012] WASC 24.

[17] *Schneider v Colhoun* 2022 SKQB 163.

[18] *Attorney General (WA) v Glew* [2014] WASC 100.

[19] *Ramsey v Skyring* [1999] FCA 907.

ideology is believed to reflect a variety of diverse extremist doctrines from groups including anti-tax protesters, militias, Christian identity and Posse Comitatus.[20] In seeking to understand the key ideological currents running through Sovereign Citizen beliefs, it is important to consider these in greater depth and their collective impact.

The anti-tax movement evolved in the 1950s as an anti-government movement asserting that income tax is illegitimate. The Anti-Defamation League states that in addition to white supremacist elements, 'the tax protest movement is a key component of the strain of extreme right-wing anti-government activism often referred to as the "patriot" movement'.[21] The Militia movement evolved in the 1990s as right-wing anti-government extremists consisting of armed paramilitary units that believed government is involved in a conspiracy (the new world order) to enslave Americans. The Christian Identity movement is a white supremacist religious movement that emerged in the 1960s and is founded on the belief that whites (people of European descent) are descended from the lost tribes of ancient Israel, and God's chosen people.[22] They consider non-whites to be created as beasts and refer to them as 'mud people'. They are highly antisemitic, believing that Jews are descended from Satan (though as the ADL notes, they are not 'Christian Fundamentalists'). The Posse Comitatus is a far-right populist social movement originating in California and Oregon in the 1970s. It held the belief that the Constitution had been undermined and that county government is the highest form of power. Consequently, county sheriffs are the highest form of power and have the ability to enforce the law.[23] As will become evident, this continues to shape sovereign citizen beliefs to this day.

There are an estimated 300,000 to 500,000 sovereign citizens in the United States, and more than 30,000 in Canada.[24] There is diversity amongst these, including the emergence of 'Moorish', African American sovereign citizens, demonstrating the significant capacity of sovereign citizen beliefs to be adapted to local context. These are all extreme anti-government movements that hold strong conspiratorial beliefs and believe that governments are illegitimate.[25] They have a strong track record of individual actions of violence against law enforcement in particular, and what Sarteschi refers to as 'paper terrorism', used to intimidate and coerce opponents.[26] Critically, as will be discussed further below, these are 'thick' ideological orientations that seek a holistic social programme to shape a new world grounded on extremist race and religion.

[20] D Alexander, 'The Sovereign Citizen Movement: Threats and Responses' *Security Magazine* (1 June 2016), www.securitymagazine.com/articles/87159-the-sovereign-citizen-movement-threats-and-responses. See Young, Hobbs and Goldwasswer, ch 6 in this volume.

[21] Anti-Defamation League, 'The Sovereign Citizen Movement in the United States' (21 December 2023), www.adl.org/resources/backgrounder/sovereign-citizen-movement-united-states.

[22] Anti-Defamation League, 'Christian Identity', extremismterms.adl.org/glossary/christian-identity.

[23] Anti-Defamation League, 'Posse Comitatus', extremismterms.adl.org/glossary/posse-comitatus.

[24] Alexander (n 20).

[25] ibid.

[26] Sarteschi (n 2) 31–57.

III. The Sovereign Citizen Movement in Australia

Sovereign citizen ideas have been present in Australia for many decades including, most notably, the declaration of the 'Principality of Hutt River' by farmer Leonard Casley in 1970. Non-academic, journalistic inquiry suggests that Australia has over 30 'micronations',[27] whilst many more – some approaching a threshold of statehood, and others falling far short – exist internationally.[28] The vast majority of sovereign citizens, however, do not tie their claims to land. It is difficult to estimate numbers in Australia and New South Wales with any certainty. In 2015 New South Wales Police considered that 300 sovereign citizens were active in New South Wales.[29] Growth in the Australian context has however been exponential, particularly in the context and aftermath of the COVID-19 pandemic.

During the COVID-19 pandemic, the City of Melbourne, Australia earned the dubious honour of having more lockdowns than any other city in the world,[30] with 262 total days of public health-driven 'stay at home orders' between 2020 and 2021 enforced by a so-called 'ring of steel' around Melbourne. Whilst the city would subsequently have one of the highest vaccination rates (over 90 per cent) of anywhere in the world, the social conditions created by lockdown policies in a city of over five million inhabitants saw the emergence of significant anti-lockdown protests and the evolution of a loose coalition of anti-lockdown actors calling themselves the 'Freedom Movement'.

This consisted of a blend of protesters ranging from anti-vaxxers and evangelical Christians to far-right actors and conspiracy theorists. The prominence of the 'red ensign' at protests, often flown upside down, was a prominent characteristic of many of these protests and subject to media and scholarly attention alike as they tried to make sense of its use before determining that sovereign citizens were behind its deployment.[31] The use of the ensign appeared to grow as the protests evolved and spread to other state capitals. It was in Canberra in December 2021 that sovereign citizen activists would attempt to connect their struggle to that of the Aboriginal Tent Embassy, a permanent protest site against

[27] M Siegal, 'The Royal Me: What's with Australia's Secession Obsession?' *The Atlantic* (15 April 2012), www.theatlantic.com/magazine/archive/2012/04/the-royal-me/308912/.

[28] H Hobbs and G Williams, *Micronations and the Search for Sovereignty* (Cambridge University Press, 2022) 20–81.

[29] M Elias, 'Robert says Being a Sovereign Citizen is like Having a "Mind Virus". It's a Movement the Pseudo-Law Expert Knows Well' The Feed (18 December 2022), www.sbs.com.au/news/the-feed/article/robert-says-being-a-sovereign-citizen-is-like-having-a-mind-virus-its-a-movement-the-pseudo-law-expert-knows-well/h9ftkonin.

[30] I Macreadie, 'Reflections from Melbourne: The Worlds most Locked-Down City, through the Covid-19 Pandemic and Beyond' (2022) 43 *Microbiology* 3, 3–4.

[31] J McIntyre, 'What is the Australian Merchant Navy Flag, the Red Ensign? And why do Anti-Government Groups use it?' The Conversation (12 November 2021), theconversation.com/what-is-the-australian-merchant-navy-flag-the-red-ensign-and-why-do-anti-government-groups-use-it-170270.

Australia's treatment of Indigenous peoples, linking with fringe Indigenous activists the 'Aboriginal Sovereign movement', of whom one activist would set fire to the old Australian Parliament House, causing over AUSD five million damage.[32] There have been many instances of sovereign citizens being arrested for failing to comply with police. Also in 2021, Western Australian and Queensland Police confiscated 470 fake sheriff badges,[33] demonstrating the intellectual lineage of the movement in the Posse Comitatus movement. Numerous sovereign citizens have been arrested after failing to comply with police officers, whilst in Queensland, a sovereign citizen had his gun licence revoked after attending a police station and demanding that the officer in charge be arrested.[34]

The deployment of pseudolegal paperwork directed at courts and government agencies has had a significant impact, delaying the administration of justice and resulting in a significant associated financial impact. In May 2023, ABC reported New South Wales magistrate Mark Douglas's claims that New South Wales courts had dealt with 300–400 sovereign citizen matters employing pseudolegal arguments in the period December 2022 to May 2023, with a detrimental impact on the timely administration of justice in the courts and wider legal system.[35] This impact has been felt across local, state and federal governments. Yet due to the disjointed nature of Australia's various sovereign citizen movements and, as noted above, their loose affiliations and lack of centralised decision-making, it is difficult to determine who precisely has been responsible. It is possible to instead examine three case studies of sovereign citizens deploying and/or spreading sovereign citizen tactics to gain a deeper insight into who is attracted to these movements. I look here at three core categories: grifters; the old sovereign citizens; and the new.

As has become clear, there are many sovereign citizen movements operating across the Australian continent. Historically, and somewhat ironically, these have been restricted to state lines, with different movements operating in their local territories. This has in recent years, particularly post-pandemic, changed. The below examples are broadly representative of this change and, importantly, indicative of the support base for sovereign citizen beliefs in Australia.

[32] M Day and B Carlson, 'So-Called Sovereign Settlers: Settler Conspirituality and Nativism in the Australian Anti-Vax Movement' (2023) 12 *Humanities* 112; P Taplin, C Holland and L Billing, 'The Sovereign Citizen Super Conspiracy: Contemporary Issues in Native Title Anthropology' (2023) 34 *The Australian Journal of Anthropology* 110; T Hassan, 'Who are the Original Sovereigns Who were Camped out at Old Parliament House and What are their Aims?' The Conversation (17 January 2022), theconversation.com/who-are-the-original-sovereigns-who-were-camped-out-at-old-parliament-house-and-what-are-their-aims-174694.

[33] Elias (n 29).

[34] A Utting, 'Queensland Sovereign Citizen Loses Bid to Carry Guns after Rockhampton arrest' ABC News (27 May 2023), www.abc.net.au/news/2023-05-27/qld-sovereign-citizen-loses-bid-to-carry-gun-police/102398316.

[35] S Kesteven, and D Carrick, 'Magistrates Witness a 'Sharp Rise' in Sovereign Citizen Cases Brought Before Local Courts' ABC News (8 May 2023), www.abc.net.au/news/2023-05-08/nsw-magistrates-report-sharp-rise-in-sovereign-citizen-cases/102285772.

A. Traditional Sovereign Citizens: Advance Australia HQ (Restore Australia 2012)

It may appear strange to refer to a movement that has been around for just a dozen years as an 'old' or 'traditional' form of Sovereign Citizen activism, however the pace of change, particularly post-pandemic, makes this an apt description for the Advance Australia movement led by Mike Holt. Originally started as the Restore Australia movement in 2012, the name change occurred in 2017, coinciding with the emergence of a series of nativist and far-right patriot-style movements that emerged in the aftermath of the election of US President Donald Trump.

Advance Australia under Holt's leadership is a 'common law' group. Holt explained in an interview in 2021, 'Common law is the law of man, of God, of the universe, so it's a natural law.'[36] Holt aims to 'tear down' the 'corrupt' political party system and replace it with Citizen Initiated Referendums, in which the Government is replaced in its entirety by votes by and for the people. The website notes 'Common law assemblies would be set up across the land, creating local governments of the people.'[37] Other elements of his proposed programme include tax reform, elearning courses about common law rights featuring modules such as 'Four Acts of Treason' and 'Lawful Rebellion', books on 'how to fight fines' featuring pseudolegal concepts, and conspiratorially laden information sheets about the 'new world order'. Website visitors can also 'Book a phone consultation' at AUSD 100 per hour.[38] Interestingly, despite the anti-government, anti-tax beliefs of this movement it appears to be registered for Goods and Services Tax (GST), meaning that it not only pays tax, but actively contributes to the Government it claims to reject.

It is difficult to estimate the size of the movement. Holt's X (Twitter) profile has 851 followers, though does not appear to have been used since January 2021. The group seems to operate primarily in Queensland and remains active to the time of writing.

B. The Grifters: Know Your Rights

The Know Your Rights Group is a key hub for pseudolegal information and critically, templates that assist sovereign citizens seeking to avoid their societal obligations. This includes payment of tax, fines and, while they existed, mandatory vaccinations during the COVID-19 pandemic. Know Your Rights states that its

[36] E Tlozek, 'Covid-19 is Accelerating the Rise of Conspiracy and Sovereign Citizen Movements in Australia' ABC News (21 August 2021), www.abc.net.au/news/2021-08-21/covid-19-accelerating-rise-of-conspiracy-movements-in-australia/100393666.

[37] Advance Australia, 'Citizens Initiated Referendums (Binding CIR)', advance-australia.com.au/step-1-cir.

[38] Advance Australia, 'Contact Us', advance-australia.com.au/contact-us.

first aim is to 'wake people up to the TRUTH that the governments and those who are REALLY in power have been suppressing for many years'.[39]

The website, run by 'Daryl' and 'Mike', features 17 headings including 'Fines', 'Tax', 'Banking', 'Strawman', 'COVID & vaccinations' and 'Financial protection'. It becomes clear that the group is focused primarily on escaping financial responsibilities and deploy sovereign citizen concepts and pseudolaw to attract the economically vulnerable. Accompanying this material is a focus on political elements, including 'Constitution', 'Local Government' and 'Conspiracy???', implying that financial stresses are caused by the Government.

Importantly, the founders offer immediate solutions to these financial problems; inside knowledge that can be purchased online. Products range from their digital e-book (AUD 67), DVD packs ranging from AUD 24 for a CD documenting the 'Almanac of Evil' and a CD featuring a 584-page PDF document titled 'Invisible Contracts', to an AUD 647 'Ultimate Platinum Combo Pack' featuring all CDs and books.[40] Signalling their higher-ranking status in the Sovereign Citizen hierarchy, coaching with Daryl or Mike is available for AUD 247 an hour (this is almost 2½ times the cost of coaching by Mike Holt). Memberships are available for AUD 19.95 a month, offering access to 'fully edited weekly podcasts' and tickets to three-day seminars including the 'Advanced Mastermind Workshop' and slides on 'debt slavery' and 'personal tax is voluntary', and can be purchased in capital cities for AUD 567.00. Affiliate memberships offer those who refer others a 20 per cent commission on sales. Videos posted to the website interview passers-by about their 'knowledge' and feature recommendations from happy seminar attendees who share their enthusiasm (before they have tried the pseudolegal tactics offered).

'Mike' and 'Daryl' are charismatic and strongly spoken and appear to offer solutions for those in debt and facing immense economic challenges in their lives. In this sense, they cloak their graft in a sovereign citizen belief system as a saleable product to the weak and desperate.

C. The New Sovereign Citizens: My Place

In contrast to traditional 'old' sovereign citizen groups and grifters, My Place is more a movement than a group and frames its recruitment narrative in a positive casing. Its motto is to 'put UNITY back into CommUNITY' and to promote the notion that 'My place is your place'.[41] Its stated aims are to 'Do no Harm' and only to 'Do Good'. Amongst a wide array of values listed are 'truth', 'integrity', 'respect', transparency', 'love', gratitude', 'courage', 'responsibility' and 'collaboration'.[42]

[39] Know Your Rights Group, 'About Us', www.knowyourrightsgroup.com.au.
[40] Know Your Rights Group, 'Products', www.knowyourrightsgroup.com.au/products.
[41] My Place, web.myplaceaustralia.org.
[42] ibid.

Superficially, the group appears to offer an inclusive and collaborative space for community members to join and belong to something larger than themselves.

The My Place Frankston website home page, which constitutes the 'home base' for the movement, starts by listing times and dates for town hall meetings, including an 'Organic Food order pick up', a workshop on 'Frequency and Essential Oils', community markets, and a wine and cheese tasting night. On first appearances, the movement offers a salve for the often atomised, digital media-centric society that we have become, emphasising face-to-face contact and community. However, the 'General information' tab on the home page takes the visitor to information on a raft of wider social and political issues, indicating a strong intersection with right-wing and conspiratorial politics. Information includes a 'Vote no to Apartheid' link (referring to the referendum to recognise Aboriginal and Torres Strait Islander peoples by establishing a Voice to Parliament), conspiratorial material about 'smart cities', '5G' information and a 'Timeline to Treason'.[43] On clicking a link to the Frankston People's Council, the visitor is taken to an independent website featuring the red ensign and outlining the 'alternative local government of Frankston's' platform and links to pseudolegal material including 'withdrawal of consent' forms.

The tactics employed by the My Place movement are often referred to by those countering violent extremism as 'breadcrumbing' (derived from the folk tale *Hansel and Gretel*). That is, moderate and even socially inclusive material might be deployed before gradual increases in exposure to more hardline and extremist material that reveals the true ideological disposition of the movement. Public statements by the founder of My Place include references to traitors 'hanging' and indicate hatred for government and the police. The founder, Darren Bergwerff, has also been the subject of an Australian Broadcasting Corporation expose, sharing extreme antisemitic material online and associating with far-right political actors from within the Freedom Movement.[44]

Digging deeper into the My Place website, the visitor is taken to the ideological heart of the movement, including a stated belief that we are already living in World War Three, that a cabal of bankers operates behind the scenes, pulling the strings, and that the United States and Jews hold the real power and must be opposed.[45] It identifies three stages of 'revolution'. The first is 'ideological resistance' to 'wake up as many people as possible'. The second is civil disobedience (non-violent resistance), or as the website states, 'put your money where your mouth is'. The third stage is 'direct physical resistance'. The website advises that this is to be delayed for as long as possible as the other two stages need to be firmly in place first.

My Place Australia has grown its online profile exponentially in the aftermath of the COVID-19 pandemic. From its base in Frankston, Victoria, as of May 2024,

[43] My Place, 'My Place Website: Frankston', www.myplacefrankston.com.

[44] E Baker, 'Video: "Extreme" Groups have a Strategy to Influence Local Councils' ABC 7:30 Report (2 April 2023), www.abc.net.au/news/2023-04-03/'extreme'-groups-have-a-strategy-to-influence/102182806.

[45] My Place (n 41).

they have 185 My Place chapters including 60 in Victoria, 51 in Queensland, 44 in New South Wales, 17 in South Australia, eight in Western Australia and three in Tasmania. The location of chapters is primarily outer suburban and regional, with some large regional cities such as Geelong (899 members) and Bendigo (458 members) in Victoria, Newcastle (2,000 members) in New South Wales, and Townsville (1,200 members) in Queensland. This group would likely exercise much greater influence in these smaller areas than with a similar number of members in a capital city.

My Place has given rise to an indigenisation of the sovereign citizen movement in the Australian context. The narrative arc of My Place posits that government is fundamentally corrupt, and that the people are being exploited by a global agenda and must rise up against both their financial exploitation and coercion by the Government. Yet in contrast to many other sovereign citizen movements framed primarily in a negative and reactionary sense, My Place wraps this ideological package up in messaging about belonging, inclusion and community. This appears to resonate for those in the outer suburbs and, in particular, regional Australia. An analysis of My Place in its home state of Victoria reveals that over 12 per cent of its online chapters are located in inner suburban areas. This more than doubles to just over 26 per cent for outer suburban areas. However, it is regional Victorians who appear most likely to be attracted to these movements. Just over 61 per cent of chapters are located in regional cities and towns.[46] This high figure contrasts with the fact that just 23 per cent of Victorians live in rural and regional Victoria. The *Index of Relative Socioeconomic Disadvantage* demonstrates that rural local government areas in Victoria are more likely to be classified as 'most disadvantaged'.[47] Furthermore, the average age of Victorians aged over 60 in rural and regional Victoria (26 per cent) is higher than in Greater Melbourne (18 per cent),[48] and residents are more likely to be white and speak English as a first language.[49]

Whilst there is more research to be done on the precise demographics of Sovereign Citizen movements, it can be noted that the most successful recruitment terrain for My Place in the state of Victoria is in regional and rural areas where there is significantly higher socio-economic disadvantage amongst populations who are older and less culturally diverse than in the City of Greater Melbourne.

[46] ibid.

[47] Victorian Government Department of Health 'Your Health Report: Rural and Regional Victorians' (18 April 2023), www.health.vic.gov.au/your-health-report-of-the-chief-health-officer-victoria-2018/health-inequalities/rural-and-regional#; see also Australian Bureau of Statistics, 'Socio-Economic Indexes for Areas' (2023), www.abs.gov.au/websitedbs/censushome.nsf/home/seifa.

[48] Victorian Government, 'Victoria's Seniors' (28 June 2022), www.vic.gov.au/ageing-well-action-plan/victorias-seniors.

[49] Australian Bureau of Statistics, 'Cultural Diversity of Australia' (20 September 2022), www.abs.gov.au/articles/cultural-diversity-australia.

IV. Why are People Attracted to Sovereign Citizen Movements and to the Use of Pseudolaw?

The above exploration tells us where one Sovereign Citizen movement, My Place, is likely to gain more traction and suggests some contributing factors, socio-economic disadvantage being primary amongst them. The pseudolegal fabrication of the 'Strawman' and the apparent opportunity to reject their debt and imposed constraints on their lives appears to offer something to them. It is in this context that pseudolegal mechanisms, which I consider here as a form of extremism (not in and of themselves 'violent' extremism), and the violent potential of the Sovereign Citizen movement become apparent. However, to understand this in greater depth, we need to draw convergences in various theoretical perspectives across the radicalisation literature, social sciences and legal theory.

A. Push, Pull and Personal Factors to Radicalisation

The framing of 'push', 'pull' and personal factors as contributors to radicalisation, developed by Vergani, Iqbal, Ilbaha and Barton and based on their systematic scoping review of literature,[50] provides a valuable starting point to understanding both structural and external factors shaping the appeal of Sovereign Citizen movements.

Push factors are structural factors that drive individuals toward violent extremism, including loss of legitimacy, geopolitical factors, relative deprivation, inequality and violence. These may include unemployment and education, though also more tangible factors including experiences of injustice, inequality, marginalisation and social exclusion. Grievance, frustration, victimisation and stigmatisation may also play a role.[51] Emotion plays an important role in driving people toward extremist narratives, in particular anger. Whilst anger can be a positive mobilising force toward social change, it can also accompany feelings of shame, humiliation, resentment and dishonour.[52]

Pull factors identified by Vergani et al include cognitive factors such as consumption of propaganda and online material, and the perceived morality of a group. Also important are social mechanisms and group processes such as identity fusion and identification, group dynamics including peer pressure, the formation of strong bonds with resultant fulfilment and belonging, total identification with a group and family and kinship ties, and leadership, including the role of

[50] M Vergani et al, 'The Three Ps of Radicalization: Push, Pull and Personal: A Systematic Scoping Review of the Scientific Evidence about Radicalization into Violent Extremism' (2020) 43 *Studies in Conflict & Terrorism* 854, 854.

[51] ibid 858, 861.

[52] J Roose et al, *Masculinity and Violent Extremism* (Palgrave, 2022).

charismatic leadership and emotional and material incentives.[53] Finally, personal factors contributing to radicalisation identified by Vergani et al include individual psychological vulnerabilities independent of push and pull factors (mental health conditions, depression, trauma), personality traits (narcissism and impulsivity) and specific individual characteristics (age, gender nationality) that may contribute to make an individual more susceptible to extremism.[54]

Due to the often-secretive nature of sovereign citizen movements, there is not currently a great deal known about their dynamics. However, based on the above case studies of traditional and new forms of sovereign citizenship movements and associated grifters for whom the commodification of pseudolaw appears to be profitable, it is possible to suggest that push factors toward the movement may include socio-economic deprivation, and sense of injustice, frustration and victimisation.

British labour economist Guy Standing has written extensively on what he terms 'the precariat'. Standing asserts that 'the precariat is the new dangerous class because all elements in it reject mainstream political establishments'.[55] It is a class with 'no occupational identity, no occupational narrative that they can give to their lives' and who are exploited outside the workplace as well as in it,[56] that is, when indeed they are in it at all. The precariat, he notes, is 'defined by distinctive relations to the state: they are losing rights taken for granted by full citizens'; they are 'denizens who inhabit a locale without civil, cultural, political, social and economic rights'.[57] Whilst legal rights remain in place in theory, legal services are significantly under-resourced[58] and other forms of legal recourse are cost-prohibitive. Further, the law is very often understood as embedded in a system of hostile government that is incapable of meeting their needs and indeed, actively hostile to their interests.

This set of experiences goes hand in glove with the feeling of political emotions, or what Standing refers to as a 'consciousness of relative deprivation'.[59] These are defined by the 'Four A's': Anger, Anxiety, Anomie and Alienation. If anxiety is a future focused emotion and anomie (despair) and alienation (social frustration) are reactions, anger is a present focused emotion that drives social change in the present.

However, the role of charismatic leadership, particularly amongst the 'grifters' charging significant amounts for secret pseudolegal knowledge and advice, must also be understood as a key 'pull factor'. Almost always middle-aged white men, these charismatic leaders possess a self-assuredness arguably unique to those who occupy a hegemonic position in society and of individuals who it might be

[53] Vergani et al (n 50) 858, 863.
[54] ibid 858–59.
[55] G Standing, 'The Precariat' (2014) 13 *Contexts* 10, 11.
[56] ibid 12.
[57] ibid 11.
[58] Impact Economics and Policy, 'Justice on the Brink: Stronger Legal Aid for a Stronger Legal System' (November 2023), www.nationallegalaid.org/resources/justice-on-the-brink.
[59] ibid.

hypothesised, have never been told 'no'. Videos feature these men front and centre of the camera as they confidently assert the need for their product, be it a template or their political movement. The self-assuredness and confidence of these grifters, who position themselves at the apex of what are hierarchical organisations, appear to be key for those searching for an alternative solution to their current struggles.

Little is known about the personal factors including possible mental health challenges drawing adherents towards Sovereign Citizen movements. Mental illness does not preclude the capacity to subscribe to and act upon an ideological belief. There are numerous dimensions of these personal factors contributing to the uptake of Sovereign Citizen beliefs that must be better understood.

B. Sovereign Citizens as Social Movement

Social movement theory can offer a useful framework for understanding the attraction of individuals to extremism. As Beck notes, this theory, 'due to its integrative and interdisciplinary nature is uniquely positioned to contribute a necessary conceptual framework for the study of political violence and terrorism'.[60]

Extremist movements, like all social movements, incorporate the same factors – 'personal and collective grievances, political and religious ideologies, networks and interpersonal ties, and enabling environments and support structures' – as any other type of movement.[61] Social movement theory may be understood as attempting to explain the 'origins, growth, decline and outcomes of social movements, including the social, cultural, and political manifestations and consequences of such movements including violence'.[62]

The concept of relative deprivation (a pull factor within Vergani et al's theory of radicalisation) is important within social movement theory, explaining why emotional responses and actions are triggered when an individual's expectations or anticipated trajectory is not attained in comparison with that of another social group. This may include a sense of deprivation in relation to economic resources, power and social status, resulting in feelings of resentment, humiliation and anger. Individual subjective levels of deprivation can also engender grievance and can play a role in the development of social movements as well as opening political opportunities for protest and anti-government action. This is evident when considering the broad patterns of attraction to the Sovereign Citizen movement My Place outlined above, where the more socio-economically challenged outer suburban

[60] C Beck, 'The Contribution of Social Movement Theory to Understanding Terrorism' (2008) 2 *Sociology Compass* 1565.

[61] R Futrel, P Simi and A Tan, 'Political Extremism and Social Movements' in D Snow et al (eds), *The Wiley Blackwell Companion to Social Movements* (Wiley, 2018) 618.

[62] S Flynn, 'Types of Social Movements' in Salem Press (eds), *Sociology Reference Guide: Theories of Social Movements* (Salem Press, 2011) 26.

and regional areas have demonstrated a greater attraction, at least online, to the movement than is evident in the inner suburbs.

In a similar vein, the concept of social isolation and its impact on emotions stemming from the 'mass society' also resonates here. Amidst rapidly increasing social and economic inequalities, the COVID-19 pandemic and resultant lockdowns had the contrary impact of legally requiring citizens to stay in one place for prolonged periods, resulting in an immense psychological and social upheaval and uprooting of daily life. It is in the context of this disruption that people would increase their online activity, seeking alternative cognitive and social structures and gaining significantly increased exposure to conspiracy theories. This created a political opportunity for activists and grifters alike to advance a set of claims that can prove beneficial to their own standing and the social trajectory. Variables including the form and substance of the grievance(s), the mode of their transmission, and government or institutional actions and responses combine to play an important role in shaping the development of the social movement and their actions to shape society.

C. Tyler's Theory of Procedural Justice, Legitimacy and the Effective Rule of Law

Tom Tyler's theorising on procedural justice, legitimacy and the effective rule of law provides an important accompaniment to the social scientific theoretical frames deployed above.[63] Tyler asserts that people's perceptions of procedural justice play a critical role in their willingness to comply with laws and accept the authority of legal institutions, even when outcomes are unfavourable for them.[64] He states:

> We would expect, based on theories of legitimacy, that people who view legal authorities as more legitimate, and hence more entitled to be obeyed, would be more likely to defer to legal authorities, accepting their decisions about how to resolve problems or restrict their own behaviour.[65]

As Meyerson, MacKenzie and MacDermott argue, in their relational approach to procedural justice, proper treatment imbuing legitimacy can 'cushion' the impact of detrimental outcomes.[66]

When legal procedures are perceived as fair, respectful and unbiased, citizens are more likely to bestow them with legitimacy, which is essential for the

[63] T Tyler, 'Procedural Justice, Legitimacy, and the Effective Rule of Law' (2002) 30 *Crime and Justice* 283.

[64] ibid 297.

[65] ibid 319.

[66] D Meyerson, C MacKenzie and T MacDermott, 'Procedural Justice in Law, Psychology, and Philosophy' in D Meyerson, C MacKenzie and T MacDermott (eds), *Procedural Justice and Relational Theory: Empirical, Philosophical and Legal Perspectives* (Routledge, 2020) 3.

maintenance of social order. This ties into the sociological work on crisis developed by Jurgen Habermas in the mid-1970s, which explores how political, economic and cultural institutions and structures maintain their power.[67] A 'legitimation crisis' refers to the failure of governments to attract loyalty from the public, undermining the government's capacity to act.

A crisis of legitimacy and belief in the legal process is proclaimed every generation. Writing in 1982, Friedrichs noted that the claim that society is experiencing a legitimacy crisis or 'crisis of confidence' in its institutions had been held for at least two decades.[68] In the context of the COVID-19 pandemic and associated public health orders and lockdowns, a similar crisis of legitimacy has plagued western governments. The work of Hobbs and Williams, for example, indicates that key institutions, including Australian parliaments, which should have played a critical role during the pandemic, including the ventilation of grievances, often performed poorly.[69] Yet the legal system, with more permanence for employees (than politicians) and without the need for political point-scoring, may have been anticipated to have done better. If it was to merely perform as expected and enact procedural fairness and be transparent and accessible, a 'cushioning effect' should have occurred.

Yet the anticipated cushioning effect that we would expect to see from an impartial and procedurally just court system does not appear to have translated into greater trust from those at the margins. The legal system has become conflated with the perceived failures of democratic governance. Those who have felt themselves to have been alienated from the system have instead sought to not only claim sovereignty, but to replace the system entirely with their own pseudolegal order that they believe will develop the justice and fairness lacking in their lives. Through this process, they experience a transformation, an evolution, moving from living within the shadow of the law in a system they do not believe in, to becoming the arbiter of the law. As is common in other forms of extremism, whereby upon adopting a narrative, young men transform from 'zero to hero', becoming warriors fighting for a cause, in this case this metamorphosis sees those at the alienated and excluded fringe of society become 'sovereign', possessing ultimate power over their destiny.

We know, as the theoretical paradigms above suggest, that there are a number of key push and pull factors including rapidly growing economic inequalities, a cost-of-living crisis and housing affordability crisis (a sense of 'relative deprivation'), that have combined with the severe application of state powers during the pandemic, shaping the attractiveness of extremist narratives. We also know

[67] J Habermas, 'What Does a Crisis Mean Today? Legitimation Problems in Late Capitalism' (1973) 40 *Social Research* 643.

[68] D Friedrichs, 'The Law and the Contemporary Legitimacy Crisis: A Programmatic Statement and A Selective Bibliography of Recent Sources' (1982) 11 *ALSA Forum* 95.

[69] H Hobbs and G Williams, 'Australian Parliaments and the Pandemic' (2023) 46 *UNSW Law Journal* 1314, 1318.

that personal and collective grievances and their associated political emotions, in particular anger, have been mobilised and exploited by key actors for both financial profit and political capital. This goes a long way to explaining the appeal of the sovereign citizen narrative, particularly in its indigenised form in groups such as My Place, concentrated as they are in key areas experiencing greater socio-economic challenges, and offering a sense of community, inclusion, solidarity and empowerment. Yet we need to look a little further to adequately grasp both the cohering elements of the Sovereign Citizen movement and their potential for violent escalation beyond the individual level to collective mobilisation. It is important in determining the potential for sovereign citizens to mobilise collectively to violence to consider whether their beliefs can be considered to constitute an ideology.

V. Sovereign Citizen Ideology and the Potential for Violence

Sovereign citizens are often considered to adhere to an 'ideology', which would mean that beyond requiring a 'body of doctrine, myth, and symbols of a social movement, institution, class, or large group',[70] they possess a 'political and cultural plan' to shape the world. As the *Oxford Reference Dictionary* makes clear, 'an ideology is a conceptual scheme with a practical application'.[71] An ideology must be animated by a core idea about how the world should be structured to which adherents collectively mobilise.

It is important to understand the extent to which sovereign citizens may be considered to constitute an ideological movement working according to a political and cultural plan to shape the world and its institutions, or a set of grievance-fuelled interconnected beliefs. This can give us insights into both the reasons people are joining (political activism or personal grievance) and the potential of the Sovereign Citizen movement for different forms of violence (mass violence or individual actors). It is thus important to look at the specific belief system of sovereign citizens and their characteristics.

The key beliefs of sovereign citizens are encapsulated in their pseudolaw, and reflected in the concepts outlined above. These include the concept of the Strawman and the beliefs that legislative authorities require consent, and that the current government lacks legitimacy.

The concept of sovereign citizen intellectuals may initially appear oxymoronic, yet key actors have developed core ideas that have become influential within these movements. David Wynn Miller, for example, developed the unique grammar and syntax system that he claimed could unlock the real meaning and truth of

[70] *Macquarie Dictionary* (2023), 'Ideology'.
[71] *Oxford Reference Dictionary* (2023), 'Ideology'.

legal documents, whilst Roger Elvick, a 'prominent sovereign citizen guru'[72] and white supremacist, developed the 'redemption theory', in which the concept of the 'strawman' was central.

Broadly speaking, then, sovereign citizens may be understood as sharing conspiratorial anti-government ideas about society, power and who determines the allocation of resources within society. Yet the question must be posed: what is their plan for society? What does a sovereign citizen-based society of 'free men and free women' look like? Sovereign citizens 'have no leader, no central repository for ideas, and no unifying collective mission'.[73] They generally operate independently or in small groups that mobilise for training seminars, to assist one another with paperwork, and to socialise or protest based on their sovereign citizen beliefs.[74] Sovereign citizen beliefs are, due to their conspiratorial basis, complex and often difficult to unravel. Because there is no centralised leadership or cohesive text,[75] some aspects of belief and practices evolve based on local contexts whilst others remain consistent across international borders. It is difficult to conceive of sovereign citizens as offering any holistic view of how the world should be structured. They know what their grievances are and what they stand against – government and perceive powerful elites. However, they do not commonly articulate what they stand for, other than an anarchic realm, without states, in which individual actors determine their own futures. To this extent, it is difficult to conceive of the Sovereign Citizen movement as, at best, a 'thin' ideology based on grievance rather than as offering any coherent ideology to inform social change.

Yet we have seen important developments in the Australian context, where groups such as My Place, the 'new' sovereign citizens, are actively seeking the establishment of a 'parallel society' that has more in common with 'thick' ideological movements grounded in a more holistic political and moral worldview.[76] This has manifested in the group's leader Darren Bergwerf declaring himself the mayor of the People's Council of Frankston, an alternative to the local council, seeking to contest elections to gain access to power and the group's manifesto, articulating its three-stage plan for revolution, which will ultimately require violence. In this alternative vision, 'Lore' (pseudolaw) will replace 'law', and the spiritual war 'between GOD and Satan' will be won.[77] Pseudolaw in this context, irrespective of its complete lack of consistency and legal credibility, scaffolds this thicker, future-focused, ideology, tying into the narrative arc of the movement as combatting treason and globalist evil, dissolving political and economic power to the people and forming the base of a new social order. These ideas intersect with

[72] M Pitcavage, 'Winston Shrout: The Rise and Fall of a Sovereign Citizen Guru' Anti-Defamation League (21 March 2016), www.adl.org/resources/blog/winston-shrout-rise-and-fall-sovereign-citizen-guru.

[73] Kalinowski IV (n 1) 155.

[74] Federal Bureau of Investigations (n 3) 3.

[75] Kalinowski IV (n 1) 155; Young, Hobbs and McIntyre (n 4).

[76] See Sarteschi's work on American State Nationals in ch11 of this volume.

[77] My Place, 'National Action' (2024), static1.squarespace.com/static/62983d52138786320f0e6022/t/65e9447019a10d5c5eb55da1/1709786225141/Doc+5+%281%29.pdf.

other movements, with which sovereign citizens share a common ideological lineage, including the far right and Christian Identity movements. The movement's vocabulary and agenda have a strong violent potential not necessarily immediately visible to those drawn to the movement, though likely to be communicated to them as they become acculturated. It demonstrates the potential for those at the margins of society experiencing anger, though also emotions including disempowerment, dislocation, shame, humiliation, frustration and isolation, to be drawn into extremist and violent extremist movements.

VI. Final Thoughts: Vulnerability, Malevolence and Disengagement

Sovereign Citizen movements in Australia bear little resemblance to movements in North America. Whilst much of the anti-government rhetoric and use of pseudolegal mechanisms is similar, the Australian governance framework does not feature 1st and 2nd Amendment rights pertaining to complete freedom of speech and the right to bear arms that have arguably contributed to the challenges posed by armed militias and Sovereign Citizen movements seen in the United States.

Australian Sovereign Citizen movements are characterised by charismatic leaders, not by masculine strength. In the most successful of these movements, which seek political rather than economic gain, leaders express a genuine concern about helping their followers and emphasise inclusion and solidarity in the face of a perceived corrupt, out-of-touch government. The most successful of these has been the My Place movement, emphasising 'unity', 'community' and 'doing good'. For the socially and economically vulnerable citizens drawn to these movements, pseudolegal mechanisms offer empowerment and hope, and the wider group offers belonging that otherwise appears to escape them in their daily lives. The application of pseudolaw and associated language is experienced by those on the other end as inherently hostile, threatening and malevolent, and viewed by scholars and security analysts as extremist and, at times, crossing a line from rhetorical and symbolic violence into violent extremism. It is psychologically unsettling, expensive and difficult to deal with.

When a group or movement is labelled as violent extremists, this triggers a highly securitised response. The arms of government tasked with countering violent extremism and counterterrorism quickly swing into action. Groups are subject to surveillance, with massively increased scrutiny of their communications. A much lower threshold is considered acceptable when individuals or the group commit even minor infractions of the law and the media and wider community often mobilise against the group as well, contributing to the sense of being under constant attack. Some of this is indisputably the case for Australian sovereign citizens, who very often face arrest and dismissive or negative media scrutiny for their actions.

It is tempting to view them as having brought such societal and security pressure upon themselves, and it is indeed critical to take the security threat seriously. However, in seeking to assist in the disengagement of those drawn to these movements in the first place, we must look at those societal push factors that have contributed to their vulnerability, including socio-economic marginalisation and inequalities, and a perception of the government and the legal process as having failed them, which contribute to a lack of trust. This does not excuse uncivil and illegal behaviour; however, it is critical to view this as a social movement centred on a perception of victimhood. We must then also vigorously target those political and financial opportunists and grifters sharing narratives that both seek to delegitimise democratic institutions, and who financially and politically profit from the sale of pseudolegal templates and recruitment of large swathes of people.

Addressing the challenge requires a whole-of-government approach to addressing inequalities in outer suburban and regional Australia. It also requires asserting alternative narratives that aim to rebuild a sense of trust and social inclusion, particularly amongst Australians facing financial difficulties who may feel left behind. The legal and court processes must work to become more transparent and accessible. To this end, governments may want to reconsider consistent cuts to legal aid, particularly in areas where pseudolegal mechanisms have become part of an established conversation about alternatives. The legal system can aim to become more approachable and transparent, and adopt an educative model for those at the margins. The recent growth in sovereign citizen movements in Australia and across western contexts in the context of the pandemic must be understood as a symptom of a deeper set of social and economic circumstances and treated accordingly.

16

Responding to Pseudolaw

HARRY HOBBS, STEPHEN YOUNG AND JOE McINTYRE

I. Introduction

In the Introduction to this volume, we began with a story. We related the experience of James Jones, who had run into trouble with the authorities in Whanganui, New Zealand over failing to register his dog with the local government. In successive court hearings, Jones made clear that he did not regard himself as bound by the laws of New Zealand. He was a sovereign man born free who had not consented to abide by statutory law, and he had not contracted with the corporation known as the New Zealand Government. Jones did not succeed at any stage. Nevertheless, he persisted in his claims. Why?

From our vantage point, it is impossible to answer this question with precision. It is clear, however, that Jones's pseudolegal beliefs are strongly held. Several years earlier, in January 2014, he served a document he describes as a 'Claim of Right' on the 'Crown Corporation of New Zealand', addressed to Prime Minister John Key, Attorney-General Christopher Finlayson, the Solicitor-General and the Commissioner of Police.[1] The document repeats a range of sovereign citizen pseudolegal tropes that give an insight into Jones's subsequent actions. It asserts that 'the basis of all Law in New Zealand is that of Common Law, which is derived from the law of the creator', that 'all law is a contract' and that 'a contract requires an Offer, Consideration and Acceptance'. It notes further that a contract can only be made 'between like entities; real human to real human or fictional person to fictional person', that the Births Deaths and Marriages Act 1933 'created a legal person by way of a legal fiction' and that the New Zealand Government is a corporation. Jones explains that, given these truths, any person can 'exist free of government control and statutory restraints', including by disobeying statutes and court orders. Jones concludes:

> 57. Therefore be it resolved *and* known to any and all concerned and affected parties, that I, James a Freeman-on-the-Land, do hereby state clearly, specifically and unequivocally my intent;

[1] Quotes from these passages are drawn from, James Son of James, 'Claim of Right of James', www.jamessonofjames.com/claim-of-right-of-james.

> 58. To peacefully and lawfully exist free of all statutory obligations and/or restrictions, and maintain all rights at law to trade or barter, and,
>
> 59. To travel peacefully and lawfully on the geographical area commonly known as New Zealand and the Commonwealth by whatever means I deem necessary, and;
>
> 60. To be a steward of the land and waters of the geographical area commonly referred to as New Zealand and the Commonwealth and to any land for which I may lay claim.

In an addendum to his Claim of Right, Jones gestures towards two elements within the pseudolaw matrix that are paradoxical and concerning. First, despite disclaiming any obligation to abide by state law or accept the authority of Parliament, the Government and the courts, Jones reserves the right 'to use any service provided by the Government of New Zealand that I deem necessary without it affecting my status as a Freeman-on-the-Land'. In essence, he declares that he will have his cake and eat it too. Second, and more seriously, Jones explicitly raises the latent potential for violence inherent in these arguments. He assumes for himself 'the inalienable right to use deadly force to protect my life, family and property' if his person is interfered with in any way. Given the intensely personal nature of sovereignty claimed by Jones, his understanding of interference is likely esoteric and erratic.

Of course, Jones is not correct about the law. The document he issued has no legal force. One cannot abrogate for themselves the right to pick and choose what law to follow. Nonetheless, the Claim of Right is relatively sophisticated. In addition to echoing John Locke's theory on the right of revolution,[2] it also includes a notice providing parties who wish to dispute his claims 10 days to respond. When Jones did not receive a response from the Prime Minister, Attorney-General, Solicitor-General or Commissioner of Police, he believed they had acquiesced. Jones then mailed a 'Default Judgment' to the original addressees confirming this point.[3] Thus, according to his pseudolegal processes, Jones was and is a Freeman. He did not have to register his dog if he did not want to. Perhaps this is why he continued to litigate what looks to us – from outside his legal universe – like a claim that is 'utterly hopeless'.[4] He believes he was in the right.

But even if we attempt to recreate his (mis)understanding of legality, it only gets us part of the way to an answer. We do not know how or why Jones first engaged with pseudolaw. We do not know if Jones was triggered by some incident or event that inspired him to delve deeper into pseudolaw and made its fantastical claims appear credible. What is clear is that the language and terms littered throughout his Claim of Right reveal a mature and complex understanding of pseudolaw. He has spent time educating himself. He may well be supporting others in their schooling.

[2] J Locke, *Second Treatise of Government* (Hackett Publishing, 1980) 111.
[3] James Son of James, 'Default Judgment', www.jamessonofjames.com/wp-content/uploads/2017/08/Default-Judgement-CoR.pdf.
[4] Transcript of Proceedings, *Citta Hobart Pty Ltd v Cawthorn* [2022] HCA Trans 1 [960] (Edelman J).

Understanding the motivations of pseudolegal actors and adherents is critical to developing appropriate responses,[5] but the diversity of pseudolaw complicates this task. On the one hand, responses may be too blunt, broad, and brutal, fuelling gurus and conspiracists who believe the state is despotic. At the same time, failing to act and allowing pseudolegal gurus and adherents to proselytise can hasten its spread. Striking the right balance in the right case requires a clear understanding of the phenomenon as well as the ways it manifests across law, government and society. It also requires understanding how the phenomenon is connected to and emerges out of our systems of law and governance.

Pseudolaw holds up a mirror – often distorted and partial – to the legal system itself. It invites reflection on the power that adherents presume law has, the power it actually has, and how law operates, is misused, and can catalyse pseudolaw. In this example, though we might see Jones as a strange adherent of a cult, deploying gobbledygook and arcane rituals to further misguided delusions, he is also a representative of a section of the population for which law remains a foreign language. For this (large) part of the population, law is inaccessible, arcane and partisan. It favours the rich and powerful who employ legal translators,[6] and leaves everyone else without a clear role.[7] Studying pseudolaw invites us to consider the weaknesses inherent in the legal system.

In this final chapter, we reflect on how our understanding of pseudolaw and the rise of sovereign citizens as the most prominent contemporary pseudolaw proponents inform the development of appropriate responses. We focus on two primary actors that are most likely to encounter pseudolegal adherents and thus have the greatest opportunity to mitigate its harms and ameliorate its attractiveness to individuals: legal actors and government actors. Although we focus on these two institutional players, it is important to acknowledge that the most effective response may be located at the individual level. We conclude with reflections on a theme that appears to connect all pseudolegal adherents: alienation.

II. The Role of Legal Actors

Legal actors are in some ways best suited to respond to pseudo*law*. The legal actors we have in mind here are those who apply or uphold the state (or international) law. They may work in institutional settings, like courts or law/bar societies, or they may be sole practitioners who assist clients. Those with legal training and expertise are well positioned to do this because they have ethical and professional responsibilities to individuals and the legal system to protect them from legal arguments that have no prospect of success. That the claims investigated in this

[5] SP Koniak, 'The Chosen People in Our Wilderness' (1997) 95 *Michigan Law Review* 1761, 1797.
[6] See M O'Sullivan, ch 3 in this volume.
[7] See K Leader, ch 5 in this volume.

volume have no prospects of winning in state or international fora is, after all, one of the factors that makes it both *pseudo* and *law*. When legal actors uphold their responsibilities, they can help mitigate pseudolaw's harmful effects.

There are four primary roles legal actors can play in mitigating the harms of pseudolaw. They can: minimise the disruption caused by pseudolaw through the adoption of procedures and approaches; educate and inform the adherents about law and pseudolaw; support legal literacy in society; and use law or bar societies to regulate and discipline individuals who are providing harmful legal information. We consider each in turn.

A. Minimising the Disruption of Pseudolaw

Courts are busy places and pseudolaw can be disruptive to the efficient administration of justice. A litigant that files hundreds of pages of irrelevant legal information, or makes submissions littered with confusing stamps, sigils and fingerprints, may frustrate registry staff and put a strain on limited court resources. Similarly, a litigant that refuses to appear in the ordinary manner,[8] or attends court with a train of followers, whether to support the litigant present their case as a McKenzie friend or to witness (and take part in) a performance,[9] can derail the smooth operation of justice. Thankfully, there are many procedural and substantive options open to courts.

It can sometimes be difficult to tell whether an argument is hopeless because it misunderstands or misconstrues legal authority, or that it is hopeless because it is pseudolaw. Pseudolaw has no unifying doctrine or catechism, nor any single leader, so individuals are free to adopt and adapt any claim they choose. Nevertheless, as this edited collection has made clear, pseudolaw adherents and litigants tend to share tropes and patterns of argument across jurisdictions. Courts can use this to their advantage. Indeed, the simplest approach, as Bridgette Toy-Cronin notes, is to forestall pseudolaw adherents and advocates 'before they enter the court'.[10] In the Canadian province of Alberta, for instance, the Court of the King's Bench has made a list of 'stereotypic and unique pseudolaw motifs' such as unusual name formatting and ink fingerprints.[11] The Court has issued a 'Master Order' that allows clerks to reject any filings with those motifs, 'circle the prohibited defect on a list' and return the filing to the litigant.[12] As Rooke ACJ explained in *Re Gauthier*, this arrangement

> is designed to intercept OPCA [Organized Pseudolegal Commercial Argument] litigation at the earliest possible point so that persons attempting to file such are directed

[8] *Kelly v Fiander* [2023] WASC 187; *R v Duncan*, 2013 ONCJ 160; *US v Hansen*, 929 F 3d 1238 (10th Cir, 2019). For analysis see, J McIntyre, H Hobbs and S Young, 'The Strawman Trap: Non-Appearance and the Pitfalls of Pseudolaw' (2024) *Australian Law Journal* (forthcoming).

[9] B Toy-Cronin, ch 14 in this volume.

[10] ibid.

[11] Personal Communication from DJ Netolitzky, 5 December 2022 (copy on file with the authors).

[12] ibid.

> to *Meads v Meads*, given notice of the irregular and legally incorrect nature of OPCA schemes, and then have the opportunity to abandon pseudolegal concepts before those misconceptions lead to unnecessary, abusive, and futile litigation, and the expenditure of litigant and court resources.[13]

The rule has proven successful. According to 'unpublished data … "90% of the persons who had their documents rejected this way never returned"'.[14]

Courts may achieve similar results through different procedures. The High Court of Australia's Rule 6.07 allows a Registrar to seek the direction of a Justice if a writ, application, summons, affidavit or other document appears on its face to be an abuse of process, frivolous or vexatious.[15] In these circumstances, the Justice may direct the Registrar to refuse to issue or file the document until and unless the party seeking to issue or file it obtains the leave of a Justice. Because these applications for leave are determined without an oral hearing, the Court has been clear that 'exercise of the discretion to nip a proceeding in the bud is appropriate only in the clearest of cases'.[16] While the boundaries of what constitutes frivolous or vexatious claims is open, the rule has been applied in cases adorned with pseudolegal language and tropes. In 2023, Gageler ACJ refused an application for leave to issue or file an application for a constitutional or other writ under rule 6.07.3. His Honour determined that the proposed application to order the Attorney-General instruct the Crown to grant the applicant the title of 'Sovereign Empress of Australia' was 'unintelligible'.[17]

In the Court of King's Bench of Alberta and the High Court of Australia rules have been established to restrict access to the Court for pseudolegal and other hopeless cases. Both courts are, however, appellate courts, and thus see far less pseudolegal activity than courts of first instance. It is unclear if courts of first instance can or should adopt similar processes as they may well be the most appropriate venue for ventilating all sorts of legal claims, including those involving pseudolaw (to ascertain whether they contain a real legal issue). As we have noted elsewhere, adopting mechanisms that prevent pseudolegal claims from being filed is a broad-brush approach that can have unintended consequences, including dismissing meritorious cases that an impecunious individual has inadvertently dressed up in pseudolaw.[18]

This strikes at the heart of a key challenge posed by pseudolaw to the administration of justice. In clear cases – where no colourable claim is present – the most appropriate way to mitigate the harms and delays associated with pseudolaw is to dispense with them quickly and judiciously. But where the line is drawn is

[13] *Re Gauthier*, 2017 ABQB 555 [6].

[14] C McRoberts, 'Tinfoil Hats and Powdered Wigs: Thoughts on Pseudolaw' (2019) 58 *Washburn Law Review* 637, 659, citing Email from DJ Netolitzky, 1 March 2019.

[15] High Court Rules 2004, r 6.07.

[16] *Re Young* (2020) 94 ALJR 448 [11].

[17] *Taylor, In the matter of an application for leave to issue or file* [2023] HCA Trans 63 (18 May 2023).

[18] S Young, H Hobbs and J McIntyre, The Growth of Pseudolaw and Sovereign Citizens in Aotearoa New Zealand Courts' (2023) *New Zealand Law Journal* 6, 10.

not always clear. And adopting processes to pursue efficiency may limit access to justice and exclude those who seek legal solutions.[19]

Of course, pseudolegal tropes and language may not always be present in written submissions. Sometimes, these arguments do not appear until an oral hearing, perhaps after a litigant has dispensed with representation. For judicial officers unfamiliar or unprepared for such submissions, bench books are increasingly providing valuable overviews – and rebuttals – of pseudolegal tropes and arguments. The Judicial College of Victoria, for example, has created a list of 'common pseudo-legal arguments' with reference to case law. It includes common elements such as the 'strawman duality', and the notion that legislation is of no effect because of some defect in state authority.[20] The Judicial Commission of New South Wales has a similar but longer list of common arguments, which includes Indigenous sovereignty arguments.[21] These documents are useful. They provide summary backgrounds and clear responses for judicial officers who engage with pseudolegal arguments. Nevertheless, care should always be taken to assess the argument made in the instant case. Strawman arguments will invariably be properly characterised as pseudolegal and ought to be rejected outright. However, not all claims of First Nations sovereignty are necessarily pseudolaw (even if magistrates do not have legal authority to address them).[22] Pseudolaw and Indigenous sovereignty are categories that overlap,[23] but they are also grounded in distinct normative universes.

The bench books demonstrate that legal actors are responding and developing ways to address the harms caused by pseudolaw. It is vital that judges dismiss pseudolegal arguments without 'dignifying them'[24] or wasting time.[25] Judges may need to be strict to ensure the effective administration of justice and courts can use their inherent powers to regulate processes and control the courtroom. Where a pseudolegal advocate is engaging in abusive litigation strategies, courts can exclude that person, hold them in contempt and even declare them vexatious, thus placing restrictions on their ability to access the court in the future.

These are extreme powers that should be used only in the clearest cases. Consider the fine balance struck by Wisconsin Circuit Court Judge Dorow in the

[19] M McMahon, ch 9 in this volume.

[20] Judicial College of Victoria, 'Tip Sheet: Sovereign Citizens, Querulant Litigants and High-Conflict Behaviours', www.judicialcollege.vic.edu.au/resources/tip-sheets (on file with authors).

[21] Judicial Commission of New South Wales, *Equality before the Law Bench Book*, s 10.5, www.judcom.nsw.gov.au/publications/benchbks/equality/section10.html#p10.5.

[22] S Young and H Hobbs, 'The Illegitimate State: The Alarming Intersection between Sovereign Citizen and Indigenous Sovereignty Claims' (draft, on file with authors); F Te Aho and J Tolmie, 'Māori Rejections of the State's Criminal Jurisdiction Over Māori in Aotearoa New Zealand's Courts' (2023) 30 *New Zealand Universities Law Review* 409, 421–22.

[23] See, for example, *Anderson v Kerslake* [2013] QDC 262.

[24] *Wnuck v Commissioner of Internal Revenue*, 136 TC 498, 512 (Tax Ct, 2011); *Smadu v Stone* [2016] WASC 80.

[25] *Re Magistrate M M Flynn; ex parte McJannett* [2013] WASC 372 [15]; *Scordo v Commonwealth Bank of Australia* [2024] FCA 359; H Hobbs, S Young and J McIntyre, 'The Internationalisation of Pseudolaw: The Growth of Sovereign Citizen Arguments in Australia and Aotearoa New Zealand' (2024) 47 *UNSW Law Journal* 309, 337.

trial of Darrell Brooks Jr, who drove his vehicle through a Christmas parade in 2021 killing six people and injuring 62.[26] After Brooks fired his public defender so he could 'represent [him]self as a sovereign citizen',[27] Judge Dorow expertly managed his erratic and vituperative litigation strategy. Judge Dorow prevented him from arguing he was a 'sovereign citizen'; managed his outbursts and attempts to introduce evidence; temporarily paused the trial after Brooks pounded his fist and attempted to 'stare down' the judge; and had officers place him in an adjacent room with audio and visual connections for him to continue participating in the trial despite his threats of violence.[28] In doing so, Judge Dorow allowed Brooks to represent himself in the manner he deemed appropriate while ensuring the safety of everyone in the courtroom and providing a fair and balanced trial. This is an extreme scenario, but it demonstrates the difficulty judges may face in balancing the rights of an accused and the need to ensure the proper administration of justice.

Care must be taken to preserve the function of the courts while conserving sparse judicial resources. However, in rare cases – depending on the particular litigant – it may be appropriate for judges to spend some time explaining clearly why their submissions are unhelpful. This can be done in and outside court.

B. Direct Education of Adherents

Judicial officers can manage adherents. They may also be able to educate them. By engaging with litigants calmly and patiently, judicial officers may be able to prise open small cracks of doubt, helping to pull an adherent out of their conspiratorial beliefs. Consider the case of Robert Sudy, a former pseudolaw adherent in New South Wales, who now runs the most significant database tracking pseudolaw in Australia.[29] Charged with driving a motor vehicle without registration or a licence, Sudy appeared before Magistrate David Heilpern at Grafton Local Court. Over the following three and a half hours, Sudy offered all manner of pseudolegal arguments, addressing both the magistrate and the gallery. Sudy reflects on the audience he received:

> The one thing Dave did impress me with, was his attitude. He was not belittling or dismissive, he tried to empathise with my argumentation, and I felt comfortable there despite the induced paranoia of the ideology. He told me he'd read all my materials and found them interesting, to which I felt heard and complimented, despite him informing me in the same breath that he could not see it as a contract.[30]

[26] Associated Press, 'A Wisconsin Man is Convicted of Killing 6 with an SUV in a Christmas Parade' NPR (26 October 2022), www.npr.org/2022/10/26/1131614524/wisconsin-christmas-parade-suv-guilty.

[27] Law and Crime Network, 'Accused Waukesha Parade Attacker Says He's a "Sovereign Citizen", Wants to Rep Himself' YouTube (28 September 2022), www.youtube.com/watch?v=MZVJxA8gnNE.

[28] Law and Crime Network, 'Bizarre Trial of Darrell Brooks: Outbursts and Oddities of the Waukesha Parade Attacker's Case' YouTube (28 October 2022), www.youtube.com/watch?v=97QPwFW-sAs.

[29] R Sudy, 'Freeman Delusion', www.freemandelusion.com.

[30] Personal communication from R Sudy, email (11 June 2024) (on file with authors).

This sort of direct intervention will not be appropriate in all cases, especially when adherents threaten or abuse court staff, parties, witnesses and others. It does suggest, however, that some alienated individuals can be encouraged – with patience and respect – to step away.

More commonly, judicial officers can explain why pseudolaw does not work in their judgments. We are not suggesting that judges should – in every case it arises – set out in chapter and verse why the strawman argument is untenable or why the King James Version of the Bible is not higher law than statutes passed by Parliament. The efficient administration of justice demands otherwise. Rather, drawing on scholarship that has found a 'thorough and explicit [rejection]' of pseudolaw arguments can have an effect in diminishing their prevalence,[31] we contend that there is value in a clear and comprehensive dismantling of pseudolaw. The best example is the Canadian decision of *Meads v Meads*.[32]

In *Meads*, Rooke ACJ of the Alberta Court of Queen's Bench granted an application to move a contentious family law dispute into case management. One of the parties, Dennis Larry Meads, had submitted a collection of pseudolegal tropes and arguments. In a 736-paragraph decision, Rooke ACJ responded, providing a 'magisterial'[33] overview and refutation of pseudolaw as it existed in Canada. Reviewing the impact of the *Meads* decision, Donald Netolitzky concludes that it accomplished several goals.[34] First, it convinced Dennis Meads to abandon his pseudolegal claims. Second, in providing courts and judges a 'field guide' to the theory and manifestations of pseudolaw, the judgment has served as a 'much referenced resource to understand and then respond to the abusive litigants who use [these] strategies'.[35] Indeed, *Meads* has been cited as authority to dispose of strawman arguments in countries all over the world. As one UK lawyer remarked, *Meads* has 'done many judges around the world a huge favour by exploding the movement's ideas and leaders'.[36] But, the impact of *Meads* is even broader than simply a resource for judges.

C. General Legal Information

Pseudolaw thrives, in part, because of the poor general levels of legal literacy amongst the population, making it difficult for potential adherents to distinguish between law and *pseudo*law. Improving access to legal information can help mitigate the spread and influence of this phenomenon. *Meads*, again, illustrates how.

[31] McRoberts (n 14) 664.
[32] *Meads v Meads* [2012] ABQB 571.
[33] Hobbs, Young and McIntyre (n 25) 316.
[34] DJ Netolitzky, 'After the Hammer: Six Years of *Meads v. Meads*' (2019) 56 *Alberta Law Review* 1167.
[35] ibid 1168.
[36] A Wagner, 'Freemen on the Land are "Parasites" Peddling "Pseudolegal Nonsense": Canadian Judge Fights Back' UK Human Rights Blog (30 September 2012), www.ukhumanrightsblog.com/2012/09/30/freemen-of-the-land-are-parasites-peddling-pseudolegal-nonsense-canadian-judge-fights-back.

Meads, Netolitzky explains, 'is that most exotic of creatures – a court judgment read by the public for educational and informational purposes'.[37] By providing 'a useful, practical, and highly readable' explanation as to why pseudolaw will not succeed,[38] *Meads* gained 'a cult following'[39] and has contributed to the decline of the phenomenon in Canada. In his contribution to this collection, Netolitzky explains further:

> Canadian case law that responds to pseudolaw is not simply a legal response, but a social one as well, with written court decisions obviously designed to be accessible to the general public. These 'weaponised judgments' were intended to communicate with both pseudolaw populations and the general layperson population, and shape public dialogue and perceptions.[40]

Meads has demonstrated that when judges write decisions 'with an eye to the wider context',[41] they may disarm the attractiveness of pseudolaw.

The wider social effectiveness of *Meads* relies on its accessibility. The judgment is clear and crisp, but it is also available on the Canadian Legal Information Institute (CanLII) website. Funded by the Federation of Law Societies of Canada, CanLII provides no-cost access to many cases, statutes and secondary legal sources. It allows individuals – whether attracted to pseudolaw or not – to gain an insight and understanding into what otherwise is a mysterious and arcane field.[42]

CanLII is part of the broader Free Access to Law Movement (FALM), which has sought to provide free access to legal information since the early 1990s.[43] These projects were driven by legal academics, initially at Cornell University, then at the University of Technology Sydney and the University of New South Wales, before being replicated worldwide.[44] Prior to these projects, legal materials – both legislation and case law – was largely inaccessible to the public. The availability of legal resources is likely to have had an impact on the evolution of pseudolaw. Even if pseudolegal advocates only read legal instruments in ways that conform to their favoured narratives, the fact remains that they do legal research. This provides a space for legal actors to engage directly with pseudolaw adherents through legal sources. As *Meads* highlights, thorough and authoritative case law that explains why pseudolaw will not work appears to be helpful in leading many to discard their pseudolegal claims.

[37] Netolitzky (n 34) 1169.

[38] McRoberts (n 14) 664.

[39] C Gillis, 'Court Decision with a Cult Following' Maclean's (6 March 2013), www.macleans.ca/news/canada/court-decision-with-a-cult-following.

[40] DJ Netolitzky, ch 7 in this volume.

[41] McRoberts (n 14) 665.

[42] K Leader, ch 5 in this volume.

[43] G Greenleaf, 'Free Access to Legal Information, LIIs, and the Free Access to Law Movement' in R Danner and J Winterton (eds), *The IALL International Handbook of Legal Information Management* (Routledge, 2011) 201.

[44] ibid.

Accessibility is different from understanding. Understanding law requires a degree of legal literacy, which requires, in turn, a conceptual infrastructure for engaging with and understanding authoritative sources.[45] It is not enough to simply provide access to legal sources, materials need to be presented in ways that can be understood by the public. Again, this is a role where legal actors, particularly legal academics, can contribute to minimising the impacts of pseudolaw by countering misinformation with accessible information and resources. In the lead-up to the 2023 'Voice' Referendum in Australia, for example, many legal academics across the country rallied to provide clear, concise and accessible information to counter the misinformation – some of which was pseudolaw-related – and disinformation that was rife throughout the campaign.[46] One initiative was the Voice Legal Literacy Project,[47] which set out to provide extensive, accurate and impartial legal information about the referendum, and the broader constitutional context, in a way that was accessible to the public. This involved using a range of media and sources and furnishing links and primary sources to enable the public to undertake further research. Similar resources could be designed to respond to the claims of pseudolaw.

Changing patterns in how people learn suggest that the source-only text-based model of FALM needs an update. In his chapter, Netolitzky noted that the first wave of pseudolaw adherents in Canada conducted their own legal research online, but that more recent adherents 'prefer Internet videos'.[48] There likely is a cultural shift occurring. Notable and apex judicial opinions are now released with summaries and press releases. Short communications, especially in bite-sized videos, instead of turgid and technical legal jargon sprawling over hundreds of pages, are easier to access, digest and learn from. Some legal actors, including scholars, have recognised this reality. Professor Emerita Anne Twomey's Constitutional Clarion YouTube channel provides a valuable student-focused overview of a range of public law matters,[49] some of which have covered responses to pseudolegal arguments.[50] Law societies (and scholars) should take note.

D. Professional Discipline

The fourth primary response available to the legal profession is investigatory and regulatory. The advocates and gurus who promote and sell pseudolegal information

[45] LJ Ax-Fultz, 'Igniting the Conversation: Embracing Legal Literacy as the Heart of the Profession,' (2015) 107 *Law Librarian Journal* 421, 427–30; AR Gomez, 'Demand Side Justice' (2021) 28 *Georgetown Journal on Poverty Law and Policy* 411, 427.

[46] See J McIntyre and J Charles, Submission No 92 to Joint Standing Committee on Electoral Matters, 'Inquiry into Civics Education, Engagement, and Participation in Australia' (29 May 2024) 29.

[47] The Voice Legal Literacy Project, www.referendum-voice.com.au.

[48] D Netolitzky, ch 7 in this volume.

[49] Anne Twomey, Constitutional Clarion, YouTube, www.youtube.com/@constitutionalclarion1901.

[50] Anne Twomey, Constitutional Clarion, 'What Colour is the Constitution?' YouTube (26 September 2023), www.youtube.com/watch?v=IE6SCmeUMUc.

and their services online may charge thousands of dollars. Some who do so are clearly not lawyers. For instance, American 'non-citizen' Brandon Joe Williams, spreads a variation of the strawman argument through his 'Contract Killer Course', available on YouTube.[51] As part of his 'Williams & Williams Law Group', Williams offers services as an 'attorney-in-fact' (not law), who can assist clients with their legal issues.[52] For a non-negotiable donation of USD 20,000 Williams will support his clients obtain 'diplomatic immunity'.[53] Many others exist. David Heilpern discussed two in his contribution to this collection. As Heilpern noted, these individuals are engaged in consumer fraud and should be investigated and prosecuted.[54]

Sometimes, legal professionals became ensnared in pseudolaw activities. In 2017, Canadian lawyer Glenn Bogue had his licence suspended by the Law Society of Upper Canada for using litigation techniques that could harm the administration of justice. Bogue had adopted a range of pseudolegal arguments, including referring to 'non-existent or self created tribunals' which had allegedly indicted and convicted the Prime Minister, the Pope and the Queen.[55] Similarly, in 2021, a New South Wales solicitor had his practising certificate suspended for making statements likely to mislead and undermine confidence in the administration of justice. Nathan Buckley had encouraged the public to breach public health laws imposed in response to the COVID-19 pandemic by 'deliberately providing false information'.[56] The response of the Law Societies in these cases is admirable – and capable of replication.

These examples, two among many, raise the following questions: what does it mean that individuals with legal training can become entangled with pseudolaw? Does it suggest that some people are susceptible even if they have sufficient training, or does it indicate they were poorly trained, underwent a traumatic incident, or something else? Many aspects of this phenomenon require additional research. It also indicates that actors from other sectors in society have important roles to play.

III. The Role of Government Actors

Pseudolaw is a legal phenomenon, but it pervades any space where law operates. Adherents routinely use pseudolegal arguments in their interactions with, among

[51] BJ Williams, 'Contract Killer Course' YouTube, www.youtube.com/playlist?list=PLAvMnawbCOrYHaqiPNkJzPx_-JWBp7n-m.

[52] Williams & Williams Law Group, 'About', www.williamsandwilliamslawfirm.com/about.

[53] Williams & Williams Law Group, 'Services', www.williamsandwilliamslawfirm.com/services.

[54] D Heilpern, ch 12 in this volume.

[55] A Robinson, 'Lawyer Suspended Over Allegedly Vexatious Conduct' *Law Times* (26 June 2017), www.lawtimesnews.com/news/general/lawyer-suspended-over-allegedly-vexatious-conduct/262608.

[56] G Mitchell and S McPhee, 'Lawyer who Brought Anti-Vaccine Case has Practising Certificate Suspended' *Sydney Morning Herald* (12 November 2021), www.smh.com.au/national/nsw/lawyer-who-brought-anti-vaccine-case-has-practising-certificate-suspended-20211112-p598ja.html.

other institutions, police, local councils and authorities, tax offices and health departments. It follows that any response to pseudolaw must look beyond the actions of legal actors to consider the benefits of a 'whole of government' approach. In discussing government actors, we have in mind those who are primarily public-facing administrators, elected officials, educators and others, even if they are also involved in law enforcement or adjudication. In this part, we suggest ways that government can respond by increasing regulatory enforcement and criminalising well-known pseudolegal means of harassment.

Pseudolaw commonly operates where consumer and professional regulators could become involved but largely do not. We have already noted that pseudolegal operators who market products and services to consumers are engaging in fraud. In many cases, however, authorities appear largely to tolerate pseudolegal businesses and organisations.[57] It is not clear why this is the case. It might reflect a combination of moral and practical considerations. Perhaps there is a feeling that any consumer who is defrauded is not an innocent party, given they purchased a product or service in a hopeless – and criminal – attempt to avoid the law. Similarly, although these businesses are advertised extensively on particular social media channels, they engage relatively low-level issues, such as traffic offences, such that they do not attract significant attention from legitimate authorities.

This is not always the case. Colin McRoberts' chapter reveals that pseudolegal businesses can cause significant harm where they purport to regulate unlicensed medical practitioners.[58] Similarly David Heilpern's contribution to this volume notes that relatively small-scale pseudolegal operations can act as a gateway to broader and deeper engagement with pseudolaw.[59] These operations can also make significant income. A recent report from Tax Policy Associates exposes a fraudulent pseudolegal business in the United Kingdom called 'Matrix Freedom' that promises to make clients' mortgages disappear, and which is making GBP 500,000 a month.[60] Despite a devastating judgment from the England and Wales High Court noting that the scheme has 'every appearance of deceit, of abuse and contempt of court',[61] the police do not appear to have commenced a criminal investigation. One of the motivations of this collection is to encourage authorities to understand pseudolaw and to take its harms seriously. Better enforcement of existing regulatory regimes has the potential to dramatically restrain the growth of pseudolaw.

Depending on the pseudolaw tactics, statutory reform may be necessary to achieve effective regulation. In the United States, for example, where the issue of

[57] Though not in Austria where, Anna Löbbert points out, 'state deniers' are criminalised: A Löbbert, ch 10 in this volume.

[58] C McRoberts, ch 13 in this volume.

[59] D Heilpern, ch 12 in this volume.

[60] D Neidle, 'How a Conspiracy Theory Makes £500k a Month from the Vulnerable' Tax Policy Associates, www.taxpolicy.org.uk/2024/06/08/matrix_freedom_scamming_vulnerable_people/?a=1%2F.

[61] *Iain Clifford Stamp v Capital Home Loans T/A/ CHL Mortgages* [2024] EWHC 1092 [37].

paper terrorism has been especially prominent, 24 states have adopted legislation making filing fraudulent liens illegal. A range of approaches have been taken from pre- and post-filing administrative remedies, post-filing judicial relief, and the imposition of criminal and civil penalties.[62] In California, the Secretary of State can refuse to file a lien if they believe the request is unlawful, false or fraudulent, or that it promotes illegitimate objects or purposes.[63] Similarly for the post-filing stage, in Illinois, the Secretary of State may terminate a record that has been filed if they have a reasonable basis for determining it violates applicable law.[64]

The majority of these legislative regimes impose civil penalties, but in some cases legislative responses have created the potential for criminal sanctions. Thus while Colorado allows for post-filing judicial relief when a spurious lien has been filed by permitting the court to subsequently declare it invalid,[65] Georgia additionally allows criminal sanctions to be imposed against the party filing the fake lien.[66] A similar law exists at the national level, with specific penalties targeted at those who file false liens in retaliation against federal judges or law enforcement officers.[67] Nevertheless, this regime of criminalisation and increased regulation is not consistent across all states.

Criminalisation may be necessary in certain contexts to address issues arising from the growth of pseudolaw. However, caution should underpin any expansion of the criminal law, as criminalisation can have unintended effects. As Stephen Young, Harry Hobbs and Rachel Goldwasser have noted, incarceration of militia members and others involved in the Common Law movement facilitated the spread of sovereign citizen pseudolaw through prison populations across the United States.[68] Criminalisation can also turn adherents into martyrs and prophets – it is only a short leap for a guru to explain to their flock how their imprisonment reveals the state will do anything to prevent people from learning the truth. Equally, criminalisation is not suitable in all instances. It is difficult, impractical, and perhaps even unconstitutional to criminalise gurus who only share their 'knowledge' about the law and never act upon it.

Legal and government actors can respond to pseudolaw in ways that dampen its growth and spread. These are not, however, the only or even the most meaningful actors. Many people fall into pseudolaw because they are seeking support and community. They may start with a complaint about a personal injustice – mask

[62] National Association of Secretaries of State, 'State Strategies to Subvert Fraudulent Uniform Commercial Code (UCC) Filings: A Report for State Business Filing Agencies' (June 2019) appendixes I–IV, 12–32, www.nass.org/sites/default/files/bogus%20filing/final-nass-report-bogus-filings-june19.pdf.

[63] Cal Govt Code Ann § 12181 (2019).

[64] 810 Ill Comp Stat §§ 5/9-516(b)(3)(B)-(e), (3.5).

[65] Colo Rev Stat § 38-35-204 (2023); see also Kan Stat Ann § 58-4302 (2023).

[66] Ga Code § 16-10-20.1 (2023–24).

[67] Court Security Improvement Act of 2007, 18 USC § 1521 (2008).

[68] S Young, H Hobbs and R Goldwasser, ch 6 in this volume.

mandates, vaccines, zoning regulations, mortgagee repossession – but quickly find themselves supported by a group of empathetic individuals. This community may even offer to provide practical pseudolegal help to resolve the initial challenge. It is easy to see how pseudolegal narratives can propagate and grow. Broader individual and social responses are needed.

IV. Addressing Alienation

The primary theme that emerges from this discussion – and the contributions in this volume – is that pseudolaw adherents often feel excluded or alienated from the legal system.[69] Underlying the anti-authoritarianism and conspiratorial thinking of adherents is a belief that the legal system does not operate for them, that it is a domain for the wealthy, the elite and the powerful. Pseudolaw offers individuals a mode of engaging with the law on terms that work for them, and which, on a generous reading, might be viewed as an attempt to reclaim the law, to return to a time when it was Good and Just. On such a view, deriding these individuals is unhelpful and may, in fact, further encourage them. Instead, always bearing in mind that these pseudolegal claims are without legal merit, it is worth considering whether our legal systems are accessible and comprehensible to our communities.

Alienation is not merely a matter of perception, but one of hard reality. In Australia, more than 25 per cent of people experience a 'substantial' legal problem every year,[70] but only three to four per cent of these serious disputes are resolved, directly or indirectly, through the justice system. Of that number, only around one per cent end in a trial and final judgment. The formal justice system plays an extraordinarily marginal role in resolving serious legal problems.[71] Not everyone desires to resolve their issues through the courts, but these numbers suggest that another reason why many legal issues remain outside the justice system is that the majority of Australians are alienated from it. What has been described as the 'unspoken, unexamined controversy facing the civil justice system'[72] is the reality that the legal system 'is slowly strangling itself'.[73] Soaring costs make its access prohibitive for all but the very wealthy. Where meaningful access to the law is beyond one's grasp, the promise of pseudolaw becomes beguiling. The rise of pseudolaw and its detrimental impacts should compel the state to reform access

[69] See M O'Sullivan, ch 3; K Leader, ch 5; J Roose, ch 15, all in this volume.

[70] C Coumarelos, et al, 'Legal Australia-Wide Survey Legal Need in New South Wales' Law and Justice Foundation NSW (2012) 61, www.lawfoundation.net.au/wp-content/uploads/2023/11/32PJR_Legal-Australia-Wide-Survey-Legal-need-in-New-South-Wales_2012.pdf.

[71] J McIntyre, 'The Ur-Controversy of Civil Courts' in M Camilleri and A Harkness (eds), *Australian Courts: Controversies, Challenges and Change* (Springer, 2022) 345, 350–51.

[72] ibid 348.

[73] L McNamara, 'Civil Litigation Costs are Cause for Concern' (2012) 34 *Bulletin* 16, quoting South Australian Chief Justice John Doyle.

to justice.[74] Pseudolaw is a symptom of a sick system and its spread and continued growth invite reflection on how to genuinely democratise the legal system.

One step towards this goal focuses on enhancing legal literacy. Pseudolaw can only flourish where there is a lack of sufficient understanding of the law, its authorities, its systems and its processes. The problem is that without a firm grounding, engagement with the law can have the opposite effect, pushing certain individuals towards pseudolaw. Indeed, Kate Leader has noted that many litigants in person are exposed to networks that advance conspiracist ideation on the internet because of the 'absence of formal and accessible legal advice'.[75] The litigants she studied developed conspiracy ideation as a result of their interaction with the court system. They perceived its rules and processes as operating behind closed doors and ultimately denying them justice. It seems reasonable to posit that individuals may be attracted to pseudolaw because it provides an answer to questions they have about how government or the world operates. That answer is incorrect, but it fulfils an epistemic need.

The challenge for many societies is that citizens generally have little awareness and understanding of key features and concepts that underlie their system of government. This is certainly true for Australia. Professor Emerita Twomey has recently acknowledged this point. In a submission to a parliamentary inquiry into civics education, engagement and participation in Australia, Twomey notes that she is often contacted by people alleging 'all kinds of constitutional conspiracies and legal "errors" … which magically cause all law to be invalid in Australia and all courts to have no authority'.[76] She explains further:

> The problem is that by the time I try to explain the misconceptions or falsities that are at the root of their arguments, the people making them are so far down the rabbit-hole and so committed to this fantasy world, that they cannot be brought back to reality. The only way that this can be headed off is for Australians, when they are young, to be given a sound understanding of the basics of the system of governance and law, so that they can easily recognise and dismiss pseudo-legal nonsense when they see it. Essentially, we need to be inoculating people by giving them knowledge and the skills to engage in logical reasoning, so they can make a rational assessment of the vast array of material that they are now exposed to on the internet, and discern what is authoritative and sensible as opposed to what is false and manipulative and derived from dubious sources.[77]

Twomey is correct. One way of 'inoculating people' is to ensure that individuals have the knowledge and skills to deal with materials presented online.

[74] For commentary on a principled approach for reform in Australia, see J McIntyre, 'A Framework for Civil Justice Reform Pt I: Theory' (2013) 35 *The Law Society Bulletin* 12; J McIntyre, 'A Framework for Civil Justice Reform Pt II: Politics and Practice' (2013) 35 *The Law Society Bulletin* 18.

[75] K Leader, 'Conspiracy! Or When Bad Things Happen to Good Litigants in Person' (2024) *Legal Studies*, doi.org/10.1017/lst.2024.18; Leader (n 29) 35.

[76] A Twomey, Submission No 31 to Joint Standing Committee on Electoral Matters, Inquiry into Civics Education, Engagement and Participation in Australia (21 May 2024) 3.

[77] ibid.

To deradicalise adherents and limit new recruitment, it may be necessary to enhance general legal literacy, giving people the tools to directly engage with our legal system.

There is growing research on the concept of legal literacy. It refers to the idea that it is necessary to master legal discourse at a level to conduct 'a meaningful and active life in a world saturated with a legal culture'.[78] It involves developing a sufficient set of legal knowledge and skills to be aware of the role of law in everyday life,[79] as well as some capacity to engage with legal issues that arise.[80] It can be defined as

> the background information stored in one's mind that enables them to take up a legal document, read an article in the newspaper on a law-related event, with an adequate level of comprehension, getting the point, grasping the implications, relating what they read to the unstated context which alone gives meaning to what they read.[81]

Without legal literacy citizens may feel unable to make a decision, or may struggle to discern accurate information in the midst of legal and political debate. People will feel 'intimidated and alienated' from the law,[82] and from the political discourse that takes that legal context for granted. Archie Zariki, one of the leading scholars on legal literacy, likens the concept to learning the language of a foreign society to be able to operate effectively within it: 'For those who lack legal literacy, the world of lawyers and judges feels just as foreign as an unfamiliar country'.[83]

Enhancing legal literacy has many positive effects. It is most 'profoundly associated with the concept of meaningful access to justice'.[84] Yet, it can improve lives in many ways. Because a lack of legal literacy has a disproportionate effect on disadvantaged and marginalised populations,[85] developing such literacy helps address social disadvantage and improve social and economic welfare. As Jo Watson Hackl notes, 'Education in legal literacy helps low-income people become effective self-advocates, access available resources, and identify and work with legal professionals to attend to legal problems at their earliest, most easily resolved stage.'[86]

The absence of legal literacy has the opposite effect. It hampers legal and political engagement, embeds social and economic disadvantage and undermines access to justice. Alienation from legal discourse can radicalise individuals and lead to

[78] Y Roznai and N Mordechay, 'Access to Justice 2.0: Access to Legislation and Beyond' (2015) 3 *Theory and Practice of Legislation* 333, 359.

[79] See Coumarelos et al (n 70) 29–30.

[80] ME Manley-Casimir, WM Cassidy and S de Castell, 'Legal Literacy: Toward a Working Definition, Report Submitted to the Canadian Law Information Council' (Canadian Law Information Council, 1986) 90.

[81] Ax-Fultz (n 45) 427–30; Gomez (n 45) 427.

[82] S Freudenberg, 'Beyond Lawyers: Legal Literacy for the Future' (2017) 45 *Australian Business Law Review* 387, 387 fn 1, citing Canadian Bar Association, 'Reading the Legal World: Literacy and Justice in Canada, Report of the Canadian Bar Association Task Force on Legal Literacy' (1992).

[83] A Zariki, *Legal Literacy: An Introduction to Legal Studies* (Athabasca University Press, 2014) 21.

[84] Freudenberg (n 82) 389.

[85] Roznai and Mordechay (n 78) 359.

[86] JW Hackl, 'A New Generation in Legal Literacy' (2012) 46 *Clearinghouse Review* 367, 367.

conspiratorial and pseudolegal thinking.[87] Enhanced civics education is vital in giving citizens the tools they need to inoculate themselves against the 'obvious nonsense'[88] that is pseudolaw.

Alas, as much as increasing legal education and literacy is necessary, it is not enough. The spread of pseudolaw 'is indicative of growing social problems, including social unrest, dissatisfaction, disaffection, stratification and inequality'.[89] While every person picks up pseudolaw for their own reasons, a range of factors make the phenomenon more attractive to larger subsections of society. In this collection, Josh Roose explored this point through a discussion on the 'paradox of pseudolaw'.[90] As Roose explained, individuals have personal reasons for adopting pseudolaw, but their reasons are influenced by broader structural factors. For those at the margins of society, exploited in and out of the workplace and bombarded by a feeling of loss, our legal and governance system appears hostile.

Adherents articulate their issues in the language of personal sovereignty and empowerment, because they feel disempowered. Pseudolaw is a language about individual rights to property, contract and sovereignty, but it can be read also as a critique of the state's inability or unwillingness to protect socio-economic and cultural resources. Unfortunately for the believer, given pseudolaw fails and is liable only to make their legal problems worse, though these individuals are searching for utopias,[91] they end up contributing to the dystopia they are challenging. Pseudolaw is an example of 'cruel optimism', where the element desired for one's flourishing is an obstacle to that flourishing.[92] Perhaps ultimately, then, the best response is to work towards making society more equal, equitable and fair.

[87] Hobbs, Young and McIntyre (n 25) 341–42.
[88] *Bradley v The Crown* [2020] QCA 252 [1] (Sofronoff P).
[89] Hobbs, Young and McIntyre (n 25) 322.
[90] J Roose, ch 15 in this volume.
[91] BB Arnold, ch 4 in this volume.
[92] Lauren Berlant, *Cruel Optimism* (Duke University Press, 2011) 1.

INDEX

www.ingramcontent.com/pod-product-compliance
Ingram Content Group UK Ltd.
Pitfield, Milton Keynes, MK11 3LW, UK
UKHW020234290926
15470UKWH00002B/533

9 781509 978915